Qualitative Research in Sport Management

D1245622

Good qualitative research can help sport management researchers and industry professionals solve difficult problems and better understand their organisations, stakeholders, and performance. Now in a fully revised and extended new edition, this book is a user-friendly introduction to qualitative methods in sport management. Covering the full research process from research planning to reporting results, this edition includes expanded coverage of cutting-edge areas, including digital and social media research, critical realism, and social network analysis.

The book examines the reflective and interrogative processes required for developing effective qualitative research questions and includes a deeper discussion of ontology and epistemology in the light of today's rapidly changing society. It takes the reader step-by-step through essential and emerging qualitative methods, from actor network theory and ethnography to computer-assisted data analysis and sampling typologies. Every chapter includes examples of real qualitative research, including shorter "research briefs" and extended case studies, reflecting the exciting qualitative research that is currently occurring in sport business and management, and highlighting the links between research and sport management practice.

This is essential reading for courses in sport management, sport business, sport policy, sport marketing, sport media, and communications. It provides students, researchers, and practitioners with the knowledge and skills to undertake qualitative research while deepening their understanding of how the social world can be perceived and interpreted through a particular theoretical lens.

Useful online materials include recommended readings and PowerPoint slides.

James Skinner is Director of the Institute for Sport Business and a Professor of Sport Business at Loughborough University London, UK. James has published numerous books and journal articles on research methods and teaches research method courses to postgraduate students across the globe.

Allan Edwards has held numerous academic appointments within Australia and internationally. His most recent position before his retirement was as Reader in Sport Business at Loughborough University London, UK. Allan has a passion for qualitative research, and this is reflected by his extensive use of qualitative methods in his research.

Aaron C.T. Smith is Professor of Sport Business at Loughborough University London, UK. Aaron has published extensively in qualitative research methods and conducted research employing qualitative methodologies with organisations across the Asia-Pacific region, Europe, North America, and the Middle East.

Qualitative Research in Sport Management

Second Edition

James Skinner, Allan Edwards
and Aaron C.T. Smith

LONDON AND NEW YORK

Second edition published 2021
by Routledge
2 Park Square, Milton Park, Abingdon, Oxon, OX14 4RN

and by Routledge
52 Vanderbilt Avenue, New York, NY 10017

Routledge is an imprint of the Taylor & Francis Group, an informa business

First edition published by Elsevier Ltd. 2009

British Library Cataloguing-in-Publication Data
A catalogue record for this book is available from the British Library

Library of Congress Cataloguing-in-Publication Data
A catalogue record has been requested for this book

ISBN: 978-0-367-42659-0 (hbk)
ISBN: 978-0-367-42660-6 (pbk)
ISBN: 978-0-367-85424-9 (ebk)

Typeset in Trump Mediaeval LT Std
by KnowledgeWorks Global Ltd.

Visit the eResources: www.routledge.com/9780367426606

Contents

Part 1: The context of sport management research

Part 2: Planning the sport management research process

Part 3: Foundations of sport management research

Part 4: Analysing the sport management data

Part 5: Paradigms used in sport management research

Figures

Tables

The context of sport management research

CHAPTER 1

The nature and usefulness of qualitative research for sport management

LEARNING OUTCOMES

By the end of this chapter you should be able to:

- Provide an introductory understanding of qualitative sport management research.

- Have sufficient information to appreciate how qualitative sport management research is undertaken.

- Highlight different types of qualitative research.

- Describe in brief the characteristics, strengths and weaknesses, advantages, and importance of qualitative sport management research.

CHAPTER OVERVIEW

Every research project is guided by what a researcher wants to achieve, what they believe is good research, and what it means to conduct research into sport management. Each researcher, therefore, has particular priorities and orientations that direct the research project. However, the adequacy of the answers we get from our research is always reliant on how willing we are as researchers to peer into the unknown. This means we have to look at things in often unconventional ways or from different vantage points. When a range of methodologies and theoretical perspectives are employed by researchers working within an academic discipline, then new knowledge is generated, and the discipline is able to progress in its development. According to Denzin and Lincoln (1994), qualitative research focuses on interpretation of phenomena in their natural settings to make sense in terms of the meanings people bring to these settings. Qualitative research involves collecting information about personal experiences, introspection, life story, interviews, observations, historical, interactions, and visual text, which are significant moments and meaningful in peoples' lives. Patton (2002) stated that the purpose of qualitative research is not necessarily to predict what might occur, but rather to understand in depth the characteristics of the situation and the meaning brought by participants and what is happening to them at the moment. The aim of qualitative research is to truthfully present findings to others who are interested in what you are doing. If you are a research student, then you have a role to play in this process of developing knowledge not only for yourself but also for future practitioners, academics, and students of sport management. This chapter addresses the distinctiveness of qualitative research and the benefits it holds for sport management research. The chapter covers the characteristics of qualitative research; how these compare with those of quantitative research; and the value of qualitative research for sport management inquiry.

INTRODUCTION

Sport research should systematically advance knowledge about the discipline and thus be relevant to both academics and practitioners. Research methods play an important role in advancing knowledge, and continuous efforts to develop and apply new research methods that are essential for sport management research to capture the complexities of the contemporary sporting landscape (Smith & Stewart, 2010). Important but complex research issues have emerged as sport continues to globalise and further embed itself in the social, cultural, and economic fabric of society. In many cases, addressing these research problems challenges research designs and methods in which sport management researchers have been trained. However, it is clear that when investigating the diverse, complex, and changing contemporary field of sport, we need to recognise there is no longer a single methodology that meets the needs of all sport management related research (Hoeber & Shaw, 2017).

Diversity in methods and approaches can facilitate the development of the sport management discipline. Historically, under the influence of the dominant positivist paradigm, sport-related research predominately focused on scientific explanation and prediction through a value-free lens as possible (Glesne, 2006). Positivists usually embraced an ontological view that there is one reality that can be quantified and measured. Epistemologically, positivists believed that reality consists of facts and with appropriate methods scientists can ascertain those facts (Denzin & Lincoln, 2008). As such, positivists were usually characterised by a belief that, if an investigation follows the rigid methods set forth, and establishes a degree of methodological validity and reliability, the results can be considered objective and value-free facts of the world (Kuhn, 1962).

Sport management research to a large extent grew out of the view that researchers should use research methods that were similar to those that had seemed to lead to the discovery of objective laws and regularities in the natural sciences (Skinner & Edwards, 2005). The appropriate way of knowing about knowledge production is thought to be by means of the hypthetico-deductive method in which the sport researcher begins with a clearly articulated theory, deduces hypotheses which are logically consistent with the theory, and then tests the hypotheses under experimental conditions. Such methodology assumes that through observation and precise measurement, social reality (Kuhn, 1962), which is external to and independent of the mind of the observer, may be rendered comprehensible to the sport management researcher (van Manen, 1997).

According to Sharp and Green (1975), it is in approaches to theorisation, as much as in the methodology itself, that the "inherent weakness" of such deductive research is revealed. Critical sport management theorists challenged the positivist logical empiricist tradition and argued that while "fact finding" and "head counting" produces voluminous statistical data, it does not address the social circumstances out of which such data arise (Frisby, 2005). Criticism of the separation of the individual from social structures, which is a characteristic of the positivist tradition, coupled with a philosophical attack upon the tenets of positivism, and the realisation that social advances do not necessarily follow any correct scientific manner (Kuhn, 1962), led to the emergence of more interpretive research (Woods & Hammersley, 1977). This approach shares a common concern with the investigation of ways in which human actors themselves construct the social world through the interpretation of the interaction with other human actors. This relationship between the research and informant prompted the emergence of new paradigms emerging in sport management research. Sport management researchers embracing these new research paradigms signalled a growing awareness in the sport management research community that there is no single or right way to understand social reality (Smith & Sparkes, 2016).

What the above discussion indicates is that the sport management researcher should determine which approach will be most effective given the research question. As these questions become more complex, there is a need for more innovative qualitative methods and approaches to explore new emerging sport management phenomena, for example the social and economic influence of the growth of E-Sports. Conducting and publishing research with real implications for sport management practice has long been a challenge for sport management researchers (Frisby, 2005), the challenge looms even larger as the sport industry continues to evolve and expand rapidly. One way to address emerging new research phenomena is through innovative qualitative research methods or approaches. Innovation in this sense might mean the development of new methods, approaches, or procedures or the integration of multiple qualitative methods in innovative ways. This book therefore aims to provide examples of a range of innovative research qualitative methodologies that can be applied in sport management research. In doing so, the chapters within the book aim to advance our theoretical understanding and practical application of research in sport management.

WHY DO SPORT MANAGEMENT RESEARCH?

Research and reflection are essential in any discipline if that discipline wants to grow in a positive and beneficial way. Thomas, Nelson, and Silverman (2005) asserted:

> one of the primary distinctions between a discipline or profession and trade is that the trade deals only with how to deal with something, whereas the discipline or profession concerns itself not only with how but also with why something should be done in a certain manner and why it should even be done. (p. 6)

Sport management research can add important information to the discipline's knowledge base. Such information, where relevant, can be drawn on by other researchers, practitioners, policy makers, and even other stakeholders such as club members, athletes, fans, existing and potential sponsors, advertisers, marketers, and any other interested member of the general public. For the sport management researcher, a particular research study may be on a topic or issue previously ignored, or perhaps on a "new" topic that had never been considered before. The research may also build on previous research studies, providing results to confirm or extend the previous study, or even to question its findings. This is true of any academic discipline and sport management is no exception. A research report might provide a study that has not been conducted and thereby fill a void in existing knowledge. It can also provide additional results to confirm or disconfirm results of prior studies.

Research can assist in advancing organisational practices through suggesting new ideas to improve organisational effectiveness and efficiencies. It can help practitioners evaluate approaches that they hope will work in their own management settings and at a broader level create relationships between sport managers who may be trying out similar ideas in different locations. Research also informs conversations, for example by influential policy makers, which might directly impact on sport managers. For example, policy decisions relating to drugs in sport or the funding of youth sport in deprived areas. Research can help the policy makers weigh up various perspectives and make informed decisions: decisions that therefore should be fair, contextualised, responsible, and (hopefully) effective.

SPORT MANAGEMENT RESEARCH

Types of research

In this book, we refer to two main types of research: *basic research* and *applied research*. *Basic research* is theoretical in nature, and deals with theoretical problems. It tries and makes sense of the world and the way in which the world operates. In general, the research takes place in a controlled setting such as a laboratory, but for the sport manager this could be an interview room or any other venue where the researcher can control the conditions under which the research takes place. In this situation, the results of research may have little direct application for the sports manager (i.e. a team manager or community sport organisation). The research may yield important data for the researcher and other academics interested in the same theory or problem. However, the form in which the research is reported/conveyed, i.e. academic journals, and the types of data collected make it unlikely to be of direct relevance to a sport management setting. *Applied research* on the other hand takes place in the real world, or real-world settings such as the sporting organisation, and therefore, if undertaken well, it can produce results that are relevant to the sport management practitioner and can be implemented back within the specific sporting organisation to improve practice. Most sport management research is neither purely applied nor purely basic, but incorporates some aspects of both.

METHODOLOGICAL FEATURES OF RESEARCH

The distinctive methodological features of the research are twofold: (1) organisational and design concerns such as whether or not the proposed research is exploratory or highly structured; and (2) the conceptual and theoretical frame of reference that will guide the research – that is, qualitative or quantitative research. Manheim and Rich (1995) define *exploratory research* as:

> *research intended only to provide greater familiarity with the phenomena one wants to investigate so that one can formulate more precise research questions and perhaps develop hypotheses. Such studies can be essential when a sport management researcher is investigating new phenomena or phenomena that have not been studied before. (p. 89)*

In contrast, *structured research* refers to a research process that follows a relatively familiar patterned arrangement. For example, in a structured study, the researcher organises or *structures* what one is looking for according to a protocol that guides him/her in terms of "What to look for, the order in which to make observations and the way to record the results" (Manheim & Rich, 1995, p. 202). These types of approaches influence research questions and the research design.

RESEARCH PARADIGMS

We believe that it is important that sport management researchers understand research paradigms and that they have an understanding of the major frameworks that they will come across in their reading. This is because it is not a matter of having a theory and putting it into practice, nor of doing something and deriving a theory from it, but of both theory and practice happening simultaneously, interactively, and continuously. Understanding the range of possible frameworks, and how others have used them is key to understanding your own processes of thought. Paradigms can be considered as ways of seeing the world in terms of perceiving, understanding, and interpreting a theory, explanation, model or map. Edwards and Skinner (2009) suggested that most sport management researchers have an intellectual framework that governs the way they perceive the world, and their own place within it, even if they are unable to articulate just what that framework is.

This paradigm, or framework, shapes research from the beginning to the end, because it provides the structure within which choices (including the initial choice of a research subject) are made. This framework comes partly from the institutional setting within which research takes place – the position taken by employers or those who commissioned the research, or by supervisors, by the department within which researchers work and by the university/college that employs them. Part of it will come from the personal position of the sport management researcher that may have been shaped by their biography of experiences as well as their previous education, political and religious beliefs, gender, sexual preference, race, and/or class affiliations. So, your choice of a research topic, its conduct, and its results will be governed by your own beliefs about your understanding of what constitutes knowledge and knowing. Research paradigms can shape our thinking (and research) processes as they allow us to understand what kinds of knowledge are possible, and how we can ensure they are both adequate and legitimate (Maynard & Purvis, 1994). We shall explore research paradigms in greater detail in Chapter 2 of this text, as sport management research embraces a diverse array of practices driven by varying knowledge constituting assumptions.

Research brief

Title: Contemporary qualitative research methods in sport management
Authors: Hoeber, L., *University of Regina* & Shaw, S., *University of Otago* (2017)
Reference: Hoeber, L. & Shaw, S. (2017). Contemporary qualitative research methods in sport management. *Sport Management Review*, 20(1), 4–7.
Qualitative research methods in sport management scholarship are largely defined by a formulaic approach in which case studies, semi-structured interviews, and coding are often used. Alternative qualitative approaches, which may open up research to new audiences and research participants, and challenge assumptions about "good research", appear to be largely absent. This article considered contemporary qualitative research methods in sport management which include conceptual advances in community-based research approaches, Indigenous methodologies, participatory action research, autoethnographies, and narratives. In addition, the authors presented empirical papers that illustrated the use of autoethnography, narrative, digital ethnography, and phenomenology in the field.

SPORT MANAGEMENT RESEARCH METHODOLOGIES

Today, a growing number of sport managers are examining and exploring new methods for sport management research. Historically, positivistic, quantitative methodologies have served as the dominant approaches for research exploration in the field of sport management (Amis & Silk, 2005). There is a move towards a consideration of what these other methods can offer to sport management. Recently, an increasing number of scholars have acknowledged the need to consider and embrace alternative worldviews and eclectic methodological approaches to examine questions about the social world (Hoeber & Shaw, 2017).

This perhaps represents a departure from historical quantitative trends and a desire to seek deeper meaning and a greater understanding of the research issue under investigation. As a result of such critical analyses, it could be suggested that many of the longstanding beliefs and values pertaining to arguments of what makes scientific research are being challenged even more. At the core of these deliberations are perhaps deeply rooted philosophical questions such as what constitutes justifiable knowledge; in what ways is knowledge recognised and understood; and how is knowledge stored, distributed, and put into use (Stewart-Withers, Sewabu, & Richardson, 2017)? Likewise, questions about the generation of knowledge claims and specifically how people can go about producing value-free facts about the world have spurned further debate (Glesne, 2006). As Amis and Silk (2005) lamented: "too often our work in sport has been presented as neutral and value free, with little regard for the historical, social, political, and cultural context in which the work takes place" (p. 357).

Concerns have also long been expressed about the lack of domain diversity and limited range of topics being explored (Pitts, 2001; Slack, 1998). Wendy Frisby in her acceptance speech of the 2004 Earle F. Zeigler award challenged the sport management research community to embrace multiple research paradigms. Frisby (2005) wrote:

> The paradigm we operate from as researchers, whether it be positivism, pragmatism, interpretivism, critical social science, postmodernism or a combination of these paradigms, shape the questions we ask, the methods we use, and the degree to which our findings will have an impact on society. (p. 2)

Frisby (2005) while not making judgements concerning certain paradigms speaks of the importance in writing with paradigmatic lenses in mind. Although this can be a complex undertaking, it is the foundation of qualitative research. At the time, others supported Frisby's contentions (Amis & Silk, 2005; Skinner & Edwards, 2005) that the field of sport management tends to be overly focused on the same theories and paradigms (Quatman, 2006). Quatman, however, suggested that the rate at which these approaches were being embraced implied "a culture of guarded optimism at best toward these new approaches" (p. 14). As Amis and Silk (2005) articulated:

> There is little doubt that some related disciplines – such as education, cultural studies, leisure studies, and the sociology of sport – have progressed more rapidly than sport management in their acknowledgment of the value of different ideological, epistemological, and methodological approaches. (cited in Quatman, 2006, p. 14)

Quatman (2006) indicates that the 2005 special issue in the *Journal of Sport Management* reflected on the "constrained idea space (i.e. content and diversity of knowledge circulating) in the field and focused on 'expanding the horizons' of sport management research through critical and innovative approaches" (p. 2). The special edition raised hopes that future sport management research would lead to a range of counter-hegemonic approaches. By recognising, and in essence advocating for the alternative methods presented, Amis and Silk (2005) sought to "aid the power of those in the academy to apply research so that it impacts, and is meaningful to, the various communities that sport management has the potential to touch" (cited in Quatman, 2006, p. 2). There is a need to move beyond current research practices and embrace socially inclusive approaches to understanding the lived experiences of sport managers in order to promote a more inclusive culture for the generation of knowledge in the field. Despite these calls to embrace new paradigms, there remained considerable institutional pressure on sport management researchers to remain within a quantitative framework approach so as to maintain an aura of academic respectability.

We are however now seeing a significant use of *qualitative methods*. This has led to many sport management researchers embracing qualitative methods in sport management and acknowledge they can stand alongside and complement quantitative methods. This is important, since both qualitative and quantitative methods have value to the researcher and each can complement the other albeit with a different focus. While this is a welcomed shift, Hoeber and Shaw (2017) have argued that despite calls from a number of academics within sport management (Amis & Silk, 2005; Edwards & Skinner, 2009; Frisby, 2005; Skinner, Edwards, & Corbett, 2015) for a more diverse range of qualitative research approaches there is still a lack of variety in the current approaches (Shaw & Hoeber, 2016). Hoeber and Shaw suggested:

> We would like to see more use of methodological approaches such as critical race theory, post- colonial methodologies and critical management studies, that question and draw attention to dominant ideologies and practices within the sport industry. (p. 4)

They further suggest that methodologies like Participatory Action Research (PAR), Feminist Action Research (FAR), and community-based research take

Table 1.1	Different qualitative methods	

■ Action research	■ Interviews
■ Analytic induction	■ Life histories
■ Attributional coding	■ Matrices
■ Case studies	■ Metaphors
■ Cognitive mapping	■ Narratives
■ Conversation analysis	■ Participant observation
■ Co-research	■ Pictures (video etc.)
■ Critical analysis	■ Repertory grid
■ Critical incident technique	■ Search conferences
■ Diary studies	■ Soft systems analysis
■ Discourse analysis	■ Story analysis
■ Document analysis	■ Template analysis
■ Electronic interviews	■ Twenty Statements Test
■ Ethnomethodology	■ Tracer studies
■ Ethnography	■ Group methods
■ Grounded theory	■ Hermeneutics

some time to establish, develop, and coordinate, but have so much potential to positively affect communities beyond the academy (p. 4).

The aim of quantitative research grounded in positivism is to examine questions about cause and effect or to measure and evaluate. The assumptions of positivist research make it less suited to investigating the complexity of contemporary sport management. Qualitative methods can provide greater insights to study sport management in a holistic or critical sense. This is because there is a more natural fit between qualitative research, with its ability to delve into meaning, and the critical or interpretive ways of thinking which are concerned with the social construction of reality. Table 1.1 provides an overview of the range of different qualitative research methods available to the sport management researcher.

The central interest of this book is in qualitative research, including not only qualitative methodologies and methods but also qualitative thinking. We present below some of the tenets of qualitative thinking and research, acknowledging that they are primarily associated with the assumptions of an interpretive orientation. After this, we outline some of the differences with quantitative research, noting how qualitative and quantitative sit on an interactive continuum of thinking about research in sport management.

Research brief

Title: Changing methods and methods of change: Reflections on qualitative research in sport for development and peace
Authors: Darnell, S.C., *University of Toronto*, Whitley, M.A., *Adelphi University*, & Massey, W.V., *University Wisconsin* (2016)
Reference: Darnell, S.C., Whitley, M.A., & Massey, W.V. (2016). Changing methods and methods of change: Reflections on qualitative research in sport for development and peace. *Qualitative Research in Sport, Exercise and Health, 8* (5), 571–577.
This collection of papers consisted of diverse, contemporary, and thought-provoking examples of qualitative methods in the study of Sport for Development and Peace (SDP). In this conclusion, the authors reflected on some of the key themes that cut across the contributions. Four main topics were discussed: Interpretation (the subjects and voices at the centre of SDP research), Outcomes (the variety of results that are likely to emerge from SDP research), Creativity and Diversity (the need for SDP research that is novel, nuanced, and sometimes messy), and Hope (the productive tension between critique and optimism in SDP research). Through this deliberation, the authors advocated for an ongoing and even renewed commitment to the qualitative study of SDP, one that moves beyond the rather strict confines of Monitoring and Evaluation, and embraces the full range of social and political implications that emerge from the activities of SDP.

A QUALITATIVE APPROACH TO SPORT MANAGEMENT RESEARCH

Qualitative research is difficult to define clearly. It has no theory or paradigm that is distinctively its own. Nor does qualitative research have a distinct set of methods or practices that are entirely its own (Denzin & Lincoln, 2011). Qualitative methods aim to answer questions about the **"what"**, **"how"**, or **"why"** of a phenomenon rather than **"how many"** or **"how much"**, which are answered by quantitative methods. Saldana (2015) suggests quantitative analysis calculates a *mean*. Qualitative analysis calculates *meaning*. Table 1.2 outlines the differences between qualitative and quantitative approaches.

WHY QUALITATIVE RESEARCH?

There are probably two main inter-related answers to this question. The first is that qualitative research can be valuable for studying *meaning*: what is important to people based on their knowledge and experience and why, since meaning influences social interactions on an individual and collective level. In studying meaning, qualitative research is humanistic because it focuses on the personal, subjective, and experiential basis of knowledge and practice. It is also holistic because it seeks to situate the meaning of particular behaviours and ways of thinking about or doing things in a given context (Kielmann, Cataldo, & Seeley, 2012). The second answer is that the interpretive and *reflexive* approach that qualitative research takes can reveal what is important about *processes*: of

Table 1.2	Qualitative versus quantitative research	
Criteria	**Qualitative research**	**Quantitative research**
Purpose	To understand and interpret social interactions	To test hypotheses, look at cause and effect, and make predictions
Definitions	A systematic subjective approach used to describe life experiences and give them meaning	A formal, objective, systematic process for obtaining information about the world. A method used to describe, test relationships, and examine cause and effect relationships
Research questions	■ What? ■ How? ■ Why?	■ How much? ■ How many? ■ Is there a statistical difference between…? ■ Is there a correlation? ■ Which are the strongest predictors of…?
Group studied	Smaller and not randomly selected	Larger and randomly selected
Type of research	Exploratory	Descriptive or causal
Approach	■ Holistic ■ Study design can be flexible, allowing exploration of ideas which emerge during the study ■ Understanding of a phenomenon from the subject's perspective ■ Focus on subjective meaning, understanding, and process	■ Reductionist ■ Study design is predetermined ■ Understanding of a phenomenon from the researcher's perspective ■ Focus on objective measurement
Characteristics	■ Soft science ■ Focus: complex and broad ■ Subjective ■ Dialectic, inductive reasoning ■ Develops theory ■ Uniqueness	■ Hard science ■ Focus: concise and narrow ■ Objective ■ Logistic, deductive reasoning ■ Tests theory ■ Generalisation
Variables	Study of the whole, not variables	Specific variables studied
Research instrument	The primary research instrument is the researcher	Validated instrument, measure, rating scale or questionnaire

(Continued)

Table 1.2	Qualitative versus quantitative research *(Continued)*	
Criteria	**Qualitative research**	**Quantitative research**
Sampling	■ Purposeful or theoretical sampling ■ Reflects the population's diversity ■ Flexible enough to be propelled by emerging theory ■ In the ideal case the size of the sample is determined by data saturation	■ Random or probability sampling ■ Representative of population ■ Predetermined by power calculations
Type of data collected	Textual – Words, images, or objects	Numerical – Numbers and statistics
Form of data collected	Qualitative data such as open-ended responses, interviews, participant observations, field notes, and reflections	Quantitative data based on precise measurements using structured and validated data-collection instruments
Reliability and validity	Reliability and validity determined through multiple sources of information	Reliability and validity determined through statistical and logical methods
Type of data analysis	■ Non-statistical analysis ■ Themes are the units of analysis ■ Analysis and data collection can be undertaken concurrently	■ Statistical analysis ■ Variables are the units of analysis ■ Analysis after collection of data
Objectivity and subjectivity	Subjectivity is expected	Objectivity is critical
Role of researcher	Researcher and their biases may be known to participants in the study, and participant characteristics may be known to the researcher	Researcher and their biases are not known to participants in the study, and participant characteristics are deliberately hidden from the researcher (double blind studies)
Results	Particular or specialised findings that is less generalisable	Generalisable findings that can be applied to other populations
Scientific method	Exploratory or bottom-up: the researcher generates a new hypothesis and theory from the data collected	Confirmatory or top-down: the researcher tests the hypothesis and theory with the data
View of human behaviour	Dynamic, situational, social, and personal	Regular and predictable

Table 1.2	Qualitative versus quantitative research *(Continued)*	
Criteria	**Qualitative research**	**Quantitative research**
Most common research objectives	Explore, discover, and construct	Describe, explain, and predict.
Focus	Wide-angle lens: examines the breadth and depth of phenomena.	Narrow-angle lens: tests a specific hypotheses
Nature of observation	Study behaviour in a natural environment	Study behaviour under controlled conditions; isolate causal effects
Nature of reality	Multiple realities: subjective	Single reality: objective
Final report	Narrative report with contextual description and direct quotations from research participant	Statistical report with correlations, comparisons of means, and statistical significance of findings
Quality/rigour	Trustworthiness, authenticity Validity	Internal/external validity, reliability Generalisability

Source: Adapted from Holloway and Wheeler (2010); Johnson and Christensen (2008) Lichtman (2006).

social behaviour, interventions and research methods themselves. According to an interpretive approach, the aim of qualitative research is to explain (e.g. an intervention's apparent success, or otherwise) rather than to merely describe (Kielmann et al., 2012). Further, by adopting a reflexive position to research as a social interaction, qualitative researchers are explicit about highlighting the interconnection between the nature of enquiry (e.g. how a survey question is asked) and the conclusions that are drawn, especially when the outcomes can only be understood through reference to that process (Walker & Dewar, 2000).

Lindlof and Taylor (2002) write that the questions which animate qualitative enquiry are: what's going on here? What is the communicative action that is being performed? How do they do it? What does it mean to them? How do they interpret what it means to others? How do we interpret and document how they act, what they tell us about what they know, and how they justify their actions? What is the relation of us to them, of self to other?

Eisner (1991) and Patton (1990) identified what they considered to be the ten prominent characteristics of qualitative or naturalistic research. The list that follows represents a synthesis of these authors' descriptions of qualitative research:

1. Qualitative research uses the natural setting as the source of data. The researcher attempts to observe, describe, and interpret settings as they are maintaining what Patton (1990) calls an "empathic neutrality" (p. 55).

2. The researcher acts as the "human instrument" of data collection.

3. Qualitative researchers predominantly use inductive data analysis.

4. Qualitative research reports are descriptive, incorporating expressive language, and the "presence of voice in the text" (Eisner, 1991, p. 36).

5. Qualitative research has an interpretive character, aimed at discovering the meaning events have for the individuals who experience them, and the interpretations of those meanings by the researcher.

6. Qualitative researchers pay attention to the idiosyncratic as well as the pervasive, seeking the uniqueness of each case.

7. Qualitative research has an emergent (as opposed to predetermined) design, and researchers focus on this emerging process as well as the outcomes or product of the research.

8. Qualitative research is judged using special criteria for trustworthiness (these will be discussed in some detail in a later section).

9. Typically, the findings are in the form of themes, categories, concepts, or tentative hypotheses or theories.

10. The researcher is an integral part of the research process. The issue is not one of minimising the influence of the researcher, but of knowing how the researcher was involved in data collection and analysis in order to assess better the information they provide.

WHAT ARE THE CRITICISMS OF QUALITATIVE RESEARCH?

Despite its strengths, qualitative enquiry is not without its limitations, many of which are noted through the course of this book. We would argue that qualitative research methods have much to offer sport management research, however, as with any research approach, there are *strengths and weaknesses*. These should be carefully and systematically weighed up and assessed by the researcher before any firm decision is made. The methodology selected needs to be fitted to the aims and objectives of the research proposed. Table 1.3 outlines some of these *strengths and weaknesses*.

THE ROLE OF THE SPORT MANAGEMENT RESEARCHER IN QUALITATIVE INQUIRY

Denzin and Lincoln (2008) define qualitative researchers as people who usually work in the "real" world of lived experience, often in a natural setting, rather than a laboratory based experimental approach. The qualitative researcher tries

Table 1.3	Strengths and weaknesses of qualitative research

Strengths	Weaknesses
■ Open-ended questioning reveals new or unanticipated phenomenon, and raises more issues through broad and open-ended inquiry.	■ Difficult to demonstrate the scientific rigor of the data collection exercise.
■ Includes a diverse and representative cross-section of affected persons.	■ It is generally open-ended; the participants have more control over the content of the data collected.
■ It is in-depth analysis of the impact of an emergency.	■ It does not have a preconceived, finite set of issues to examine.
■ It is rich and detailed information about affected populations.	■ Results in data are not objectively verifiable.
■ It allows researchers to explore the views of homogenous as well as diverse groups of people help unpack these differing perspectives within a community.	■ Collection of the data can be time consuming and costly. Therefore, the time required for data collection, analysis, and interpretation is lengthy.
■ As statistics are not used in it, and uses a more descriptive, narrative style, and gains new insight.	■ It needs skilled interviewers to successfully carry out the primary data collection activities.
■ It can play the important role of suggesting possible relationships, causes, effects, and dynamic processes.	■ It requires a labour intensive analysis process, such as, categorisation, recoding, etc.
■ It allows people to open up and allows for new evidence that was not even initially considered.	■ The important issue could be overlooked and go unnoticed.
■ It provides a rich picture of social phenomena and in its specific contexts reveals critical incidents.	■ Low levels of standardisation; and definitions/criteria, etc., vary from researcher to researcher.
■ It provides a holistic interpretation of the detailed processes that have, and shapes people's lives.	■ Contexts, situations, events, conditions, and interactions cannot be replicated to any extent, nor can generalisations be made to a wider context than the one studied with any confidence.
■ Its cultural assessment is the ability to probe for underlying values, beliefs, and assumptions.	■ The viewpoints of both researcher and participants have to be identified and elucidated because of issues of bias.
■ It provides insights into intra-household relations and processes.	■ All researchers' interpretations are limited and positioned subjects; personal experience and knowledge influence the observations and conclusions.
■ It offers deeper insights into causes and direction of causal processes.	■ It needs skilled interviewers to successfully carry out the primary data collection activities.
■ It permits researchers to access data on difficult issues, e.g. domestic violence.	■ Completion of research is often dependents on a single individual.
■ The data collection process requires limited numbers of respondents, which can be carried out with limited resources.	

(*Continued*)

Table 1.3	Strengths and weaknesses of qualitative research (*Continued*)
Strengths	**Weaknesses**
■ Data on marginal groups that surveys often cannot locate can be collected, e.g. illegal migrants, the homeless, child-headed households.	■ Often results cannot be generalised as it is unclear, whom they represent.
■ Because of close researcher involvement, the researcher gains an insider's view of the field, which allows the researcher to find issues that are often missed by the scientific, more positivistic enquiries.	■ Findings less likely to influence policy as they lack the legitimacy of science, and the precision of numbers.
■ It encourages creativity and innovative explanatory frameworks.	■ Datasets are rarely made publicly available so that findings cannot be tested, and other researchers cannot use the dataset.
■ Data analyst is usually heavily involved in data collection and knows its strengths.	■ Because of the subjective nature of qualitative data and its origin in single contexts, it is difficult to apply conventional standards of reliability and validity.
■ Participatory methodologies empower, rather than objectify respondents.	■ No objectively verifiable results obtained.
■ It adds flesh and blood to social analysis.	

Source: Adapted from Bowen (2006); Creswell (2014); Yauch & Steudel (2003).

to make sense of social phenomena and the meanings people bring to them. In qualitative research, it is acknowledged that the researcher is an integral part of the process and who may reflect on their own influence and experience in the research process. The qualitative researcher accepts that they are not "neutral". Instead they themselves in the position of the participant or "subject" and attempt to understand how the world is from that person's perspective. As this process is re-iterated, hypotheses begin to emerge, which are "tested" against the data of further experiences e.g. people's narratives. One of the key differences between quantitative and qualitative approaches is apparent here: the quantitative approach states the hypothesis from the outset, (i.e. a "top down" approach), whereas in qualitative research the hypothesis or research question, is refined and developed during the process. This may be thought of as a "bottom-up" or emergent approach.

Before conducting a qualitative study, it is recommended that a sport management researcher does *three* things: First, they must adopt the stance suggested by the characteristics of the naturalist paradigm. Second, the researcher must develop the level of skill appropriate for a human instrument, or the vehicle through which data will be collected and interpreted. Finally, the researcher must prepare a research design that uses accepted strategies for naturalistic inquiry (Lincoln & Guba, 1985).

Glaser and Strauss (1967) and Strauss and Corbin (1990) refer to what they call the *"theoretical sensitivity"* of the researcher. Theoretical sensitivity refers to a personal quality of the researcher. It indicates an awareness of the subtleties of meaning of data. It refers to the attribute of having insight, the ability to give meaning to data, the capacity to understand, and capability to separate the pertinent from that which isn't (Strauss & Corbin, 1990, p. 42). Strauss and Corbin believe that theoretical sensitivity comes from a number of sources, including professional literature, professional experiences, and personal experiences. The credibility of a qualitative research report relies heavily on the confidence readers have in the researcher's ability to be sensitive to the data and to make appropriate decisions in the field (Eisner, 1991; Patton, 1990). Lincoln and Guba (1985) identified the characteristics that make humans the "instrument of choice" for naturalistic inquiry. Humans are responsive to environmental cues, and are able to interact with the situation; they have the ability to collect information at multiple levels simultaneously; they are able to perceive situations holistically; they are able to process data as soon as they become available; they can provide immediate feedback and request verification of data; and they can explore atypical or unexpected responses.

THE MIXED METHOD APPROACH TO SPORT MANAGEMENT RESEARCH

The emergence of mixed methods design was a recognition of how the positivist and interpretative paradigms could be used together. In following a mixed method approach the sport management researcher collects both quantitative data (quantifiable data) as well as qualitative data (images, interviews, stories). This is not simply a process of collecting two distinct types of data – quantitative and qualitative. The research method integrates, links or embeds both strands. The strength of this design is that it combines the advantages of each form of data – that is, quantitative data provides for generalisability whereas the qualitative data offers information about the context or setting. This design enables a sport management researcher to gather information that uses the best features of both quantitative and qualitative data collection (Skinner et al., 2015).

One form of mixed method design that can be successfully utilised by the sport management researcher is *triangulation mixed methods*. In a *triangulation* study the researcher gathers both quantitative and qualitative data, analyses both datasets separately, compares the results from the analysis of both datasets, and makes an interpretation as to whether the results support or contradict each other. The direct comparison of the two data sets by the researcher provides a more reliable perspective on the problem being studied: a "triangulation" of data sources. The strength of this design is that it combines the advantages of each form of data – i.e. quantitative data provides for generalisability, whereas the qualitative data offers information about the context or setting. This design enables a researcher to gather information that uses the best features of both quantitative and qualitative data collection. It can be difficult, however, to transform one form of data into the other form in order to integrate and compare data. Additionally, even if integration of the data is possible, inconsistent results may emerge, making it necessary to collect additional data or revisit the collected databases to reconcile the differences.

Research brief

Title: Using a mixed method audit to inform organizational stress management interventions in sport

Authors: Rumbold, J.L., *Sheffield Hallam University*, Fletcher, D., *Loughborough University*, & Daniels, K., *University of East Anglia* (2018)

Reference: Rumbold, J.L., Fletcher, D., & Daniels, K. (2018). Using a mixed method audit to inform organizational stress management interventions in sport. *Psychology of Sport and Exercise, 35,* 27–38.

The purposes of this study were twofold: to conduct a mixed method organisational-level stress audit within a sport organisation and to explore recommendations for organisational stress management. Semi-structured interviews, focus groups, and surveys were conducted with 47 participants (professional sportsmen, coaches, sport science support, and administrative staff) who represented a professional sport organisation. In addition, content analysis was employed to analyse the data. The findings indicated a wide range of organisational stressors (e.g. cultural and academy issues), appraisals, and coping behaviours (e.g. emotion-focused behaviours), and stressor outcomes (e.g. emotional responses) for sport performers.

CONCLUSION

This book represents a departure from historical quantitative trends and a desire to seek deeper meaning and a greater understanding of the research issue under investigation. Despite the qualitative focus of the book we advocate that there is no one best research approach: quantitative, qualitative, or mixed methods approaches all have a place in sport management research. It is vital that sport management researchers use designs that are the most applicable to their research and legitimises the distinctiveness of sport management research perspectives and agendas. Sport management research can be considered a convergence of disciplines that include management, philosophy, economics, marketing, politics, governance, and policy. As such, to explore the complex nature of the different specialisations associated with sport management the application of innovative qualitative research methodologies are essential. In endeavouring to emulate rigorous standards of research sport management researchers should take methodological "risks" and embrace more eclectic qualitative research approaches. Expanding the scope of a method (its associated concepts and practices) within a sport management context can respond to the changing concerns of the sport management discipline, raise new research questions, enhance a method's contribution, and be a step toward further methodological innovation (Chang, 2017).

New methods or research approaches can solve controversial issues and facilitate the development of new theories (Greenwald 2012). Sport management researchers should take advantage of innovative qualitative approaches from other fields to explore emerging phenomena or innovatively advance scholarly sport management research approaches. For example, technology, globalisation, and commercialisation may be the principal trends, however they are not the only trends in sport. Sport management researchers have the opportunity to study other trends, including the modernisation of sport organisations, changing governance practices, regulatory changes, innovation, merchandising, socio demographic influences (i.e. aging populations, change in employment patterns, increasing diversity), sport for development, physical activity, and sport participation changes. As such, the use of innovative qualitative methods discussed in this book should be central to the sport management discipline. Without new methodological insights sport management researchers may only use those research approaches they are comfortable with or have been trained to do. This limits the scope of their exploration, as well as the development of sport management research. Most importantly, qualitative method innovation requires developing a good command of multiple methods and for the future a close collaboration among researchers in different disciplinary fields (Faber, 2015). As sport continues to expand across the globe sport management researchers will need to equip themselves with multiple research skills and innovative methodologies to address the research problems of a fluid and dynamic sporting terrain. We present these methodological approaches and techniques in the following chapters.

STRUCTURE OF THE BOOK

In Chapter 2 – "Research Paradigms and Methodology in Qualitative Sport Management Research" – of Part 1, we explain the philosophical underpinnings, history and traditions of qualitative research. We argue that sport management researchers need to look carefully at the claims of others, judging for themselves whether they are convincing. To do that, they need to understand the process by which other researchers have come to their conclusions, and this means understanding both their methodologies and the intellectual frameworks within which they have operated. In Part 2, Chapter 3 – "Sampling in Qualitative Research" – we explore the sampling options available to sport management researchers, their relationship to sample size, and the criticism of sampling practices used in qualitative research. Chapter 4 – "Establishing Reliability and Validity in Qualitative Inquiry" – clarifies the meaning and use of reliability and validity in the qualitative research paradigm and how it is applied. Chapter 5 – "Reflexivity in Sport Management Research" – discusses the various interpretations of reflexivity and outline its application to sport management research. In Chapter 6 – "Research Ethics for Qualitative Sport

Management Research" – we examine the common ethical concerns that qualitative sport management researchers confront and highlight the ethical principles that can guide research and researchers. Part 3 of the book addresses the Foundations of sport management research. To do this, Chapter 7 – "Methods of Data Collection for Sport Management Research" – discusses how the sport management researcher should approach fieldwork and the need to use a range of data collection techniques. Part 4 of the book, Chapter 8 – "Modes of Analysis in Sport Management Research" – discusses qualitative data analysis discusses in sport management research. It notes that the purpose of qualitative data analysis is to make sense of the data so that evidence can be obtained to answer the research question.

Part 5 of the book presents an analysis and discussion of "Paradigms Used in Sport Management Research." Chapter 9 – "Action Research in Sport Management Research" – commences this section and explores the various methodologies of Action Research, particularly Emancipatory and PAR, both of which have features that make them applicable to the field of sport management research. Chapter 10 – "Deconstruction in Sport Management Research" – examines deconstruction as a way of understanding and critiquing sport management theory and practice. Chapter 11 – "Case Study in Sport Management Research" – maps the value of case study in sport management research. In particular, it deals with the paradigmatic aspects of case study as a research strategy. Chapter 12 – "Discourse and Critical Discourse in Sport Management Research" – explores the methodology of discourse, discourse analysis and critical discourse analysis, and their possible applications to the field of sport management research. Chapter 13 – "Ethnomethodology and Sport Management Research" – examines some of the basic tenets of ethnomethodology and how these can be applied to the field of sport management research in useful and practical ways that can facilitate the development of practices that enhance sport management education. Chapter 14 – "Ethnography and Sport Management Research" – provides an introduction and overview to the concepts of ethnography, and provides some examples of critical and postmodern frameworks that ethnographic researchers can use in the sport management research. Chapter 15 – "Emerging Ethnographies and Sport Management Research" – highlight some emerging ethnographical methodologies and demonstrates how they can be situated in the sport management research field. "Gender Theories and Sport Management Research" is the focus of Chapter 16. This chapter explores gender research methodologies and their application in sport management research. Chapter 17 – "Grounded Theory and Sport Management Research" – examines the debates surrounding the application of grounded theory to research and identifies and discusses the principles that underpin grounded theory approaches to research in sport management settings. Chapter 18 – "Narrative Inquiry in Sport Management Research" – reviews the qualitative research methods of "narrative", "story", and "voice", and highlights how they can provide rich descriptions of the sport management environment and at the same time provide an alternative research approach. Chapter 19 – "Phenomenology and Sport Management Research" – identifies that phenomenology offers researchers a different perspective, while providing the opportunity to explore previously unchartered waters, as it aims to investigate and comprehend the lived experience of its participants. Chapter 20 – "New Directions for Sport Management Research" – charts the new directions that are evolving in sport management research and demonstrates how they can be situated in the sport management research field.

Part 6 of the book, "Digital Tools for Qualitative Research," provides deep insight into the digital age of qualitative research and how to utilise these platforms for research. Chapter 21 – "Social Media Research Methods in Sport Management" – explores the opportunities and barriers associated with social media research, paying particular attention to the features that differentiate it from traditional qualitative methods. Part 7 of the book presents the final chapter. Chapter 22 – "Research Preparation and the Sport Management Research Report" – identifies that from the initial idea that sparks the sport management researcher's interest, the sport management researcher must carefully review and plan each step of the research journey. It provides insight into the format used in writing a research report and seeks to guide the researcher in writing up a report in a systematic way.

REFERENCES

Amis, J., & Silk, M. (2005). Rupture: Promoting critical and innovative approaches to the study of sport management. *Journal of Sport Management, 19,* 355–366.

Bowen, G.A. (2006). Grounded theory and sensitizing concepts, *International Journal of Qualitative Methods, 5*(3), 12–23.

Creswell, J. W. (2014). *Qualitative Inquiry & Research Design: Choosing among Five Approaches (4th Ed.).* Thousand Oaks, California: Sage Publications.

Denzin, N. K., & Lincoln Y. S. (Eds.). (1994). Introduction: The discipline and practice of qualitative research. In Norman Denzin & Yvonna Lincoln (Eds), pp 1–21. *Handbook of qualitative research.* (1st Ed): Thousand Oaks, California: Sage Publications.

Chang, C. (2017). Methodological issues in advertising research: Current status, shifts, and trends. *Journal of Advertising, 46*(1), 2–20.

Denzin, N. K., & Lincoln, Y. S. (Eds.) (2008). *The landscape of qualitative research* (3rd ed.). London: Sage Publications.

Denzin, N. K., & Lincoln, Y. S. (Eds.) (2011). *Handbook of qualitative research* (5th ed.). Thousand Oaks, CA: Sage Publications.

Edwards, A., & Skinner, J. (2009). *Qualitative research in sport management.* Oxford: Elsevier.

Eisner, E. W. (1991). *The enlightened eye: Qualitative inquiry and the enhancement of educational practice.* New York, NY: Macmillan Publishing Company.

Faber, R. J. (2015). Peeking under the curtain and over the horizon: The reflections of another former editor. *Journal of Advertising, 44*(3), 289–295.

Frisby, W. (2005). The good, the bad, and the ugly: Critical sport management research. *Journal of Sport Management, 19*(1), 1–12.

Glaser, B. G., & Strauss, A. (1967). *The discovery of grounded theory: Strategies for qualitative research.* New York, NY: Aldine De Groyter.

Glesne, C. (2006). *Becoming qualitative researchers: An introduction.* Boston: Pearson, Allyn, & Bacon.

Greenwald, A. G. (2012). There is nothing so theoretical as a good method. *Perspectives on Psychological Science, 7*(2), 99–108.

Hoeber, L., & Shaw, S. (2017). Contemporary qualitative research methods in sport management. *Sport Management Review, 20,* 4–7.

Holloway I, Wheeler S (2010) *Qualitative research in nursing and healthcare.* UK: Wiley-Blackwell.

Johnson, R. B., & Christensen, L. B. (2008). *Educational research: Quantitative, qualitative, and mixed approaches* (3rd ed). Boston, MA: Allyn & Bacon.

Kielmann, K., Cataldo, F., & Seeley, J. (2012). *Introduction to Qualitative Research Methodology: A Training Manual.* Produced with the support of the Department for International Development (DfID), UK.

Kuhn, T. S. (1962). *The structure of scientific revolutions.* Chicago: University of Chicago Press.

Lichtman, M. (2006). *Qualitative Research in Education: A User's Guide.* Thousand Oaks, California: Sage Publications.

Lincoln, Y. S., & Guba, E. G. (1985). *Naturalistic inquiry.* Beverly Hills, CA: Sage.

Lindlof, T. R., & Taylor, B. C. (2002). *Qualitative communication research methods* (2nd ed.). Thousand Oaks, CA: Sage.

Manheim, J. B., & Rich, R. C. (1995). *Empirical political analysis: Research methods in political science.* White Plains, N.Y: Longman.

Maynard, M., & Purvis, J. (1994). *Methods, practice and epistemology: The debate about feminism and research.* New York: Taylor & Francis.

Patton, M. Q. (1990). *Qualitative evaluation and research methods.* London: Sage Publications.

Patton, M. Q. (2002). *Qualitative evaluation and research methods,* (3rd ed). Newbury Park, CA: Sage Publications.

Pitts, B. G. (2001). Sport management at the millennium: A defining moment. *Journal of Sport Management, 15,* 1–9.

Quatman, C. (2006). *The Social Construction of Knowledge in the Field of Sport Management: A Social Network Perspective.* Unpublished doctoral dissertation, The Ohio State University, Columbus.

Saldana, J. (2015). *The coding manual for qualitative researchers.* Thousand Oaks, California: Sage Publications.

Sharp, R., & Green, A. (1975). *Education and social control.* London: Routledge & Kegan Paul.

Shaw, S., & Hoeber, L. (2016). Unclipping our wings: Ways forward in qualitative research in sport management. *Sport Management Review, 19,* 255–265.

Skinner, J., & Edwards, A. (2005). Inventive pathways: Fresh visions of sport management research. *Journal of Sport Management, 19,* 404–421.

Skinner, J., Edwards, A., & Corbett, B. (2015). *Research methods for sport management.* Oxford: Routledge.

Slack, T. S. (1998). Is there anything unique about sport management? *European Journal for Sport Management, 5,* 21–29.

Smith, B., & Sparkes, A.C. (2016). *Routledge handbook of qualitative research in sport and exercise.* New York: Routledge.

Smith, A., & Stewart, B. (2010). The special features of sport revisited. *Sport Management Review, 10*(1), 1–11.

Stewart-Withers, R., Sewabu, K., & Richardson, S. (2017). Talanoa: A contemporary qualitative approach for sport management. *Sport Management Review, 20*(1), 55–68.

Strauss, A., & Corbin, J. (1990). *Basics of qualitative research: Grounded theory procedures and techniques*. London: Sage.

Thomas, J. R., Nelson, J. K., & Silverman, S. J. (2005). *Research methods in physical activity*. Champaign, IL: Human Kinetics.

van Manen, M. (1997). *Researching lived experience* (2nd ed.). London: The Althouse Press.

Walker, E., & Dewar, B. J. (2000). Moving on from interpretivism: An argument for constructivist evaluation. *Journal of Advanced Nursing, 32*(3), 713–720.

Woods, P., & Hammersley, M. (1977). *School experience*. London: Croom Hel.

Yauch, C.A., & Steudel, H.J. (2003). Complementary Use of Qualitative and Quantitative Cultural Assessment Methods. *Organizational Research Methods, 6*(4), 465–481.

CHAPTER 2

Research paradigms and methodology in qualitative sport management research

LEARNING OUTCOMES

By the end of this chapter you should be able to:

- Explain the assumptions about the nature of knowledge and reality that underlie research paradigms.

- Describe the research paradigms the sport management researcher can draw on to frame their research.

- Comment on how the sport management research process can be shaped by applying different theoretical perspectives.

KEY TERMS

1. **Positivism:** a theoretical perspective based on notions of impartiality and objectivity and assumptions that the researcher can remain separate from, and not influence, the research field.

2. **Constructivism:** a construction of the human mind shaped by experiences of the world.

3. **Crisis of representation:** how to locate the sport management researcher and their subjects in reflective texts.

4. **Structuralism:** decisive shaping factors in structural forms discoverable within society or the unconscious, or both.

5. **Post-structuralism:** challenges the very idea of structure, including the idea of a centre, a fixed principle, a hierarchy of meaning and a solid foundation.

6. **Ontology:** refers to how one sees the world and the nature of one's reality.

7. **Epistemology:** what is the relationship between the enquirer and knowledge?

8. **Paradigm:** is a set of prepositions that explain how the world is perceived, and it contains a worldview, a way of breaking down the complexity of the real world, telling researchers and social scientists in general what is important, what is legitimate, and what is reasonable.

KEY THEMES

1. How has qualitative research been shaped by differing theoretical perspectives?

2. How are Ontology, Epistemology, and Methodology related to the sport management research process?

3. How does who we are influence the research process?

CHAPTER OVERVIEW

In this chapter, we begin with a brief introduction of the philosophical under-pinnings, history, and traditions of qualitative research. This is not intended as a comprehensive account but rather to highlight some key issues for the sport management researcher. Sport management researchers spend a great deal of time evaluating other people's research, deciding what the strengths and weaknesses are in each case, and hoping to apply their conclusions to their own reading and to the procedures they follow in their research. In this chapter, we recognise that sport management researchers' own value systems inevitably come into play. We also argue that sport management researchers therefore need to look carefully at the claims of others, judging for themselves whether they are convincing. To do that, they need to understand the process by which other researchers have come to their conclusions, and this means understanding both their methodologies and the intellectual frameworks within which they have operated.

INTRODUCTION

To begin, it is useful to sketch of brief history of qualitative research in the human disciplines. Denzin and Lincoln (2000) do this by identifying *seven* moments: the first one is the *traditional period* (1900–1950), which represents a time when qualitative researchers were firmly entrenched within the positivist paradigm. Accounts from these researchers were bound within the language and objectives of this paradigm. Denzin and Lincoln associate the traditional period with discussions of the scientific principles of objective ethnography espoused by researchers such as Malinowksi, as well as the urban ethnography practiced by the Chicago School. The second moment, known as *"the modernist"* or the *"golden age"* (1950–1970), is associated with the formalisation of qualitative methods as a rigorous equal to its quantitative counterpart. Researchers within this period were still heavily engaged with the language of positivism that is also known as post-positivism. The gradual necessity for a "bilingual" diction-ary of methodologies emerged with the onset of what Denzin and Lincoln call the "*blurred genres*" (1970–1986). Here the approaches of the human disciplines were slowly opening-up to a more pluralistic, interpretative, and open-ended perspective. It was during this time period that the privileged voice of the observer and his/her interpretations were challenged. The next period, the "*crisis of representation*" (1986–1990) involved research that called into question the issues of class, race and gender, and notion of the reflexivity. Books such as *Writing Culture* (Clifford, 1986), *Works and Lives* (Geertz, 1988), and *The Predicament of Culture* (Clifford, 1988) critiqued the premise of the "objective" ethnography, and accordingly new methods, models of truth, and representation were sought. It was during this period that "issues such as validity, reliability, and objectivity, previously believed settled, were once more problematic" (Denzin & Lincoln, 2000, p. 26). The *post-modern period* (1990–1995) is characterised by experimental and new ethnographies, which give rise to different ways of knowledge and also gives space to other voices. Denzin and Lincoln make reference to Ellis and Bochner's (1996) work *Composing Ethnography: Alternative Forms of Qualitative Writing* to highlight the triple crisis of representation, legitimation, and praxis that researchers were grappling with. Denzin and Lincoln discuss the "*post-experimental stage*" (1995–2000); and, the last stage, "*the future*" (2000–present) together. The authors present a time period where fictional ethnographies, ethnographic poetry, and multimedia texts are taken for granted. It is in the present, the authors argue, that the post-experimental writer seeks to "connect their writings to the needs of a free democratic society. The demands of a moral and sacred qualitative social science are actively being explored by a host of new writers from many different disciplines" (Denzin & Lincoln, 2000, p. 29). A summary of these seven moments is provided in Table 2.1.

The attempt to map qualitative research methods and situate them within historical moments is a useful tool when analysing the various epistemologies that have developed over time, which in turn have impacted on research

Table 2.1	Seven moments of qualitative research
Seven moments of qualitative research	
The Traditional Period (1900–1950)	
The Modernist or Golden Age (1950–1970)	
Blurred Genres (1970–1986)	
The Crisis of Representation (1986–1990)	
The Post-Modern: A Period of Experimental and New Ethnographies (1990–1995)	
Post- Experimental Inquiry (1995–2000)	
The Future (2000–Present)	

methodologies. Denzin and Lincoln's (2000) framework provides details of the different major directions that qualitative methodology debates have witnessed. Accordingly, the framework can readily be applied to sport management, especially when considering how the social sciences have seen a gradual reorganisation of information flows within the global community of the human disciplines (Alasuutari, 2004).

This evolution of qualitative research suggests that the social world could be explored in different ways. The concept of a *paradigm* suggests that there is no single, accepted way of carrying out qualitative research. The discussion suggests that how researchers proceed depends upon a range of factors, including how one sees the world and the nature of one's reality (*ontology*), the relationship between the inquirer and knowledge (*epistemology*), and what technique can be used to measure the perceived reality (*methodology*). Differences in the mix of these factors have led to numerous variations in approaches to qualitative research. Some writers argue that different methodological approaches are underpinned by particular philosophical or theoretical assumptions and that researchers should maintain consistency between their philosophical starting point and the methods they adopt. Indeed, maintaining consistency is seen as one way of producing more "valid" findings (Morse, Barrett, Mayan, Olson, & Spiers, 2002). In contrast, others believe that each method associated with a range of philosophical positions has something to offer. Thus, they argue that better-quality work is produced if a range of approaches and methods are considered, and choices made according to the aims and context of the research (Patton, 2002; Seale, Silverman, Gobo, & Gubrium, 2007). Either way there is general agreement that an understanding of the background from which different methods originate will contribute to better research practice.

A useful starting point in examining research philosophies is the consideration of research questions. It is a fundamental axiom of "good" research that the methods chosen to use in a study should be driven by, and appropriate to, the research question/s (Abernethy, Chua, Luckett, & Selto, 1999). However, specific research questions and the research method/s used in answering those questions presume a particular methodological perspective. Methodology, in turn, reflects an underlying philosophy comprising an ontological view and associated epistemological assumptions. Thus, the most fundamental consideration in posing and answering research questions is the researcher's philosophical or meta-theoretical position.

PARADIGM DEFINITION

The concept of *paradigm* has been strongly associated with Thomas Kuhn who through his own enquiring activity began to question how "the practice of astronomy, physics, chemistry, or biology normally failed to evoke the controversies over fundamentals that today often seem endemic among, say, psychologists or sociologists" (Kuhn, 1962, p. 9). Kuhn coined the word *paradigm* as a framework to assist in the true understanding of past research enquiry, emerging practices, and as a means of identifying "models from which spring particular coherent traditions of scientific research" (Kuhn, 1962, p. 10). He defined a paradigm as, "a set of values and techniques which is shared by members of a scientific community, which acts as a guide or map, dictating the kinds of problems scientists should address and the types of explanations that are acceptable to them" (Kuhn, 1970, p. 175). Other researchers have joined the paradigm discussion. Senge (1990) called paradigms mental models and describes them as: "deeply ingrained assumptions and generalisations that influence how people see the world and behave" (p. 8). People are not always aware of their mental model. Senge, Kleiner, and Roberts (1994) suggested that people cannot steer through the environment of life without a mental model, and that all mental models are, in some way, flawed. Pascale (1990) preferred the term paradigm to a mindset because it encompasses the sharing of a belief system by a community, whereas a mindset or worldview refers to an individual. Guba and Lincoln (1994) described a paradigm as a set of basic beliefs dealing with first principles. It is a worldview describing the nature of the world, a person's place in it, and their relationship with the world.

In simple terms, a paradigm is a set of prepositions that explain how the world is perceived, and it contains a worldview, a way of breaking down the complexity of the real world, telling researchers and social scientists in general what is important, what is legitimate, and what is reasonable (Patton, 1990; Sarantakos, 2002). Paradigms allow researchers to identify the relationship between variables and to specify appropriate methods for conducting particular research (Guba & Lincoln, 1994; Lincoln & Guba, 2000). A paradigm may therefore be viewed as a set of basic beliefs that deals with ultimates or first principles. It is the basic belief system or *worldview* that guides enquiry, or the individual, regarding their place in that world, the range of possible relationships in it and its parts (Guba & Lincoln, 1994, 1998). Guba (1990) suggested, there are many paradigms that we use in guiding our actions: the adversarial paradigm that guides the legal system, the judgemental paradigm that guides the selection of Olympic winners, the religious paradigms that guide spiritual, and moral life, as well as those that guide disciplined inquiry.

Uniformity is lacking in various textbooks and scholarly work on the different paradigms in use, as well as the philosophical nature of its origins. Therefore, many sport management researchers find discussions on paradigms difficult to follow and understand. We believe that it is important that sport management researchers understand research paradigms and that they have an understanding of the major frameworks that they will come across in their reading. This is because it is not a matter of having a theory and putting it into practice, nor of doing something and deriving a theory from it, but of both theory and practice happening simultaneously, interactively, and continuously. Understanding the range of possible frameworks, and how others have used them is key to understand your own processes of thought.

THE THREE PERSPECTIVES: ONTOLOGICAL, EPISTEMOLOGICAL, AND METHODOLOGICAL

Reflecting on the emergence, perception, and employment of new qualitative research in sport management, it is necessary to not only review the nature of that enquiry with its various *epistemological, ontological,* and *methodological* underpinnings, but also to consider the conditions outside of academic walls under which this kind of research is possible. Over the past few decades, sport management has witnessed changing conditions under which qualitative research has been conducted, including political and economic contexts that have impacted on the general perception of qualitative research as well as framing the work of researchers generally. Lincoln and Guba (2000) offer the following useful explanation of how a paradigm shapes our thinking processes:

> *A paradigm encompasses four concepts: ethics, epistemology, ontology and methodology. Ethics asks, How will I be as a moral person in the world? Epistemology asks, How do I know the world? What is the relationship between the inquirer and the known? Ontology raises basic questions about the nature of reality and the nature of the human being in the world. Methodology focuses on the best means for gaining knowledge about the world. (p. 167)*

While this explanation is quite comprehensive, we argue that *axiology* (what is the role of researcher's values in this quest?) should be considered when considering what shapes out thinking processes.

We will now discuss briefly three aspects: *ontology, epistemology,* and *methodology.* At the most fundamental level, choosing an ontological and epistemological paradigm and associated methodology for a sport management study needs to be driven by the objective of finding the most appropriate way to answer the research question. Most research questions in our discipline are not answerable independently of the human behaviour and perceptions within which they are embedded. Sport management has both "behavioural and political dimensions". These dimensions suggest that naturalistic and qualitative approaches to the collection and analysis of sport management research data are required (perhaps as a first step in the research process), in order to describe and gain some understanding of the complexities of producing and using that information.

The ontological perspective

Ontology refers to how one sees the world and the nature of one's reality. An underlying ontological question concerns whether the social and natural worlds exist in similar ways or whether the social world is fundamentally different because it is open to subjective interpretation. Ontology poses questions such as: (1) What is the nature of reality?; (2) What is already known about this reality?; (3) What is already known about the real world?; and (4) Is this how things really work? (Perry, Riege, & Brown, 1999). In broad terms, social science has been shaped by two overarching ontological positions in relation to these issues – *realism* and *idealism*. Realism is based on the idea that there is an external reality that exists independently of people's beliefs about or understanding of it. In other words, there is a distinction between the way the world is, and the meaning and interpretation of that world held by individuals. Variants of realism include: *naive realism* (Madill, Jordan, & Shirley, 2000), or *shallow realism* (Blaikie, 2007) – reality can be observed directly and accurately; *cautious realism* (Blaikie, 2007) – reality can be known approximately or imperfectly rather than accurately; *depth realism* (Blaikie, 2007); *critical or transcendental realism* (Bhaskar, 1979; Robson, 2002) – reality consists of different levels – the empirical domain that is made of up what we experience through our senses, the actual domain that exists regardless of whether or not it is observed, and the real domain that refers to underlying processes and mechanisms; *subtle realism* (Blaikie, 2007; Hammersley, 1992) – an external reality exists but is only known through the human mind and socially constructed meanings; *critical realism* – a specific form of scientific realism in which the objects of science are distinct from the practice of science (Brown, 1999) (we discuss critical realism later in the chapter); *materialism* is a variant of realism which recognises only material features, such as economic relations, or physical features of the world as holding reality. Values, beliefs, or experiences are "epiphenomena" – features that arise from, but do not shape, the material world. Idealism, on the other hand, asserts that reality is fundamentally mind dependent: it is only knowable through the human mind and through socially constructed meanings, no reality exists independently of these, and no external reality exists independent of our beliefs and understandings. Variants of idealism include; *subtle or contextual or collective idealism* (Hughes & Sharrock, 1997; Madill et al., 2000; Shaw, 1999) – the social world is made-up of representations constructed and shared by people in particular contexts; and *relativism or radical idealism* (Hughes & Sharrock, 1997; Madill et al., 2000; Shaw, 1999) – there is no shared social reality, only a series of different (individual) constructions.

The epistemological perspective

The second question is the *epistemological* question. This asks what is the relationship between the inquirer and knowledge? Guba and Lincoln (1994) postulate that no one answer can be given to this question; the answer is dependent on the answer to the ontological question. For example, if the world is considered "real" then the researcher's position is one of objective separation from the object of research.

Epistemology refers to the relationship researchers have with the reality they have created, their justified belief and the truth of their final research findings (Guba & Lincoln, 1994). Therefore, epistemology poses the social questions such as; (1) What is the relationship between the sport management researcher and the reality, as they perceive it?; (2) Is the reality shared by others or only by the sport management researcher?; and (3) Has the perceptions of the sport management researcher, shaped the desired reality, or is it a "true" representation of the reality? (Guba & Lincoln, 1994).

Krug and Hepworth (1997) argued that the epistemological dog wags the methodological tail, and epistemologies are always grounded within larger social practices. Spencer et al. (2003, pp. 45–46) outlined a range of epistemological positions, which might be organised into a spectrum as follows:

- **Subjective Idealism:** there is no shared reality independent of multiple alternative human constructions;

- **Objective Idealism:** there is a world of collectively shared understandings;

- **Critical Realism:** knowledge of reality is mediated by our perceptions and beliefs;

- **Scientific Realism:** it is possible for knowledge to approximate closely an external reality;

- **Naïve Realism:** reality exists independently of human constructions and can be known directly.

Some key issues dominate epistemological debates. The *first* of these relates to the way in which knowledge is best acquired. One view holds that knowledge is based on *induction*, a "bottom-up" process through which patterns are derived from observations of the world. In contrast, those who argue that knowledge is acquired through *deduction* view knowledge acquisition as a "top down" process, whereby logically derived propositions or hypotheses are tested against observations. *Inductive* processes involve using evidence as the genesis of a conclusion – evidence is collected first, and knowledge and theories built from this. *Deductive* processes use evidence in support of a conclusion – a hypothesis is first developed and evidence is then collected to confirm or reject it.

A *second* key epistemological issue concerns the relationship between the researcher and the researched and how this influences the connection between "facts" and "values". In one model, the phenomena being researched are seen as independent of and unaffected by the behaviour of the researcher. The researcher can be objective in their approach and the investigation can be viewed as value free. In contrast others believe that in the social world people are affected by the process of being studied and that the relationship between the researcher and social phenomena is interactive. In this case, the researcher cannot be neutral and cannot produce an objective or "privileged" account. In this context, *reflexivity* in qualitative research is considered particularly important.

A *third* key epistemological issue relates to a focus on what it means to accept particular claims as accurate or "true". The dominant theory of truth has been held to be one of *correspondence* – that is, there is a match between observations or readings of the natural world and an independent reality. An alternative view, known as the *intersubjective* or *coherence* theory of truth, and proposed as more appropriate for the study of the social world, suggests that this "independent" reality can only be gauged in a consensual rather than an absolute way. If several reports confirm a statement then it can be considered "true" as a representation of a socially constructed reality. Finally, there are those who argue for a pragmatic theory of truth, which rests on the premise that an interpretation is true if it leads to, or provides assistance to take, actions that produce the desired or predicted results.

Research brief

Title: Olympic and international level sports coaches' experiences of stressors, appraisals, and coping

Author: Didymus, F. F., *Leeds Beckett University* (2017)

Reference: Didymus, F. F. (2017). Olympic and international level sports coaches' experiences of stressors, appraisals, and coping. *Qualitative Research in Sport, Exercise and Health*, 9(2), 214–232.

The aim of this study was to explore psychological stress with Olympic and international level sports coaches. In particular, the study aimed to explore situational properties of stressors and coaches' appraisals to address voids in the published literature. Guided by a constructionist epistemological position that contained traces of post-positivism and a relativist view of reality, the author conducted semi-structured interviews with six women and nine men. The author applied abductive logic during latent thematic analyses to organise and analyse the data. The findings suggested that the coaches experienced many stressors that related to 10 themes (e.g. athlete concerns, performance) and that these stressors were underpinned by seven situational properties (e.g. ambiguity, imminence, novelty).

The methodological perspective

The third question is the *methodological* question. Guba and Lincoln (1994) write that this asks how the researcher will go about the research. This leads to the following question: "What technique can be used to measure the perceived reality"? *Methodology* refers to the ways in which knowledge is acquired, including the ideas that govern the principles, rules, and procedures of a particular field of study or discipline such as public relations. The key question here is "How do we know?" "Methodology" is sometimes confused with "method" but they are not synonymous. Methodology as compared to the term *"methods"* refers to the strategy, the plan and action, the process or design lying behind the choice, and use of a particular method. Furthermore, there is a theoretical perspective, a philosophical stance that informs a methodology grounding its logic and criteria (Crotty, 1998). Given this definition, positivism, symbolic interactionism, phenomenology, hermeneutics, interpretivism, or critical theory, are theoretical perspectives. Survey research, ethnography, Grounded Theory (GT), and discourse analysis are methodologies. Analysis methods derived from these various frameworks are statistical procedures, theme identification, constant comparison, document analysis, content analysis, or cognitive mapping. GT may also be classified as method, if understood and used as a series of procedures. Research *methods* are the step-by-step techniques that researchers adopt in a systematic process. They can be employed within any paradigm because they are common to almost all epistemologies and methodologies. While methods are the procedures and tools for doing the research, methodology refers to the principles, concepts, and theories that underpin these methods.

NATURE AND CONTEXT OF RESEARCH QUESTIONS

At the most fundamental level, choosing an ontological and epistemological paradigm and associated methodology for a sport management study needs to be driven by the objective of finding the most appropriate way to answer the research question.

Conceptualising paradigms

The outcome of "good research" is the satisfactory achievement of a desired result or outcome. The determination of what upholds good research has been the issue that drives the paradigm debate. Guba and Lincoln (1989) suggested:

> *Inquiry paradigms define for inquirers what it is they are about, and what falls within and outside the limits of legitimate inquiry. The basic beliefs that define inquiry paradigms can be summarized by the responses given by proponents of any given paradigm to three fundamental questions, which are interconnected in such a way that the answer given to any one question, taken in any order, constrains how the others may be answered. (p. 108)*

Such development is further preceded by the nature of the inquiry itself, the question being asked, "what is available in the context, and what the researcher can do in that setting" (Denzin & Lincoln, 1994, p. 2), and the worldview of the researcher. Many researchers find discussions on paradigms difficult to follow and understand. A lack of uniformity in various textbooks and scholarly work on the different paradigms have made the process confusing as the following example indicate. Rynes and Gephart (2004) refer to positivism, post-positivist, interpretive paradigms, and critical post-modernism; Creswell (2014) points to the positivist, post-positivist, constructivist, critical, and feminist-post-structural approaches; Lincoln and Guba's (2000) categories are positivism, post-positivism, critical theory, constructivism, and participatory and suggest paradigms are widely accepted as a working framework.

This book does not intend a comprehensive discussion of similarities, differences, and history among all paradigms. However, we will discuss what we believe are the basic premise of some paradigms most relevant to sport management research. These are: positivism, post-positivism, constructivism, interpretivism, participatory, critical theory, post-structuralism, post-modernism, and pragmatism.

Positivism

Positivism as a theoretical perspective is based on notions of impartiality and objectivity, and assumptions that the researcher can remain separate from, and not influence, the research field in uncovering a single truth. A positivist perspective presents the social world as existing independent of human consciousness and therefore data are not affected by the participants' or the researcher's interpretation. Internal and external validity are sought with the results being presented in the form of scientific report (Denzin & Lincoln, 2018). The aim of such research is to uncover underlying laws that account for the how and why of certain behaviours and events, and is, therefore, useful in developing predictive models of behaviour. Positivists also believe scientists can accurately portray the truth that is "out there" (Willig, 2013).

In the positivist tradition, there is a concern with measurement, reliability, prediction, and replicability. The appropriate way of going about knowledge production is thought to be by means of the hypthetico-deductive method in which the researcher begins with a clearly articulated theory, deduces hypotheses that are logically consistent with the theory, and then tests the hypotheses under experimental conditions. But since social science hypotheses do not often lend themselves to laboratory experimentation, statistical analysis of large samples usually counts as objective testing. Such methodology assumes that through observation and precise measurement, social reality, which is external to and independent of the mind of the observer, may be rendered comprehensible to the social scientist.

It is in approaches to theorisation, as much as in the methodology itself, according to Sharp and Green (1975), that the "inherent weakness" of such deductive research is revealed. Critical theorists argue that while "fact finding" and "head counting" produces voluminous statistical data, it does not address the social circumstances out of which such data arise. Quantitative, positivist sport management studies assume the existence of a natural social order with an underlying value consensus. According to Sharp and Green, this limits both the formulation of problems to be studied and the conceptualisation of possible solutions:

> *Methodologically, this tradition tends to engage in positivistic 'fact finding' procedures with arbitrarily imposed categories for differentiating the data. It fails to do justice to the complexity of social reality, which cannot be 'grasped' by merely reducing sociologically significant characteristics of men to their external and objective indicators. (pp. 2–3)*

In sum, the main contemporary criticisms of positivism are well summarised by Burrell and Morgan (1979) as follows:

> *Science is based on 'taken for granted' assumptions, and thus, like any other social practice, must be understood within a specific context. Traced to their source all activities which pose as science can be traced to fundamental assumptions relating to everyday life and can in no way be regarded as generating knowledge with an 'objective', value- free status, as is sometimes claimed. What passes for scientific knowledge can be shown to be founded upon a set of unstated conventions, beliefs and assumptions, just as every day, common-sense knowledge is. The difference between them lies largely in the nature of rules and the community which recognises and subscribes to them. The knowledge in both cases is not so much 'objective' as shared. (p. 255)*

Positivism was probably the most powerful intellectual framework of the nineteenth and twentieth centuries, across all disciplines. It was built upon a realist assumption that the world is out there waiting to be known. It has faith in the scientific method, which it sees as leading to the growth of objective and verifiable knowledge (rather than mere superstition and guesswork). The grip of positivism on the scientific world has been weakening over recent decades, as scientific research methodology begins to shift away from the goal of absolute truth, based on claims to objectivity, generalisation, and prediction, and find ways to deal with concepts such as "uncertainty" and "chaos". Positivism could be viewed as excessively narrow and inflexible and therefore unlikely to successfully capture either the hidden complexities or the commercial and cultural contexts of sport or the sport management environment. What is required is the means to provide sport management researchers with a more sophisticated understanding of the epistemological and sociological sciences. Table 2.2 outlines the features of positivism.

Table 2.2	Features of positivism

Features of positivism

Knowledge is produced through the senses based on careful observation.

Regularities and "constant conjunctions" are identified.

Inductive reasoning is used after data have been collected to generalise from empirical instances to general laws.

Reality is unaffected by the research process, facts and values are separate, objective value-free inquiry is possible.

The methods used in the natural sciences are appropriate for studying the social world.

Reality can be known accurately (knowledge is foundational, correspondence theory of truth).

Post-positivism

The term "post-positivism" is harder to define than positivism. There are, broadly speaking, two families of definition. The more limited definition is represented by Lincoln and Guba (2000). They attribute to post-positivism an ontology of *critical realism*, an epistemology that still seeks knowledge (but admits that verification is not achievable and judges success of Popper's principles and the search for relative objectivity through the critical community of scholars), and a methodology more open to qualitative methods. Realism provides a world view in which an actual social phenomenon can be ascertained even though it is imperfect and probabilistically comprehendible (Guba & Lincoln, 1994; Merriam, 1998; Perry & Coote, 1994; Perry et al., 1999). That is, for realists the means to determine the reality of a social phenomenon is through the triangulation of cognition processes.

A more inclusive definition proposes post-positivism as the covering term for all the intellectual frameworks that have positioned themselves against positivism. Researchers from this perspective (Lather, 1991) see the research process to some degree as circular or spiral or cumulative (rather than linear and sequential), prefer qualitative over quantitative methods of research, and apply hermeneutic and contextual explanatory systems within a constructivist epistemology. Post-positivism differs from positivism by its view that the truth lies only in probability that is not verifiable, which results in the falsification of the hypothesis (Rynes & Gephart, 2004). Similar to the pure positivist assumptions, this approach is deterministic (logically linking effects and outcomes) and reductionist (reduces phenomena to small, testable sets) (Creswell, 2014). The aim of research within a post-positivist framework is to gain as thorough an understanding of reality as possible by subjecting it to comprehensive and critical examination (Guba & Lincoln, 1994). Rynes and Gephart (2004) pointed

Table 2.3	Features of post-positivism

Features post-positivism

Knowledge of the world is produced through testing propositions: hypotheses about causal relationships are derived from scientific theories and then evaluated empirically against observations.

Deductive reasoning is used to postulate possible relationships and models before data are collected.

Reality is unaffected by the research process, facts and values are separate, objective value-free inquiry is possible.

The methods used in the natural sciences are appropriate for studying the social world.

Reality can be known approximately, hypotheses can be rejected or provisionally confirmed, but not definitively proved to be true (knowledge is provisional and fallibilistic, coherence theory of truth).

out that "well developed post-postivist qualitative methods can uncover facts and compare facts to hypotheses or prior findings in an attempt to falsify prior hypotheses or to contradict previous knowledge" (p. 456). Qualitative research through this approach is also sometimes referred to as "modernist" qualitative research (Locke & Golden-Biddle, 2002). Table 2.3 outlines the features of post-positivism.

Constructivism

Constructivism or social constructivism concurs that reality is constructed in the social and cultural context and is almost impossible to discern (Blustein et al., 2005). Constructivism moves away from the traditional positivist criteria of internal and external validity and seeks instead trustworthiness and authenticity (Denzin & Lincoln, 2018). The constructivist paradigm assumes a relativist ontology (there are multiple realities), a subjectivist epistemology (knower and respondent co-create understandings), and a naturalistic (in the natural world) set of methodological procedures (Denzin & Lincoln, 2018). Constructivism sees knowledge as pertaining to the world we experience (von Glasersfeld, 1997) and all theory as lacking in certainty.

Crotty (1998) argued that we cannot be both objectivist, that is, take the "view that things exist as *meaningful* entities independently of consciousness and experience, that they have truth and meaning residing in them as objects" (p. 5). Constructivism posits that truth, or meaning, comes into existence in and out of our engagement with the realities of our world. Meaning is not discovered, but constructed. Different people may construct meaning in different ways, even in relation to the same phenomenon. Subject and object emerge as partners in the generation of meaning, and therefore meaning or "truth" cannot be described as "objective". As such, constructivism is interested in the values which are beneath the findings. Thus it uses inductive methods. The inductive methods of constructivism require the sport management researcher to be a "passionate participant" (Guba & Lincoln, 1994) during fieldwork. Like critical theory (discussed later in this chapter), the data depends on the interaction between the interviewer and respondent (Anderson, 1992). Both critical theory and constructivism require the researcher to be subjective to develop knowledge in this interaction (Anderson, 1992; Guba & Lincoln, 1994).

Research brief

Title: Experiences of bullying victimisation in female interuniversity athletes
Author: Jewett, R. *Ryerson University*, Kerr, G. *University of Toronto*, MacPherson, E. *University of Toronto* & Stirling, A. *University of Toronto* (2019)
Reference: Jewett, R., Kerr, G., MacPherson, E., & Stirling, A. (2019). Experiences of bullying victimisation in female interuniversity athletes. *International Journal of Sport and Exercise Psychology*, 1–15.
The purpose of the study was to explore interuniversity student–athletes' experiences with bullying victimisation. Eleven female athletes from a range of individual and team sports volunteered to be interviewed about their personal experiences as targets and witnesses of bullying behaviours from their teammates. The study design and implementation were informed by a social constructivist research paradigm in order to acknowledge human experiences as a complex interplay of social, cultural, historical, and individual influences. The interviews elicited stories that were analysed using narrative thematic analysis. The authors concluded that bullying represents a form of peer-to-peer interpersonal conflict in the sport context that has serious negative effects on athlete mental health and well-being.

Interpretivism

Interpretivism also arose as a reaction to positivism. Denzin and Lincoln (2000) summarise this as a difference in the view of science as a means of providing causal explanations (positivism) or of developing understanding of human action (interpretivism). The authors state that from an interpretivist perspective "what distinguishes human (social) action from the movement of physical objects is that the former is inherently meaningful" (p. 191). Interpretivists take the view that objectivity can be achieved believing that "it is possible to understand the subjective meaning of action. The interpreter reproduces or reconstructs, the original meaning of the action" (Denzin & Lincoln, 2003, p. 193). To achieve this level of objectivity, interpreters must employ methods that enable them to step outside their own frames of reference and take a theoretical attitude as a neutral observer. This paradigm sees reality as created by people assigning meaning; however, patterns of behaviour "emerge" due to social conventions. Interpretive research aims to explain and understand social life, using an inductive approach, and presenting reality symbolically. Understanding subjective meaning is important and "value neutrality is neither necessary or possible" (Sarantakos, 1998, p. 38).

The interpretivist stance requires the use of qualitative research methodologies as these enable researchers to explore how people make sense of their lives (Miles & Huberman, 1994), their experiences, and reactions to those experiences. These research methods allow for in-depth exploration of the issues as perceived by the participants, to ascertain their view of events and hear their story. An interpretivist approach involves:

> ....the systematic analysis of socially meaningful action through the direct detailed observation of people in natural settings in order to arrive at understandings and interpretations of how people create and maintain their social worlds. (Neuman, 2000, p. 71)

Interpretive approaches to research posit that research cannot be value free. It is not possible to "suspend values in order to understand" (Maykut & Morehouse, 1994, p. 12), as values are embedded in all aspects of the research, from what is chosen as the topic, how it is examined, and the relationship between researcher and research (Maykut & Morehouse, 1994). Moreover, the relationship between the researcher and the informant affects the gathering, interpretation, and writing up of data (Denzin, 1989; Fraenkel & Wallen, 1993). The constructivist–interpretivist paradigm is embodied in many theoretical perspectives including symbolic interactionism (Crotty, 1998), which was particularly influential in the development of GT.

Symbolic interactionism

Symbolic interactionism "sees meanings as social products, as creations that are formed in and through the defining activities of people as they interact" (Blumer, 1969, p. 4). It differs from behaviourist models, based in objectivist epistemologies, in its belief that people act reflectively, consciously construct what they do and are able to modify or alter the meanings and symbols they use in their interactions. It is therefore the patterns of action and interaction that make up groups and societies (Ritzer, 1996), and interactionists "study how people produce their situated versions of society" (Denzin, 1992, p. 23). The focus is on the generation of meaning and its interpretation. Symbolic interactionism rests on three main premises: (1) that human beings act toward things on the basis of the meanings that the things have for them; (2) that the meaning for such things is derived from, or arises out of, the social interaction that one has with one's fellows; and (3) that these meanings are handled in, and modified through, an interpretative process used by the person in dealing with the things he encounters (Blumer, 1969). The basic principles of symbolic interactionism are set out by Ritzer (1996) and are shown in Table 2.4.

Table 2.4	The basic principles of symbolic interactionism

Basic principles of symbolic interactionism

Human beings are endowed with the capacity for thought.

The capacity for thought is shaped by social interaction.

In social interaction, people learn the meanings and the symbols that allow them to exercise their distinctly human capacity for thought.

Meanings and symbols allow people to carry on distinctly human action and interaction.

People are able to modify or alter the meanings and symbols that they use in action and interaction on the basis of their interpretation of the situation.

People are able to make these modifications and alterations because, in part, of their ability to interact with themselves, which allows them to examine possible causes of action, assess their relative advantages and disadvantages, and then choose one.

The intertwined patterns of action and interaction make up groups and societies.

In short, symbolic interactionism's most important methodological premise is that all social inquiry must be grounded in the particular empirical world studied (Locke, 2001), and from the detailed description gained by observing behaviour researchers can formulate interpretations.

PARTICIPATORY PARADIGM

The *participatory paradigm* is mostly associated with *co-operative inquiry:* a person centred inquiry that does research *with* people, not *on* them or *about* them. This means people become co-researchers involved in all levels of the research design (Heron, 1996). The participatory paradigm allows researchers and participants to "be co-participants in defining and altering' situations" (Joyappa & Martin, 1996, p. 2). It is an approach that seeks to empower both individuals and communities in a way that allows and perhaps even facilitates eventual social change (Joyappa & Martin, 1996). As argued by Heron and Reason (1997), the participatory worldview allows us, as researchers, to unite with other persons in a collaborative approach to inquiry. An important aspect of participatory research is its attempt to share control of the actual research process with those involved in it. What becomes important in this research approach is who produces, validates, and is empowered by knowledge. Participatory research is ultimately a bottom-up approach that is participant driven and favours individual meaningful outcomes over a broader generalisability of findings (Joyappa & Martin, 1996).

In terms of how we view the world, the participatory paradigm asserts that in no way can we ever have absolute experiential knowledge, and as such, what must be remembered about experiential knowing is that the very process of perceiving is also a meeting, a transaction (Heron & Reason, 1997). Heron and Reason stated: "To experience anything is to participate in it, and to participate is both to mould and to encounter; hence experiential reality is always subjective-objective" (p. 278). This relationship means that we come to know a world at an interactive interface, which exists between one and what is encountered. Heron and Reason describe that a knower comes to know in four different ways; that is an experiential, presentational, propositional, and practical way. The first kind of knowing, experiential, stems from an "empathic resonance with a being. It is also the creative shaping of a world" (p. 280). There inherently is an acceptance of our perspective of knowledge, and while authentically valuing that, we recognise its biases and articulate this consciousness and awareness. They go to suggest that from a participatory worldview, methodologies need to reflect this democratic dialogue creation between both the participants and the researchers through co-operative methods of inquiry. They also posit that a co-operative method means that:

> People collaborate to define the questions they wish to explore
> and the methodology for that exploration (propositional knowing);
> together or separately they apply this methodology in the world
> of their practice (practical knowing); which leads to new forms of
> encounter with their world (experiential knowing); and they find ways
> to represent this experience in significant patterns (presentational
> knowing) which feeds into a revised propositional understanding of
> the original question. (p. 282)

Critical theory

Critical inquiry, unlike positivism and constructivism–interpretivism, seek to challenge the status quo. Critical theorists do not share the confidence of interpretivists in people's accounts of experience: Where most interpretivists today embrace such accounts as descriptions of authentic "lived experience", critical researchers hear in them the voice of an inherited tradition and prevailing culture (Crotty, 1998). Critical research views claims to truth as always discursively situated and implicated in relations of power (Kincheloe & McLaren, 2005) with each set of meanings supporting particular power structures and resisting change toward greater equity (Crotty, 1998).

Critical theory was developed in Germany by the Frankfurt school over 70 years ago. It follows the tradition of Marx, Kant, and Hegel (Kincheloe & McLaren, 1994, 2000). Kincheloe and McLaren (1994, 2000) define a criticalist as a researcher who uses research as a social or cultural criticism. A critical researcher aims to produce a social or cultural criticism within certain assumptions. The assumptions of critical theory, write Kincheloe and McLaren (1994, 2000), are that:

- thought is modified by power relations;
- facts are value mediated;
- the relationship between concept and object is mobile;
- language is central to developing subjectivity;
- society has a social status hierarchy;
- there are many faces of oppression; and
- research often, unwittingly, reproduces the class system.

Moreover, Kincheloe and McLaren (1994, 2000) suggested that modern critical analysis is hybrid and not confined to a specific school of analysis. Critical researchers try to understand the ideologies that inform their research so that assumptions can be transparent. Information for critical theorists is an act of human judgement or interpretation, knowledge that must be interpreted by people. This interpretation and development of theory requires an understanding of the relationship between the parts of the whole (Wack, 1985a, 1985b). Critical theories include radical humanism, radical functionalism, structuralism, and post-structuralist tendencies (Nieuwenhuis, 2016). Among the assumptions that differentiate critical theory from the constructivist notion, is the belief that social power shapes reality and the action agenda needed for its reform (Creswell, 2014; Nieuwenhuis, 2016). From the critical stance, research is used to challenge traditions, power structures, and the status quo (Blustein et al., 2005).

Creswell (2014) noted that there are a number of themes for the critical researcher; one of the core themes is to critique and imagine a different society. Critical research aims to confront issues in a society or part of it and to change the wrongs that emerge from the research as perceived by the researcher. To just increase knowledge is not enough for the critical researcher (Kincheloe & McLaren, 1994, 2000). In contrast to empirical research, critical research depends on meaning being derived from interpretation of data (Kincheloe & McLaren, 1994), in this sense "what we see is not what we see but what we perceive" (p. 144). According to Kincheloe and McLaren (1994, 2000), knowledge comes from interpreting data by people who are part of the world and understanding the relationships between parts of the world. Critical theory researchers in sport management critique and transform social, political, economic, ethnic, and gender values. Research inquiries can entail long-term ethnographic and historical research of organisational processes and structures. Critical theory accepts that there are multiple social realities, which are constructed by groups involved in the research. Thus, truth is only known within a particular social group's constructed reality (Easton, 1982).

Research brief

Title: Women Ice Hockey Officials and Gender Relations in Officiating
Author: Danford, M. *University of Toronto* (2019)
Reference: Danford, M. (2019). Women Ice Hockey Officials and Gender Relations in Officiating. *Doctoral dissertation University of Toronto.*
This study explored the current experiences of women ice hockey officials in Canada. To guide this research, the author applied a Critical Feminist Theory framework to data from document analyses, observations of hockey games, and semi-structured interviews with women ice hockey officials from across Canada. The results showed that women ice hockey officials face numerous challenges in obtaining higher certification levels and having opportunities to officiate higher level hockey games. The career paths and career contingencies for women ice hockey officials differed from their men colleagues due to the hegemonic structures that construct hockey as a masculine space, and as a result, these structures directly influenced the participating women's ability to advance in officiating in Canada. The participants shared experiences of exclusion at sites of training and education, limitations to advancing, and disinvolvement such as quitting/dropping-out, and retirement.

Post-structuralism

Post-structuralism emerges as clearly different from positivist paradigms and structuralism. Structuralism "looks for decisive shaping factors in structural forms discoverable within society or the unconscious, or both" (Crotty, 1998, p. 204), whereas post-structuralism "challenges the very idea of structure, including the idea of a centre, a fixed principle, a hierarchy of meaning and a solid foundation" (Alvesson, 2002, p. 30).

Post-structuralism places a strong focus on the origins of language linking language, subjectivity, social organisation, and power. Language produces meaning and creates social reality. Language is how "social organisation and power are defined and contested and the place where one's sense of self – one's subjectivity – is constructed" (Richardson & St Pierre, 2005, p. 961). Richardson and St Pierre view post-structuralism as a particular kind of post-modernist thinking, a view also taken by authors who see post-structuralism as a more specific form of thought (Crotty, 1998) and therefore subsumed under post-modernism. An alternate view holds that post-structuralism, which was developed in France, provides the orientations and ideas that post-modernism, a much broader movement geographically and conceptually, has made its own, enlarged, and extended range of subject areas (Crotty, 1998). In this view, post-structuralism provided the foundations for post-modernism. Alvesson (2002) suggests that it is almost impossible to establish a clear relationship between post-structuralism and post-modernism as authors use the terms in different ways, but that post-modernism tends to be used more frequently due to the familiarity emanating from the term's use in the most varied of contexts.

Post-modernism

Post-modernist research, in a similar vein to critical theory, seeks to expose the hidden structure of the social world and aims to deconstruct or dissolve all distinctions by breaking down boundaries. This similarity to the critical theory may be the reason why some scholars do not refer to post-modernism as such, but include it in the field of critical theories. Post-modernism is rooted in understanding that knowledge is constructed, culturally situated, and the lives of participants is ultimately incomprehensible. This leads to a view of multiple realities. Reality is "constructed by the discourse of each social and historical context so what is 'real' is 'what is represented as such'" (Locke, 2001, p. 11).

Post-modernists break down boundaries within research seeing research as a form of art in which the presence of the researcher must be evident. The value of research is to stimulate thought in others. It is certainly not to make predictions or reinforce existing power relations (Neuman, 2000).

Researchers from a post-modern worldview may not represent a single paradigm, although certain features are similar for post-modern research (Nieuwenhuis, 2016). These features entail: (1) challenging the conventional; (2) mixing styles; (3) tolerating ambiguity; (4) emphasising diversity; (5) accepting innovation and change; and (6) focusing on multiple realities that is socially constructed. Post-modernism is often associated with creative approaches of representation, for instance organisational autoethnography and art-based research (Wertz, 2011). With the incorporation of critical and post-modern views into the field of sport management, sport management scholars have emphasised "the need to understand sport management in its wider, political, economic, and ideological context and be concerned with exposing patterns of inequality and intervening in local communities" (Amis & Silk, 2005, p. 357). While this is of course important in a grander sociological sense, it is also important to recognise the significance that these needs hold within the sport management research. That is, researchers in the field of sport management need to be concerned with the political, economic, and ideological patterns of inequality that may exist in terms of scholarly interactions with one another. Certainly, the dream of an open-minded and diverse culture of scholarship is not an uncommon goal for researchers in the field. As Amis and Silk expressed: "In keeping with a field that is inherently multidisciplinary in nature, we envision an academic landscape that is not dominated by any single overarching meta-narrative that marginalises and obfuscates alternative approaches" (p. 358). Despite this commentary, critical and post-modern approaches, at this time, still remain at the fringes of sport management research (Skinner & Edwards, 2005).

Pragmatism

Pragmatism is not always referred as a paradigm or philosophy of science since is not committed to a single philosophy. It is rather concerned with the best practical way to answer a research question (Frost, 2011). As such the research question is the pivotal point for the selection of method. As a result, methods from different, often opposing, traditions are deemed acceptable to answer a research question. Although pragmatism is mostly associated with mixed methods research (Creswell, 2014), it is also common to the bricolage approach to qualitative research (Denzin & Lincoln, 2000). This approach advances the adapting and combining of different ontologies and qualitative methods to answer research questions from various perspectives, and thus giving way to methodological pluralism (Frost, 2011; Willig, 2013).

CRITICAL REALISM

This section presents an overview on the post-positivist philosophy of critical realism. Critical realism is advocated as an alternative research paradigm for sport management, one which has been largely overlooked or ignored. A critical realist stance offers the potential to investigate not only the economic consequences of sport management, but also the perceptions and perceptual biases of sport managers, decision-makers, and other stakeholders.

Basis of critical realism

The philosophy of critical realism can be said to straddle two independent, but not mutually exclusive schools of thought. The first is American critical realism (see Preston 1965), a relatively short-lived movement of the early twentieth century, and the second is a contemporary and arguably more critical philosophical movement (also dubbed critical realism), and represented principally by the works of Bhaskar (1978, 1979, 1989) see also (Collier, 1994). Despite Bhaskar's evolving stance on the emancipatory nature of critical realism and the commonalities of contemporary critical realism with critical theory perspectives, critical realism is still scientifically favoured (Bhaskar, 1978) and arguably less radical.

Modern critical realism is a school of thought in its own right, distinct from naive realism and from idealistic, radical, and constructivist conceptions (Tholey, 1989). Critical realism may be viewed instead as a specific form of scientific realism in which the objects of science are distinct from the practice of science (Brown, 1999) or, as Bhaskar (1975) articulated: "I have argued that the concept of natural necessity is the concept of a real generative mechanism at work, a concept which is applicable to the world quite independently of men" (p. 183). Situated under the umbrella of post-positivism, and offering a modified objectivist view, critical realism is:

> Any doctrine reconciling the real, independent, objective nature of the world (realism) with a due appreciation of the mind-dependence of the sensory experiences whereby we know about it (hence critical). In critical, as opposed to naive, realism the mind knows the world only by

means of a medium or vehicle of perception and thought; the problem is to give an account of the relationship between the medium and what it represents. (Blackburn, 1996, p. 88)

While positivism concerns a single, concrete reality, and constructivist interpretivism embraces multiple realities, critical realism concerns multiple perceptions about a single, mind-independent reality (Healy & Perry, 2000). Critical realists presume that a reality exists, but that it cannot be fully or perfectly apprehended (Guba, 1990). Both constructivists and critical realists reject logical positivism (Firestone, 1990) because of its causal reductionism, and both schools of thought reflect disillusionment with the objectivity and truth positions espoused by positivists.

The aim of critical realist research is the "identification and verification of underlying generative mechanisms" or structures that give rise to actions and events that can be experienced in the empirical domain (Wollin, 1996, p. 1). Within a critical realism framework, both qualitative and quantitative methodologies are deemed appropriate (Healy & Perry, 2000) for researching the underlying mechanisms that drive actions and events. Critical realism's combination of quantitative and qualitative methodologies complements the provision of an elaborated view of issues and phenomena studied, and establishes the validity of findings. Critical realist research may be initially qualitative and inductive, enabling issues, propositions, and models to be developed, clarified, and modified, then followed by the hypothetico-deductive approach (most commonly used in quantitative research) to unearth knowledge concerning broader mechanisms and tendencies. Sport management research conducted within a critical realist paradigm thus has its basis in replicability, coherence, and consensus, since results obtained from applying both qualitative and quantitative methodologies can be judged on these bases.

According to critical realism, the social world is comprised of four levels of reality: material, ideal, artefactual, and social. The levels of reality correspond to the depth of reality being considered ranging from the superficial material reality to the deeply embedded social reality. Critical realism also suggests a unique relationship among structures and agents when seeking to understand this multi-reality. Criticisms of the critical realism perspective can be found in post-structuralist readings on management (see, Willmott, 2005). Broader debates around theory development have included critical realism and suggest that the perspective is useful for theory verification, a much neglected area of sport management research.

CHOOSING A THEORECTICAL APPROACH

We now consider the role of "theory" in qualitative research in the sense of whether or not researchers must conduct their inquiry under the banner of, and in conformity with, a particular theoretical tradition or paradigm. It is common to find researchers who are bewildered by which approach they should take. While it is advisable for researchers to have an understanding of different epistemologies, paradigms or traditions as a way of understanding the range of approaches available, we would argue against "epistemological determinism". Hammersley (2004), for example, says that researchers should be encouraged to become "neither ostriches nor fighting cocks" (p. 557). We would argue that polarisation between traditions is dangerous and caution against unthinking alignment with any one tradition.

We do not propose that all these paradigms are equal, or even equally valid, only that all are currently in use, so you are likely to find them represented in the reading you do, and you are likely to have absorbed some at least of this into your own ways of thinking. We have in this chapter, provided a brief map of the terrain – a way of understanding how all these various philosophical frameworks, the fundamental methodological approaches, and the practical methods within each relate to each other. With this knowledge, we hope you will be empowered to understand your own framework(s) and so to select your methodology wisely – choosing those methods that are appropriate for your research project, and understanding the implications of your choices. If sport management researchers are comfortable making an ideological commitment to a particular tradition, regardless of their research topic, then that is their choice, but they should not be forced into a theoretical or methodological straitjacket. We advocate a flexible approach to research design. We believe that it is more important to choose the appropriate method or methods to address specific research questions than to align with a specific epistemological stance. As such we believe that quality in research practice has more to do with choosing the right research tools for the task rather than with methods that are confined to specific traditions.

CONCLUSION

Sport management researchers embracing these new research paradigms signal a growing awareness in the sport management research community that there is no single or right way to understand social reality. Qualitative methods, and more recently the support for emergent theoretical approaches to sport management research, have provided an alternative to the positivistic testing of formal theories developed by empirical researchers. Moreover, our understanding of how social reality is depicted is being continually challenged and subsequently, as Richardson (2000) suggested, the research process is becoming harder to master. It is therefore important that as sport management academics and students we grapple with questions regarding the nature of the knowledge that informs our discipline and we assess particular research practices before they adopt them. A failure to do so may lead us to unwittingly generate knowledge that is inimical to their particular quest. In endeavouring to emulate rigorous standards of research, sport management researchers should be encouraged to take more methodological "risks" and embrace more eclectic research approaches. Through embracing such concerns, the sport management researcher will increasingly identify dimensions of the reflexive nature of researcher and participant intersubjectivity and the reflexive moments of research interaction. Because of their vantage point in interacting intensively at multiple levels and in an enduring way with people from all walks of life sport management researchers are well positioned to take up many of the challenges that qualitative research paradigms can offer.

Against this backdrop, this chapter has outlined the major paradigms in qualitative research which may be utilised by sport management researchers. We have suggested that there is no single paradigm, and/or methodology, that meets the needs of all sport management researchers and all research questions, when investigating our diverse, complex and evolving contemporary field. Therefore, it is crucial that the most appropriate paradigm and thereby the most appropriate methodology to conduct the research is adopted by the sport management researcher.

REVIEW AND RESEARCH QUESTIONS

1. Summarise the historical moments in qualitative research and the related theoretical paradigms.

2. Distinguish among Ontological, Epistemological, and Methodological perspectives in the context of sport management research.

3. Explain what is meant by the term "paradigm" and the different types of paradigms that are associated with sport management research.

4. Provide an example of how Critical Realism could be used in sport management research?

REFERENCES

Abernethy, M. A., Chua, W. F., Luckett, P. F., & Selto, F. H. (1999). Research in managerial accounting: learning from others' experiences. The scientist has no other methods than doing his damnedest. *Accounting and Finance, 39*(1), 1–27.

Alasuutari, P. (2004). *Social theory and human reality*. Thousand Oaks, CA: Sage Publications.

Alvesson, M. (2002). *Understanding organizational culture*. London: Sage.

Amis, J., and Silk, M. (2005). Rupture: Promoting critical and innovative approaches to the study of sport management. *Journal of Sport Management, 19*, 355–366.

Anderson, O. R. (1992). Some interrelationships between constructivist models of learning and current neurobiological theory with implications for science education. *Journal of Research in Science Teaching, 29*, 1037–1058.

Bhaskar, R. (1975). *A realist theory of science* (1st ed.). Leeds: Leeds Books.

Bhaskar, R. (1978). *A realist theory of science* (2nd ed.). Brighton: Harvester Press.

Bhaskar, R. (1979). *The possibility of naturalism: a philosophical critique of the contemporary human sciences.* Brighton: Harvester Press.

Bhaskar, R. (1989). *Reclaiming reality: A critical introduction to contemporary reality.* London: Verso.

Blaikie, N. (2007). *Approaches to social enquiry* (2nd ed.). London: Polity Press.

Blackburn, S. (1996). *Oxford dictionary of philosophy.* Oxford: Oxford University Press.

Blumer, H. (1969). *Symbolic interactionism: Perspective and method.* Englewood Cliffs, NJ: Prentice-Hall.

Blustein, D. L., Kenna, A. C., Murphy, K. A., DeVoy, J. E., & DeWine, D. B. (2005). Qualitative research in career development: Exploring the center and margins of discourse about careers and working. *Journal of Career Assessment, 13,* 351–370.

Brown, A. (1999). *Developing realistic methodology: How new dialectics surpasses the critical realist method for social sciences.* Middlesex University Business School Discussion Paper.

Burrell, G. & Morgan, G. (1979). *Sociology of paradigms and organizational life: Elements of the sociology of corporate life.* London: Heinemann.

Clifford, J. (1986). Introduction: Partial truths. In J. Clifford & G. E. Marcus (Eds.), *Writing Culture: The Poetics and Politics of Ethnography,* pp. 1–26. Berkeley, CA: University of California Press.

Clifford, J. (1988). *The predicament of culture: Twentieth-century ethnography, literature and art.* Cambridge, MA: Harvard University Press.

Collier, A. (1994). *Critical realism: An introduction to the philosophy of Roy Bhaskar.* London: Verso.

Creswell, J.W. (2014). *Qualitative inquiry & research design: Choosing among five approaches* (4th ed.). Thousand Oaks, CA: Sage Publications.

Crotty, M. (1998). *The foundations of social research: Meaning and perspective in the research process.* Sydney, NSW: Allen & Unwin.

Denzin, N. K. (1989). *Interpretive interactionism.* Newbury Park, CA: Sage.

Denzin, N. K. (1992). *Symbolic interactionism and cultural studies: The politics of interpretation.* Cambridge, MA: Blackwell.

Denzin, N. K., & Lincoln, Y. S. (1994). Introduction: The discipline and practice of qualitative research. In N. Denzin & Y. Lincoln (Eds.), *Handbook of Qualitative Research* (1st ed.), pp. 1–21. Thousand Oaks, CA: Sage Publications.

Denzin, N. K., &Lincoln, Y. S. (2000). Introduction: The discipline and practice of qualitative research. In N. Denzin & Y. Lincoln (Eds.), *Handbook of Qualitative Research* (2nd ed.), pp. 1–29. Thousand Oaks, CA: Sage Publications.

Denzin, N.K., & Lincoln, Y.S. (Eds.) (2003). *The landscape of qualitative research: Theories and issues* (2nd ed.). London: Sage Publications.

Denzin, N. K., & Lincoln, Y.,S. (2018). Introduction: The discipline and practice of qualitative research. In Norman Denzin & Yvonna Lincoln (Eds.), *Handbook of Qualitative Research* (5th ed.), pp. 1–27. Thousand Oaks, CA: Sage Publications.

Easton, G. (1982). *Learning from case studies.* Englewoods Cliffs, NJ: Prentice Hall International.

Ellis, C., & Bochner, A. P. (Eds.) (1996). *Ethnographic alternatives book series* (Vol. 1). *Composing Ethnography: Alternative Forms of Qualitative Writing.* Walnut Creek, CA: AltaMira Press.

Firestone, W. A. (1990). Accommodation: towards a paradigm-praxis dialectic. In E. G. Guba (Ed.), *The Paradigm Dialog,* pp. 105–124. Newbury Park, CA: Sage Publications.

Fraenkel, J. R., & Wallen, N. E. (1993). *How to design and evaluate research.* New York, NY: McGraw-Hill.

Frost, N. (2011). *Qualitative research methods in psychology: Combining core approaches.* Maidenhead: Open University Press.

Geertz, C. (1988). *Works and lives: The anthropologist as author.* Stanford, CA: Stanford University Press.

Guba, E. G. (Ed.) (1990). *The paradigm dialog.* Newbury Park, CA: Sage Publications.

Guba, E. G., & Lincoln, Y. S. (1989). *Fourth generation evaluation.* Newbury Park, CA: Sage.

Guba, E. G., & Lincoln, Y. S. (1994). Competing paradigms in qualitative research. In N.K. Denzin, & Y.S. Lincoln (Eds.). *Handbook of Qualitative Research,* pp. 105–117. Thousand Oaks, CA: Sage Publications.

Guba, E. G., & Lincoln, Y. S. (1998). Competing paradigms in qualitative research. In N. K. Denzin, & Y. S. Lincoln (Eds.), *The Landscape of Qualitative Research,* pp. 195–222. Thousand Oaks, CA: Sage Publications.

Hammersley, M. (1992). Some reflections on ethnography and validity. *Qualitative Studies in Education, 5*(3), 195–203.

Hammersley, M. (2004). Action research: a contradiction in terms. *Oxford Review of Education 30*(2), 165–181.

Healy, M., & Perry, C. (2000). Comprehensive criteria to judge validity and reliability of qualitative research within the realism paradigm. *Qualitative Market Research – An International Journal, 3*(3), 118–126.

Heron, J. (1996). *Co-operative inquiry: Research into the human condition.* Newbury, CA: Sage Publications.

Heron, J., & Reason, P. (1997). *Qualitative inquiry.* London: Sage Publications.

Hughes, J., & Sharrock, W. (1997). *The philosophy of social research.* Essex: Pearson Publishing.

Joyappa, V., & Martin, D. (1996). Exploring alternative research epistemologies for adult education: participatory research, feminist research, and feminist participatory research. *Adult Education Quarterly, 47* (1), 1–14.

Kincheloe, J. L., & McLaren, P. L. (1994). Rethinking critical theory and qualitative research. In N.K. Denzin & Y.S. Lincoln (Eds.), *Handbook of Qualitative Research,* pp. 138–157. Thousand Oaks, CA: Sage Publications.

Kincheloe, J. L., & McLaren, P. L. (2000). Rethinking critical theory and qualitative research. In N. K. Denzin, & Y. S. Lincoln (Eds.), *Handbook of Qualitative Research,* (2nd ed.), pp. 279–313. Thousand Oaks, CA: Sage Publications.

Kincheloe, J. L., & McLaren, P. L. (2005). Rethinking critical theory and qualitative research. In N. K. Denzin, & Y. S. Lincoln (Eds.), *Handbook of Qualitative Research* (3rd ed.), pp. 303–342. Thousand Oaks, CA: Sage Publications.

Krug, G., & Hepworth, J. (1997). Poststructuralism, qualitative methodology and public health: Research methods as a legitimation strategy for knowledge. *Critical Public Health, 7*(1–2), 50–60.

Kuhn, T. S. (1962). *The structure of scientific revolutions.* Chicago: University of Chicago Press.

Kuhn, T. S. (1970). *The structure of scientific revolutions* (2nd ed.). Chicago: University of Chicago Press.

Lather, P. (1991). *Getting smart: Feminist research and pedagogy with/in the postmodern.* New York: Routledge.

Lincoln, Y. S., & Guba, E. G. (2000). Paradigmatic controversies, contradictions, and emerging confluences. In N. Denzin & Y. Lincoln (Eds.), *Handbook of Qualitative Research* (2nd ed.), pp. 163–188. Thousand Oaks, California: Sage Publications.

Locke, K. (2001). *Grounded theory in management research.* London: Sage Publications.

Locke, K., & Golden-Biddle, K. (2002). An introduction to qualitative research: its potential for industrial and organizational psychology. In Rogelberg, S. (Ed.), *Handbook of Research Methods in Industrial and Organizational Psychology*, pp. 99–118. Malden, MA: Blackwell.

Madill, A., Jordan, A., & Shirley, C. (2000). Objectivity and reliability in qualitative analysis: Realist, contextualist and radical constructionist epistemologies. *British Journal of Psychology, 91*, 1–20.

Maykut, P., & Morehouse, R. (1994). *Beginning qualitative research: A philosophic and practical guide*. London: Routledge.

Merriam, S. B. (1998). *Qualitative research and case study applications in education. Revised and expanded from "Case Study Research in Education"*. San Francisco, CA: Jossey-Bass Publishers.

Miles, M. B., & Huberman, M. A. (1994). *Qualitative data analysis*. Thousand Oaks, CA: Sage.

Morse, J. M., Barrett, M., Mayan, M., Olson, K., & Spiers, J. (2002). Verification strategies for establishing reliability and validity in qualitative research. *International Journal of Qualitative Methods, 1*(2), 13–22

Nieuwenhuis, J. (2016). Introducing qualitative research. In K. Maree (Ed.), *First Steps in Research* (2nd ed.). Pretoria, South Africa: Van Schaik Publishers.

Neuman, W. L. (2000). *Social research methods: Qualitative and quantitative approaches* (4th ed.). Boston: Allyn & Bacon.

Pascale, P. (1990). *Managing on the Edge*. New York: Touchstone.

Patton, M. Q. (1990). *Qualitative evaluation and research methods*. Newbury, CA: Sage Publications.

Patton, M. Q. (2002). *Qualitative evaluation and research methods* (3rd ed.). Newbury Park, CA: Sage Publications.

Perry, C., & Coote, L. (1994). Processes of case study methodology: Tool for management development. *Paper presented at the Australian and New Zealand Academy of Management (ANZAM) Conference*. Wellington, New Zealand: Victoria University of Wellington.

Perry, C., Riege, A., & Brown, L. (1999). Realism's role among scientific paradigms in marketing research. *Irish Marketing Review, 12*(2), 16–23.

Preston, W. W. (1965). The mote in the eye of the critic of critical realism. *Philosophy and Phenomenological Research, 26*(1), 35–50.

Richardson, L. (2000). Writing: A method of inquiry. In N. K. Denzin and Y. S. Lincoln (eds), *Handbook of qualitative research* (2nd edn, pp. 923–948). Thousand Oaks, CA: Sage Publications.

Richardson, L., & St Pierre, E. A. (2005). Writing: a method of inquiry. In N. K. Denzin, & Y. S. Lincoln (Eds.). *Handbook of Qualitative Research*, (3rd ed.), pp. 959–978. Thousand Oaks, CA: Sage Publications.

Ritzer, G. (1996). *The McDonaldization of society: An investigation into the changing character of contemporary social life*. Newbury Park, CA: Pine Forge Press.

Robson, C. (2002). *Real world research* (2nd ed.). Oxford: Blackwell.

Rynes, S., & Gephart, R. P. Jr (2004). Qualitative research and the academy of management journal. *Academy of Management Journal, 47*, 454–462

Sarantakos, S. (1998). *Social Research*. Melbourne: Macmillan Education Australia.

Sarantakos, S. (2002). Beyond domestic patriarchy: marital power in Australia. *Nuance, 4*, 12–34.

Seale, C., Silverman, D., Gobo, G., & Gubrium, J.F. (Eds.) (2007). *Qualitative research practice*. Thousand Oaks, CA: Sage Publications.

Senge, P. (1990). *The fifth discipline: The art and practice of the learning organization.* New York: Doubleday.

Senge, P., Kleiner, A., & Roberts, C. (1994). *The fifth discipline fieldbook.* London: Nicholas Brealey.

Sharp, R., & Green, A. (1975). *Education and social control.* London: Routledge & Kegan Paul.

Shaw, I. (1999). *Qualitative evaluation: Introducing qualitative methods.* Thousand Oaks, CA: Sage Publications.

Skinner, J., & Edwards, A. (2005). Inventive pathways: Fresh visions for sport management research. *Journal of Sport Management, 19*(4), 404–421.

Spencer, L., Ritchie, J., Lewis, J., & Dillon, L. (2003). *Quality in qualitative evaluation: A framework for assessing research evidence.* London: National Centre for Social Research. Government Chief Social Researcher's Office, UK.

Tholey, P. (1989). Overview of the development of lucid dream research in Germany. *Lucidity Letter, 8*(2), 1–30.

von Glasersfeld, E. (1997). Amplification of a constructivist perspective. *Issues in Education, 3* (2), 203–209.

Wack, P. (1985a). The gentle art of reperceiving scenarios: Uncharted waters ahead (part 1 of a two-part article). *Harvard Business Review,* 73–89.

Wack, P. (1985b). The gentle art of reperceiving scenarios: Shooting the rapids (part 2 of a two part article). *Harvard Business Review,* 2–14.

Wertz, F. J. (2011). A phenomenological psychological approach to trauma and resiliency. In F. J. Wertz, K. Charmaz, L. McMullen, R. Josselson, R. Anderson, & E. McSpadden (Eds.), *Five Ways of Doing Qualitative Analysis: Phenomenological Psychology, Grounded Theory, Discourse Analysis, Narrative Research, and Intuitive Inquiry,* pp. 124–164. New York, NY: Guilford Press.

Willig, C. (2013). *Introducing qualitative research in psychology.* London: Open university Press/McGraw-Hill Education.

Willmott, H. (2005). Theorizing contemporary control: Some post-structuralist responses to some critical realist questions. *Organization, 12*(5), 747–780.

Wollin, D. (1996). *Rigor in theory-building from cases.* Paper presented at ANZAM '96 Conference, Wollongong, NSW, 6–8 December, 1996.

PART 2

Planning the sport management research process

Sampling in qualitative research

CHAPTER OVERVIEW

For the qualitative researchers, sampling is based upon their relevance in the research topic as opposed to their representativeness, which determines the way in which the participants to be studied are selected. Sport management researchers can utilise various sampling techniques as they aim to select participants with a connection to, involvement in, or interest in the research topic under investigation. This chapter explore the sampling options available to sport management researchers, their relationship to sample size, and the criticism of sampling practices used in qualitative research.

INTRODUCTION

Sampling is the process of systematically selecting the data that will be examined during the course of a study. Sampling involves decisions about what data to collect and analyse, and where these can be accessed. Sampling decisions begin during the early stages of research. These depend on the focus and topic of the research but include: (1) *where to sample?*: at the broadest level, the setting or site for your study; (2) *what to sample?*: within the above context, the time period, activities, events, processes or issues; and (3) *whom or what to sample?*: at a micro-level, the group of people or cluster of materials or artefacts (Hammersley & Atkinson, 2007). Sampling is complex, it can be structured but in many cases such as in qualitative research it is flexible and evolves and develops during the study. It can be sequential in its process, for example the selection of the sampling units is not made before fieldwork begins but develops as discoveries are made. In this sense, sampling is guided by theoretical development and it becomes progressively more focused. This continuous development carries on throughout the study until no new relevant data arises as the researcher searches for negative or deviant cases. This chapter therefore deals with the important issue of sampling in sport management research.

SAMPLING IN QUALITATIVE RESEARCH

Researchers always try to draw a representative sample to draw any conclusion about the "real world". This is a part of the researcher's responsibility. There are two basic sampling techniques: ***probability*** and ***non-probability*** sampling. A probability sample is defined as a sample in which every element of the population has an equal chance of being selected. Alternatively, if sample units are selected on the basis of personal judgement, the sample method is a non-probability sample.

For the qualitative researcher, sampling is based upon their relevance to the research topic as opposed to their representativeness, which determines the way in which the participants to be studied are selected. Sport management researchers will in general utilise techniques that are defined as *"non- probability"* sampling techniques, as they aim to select participants with a connection to, involvement in, or interest in the research topic under investigation.

In a *non-probability* sample, some subjects have a greater, but unknown, chance (probability) than others of selection. Non-probability sampling is frequently used in qualitative research where in-depth understanding of particular groups or individuals' experiences are more important than representativeness. Qualitative researchers aim to find cases that enhance what the researcher will learn within a specific context – for the sport management researcher, a sample drawn from a specific group who are involved in or have an interest in an area related to the research study – i.e. individual athletes, spectators at specific sporting events, employees of sport management enterprises, families of athletes – will be more likely to provide relevant data and a deepened understanding of the research topic, rather than a random sample drawn from the general public that may provide no relevant information about the topic at hand. When choosing the sample population, the sport management researcher aims to obtain a range of responses or ideas, and seeks to explore issues to generate research questions/hypotheses; the sample therefore aims to include a wide variety of people likely to be able to share experiences relating to a given topic.

There are many different types of *non-probability* sampling, some of which are more applicable to the sport management researcher than others. *Purposive* sampling, for example, has definite applicability to the sport management research context, whereas *convenience* or *quota sampling* have flaws that make them less suited for sport management research. There are a number of different types of sample and sampling. The following are the most important and most often used types of sampling, although many sampling types overlap.

Non-probability sampling

Purposive samples are often referred to as "judgement samples", because researchers select participants subjectively. The sport management researcher would use purposive sampling in studies where unique cases are required to provide especially informative data – for example senior managers responsible for specific portfolios. Also, the researcher may use purposive sampling when aiming to identify particular types of cases for further in-depth investigation. With purposive sampling the sport management researcher is thinking and planning ahead about the analysis process and the social explanations or interpretations they intend to construct.

Snowballing is a technique to identify further respondents who fit the characteristics of the research focus or situation. In snowball sampling, the researcher obtains additional samples by their connection to or referral from the original sample source. *Snowball sampling* is particularly useful when researchers are investigating aspects of organisations or people that are interconnected in some way – and for the sport management researcher this could relate to branches of a worldwide sporting agency, or athletes that have been convicted of doping violations. The cases may not know or even interact with other cases in the sample, but they have a link – either direct or indirect. Snowball sampling is a multistage technique – it starts with either one, or a few cases, and then "snowballs" to include other cases, based on their links to the original cases.

Convenience sampling is frequently used in qualitative research concerned with exploring views and experiences. In this type of sample, anyone from the study population who is available can be interviewed. Although this method can save time, money, and effort, it does so at the expense of information and credibility (Miles & Huberman, 1994; Pope & Mays, 2000). An example of a sport management researcher using this type of sampling would be to conduct interviews on the street or in a shopping centre – the people interviewed are convenient, but they do not represent everyone, and will not necessarily have any knowledge of, or interest in, the research topic. Another example would be the sport management researcher distributing a survey via a letter box drop or via publication in a newspaper, and asking people to complete the survey and mail it in. Not everybody reads the newspaper or unsolicited mail, and those that do may or may not have an interest in the topic. Some people will respond, but a sample obtained this way could not be used to generalise accurately. It therefore tends to produce ineffective, unrepresentative samples, and is not recommended for the sport management researcher. An overview of a whole range of sampling approaches can be found in Patton (2002) and Marshall and Rossman (2006). Table 3.1 provides a full list of sampling approaches.

Research brief

Title: A coach perspective on the use of planned disruptions in high-performance sports
Authors: Kegelaers, J., *Vrije Universiteit Brussel & Amsterdam University of Applied Sciences*, Wylleman, P., *Vrije Universiteit Brussel*, & Oudejans, R. R., *Amsterdam University of Applied Sciences & Vrije Universiteit Amsterdam* (2020)
Reference: Kegelaers, J., Wylleman, P., & Oudejans, R. R. (2020). A coach perspective on the use of planned disruptions in high-performance sports. *Sport, Exercise, and Performance Psychology, 9*(1), 29.

In elite sports, a case is increasingly made for the structural inclusion of what is labelled as planned disruptions. These are structured and deliberate training activities whereby athletes are exposed to increased and/or changing demands under controlled circumstances. The present study aimed at exploring the different types of planned disruptions high-performance coaches use and the desired outcomes of these disruptions. To this end, thematic analysis was used to analyse semi-structured interviews with nine talent development and elite-level coaches. Using a combination of purposeful criterion and opportunistic sampling, participants were selected based on the following criteria: (a) be employed as a coach by their national sport governing body, (b) coach athletes who received a high performance athlete statute from their National Olympic Committee, and (c) already utilise some form of planned disruptions in their coaching. Results indicated that these coaches used a combination of nine types of planned disruptions (i.e. location, competition simulation, punishments and rewards, physical strain, stronger competition, distractions, unfairness, restrictions, and outside the box). These strategies were used to familiarise athletes to pressure, create awareness, develop or refine personal resources, and promote team processes.

Table 3.1	Sampling approaches

Types of sampling approaches

Type of sampling	Purpose
Intensity sampling	The researcher selects a small number of rich cases that provide in-depth information and knowledge of a phenomenon of interest. As Patton (2001) points out, **intensity sampling** requires prior information and exploratory work to be able to identify intense examples.
Extreme or deviant case sampling	The process of selecting or searching for highly unusual cases of the phenomenon of interest or cases that are considered outliers, or those cases that, on the surface, appear to be the "exception to the rule" that is emerging from the analysis.
Snowball or chain sampling	Snowball or chain sampling involves utilising well informed people to identify critical cases or informants who have a great deal of information about a phenomenon.
Maximum variation sampling	To document diverse variations; can help to identify common patterns that cut across variations.
Convenience sampling	A process of selecting subjects or units for examination and analysis that is based on accessibility, ease, speed, and low cost.
Criterion sampling	Criterion sampling involves selecting cases that meet some predetermined criterion of importance (Patton, 2001, p. 238).
Random sampling	A systematic process of selecting subjects or units for examination and analysis that does not take contextual or local features into account.
Homogenous sampling	The process of selecting a small homogeneous group of subjects or units for examination and analysis.
Critical case sampling	The process of selecting a small number of important cases – cases that are likely to "yield the most information and have the greatest impact on the development of knowledge" (Patton, 2001, p. 236).
Theory-based or theoretical sampling	The process of selecting "incidents, slices of life, time periods, or people on the basis of their potential manifestation or representation of important theoretical constructs" (Patton, 2001, p. 238).
Confirming and disconfirming cases	Identifying confirming and disconfirming cases is a sampling strategy that occurs within the context of and in conjunction with other sampling strategies.
Typical cases	The process of selecting or searching for cases that are not anyway atypical, extreme, deviant, or unusual.
Intensity sampling	The process of selecting or searching for rich or excellent examples of the phenomenon of interest. These are not, however, extreme, or deviant cases.

(*Continued*)

Table 3.1	Sampling approaches (*Continued*)	
Types of sampling approaches		
Type of sampling	**Purpose**	
Politically important cases	The process of selecting or searching for a politically sensitive site or unit of for analysis.	
Purposeful random sampling	The process of identifying a population of interest and developing a systematic way of selecting cases that is not based on advanced knowledge of how the outcomes would appear.	
Stratified purposeful sampling	Patton (2001) describes these as samples within samples and suggests that purposeful samples can be stratified or nested by selecting particular units or cases that vary according to a key dimension.	
Opportunistic or emergent sampling	Opportunistic or emergent sampling occurs when the researcher makes sampling decisions during the process of collecting data.	
Theoretical sampling	Theoretical sampling develops as the study proceeds and cannot be planned beforehand (Glaser and Strauss, 1967).	
Heterogeneous sample	Heterogeneous sampling is also called *maximum variation sampling* (Patton, 2002) because it involves a search for variations in settings and for individuals with widely differing experiences of a particular phenomenon.	
Combination or mixed purposeful sampling	Combination of above approaches meets multiple interests and needs.	

DEFINING YOUR SAMPLE

Sample criteria

Sample criteria outline the demographics, characteristics or attitudes research-ers want the sample to possess. In some cases, it may be a combination of demo-graphically, behaviourally, and attitudinal criteria. Some examples of sample criteria include:

1. *Demographically defined*: gender, age, ethnicity, socio-economic group (SEG), or location. For example, you may be interested in the opinions of women, so your sample would be only female, or you may only want to talk to Londoners.

2. *Behaviourally defined*: activity, ownership, or other common lifestyle traits. For example, you could be interested only in the opinions of people who have/have not taken part in a particular activity, or bicycle owners, or only people who regularly visit a fitness centre.

3. *Attitudinally defined*: those with a particular attitude. For example, those who are dissatisfied with a product or people's attitudes towards anti-doping.

Best practice is to define the sample criteria as clearly as possible. Sometimes it's beneficial to set quotas within a sample. A quota is a maximum limit that is assigned to one or more sample criteria to make sure different groups are equally or reasonably represented in your results.

SAMPLE SIZE

Unlike in quantitative research, where there is a formula for determining the sample size needed for statistical power at a given level of confidence, there is no formula for determining the "correct" size of a qualitative sample. Sample size in qualitative research is not judged by the same criteria as it is in quantitative research because statistical power is not the goal (Patton, 2002). Instead, the researcher needs to consider the trade-offs between breadth and depth, and that can be done only by considering the purposes of the qualitative portion of the study. If the goal is to capture variation – i.e. breadth – across cases (programmes, individuals) that may call for a larger sample than one intended to explore a narrow phenomenon in depth. The sample size should provide what Patton terms "reasonable coverage" of whatever is to be studied. This number can be increased if "saturation" is not reached once data from the minimum sample has been collected. Sample "saturation" is reached when data collected from additional subjects no longer contributes any new information. It is important to keep in mind that saturation or informational redundancy can be reached prematurely if: (1) one's sampling frame is too narrow; (2) one's analytical perspective is skewed or limited; (3) the method employed is not resulting in rich, in depth information; and (4) the researcher is unable to get beyond the surface or "status quo" with respondents.

Recent methodological developments in the literature offer some new insights into qualitative sample sizes that can achieve saturation and are applicable across most qualitative study designs. Historically, most researchers would agree it takes about 18–20 interviews for most studies to achieve saturation (Patton, 2015). Hennink, Kaiser, and Marconi (2017), however, conducted an in-depth analysis of qualitative coding and thematic harmonisation processes to provide better parameters for appropriate sample sizes, which can maximise the ability of a researcher to achieve data saturation. Their work built on two earlier studies by Guest, Bunce, and Johnson (2006) and Namey, Guest, McKenna, and Chen (2016). The team's findings suggest in most qualitative study designs researchers should consider a sample of between 4 and 40 participants that suits their research purpose.

The appropriate number of participants chosen for research will depend on the type of research question, the type of qualitative approach used in the study, material, time, and resources. Sandelowski (1995) suggested, when determining an adequate sample size in qualitative research, it is ultimately a matter of judgement, experience, and researchers. They will need to evaluate the quality of the data collected in light of the uses to which it will be put and the research method, sampling and analytical strategy employed. As Silverman (2010) citing Mitchell (1983), stated "the validity of qualitative analysis depends more on the quality of the analysis than on the size of the sample" (p. 54). There are a number of questions the sport management researcher should consider when considering sampling. These include: (1) Can they explain how the sampling strategy meets the goals of the study?; (2) Does the sampling strategy make intuitive sense? That is, does it seem likely to include the most information-rich cases or participants and do so in an organised, systematic manner?; (3) If the research plan or proposal calls for a convenience sample, can you explain why a more systematic approach to sampling was not adopted?; (4) Have you secured a minimum sample size for the qualitative data collection?; Can you explain how this size of sample will provide reasonable coverage, achieve representation of the individuals/cases to be studied, or achieve saturation?

Research brief

Title: Qualitative investigation of athletes' perceptions of cheating in sport
Authors: Šukys, S., *Lithuanian Sports University*, Karanauskienė, D., *Lithuanian Sports University*, & Šmigelskaitė, J., *Lithuanian Sports University* (2019)
Reference: Šukys, S., Karanauskienė, D., & Šmigelskaitė, J. (2019). Qualitative investigation of athletes' perceptions of cheating in sport. *Baltic Journal of Sport and Health Sciences, 3* (114).
The aim of the present study was to give voice to elite athletes exploring their perceptions of cheating in sport. Utilising a purposeful sampling technique, 11 athletes were interviewed – one woman and 10 men from football (F, $n = 6$), rugby league (R, $n = 2$), and three from athletics (A).

Athletes' perceptions related to cheating in sport were explored by individual semi-structured interviews. Interpretive thematic data analysis was conducted in several stages, beginning with the exploration of the recorded materials. The analysis of the interview data allowed to distinguish the following broad themes: the perceived forms of cheating in sport, causes of cheating, initiators of cheating, and athletes' views on the evaluation of cheating, and as a separate theme – athletes' insights on cheating in children's sport. The athletes were aware of the prevalence of cheating in all sports, emphasising that it is an illegal phenomenon and associated it with the potential financial benefits, corruption, match fixing, and the use of doing.

IDENTIFYING PARTICIPANTS

Without the right sample to represent the phenomenon of interest, a qualitative study cannot achieve data saturation, meet its goals, or make a meaningful contribution to the literature. With these issues in mind it is important to consider the *inclusion and exclusion criteria* for participants. When considering this it should be specified for each particular research question/objective. You should also consider the *identification of sub-groups*. This is necessary in order to form suitable focus groups (focus groups are discussed in greater detail in Chapter 7) that will represent the range of experiences and opinions in a wider study population. The composition of focus groups needs to be carefully considered in relation to differences in experiences or behaviours of interest to the study across social groups as well as to power relations and sensitivities that may be involved in being asked to discuss particular research topics in a semi-public manner.

CRITICISM OF SAMPLING APPROACHES

Qualitative samples continue to come in for criticism; as Gobo (2007) aptly noted: "sampling in qualitative research has had a hard time" (p. 425). Qualitative researchers are often assailed for producing samples that lack representativeness and are non-probabilistic, while too small a sample is said to lead to results devoid of credibility. Critics of non-random samples, opportunistic samples, purposive samples, and snowball samples argue that they lack statistical power and lead to findings that are meaningless without extrapolation to wider populations. This line of thinking has tended to denounce qualitative data for its lack of generalisability. Without generalisability, it is said, there can be no validity, and without validity, there is no opportunity to apply findings to other settings. Thus, the data is considered unreliable (reliability and validity are discussed in more detail in Chapter 4).

Much of this criticism rests on misunderstandings or lack of knowledge. Rapport et al. (2018) offer a rebuttal to this position through six points. First, they note that qualitative researchers have always welcomed variance and the insights that variance affords. This provides a unique opportunity to explore a phenomenon in greater detail. This is because social research does not aim to control conditions where social phenomenological observations take place. Indeed, qualitative researchers refute the possibility of controlling for social conditions. This leads to a deep-seated understanding of a phenomenon in all of its complexity that can be both qualified and nuanced. Second, they suggest smaller samples reap the benefits of more extensive and in-depth data examination, leading to a greater level of understanding, including not only what data to share but also what data they do not share, in statistical terms the outliers that are the exception to the rule. Third, they posit that qualitative samples can lead to unexpected disclosures, unplanned situations that are extremely valuable. Qualitative research has an inbuilt flexibility to manage changes in the research setting, for example, if there is a sudden change in consumer purchasing behaviour or views due to unforeseen factors. They can explain these sudden changes and its consequences. Fourth, they argue that qualitative samples are able to achieve theoretical legitimacy and social significance, rather than generalisability and statistical logic. Theoretical legitimacy helps qualitative researchers answer complex questions by ensuring that theory is derived from data using inductive rather than deductive methods. For this to occur they note there must be a "reciprocal relationship" between sampling methods, sample sizes, data mining, and theory development. This reciprocal relationship is premised on the need for theoretical rigour rather than statistical causal explanation. Theoretical sampling leads to emergent hypotheses, created through small samples of similar cases, which once created, can be tested for confirmation or refutation. Fifth, they point out that small samples lend themselves to group-working activity. Here, qualitative researchers are equally responsible for the data, and aim for "consensus-agreement" on key issues arising. Group-work supports a search for data's commonality and difference, and highlights discrepancies in group thinking. It reveals patterns in the data and indicates both what people say they do, and what they actually do. Group-work also helps to confirm whether findings are valid, reliable, and the trustworthy representations of raw data. Small samples help ease data handling and ensure that a group of qualitative researchers can cohere to provide evidence of what is effective and what needs redressing. The level of collaboration needed to achieve this is simply impossible with large datasets, where data uniformity is paramount. Finally, they suggest that small sample sizes apply a subjective prism to sense making. Thus, subjectivity adds a "positive bias" to a researchers' understanding.

Research brief

Title: Exploring athletes' perceptions of the relationship between mental toughness and dispositional flow in sport
Authors: Jackman, P. C., *University of Lincoln*, Swann, C., *University of Wollongong*, & Crust, L. *University of Lincoln* (2016)
Reference: Jackman, P. C., Swann, C., & Crust, L. (2016). Exploring athletes' perceptions of the relationship between mental toughness and dispositional flow in sport. *Psychology of Sport and Exercise, 27*, 56–65.
Despite considerable scholarly attention over the last two decades, little is known about the influence of dispositional attributes on flow in sport. In achievement settings, mental toughness (MT) is a personal capacity supporting the process of high performance. Based on common overlaps with peak performance, confidence, control, concentration, and thriving in demanding situations, the present research aimed to explore the relationship between MT and dispositional flow and to elucidate the psychological variables underlying dispositional flow. A mixed method explanatory participant-selection design was adopted, whereby a quantitative approach was used to identify individuals for a qualitative follow-up phase to explore the relationship between MT and dispositional flow. An intensity sampling strategy was used to identify individuals with higher/lower MT and dispositional flow. Semi-structured interviews were conducted with 16 athletes. Seven general dimensions describing the psychological attributes related to dispositional flow in athletes with higher and lower MT emerged. Specifically, differences in confidence, perfectionism, goal orientation, coping mechanism selection, locus of control, optimism, and concentration were apparent and could account for differences in dispositional flow.

CONCLUSION

This chapter has highlighted that for the qualitative researcher, sampling is based upon its relevance to the research topic. As such, qualitative researchers use different sampling techniques from the randomly selected and probabilistic sampling techniques that quantitative researchers generally use. Sampling techniques used by qualitative researchers are less rigid and do not adhere to a strict sampling frame as in quantitative studies. This is because qualitative sampling can develop during the research process. In this sense, sampling is guided by theoretical development and it becomes progressively more focused.

REVIEW AND RESEARCH QUESTIONS

1. How do you decide on *who* and *how many* participants to include in your sample?

2. Selection of a sample in qualitative research is determined by convenience and representativeness. Discuss.

3. Explain when the sport management researcher achieves sample saturation?

REFERENCES

Glaser, B. G. & Strauss, A. S. (1967). *The Discovery of Grounded Theory: Strategies for Qualitative Research*. New York: Aldine de Gruyter.

Gobo, G. (2007). Sampling, representativeness and generalizability. In C. Seale, G. Gobo, J. F. Gubrium, & D. Silverman D. (Eds.), *Qualitative Research Practice*, pp. 405–426. London: Sage Publications.

Guest, G., Bunce, A., & Johnson, L. (2006). How many interviews are enough? An experiment with data saturation and variability. *Field Methods, 18*, 59–82.

Hammersley M., & Atkinson P. (2007). *Ethnography: Principles in practice* (3rd ed.). London: Routledge.

Hennink, M. M., Kaiser, B. N., & Marconi, V. C. (2017). Code saturation versus meaning saturation: How many interviews are enough? *Qualitative Health Research, 27*(4) 591–608.

Marshall, C., & Rossman, G. B. (2006). *Designing qualitative research* (4th ed.). Thousand Oaks, CA: Sage Publications.

Miles, M. B., & Huberman, M. A. (1994). *Qualitative data analysis*. Thousand Oaks, CA: Sage Publications.

Mitchell, J. (1983) 'Case and Situational Analysis'. *Sociological Review, 31*(2), 187–211.

Namey, E., Guest, G., McKenna, K., & Chen, M. (2016). Evaluating bang for the buck: A cost-effectiveness comparison between individual interviews and focus groups based on thematic saturation levels. *American Journal of Evaluation, 37*, 425–440.

Patton, M. Q. (2002). Two decades of development in qualitative inquiry: A personal, experimental perspective. *Qualitative social work, 1*(3), 261–283.

Patton, M. Q. (2015). *Qualitative research and methods: Integrating theory and practice.* Thousand Oaks, CA: Sage Publications.

Pope, C., & Mays, N. (2000). *Qualitative research in health care.* London: Blackwell.

Rapport, F., Hogden, A., Faris, M., Bierbaum, M., Clay-Williams R., Long, J., Shih, P., Seah, R., & Braithwaite, J. (2018). *Qualitative research in healthcare: Modern methods, clear translation: A White Paper.* Sydney, Australia: Australian Institute of Health Innovation, Macquarie University.

Sandelowski, M. (1995). Sample size in qualitative research. *Research in Nursing and Health, 18,* 179–183.

Silverman, D. (2010). *Qualitative research.* London: Sage Publications.

CHAPTER 4

Establishing reliability and validity in qualitative inquiry

LEARNING OUTCOMES

By the end of this chapter you should be able to:

- Define reliability and validity in qualitative research.

- Discuss the importance of establishing validity.

- List strategies used by researchers to improve reliability and validity.

KEY TERMS

1. **Reliability:** consistency, dependability. The results can be replicated.

2. **Validity:** truthfulness of the research outcomes.

3. **Authenticity:** how "real" are the results.

4. **Credibility:** how believable or credible something is.

5. **Trustworthiness:** a set of criteria that have been offered for judging the quality or goodness of qualitative enquiry.

6. **Authenticity:** when strategies used are appropriate for the true reporting of participants' ideas.

7. **Auditability:** the documentation or paper-trail of the researcher's thinking, decisions, and methods related to the study.

8. **Rigor:** how the researcher establishes the trustworthiness of the findings.

KEY THEMES

- Validity and reliability do not make sense in qualitative research.

- Trustworthiness refers to a set of criteria that have been offered for judging the quality of qualitative inquiry.

- Validating qualitative research may include credibility, transferability, dependability, and confirmability.

- For qualitative research, claims of generalisability have never been strong.

CHAPTER OVERVIEW

This chapter discusses the issues and meaning of reliability and validity in qualitative research. In the context of qualitative research, many perspectives, terms, and procedures have been developed to establish reliability and validity like internal validity, external validity, reliability, objectivity (LeCompte & Goetz, 1982); credibility, transferability, dependability, conformability (Lincoln & Guba, 1985); and credibility, authenticity, integrity, explicitness, vividness, creativity, thoroughness, congruence, and sensitivity (Whitternore, Chase & Mandle, 2001 as cited in Creswell, 2012). Depending on their philosophical perspectives, some qualitative researchers reject the framework of validity that is commonly accepted in more quantitative research in the social sciences. They reject the basic realist assumption that there is a reality external to our perception of it. A major dispute involving qualitative research is whether validity and rigor are appropriate terms. In addition, there has been a proliferation of terminology that has led to controversy. This chapter clarifies the meaning and use of reliability and validity in the qualitative research paradigm. It uses the widely accepted constructs on qualitative paradigm and explains the techniques that can be used by the researchers to ensure the reliability and validity in a qualitative sport management research.

RELIABILITY AND VALIDITY

The notion of *validity*, especially in quantitative research, is generally linked to a concern with *objectivity*. Objectivity means that the human element and biases are supposedly removed, including eradication of any influence on the data by researchers' own value systems. Thus, the research is supposedly more valid and accurate. However, no research is wholly value neutral or objective. Qualitative researchers stress that their research is not about measurable facts but is instead based on subjective, interpretive, and contextual data; whereas, quantitative research attempts to control and/or exclude those elements (Auberbach & Silverstein, 2003; Glaser & Strauss, 1967; Maxwell, 1992; Strauss & Corbin, 1998). In quantitative research, reliability (also referred to as *Auditability*) is the extent to which a research instrument such as a questionnaire, when used more than once, will reproduce the same results or answer. In qualitative research, the idea of replicability and reliability is rarely used because of the subjective nature of qualitative research.

The actual understanding of validity in qualitative research in the literature is confusing. Despite criticism, Kvale and Brinkmann (2009), Maxwell (2005), and Silverman (2010) are among the leading research scholars who continue to promote the use of **reliability** and **validity** within a qualitative framework. They argue that these offer the most effective means of evaluating the quality of research, and that researchers have a general understanding of these terms even though they are used differently in qualitative and quantitative research. For

Lincoln and Guba (1985), *rigor* and *trustworthiness* in qualitative research are analogous to *validity* and *reliability* in quantitative research. Rigor in qualitative research is defined as how the researcher establishes the trustworthiness of the findings (Morse, 2015). Rigorous qualitative research reflects how well the study was implemented and managed unforeseen circumstances. *Trustworthiness*, on the other hand, ensures that the study findings are representative of the experiences of participants in relation to the study processes and procedures, and that these experiences are offered by the participants themselves.

TWO MAJOR TRENDS IN THE RELIABILITY AND VALIDITY DEBATE

It is important that we examine the two major trends in this debate around reliability and validity, as it has implications for the research process. The ***exclusive trend***, for which the qualitative paradigm is radically different from the quantitative paradigm, requires that a new language must be used to express its rigor and validity (Guba & Lincoln, 1981, 1982, 1989). The ***inclusive trend***, which argues that the credibility of qualitative research, can only be widely accepted if the language of mainstream (quantitative) research is maintained, although operationalised to meet the new conditions and circumstances (Creswell, 2009; Morse et al., 2002; Yin, 1994).

THE EXCLUSIVE TREND

The proponents of the exclusive trend claim that the terms "validity" and "reliability" from quantitative research do not make sense in qualitative research, so they should be replaced. Trochim and Donnelly (2008) described the belief of some researchers that a purpose of the qualitative approach is to reject validity as no single reality exists. However, instead of seeking objective reliability and validity, alternative criteria for validating qualitative research may include "credibility, transferability, dependability, and confirmability" (p. 149). Table 4.1 compares these criteria against those that are most commonly used in quantitative research that are discussed further in the next section.

Trustworthiness

Trustworthiness is the umbrella term coined by Lincoln and Guba (1985). They use this term to refer to a set of criteria that have been offered for judging the quality or goodness of qualitative inquiry. Lincoln and Guba and many others have argued that these criteria are more appropriate than the traditional quantitative criteria of validity and reliability. There are four major components that comprise trustworthiness criteria, these are: *credibility, transferability, dependability,* and *confirmability*.

Table 4.1	Criteria commonly used in validating qualitative and quantitative research	
Quantitative research	**Qualitative research**	
Internal validity	*Credibility* – can the research findings be trusted? Was the process robust and transparent?	
External validity	*Transferability* – do the findings extend to other areas and offer useful insights for others?	
Reliability	*Dependability* – are the findings repeatable, or would other researchers report similar interpretations?	
Objectivity	*Confirmability* – is there any way of testing the findings for "truth"? Even if the study cannot be repeated, is there an auditable trail we can follow from raw data to final analysis.	

ENSURING TRUSTWORTHINESS IN QUALITATIVE RESEARCH

Lincoln and Guba (1985) proposed four criteria for judging the soundness of qualitative research and explicitly offered these as an alternative to more traditional quantitatively oriented criteria. They felt that their four criteria better reflected the underlying assumptions involved in much qualitative research. Their criteria for evaluating trustworthiness are: (1) *credibility*; (2) *transferability*; (3) *dependability*; and (4) *confirmability*; more recently the concept of *authenticity* has been introduced.

Credibility rather than internal validity should be the aim of qualitative researchers (Lincoln & Guba, 1985). According to Merriam (1998), credibility deals with the question of how congruent are the findings with reality? Credibility in qualitative research is like internal validity in quantitative research. Credibility involves ensuring that the participants, setting, and processes are accurately identified and described for the research to be meaningful. Techniques for establishing credibility include: prolonged engagement, persistent observation, triangulation, peer debriefing, negative case analysis, referential adequacy, and member checking. For example, a sport management researcher investigating concussion policies in a football team may enhance credibility by interviewing several people at different levels and positions in the organisation to encompass any different and consistent viewpoints.

Transferability replaces the notion of external validity and is close to the idea of theory-based generalisability. Transferability refers to the degree to which the results of qualitative research can be generalised or transferred to other contexts or settings. From a qualitative perspective, transferability is primarily the responsibility of the one doing the generalising. The researcher describes in detail the context and underlying assumptions of the research (thick description), so that transferability is possible, but the person who transfers the results to a different context is responsible for the transfer. The notion of transferability raises the question of whether we can we apply these findings to other contexts or groups of people? In a sport management context, will fans of one sport studied have similar viewpoints or actions of fans in other sports? All steps of the methods used to collect and analyse data should be documented and traceable in order to allow for *auditability* (Padgett, 2008). To reduce *researcher bias*, a process of reflexivity, or a systematic self-awareness, where the researchers would reflect on their analysis of the data and discuss the differences in coding after cross-checking, is important.

Dependability emphasises the stability of the data over time. Dependability is often another word for reliability. It is when the researcher attempts to account for changing conditions in the phenomenon chosen for the study as well as changes in the design created by increasingly refined understanding of the setting. Dependability in qualitative research is often achieved by the researcher allowing cross-checking of codes (also known as inter-coder agreement or inter-rater reliability – discussed in Chapter 8) by other research experts to see whether these experts would code in the same way as the researcher (Creswell, 2009). As a sport management researcher, if you have coded interviews with team managers, coaches, and athletes that reflect particular values over doping allegations, by then asking an external expert to code segments of the interviews tests dependability if those same particular values arise. The researcher must be able to account for the permanently changing context in which the research takes place, describing any changes that occur and how these changes affect the research.

Confirmability demonstrates that the inquiry is free of bias, values, and prejudice; that is the data interpretations and outcomes are rooted in contexts and persons apart from the researcher and are not mere products of the researcher's imagination. The researcher must document the procedures, so that others can check and recheck the data throughout the study. Like *credibility*, techniques that may be used to strengthen confirmability include: prolonged engagement, persistent observation, peer debriefing, negative case analysis, and triangulation. Continuing the example above, if the sport management researcher has a biased opinion of doping in sport and allows that bias to creep into the coding process, they may "uncover" values from the managers, coaches, and athletes that match their own values. A first external expert may code the data to test dependability, and a second external expert may code portions of the data to confirm the findings. After the study, a data audit or external audit should be conducted by a researcher not involved in the research process, to examine both the process and product of the research study. This process "will ensure the truth value of the data" (Creswell, 2009, p. 199).

The concept of *authenticity*, which includes fairness, the sharing of knowledge and action, has not yet become as widely known and debated as the concept of trustworthiness. This concept was added to the Lincoln and Guba (1985) original framework. A study is authentic when the strategies used are appropriate for the "true" reporting of participants' ideas, when the study is fair, and when it helps participants and similar groups to understand their world and improve it. Authenticity is usually evident in participatory research when researchers and members of a team or organisation cooperate to build together strategies to bring about social change.

THE INCLUSIVE TREND

Many interpretations exist within the inclusive trend. The approach discussed here is proposed by Creswell (2009). According to Creswell, qualitative validity refers to the different procedures the researcher employs to ensure findings are accurate, whereas qualitative reliability refers to whether a particular research approach is consistent across different projects and different researchers. Qualitative generalisation is a term that is not often discussed in contexts of qualitative research, since the findings achieved from qualitative research methods are normally not intended for generalisation (Creswell, 2009). The following discussion will outline this trend.

QUALITATIVE VALIDITY

Creswell (2009) recommended the use of multiple strategies that enhance the researcher's ability to assess the accuracy of findings, as well as convince the readers of that accuracy. According to Creswell, one advantage of qualitative research can be high validity. Validity, in Creswell's interpretation, means that "the researcher checks for the accuracy of the findings" (p. 190) by using multiple strategies to enhance the researcher's ability to evaluate the precision of findings. Creswell also suggested that "good qualitative research contains comments by the researchers about how their interpretation of the findings is shaped by their background" (p. 192).

Creswell (2009) suggests: that *qualitative validity* does not have the meaning used in quantitative research: it just means that that the researcher checks for the accuracy of the findings by employing adequate procedures. *Qualitative reliability* indicates that the researcher's approach is consistent across different researchers and different projects.

While *qualitative generalisation* is a term used in a limited way in qualitative research, since the intent is not to generalise finds, but rather to explore particular phenomena in the context where they occur.

Creswell (2009) argued that it is a prime imperative to check for the accuracy of the findings and he listed eight strategies to avoid validity issues that should also improve the researcher's capability to evaluate the truthfulness of the given information. These are:

- Triangulation

- Member checking

- Rich, thick description

- Avoidance of researcher bias

- Negative case analysis

- Prolonged engagement

- Peer debriefing

- External auditing

Maxwell (1992) is yet another researcher who has examined the issue of validity. He developed **five** categories to judge the validity of qualitative research: (1) descriptive validity, (3) interpretive validity, (3) theoretical validity, (4) evaluative validity, and (5) generalisability. These five categories will now be discussed.

- *Descriptive validity*: This is defined as the accuracy of the behaviours, events, objects, settings, and others reported by the researcher. For example, that which is reported is actually what happened or what was heard or observed. Descriptive validity forms the base on which all the other forms of validity are built upon. Without an accurate account of the formative data all else is irrelevant (Glaser & Strauss, 1967).

- *Interpretive validity*: This is defined as the accuracy of interpretation as to what happened in the minds of subjects and the extent to which the researcher understands exactly the opinions, thinking, feelings, intentions, and experiences of subjects. Interpretive validity captures how well the researcher reports the participants' meaning of events, objects, and/or behaviours (Maxwell, 1992). The key here is that the interpretations are not based on the researcher's perspective but that of the participant.

- *Theoretical validity*: This is defined as the extent to which the theoretical explanations developed are in congruent with the data and is reliable and can be defended. Theoretical validity "goes beyond concrete description and interpretation and explicitly addresses the theoretical constructions that the researcher brings to, or develops during, the study" (Maxwell, 1992, p. 50).

- *Evaluative validity*: This moves away from the data itself and tries to assess the evaluations drawn by the researchers (Maxwell, 1992). Claims may be drawn from the researchers own understanding of the situation and not on the data. For example, if the researcher studying a sport organisation declared that the employees were wrong about their feelings regarding management policies based upon their personal interpretation of the situation then the validity of the participants responses are problematic. However, the problem of how the researcher evaluates the data they receive may raise questions from other researchers on the quality of data and research methods utilised.

- *Generalisability*: This refers to the extent to which one can extend the account of a particular situation or population of other persons, times, or settings than those directly studied. Maxwell (1992) suggests that this issue plays a different role in qualitative research than it does in quantitative or experimental research, because qualitative studies are usually not designed to allow systematic generalisations to some wider population. Generalisation in qualitative research usually takes place the development of theory that only makes sense of the particular persons or situations studied, but also show how the same process, in different situations, can lead to different results. Maxwell argues that in qualitative research, there are two aspects to generalisability; "generalizing within the community group or institution studied to persons, events and settings that were not directly observed or interviewed; and generalizing to other community, groups, or institutions" (p. 293).

According to Maxwell (1992), by applying these five categories of validity, qualitative researchers and readers can assess the validity of the findings.

ENSURING TRUSTWORTHINESS IN QUALITATIVE RESEARCH

Patton (2002) notes that a significant "barrier to credible qualitative findings stems from the suspicion that the analyst has shaped findings according to predispositions and biases" (p. 553). However, there are strategies that qualitative researchers can and should employ to ensure that their conclusions present as full and accurate a picture of what is being studied as possible. Conclusions must be supported by the data, and the interpretive process needs to be rigorous. Rigor in interpretation rests on several strategies including considering rival conclusions, looking for negative or disconfirming cases, using triangulation, and getting feedback from study participants (Patton, 2002).

As discussed previously, the *exclusive trend* in the qualitative paradigm is so radically different from the quantitative paradigm that a new language must be used to express its rigor and validity (Guba & Lincoln, 1981, 1982, 1989).

As discussed previously in this chapter, Lincoln and Guba (1985) proposed four criteria for evaluating trustworthiness of qualitative research findings. Lincoln and Guba's (1985) approach is widely accepted as the best approach so

Table 4.2	Techniques for establishing trustworthiness
Criteria and techniques for ensuring trustworthiness in qualitative research	
Techniques for establishing *credibility*	■ Prolonged engagement
	■ Persistent observation
	■ Triangulation
	■ Peer debriefing
	■ Negative case analysis
	■ Referential adequacy
	■ Member checking
Techniques for establishing *transferability*	■ Thick description
Techniques for establishing *dependability*	■ Inquiry audit
Techniques for establishing *confirmability*	■ Confirmability audit
	■ Audit trail
	■ Triangulation
	■ Reflexivity

we will return to these criteria and unpack the techniques used to ensure the trustworthiness of the research findings. The four criteria and the techniques associated with them are highlighted in Table 4.2 and will be subsequently discussed in more detail.

Research brief

Title: Mediating peer teaching for learning games: An action research intervention across three consecutive sport education seasons
Authors: Farias, C., *University of Porto*, Mesquita, I., *University of Porto*, Hastie, P. A., *Auburn University*, & O'Donovan, T., *University of Bedfordshire* (2018)
Reference: Farias, C., Mesquita, I., Hastie, P. A., & O'Donovan, T. (2018). Mediating peer teaching for learning games: An action research intervention across three consecutive sport education seasons. *Research Quarterly for Exercise and Sport, 89*(1), 91–102.
The purpose of this study was to provide an integrated analysis of a teacher's peer-teaching mediation strategies, the student–coaches' instruction, and the students' gameplay development across three consecutive seasons of sport education. Twenty-six 7th-grade students participated in three consecutive sport education seasons of invasion games (basketball, handball, and soccer). The research involved three action research cycles, one per season, and each cycle included the processes of planning, acting and monitoring, reflecting, and fact finding. Data collection consisted of videotape and audiotape records of all 47 lessons, a reflective field diary kept by the first author in the role of teacher–researcher, and a total of 24 semi-structured focus-group interviews. Trustworthiness criteria for assuring the quality of qualitative research included extensive data triangulation, stakeholders' crosschecking, and collaborative interpretational analysis.

The techniques mentioned below may be used by the researchers to ensure credibility in qualitative research.

Prolonged engagement

Lincoln and Guba (1985), Erlandson and his colleagues (Erlandson, Harris, Skipper, & Allen, 1993), and Merriam (1995) are among the many others who recommend "prolonged engagement" between the researcher and the participants in order to gain an adequate understanding of an organisation and to establish a relationship of trust between the researcher and the participants. The important issue here is spending sufficient time in the field to learn or understand the culture, social setting, or phenomenon of interest. Such involvement gives the researcher time to check and recheck the quality of the observations and interpretations they have made, enabling them to distinguish the important issues from trivialities. Some of the benefits of prolonged engagement in the setting are:

- researchers gain a good understanding of the context and are more likely to present a convincing account of participants' perspectives;

- participants learn to trust the researcher and are more likely to tell the truth;

- over a prolonged period, the researcher is more likely to examine and reflect on their own assumptions and the role they play in how they relate to the data.

Persistent observation

A subset of prolonged engagement is the idea of persistent observation. Lincoln and Guba (1985) suggest if the purpose of prolonged engagement is to render the inquirer open to the multiple influences and contextual factors that impinge upon the phenomenon being studied, the purpose of persistent observation is to identify those characteristics and elements in the situation that are most relevant to the problem and focusing on them in detail. In this sense, while prolonged engagement provides scope, persistent observation provides depth.

Triangulation

Qualitative researchers generally use this technique to ensure that an account is rich, robust, comprehensive, and well developed. Triangulation involves using multiple data sources in an investigation to produce greater understanding (Merriam, 1995). Triangulation rests upon the belief that a single method can never adequately explain a phenomenon. Using multiple methods can help to facilitate a deeper understanding. The concept has been aptly captured by

Tracy (2010) and it refers to Denzin (1978) who argues that triangulation in qualitative research assumes that if two or more sources of data, theoretical frameworks, types of data collected, or researchers converge on the same conclusion, then the conclusion is more credible. Denzin (1978) and Patton (1999) identify *four* types of triangulation:

- **Methods triangulation** – checking out the consistency of findings generated by different data collection methods. Triangulation by method uses several approaches to collect data and information about the topic being explored. Here the researcher chooses the method of inquiry according to the question being researched, e.g. by observing behaviours (an observational approach) or exploring how participants feel e.g. using interviews. Multiple methods help avoid any problems of the research findings being an artefact of the particular method used (Banister et al., 2011). This can help resolve issues around any questions of validity or distortion (Flick, 1992, 2007). It is becoming more common to have qualitative and quantitative data in a study to address this issue as mixing approaches elucidates complementary aspects of the same phenomenon. It is often the points where these data diverge that are of great interest to the qualitative researcher and provide the most insights.

- **Triangulation of sources** – examining the consistency of different data sources from within the same method. For example, at different points in time, in public versus private settings and comparing people with different viewpoints.

- **Analyst triangulation** – using multiple analyst to review findings or using multiple observers and analysts. This can provide a check on selective perception and illuminate blind spots in an interpretive analysis The goal is **not** to seek consensus, but to understand multiple ways of seeing the data.

- **Theory/perspective triangulation** – using multiple theoretical perspectives to examine and interpret the data. This approach aims to explore the diversity and complexity that is frequently the reality of research particularly when examining human behaviours. Theoretical triangulation acknowledges, and allows for, the broad range of theories, complexity, and diversity of the real world and how different theories may be accounted for in research (Kok et al., 2004).

Peer debriefing

It is suggested that the sport management researcher discuss the interpretations and conclusions of the findings with a peer. Through analytical probing, a peer debriefer can help uncover taken for granted biases, perspectives, and assumptions on the researcher's part. Lincoln and Guba (1985) note: "It is a process of exposing oneself to a disinterested peer in a manner paralleling an analytical sessions and for the purpose of exploring aspects of the inquiry that might otherwise remain only implicit within the inquirer's mind" (p. 308).

A peer review or debriefing is a process of exposing oneself to a disinterested peer in a manner paralleling analytical sessions and for the purpose of exploring aspects of the inquiry that might otherwise remain only implicit within the inquirer's mind. A peer reviewer provides support, plays devil's advocate, challenges the researchers' assumptions, pushes the researchers to the next step methodologically, and asks hard questions about methods and interpretations (Lincoln & Guba, 1985).

In the peer debriefing strategy, the lens for establishing credibility is someone external to the study, and a critical paradigm is operating because of the close collaboration between the external reviewer and the qualitative researcher. This procedure is best used over time during the process of an entire study. Peer debriefers can provide written feedback to sport management researchers or simply serve as a sounding board for ideas. The ultimate purpose of peer debriefing is to enhance the credibility, or truth value, of a qualitative study, by providing "an external check on the inquiry process" (Lincoln & Guba, 1985, p. 301). Peer debriefing is particularly advisable because of a distinctive characteristic of qualitative research – "the researcher-as-instrument".

Individual researchers are the primary means for data collection and analysis. This also provides an opportunity for the researcher to test and defend emergent hypotheses and see if they seem reasonable and plausible to a disinterested peer debriefer. The benefits of peer debriefing are:

- peers may detect bias or inappropriate subjectivity;

- peers might provide alternative explanations to your own;

- peers may warn against inappropriate attempts to produce interpretations that are not substantiated by the data;

- peers keep you "honest" about the meanings and interpretations you assign to participants' statements.

(Onwuegbuzie and Leech, 2007).

An example of peer debriefing could be if the sport management researcher is conducting an investigation at an English Premier League club, the researchers may have developed abstract concepts and a provisional theory concerning corporate threats to club image and identity. They would then submit their tentative framework to academic colleagues involved in similar research, receiving comments from them, which would lead them to examine alternative explanations for the evidence that they had not considered previously. This would assist them in refining their provisional interpretations.

Negative case sampling

Negative or deviant case analysis is recommended by several qualitative investigators including Miles and Huberman (1994) and Creswell (1998). According to Strauss and Corbin (1990), negative case analysis enhances rigor in qualitative research and is used in the quest for verification. A negative case analysis is an ongoing and deliberate attempt to refute or challenge developing themes/ideas. Negative case analysis refers to the process of testing out sampling strategies and/or analysis to look for alternative explanations or different cases that are in contrast to the researcher's own theories or explanations. The aim is to confirm or disconfirm the findings of research by comparing it with the findings of cases that are opposite or different. For example, if a sport management researcher studied the leadership behaviour of a sport manager based on interviews with selected staff and the findings indicate the sport leader studied is autocratic. To enhance the validity of findings, the researcher might interview staff from another sport organisation, where they suspect the leadership of the manager is less autocratic and compare the opinions of staff at this location.

Negative case analysis may involve a re-examination of every case, after the initial analysis is completed, to see whether the characteristics or properties of the emergent themes (thematic analysis is discussed in Chapter 8) were applicable to all cases. Searching for negative cases and alternative explanations always presents challenges. It is not easy to become aware of discrepant data and negative or alternative cases.

Referential adequacy

This involves identifying a portion of data to be archived, but not analysed. The sport management researcher would then conduct the data analysis on the remaining data and develops preliminary findings. The researcher then returns to this archived data and analyses it as a way to test the validity of their findings. Finally, the researcher returns to this archived data and analyses it as a way to test the validity of their findings.

Member checking

Lincoln and Guba (1985) consider member checks as the single most important provision that can be made to strengthen a study's credibility. This can be done both formally and informally as opportunities for member checks may arise during the normal course of observation and conversation. Participants may also be asked to read any transcripts of dialogues in which they have participated. Here the emphasis should be on whether the participants consider that their words match what they actually intended. Merriam (1995) further elaborates that it is not only about taking data collected from the study participants, but also the tentative interpretations of these data, back to the people from whom they were derived and asking if the interpretations are plausible, if they "ring true". The specific purposes of member checking are:

- to find out whether you are presenting the reality of the participants in a way that is credible to them;

- to provide opportunities for them to correct errors which they might have made in their discussions with you;

- to assess your understanding and interpretation of the data;

- to challenge your ideas;

- to gather further data through participants' responses to your interpretations.

To enhance internal validity, or in qualitative terms *Credibility*, a sport management researcher could return to the participants who were interviewed and check whether what you had recorded was what they had said in the interview. For example, "Is this what you meant when you said ….?" Or go back to the subjects you had observed and ask them whether what you had recorded about their behaviour is accurate. For example, "Did you do this?" Through this process of verification, the credibility of qualitative research can be enhanced. Lincoln and Guba (1985) posit that this is the most crucial technique for establishing credibility. However, this technique is controversial. Table 4.3 provides an overview of member checking techniques that can be carried out.

Member checking relies on the assumption that there is a fixed truth of reality that can be accounted for by a researcher and confirmed by a participant. From an interpretive perspective, understanding is co-created and there is no objective truth or reality to which the results of a study can be compared. The process of member checking may therefore lead to confusion rather than confirmation because participants may change their mind about an issue, the interview itself may have an impact on their original assessment, and new experiences (since the time of contact) may have intervened. Respondents may also disagree with researcher's interpretations. Then the question of whose interpretation should stand becomes an issue. It should also be remembered both researchers and members are stakeholders in the research process and have different stories to tell and agendas to promote. This can result in conflicting ways of seeing interpretations. Morse (1994), Angen (2000), and Sandelowski (1993) offer a comprehensive critique of the use of member checks for establishing the validity of qualitative research, these are:

- Members struggle with abstract synthesis.

- Members and researchers may have different views of what is a fair account.

- Members strive to be perceived as good people; researchers strive to be seen as good scholars. These divergent goals may shape findings and result in different ways of seeing and reacting to data.

- Members may tell stories during an interview that they later regret or see differently.

- Members may deny such stories and want them removed from the data.

- Members may not be in the best position to check the data. They may forget what they said or the manner in which a story was told.

- Members may participate in checking only to be "good" respondents and agree with an account in order to please the researcher.

- Different members may have different views of the same data.

Table 4.3	Techniques for carrying out a member check	
Technique	**Problems**	**Comments**
1. Present participants with a transcript of their interview or fieldnotes on your observations.	1. Time consuming 2. Participants do not see your interpretation of your data	1. An acceptable technique but is time consuming for the novice researcher
2. Present participants with a summary of their interview and your observations, plus your interpretation of their words and actions.	1. Requires you to write summaries and accounts specifically for the purpose of member checking	1. Useful for confirming idea and the meaning of your account 2. Participants can suggest adaptations to your interpretation 3. Their comments can clarify, trigger, or extend your ideas that can be fed back into your final report
3. Present a copy of the final report or substantial section of it to the participants	1. Lengthy process 2. Demands commitment from participants 3. Value of feedback on academic reports depends on the participants familiarity with the style of presentation	1. It has the potential to be very valuable, as it allows participants to read the study in its entirety and comment 2. A risk that some sport organisations will draw funding or support if they consider your conclusions to be unfavourable

Research brief

Title: Personal and social responsibility development: Exploring the perceptions of Portuguese youth football coaches within competitive youth sport
Author: Santos, F., *University of Porto*, Corte-Real, N., *University of Porto*, Regueiras, L., *Nun'Alvres Institute*, Dias, C., *University of Porto*, & Fonseca, A., *University of Porto* (2017)
Reference: Santos, F., Corte-Real, N., Regueiras, L., Dias, C., & Fonseca, A. (2017). Personal and social responsibility development: Exploring the perceptions of Portuguese youth football coaches within competitive youth sport. *Sports Coaching Review*, 6(1), 108–125.
Youth sport is a valuable context to foster the development of personal and social responsibility (PSR). Within competitive youth sport, coaches face many challenges promoting PSR while still being required to win. The purpose of this study was to analyse the perceptions of youth coaches on delivering and barriers to delivering PSR in competitive youth sport. The data were collected through semi-structured interviews conducted with 17 youth coaches who coached under-15 football teams in Portugal. A thematic analysis was performed which generated high (e.g. coaching practice) and low order categories (e.g. positive transference). The findings showed that coaches considered PSR development important in different developmental stages. The relationship between parents and coaches was identified as a key factor. A negative case analysis was also used to reflect the data obtained with rigour, more specifically to portray certain cases that diverged from the general tendency.

TECHNIQUES FOR ESTABLISHING TRANSFERABILITY

Following techniques may be used by the researchers to ensure transferability in qualitative research.

Thick description

A term coined originally by the philosopher Ryle and borrowed by Geertz (1973), it means not only a detailed description of the context, people, and process of the research, but also the meaning and intentions of the participants. Thick description is provided by Lincoln and Guba (1985) as a way of achieving a type of external validity. It requires that the researcher accounts for the complex specificity and circumstantiality of their data. By describing a phenomenon in sufficient detail, one can begin to evaluate the extent to which the conclusions drawn are transferable to other times, settings, situations, and people.

Rich, thick description lends itself to establish credibility. According to Denzin (1989), "thick descriptions are deep, dense, detailed accounts … thin descriptions, by contrast, lack detail, and simply report facts" (p. 83). The purpose of a thick description is that it creates a level of trust in the data, so that the reader can see and feel how well the quotes have been analysed and organised. The process of writing using thick description is to provide as much detail as possible. It may involve describing a small slice of interaction, experience, or action; locating individuals in specific situations; bringing a relationship or an interaction alive between two or more persons; or providing a detailed rendering of how people feel (Denzin, 1989). So, instead of just describing themes related to match fixing from several data sources, the sport management researcher might explicitly describe the emotions, context, and dialogue of the interview sessions with sport managers affected by match fixing.

According to Creswell (1998), rich, thick descriptions allow the reader to see connections and patterns (as well as the researcher) and make decisions regarding transferability because the writer describes in detail the participants or settings under study. With such detailed description, the researcher enables readers to transfer information to other settings and to determine whether the findings can be transferred "because of shared characteristics" (p. 203).

TECHNIQUES FOR ESTABLISHING DEPENDABILITY

The following techniques may be used by the researchers to ensure dependability in qualitative research.

Inquiry audit

Lincoln and Guba (1985) emphasise "inquiry audit" as one measure that may enhance the dependability of qualitative research. It involves having a researcher not involved in the research process to examine both the process and product of the research study (Hoepfl, 1997). Merriam (1995) uses the term "audit trial" as one of the techniques to establish dependability. According to Merriam, in order for an audit to take place, the researcher must describe in detail how data were collected, how categories were derived, and how decisions were made throughout the inquiry. The purpose is to evaluate the accuracy and evaluate whether or not the findings, interpretations, and conclusions are supported by the data. It provides an opportunity for an outsider to challenge the process and findings of a study. Important feedback from an external researcher or expert can lead to additional data gathering and the development of stronger and better articulated findings.

TECHNIQUES FOR ESTABLISHING CONFIRMABILITY

Following techniques may be used by the researchers to ensure confirmability in qualitative research.

Audit trail

An audit trail is a transparent description of the research steps taken from the start of a research project to the development and reporting of findings. These are records that are kept regarding what was done in an investigation. Such records should be documented and organised appropriately for retrieval purposes. These records should be made available as evidence of data collected when challenged as well as validation of the interpretation of data.

Lincoln and Guba (1985, pp. 309–310) cite Halpern's (1983) categories for reporting information when develop an audit trail, these are:

- *Raw data* – including all raw data, written field notes, unobtrusive measures (documents).

- *Data reduction and analysis* products – including summaries such as condensed notes, unitised information, quantitative summaries, and theoretical notes.

- *Data reconstruction and synthesis products* – including structure of categories (themes, definitions, and relationships), findings and conclusions, and a final report including connections to existing literatures and an integration of concepts, relationships, and interpretations.

- *Process notes* – including methodological notes (procedures, designs, strategies, rationales), trustworthiness notes (relating to credibility, dependability, and confirmability), and audit trail notes.

- *Materials relating to intentions and dispositions* – including inquiry proposal, personal notes (reflexive notes and motivations), and expectations (predictions and intentions).

- *Instrument development information* – including pilot forms, preliminary schedules, observation formats.

An audit trail is established by sport management researchers documenting the inquiry process through journaling and memoing, keeping a research log of all activities, developing a data collection chronology, and recording data analysis procedures clearly.

Reflexivity

Reflexivity is an attitude of attending systematically to the context of knowledge construction, especially to the effect of the researcher, at every step of the research process. Malterud (2001) suggests: "a researcher's background and position will affect what they choose to investigate, the angle of investigation, the methods judged most adequate for this purpose, the findings considered most appropriate, and the framing and communication of conclusions" (pp. 483–484).

Understanding something about the position, perspective, beliefs, and values of the researcher is an issue in all research, but particularly in qualitative research where the researcher is often constructed as the "human research instrument" (the concept of "reflexivity" is explored in more detail in Chapter 5).

QUALITATIVE GENERALISABILITY

Once a study's conclusions have been accepted as credible, a logical next step is to ask if they can be generalised beyond the settings or individuals studied. *"Generalisability"* refers to the ability to apply the findings or theory resulting from the study universally (Auerbach & Silverman, 2003; Maxwell, 1992), which Walsh (2003) puts under the heading of *"transferability"*. For qualitative research, generalisability is problematic. Qualitative research is concerned with the concepts and idiosyncratic characteristics of a select group; therefore, the findings or theory may only applicable to a similar group (Auerbach & Silverman, 2003; Maxwell, 1992; Strauss & Corbin, 1998).

Generalisability is a term that is not discussed often in contexts of qualitative research, since the findings achieved from qualitative research methods are normally not intended for generalisation (Creswell, 2009). Therefore, "qualitative generalisation is a term that is used in a limited way ... since the intent of this form of inquiry is not to generalise findings ... 'particularity' rather than 'generalisability' is the hallmark of qualitative research" (pp. 192–193). Generalisability can also be referred to as external validity. Threats to external validity occur if the researcher develops inaccurate inferences from the sample and generalises these findings to the larger population.

The term has its origin in quantitative research, with its random statistical sampling procedures and search for law-like patterns. However, this type of generalisability is difficult to achieve in qualitative research, where there is no search for law-like generalities as each study has specificity and uniqueness. This is because the interpretive worldview prefers to focus on specific instances or cases that are not necessarily representative of other cases or populations.

Generalisations are tentative at best, and this holds true for both qualitative and quantitative research findings. For qualitative research in particular, claims of generalisability have never been strong (Firestone, 1993). Some qualitative researchers are sceptical, or even dismissive, of generalisation, preferring to focus on understanding specific phenomena as they interact with a specific context, rather than looking for typical or average outcomes across settings (Firestone, 1993; Miles & Huberman, 1994; Stake, 1978 as cited in Patton, 2002). Many qualitative researchers recognise that the question of whether or not findings from a specific study have any applicability to other settings remains an important one that does not go away (Miles & Huberman, 1994).

Some qualitative researchers still believe that efforts should be made to generalise findings of qualitative research. These researchers argue that the in-depth description of a particular phenomenon is sufficient for the researcher to make generalisations to other individuals or individuals. To enable the findings of qualitative research to generalised, researchers have proposed ways in which validity can he enhanced. Benz and Newman (1998) proposed the following terms while discussing the issue of *generalisation* of qualitative research findings:

- *Applicability*: Can the study be applied to another sample? It should be remembered that there are no "significant differences", and it is difficult to generalise to the population based on the findings of a sample. For example, if you observe three sport managers from different sport organisations. Can you generalise what you observed about all sport managers in the country? The greater the similarity between subjects, the higher is the possibility of making generalisations.

- *Context dependent*: Can the findings of a study be generalised to another setting or context? For example, if what was observed was not so much context dependent, then the findings may be "transferred" (Guba & Lincoln, 1989) to another context or situation. It may then be able to generalise the findings.

- *Replicability*: What is the likelihood of a particular product or event that will occur under similar conditions? It is difficult to replicate or repeat a qualitative research because the natural setting is constantly changing. Researchers are therefore advised to be cautious when making claims that a study can be replicated.

The foregoing discussion suggests that the concept of generalisation is subtle and complex, and much debated among both quantitative and qualitative researchers. A full discussion is well beyond the scope of this book. Our advice is that *generalisability* should be viewed with extreme caution in qualitative sport management research. Nevertheless, if that is still something that you wish to explore then the following questions need to be addressed.

Questions to ask about generalisability:

1. How do the sampling plan and analytic approach incorporate strategies that will strengthen the generalisability of the study's findings?

2. Does the final report discuss what reasonably can be generalised from this study? On what basis is the researcher claiming generalisability?

3. Does the report explore how the sampling or analytic approach may have limited generalisability and in what ways?

4. Which processes and outcomes described in the report are generic enough that they may be applicable in other programmes and settings?

5. Have similar findings been replicated in other studies? Are the findings in agreement with or otherwise confirmatory of prior theory?

6. Does the final report suggest other settings that might provide a useful test of the findings? (Miles & Huberman, 1994, p. 279).

QUALITATIVE RELIABILITY

Reliability is commonly used in relation to the question of whether the measures devised for concepts in the social sciences are consistent. *Qualitative reliability* differs from validity in that reliability indicates the "researcher's approach is consistent across different researchers and different projects" (Creswell, 2009, p. 190). In order to do this, Creswell and Yin (2009) suggest documentation of as many steps of the procedure as possible and other reliability procedures, including cross-checking codes, checking transcripts and writing definitions of codes, and constantly comparing data with those definitions of the codes.

Creswell (2009) suggests four procedures that can be used as a means of ensuring *reliability* for single researcher studies: (1) ensure appropriate preparation (skill/knowledge level) of the researcher; (2) ensure appropriate review of the literature; (3) ensure coding reliability; and (4) ensure transcripts do not contain obvious errors. Gibbs (2007) similarly suggests the following reliability procedures: (1) check transcripts for mistakes; (2) check the persistence of the meaning of the codes; (3) coordinate communication among coders; and (4) cross-check codes developed by different researchers. Other reliability control measures used included having backup copies of both recorded interviews and transcripts. In addition, repetition of certain questions may lead to misinterpretation of the findings, and should be clarified during and after the interviews. This probing is also a technique of getting a deeper understanding of responses.

AVOIDANCE OF RESEARCHER BIAS

Creswell (1998) asserts that avoiding, or at least clarifying, researcher bias from the outset of a study is a validity issue. In this strategy, the sport management researcher notes past experiences, biases, prejudices, and orientations that may influence the study. For example, if the sport management researcher was an athlete who personally experienced a drastic change in team policies that affected their career, this should be noted if they are studying post-athletic career pathways for athletes. Hatch (2002) also advises researchers to submit a self-disclosure statement detailing any potential biases that may be relevant to the topic of the study. McMillan (2004) adds that attributes of the researcher such as age, gender, race, hostility, and physical appearance may influence research results. Two strategies to avoid researcher bias are reflexivity (researcher self-awareness and self-reflection) and researcher journaling (detailed and timely documentation of the researcher thoughts). Reflexivity (discussed in greater detail in Chapter 5) is a validity procedure whereby researchers report on (and may even try to modify) personal beliefs, values, and biases that may shape their inquiry. This validity procedure uses the lens of the researcher but to reflect on the social, cultural, and historical forces that shape their interpretation.

CONCLUSION

This chapter has explained the concept of *reliability* and *validity* based upon the seminal work of Lincoln and Guba (1985), which has shaped the understanding of reliability and validity in qualitative research paradigm. Researchers' adopting Lincoln and Guba's qualitative paradigm should seek to satisfy four criteria of trustworthiness; namely credibility, transferability, dependability, and confirmability. A series of techniques that can be used to conduct qualitative research that achieves these criteria has also been discussed. The importance of acknowledging the potential for researcher bias was also raised.

REVIEW AND RESEARCH QUESTIONS

1. Discuss the issues of reliability and validity in qualitative research?

2. To what extent can you generalise the findings of qualitative studies?

3. What should a researcher do to enhance the internal validity of qualitative research?

REFERENCES

Angen, M. J. (2000). Evaluating interpretive inquiry: Reviewing the validity debate and opening the dialogue. *Qualitative Health Research, 10*(3), 378–395.

Auberbach, C. F., & Silverstein, L. B. (2003). *Qualitative data: An introduction to coding and analysis.* New York: New York University Press.

Banister, P., Dunn, G., Burman, E., Daniels, J., Duckett, P., Goodley, D., Lawthom, R., Parker, I., Runswick-Cole, K., Sixsmith, J., Smailes, S., Tindall, C., & Whelan, P. (2011). *Qualitative methods in psychology: A research guide* (2nd ed.). Maidenhead: Open University Press/McGraw Hill.

Benz, C. and Newman, I. (1998). *Qualitative-Quantitative Research Methodology: Exploring the interactive continuum.* Carbondale, IL: Southern Illinois University Press.

Creswell, J. W. (1998). *Qualitative inquiry and research design: choosing among five traditions.* Thousand Oaks, CA: Sage Publications.

Creswell, J. W. (2009). *Research design: Qualitative, quantitative and mixed method approaches* (3rd ed.). Los Angeles, CA: Sage Publications.

Creswell, W. (2012). *Qualitative inquiry and research design: Choosing among five approaches.* London: Sage Publications.

Denzin, N. K. (1978). *The research act: A theoretical introduction to sociological methods.* New York: McGraw-Hill.

Denzin, N. K. (1989). *Interpretive interactionism.* Newbury Park, CA: Sage Publications.

Erlandson, D., Harris, E., Skipper, B., & Allen, S. (1993). *Doing naturalistic inquiry.* Newbury Park, CA: Sage Publications.

Firestone, W. A. (1993). Alternative arguments for generalizing from data as applied to qualitative research. *Educational Researcher, 22,* 16–23.

Flick, U. (1992). Triangulation revisited: Strategy of or an alternative to validation of qualitative data. *Journal of Theory of Social Behavior, 22,* 175–197.

Flick, U. (2007). *Managing quality in qualitative research.* London: Sage Publications.

Glaser, B., & Strauss, A. (1967). *The discovery of grounded theory: Strategies for qualitative research.* New York: Aldine.

Geertz, C. (1973). *The interpretation of cultures.* New York: Basic Books.

Gibbs, G. R. (2007). *Analyzing qualitative data* (2nd ed.). London: Sage Publications.

Guba, E. G., & Lincoln, Y. S. (1981). *Effective evaluation: Improving the usefulness of evaluation results through responsive and naturalistic approaches.* San Francisco, CA: Jossey-Bass.

Guba, E. G., & Lincoln, Y. S. (1982). Epistemological and methodological bases of naturalistic inquiry. *Educational Communication and Technology Journal, 30,* 233–252.

Guba, E. G., & Lincoln, Y. S. (1989). *Fourth generation evaluation.* Newbury Park, CA: Sage Publications.

Halpern, E. S. (1983). *Auditing Naturalistic Inquiries: The Development and Application of a Model.* Unpublished Doctoral Dissertation, Indiana University.

Hatch, J. A. (2002). *Doing qualitative research in educational settings.* Albany: State University of New York Press.

Hoepfl, M. C. (1997). Choosing qualitative research: A primer for technology education researchers. *Journal of Technology Education, 9*(1), 47–63.

Kok, G., Schaalma, H., Ruiter, R. A. C., & Van Empelen, R. (2004). Intervention mapping: A protocol for applying health psychology theory to prevention programmes. *Journal of Health Psychology, 9*(1), 85–98.

Kvale, S., & Brinkmann, S. (2009). *Interviews: Learning the craft of qualitative research interviewing.* London: Sage Publications.

LeCompte, M. D., & Goetz, J. P. (1982). Problems of reliability and validity in ethnographic research. *Reviews of Education Research, 52*(1), 31–60

Lincoln, Y. S., & Guba, E. G. (1985). *Naturalistic inquiry.* Beverly Hills, CA: Sage Publications.

Malterud, K. (2001). Qualitative research: Standards, challenges and guidelines. *The Lancet, 358,* 483–488.

Maxwell, J. A. (1992). Understanding and validity in qualitative research. *Harvard Educational Review, 62,* 279–299.

Maxwell, J. A. (2005). *Qualitative research design: An interactive approach* (2nd ed.). Newbury Park, CA: Sage Publications.

McMillan, J.H. (2004). Qualitative and mixed-method research designs. In A. Burvikovs (Eds.), *Educational Research: Fundamentals for the Consumer.* (pp. 255–292). Boston, MA: Pearson Education, Inc.

Miles, M. B., & Huberman, M. A. (1994). *Qualitative data analysis.* Thousand Oaks, CA: Sage Publications.

Merriam. S. (1995). What can you tell from an N of 1?: Issues of validity and reliability in qualitative research. *PAACE Journal of Lifelong Learning, 4,* 50–60.

Merriam, S. (1998). *Qualitative research and case study applications in education.* San Francisco, CA: Jossey-Bass Publishers.

Morse, J. M. (1994). *Critical issues in qualitative research methods.* Thousand Oaks, CA: Sage Publications.

Morse, J. M., Barrett, M., Mayan, M., Olson, K., & Spiers, J. (2002). Verification strategies for establishing reliability and validity in qualitative research. *International Journal of Qualitative Methods, 1*(2), 13–22.

Morse, J. M. (2015). Critical analysis of strategies for determining rigor in qualitative inquiry. *Qualitative Health Research, 25*(9), 1212–1222.

Onwuegbuzie, A. J., & Leech, N. L. (2007). Validity and qualitative research: An oxymoron? *Quality & Quantity: International Journal of Methodology, 41*(2), 233–249.

Padgett, D. (2008). *Qualitative methods in social work research.* Los Angeles, CA: Sage Publications.

Patton, M. Q. (1999). Enhancing the quality and credibility of qualitative analysis. *HSR: Health Services Research, 34*(5), 1189–1208. Part II.

Patton, M. Q. (2002). *Qualitative evaluation and research methods* (3rd ed.). Thousand Oaks, CA: Sage Publications.

Sandelowski, M. (1993). Rigor or rigor mortis: The problem of rigor in qualitative research revisited. *Advances in Nursing Science, 16*(2), 1–8.

Silverman, D. (2010). *Qualitative research.* London: Sage Publications.

Strauss, A., & Corbin, J. (1990). *Basics of qualitative research: Grounded theory, procedures and techniques.* Newbury Park, CA: Sage Publications.

Strauss, A., & Corbin, J. (1998). *Basics of qualitative research.* Thousand Oaks, CA: Sage Publications.

Tracy, S. J. (2010). Qualitative quality: Eight 'big-tent' criteria for excellent qualitative research. *Qualitative Inquiry, 16*(10), 837–851.

Trochim, W. M. K., & Donnelly, J. P. (2008). *The research methods knowledge base* (3rd ed.). Mason, OH: Atomic Dog/Cengage Learning.

Walsh, K. (2003). Qualitative research: Advancing the science and practice of hospitality. *Cornell Hotel and Restaurant Administration Quarterly, 44*(2), 66–74.

Yin, R. K. (1994). *Case study research: Design and methods.* Thousand Oaks, CA: Sage Publications.

Yin, R. K. (2009). *Case study research: Design and methods* (5th ed.). Thousand Oaks, CA: Sage Publication.

CHAPTER 5

Reflexivity in sport management research

LEARNING OUTCOMES

By the end of this chapter, you should be able to:

- Examine the emerging development of reflexivity in qualitative research.

- Identify the various interpretations of reflexivity and outline its application in sport management research.

- Understand that reflexivity is an important component in qualitative research.

- Recognise that reflexivity can assist researchers to become aware of how the values, opinions, and experiences they've brought to the research can be a positive thing.

KEY TERMS

1. **Reflexivity:** a way to reflect on one's own position.

2. **Relational reflexivity:** prioritises a connectedness between researchers and participants.

3. **Prospective reflexivity:** the effects of the researcher on the study.

4. **Retrospective reflexivity:** the effects of the study on the researcher.

5. **Positionality:** how researchers are situated.

6. **Methodology:** a particular social scientific discourse (a way of acting, thinking, and speaking).

KEY THEMES

- There are various interpretations of reflexivity.

- The application of reflexivity in sport management research is important.

- Reflexivity challenges the view of knowledge production and is independent of the researcher producing the knowledge.

- Reflexivity needs to occur in all stages of the research process.

CHAPTER OVERVIEW

Often described with terms such as "critical reflection", "self-critical dialogue", and "reflexive practice" (Kippax & Kinder, 2002), reflexivity is a ubiquitous, varied, and, at times, contentious approach in qualitative inquiry that presents challenges as we strive to understand and use the concept in our work. Reflexivity stems from reflective practice, a concept principally articulated by Schön (1983). Reflective practice implies that the product of reflection is reinvested in professional's actions, allowing them to better cope with complex practice situations and problems (Bleakley, 1999; Schön, 1983). Lindlof and Taylor (2011) have described reflexivity as the "heartbeat of qualitative research" (p. 72).

Reflexivity is commonly addressed in qualitative methodology as a way to reflect on one's own position. In doing so, the researcher engages in the practice of self-reflection in order to better understand how a researcher's lens affects the research project, particularly because qualitative research often includes interactions with participants. Based upon the notion that research is an interpretive activity, positivist notions of objectivity and empirical facts are rejected. The research process is regarded as being subjected to a variety of influences, which impact upon the interpretations generated, thus a reflexive stance is required in order to identify and understand what these influences are. In this sense, reflexivity is "a way of emphasising the importance of self-awareness, political/cultural consciousness, and ownership of one's perspective" (Patton, 2002, p. 64), all of which are relevant to sport management research. The aim of this chapter is to discuss the various interpretations of reflexivity and outline its application to sport management research.

REFLEXIVITY AND POSITIONALITY

In research, the consideration of a researcher's lens is often discussed as researcher *reflexivity* and *positionality*. Reflexivity pertains to the "analytic attention to the researcher's role in qualitative research" (Gouldner, 1971, p. 16, as cited in Dowling, 2006). It is both a *concept* and a *process* (Dowling, 2006). As a **concept**, it refers to a certain level of consciousness. Reflexivity entails self-awareness (Lambert, Jomeen, & McSherry, 2010), which means being actively involved in the research process. It is about the recognition that as researchers, we are part of the social world that we study (Ackerly & True, 2010; Frank, 1997; Morse, 1991).

Reflexivity as a **process** is introspection of the role of subjectivity in the research process. It is a continuous process of reflection by researchers on their values (Parahoo, 2006) and of recognising, examining, and understanding how their "social background, location, and assumptions affect their research practice" (Hesse-Biber, 2007, p. 17). The key to reflexivity is "to make the relationship between and the influence of the researcher and the participants explicit" (Jootun, McGhee, & Marland, 2009, p. 45). This process determines the filters through which researchers are working (Lather, 2004), including the "specific ways in which our own agenda affect the research at all points in the research process" (Hesse-Biber, 2007, p. 17). As such, reflexivity means being aware of and acknowledging the researcher's contribution to the construction of meanings throughout the research process. It means acknowledging the impossibility of remaining outside of one's subject matter. At the heart of the concept of reflexivity, then, the researcher is viewed as an instrument of the research process. Thus, the researcher needs to acknowledge how they incorporate into their work a certain set of preconceived behaviours, attitudes, and beliefs, and in fact, we argue that these personal experiences enrich the research endeavour.

Practicing reflexivity is a significant component of qualitative research (Morse, Barrett, Mayan, Olson, & Spiers, 2002), but as a process, it should be embedded in all the principles (van der Riet, 2012) and relate to the degree of influence that the researchers exert, either intentionally or unintentionally, on the findings (Jootun et al., 2009). Jootun et al. also expressed, "inclusion of a reflexive account increases the rigour of the research process" (p. 1). Reflexivity "requires researchers to come from behind the protective barriers of objectivity" (Etherington, 2007, p. 599) and, as a result, researchers can connect with others as a way to humanise and relate to participants in the research relationship. The invitation to others allows for an interactive relationship when practicing relational reflexivity (Hibbert, Sillince, Diefenbach, & Cunliffe, 2014). *Relational reflexivity* prioritises a connectedness between researchers and participants in an attempt to build theory through engaging otherness and enacting connectedness (Hibbert et al., 2014). By doing so, the practice and idea of reflexivity is more inclusive of the participants and their communities, particularly those who come from different cultures and backgrounds.

The idea of reflexivity challenges the view of knowledge production as independent of the researcher producing the knowledge and of knowledge as an objective entity (Berger, 2015). The researcher is therefore not only engaged with the *process*, but also a critical part of that process. In order to ensure quality in qualitative research, reflexivity needs to occur on all stages of the research process. Berger notes that being reflexive as a qualitative researcher means turning of the researcher lens back onto oneself to recognise and take responsibility for one's own situatedness within the research. It is important to analyse the effect that our situatedness has on the participants we study, the questions we ask, as well as the data we collect and interpret (Berger, 2015). Reflexivity is thus considered essential, potentially facilitating understanding of both phenomenon under study and the research process itself (Watt, 2007). Reflexivity involves reflecting on the way in which research is carried out and understanding how the process of doing research shapes its outcomes (Hardy, Phillips, & Clegg, 2001).

Reflexivity works in tandem with *positionality*, which is described as how researchers are situated. Understanding where the researcher stands "in relation to 'the other'" (Merriam et al., 2001, p. 411) is considered when questioning one's positionality during the research process. The researcher's positionality/ies does not exist independently of the research process nor does it completely determine the latter. Instead, this must be seen as a dialogue – challenging perspectives and assumptions both about the social world and of the researcher him/herself. This enriches the research process and its outcomes. In brief, reflexivity is an internal understanding of one's perspective, and positionality is how one is positioned in contrast to those being studied. Researchers must understand that there are multiple ways of producing knowledge. By understanding their **positionality** and incorporating reflective processes when conducting research, sport management researchers can have a better sense of who they are and how they think about research influences their research activities.

Research brief

Title: Reconstructing athletic identity: College athletes and sport retirement
Author: Menke, D. J., *University of Memphis* & Germany, M. L., *University of Memphis* (2019)
Reference: Menke, D. J. & Germany, M. L. (2019). Reconstructing athletic identity: College athletes and sport retirement. *Journal of Loss and Trauma, 24*(1), 17–30.
This phenomenological study examined the transition out of sport for former college athletes from revenue-producing sports. Previous studies presented mixed results on factors that impact this transition. Findings indicated that Coping with Transition, Gains or Strengths, and Loss of Identity are salient themes when sports careers end. Implications of the study suggested that college athletes will benefit from coping skills to deal with the loss of sport, and interest in activities outside of sport can prevent significant distress during the transition. This study suggested that counsellors and others working with college athletes can prepare college athletes for a smooth sport retirement.

TYPES OF REFLEXIVE PRACTICES REFLECTED IN CONTEMPORARY QUALITATIVE RESEARCH

The rationale for the use of reflexivity varies with the *research traditions*. For a phenomenologist, the same phenomenon will have different interpretations depending on the subject itself, and hence the data of the subject is as important as the data of the object. On the other hand, from a social constructionist perspective, a reflection on our own history may help to change the course of the history. Reflexivity can be used with different objectives namely: of knowing the self or others, knowing the truth, and also for transcending these (Pillow, 2003).

Finlay (2002) noted the challenges associated with reflexivity in research and the importance of the researcher negotiating a path through this complicated landscape, and by virtue of the journey, the researchers making "interesting discoveries" during their research activities. Finlay developed a classification, or maps, of **five** types of reflexive practices reflected in contemporary qualitative research: (1) *introspection*, (2) *intersubjective reflection, (3) mutual collaboration*, (4) *social critique*, and (5) *discursive deconstruction*. These five perspectives of reflexivity in qualitative research can overlap or be used at the same time by the researcher.

Explaining reflexivity as ***introspection***, Finlay (2002) notes "insights can emerge from personal introspection which then forms the basis for a more generalised understanding and interpretations" (p. 214). Introspection should not only be viewed as self-reflection, but also as an opportunity to become more explicit about the link between knowledge claims, personal experiences of both participant and researcher, and the social context. Reflexivity as ***intersubjective reflection*** refers to when researchers explore the mutual meanings emerging within the research relationship and at the same time focus on the situated and negotiated nature of the research encounter (Finlay, 2002). Involving more than reflection, this perspective is underscored by the researcher focusing on the "self-in-relation-to-others [which] becomes both the aim and object" of the analysis (p. 216). The researcher considers the potential challenges within the research relationship while looking at both inward meanings and outward into the realm of shared meanings in order to examine the research relationship and the potential challenges that may arise with the participant. When describing reflexivity as ***mutual collaboration***, Finlay explained that collaborative reflexivity "offers the opportunity to hear, and take into account, multiple voices and conflicting positions" (p. 220). By incorporating the voices of the researched in the process of self-reflection, the researcher acknowledges that the research participant is also a "reflexive being" who mutually contributes to the data analysis component of the research process. Power imbalance can exist between researchers and those they research based on their social positions at the time of the research. A concern for researchers who use reflexivity as ***social critique*** is determining how to manage the power imbalance between researcher and participant (Finlay, 2002). By incorporating a social critique in one's research reflection, the researcher is able to acknowledge and address the "social construction of power" and the positionality of the researcher and the research participant during the research process. ***Discursive deconstruction*** refers to researchers understanding that language is ambiguous, and reflection during and after their research activity can be helpful for interpreting the voices of their research participants. In reflexivity as *discursive deconstruction*, "attention is paid to the ambiguity of meanings in language used and how this impacts on modes of presentation" (p. 222). Because language itself, the use of certain language, and the emphasis on certain aspects of language represents those being researched, the researcher will have to contend with representing the dynamic, multiple meanings embedded in language used during the research process. In other words, the researcher will have to carefully deconstruct what the participant said while ensuring the language used does not lose its meaning during the researcher's interpretation and representation of what was said.

PROSPECTIVE AND RETROSPECTIVE REFLEXIVITY

Reflexivity can be divided into two types: **prospective** and **retrospective**. *Prospective reflexivity* refers to the effects of the researcher on the study, whereas *retrospective reflexivity* refers to the effects of the study on the researcher (Attia & Edge, 2017). ***Prospective reflexivity*** has been more frequently accounted for in the literature; for example, in relation to considering how to handle researcher status, insider/outsiderness, gender, or ethnicity. Rather than seeing such influences as potential contamination of the data to be avoided or allowed for by achieving competence in an appropriate methodological procedure, prospective reflexivity seeks to help researchers grow their capacity to understand the significance of the knowledge, feelings, and values that they brought into the field to the research questions that they came to formulate, to the analytical lenses that they chose to employ, and to their findings.

   Retrospective reflexivity is summed up in Sandywell's (1996) observation: "...reflexive action changes the form of the self: a reflexive practice never returns the self to the point of origin" (p. xiv). The significance of this assertion with regard to a developmental approach is that it establishes a metaphorical sense of movement of distance travelled. The interpretation of that trajectory, including its consequence, indexes the individual development experienced. Once again, we see the recording of this development as intrinsic to sport management research. Retrospective reflexivity entails several challenges. For instance, van der Riet (2012) identifies the challenge of how to manage the emotions of our research participants. She argues that total detachment is unrealistic and can hinder the research process. Moreover, she posits that researchers should be mindful of their behaviours and actions and should be aware of the "Hollywood plot" that makes the research findings seem more positive than they actually are. Jootun et al. (2009) also acknowledges that it is difficult not to influence and be influenced by the research participants. Nevertheless, the reflexive research recognises that any finding is the product of the researcher's interpretation. Understanding the bidirectional relationship between researcher and research is an important concept in qualitative methodology. As Smyth & Shacklock (1998) indicate:

> *Reflexivity in research is built on an acknowledgement of the ideological and historical power dominant forms of inquiry exert over the researcher and the researched. Self-reflection upon the constraining conditions is the key to the empowerment `capacities of research and the fulfilment of its agenda. ... As we see it, the process of reflexivity is an attempt to identify, do something about, and acknowledge the limitations of the research: its location, its subjects, its process, its theoretical context, its data, its analysis, and how accounts recognize that the construction of knowledge takes place in the world and not apart from it. (pp. 6–7)*

Through reflexivity, we become aware of our contribution to the construction of meanings and of lived experiences throughout the research process (Ackerly & True, 2010; Denzin & Lincoln, 2011; Pillow, 2003; Reay, 2007). Our reflexivity notes/insights reveal how we explored the ways in which our involvement in the various researches influenced, acted upon, and informed the very studies we engaged in. Fieldwork is intensely personal; our positionality (i.e., position based on class, sex, ethnicity, race, etc.) and who we are as persons (shaped by the socio-economic and political environment) play a fundamental role in the research process, in the field as well as in the final text. Reflexivity must then be a part of our commitment. It must become a duty of every researcher to reveal and share these reflexivities, not only for learning purposes but towards enhancing theory building.

REFLEXIVITY IN THE RESEARCH PROCESS

The concept of reflexivity challenges the assumption that there can be a privileged position where the researcher can study social reality objectively, that is, independent from it through value-free inquiry. But it should be noted that objectivity pertains to adopt appropriate methodological tools and techniques for qualitative research. Ackerly and True (2010) posit that researchers have to take seriously this commitment of reflexivity. There is a need for constant reflections and the review of theoretical approaches and perspectives. A number of researchers have attempted to further unpack *reflexivity.* For example, according to Dowling (2006), reflexivity in the research process can take on several forms: *personal, epistemological, methodological critical,* and *feminist*. These types are discussed more thoroughly in the following section.

Personal reflexivity

Qualitative research aims to understand how meanings are constructed and probe into how the participants utilise experience to construct reality (Jootun et al., 2009). In qualitative studies, researchers locate themselves with how their participants view the world (Lambert et al., 2010). Reay (2007) argues that reflexivity is about giving as full and honest an account of the research process as possible, in particular explicating the position of the researcher in relation to the research. Jootun et al. suggest that qualitative researchers are prone to a degree of subjectivity as the "interpretation of the participants" behaviour and collected data is influenced by the values, beliefs, experience, and interest of the researcher. Reflexivity contributes in making the research process open and transparent. The awareness of the reciprocal influence of both participants and researcher/s on the process and outcome is important to ensure rigour in qualitative research.

Epistemological reflexivity

The concept of reflexivity has serious epistemological implications. According to Johnson and Cassell (2001), we become more consciously reflexive by thinking about our own thinking, by noticing and criticising our own epistemological pre-understandings and their effects on research, and by exploring possible alternative commitments. Willig (2001) and Dowling (2006) suggest that researchers may find themselves asking one question after the other in the process of conducting the research. These questions may include: How has the research question defined and limited what can be "found"?; How has the design of the study and the method of analysis "constructed" the data and the findings?; How could the research question have been investigated differently?; To what extent would this have given rise to a different understanding of the phenomenon under investigation? These questions encourage or push the researcher to reflect upon the assumptions (about the world, about knowledge) that we have made in the course of the research, and it helps us think about its implications to the research and its findings. Being reflexive about epistemological assumptions involves an analysis of: (1) What our measures can actually tell us about the nature of the world and human action?; (2) What our aims are in conducting the research?; and (3) What assumptions are implicated in the theories that drive our research and are produced as a result of our research?

Methodological reflexivity

Methodology is defined by Schwandt (2001) as "a particular social scientific discourse (a way of acting, thinking, and speaking) that occupies a middle ground between discussions of method and discussions of issues in the philosophy of social science" (p. 161). This notion of methodology raises two issues in relation to methodological reflexivity. The first is concerned with what roles the researcher plays in relation to the negotiation of method and discussions of the philosophy of social science. The second is the dichotomy between objectivity and subjectivity. What roles does the researcher play in relation to the negotiation of method and discussions of the philosophy of social science? Methodological *reflexive* critique is a "localised critique" and evaluation of the "technical" aspects of a particular methodology. This involves a critique of: (1) how the research should be designed or conducted in order to provide a convincing account; (2) alternative interpretations and their refutation; (3) the role researchers play in producing results; and (4) the choices that were made and reasons for them.

Critical reflexivity

Reflexivity from a critical standpoint examines the political and social constructions that inform the research process (Koch & Harrington, 1998).

This type of reflexivity is often employed in critical ethnography where the ethnographer is inevitably involved throughout the text and its creation (Muecke, 1994). Critical reflexivity posits that the production of knowledge is entrenched in certain socio-political and cultural contexts. It is the task of the researcher to address ethical and political questions that shape the research process.

Reflexivity from this perspective allows us to be critical about what we hear, write, and interpret. This raises an issue of just how far the researcher can go to interpret other people's lives and experiences. Critical reflexive researchers not only listen for everyday processes and translation (DeVault, 1990), but must be able to give more voice to the participants, get close enough to what they are saying, and their representation about themselves. The form of reflexivity aligns with the critical research paradigm, which is one of the fundamental research paradigms in sport management research. It is the only approach amongst interpretive, critical, and positivist approaches that stresses emancipation, empowerment, and transformation of research subjects as well as the researcher. Such transformation is brought through the use of reflexivity – an essential ingredient of critical research. However, this approach has remained an under-represented paradigm in sport management research.

Feminist reflexivity

Reflexivity from a feminist standpoint is also called a "performed politics" (Marcus, 1994). Recent discussions on reflexivity employed in feminist research look into power differentials within the various stages of the research process (Hesse-Biber & Piatelli, 2007). This refers to how gender-based differences shape the research process. According to Dowling (2006), reflexivity is important in feminist research because the researcher has to identify with the female research participants and must be constantly aware of how her values, beliefs, and perceptions are shaping the research process. This type of reflexivity assumes a partnership between the researchers and the research participants as it offers the opportunity for raising new questions, engaging in new kinds of dialogue, and organising different kinds of relations (Hesse-Biber & Piatelli, 2007). Pillow (2003) calls this "reflexivity of discomfort" since it can disrupt the process of discovery. Reciprocity and reflexivity are therefore critical aspects of feminist research. Nevertheless, this type of reflexivity does not suggest an intimate reciprocity between the researcher and the participants. Researchers claim (Denzin & Lincoln, 2011; Mayo, Candela, Matusov, & Smith, 2008) that feminist research must take into account reciprocity. Researchers have to write and share how they experienced research, how they do their work, be it good or bad, and make visible the questions, complexities, and processes of ding research (Pillow & Mayo, 2007).

Research brief

Title: An examination of women's sport sponsorship: a case study of female Australian Rules football
Author: Morgan, A., *Edith Cowan University* (2019)
Reference: Morgan, A. (2019). An examination of women's sport sponsorship: A case study of female Australian Rules football. *Journal of Marketing Management, 35*(17–18), 1644–1666. In recent years, there has been an increase in corporate and media interest in women's sport leagues and events. Despite the increase in commercialism and professionalism of women's sport, there is a lack of research focusing on the marketing of and through women's sport. This current study addressed this gap, examining the motivations of sponsors involved in the women's Australian Rules football national league. Exploratory in outlook, this paper presented reflective insights from key sponsorship decision makers. It was found that sponsorship was motivated by a desire to promote gender equality at a firm, industry, and broader societal level.

REFLEXIVITY IN SPORT MANAGEMENT RESEARCH

In sport management research, the call for reflexivity has emerged relatively recently compared to other social science disciplines (Edwards, 1999). Alvesson and Skoldberg (2000) suggest that promoting a more reflective approach by incorporating ideas from the philosophy of science (such as epistemic considerations), represents an attempt to "raise the level of qualitative method" through its "intellectualisation" (p. vii). Reflexivity in this context enables both in-depth thinking about the methods we use and the epistemological commitments that underlie them. Other authors have also pointed to the benefits of reflexivity for the qualitative researcher. Finlay (2002), for example, suggests that apart from the advantages of enhanced trustworthiness of the data and an enhanced understanding of the role of the researcher, reflexivity in itself can be empowering.

Reflexivity and *positionality* are essential in sport management fieldwork because the production of knowledge and the power relations that are inherent in research processes in order to undertake ethical research (Sultana, 2007) should always be at the foundation of the researcher's project. Reflexivity can be a helpful tool for understanding and applying ethical considerations to qualitative research (Guillemin & Gillam, 2004). Researchers can utilise reflexivity as a "sensitising notion that can enable ethical practice to occur in the complexity and richness of social research" (Guillemin & Gillam, 2004, p. 278). Engaging in introspection and awareness as a component of reflexivity may assist in transparent and ethical research practices. The act of being transparent with the research process "calls for a positioning of reflexivity not as clarity, honesty, or humility, but as practices of confounding disruptions" (Pillow, 2003, p. 192). By embracing reflexivity, researchers allow for emancipation of the self and understanding of the studied population when navigating international contexts.

A further benefit can be seen in the impact of theory development. Weick (2002) suggests that theory construction in the new millennium is partly an exercise in disciplined reflexivity and that this newer attention to self-as theorist makes for better theory in the field, with the caveat that the attention is directed towards spotting excluded voices and thinking more deeply about topics. Moreover, reflexivity can be seen as an ongoing process in relation to learning as reflexivity encourages us to strive not to be complacent and to continue to review and critique our own research practice (Cassell & Symon, 2004). Given the benefits of increased reflexivity for the sport management research, it is perhaps surprising that there is little information available about how we can actually do reflexivity in practice. Finlay (2002) suggests that reflexive analysis is always problematic as the complex and often ambiguous nature of research means that those processes are often difficult to unfold.

Within the field of sport management research, there are few discussions about the issues involved in reflexive research practice. Consequently, as Lynch (2000) argues "What reflexivity does, what it threatens to expose, what it reveals and who it empowers depends upon who does it and how they go about it" (p. 36). Such comments are consistent with Johnson and Duberley's (2003) assertion that any reflexive researcher needs an understanding of their own epistemological assumptions in relation to reflexivity. Dr Christina Hughes form the University of Warwick has proposed a number of research issues to reflect upon. We have slightly modified her list so as to provide a guideline for sport management researchers. These issues include:

- Reflect on the wider relevance of the setting and the topic, and the grounds on which empirical generalisations are made, if any, such as establishing the representativeness of the setting, its general features or its function as a special case study with a broader bearing.

- Reflect on the features of the topic or setting left unresearched, discussing why these choices have been made and what implications follow from these decisions for the research findings.

- Reflect on the theoretical framework they are operating within, and the broader values and commitments (political, religious, theoretical, and so on).

- Critically assess their integrity of the researchers by considering:

  - The grounds on which knowledge claims are being justified (length of fieldwork, the special access negotiated, discussing the extent of the trust and rapport developed with the participants)

  - Their background and experiences in the setting and topic.

  - Their experiences during all stages of the research, especially mentioning the constraints imposed therein.

  - The strengths and weaknesses of their research design and strategy.

■ Critically assess the data, by:

- Discussing the problems that arose during all stages of the research.

- Outlining the grounds on which the researchers developed the catego-risation system used to interpret the data, identifying clearly whether this is an indigenous one used by respondents themselves, or an ana-lyst-constructed one, and, if the latter, the grounds which support this.

- Discussing rival explanations and alternative ways of organising the data;

- Providing sufficient data extracts in the text to allow readers to evaluate the inferences drawn from them and the interpretations made of them.

- Discussing power relations within the research, between researcher(s) and participants, and within the research team, in order to establish the effects of class, gender, race, and religion on the practice and writing up of the research.

■ Show the complexity of the data, avoiding the suggestion that there is a simple fit between the social world under scrutiny and the ethnographic representation of it, by:

- Discussing negative cases which fall outside the general patterns and categories employed to structure the ethnographic description, which often serve to exemplify and support positive cases.

- Showing the multiple and often contradictory descriptions proffered by the participants themselves.

- Stressing the contextual nature of participants' accounts and descrip-tions, and identifying the features that help to structure them.

In order to address some of these issue proposed by Hughes, sport management researchers must engage in the process of reflexivity throughout the data col-lection phase. Keeping a research diary is an essential part of undertaking qual-itative research. It is useful to separate this into four sections in order that you are prompted to reflect on different aspects of doing research and your role within the construction of research knowledge. The four section would include: (1) *Observational notes*: these are descriptive notes of an event such as an inter-view, chance encounter, observation; they contain as little interpretation as pos-sible and are as reliable as you can construct them. (2) *Methodological notes*: this is where you reflect on the methodological aspects of the research and your actions in undertaking an interview, survey, observation, etc. You may ask yourself: how did the interview go? what was your role within it? (3) *Theoretical notes*: it is here that you begin to make meaning about your data. What are your initial explanations? What is your data telling you? (4) *Analytic memos*: this is the place where you are trying to bring several inferences together. You might, for example, review your theoretical notes and begin to see patterns or recurrent themes in your data. You would also attempt to link your analysis.

It should also be noted that the validity of reflexivity in qualitative research is frequently challenged. Vaidya (2018) has attempted to address this issue by proposing a *Validity Framework*. This framework proposes the four phases for critically reflecting on the research results. In the first phase, coding of the data occurs. The researcher codes the data assuming that certain codes will be more frequent than others, this may be due to subjective influences. In phase 2, conclusions are drawn before reflexivity is applied. With the coding completed, the researcher now develops the themes using an approach such as constant comparative method. Based on this method, a relationship between the various constructs is developed. For example, if exploring trust formation has honesty, sincerity, and transparency related to it? In phase 3, the researcher's position is reflected. The researcher applies the same theoretical concepts to his/her persona. For example, the concepts are applied both to the research phenomenon and to the researcher. In the final phase, a comparison is made between the research results before and after reflexivity. As such, the researcher should compare the results before and after performing critical reflection. The themes that occur commonly between the two set of results can be attributed to the researcher's own biases.

Research brief

Title: Exploring issues of trust in collaborative sport governance
Author: O'Boyle, I., *University of South Australia* & Shilbury, D., *Deakin University* (2016)
Reference: O'Boyle, I. & Shilbury, D. (2016). Exploring issues of trust in collaborative sport governance. *Journal of Sport Management, 30* (1), 52–69.
This study explored how trust is manifested on the levels of collaboration that take place in sport governance networks. A case study approach was used as the guiding method to examine the contributing factors that facilitate or inhibit trusting relationships between boards within sporting networks. Three sports from Australia were employed as the population for the study and 36 in-depth interviews were conducted with participants from national and state organisations operating within those networks, two federated and one partially unified. Interviews were analysed using an interpretive process and a thematic structure relating to the issues and impact of trust and distrust within the three networks was developed. Extant levels of trust, transparency, the capacity to build trust, and leadership emerged as the key themes in the study.

ETHICAL RESEARCH

Guillemin and Gillam (2004) argue that active engagement with reflexivity helps ensure that our research practices are ethical. They argue that, "being reflexive in an ethical sense means acknowledging and being sensitised to the micro-ethical dimensions of research practice and in doing so, being alert to and prepared for ways of dealing with the ethical tensions that arise" (p. 278).

Reflexivity therefore can be a helpful tool for understanding and applying ethical considerations to qualitative research. Researchers can utilise reflexivity as a "sensitising notion that can enable ethical practice to occur in the complexity and richness of social research" (p. 278). Engaging in introspection and awareness as a component of reflexivity may assist in transparent and ethical research practices. The act of being transparent with the research process "calls for a positioning of reflexivity not as clarity, honesty, or humility, but as practices of confounding disruptions" (Pillow, 2003, p. 192). By embracing reflexivity, researchers allow for emancipation of the self and understanding of the studied population when navigating international contexts.

McGraw, Zvonkovic, and Walker (2000), in order to pinpoint the connection between reflectivity and ethics, affirm that reflectivity is a process whereby researchers place themselves and their practices under scrutiny, acknowledging the ethical dilemmas that permeate the research process. If guaranteeing the ethics of research is not a merely regulatory activity, which implies only to apply rules and codes, but it requires the researcher shapes oneself as an ethical instrument, then the reflective practice is the first and main ethical imperative, because an ethical self-forming activity implies reflectivity (Cannella & Lincoln, 2007).

CONCLUSION

This chapter has examined the emerging development of reflexivity in qualitative research. Reflexivity represents an important tool for establishing trustworthiness in qualitative research, because if we do not consider the ways in which who we are may get in the way of portraying the voice of the participant, we may miss important meanings that are being presented by our participants. Reflexivity allows researchers to increase the credibility of their work by detailing how their values, beliefs, knowledge, and biases influence this work.

REVIEW AND RESEARCH QUESTIONS

1. What is reflexivity? What conceptualisation works best for you and why?

2. How is reflexivity important for qualitative work, and your work in particular?

3. How will you incorporate your understanding of reflexivity into your work?

4. Reflect on your sport management research project, focus particularly on your research questions:

a. What insights were generated or do you hope to generate from these questions?

b. On what basis do/will these insights contribute to "knowledge"?

c. What different insights may be/have been made if a different epistemological perspective had been taken?

5. Reflect on a recent sport management research project and ask yourself the following questions:

a. What (or who) prompted the research and why?

b. How was access achieved?

c. What disciplinary assumptions were made?

d. What was the focus of the research (and what was not considered)?

e. Who was involved in the research and who was not?

f. What were the outcomes for your participants and those not directly involved?

REFERENCES

Ackerly, B., & True, J. (2010). Back to the future: Feminist theory, activism, and doing feminist research in an age of globalization. *Women's Studies International Forum*, 33, 464–472.

Alvesson, M., & Skoldberg, K. (2000). *Reflexive methodology. New vistas for qualitative researchers*. London: Sage Publications.

Attia, M., & Edge, J. (2017). Be(com)ing a reflexive researcher: A developmental approach to research methodology. *Open Review of Educational Research*, 4(1), 33–45.

Berger, R. (2015). Now I see it, now I don't: Researcher's position and reflexivity in qualitative research. *Qualitative Research*, 15(2), 219–234.

Bleakley, A. (1999). From reflective practice to holistic reflexivity. *Studies in Higher Education*, 24(3), 315–330.

Cannella, G. S., & Lincoln, Y. S. (2007). Predatory vs. dialogic ethics: Constructing an illusion or ethical practice as the core of research methods. *Qualitative Inquiry*, 13(3), 315–335.

Cassell, C., & Symon, G. (2004). *Essential guide to qualitative methods in organizational research*. Thousand Oaks, CA: Sage Publications.

Denzin, N. K., & Lincoln, Y. S. (Eds.) (2011). *Handbook of qualitative research* (5th ed.). Thousand Oaks, CA: Sage Publications.

DeVault, M. L. (1990). Talking and listening from women's standpoint: Feminist strategies for interviewing and analysis. *Social Problems*, 37(1), 96–116.

Dowling, M. (2006). Approaches to reflexivity in qualitative research. *Nurse Researcher*, 13(3), 7–21.

Edwards, A. (1999). Reflective practice in sport management. *Sport Management Review*, 2(1), 67–81.

Etherington, K. (2007). Ethical research in reflexive relationships. *Qualitative Inquiry*, 13(5), 599–616.

Frank, G. (1997). Is there life after categories? Reflexivity in qualitative research. *Occupational Therapy Journal of Research*, 17(2), 84–98.

Finlay, L. (2002). Negotiating the swamp: The opportunity and challenge of reflexivity in research practice. *Qualitative Research*, 2(2), 209–230.

Gouldner, A. (1971). *The Coming Crisis of Western Sociology*. London: Heinemann.

Guillemin, M., & Gillam, L. (2004). Ethics, reflexivity, and 'ethically important moments' in research. *Qualitative Inquiry*, 10(2), 261–280.

Hardy, C., Phillips, N., & Clegg, S. (2001). Reflexivity in organization and management theory. *Human Relations*, 4(5), 531–560.

Hesse-Biber, S. (2007). *Handbook of feminist research: Theory and praxis*. Thousand Oaks, CA: Sage Publications.

Hesse-Biber, S. N., & Piatelli, D. (2007). Holistic reflexivity: The feminist practice of reflexivity. In S. Hesse-Biber (Ed.), *The handbook of feminist research: Theory and praxis*, pp. 493–511. Thousand Oaks, CA: Sage Publications.

Hibbert, P., Sillince, J., Diefenbach, T., & Cunliffe, A. L. (2014). Relationally reflexive practice: A generative approach to theory development in qualitative research. *Organizational Research Methods, 17*(3) 278–298.

Johnson, P., & Cassell, C. (2001). Epistemology and work psychology: New agendas. *Journal of Occupational and Organizational Psychology, 74*, 125–143.

Johnson, P., & Duberley, J. (2003). Reflexivity in management research. *Journal of Management Studies, 40*(5), 1279–1303.

Jootun, D., McGhee, G., & Marland, G. R. (2009). Reflexivity: Promoting rigor in qualitative research. *Nursing Standard, 23*(23), 42–46.

Kippax, S., & Kinder, P. (2002). Reflexive practice: The relationship between social research and health promotion in HIV prevention. *Sex Education: Sexuality, Society and Learning, 2*(2), 91–104.

Koch, T., & Harrington, A. (1998). Reconceptualizing rigour: The case for reflexivity. *Journal of Advanced Nursing, 28*(4), 882–890.

Lambert, C., Jomeen, J., & McSherry, W. (2010). Reflexivity: A review of the literature in the context of midwifery research. *British Journal of Midwifery, 18*(5), 321–326.

Lather, P. (2004). This *is* your father's paradigm: Government intrusion and the case of qualitative research in education. *Qualitative Inquiry, 10*, 15–34.

Lindlof, T. R., & Taylor, B. C. (2011). *Qualitative communication research methods* (3rd ed.). Thousand Oaks, CA: Sage Publications.

Lynch, M. (2000). Against reflexivity as an academic virtue and source of privileged knowledge. *Theory, Culture & Society, 17*(3), 26–54.

Marcus, G. E. (1994). What comes (just) after "post": The case of ethnography. In N. K. Denzin, & Y. S. Lincoln (Eds.), *Handbook of Qualitative Research*. Thousand Oaks, CA: Sage Publications.

Mayo, C., Candela, M. A., Matusov, E., & Smith, M. (2008). Families and school apart: University experience to assist Latina/o parents' activism. In F. Peterman (Ed.), *Urban Schools and Democratic Challenges*, pp. 103–132. Washington DC: AACTE Press.

McGraw, L., Zvonkovic, A., & Walker, A. (2000). Studying postmodern families: A feminist analysis of ethical tensions in work and family research. *Journal of Marriage and the Family, 62*(1), 68–77.

Merriam, S. B., Johnson-Bailey, J., Lee, M. -Y., Kee, Y., Ntseane, G., & Muhamad, M. (2001). Power and positionality: Negotiating insider/outsider status within and across cultures. *International Journal of Lifelong Education, 20*(5), 405–416.

Morse, J. M. (1991). Qualitative nursing research: A free for all. In J. M. Morse (Ed.), *Qualitative Nursing Research: A Contemporary Dialogue*, pp.14–22. Newbury Park, CA: Sage Publications.

Morse, J. M., Barrett, M., Mayan, M., Olson, K., & Spiers, J. (2002). Verification strategies for establishing reliability and validity in qualitative research. *International Journal of Qualitative Methods, 1*(2), 13–22.

Muecke, M. A. (1994). On the evaluation of ethnographies. In J. M. Morse (Ed.), *Critical Issues in Qualitative Research Methods*, pp. 187–209. Thousand Oaks, CA: Sage. Publications.

Patton, M. Q. (2002). *Qualitative evaluation and research methods* (3rd ed.). Thousand Oaks, CA: Sage Publications.

Parahoo, K. (2006). *Nursing research. Principles, process and issues* (2nd ed.). Basingstoke: Palgrave Macmillan.

Pillow, W. (2003). Confession, catharsis, or cure? Rethinking the uses of reflexivity as methodological power in qualitative research. *International Journal of Qualitative Studies in Education, 16*(2), 175–196.

Pillow, W. S., & Mayo, C. (2007). Toward understandings of feminist ethnography. In S.N. Hesse-Biber (Ed.), *Handbook of Feminist Research: Theory and Praxis*, pp. 155–172. Thousand Oaks, CA: Sage Publications.

Reay, D. (2007). Future directions in difference research: Recognising and responding to difference. In S. N. Hess-Biber (Ed.), *Handbook of feminist research: Theory and praxis*, pp. 605–612. Thousand Oaks, CA: Sage Publications.

Sandywell, B. (1996). *Reflexivity and the crisis of western reason*. London: Routledge.

Schwandt, T. A. (2001). *Dictionary of qualitative inquiry* (2nd ed.). Thousand Oaks, CA: Sage Publications.

Schön, D. A. (1983). *The reflective practitioner: How professionals think in action*. New York: Basic Books.

Smyth, J., & Shacklock, G. (1998). Behind the cleansing of socially critical research accounts. In G. Shacklock, & J. Smyth (Eds.), *Being Reflexive in Critical Educational and Social Research*, pp. 1–13. Hong Kong: Falmer Press.

Sultana, F. (2007). Reflexivity, positionality and participatory ethics: Negotiating fieldwork dilemmas in international fieldwork. *ACME: An International Journal for Critical Geographies, 6*(3), 374–385.

Weick, K. E. (2002). Essai: Real time reflexivity: Prods to reflection. *Organization Studies, 23*(6), 893–898.

Vaidya, R. (2018). A reflexive method for validating the results of qualitative analysis. *Social Sciences, 7*(5), 223–232.

van der Riet, P. (2012). Reflexivity: A mainstay in promoting rigor and trustworthiness in qualitative research. *Philippine Journal of Nursing, 82*, 28–32.

Watt, D. (2007). On becoming a qualitative researcher: The value of reflexivity. *The Qualitative Report, 12*(1), 82–101.

Willig, C. (2001). *Introducing qualitative research in psychology: Adventures in theory and method*. Buckingham: Open University Press.

CHAPTER 6

Research ethics for qualitative sport management research

LEARNING OUTCOMES

By the end of this chapter, you should be able to:

- Describe why adhering to ethical principles is important in sport management research.

- Explain the specific ethical issues to consider in qualitative sport management research.

- List the core ethical principles that should guide the researcher's actions in qualitative sport management research.

KEY TERMS

1. **Ethics:** a set of principles of right conduct, and the rules and standards governing the actions of a person. Generally, ethical principles exist to ensure the protection of research participants, the researchers themselves, the universities/institutes overseeing the research, and the discipline as a whole.

2. **Integrity:** steadfast adherence to a strict moral or ethical code.

3. **Beneficence:** the state of being beneficial.

4. **Consent:** acceptance or approval of what is being done or planned by another. Where possible, informed consent (giving consent in the full knowledge of planned actions and likely consequences) is viewed as preferable to simple consent.

5. **Coercion:** compelling by force of authority, by deceit, or by the use of inappropriate incentives or punishments.

KEY THEMES

- Common ethical concerns that qualitative sport management researchers confront.

- Highlight the ethical principles that can guide research and sport management researchers.

- Nature of ethical problems in qualitative research studies is different compared to problems in quantitative research.

- Ethical considerations need to be considered in every phase of the research study.

CHAPTER OVERVIEW

In this chapter, we examine the common ethical concerns that qualitative sport management researchers confront and highlight the ethical principles that can guide research and researchers. These principles cannot ensure ethical research but they can contribute to an understanding that ethical responsibility in qualitative research is an ongoing process and that sport management researchers must always respect the mandate of maintaining ethical principles as an issue of protection of human rights. The purpose of this chapter is to indicate the ethical principles that should be adhered to in order to produce quality sport management qualitative research.

WHAT ARE RESEARCH ETHICS?

Ethics that define what is or is not legitimate or moral to do. *Research ethics* deals primarily with the interaction between researchers and the people they study. *Professional ethics* deals with additional issues such as collaborative relationships among researchers, mentoring relationships, intellectual property, fabrication of data, and plagiarism, among others. While we do not explicitly discuss professional ethics here, they are obviously as important for qualitative research as for any other endeavour.

The nature of ethical problems in qualitative research studies is different compared to problems in quantitative research. Qualitative studies are frequently conducted in settings involving the participation of people in their everyday environments. Therefore, any research that includes people requires an awareness of the ethical issues that may be derived from such interactions. Qualitative researchers observe and describe conditions rather than control them. A basic ethical principle for qualitative researchers is this: *Do not interfere with the natural setting under study.*

Given the importance of ethics for the conduct of research, it should come as no surprise that many different professional associations, government agencies, and universities have adopted specific codes, rules, and policies relating to research ethics. Dissertation and thesis researchers at universities typically have their research applications vetted by an "Ethics Committee" to ensure that they comply with strict standards.

Ethical considerations need to be considered in every phase of the research study, not just in the research design or when the researcher receives any required ethical clearance and authorisation to commence the research. The researcher needs to consider and act upon ethical responsibilities and considerations continue right through a project, even beyond the data collection phase into analysis, write up, and publication.

According to Cohen, Manion, and Morrison (2000, p. 49), ethical issues can arise at any stage of a research project and include such factors:

- The nature of the project itself;

- The context of the research;

- Procedures adopted;

- Methods of data collection;

- Nature of the participants;

- The type of data collected;

- What is done with the data and how it is disseminated?

Ethical approaches to research do not reduce the *validity* and *reliability* of it but highlight the contextual complexities within which it is carried out (Kelly, 1989). To be ethical, a research project needs to be designed to create *trustworthy* (valid) outcomes if it is to be believed to be pursuing truth. The *generalisability* of findings from one situation to another is dependent on research being carried out ethically.

Research brief

Title: Coaching Athletes with Disability: Preconceptions and Reality

Author: Wareham, Y., *University of the Sunshine Coast*, Burkett, B., *University of the Sunshine Coast*, Innes, P., *University of the Sunshine Coast*, & Lovell, G. P., *University of the Sunshine Coast* (2017)

Reference: Wareham, Y., Burkett, B., Innes, P., & Lovell, G. P. (2017). Coaching athletes with disability: Preconceptions and reality. *Sport in Society, 20* (9), 1185–1202.

It is now widely recognised that athletes with disability compete at an elite level which parallels that experienced by non-disabled athletes. The importance of quality coaching to develop an athlete's full potential is similarly recognised. However, research in the area of coaching athletes with disability is still lacking compared to its counterpart in non-disabled sport. This research explored the holistic experience of coaching elite athletes with disability, and therefore encompassed not only the coaches' preconceptions, but the rewards and challenges of their coaching experience. Semi-structured interviews were held with 12 coaches of elite athletes from sports including swimming, athletics, cycling, canoeing, triathlon, equestrian sport, and wheelchair basketball. The results of the study identified that, although the coaches reported their experience as being overwhelmingly positive, they were also regularly confronted with difficulties not generally faced by coaches of non-disabled athletes.

ETHICAL PRINCIPLES

The difficulties inherent in qualitative research can be alleviated by awareness and use of well-established ethical principles, specifically *informed consent, beneficence, privacy, justice,* and *deception.*

INFORMED CONSENT

Access to participants and settings

Gaining access to informants, settings, and materials for research is one of the first steps in the research process and ethically can be the most problematic in qualitative research. When seeking to gain access, the researcher must ensure that: (1) participation is voluntary, i.e. people do not feel coerced into taking part but do so willingly; (2) people in the setting (such as a geographical area, an organisation, or a particular context) are not inconvenienced or harmed (emotionally, psychologically, physically, or reputationally); and (3) resources that you use are freely committed, such as confidential company documents or personal diaries that they read. The following steps are recommended prior to starting research: (1) gain access to the setting; (2) obtain permission from gatekeepers – those who are able to give permission for the research to be carried out; (3) explain early and clearly the type of project in which they will be involved; and (4) ask participants for permission to undertake the research and explain how you will protect them.

The modern approach to the governance of ethical conduct of human research places a strong focus on obtaining voluntary and informed consent from potential participants. Consent involves the procedure by which an individual may choose whether or not to participate in a study. The researcher's task is to ensure that participants have a complete understanding of the purpose and methods to be used in the study, the risks involved, and the demands placed upon them as a participant. The participant must also understand that they have the right to withdraw from the study at any time. Human research is generally only considered to be ethically justifiable and sound where informed consent is obtained from participants.

From a legal standpoint, informed consent involves three elements: **capacity, information,** and **voluntariness**. All three elements must be present for consent to be effective (Drew & Hardman, 2007).

1. *Capacity* – Capacity is a participant's ability to acquire and retain knowledge. The ability of a participant to competently evaluate the information received and make a choice based on this evaluation is fundamental to the element of capacity.

2. *Information* – Information must be planned and presented so it can be completely understood by the participant. This places responsibility on a researcher to make a full disclosure about the research aims.

3. *Voluntariness* – Voluntary consent is concerned with each individual's ability to exercise the free power of choice without the intervention of force, fraud, deceit, duress, or other forms of constraint or coercion. This right to exercise choice must be present throughout the entire

research process. The intent of this interpretation is that no such "constraint or coercion" must be either explicit or implicit on the part of the researcher.

How should consent be obtained?

The method of obtaining consent will vary greatly depending on the situation involved and the degree of potential risk for participants. Consent may be obtained less formally (i.e. verbally), if the study creates little or no risk or potential invasion of privacy. In such circumstances, participants may be verbally informed of the nature of the investigation (assuming that the capacity element is present) and give consent verbally. *Verbal consent* means that a person receives all of the information needed for consent either verbally or in writing and then verbally consents to participate. The participant does not sign a consent form; therefore, this is often described as waiving the requirement for documentation of informed consent. This does not mean that the requirement for informed consent is waived. Most ethics committees require the researchers to maintain accurate records of how and when consent was obtained for each participant. Oral consent is generally acceptable form research with minimal risk, or where a loss of confidentiality is the primary risk and a signed consent form would be the only piece of identifying information for study participation. During the research process, sport management researchers have a responsibility to inform participants about:

1. The purpose of the research, expected duration, and procedures.

2. Their right to decline to participate and to withdraw from the research once participation has begun.

3. Reasonably foreseeable factors that may be expected to influence their willingness to participate such as potential risks, discomfort, or adverse effects.

4. Any prospective research benefits.

5. Limits of confidentiality.

6. Benefits or incentives for participation.

7. Whom to contact for questions about the research and research participants' rights.

Consent should be obtained in writing in other situations when participants are placed in a "at risk situation" (e.g., potential harm, stress, substantial invasion of privacy). *Written consent* means that a person receives a written form that describes the research and then signs that form to document his or her consent to participate. For illiterate participants, the form is read to them, they make some kind of mark in place of a signature, and then a witness usually signs as testimony that the consent is authentic. Written informed consent may also be described as *documented informed consent.* An example of an *assent to participate* in research agreement form is shown below.

Assent to participate example

Purpose of research

We are asking you to take part in a research study because we are trying to learn more about ... (Outline what the study is about in language that is appropriate.)

Procedures

If you agree to be in this study you will ... (Describe the procedures and the duration of participation. Describe what will take place in a language that is appropriate.)

Risks

(Describe any risks to that may result from participation in the research.)

Benefits

Your involvement in this study will help us to understand ... (Describe any benefits from participation in the research.)

Alternative procedures and voluntary participation

If you don't want to participate in this study, you don't have to participate. Remember, being in this study is up to you and no one will be upset if you don't want to participate or even if you change your mind later and want to stop. Please think this over before you decide whether or not to participate.

Confidentiality

All of your records about this research study will be kept locked up so no one else can see them. (Explain how the records will be kept confidential.)

Person to contact

You can ask any questions that you have about the study. If you have a question later that you didn't think of now, you can call the lead researcher (insert your name and telephone number) *or ask when you next see them* (If applicable: *You may call me during office hours to ask questions*).

Consent

Signing my name at the bottom means that I agree to be in this study.
  Signature of Participant: Date
  Signature of Witness: Date

Dealing with gatekeepers

Participants often have to be approached through the mediation of "gatekeepers", that is, people who have the power to grant or withhold access. They control information and grant formal or informal (sometimes verbal) entry to the setting and participants; they may also impose certain conditions for access. Gatekeepers may hold official positions, such as the general manager of a sport organisation or the Director of a sport club, or they may have an unofficial gatekeeping role, such as those persons with the informal power and influence to grant and deny access or information. Secretaries and personal assistants are often powerful, but unrecognised, gatekeepers in sport organisations.

BENEFICENCE

A second ethical principle closely linked with research is beneficence – *doing good for others and preventing harm*. Beneficence is expressed in researchers' responsibility to minimise risks of harm or discomfort to participants in research projects. Each research protocol must be designed to ensure that respect for the dignity and well-being of the participants takes precedence over the expected benefits to knowledge. As such, the design of a human research protocol that involves the participation of persons who should be considered vulnerable, disadvantaged or powerless, must adequately negate, minimise or manage any risks to the participants. Risks to such participants can be especially acute, and their ability to themselves address such risks or take actions against those who cause them harm can be severely limited.

 When considering an application for ethical clearance for a protocol that involves the participation of persons who should be considered vulnerable, disadvantaged, or powerless. An Ethics Committee will expect that the applicant(s) will take special care to identify and address any risks. If researchers are maintaining the principle of beneficence, overseeing the potential consequences of revealing participants' identities is a moral obligation. The use of pseudonyms is recommended. However, this strategy may not be sufficient if the study is conducted in a small community where participants could be easily recognised. In such cases, circulation of the study may need to be restricted. Protection of participants' identities also applies to publications. Participants should be told how results will be published. Quotations or other data from the participants, even though anonymous, could reveal their identity. Ideally, participants would approve the use of quotations used in publications.

PRIVACY

A third ethical principle closely linked with beneficence is privacy. Privacy as an ethical issue relates to the ethical principles of respect for persons and beneficence. These ethical principles require that a researcher: (1) have regard for the welfare, rights, beliefs, perceptions, customs, and cultural heritage, both individual and collective, of persons involved in research; (2) minimise risks of harm or discomfort to participants in research projects; and (3) ensure that the research protocol is designed to ensure that respect for the dignity and well-being of the participants takes precedence over the expected benefits of knowledge. In practice, any proposed access to identified personal information, the use of identified personal information, and the disclosure of personal information, need to be considered in terms of whether it compromised the ethical principle of respect for persons, whether it exposed participants to risk, and whether it placed the imperative of the expected benefits to knowledge ahead of the rights of the participants.

Issues in research affecting privacy

As with other ethical considerations, privacy has become an increasingly valued right and should be protected as much as possible. In considering privacy related to the conduct of research, several factors must be addressed. First, the *sensitivity* of the data in the view of the individual or group being studied must be considered. For example, certain types of information may be viewed as personally or situationally sensitive. Second, privacy also involves how public the *information* is made. The researcher must remain very alert concerning the degree to which private information remains confidential, particularly when such information is of a sensitive nature. The *setting* in which research is being conducted may also be an important factor in considering a potential invasion of privacy. On one end of the continuum, there are those settings that are nearly always considered private, such as a person's home. The other end of the continuum might be represented by a setting in which privacy is not generally assumed, such as collecting data from a community sport forum.

Concerns about privacy are quite often at the root of complaints about the ethical conduct of research. For example, complaints can occur due to: (1) information about a person being accessed without their knowledge and consent; (2) disclosure of results and the potential harm to participants; and (3) third parties being aware of who participates, or who has been excluded, and this being a source of potential harm.

In many cases, the most appropriate and effective way to address the ethical issues relating to privacy is by protecting the confidentiality of participants. Strategies to protect confidentiality will need to address all stages of a research project (e.g. identification of participants, recruitment, during data collection, during analysis, in reporting and publication, and in storage and any subsequent use). The issues to be considered relate to those governed by privacy regimes but can be quite different. Generally, confidentiality strategies will relate to the degree to which individual comments or data can be attributed to individual participants. Confidentiality is not an absolute ethical requirement; indeed, some research participants will very much want their comments attributed to them. However, key ethical considerations are the degree to which potential participants understand whether they will be identifiable, whether they have consented to this identification, the degree to which they should be considered a vulnerable group, and whether their identification exposes them to any risks.

Anonymity refers to a situation that exceeds confidentiality where the identity of participants is not known. Unlike confidentiality measures, where the measures to protect confidentiality might only be limited to some parts of the research process (e.g. reporting/publication and storage), arrangements to protect the anonymity of participants generally apply to all parts of the research process. There is an important distinction among the three forms of anonymity, these three forms are:

1. *Completely anonymous* – research where not even the researchers will know the identity of participants (such as a questionnaire that does not seek identifying information that is distributed to a large research population).

2. *Anonymous responses* – research where the researcher will know the identity of participants, but cannot link specific data with specific respondents (such as a questionnaire that does not seek identifying information distributed to a small or specific research population).

3. *Protected anonymity* – research where the researcher will know the identity of participants, may be able to link specific data with specific respondents, but will take steps to ensure that third parties cannot determine the identity of participants (such as an interview where the data will be recorded, reported, and stored in an aggregated form).

JUSTICE

The principle of justice refers to equal share and fairness. One of the crucial and distinctive features of this principle is avoiding exploitation and abuse of participants. The researcher's understanding and application of the principle of justice in qualitative research studies is demonstrated by recognising the vulnerability of the participants and their contributions to the study. Accordingly, a researcher must:

- Avoid imposing on particular groups, who are likely to be subject to over-researching, an unfair burden of participation in research.

- Design research so that the selection, recruitment, exclusion, and inclusion of research participants is fair.

- Do not discriminate in the selection and recruitment of actual and future participants by including or excluding them on the grounds of race, age, sex, disability, or religious or spiritual beliefs except where the exclusion or inclusion of particular groups is essential to the purpose of the research.

As such, the design of a human research protocol must not include, or exclude persons who should be considered vulnerable, disadvantaged or powerless, unless for a valid scientific reason. Moreover, the researcher must consider the degree to which participation in the research might place special burdens upon participants. A human research protocol, which involves the participation of persons who should be considered vulnerable, disadvantaged, or powerless, is likely to require extra or special recruitment and consent measures. These measures will probably be necessary to ensure that the design of the protocol is consistent with the ethical principles of respect for persons, beneficence, and justice.

DECEPTION

Research deception involves an intentional misrepresentation of facts related to the purpose of an investigation. In this context, **deception** refers to either an *omission* or a *commission* on the part of the researcher in terms of interactions with participants. An omission deception could mean that the investigator does not fully inform participants about important aspects of the study. Part or all of the information is withheld. A commission involves a situation in which the researcher gives false information about the investigation, either partially or totally. Regardless of the precise nature of deception, it has become a very prominent issue for researchers concerned with the ethics of conducting research. In the next section, we will briefly discuss a number of key ethical considerations the sport management researcher needs to be aware of.

PARTICIPANT AND NONPARTICIPANT OBSERVATION

Participant and nonparticipant observations are integral components of qualitative research and are used widely in sport management research. The accepted rule of thumb for nonparticipant observation research is that consent is not necessary when (a) access to the setting is approved by the agency or institution, (b) participants who are actively involved have given informed consent, and (c) other observed behaviour is considered public and observable by anyone present in the setting. Participant observation also presents unique ethical challenges. The participant observer often lives, eats, and sleeps on a daily basis with those under observation. In such a study, a broad range of details is observed and recorded regarding participants' cultural mores, interaction patterns, social structures, and daily behaviours. The participant observer may directly probe into many facets of the lifestyle of the participant – public, private, and often sensitive. With such a pervasive scope of observation, an invasion of privacy is inevitable. This makes informed consent absolutely necessary.

ETHICS AND PROFESSIONALISM

Ethics and professionalism could easily consume an entire ethics volume, but will only receive a cursory examination in this chapter. Our focus is on three issues: (1) integrity during the study, (2) Plagiarism, and (3) sanctions for breaches of integrity.

Integrity during the study: Any breach of integrity during the execution of a research study, whether it be unintentional errors or outright falsification of the data, seriously weakens or even invalidates the investigation. Ethical problems may also arise when strong pressure leads to inaccurate data collection. For example, such pressure may occur when a researcher believes that significant results *must* be obtained and either consciously or unconsciously alters the data. Every researcher must take precautions against breaches of integrity related to the execution of research.

Plagiarism: Plagiarism involves misrepresenting someone else's work as your own and is clearly unethical. Plagiarism is defined by many universities as the following:

> *The intentional unacknowledged use or incorporation of any other person's work in, or as a basis for, one's own work offered for academic consideration or credit or for public presentation. It includes, but is not limited to, representing as one's own, without attribution, any other individual's words, phrasing, ideas, sequence of ideas, information or any other mode or content of expression.*

Plagiarism may lead to sanctions for breaches of integrity. *Sanctions for breaches of integrity:* Sanctions can be very harsh for the person who has been unethical. For students this might mean failure in their dissertation/thesis and or exclusion from the University. Each time a breach of ethics occurs, the entire sport management discipline is discredited to some degree.

Research brief

Title: A Qualitative Investigation of Young Footballers' Perceptions Regarding Developmental Experiences
Author: Gerabinis, P., *University of Thessaly* & Goudas, M., *University of Thessaly* (2019)
Reference: Gerabinis, P. & Goudas, M. (2019). A qualitative investigation of young footballers' perceptions regarding developmental experiences. *Social Sciences, 8* (7), 215.
This study examined perceptions of Greek young football players regarding sport-related developmental experiences using a model of positive youth development through sport based on results from a qualitative study as a theoretical framework. Twenty-one young football athletes (aged 12–15) gave semi-structured interviews. The young athletes identified both positive and negative developmental experiences related to the behaviours of coaches, parents and peers. They did not report any explicit teaching of life-skills; however, they identified their life-skills development by implicit processes.

ETHICAL GUIDELINES FOR SPORT MANAGEMENT RESEARCH

Based upon the previous discussion, we propose that sport management researchers follow the following ethical guidelines.

Ethical guidelines for the sport management researcher

- Research should be designed, reviewed, and undertaken to ensure integrity and quality.

- Research participants must be informed fully about the purpose, methods, and intended possible uses of the research; what their participation in the research entails and what risks, if any, are involved, including any risks or threats to anonymity that might arise during and beyond the project itself and how these might be minimised or avoided.

- The confidentiality of information supplied by research participants and the anonymity of participants must be respected.

- Research participants must participate in a voluntary way, free from any coercion. They should be informed of their right to refuse to participate or withdraw from an investigation.

- Harm to research participants must be avoided, including their kin, wider family, and community.

- Research designs should consider potential harm to the participant's organisation or business.

- The independence and impartiality of researchers must be clear and any conflicts of interest must be explicit.

■ Research should be conducted so as to ensure the professional integrity of its design, the generation and analysis of data, and the publication of results, while the direct and indirect contributions of colleagues, collaborators, and others should also be acknowledged.

ETHICS OF RESEARCHING ONLINE

A broader discussion of issues related to researching in Chapter 21 arises when we examine "social media research", we raise some key ethical issues in this section. When researching into online discussion forums, chat rooms etc., the sport management researcher needs to remain mindful of possible ethical issues. The majority of comments posted by people online, for instance, may originally have been written and uploaded to a website for a different purpose. Contributors may have intended their internet "posts" to be private, or at least their personal views and opinions were written to share with like-minded people, perhaps going through similar experiences or coping with similar situations. People may not be happy to agree to their original postings on a website/blog being analysed by researchers and used for a different purpose. Such concerns should be considered on a case by case basis. Standard ethical practices may need adapting to account for the digital age. However, where material is in the open domain, it may be easier for sport management researchers to make a case justifying its use as source material. This would still need to be checked out with your university research ethics committee.

The design of your research may also create additional issues. For example "Netnographers" must consider additional issues (Netnography is discussed in Chapter 15). For example, there is the challenge of *online confidentiality*. While a netnographer should maintain the same privacy standards as other qualitative researchers, the retention of information on the web makes it difficult to protect confidentiality with traditional mechanisms. Some users may think of their postings to some online community site as private (Markham, 2007); therefore, Netnographers, who study sensitive issues, should go to great lengths to disguise the identity of the community they have studied as well as of its participants who are quoted. Another issues relates to *gaining informed consent*: Since online community members can disguise their identities, gaining informed consent creates unique challenges. Men may masquerade as women and children as adults, and yet the research should not proceed unless an effort is made to obtain informed and voluntary consent. Netnographers must make their own identity known, state clearly their expectations for participation, provide an explicit informed consent letter that is available as discussion participants come and go (Denzin & Lincoln, 2008), and attempt to identify those whose identity is not credible through inconsistencies in their postings (Kozinets, 2010).

Research brief

Title: An Exploration of Sport Fandom in Online Communities
Author: Kirkwood, M., *Auckland University of Technology*, Yap, S. F., *Auckland University of Technology*, & Xu, Y., *Auckland University of Technology* (2019)
Reference: Kirkwood, M., Yap, S. F., & Xu, Y. (2019). An exploration of sport fandom in online communities. *International Journal of Sport Communication*, *12*(1), 55–78.
Understanding interactions between sport fans helps sport marketers customise relationships with the fans and enhance brand loyalty. This paper analysed the social exchanges that take place in an online sport community and identified possible fan roles and their influences in the community. Based on a netnography approach, the study identified four different types of role – Oracles, Hollywoods, Jokers, and Rookies – yielding a typology of sport fans that denotes their roles in the online community. The study contributed to sport communication literature by bringing together the concepts of identity, social exchange, and role theory relative to sport-fan behaviour in an online social community.

CONCLUSION

This chapter has offered an overview of the ethics process and its implications for sport management research. It is not intended to provide a fully comprehensive understanding of the place of ethics in research but to provide guidance to the sport management researcher of the issues to consider. There will be many times when the sport management researcher faces difficult choices in relation to the conduct of their research, and will need to weigh up the benefits of the research against any possible harm or detriment caused to participants in the research study. A system of research ethics will serve to guide the sport management researcher in making the moral choices that will ultimately benefit both the research study and the research participants.

REVIEW AND RESEARCH QUESTIONS

1. Consider what ethical factors could prevent you from conducting a research project on the chosen topic.

2. What is informed consent? What factors would you want to know before agreeing to participate?

3. You are preparing to do some research into the doping experiences of female youth athletes. Your research will involve you interviewing and observing the female athletes over an extended period of time so your supervisor wants you to produce a presentation on the ethical and legal issues associated with the work you are doing. Prepare a 10-minute presentation that includes the following information:

   a. A description of two ethical and legal issues associated with the research project you are going to be doing.

   b. An analysis and explanation of the implications of not working ethically and legally in a research setting.

4. Discuss the following ethical dilemmas:

    a. Your research is in a sensitive area. You are unlikely to get access if you state your real purpose. Do you hide the goals of your research from the participants and tell them you are studying something else?

    b. You are in the middle of an interview when your interviewee interrupts the conversation to take a telephone call. He presumes you have turned off your voice recorder and goes on to discuss some highly sensitive information which would be useful for your research. Do you turn off the recorder? Do you admit your error to the interviewee, or do you pretend it didn't happen?

    c. You have been given confidential information concerning the financial status of a sport franchise, which would usefully inform your research. What would be the ethical response to this situation be?

5. As the meaning of what is ethical behaviour is often subjective and may have controversial elements, think about the following questions.

    a. What does ethics in research mean for you?

    b. Why is ethical behaviour important for you?

    c. Why should ethics matter in research?

REFERENCES

Cohen, L., Manion, L., & Morrison, K. (2000). *Research methods in education* (5th ed.). London: Routledge Falmer.

Denzin, N. K. & Lincoln, Y. S. (Eds.) (2008). *The landscape of qualitative research* (3rd ed.). London: Sage Publications.

Drew, C. J., & Hardman, M.L. (2007). *Intellectual disabilities across the lifespan* (9th ed.). Upper Saddle River, NJ: Merrill-Prentice.

Kelly, A. (1989). Education or Indoctrination? The ethics of school-based action research. In R.G. Burgess (Ed.). *The Ethics of Educational Research*, pp. 100–113. London: Routledge.

Kozinets, R. V. (2010). *Netnography: Doing ethnographic research online*. Thousand Oaks, CA: Sage Publications.

Markham, A. N. (2007). Method as ethic, ethic as method: A case of reflexivity in qualitative ICT research. *Journal of Information Ethics, 15*(2), 37–55.

PART 3

Foundations of sport management research

CHAPTER 7

Methods of data collection for sport management research

CHAPTER OVERVIEW

Data collection is the process of collecting or gathering information pertaining to a specific research topic. The data collected will be used by the sport management researcher in the latter process of analysis to formulate theories, produce recommendations, or contextualise events and activities in the sport management setting. Data collection is an important aspect of any type of research study. Inaccurate data collection can impact the results of a study and ultimately lead to invalid results. This chapter discusses how the sport management researcher should approach fieldwork and the need to use a range of data collection techniques, including observation, interviews, focus groups, and documents.

DATA COLLECTION CONSIDERATIONS

The sport management researcher needs to take into account the following when deciding on the methods of data collection to be used in the research:

- What is the nature of the research?

- How is the researcher positioned in relation to the participants?

- Is the research problem outward looking – is it externalised, or does it require inner contemplation?

- What is the primary purpose of the research? Is the end result of the research intended to be beneficial to the participants or the sport management site? Or, is the research purely academic in nature, intended to be beneficial to the researcher only?

- Who will be viewing the results of the study? Will it be the academic community or members of the sport management community?

- Is the research neutral or is there a political agenda?

The answers the sport management researcher makes to these different questions can help shape how the specific data collection techniques are conceived for the study.

GAINING ENTRY

Hammersley and Atkinson (1983) suggest appropriate tactics for gaining entry to a setting which include knowing whom to approach and how. Such knowledge is based upon some prior information about the temporal work rhythms that exist and the power alignments within the sport organisation. The sport management researcher needs to garner information in order to present themselves to the right person at the right time to gain authorisation to carry out an inquiry in a setting. When multiple entries are required to meet the purpose of the research, the sport management researcher should establish credibility and enter into positive relationships.

In many cases, entry into a sport organisation or setting is gained through a contact located within that organisation or setting, and with whom the sport management researcher may have established credibility through a previous encounters. According to Loftland (1984), the use of a contact or acquaintance to gain entry is not unusual amongst field workers: "It seems quite typical for outside researchers to gain access to settings or persons through contacts they have already established. They care about among their friends, acquaintances, colleagues, and the like for someone who is already favourably regarded by the person with access control" (p. 25). In this way, the sport management researcher's contact can become and act as a "sponsor" in the organisation, providing the sport management researcher with the opportunity to develop relationships which otherwise might have been more difficult and time consuming to achieve.

GATEKEEPERS

To secure entry to a sport organisation, the researcher may be required to perform a presentation about the purpose of the research. This empowers organisational members as they can openly discuss the research and make comment. The sport management researcher's "sponsor" can also introduce the researcher to the appropriate individuals within the organisation. Attention can then shift to the official gatekeeper of the sport organisation and their support may be secured. Hammersley and Atkinson (1983) indicate that gatekeepers will generally be concerned to the "light" in which the organisation will be portrayed, and will have a desire to see themselves and their colleagues presented in a favourable manner. As a consequence of this, the sport management researcher may be required to establish a research agreement (discussed later in the chapter) with the organisation.

FIELDWORK

Fieldwork is an important stage in the data collection process. Fieldwork frequently involves the researcher working for long periods of time in a natural setting to develop *field relations*. Field relations are the complex relationships the researcher develops with others (e.g. gatekeepers, research participants) while working in the field. These relationships have logistical, procedural, ethical, and political dimensions (Schwandt, 2001). Preparation before field work data collection begins involves *sensitisation* of stakeholders about the objectives of the research project. This process involves the following elements:

- **Giving information and gaining consent**: Information sheets and consent forms should be prepared in advance and approved by ethics boards. The fieldworker should have been trained to explain what participants are consenting to and ask for and respond to any questions from participants in an open manner. The researcher should not place pressure on the invited participant to participate.

- **Sampling**: Choosing the sample (refer to Chapter 3).

- **Establishing rapport**: Fieldworkers should develop a rapport with research participants prior to commencement. Sending invitations to participate are one way to help establish this rapport. At invitation, the participant should be informed of the general topic of the research and how long, for example, the interview is likely to take (typically 30–60 minutes).

- **Research timeline**: In order to minimise disruption in the research environment, the fieldworker should consult stakeholders to develop a research timeline for the completion of fieldwork.

- **Fieldwork visit**: Once all approvals and permissions have been finalised, the field visit should be confirmed prior to the commencement date through a phone call or email message. The fieldworker should ensure they take all necessary materials and equipment, including the interview guide, consent form, pens, notebook, tape recorder, and spare batteries.

- **Field visit notes**: Regardless of the kinds of data involved, data collection in a qualitative study takes a great deal of time. The fieldworker needs to record any potentially useful data thoroughly, accurately, and systematically, using field notes, sketches, audiotapes, photographs, and other suitable means. The data collection methods must observe the ethical principles of research.

- **Data management**: A protocol for data management should be set up at the starting of the study. This needs to consider storing and transcribing notes, and recordings and potential use of computer programmes.

THE RESEARCH AGREEMENT

In research fieldwork that involves participant observation over a long period of time, the research agreement is primarily developed as a mechanism to provide guidelines in relation to the dissemination of information. In the researcher's initial discussion, it may be decided that a confidentiality agreement should be established among the researcher, the researcher's supervisors, and the organisation itself. A sport organisation may be concerned that any information that is provided to the researcher is only viewed by those directly associated with the research and is to be used for academic purposes only. For example, if the information provided is sensitive and has been developed in order to provide the sport organisation with a competitive advantage over its rivals the organisation would not want this information in the public domain. Additionally, an agreement, through the discretion of the Chief Executive Officer/President, could provide provision to terminate the study if any information was published or distributed in the broader private or public domain without prior agreement.

A verbal research agreement (in some cases a formal written contract is required) in relation to confidentiality is established. This occurs because information given by individuals may vary and as such may have potential to cause conflict between management members. In an interviewing context, one way to overcome this is prior to each interview, the researcher should remind the participants that the interview is being conducted in complete confidentiality. Each individual can be arbitrarily assigned a label so that participants can be listed as "Respondent One", "Respondent Two", and so on. Thus, the rationale for confidentiality and negotiation of accounts is based on an ethical consideration of respect for persons who have guaranteed an intrusion into their world, and access to their opinions in regards to the research issues.

PRESERVING ANONYMITY OF PARTICIPANTS

Maintaining anonymity needs to be a consideration throughout the entire research project rather than only in the write-up. This requires the sport management researcher to use various procedures to help preserve anonymity. First, as previously mentioned, each interviewee should be identified by a number and labelled as a respondent/participant. Second, the researcher should be the only person who has access to the bulk of the data during the fieldwork stage. Fieldwork notes should not be presented to anyone, but treated as highly confidential. Finally, time itself helps to protect anonymity or at least to make identification more difficult. Over time, people tend to forget what others have said. They may even forget what they themselves said. In spite of these procedures, individuals who are familiar with the sport organisation will speculate about statements made by individuals where positive identification is not possible. However, to present the information in such a way that even the people central to it are fooled by it is to risk removing the very aspects that make it relevant, insightful, and believable. The participants should be informed of this. Having been assured of confidentiality, individuals generally feel freer to talk about the organisation. This leads us to the notion of trust.

TRUST

Wax (1971) emphasises the importance of reciprocal relationships while gaining entry. Mutual trust, respect, and co-operation are dependent on the emergence of an exchange relationship in which the researcher obtains information, and participants in a setting can identify something in that setting which will make their co-operation worthwhile.

Nelson (1969), however, suggests that restrictions can exist in achieving the desired amount of trust from participants. These potential barriers were highlighted through Nelson's direct participation in ethnographic fieldwork. His work focused on the notion of foreign and domestic participation. He believed participation in one's own formal organisation is accompanied by a set of research constraints apparently not encountered if one participates in the activities of a foreign social group. The difference lies in the participants' perceptions of the researcher. While a researcher in a foreign culture might perceive him or herself as a participant, those in the group, are likely to perceive the researcher more as a guest participant rather than a full member.

Rosen (1991) related the problems raised by Nelson (1969) to the issue of secrecy. Rosen indicates that when a researcher occupies an official place in an organisation, an office located in physical and temporal space, he or they becomes part of the first-order politics of the organisation, and therefore not someone to be fully trusted by others located in the same political arena. This is opposed to how one might trust an outsider, the researcher as an observer. In this situation, the researcher is an outsider knowledgeable of the organisation, yet at the same time probably marginal to its political processes. This issue of secrecy, according to Rosen, is related to the notion of trust. Rosen believed that when the researcher occupies a place in the first-order politics of an organisation they are tied to the instrumental relations of organisation, the means-ends processes of social intercourse. However, the researcher who occupies a role solely as an observer is tied to the moral relations among individuals, friendship-like relationships are developed and pursued. Rosen suggests that the instrumental and moral dimensions of a relationship are clearly embedded within the same discourse between actors. From a means-ends perspective, the researcher as an occupier of a role in instrumental relations will be informed according to other organisational members' perceived utility or disutility of doing so. On the other hand, the researcher as part of a friendship relationship (as an observer) will be informed of the discourse of the organisation insofar as it is germane to the discourse of friendship.

Throughout a study that requires the researcher to spend a significant amount of time in a sport organisation or setting the researcher can be perceived in a dual capacity depending on the role being fulfilled. Due to this, the sport management researcher needs to be aware of developing an impression of a person who would be discrete in handling information within the research setting, and who would honour promises of anonymity when collecting and discussing data. Therefore, it would be advisable that the sport management researcher not request at the outset full access to relevant and sensitive data. The researcher should decide to leave these requests, of what seem more delicate forms of access, until field relationships had been established. For example, although the researcher may be privy to a discussion of the detail of player contracts and their implications for management, the researcher should not request to see a copy of these contacts until a relationship of trust had been established between those concerned – if it is not, and the researcher's instincts suggest it is not appropriate, then this request should not be made. This approach of obtaining data at an appropriate time can be instrumental in allowing relationships to develop. As a consequence, this process can assist in participants being more open and candid in discussions. The outcome can be the development of relationships based on mutual trust, respect, and co-operation.

DATA COLLECTION METHODS

There are *four* basic types of qualitative data collection: (1) observations (ranging from direct to participant); (2) interviews (ranging structured to unstructured interviews); (3) focus groups; and (4) document (ranging from public records to personal documents). In recent years, new forms of data collection have emerged consisting of journaling in narrative story writing, utilising text from email messages, and observation through photographs and video. In addition, Denzin and Lincoln (2005) suggest data collection using techniques such as the analysis of artefacts and cultural records, the use of visual materials and the use of personal experience. For instance, a biography, the portrait of an individual's life, is made from documents, interviews, and possible observations (Creswell, 1998). Each of these data collection methods will now be discussed.

OBSERVATION

Observational techniques are methods by which individuals gather first-hand data on the policies, programmes, projects, processes, or behaviours being studied. They provide researchers with an opportunity to collect data on a wide range of behaviours, to capture a great variety of interactions, and to openly explore the evaluation topic. Observation entails the systematic noting and recording of actions and behaviours (both verbal and non-verbal), events and objects in the location or group being researched. Observations can be useful during both the *formative* and *summative* phases of research.

Observational techniques are perhaps the most privacy-threatening data collection technique for participants. Participants may feel uncomfortable assuming that they are being judged. Much effort may be needed to assure participants

Table 7.1	Advantages and disadvantages of observations	
Advantages of observations	**Disadvantages of observations**
■ Researcher conducts fieldwork to understand situation/context.	■ High levels of observer expertise may be necessary in various settings.
■ Researcher may be able to identify unanticipated outcomes from an "insider" perspective.	■ Observer presence may contaminate data.
■ Observations are usually unstructured and flexible.	■ Selective perception of observer may compromise data.
■ Observations give insight into the behaviour of individuals and groups.	■ Observer has little control over the setting and may not get quality data.
	■ Behaviours observed may not be an accurate representation of actual setting.
	■ Fieldwork may be expensive and time consuming.
	■ Training is critical.

that they will not be adversely affected by the research and to negotiate field-worker access to specific sites. Table 7.1 summarises some of the key discussion concerning the use of observations in qualitative research.

The role of the observer

There are various methods for gathering observational data, depending on the nature of a given research project. The extent to which full participation is possible (and/or desirable) will depend on the nature of the project and its participants, the political and social context, the nature of the evaluation questions being asked, and the resources available. Patton (1990) suggests the idea is to negotiate and adopt that degree of participation that will yield the most meaningful data about the programme given the characteristics of the participants, the nature of staff–participant interactions, and the socio-political context of the programme. There are two generally recognised observation techniques: *direct* and *participant. Direct observation* is privileged in the scientific or positivist paradigm, as it is believed to be more objective and protect the neutrality of the researcher. In contrast, *participant observation*, which evolved in the field of anthropology, is more aligned with the naturalistic paradigm that argues that total objectivity is neither possible nor desirable. These forms of observation shall now be discussed.

Direct observation

In direct observation, the researcher observes without engaging or interacting with the situation or environment they are observing, in the belief that they are not disturbing the environment and are able to maintain neutrality and objectivity in the process. For example, a sport management researcher may quietly and inconspicuously observe the engagement/non-engagement of fans with sponsorship activation booths outside a sporting event. There are critiques of this belief that point out that once researchers appear on the scene, total objectivity and therefore, control of bias, is no longer possible as the presence of the researcher alone will automatically influence people's behaviour. Engaging in *covert* observation – where the participants are unaware of the researcher's presence, raises ethical concerns (deception see Chapter 6) as participants may not have given informed consent for the observation to occur. While convert observation obviates the need to negotiate access and reactivity (a phenomenon that occurs when individuals alter their behaviour due to the awareness that they are being observed). The change may be positive or negative, and depending on the situation) is not a problem there are practical difficulties in taking notes and conducting interviews, it can lead to researcher anxiety over concerns about "blowing your cover".

Participant observation

As the name "participant" suggests, the researcher participates in the activities of the persons being observed rather than being an aloof observer. Spradley (1980) asserts that participant observation has two objectives when entering a social situation: (1) to be involved in activities appropriate to the setting, and (2) to observe the activities, people, and physical elements of the setting. Jorgensen (1989) makes the point that the methodology of participant observation is inappropriate where questions relate to fairly large populations – this is better addressed via surveys or experiments. Participant observation is most suitable when minimal conditions exist such as:

- the observation pertains to human meanings and interactions as seen from the standpoint of insiders.

- the phenomenon of investigation can be surveyed in the here and now of an everyday life setting.

- the researcher is able to obtain access into the setting.

- the research problem can be addressed by qualitative information collected by participant observation pertinent to the field setting.

- the process of inquiry is open-ended and flexible providing direct experiential and observational access based on facts about human life grounded in the realities of daily existence.

- the researcher is able to use direct observation together with other techniques for collecting information (Spradley, 1980).

The role of the researcher in participant observation also involves variations in *overt* or *covert* dimensions. In terms of the *overt*, participants in the field are fully aware who the observer is and that observations are being conducted together with a complete explanation of the study. By contrast, in a *covert* position, participants are not informed or aware of anything occurring. As mentioned previously, researchers need to be aware of ethical considerations around covert observation and the absence of informed consent on the part of the unaware (and perhaps even unwilling) research participants. Hammersley and Atkinson (1983) suggested that there is the danger of the researcher "going native". This often means being too involved or having too close a rapport with the person or persons being observed to the extent that the researcher loses objectivity, or rather (given objectivity is not always the aim of such studies), loses the ability to achieve the study's aims. For example, a researcher sent to covertly observe a culture of illicit doping in a sport team may be seduced by the success of winning, and perhaps the money/fame and status. This researcher might then be very unwilling to report on the team, or may fabricate data to help exonerate the team from any wrongdoing. A special issue with regard to observations relates to the amount of observation needed. The duration of observations could range from a limited one hour to long-term months or years (De Laine, 1997). Participant observation, if handled correctly by the researcher, it can provide an opportune and creative process to gain access to otherwise inaccessible dimension of human life and experiences (Jorgensen, 1989).

Whether the observation is direct or participatory researchers may engage in *structured observations*. This type of observation requires a data collection form to ensure observations are consistently recorded. A *structured protocol* is useful, so that once the fieldworker is familiar with the format, the sheet can be filled quickly as different items are observed. The data collection form may include space for the fieldworker to draw sketches of situations. In this case, two different observation forms may be used: one for observing specific instances and another for observing general surroundings.

Observation protocol

Observations guided by a *structured protocol* can take a variety of forms, ranging from the request for a narrative describing events seen to a checklist or a rating scale of specific behaviours/activities that address the evaluation question of interest. The use of a protocol helps assure that the researcher is gathering the pertinent information. Based upon the suggestions of Lincoln and Guba (1985), the observation protocol should provide an overall context for the data. The protocol should prompt the fieldworker to:

- **Describe the setting** where the observation took place and what the physical setting was like.

- **Identify the people** who participated in those activities, i.e. characteristics of those who were present.

- **Document the interactions** between all actors (staff, participants, fieldwork, others) in the human and social setting.

- **Describe and assess** the incidents and events.

- **Be alert to** unanticipated events that might require refocusing one or more research questions.

Field notes

Typically, *unstructured observations* are noted in a fieldnotes book. Field notes are frequently used to provide more in-depth background or to help the observer remember salient events (e.g. key emotions during a data collection, or vital information that was provided outside the formal "observation"/recording). Field notes contain the description of what has been observed. The descriptions must be factual, accurate, and thorough, without being judgemental and cluttered by trivia. The date and time of the observation should be recorded, and everything that the observer believes to be worth noting should be included. No information should be trusted to future recall, as human memory is famously unreliable. The ideal observation process is supported and contextualised by keeping systematic and analytical field notes. During the data collection phase, the researcher typically keeps four types of field notes, as described by Richardson (2000):

1. *Methodological notes* on issues and decisions pertaining to the research process, such as coding labels and participant criteria.

2. *Observational notes* collected during observations made while attending events and interviews.

3. *Analytical notes* noting assumptions and the process of data analysis and interpretation.

4. *General field notes* that include anecdotal information such as contacts made for future reference.

The use of technological tools, such as a smart phone app or laptop computer can make the collection of field notes more efficient and the notes themselves more comprehensive. Informed consent must almost always be obtained from participants before any observational data are gathered, and the participants must be informed where their data will be kept, how long for, and how it will be used before they give consent (covert studies create a problem in this respect, and the "solution" is normally agreed by negotiation with a suitable ethics committee). When taking observation field notes, we make the following recommendations:

- Record notes as soon as possible after each period in the field, and do not talk with others until observations are recorded.

- Begin the record of each field visit with a new page, with the date and time noted.

- Use wide margins to make it easy to add to notes at any time. Go back and add to the notes if you remember something later.

- Record events in the order in which they occur and note how long they last.

- Make notes as concrete, complete, and comprehensive as possible.

- Record small talk or routines that do not appear to be significant at the time; they may become important later.

- Let your feelings flow, and write quickly without worrying about spelling. Assume that no one else will use the notes.

- Include diagrams or maps of the setting, and outline your own movements and those of others during the period of observation.

- Record emotional feelings and private thoughts in a separate section.

- Avoid evaluative summarising words.

- Reread notes periodically and record ideas generated by the re-reading.

Apart from these recommendations, when collecting data through observation it is important to maintain a critical attitude that involves the continual questioning of your own assumptions and biases.

INTERVIEWS

The most utilised data collection method in qualitative research studies is the interview. Two schools of thought exist with respect to interview type. Most authors classify qualitative interviews into three types: (1) structured interviews; (2) semi-structured interviews; and (3) unstructured interviews. Other researchers propose only two types of interviews in qualitative research: *structured interviews*, in which a carefully worded questionnaire is administered; and *in-depth interviews*, in which the interviewer does not follow a rigid form but simply lets the conversation flow. The following discussion outlines the use of the term interview by both schools of thought.

Structured interviews (sometimes called standardised interviews) involve the researcher asking the same set of questions, in the same order, using the

Table 7.2	Advantages and disadvantages of structured interviews	
Advantages of structured interviews	**Disadvantages of structured interviews**
■ Usually yield richest data, details, new insights.	■ Expensive and time consuming.
■ Permit face-to-face contact with participants.	■ Need well-qualified, highly trained interviewers.
■ Provide opportunity to explore topics in depth.	■ Interviewee may distort information through recall error, selective perceptions, desire to please interviewer.
■ Afford ability to experience the affective as well as cognitive aspects of responses.	■ Flexibility can result in inconsistencies across interviews.
■ Allow interviewer to explain or help clarify questions, increasing the likelihood of useful responses.	■ Volume of information too large; may be difficult to transcribe and reduce data.
■ Allow interviewer to be flexible in administering interview to particular individuals or circumstances.	

same words, to different interviewees. Structured interviews are convenient for comparing different interviewees' answers to the same questions, and when a team of researchers is involved in conducting the interviews. For instance, structured interviews may offer a source of comparison of sponsor message recall, drawing on both the subject matter and feelings generated for a particular message. This is especially helpful when several researchers are testing recall from numerous study participants. There are several advantages and disadvantages of structured interviews outlined in the Table 7.2.

Semi-structured interviews (sometimes referred to as focused interviews) involve a series of open-ended questions based on the topic areas the researcher wants to cover. The open-ended nature of the question stays true to defining the topic under investigation, as well as providing opportunities for both interviewer and interviewee to discuss some topics in more detail. If the interviewee has difficulty answering a question or provides only a brief response, the interviewer can use cues or prompts to encourage the interviewee to consider the question further.

Semi-structured interviews use an *interview guide* (discussed later in the chapter), which includes questions or issues to be asked but does not specify exact wording. Interview guides may also include optional "probe" questions to remind the interviewer to follow up on specifics as needed. These types of interviews are favoured widely by researchers. These types of interviews are often based on the knowledge of, and/or the assumption that the respondents have had a particular experience they can elaborate upon. In these types of interviews, the situation has often been analysed before the interview. Therefore, the researcher is seeking additional information. In a semi-structured interview, an interview schedule is formulated to address the topic and to guide the interview, yet "without fixed wording or fixed ordering of questions" (Minichiello, Aroni, Timewell, & Alexander, 1995, p. 65). The content of the interview is directed on matters that are foremost to the topic of the research. The manner in which questioning takes place allows room for flexibility, social interaction, exploration of ideas and "provides opportunities to observe participants in the face-to-face ongoing interaction of the focus group" (De Laine, 1997, p. 294).

The interviewer guides and specifies the topics for which information is sought. The interview focuses on the respondent's subjective experiences. This allows the participants to describe in detail the situation, as it is meaningful to them. Moreover, it allows the interviewer to freely probe and ask follow-up questions (Doyle, 1994). Judd, Smith, and Kidder (1991) suggest the major disadvantage of semi-structured interviews is that the researcher is vulnerable to the interpretations and subjective insights of the informant. As a result, the researcher may be drawn into the participant's world view. According to Burns (1997), this problem of validity is acknowledged as inconsequential if the participant's behaviour is congruent with their perception of reality.

Unstructured interviews (sometimes referred to as "depth" or "in-depth" interviews) have very little structure at all. The interviewer goes into the interview with the aim of discussing a limited number of topics, sometimes as few as one or two, and frames the questions on the basis of the interviewee's previous response. Although only one or two topics are discussed they are covered in great detail. Unstructured interviews are exactly what they sound like – interviews where the interviewer wants to find out about a specific topic but has no structure or preconceived plan or expectation as to how they will deal with the topic. The difference with semi-structured interviews is that in a semi-structured interview the interviewer has a set of broad questions to ask and may also have some prompts to help the interviewee but the interviewer has the time and space to respond to the interviewee's responses. The major disadvantage of unstructured interviews is that the researcher is vulnerable to being dragged "off topic" by the responses of the interviewee, as responses that often seem like a natural part of the conversation may, when analysed, be totally irrelevant to the actual research question. All three types of interview can be used in combination (Patton, 1990). For example, after conducting structured interviews, researchers could follow up with semi-structured interviews, and perhaps even extend to using unstructured interviews or, conversely, they may start with unstructured interviews to relax the interviewees, and move to a semi-structured interview format.

In-depth interview

As indicated previously, some researchers propose only *two* types of interview approaches in qualitative research: *structured interviews* and *in-depth interviews*. In *structured interviews* (as above), the emphasis is on obtaining answers to carefully phrased questions. Interviewers are trained to deviate as little as possible from the question wording to ensure uniformity of interview administration. In contrast, an **in-depth interview** is a dialogue between a skilled interviewer and an interviewee. Its goal is to elicit rich, detailed material that can be used in analysis (Lofland & Lofland, 1995). In-depth interviews are characterised by extensive probing and open-ended questions. Similar to semi-structures interviews, the researcher usually prepares an *interview guide* that includes a list of questions or issues that are to be explored and suggested probes for following up on key topics. The guide helps the interviewer pace the interview and make interviewing more systematic and comprehensive. Lofland and Lofland provide guidelines for preparing interview guides, conducting the interview with the guide and writing up the interview. Poor interviewing skills, poor phrasing of questions, or inadequate knowledge of the subject's culture or frame of reference may result in a data collection that obtains little useful information.

Face-to-face structured, semi-structured, and unstructured interviews are some of the most effective procedures used by the sport management researcher. There are also several more specialised forms, including ethnographic interviewing, phenomenological interviewing, and interviewing children – each requires particular levels of expertise and guidance.

OTHER INTERVIEW APPROACHES

Telephone interviews

Telephone interviews have particular advantages over face-to-face interviews such as ease of geographic coverage, the possibility of doing more interviews in the time available, and lower costs. However, some significant drawbacks also exist and these include the sense of impersonality, especially if you have not met before (which may make rapport difficult to achieve), the lack of visual contact (cannot read non-verbal signs such as body language, disdain, annoyance, etc.) and a feeling of time pressure leading to a tendency to rush through the interview. Some consider that telephoning for an interview is intrusive for the party receiving the call and the interviewer's awareness of that to be a major problem. Many people do not like their home life being disturbed by telephone calls "out of the blue" and especially by people they don't know. A main problem is that to get participants most calls need to be made in the evening, but that is when they are dining, relaxing, etc. Therefore, they tend to be annoyed by such uninvited intrusion. Also, student researchers can often be nervous about using the telephone for interviewing and transmit their nervousness to the respondents. Moreover, telephone interviews seem more prone to interruptions and early termination. All of these can affect the quality of the data obtained. There are a few strategies for overcoming these drawbacks.

- Use voice cues to compensate for the lack of visual contact (for example, "yes", "good", "have a think about that for a minute", and so on).

- Listen sensitively and do not talk too much.

- Remember the importance of your tone and the need to project warmth and friendliness.

- Remember to write and take notes as well as listen (which is easier than in face-to-face interview).

- Sum up important points from time to time.

- Arrange in advance, a mutually convenient time for the interview.

- Jot down what you wish to say; bring all necessary materials/papers to the phone.

- Do not be afraid of silence (you can always check on what is going on by asking such questions as "did you understand my last point?", "do you need to think about that?", and so on).

Online interviewing

Online interviews take the form of text, audio or video-chats, with some forms of text-based interviewing occurring asynchronously (i.e. not in real time) while other modes occur synchronously (i.e. in real time) using computers and networks with software such as AIM (AOL Instant Messenger), Windows Live Messenger, Apple iChat, Teams, Zoom, or Skype.

Some of the different forms of online interviewing include: ***One-to-one synchronous interview***: Both researcher and participant are online, responding at the same time, either in writing, via audio or face-to-face using video. This method is especially valuable for accessing people in their own environments, such as at home, work or other non-threatening environments, especially minority and professional groups that otherwise would be difficult to contact (Gruber, Szmigin, Reppel, & Voss, 2008) or those too distant for you to reach for face-to-face interviewing. ***Asynchronous communication***: is when interview chat happens in non-real time, for example in emails. Messages are written and read at different times, which may be minutes, hours, or days apart. This allows researcher and participant to choose the times that best suit for participating in the study. This is beneficial if interviewing across worldwide time zones. When email is used for asynchronous interviews, it is less immediate than real-time chat, but has the advantage of allowing participants to be more thoughtful and reflective because they can take time to respond in a more measured way. James and Busher (2006) found that one of the benefits of email interviewing was that over time participants took greater ownership of the research focus and dialogue, responding in unexpected ways and directions, and according to their own timeframes rather than those of the researchers. This led the researchers to release some of their control of the research agenda in order to pursue these interesting new lines of investigation. Thus, there was a shift in power from a researcher-driven focus and schedule to one that was more collaboratively constructed, which, they found, improved the quality of participants' input.

Research brief

Title: Managing sport volunteers with a disability: Human resource management implications
Author: Kappelides, P., *La Trobe University* & Spoor, J., *La Trobe University* (2019)
Reference: Kappelides, P., & Spoor, J. (2019). Managing sport volunteers with a disability: Human resource management implications. *Sport Management Review, 22*(5), 694–707.
In this research, the authors examined the benefits and barriers of including volunteers with a disability in three Australian sport and recreation organisations, as well as potential human resource management implications.

Semi-structured face-to-face or telephone interviews were conducted to identify the benefits, barriers, challenges, and potential solutions for people with a disability who volunteer as well as for participants receiving the service from volunteers with a disability. The results suggested that organisations need to create an environment that facilitates open, two-way communication with volunteers with a disability about their needs and wants. There also should be training and education to all volunteers and staff around an inclusive workplace culture.

INTERVIEW GUIDE

An *interview guide* should be developed based on the objectives of the research study and typically includes around five to ten key topics or questions, which are designed to elicit information about specific aspects of the issue or problem. Under each topic or question, the inclusion of probing questions which encourage participants to reflect more deeply on the meaning of their responses may help respondents to think more deeply about the problem under investigation. This may include, for example, asking participants about real events, or *"critical incidents"*, which can reveal much about beliefs, attitudes and behaviour. The following elements should form the basis of the *interview guide*:

1. *Opening question*: a general question to orientate interview to the topic

2. *Probe questions*: Types of probes commonly used by the interviewer are:

   - Repeating the question if the interviewee strays.

   - Elaboration probes (e.g. "what did you mean by that?").

   - Focused probe (e.g. "what kind of...?").

- Giving ideas (e.g. "have you tried...?", "have you thought about...?").

- Reflecting probes (e.g. "what you seem to be saying is...?").

- Detail-oriented probe (e.g. When did it happen to you? Who was with you?).

- Clarification probe (e.g. I'm not sure I understand what you mean by "hanging out". Can you explain? You said that your manager is extremely autocratic. What do you mean by autocratic?).

3. *Inviting a summary*: The interviewer can go through a quick summary of the major information or stories collected in the interview and ask the participant if the summary covered all their major points and if they have any more to add.

4. *Concluding the interview*: At the end of the interview, participants should be given an opportunity to provide any additional information or comments. This may also be a good opportunity to ask the participant for their recommendations or solutions in addressing the research problem.

TYPES OF QUESTIONS

There are a variety of techniques for asking questions and most interviews make use of a wide range. *Grand tour* and *mini tour* questions relate to overview or more specific focus (Spradley, 1979). Grand tour questions are broad. They ask a participant to reconstruct a routine, procedure, activity, event, or cycle of activity that took place at a particular time in his or her life. The participant is the tour guide, describing the steps taken and the thoughts or feelings associated with each step (Davis, 1997). Mini tour questions are more specific. The following are examples of grand tour and mini tour questions:

Grand tour questions:

- Can you describe a typical day in the sport organisation office?

- Tell me about the events that led to your winning this sponsorship account?

- Can you describe your impressions of your sport brand?

- How did your go at promoting this event – from start to finish?

Mini tour questions:

- Can you describe what happens when you have to get press releases signed off by the PR department of the sport organisation?

- Can you describe, what it is like to use your team website?

Patton (2002) offers a different set of questions on which the interview might be based. These relate to questions about experience and behaviour; opinions and values; feelings; knowledge; sensory (related to experience but more specifically to what has been seen, felt, and heard); and to a lesser extent, background, and demographics. Examples of these questions include:

Experience and behaviour questions:

- Could you tell me about your experience of using social media as part of an integrated sport communications campaign?

- When you saw the press spill and realised the repercussions for your team's reputation, how long did it take you to activate your crisis communication plan?

Opinions and values questions:

- Why does your sport organisation hold this attitude toward people from diverse backgrounds?

Feeling questions:

- How did you feel when it was announced that you had not succeeded in your pitch for the naming rights sponsorship?

- What emotions are conjured up when you recall how you handled a difficult media relations campaign?

Knowledge questions:

- How can ethnic communities in this region lobby your sport organisation for more services?

- Who told you this piece of information?

Sensory questions:

- When you see the logo for the team, what images are conjured up in your mind?

- What do you see when you look at this billboard?

Background and demographic questions:

- What is your educational background?

- How many staff are there in the club communications team?

Other questioning forms include: (1) *Idealisation question*: describe the ideal type of communications between bosses and employees in your team? The researcher then asks the participant to compare the ideal with the actual communication relationships. In this case, the gap between the ideal and the actual would provide both an evaluation and a potential direction for future internal communication programmes; (2) *Contrast questions:* aim to reveal differences in attitudes and perceptions by comparing one thing with another. "Why did you decide to give money to this charity rather than to another"?; (3) *In hypothetical-interaction questions:* participants have to imagine a situation that is based on actual or plausible relationships and describe how they would respond. "What if...?" is often a good question to start with. For example, what if the CEO of a potential sponsor is sitting across the table from you. Describe how you would feel and what you would be thinking. What type of pitch would you use for the CEO? What would you anticipate their response to your pitch might be?

Other types of questions are *direct and factual.* These are useful for providing background information or the foundation for more extensive discussion. Examples are: (1) What are the major stories you recall from reading the sport page this week? (2) What are the most important reasons why you joined this organisation. *Structural questions* are similarly straightforward but here you are aiming to understand how people organise their feelings and knowledge within a particular area. For example, what are all the different ways that you watch sport? or what are all the different ways that you use social media to update fans on team news? Neuman (2000) suggests some rules of thumb for asking questions, these include:

- Start with a general question to orientate interview to the topic.

- Gauge the level at which you need to express yourself, the type of language that you should use so that the people you speak to understand you and do not feel intimidated by complex vocabulary or patronised by a simplistic one either.

- Use everyday vocabulary, don't use technical words or overly complicated ones.

- Put more sensitive questions towards the end.

- Ask open questions, i.e. requiring more than "yes" or "no" in answer.

- Ask neutral questions. For example, do not ask: "why haven't you had your children immunised" but rather "how did you decide whether or not to immunise your children"?

- Use concrete rather than abstract questions. For example, "think about last time you attended a game. What did you like about services then? Rather than "what do you think about West Ham stadium services"?

- Use concrete events to help people remember – e.g., "After your last game of the season" rather than "May the 15th".

There are also a number of factors to consider when determining the setting for an interview, these are:

- Select a setting that provides privacy for participants.

- Select a location where there are no distractions and it is easy to hear respondents speak.

- Select a comfortable location.

- Select a nonthreatening environment.

- Select a location that is easily accessible for respondents.

- Select a facility equipped for audio or video recording.

- Stop telephone or visitor interruptions to respondents interviewed in their office or homes.

- Provide seating arrangements that encourage involvement and interaction.

THE RHETORIC OF INTERVIEWING

The increased use of interviewing as a method of data collection in the social sciences draws attention to what Atkinson and Silverman (1997) term "the rhetoric of interviewing". This, they argue, relates to the assumption that, through interviewing, researchers gain full access to the inner feelings and thoughts, and thus the private self, of their interviewees. Atkinson and Silverman question the "overuse" of the interview and claim that it is often viewed naively or uncritically by researchers, who take the words of participants at face value and do not reflect or take an analytical stance. For example, some participants may fabricate or elaborate in order to enhance their self-esteem or cover up discreditable actions, and indeed at times you may discover discrepancies between what participants say and what they actually do.

For this reason, it is beneficial to validate the evidence you have obtained from interviews. This is done by discretely checking statements or issues with others involved in the same situations, by referring to documentary evidence and also by collecting data about social action and interaction from observation. Observation not only complements interviewing but is also a form of within-method triangulation. The situation itself, therefore, also becomes a source of data.

SAMPLING

We have discussed sampling in depth in Chapter 3; however, we shall briefly touch on it in relation to interviews. Interviews with different groups of respondents for different purposes occur as part of the research process. Participants might be *key-informants* (people who possess expert knowledge) or *stakeholders* (people in decision-making positions). The choice of participants and the number chosen will depend on the research objective. For interviews with key-informants and stakeholders, it is important to include people with a wide range of backgrounds to avoid biased results and to enable analysis of varying perspectives and reveal underlying issues or problems. Typically, 3–4 in-depth interviews are conducted with each participant to attempt to gain a consensus on responses to topics. If consensus is not reached (saturation), further participants may be selected. Identification of participants can be done in a number of ways: random sampling, convenience sampling, and snowball sampling.

LENGTH AND TIMING OF INTERVIEWS

The length of an interview depends on the participant's interest and availability, and the topic of the interview. Of course, you should suggest an approximate amount of time – perhaps an hour or an hour and a half – so that participants can plan their day, but many are willing or wish to go beyond this, although do bear in mind that even experienced researchers or willing participants tend to lose concentration after a couple of hours. Other interviews may last only 20 or 30 minutes because of the work pressures of participants. Essentially, you need to use your own judgement about an appropriate length of time to explore your topic, although the wishes of participants will always have priority. Qualitative interviews are always time consuming, however, and, if possible, it is worth allowing plenty of time for interviewing. If it is not possible to accomplish your goals in one interview, you might ask to re-interview on one or more further occasion. This said, avoid scheduling multiple interviews over the course of a single day; more than two or three a day does not allow you sufficient time to be reflective after each.

RECORDING INTERVIEW DATA

Interview data can be recorded (with the permission of the participants) and/or summarised in notes. As with observations, detailed recording is a necessary component of interviews since it forms the basis for analysing the data. Typical procedures for recording and analysing the data are as follows. First, the interviewer listens to the recording and writes a verbatim account of the interview. Transcription of the raw data includes word-for-word quotations of the participant's responses as well as the interviewer's descriptions of the participant's characteristics, enthusiasm, body language, and overall mood during the interview. The major advantages of this transcription method are its completeness and the opportunity it affords for the interviewer to remain attentive and focused during the interview. The major disadvantages are the amount of time and resources needed to produce complete transcriptions and the inhibitory impact tape recording has on some participants.

Alternatively, another procedure for recording interviews draws on notes taken by the interviewer or assigned note-taker. This method is called "note expansion". As soon as possible after the interview, the interviewer listens to the recording to clarify certain issues and to confirm that all the main points have been included in the notes. This approach is recommended when resources are scarce, when the results must be produced in a short period of time, and when the purpose of the interview is to get rapid feedback from members of the target population. The note expansion approach saves time and retains all the essential points of the discussion. In addition to the drawbacks pointed out above, a disadvantage is that the interviewer may be more selective or biased in what he or she writes, and the method of expanding notes is very likely to generate unreliable and incorrect data.

Finally, the interviewer may use no recording device, but instead takes detailed notes during the interview and draws on memory to expand and clarify the notes immediately after the interview. This approach is useful if time is short, the results are needed quickly and the evaluation questions are simple. The drawbacks noted above are at their most pronounced; however, if this method is used, real care must be taken to record the outcomes of the interview. The key practices to employ in qualitative interviews are highlighted in Table 7.3.

VALIDITY AND RELIABILITY OF THE RESEARCH INTERVIEW DATA

Interviews resemble everyday conversations, although they are focused (to a greater or lesser extent) on the researcher's needs for data. They also differ from everyday conversation because the researcher is with reliability and validity (i.e. "trustworthiness"). This means that both the researchers and the users of the findings can be as confident as possible that the findings reflect what the research set out to answer, rather than reflecting the bias of the researcher, or a very atypical group. In practical terms, this means that techniques should aim to be:

- **Reproducible**: that is, someone else could use the same *interview guide* to generate similar information.

- **Systematic**: to ensure that we are not just picking interviewees or data that support our pre-existing ideas about the answers.

- **Credible**: the questions we ask, for instance, and the ways in which we ask them should be reasonable ones for generating valid (or "truthful") accounts of phenomena.

- **Transparent**: methods should be written up so that readers can see exactly how the data were collected and analysed.

Table 7.3	Good practice in qualitative interviews

Probing and cross-checking

- Questions or topics are tailored to different informants and stages of enquiry, making use of findings from previous interviews.

- Participants can be identified progressively to explore a range of different types of knowledge and perspectives.

- Findings are reduced to understandable patterns using qualitative analysis and/or diagrams.

- Findings are validated by cross-checking with other questions and information from other informants.

Good Interpersonal skills

- Sensitivity to the respondents' mood, body language, time constraints, and the different cultural norms that may shape these.

- Ability to really listen to answers, and to probe and cross-check in a thorough but sensitive manner.

- Taking notes in a discrete, non-threatening way that does not interrupt the flow of conversation.

- Recording is often a possibility.

- Using humour and personal experience to bring up sensitive issues or to challenge a response.

Careful documentation

- Continually examining one's own biases.

- As far as possible quoting an interviewee's exact words and making clear where the interviewer's own analysis and interpretation has been added.

The reliability and validity of the data collected from the interview vary with the type of interview employed, as well the experience of the interviewer. **Reliability** in interviewing refers to how consistently a technique measures the concepts it is supposed to measure, enabling other researchers to repeat the study and attain similar findings (Sekaran, 2000; Emory & Cooper, 1991). Reliability is usually achieved through four tactics: First, reliability is attained through the structured process of interviews. Second, reliability is achieved through organising a structured process for recording, writing, and interpreting data. Third, research reliability is often achieved through comparison of the research findings between the interviewer and interviewee. Finally, the use of a planning committee to assist in the design and administration of the interview programme is another way that reliability can be achieved (Guba & Lincoln, 1994). If a number of the members of the committee agree about a phenomenon, then their collective judgement is relatively objective. **Validity** in interviewing refers to the formation of suitable operational measures for the concepts being investigated (Emory & Cooper, 1991). Interviewing attempts to achieve construct validity through three tactics. First, triangulation of interview questions is usually established in the research design stage by two or more carefully worded questions that look at the subject matter under investigation from different angles. Second, the interview method usually contains an inbuilt negative case analysis where, in each interview and before the next, the technique explicitly requires that the interviewer attempt to disprove emerging explanations interpreted in the data (Dick, 1990). Finally, the flexibility of the approach allows the interviewer to re-evaluate and re-design both the content and process of the interview programme, thus establishing content validity.

FOCUS GROUPS

Focus group discussions (FGDs) are useful for collecting data about experiences, feelings, opinions, and reactions that may not be revealed in one-to-one interviews. Focus groups are semi-structured interviews with a number of participants that aim to explore a specific set of issues. Focus groups combine elements of both interviewing and participant observation. The focus group session is, indeed, an interview (Patton, 1990) not a discussion group, problem-solving session, or decision-making group. Focus groups are (usually semi-structured) interviews with a number of participants that aim to explore a specific set of issues. FGDs (or group interviews) capitalise on group interaction and communication to generate data. FGDs can help researchers explore and clarify views in ways that are not possible or accessible in one-to-one interviews. A sport management researcher may gather eight to ten fans of a team and through a series of open-ended questions, encourage discussion around issues important to fans in their own vocabulary, and explore their priorities. Tables 7.4 provide a summary of other issues to consider when planning to use focus groups in your research.

The method of interviewing participants in focus groups comes largely from marketing research but has been widely adapted to include social science and applied research. The groups are generally composed of seven to ten people (although groups range from as small as four to as large as 12) who are unfamiliar with one another and have been selected because they share certain characteristics relevant to the study's questions. The interviewer creates a supportive environment, asking focused questions to encourage discussion and the expression of differing opinions and points of view. These interviews may be conducted several times with different individuals so that the researcher can identify trends in the perceptions and opinions expressed, which are revealed through careful systematic analysis (Krueger, 1988). This method assumes that

Table 7.4	Characteristics of a focus group

Characteristics of a focus group

The recommended size of a group is six to ten people.

Several focus groups should be run in any research project.

The members of each focus group should have something in common, characteristics that are important to the topic of investigation.

Focus groups are usually specially convened groups. It may be necessary or even desirable to use pre-formed groups but difficulties may occur.

Qualitative information is collected that makes use of participants' feelings, perceptions, and opinions.

Using qualitative approaches in focus groups requires certain skills. The researcher requires a range of skills, for example, group skills in facilitating and moderating, listening, observing, and analysing.

an individual's attitudes and beliefs do not form in a vacuum: People often need to listen to others' opinions and understandings to form their own. Often, the questions in a focus-group setting are deceptively simple; the aim is to promote the participants' expression of their views through the creation of a supportive environment. Methodologically, there are similarities with in-depth interviews, including for fieldworker skills, preparation, collecting data, and for data analysis.

The *advantages* of focus-group interviews are that this method is socially oriented, studying participants in an atmosphere more natural than artificial experimental circumstances and more relaxed than a one-to-one interview. When combined with participant observation, focus groups are especially useful for gaining access, focusing site selection and sampling, and even for checking tentative conclusions (Morgan, 1997). The format allows the researcher the flexibility to explore unanticipated issues as they arise in the discussion. The results have high *"face validity"* as focus groups seem effective in terms of achieving their stated aims. Moreover, the cost of focus groups is relatively low, they provide quick results, and they can increase the sample size of qualitative studies by permitting more people to be interviewed at one time (Krueger, 1988).

The *disadvantages* are the number of questions and range of issues that can be explored is very limited; individual respondents' response time is limited to allow for others to participate; the approach is not suitable for controversial or very personal issues and the researcher needs some high-level skills to facilitate a successful FGD. In addition, the interviewer in focus groups may often have less control over a group interview than an individual one. Time can be lost while "dead-end" or irrelevant issues are discussed. The groups can vary a great deal and can be hard to assemble and logistical problems may arise from the need to manage a conversation while getting good quality data. Data may also be difficult to analyse because the context is essential to understanding the participants' comments.

WHEN TO USE FOCUS GROUPS

Focus groups are useful in answering the same type of questions as in-depth interviews, except in a social context. Specific applications of the focus group method in evaluations include (1) identifying and defining problems in project implementation; (2) identifying project strengths, weaknesses, and recommendations; (3) assisting with interpretation of quantitative findings; (4) obtaining perceptions of project outcomes and impacts; and (4) generating new ideas. It is also important to consider certain factors when considering to use a focus group. These factors are highlighted in Table 7.5.

DEVELOPING A FOCUS GROUP

As with in-depth interviews, FGDs are typically conducted with a structured *interview guide*. Topics and prompts designed to cover topics relevant to the overall research questions are listed, usually in a less structured format than for interviews in order to elicit a flexible response. Focus group

Table 7.5 Factors to consider when choosing focus groups	
Factors to consider	**Use focus groups when.....**
Group interaction	Interaction of respondents may provide deeper insight and richer data.
Sensitivity of subject matter	Subject matter is not too sensitive to prevent respondents from withholding information.
Extent of issue	The volume of issues to cover is not too extensive.
Continuity of information	A single subject area is being examined in depth.
Observation	It is desirable for stakeholders to hear what participants have to say.
Logistics	An acceptable number of target respondents can be assembled in one location.
Cost and training	Quick turnaround is critical, and funds are limited.
Availability of qualified staff	Focus group facilitators are able to control and manage groups.

Source: Adapted from Krueger (1994).

participants are typically asked to reflect on the questions asked by the researcher. Participants are permitted to hear each other's responses and to make additional comments beyond their own original responses as they hear what other people have to say. It is not necessary for the group to reach any kind of consensus, nor it is necessary for people to disagree. The researcher must keep the discussion flowing and make sure that one or two persons do not dominate the discussion. As a rule, the focus group session should not last longer than 1 1/2 to 2 hours. When very specific information is required, the session may be as short as 40 minutes. The objective is to get high-quality data in a social context where people can consider their own views in the context of the views of others, and where new ideas and perspectives can be introduced.

SAMPLING

The composition of focus groups needs to be carefully considered in relation to differences in experiences or behaviours of interest to the study across social groups as well as to power relations and sensitivities that may be involved in being asked to discuss particular research topics in a semi-public manner. Focus groups are most commonly formed through non-probability sampling methods. The objectives of the study and information concerning confidentiality should be given to participants. Oral or written consent should be finalised prior to the focus group meeting. Logistics in conducting focus groups are important. Time and place, as with interviews, should be considered and planned in advance for time of year, time of day, and location. In terms of location, more space is needed than for one-to-one interviews.

FIELD WORK FOR FOCUS GROUP

On the day of the focus group, the role of the researcher is critical in terms of providing clear explanations of the purpose of the group, helping people feel at ease, and facilitating interaction between group members. Allocating ID numbers to individual participants on a seating chart and to key verbatim statements during the discussion is particularly helpful for keeping track of individual participant contributions for transcription, later on. There are certain ground rules for group discussions. Only one person talks at a time and it is important for us to hear everyone's ideas and opinions. Participants need to be aware there are no right or wrong answers to questions – just ideas, experiences, and opinions, which are all valuable.

It is important for us to hear all sides of an issue – the positive and the negative. Confidentiality must be assured, to coin a phrase: "What is shared in the room stays in the room".

Research brief

Title: Young people's experiences of parental involvement in youth sport
Author: Strandbu, Å., *Norwegian School of Sport Sciences*, Stefansen, K., *Oslo and Akershus University College of Applied Sciences*, Smette, I., *Oslo and Akershus University College of Applied Sciences*, & Sandvik, M. R., *Norwegian School of Sport Sciences* (2019)
Reference: Strandbu, Å., Stefansen, K., Smette, I., & Sandvik, M.R. (2019). Young people's experiences of parental involvement in youth sport. *Sport, Education and Society, 24*(1), 66–77.
Recently, parental involvement in youth sport has intensified, challenging the understanding of youth sports as an arena where adolescents can develop their identity and autonomy. On this background, this study explored how adolescents understand and negotiate their parents' involvement in sport and how they define ideal and undesirable forms of parental involvement. The study was conducted in Norway and the authors drew on data from 16 focus group interviews among 13–14-year-olds ($n=92$) recruited from two lower secondary schools. The analysis showed that young people distinguish between different aspects of the sport activity when defining ideal and undesirable forms of parental involvement.

DOCUMENTS

Collecting and reviewing documents is another qualitative research strategy. Sport management researchers often supplement interviewing and observation with the analysis of documents produced in the course of everyday events. The history and context surrounding a specific organisational setting comes, in part, from reviewing documents. Marshall and Rossman (2006) suggest that "the review of documents is an unobtrusive method, rich in portraying values and beliefs of participants in a setting". As such, documents are essentially culturally standardised discourses associated with the value system an organisation wants to promote (Miller, 1997). Lincoln and Guba (1985) defined a document as any written or recorded material not prepared for the purposes of the evaluation or at the request of the inquirer. Creswell (2009) added that the term "document" includes not just texts, but also sound, photos, videos, and any materials that carry relevant messages.

Guba and Lincoln (1981) suggest that documents can be divided into two major categories: *public records* and *personal documents*. *Public records* are materials created and kept for the purpose of attesting to an event or providing an account (Lincoln & Guba, 1985). Public records can be collected from outside (*external*) or within (*internal*) the setting in which the evaluation is taking place (i.e. through an internal audit or by employing a more neutral organisation). Examples of *external* records in sport management are attendance and statistics reports, newspaper archives, and records that can assist an evaluator in gathering information about relevant trends in branding, ticket sales, athletic performances, etc. *Internal* records include documents such as transcripts, historical accounts, institutional mission statements, annual reports, budgets, reports, minutes of meetings, internal memoranda, policy manuals,

Table 7.6	Advantages and disadvantages of document studies
Advantages	**Disadvantages**
■ Freely available in most circumstances	■ Documentation may be incomplete
■ Usually an inexpensive source of data	■ In some cases, there may be inaccuracy and questionable authenticity of data
■ Provide contextual background	■ Searching for documents may pose challenges
■ Provide opportunity for study of trends over time	■ Analysis of documents may be time consuming
■ Unobtrusive	■ Access may be difficult

institutional histories, catalogues, handbooks, official correspondence, demographic material, mass media reports, and presentations. *Personal documents* are first-person accounts of events and experiences. These include diaries, portfolios, photographs, artwork, schedules, scrapbooks, letters to the paper, etc. Personal documents can help the researcher understand how the participant sees the world and what she or he wants to communicate to an audience. Collecting data from documents is relatively invisible to, and requires minimal cooperation from persons within the setting being studied. As such, the ethical issues around consent are usually handled by an ethics committee instead of approaching the individual concerned.

The use of document collection has a number of advantages and disadvantages. Some of these are outlined in Table 7.6.

SYSTEMATIC DATA COLLECTION OF DOCUMENTS

Altheide (2000) lists six steps to follow in order to carry out systematic data collection of documents:

1. Pursue a specific problem to be investigated.

2. Become familiar with the process and context of the information source.

3. Become familiar with examples of relevant documents, noting the format in particular and select a unit of analysis, for example, each article.

4. List several items or categories to guide data collection and draft a protocol (data collection sheet).

5. Test the protocol by collecting data from several documents.

6. Revise the protocol and select several additional cases to further refine the protocol.

Like most research, qualitative document collection is not separate from data analysis. This is an interpretive process. As part of the dual process of collection and analysis Altheide (1996, pp. 23–44) developed a 12-step process model involving five stages of qualitative document analysis, as follows:

Stage 1 – Document Study Development

Step 1: Pursue a specific problem to be investigated.

Step 2: Become familiar with the process and context of the information source; explore possible documents of information.

Step 3: Select a unit of analysis.

Stage 2 – Protocol Development and Data Collection

Step 4: List several items to guide data collection and draft a protocol.

Step 5: Test the protocol by collecting data from several documents.

Step 6: Revise the protocol and select several additional cases to further refine the protocol.

Stage 3 – Data Coding and Organisation

Step 7: Arrive at a theoretical sampling rationale and strategy.

Step 8: Collect the data, using preset codes, if appropriate, and many descriptive examples. Keep the data with the original documents, but also enter data in a plain text word-processing format for easier search–find and text coding. Make appropriate adjustments to other data. Complete data collection.

Stage 4 – Data Analysis

Step 9: Perform data analysis, including conceptual refinement and data coding. Read notes and data repeatedly and thoroughly.

Step 10: Compare and contrast "extremes" and "key differences" within each category or item. Make textual notes. Write brief summaries or overviews of data for each category.

Step 11: Combine the brief summaries with an example of the typical case as well as the extremes. Illustrate with materials from the protocols for each case.

Stage 5 – Final Report

Step 12: Integrate the findings with your interpretation and key concepts in another draft.

An example of a sport management researcher utilising document analysis could be a study of the salary cap breach by the Melbourne Storm National Rugby League team in Australia. The *first stage* (steps one to three) would be to find online newspaper articles based on the questions about the salary cap regulations designed for document analysis. This would involve selecting a unit of analysis (e.g. each article). In terms of sources of information that could be used in this study, the newspaper articles could be used as primary sources, secondary sources, and tertiary sources. According to Merriam (1998), primary sources are "those in which the originator of the document is recounting first-hand experience with the phenomenon of interest. The best primary sources are those recorded closest in time and place to the phenomenon by a qualified person" (p. 122). Secondary sources are reports of a phenomenon by those who have not directly experienced the phenomenon of interest; these are often compiled at a later date (Merriam, 1998). Tertiary sources comprise information that is the distillation and collection of primary and secondary sources. The *second stage* (steps four to six) would list several items to guide data collection and draft a protocol. Miles and Huberman's (1994) document summary form could be used to develop the protocol. Based on the uniqueness of this study, other items such as emerging themes and important quotations could be added to the protocol. The protocol would then be tested by collecting data from several documents, and revising the protocol and selecting several additional documents to further refine the protocol. The *third stage* (steps seven to eight) would include data coding and organisation. This stage involves collecting the data, using preset codes (Miles & Huberman, 1994), keeping the data with the original documents, but also entering data in a table format for easier search–find and text coding. The *fourth stage* (steps nine to eleven) included conceptual refinement and data coding. Notes and data would be reviewed thoroughly a number of times. In this stage, comparisons and contrasts would be conducted on the "extremes" and "key differences" within each category or item. Textual notes and brief summaries or overviews would be made on the data for each category. The last stage (step 12) would to integrate the findings with the researcher's interpretation and key concepts.

OTHER DATA COLLECTION METHODS

Audiovisual materials (comprising materials such as photographs, compact discs, and videotapes)

Creswell (1998) indicated that one type of qualitative data collection includes audiovisual materials comprising materials such as photographs and video. Visual documents are records of events that have occurred in the past (Barthes, 1981). It has also been noted that photographs and videos speak a language of emotion and meaning (Denzin, 2004). Films, photographs, videos, and any other digital forms can be used for data collection and for organising, interpreting, and validating qualitative inquiry (Szto, Furman, & Langer, 2005).

The visual record can enhance the data previously collected by a researcher, or be used as a historical background to a research topic. These visual records document a snap-shot of real life – including disasters, celebrations, and ceremonies. Major events are made available on a visual level to successive generations, and the platform also documents what may be considered minor social conflicts at the time – such as court proceedings, public speakers, etc., but which with the passage of time assume a different level of importance. Film/video is especially valuable for discovery and validation. It documents nonverbal behaviour and communication such as facial expressions, gestures, and emotions. Film/video preserves activity and change in its original form. It can be used in the future to take advantage of new methods of seeing, analysing, and understanding the process of change. Film/video is an aid to the researcher when the nature of what is sought is known but the elements of it cannot be discovered because of the limitations of the human eye. It allows for the preservation and study of data from nonrecurring, disappearing, or rare events. Interpretation of information can be validated by another researcher or by participants.

According to Denzin (2004), *four narratives or meaning structures* exist in any set of photographs and videos. These four meaning structures are: (1) the visual text; (2) the audio text, including what photographers say about their photographs; (3) the narrative that links the visual and audio text into a coherent story, or framework; and (4) the interpretations and meanings the viewer bring to the visual, audio, and narrative texts. Documents from photographs and video clips may be analysed using Collier and Collier's (1986) principles of critical analysis of visual documents. As Collier and Collier suggest, these guidelines are provisional, and should fit to the needs of the researcher. The principles are divided into four phases, the phases include the following:

Phase One: "Looking and feeling"

- Observe the visual documents as a totality.

- Look and listen to the materials. Let them talk to you. Feel their effects on you. Record these feelings and impressions.

- Write down questions that occur to you. Note patterns of meaning.

Phase Two: "What question are you asking?"

- State your research question.

- What questions does the text claim to answer?

- How does it represent and define key cultural values? And...

- Inventory the evidence, note key scenes and images.

Phase Three: "Structured microanalysis"

- Do a scene by scene, microanalysis, transcribe discourse, describe scenes, and take quotes from the text.

- Form and find patterns and sequences.

- Write detailed descriptions.

- How does the text represent objective reality, handle facts, represent experience, and dramatise truth?

- Keep a focus on the research question.

- Identify major moments in the film/text when conflicts over values occur. And...

- Detail how the film/text/image takes a position on these values.

Phase Four: "Search for patterns"

- Return to the complete record.

- Lay out all the photographs, or view the film in its entirety.

- Return to the research question. How do these documents speak to and answer your question?

- Contrast realist and subversive reading of the text.

- Write an interpretation, based on the principles of interpretation discussed above (Collier & Collier, 1986, pp. 178–179).

Research brief

Title: Leveraging community sport organizations to promote community capacity: Strategic outcomes, challenges, and theoretical considerations

Author: Jones, G. J., *Temple University*, Edwards, M. B., *North Carolina State University*, Bocarro, J. N., *North Carolina State University*, Bunds, K. S., *North Carolina State University*, & Smith, J.W., *Utah State University* (2018)

Reference: Jones, G. J., Edwards, M. B., Bocarro, J. N., Bunds, K. S., & Smith, J. W. (2018). Leveraging community sport organizations to promote community capacity: Strategic outcomes, challenges, and theoretical considerations. *Sport Management Review, 21* (3), 279–292.

In this paper, the authors analysed the outcomes and challenges of implementing community capacity building strategies in an American community sport organisation using a qualitative case study approach. The authors drew on empirical data and conducted interviews, participant observation, and document analysis to generate data. The results highlighted the outcomes of the capacity building strategies and challenges associated with implementation. In addition, the conclusion focused on theoretical contributions to community capacity theory, namely the role of sport in facilitating inter-community relations across social groups and the link with process models of organisational capacity.

CONCLUSION

This chapter has examined the data collection methods that can be utilised to acquire data, and to address the research aims. Four basic types of qualitative data collection were discussed: (1) observations (ranging from direct to participant); (2) interviews (ranging structured to unstructured interviews); (3) focus groups; and (4) document (ranging from public records to personal documents). Audiovisual materials (comprising materials such as photographs and video) were also discussed in detail as an additional data collection method.

REVIEW AND RESEARCH QUESTIONS

1. Data collection is the process of collecting or gathering information pertaining to a specific research topic that will be used by the sport management researcher in the later process of analysis to formulate theories, produce recommendations, or contextualise events and activities in the sport management setting. With this in mind:

   a. Distinguish between the different forms of observation and interviews and how these might be used by the sport management researcher.

   b. Discuss how documents can be used by the sport management researcher to collect specific data. Provide examples of the documents a sport management researcher may use in their research.

2. Explain the relationship between the issue of "gaining entry" the "research agreement" and developing "trust".

REFERENCES

Altheide, D. L. (1996). *Qualitative media analysis*. Thousand Oaks, CA: Sage Publications.

Altheide, D. L. (2000). Tracking discourse and qualitative document analysis. *Poetics*, 27, 287–299.

Atkinson, P. Silverman, D. (1997). 'Kundera's Immortality: the interview society and the invention of the self. *Qualitative Inquiry*, 3(3), 304–325.

Barthes, R. (1981). *Camera lucida: Reflections on photography*. New York, NY: Hill & Wang.

Burns, R. B. (1997). *Introduction to research methods* (3rd edn). Melbourne, Australia: Longman.

Collier, J., & Collier, M. (1986). *Visual anthropology: Photography as a research method*. Albuquerque, NM: University of New Mexico Press.

Creswell, J. W. (1998). *Qualitative inquiry and research design: Choosing among five traditions*. Thousand Oaks, CA: Sage Publications.

Creswell, J. W. (2009). *Research design: Qualitative, quantitative and mixed method approaches* (3rd ed.). Los Angeles, CA: Sage Publications.

Davis, J. (1997). *Advertising Research: Theory and Practice*. Upper Saddle River, NJ: Pearson Higher Education.

De Laine, M. (1997). *Ethnography: Theory and applications in health research*. Sydney: Maclennan & Petty.

Denzin, N. (2004). Reading film: Using film and videos as empirical social science material. In E. Flick, E. von Kardorff, & I. Steinke (Eds). *A Companion to Qualitative Research*, pp. 237–242. Thousand Oaks, CA: Sage Publications.

Denzin, N. K., & Lincoln, Y. S. (2005). Introduction: The discipline and practice of qualitative research. In N. K. Denzin, & Y. S. Lincoln (Eds.), *The Handbook of Qualitative Research* (3rd ed.), pp. 1–32. Thousand Oaks, CA: Sage Publications.

Dick, B. (1990). *Convergent interviewing.* Brisbane: Interchange.

Doyle, P. (1994). *Marketing management and strategy.* London: Prentice Hall.

Emory, C., & Cooper, D. 1991. *Business research methods.* Homewood, IL: Irwin.

Gruber, T., Szmigin, I., Reppel, A. E., & Voss, R. (2008). Designing and conducting online interviews to investigate interesting consumer phenomena. *Qualitative Market Research, 11*(3), 256–274.

Guba, E. G., & Lincoln, Y. S. (1981). *Effective evaluation: Improving the usefulness of evaluation results through responsive and naturalistic approaches.* San Francisco, CA: Jossey-Bass.

Guba, E. G., & Lincoln, Y. S. (1994). Competing paradigms in qualitative research. In N. K. Denzin, & Y. S. Lincoln (Eds). *Handbook of Qualitative Research*, pp. 105–117. Thousand Oaks, CA: Sage Publications.

Hammersley, M., & Atkinson, P. (1983). *Ethnography: Principles in practice.* London: Tavistock.

Jorgensen, D. L. (1989). *Participant observation: A methodology for human studies.* Thousand Oaks, CA: Sage Publications.

Judd, C. M., Smith, E. R., & Kidder, L. H. (1991). *Research methods in social relations.* Fort Worth, TX: Harcourt Brace Jovanovich.

Krueger, R. A. (1988). *Focus groups: A practical guide for applied research.* Thousand Oaks, CA: Sage Publications.

Krueger, R. A. (1994). *Focus groups: A practical guide for applied research* (2nd ed.). Thousand Oaks, CA: Sage Publications.

Krueger, R. A. (1994). *Focus groups: A practical guide for applied research.* Thousand Oaks, CA: Sage Publications, Elsevier.

Lincoln, Y. S., & Guba, E. G. (1985). *Naturalistic inquiry.* Beverly Hills, CA: Sage Publications.

Loftland, J. (1984). *Analysing social settings: A guide to qualitative observation and analysis.* Belmont, CA: Wadsworth.

Lofland, J., & Lofland, L. H. (1995). *Analyzing social settings.* Belmont, CA: Wadsworth.

Marshall, C., & Rossman, G. B. (2006). *Designing qualitative research* (4th ed.). Thousand Oaks, CA: Sage Publications.

Merriam, S. (1998). *Qualitative research and case study applications in education.* San Francisco, CA: Jossey-Bass Publishers.

Miles, M. B., & Huberman, M. A. (1994). *Qualitative data analysis.* Thousand Oaks, CA: Sage Publications.

Miller, G. (1997). Building bridges: the possibility of analytic dialogue between ethnography, conversation analysis and Foucault. In D. Silverman (Ed.). *Qualitative Research: Theory, Method and Practice*, pp. 45–62. London: Sage Publications.

Minichiello, V., Aroni, R., Timewell, E., & Alexander, L. (1995). *In-depth interviewing: Principles, techniques, analysis.* Melbourne: Longman.

Morgan, D. (1997). *The Focus Group Guidebook.* Thousand Oaks, CA: Sage Publications.

Nelson, R. K. (1969). *Hunters on the Northern Ice.* Chicago: University of Chicago Press.

Neuman, W. L. (2000). *Social research methods: Qualitative and quantitative approaches* (4th ed.). Boston, MA: Allyn & Bacon.

Patton, M. Q. (1990). *Qualitative evaluation and research methods*. Thousand Oaks, CA: Sage Publication.

Patton, M. Q. (2002). Two decades of development in qualitative inquiry: A personal, experimental perspective. *Qualitative Social Work, 1*(3), 261–283.

Richardson, L. (2000). Writing: A method of inquiry. In N. Denzin, & Y. Lincoln (Eds.), *Handbook of Qualitative Research*, pp. 923–948. Thousand Oaks, CA: Sage Publications.

Rosen, M. (1991). Coming to terms with the field: Understanding and doing organizational ethnography. *Journal of Management Studies, 28*(1), 1–24.

Schwandt, T. (2001). *Dictionary of qualitative inquiry* (2nd ed.). Thousand Oaks, CA: Sage Publications.

Sekaran, U. (2000). *Research methods for business* (3rd ed.). New York: Hermitage.

Spradley, J. P. (1979). *The ethnographic interview*. Belmont, CA: Wadsworth Group,

Spradley, J. P. (1980). *Participant observation*. New York: Holt, Rinehart & Winston.

Szto, P., Furman, R., & Langer, C. (2005). Poetry and photography: An exploration into expressive/creative qualitative research. *Qualitative Social Work, 4*(2), 135–156.

Wax, R. H. (1971). *Doing fieldwork: Warnings and advice*. Chicago, IL: University of Chicago Press.

PART 4

Analysing the sport management data

CHAPTER 8

Modes of analysis in sport management research

By the end of this chapter, you should be able to:

- Define qualitative data analysis

- Explain and compare approaches in analysing qualitative data

- Code and develop categories in qualitative data analysis

- Identify key methods in the coding process

- Understand the use of Computer-Assisted Data Analysis (CAQDAS)

KEY TERMS

1. **Modes of analysis:** the process by which the researcher reviews the data collected with the aim of making sense of it, so that evidence can be obtained to answer the research question.

2. **Coding:** the organisation of raw data into conceptual categories.

3. **Theme:** something that runs through all the interviews as a persistent issue or experience.

4. **Category:** when codes can be grouped under a single title.

5. **Triangulation:** examining the consistency of information generated by different data collection techniques, or examining different data gathered by the same collection technique.

6. **Crystallisation:** the process of suspending the modes of analysis process to reflect on the analysis experience itself thereby enabling the researcher to identify and articulate patterns or themes that may emerge.

KEY THEMES

- What is coding?

- Integrating data collection with qualitative analysis.

- What is Computer-Assisted/Aided Data Analysis?

CHAPTER OVERVIEW

Qualitative data consist of words, observations, pictures, and symbols. Qualitative Data Analysis (QDA) refers to the processes and procedures that are used to analyse the data and provide some level or explanation, understanding, or interpretation. QDA typically occurs simultaneously with the data collection. Therefore, meaning and understanding often develop slowly over time in a non-linear fashion as the project progresses. The goal of the analytic process in qualitative research is to tease out themes, patterns, and connections among ideas embedded in the data. There are no formulas for analysing qualitative data and fewer conventions than for quantitative analysis (Miles & Huberman, 1994; Patton, 2002). Reducing, organising, indexing/coding, and displaying the data in various ways are the main activities undertaken in an effort to uncover key insights and patterns in the data. It is not unusual for analysis to begin while field work is still in progress; indeed, doing so may allow for necessary mid-course corrections and the development of preliminary findings. Whatever analytic approaches are used, "analysts have an obligation to monitor and report their own analytical procedures and processes as fully and truthfully as possible" (Patton, 2002, p. 434). The process should be sufficiently transparent to allow for replication. This chapter discusses QDA in sport management qualitative research. It notes that the purpose of QDA is to make sense of the data so that evidence can be obtained to answer the research question.

WHAT IS QUALITATIVE DATA ANALYSIS?

QDA is the range of processes and procedures, whereby we move from the qualitative data that have been collected into some form of explanation, understanding or interpretation of the people and situations we are investigating. The main difference between qualitative and quantitative data analysis is that the data to be analysed are text, rather than numbers. Lacey and Luff (2001) note that qualitative data is mostly in the form of words, phrases, sentences, and may include visual images, audio, and video recordings. It is a mass of words obtained from recordings of interviews, fieldnotes of observations, and analysis of documents as well as reflective notes of the researcher. This mass of information have to be organised, summarised, described, and interpreted.

Since numbers are not used, the qualitative researcher looks for categories or themes from the raw data to describe and explain phenomena. As Patton (2002) suggests,

> Qualitative analysis transforms data into findings. No formula exists for that transformation. Guidance, yes. But no recipe. Direction can and will be offered, but the final destination remains unique for each inquirer, known only when—and if—arrived at. (p. 432)

QDA is an iterative and reflexive process that begins as data are being collected rather than after data collection has ceased (Stake, 1995). The researcher adjusts the data collection process itself when it begins to appear that additional concepts need to be investigated or new relationships explored. This process is termed progressive focusing (Parlett & Hamilton, 1976).

When conducting research, there is a choice between two fundamental research approaches: *induction* and *deduction*. The *inductive approach* moves from empirical observations to conclusions that are finally developed into theories. Hence, the research process begins with collecting data with the aim of using that data to develop theories or improve existing ones. *Inductive reasoning* therefore attempts to explain individual observations that appear to co-occur or "conjoin" by proposing a mechanism or theory (Figure 8.1). Induction begins from particular observations and builds towards broader generalisations. The classic example is that if a person only ever observes men in senior sport management positions, they will induce a "rule" that all senior sport managers are men. This also illustrates the inherent weakness of inductive reasoning, as a single female senior sport manager disproves the rule, and this is why we must test theories once they have been generated through induction. Following induction, the progression from the level of "proposed theory" to that of "substantiated" theory requires many individual studies that test the specific hypotheses offered by your new theory. This approach is more likely to utilise qualitative methodologies.

The *deductive approach*, on the other hand, uses existing theories as guiding frameworks, which will offer categories and a predetermined structure for the analysis. In principle, this should lead to a more detailed understanding of a theory, for example, or an understanding of how sports managers actually apply the theory in practice. *Deductive reasoning* obtains specific hypotheses

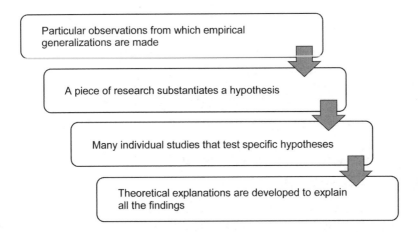

Figure 8.1 Inductive reasoning

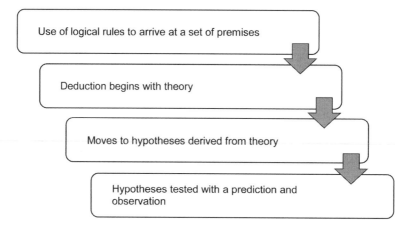

Figure 8.2 Deductive reasoning

(predictions) from a theory (Figure 8.2). This involves the use of logical if–then type rules to arrive at a set of expected observations. For example: Rule 1: All sport marketers are creative. Rule 2: Michelle is a sport marketer. Deduction: Michelle is creative. Deduction begins with theory and then develops specific, testable hypotheses derived from theory, and then tests these hypotheses by making careful and accurate observations. This approach to testing and theory is often referred to as the hypothetico-deductive method and since it emphasises on hypotheses, prediction, and testing, which is sometimes held to be the *par excellence* of science. As explained above, theories are used to derive testable predictions, or hypotheses, and then observations are carefully collected to test these predictions.

Both forms of reasoning, inductive and deductive, are useful – although the inductive approach tends to be used more in humanities-based research and adopts a qualitative methodology, while the deductive approach tends to be used more in "hard science" areas and adopts more quantitative methodologies. Some research attempts to strike a balance between *inductive* and *deductive* approaches. According to Patel and Davidson (2003), such a combination is referred to as an *abductive* approach. Hence, where an existing theory seems relevant, but may need "fleshing out" with details, an abductive approach may allow the theoretical framework to be maintained while the rich and detailed data allows new insights to be gained into how it might apply.

METHODS OF DATA ANALYSIS IN QUALITATIVE SPORT MANAGEMENT RESEARCH

Although there are many different modes of analysis in qualitative research, two approaches or modes of analysis with particular relevance to sport management research are hermeneutics and semiotics.

Hermeneutics

Hermeneutics can be treated as both an underlying philosophy and a specific mode of analysis (Bleicher, 1980). As a philosophical approach to human understanding, it provides the philosophical grounding for interpretivism (see the discussion on Philosophical Perspectives in Chapter 2). As a mode of analysis, it suggests a way of understanding textual data. The following discussion is concerned with using hermeneutics as a specific mode of analysis.

Hermeneutics is primarily concerned with the meaning of a text or text-analogue (an example of a text-analogue is an organisation, which the researcher comes to understand through oral or written text). The basic question in hermeneutics is: "what is the meaning of this text" (Radnitzky, 1970)? Taylor (1990) suggests that:

> Interpretation, in the sense relevant to hermeneutics, is an attempt
> to make clear, to make sense of an object of study. This object must,
> therefore, be a text, or a text-analogue, which in some way is confused,
> incomplete, cloudy, seemingly contradictory – in one way or another,
> unclear. The interpretation aims to bring to light an underlying coher-
> ence or sense. (p. 153)

The idea of a hermeneutic circle refers to the dialectic between the understanding of the text as a whole and the interpretation of its parts, in which descriptions are guided by anticipated explanations (Gadamer, 1976). It follows from this that we have an expectation of meaning from the context of what has gone before. The movement of understanding: "is constantly from the whole to the part and back to the whole" (p. 117). As Gadamer explains, "it is a circular relationship. The anticipation of meaning in which the whole is envisaged becomes explicit understanding in that the parts, that are determined by the whole, themselves also determine this whole" (p. 117). Ricoeur (1974) suggests that: "interpretation is the work of thought which consists in deciphering the hidden meaning in the apparent meaning, in unfolding the levels of meaning implied in the literal meaning" (p. xiv).

There are different forms of hermeneutic analysis, from "pure" hermeneutics through to "critical" hermeneutics; however, a discussion of these different forms is beyond the scope of this section. For a more in-depth discussion, see Bleicher (1980), Palmer (1969), and Thompson (1981). If hermeneutic analysis is used in an information systems study, the object of the interpretive effort becomes one of attempting to make sense of the organisation as a text-analogue. In an organisation, people (e.g., different stakeholders) can have confused, incomplete, cloudy, and contradictory views on many issues. The aim of the hermeneutic analysis becomes one of trying to make sense of the whole, and the relationship among people, the organisation, and information.

Semiotics

Like hermeneutics, semiotics can be treated as both an underlying philosophy and a specific mode of analysis. The following discussion concerns using semiotics as a mode of analysis.

Semiotics is primarily concerned with the meaning of signs and symbols in language. The essential idea is that words/signs can be assigned to primary conceptual categories, and these categories represent important aspects of the theory to be tested. The importance of an idea is revealed in the frequency with which it appears in the text. One form of semiotics is "content analysis".

Krippendorff (2013) defines content analysis as a research technique for making replicable and valid references from data to their contexts. The researcher searches for structures and patterned regularities in the text and makes inferences on the basis of these regularities. Another form of semiotics is "conversation analysis". In conversation analysis, it is assumed that the meanings are shaped in the context of the exchange (Wynn, 1979). The researchers immerse themselves in the situation to reveal the background of practices. A third form of semiotics is "discourse analysis". Discourse analysis builds on both content analysis and conversation analysis but focuses on "language games". A language game refers to a well-defined unit of interaction consisting of a sequence of verbal moves in which turns of phrases, the use of metaphor and allegory all play an important part.

Moving beyond hermeneutics and semiotics as modes of analysis in qualitative research, Madill and Gough (2008) provide a typology outlining which data analysis methods can be categorised according to the following procedures: *discursive, thematic, structured,* and *instrumental. Discursive* methods focus on the detail of the text and apply varying forms of discourse theory (i.e. conversation, discourse, metaphoric, psychoanalytically informed, and semiotic analysis). *Thematic* analyses procedures describe any form of analysis that employs clustering and thematising (e.g. analytic induction, framework analysis, grounded theory, interpretive phenomenological analysis, template analysis, thematic analysis, and theory-led thematic analysis). *Structural methods* refer to analysis following priory coding and transforming qualitative data into counts (e.g. content analysis, Q-methodology, repertory grid techniques). The most common structural method is content analysis. Although Madill and Gough categorise content analysis as a structural method, the amount of structure in question as well as the use of a priori or open coding will depend on the researcher. Traditionally, content analysis led to some form of quantification or the counting of categories. Therefore, scholars debate whether content analysis should be viewed as a qualitative or quantitative method. It can, however, have a more interpretive aim and thus indicate a stronger qualitative tendency. The last category, *instrumental methods*, include methods driven by and committed to a philosophical perspective and/or theoretical framework. This framework enables researchers to distinguish, for instance, different forms of narrative analysis or phenomenological methods. The instrumental category includes certain forms of action research, ethnography, feminist research, as well as indications of narrative and phenomenological analysis (Madill & Gough, 2008).

It is often confusing to decide which analysis method to select. The following questions may assist in decision making. First, how does the technique link in with my epistemological position? Data analysis needs to link in with the underlying philosophical stance of the research. Second, how structured are my research aims? For example, is the research aiming to develop hypotheses, answer research questions, or explore sensitising concepts? Third, what kind of data are being analysed? Fourth, what are my personal preferences, i.e., structured/unstructured techniques, and finally, will I be using a computer software package to enable my analysis?

Research brief

Title: Gatekeepers' experiences of hiring a sport psychologist: A phenomenological study
Author: Woolway, T., *Loughborough University* & Harwood, C. G., *Loughborough University* (2019)
Reference: Woolway, T. & Harwood, C. G. (2019). Gatekeepers' experiences of hiring a sport psychologist: A phenomenological study. *Journal of Applied Sport Psychology*, *31*(4), 474–493.
Within applied sport psychology, the process of gaining entry, specifically the employment interview, has received little attention relative to other stages of practice. This study, guided by an interpretative phenomenological approach, aimed to understand the experiences of gatekeepers to practice within United Kingdom elite sport who have been directly involved in the hiring of sport psychologists. Semi-structured interviews with seven participants were transcribed verbatim and analysed using interpretative phenomenological analysis. Four essences emerged: consultant affability, consultant confidence versus arrogance, consultant collaboration, and presentation of consultant competency. These findings highlighted the importance of developing interpersonal skills, interview technique, and self-promotion skills in sport psychology practitioners.

MODES OF ANALYSIS PHASES

In order to deal with data analysis, Creswell (2009) suggested three strategies should be employed. Step one requires preparing and organising the data; step two suggests reducing the data into themes through a process of coding and condensing the codes; and step three is about representing the data in figures, tables, or a discussion. Creswell also provides data analysis guidelines. These steps are interrelated and not always visited in the order presented. These guidelines or *six step* data analysis process are identified below and will be subsequently discussed:

1. *Transcription:* Transcription is the process of converting audio recorded data or handwritten field notes obtained from interviews and observations into verbatim form (i.e. written or printed) for easy reading. After transcription, it is necessary to organise your data into sections that are easy to retrieve.

2. *Thematic labelling:* Bogdan and Biklen (1982) defined qualitative modes of analysis as "working with data, organising it, breaking it into manageable units, synthesising it, searching for patterns, discovering what is important and what is to be learned, and deciding what you will tell others" (p. 145). Qualitative researchers tend to use inductive analysis of data, meaning that the critical themes emerge out of the data. Qualitative analysis requires some creativity, for the challenge is to place the raw data into logical, meaningful categories; to examine them in a holistic fashion; and to find a way to communicate this interpretation to others. This process is called thematic labelling.

3. *Coding process:* Coding is the process of examining the raw qualitative data in the transcripts and extracting sections of text units (words, phrases, sentences, or paragraphs) and assigning different codes or labels so that they can easily be retrieved at a later stage for further comparison and analysis, and the identification of any patterns. Strauss and Corbin (1990) differentiate between three **kinds of coding** procedures from the data: open, axial, and selective **coding**. Coding will be discussed in more detail later in this chapter.

4. *Individual and cross-case analysis:* This process involves applying the thematic framework to all transcripts systematically and annotating the textual data with codes.

5. *Conceptual model development:* This is the process of developing individual matrices for each key theme and entering coded sections of text (plus identifiers) into appropriate charts.

6. *Data sense making (theory extensions): This* involves using the charts to map the range and nature of responses, create typologies, identify associations between themes and attempt explanations.

Miles and Huberman (1994), however, suggest that qualitative *analysis* consist of three procedures: These are as follows:

1. **Data reduction:** This refers to the process whereby the mass of qualitative data you may obtain – interview transcripts, field notes, etc. – is reduced and organised, for example, coding, writing summaries, discarding irrelevant data, and so on. This process should begin almost as soon as you begin the data collection, and is often an ongoing process throughout much of the research.

2. **Data display:** This is where you draw conclusions from the mass of data, Miles and Huberman (1994) suggest that a good display of data, in the form of tables, charts, networks, and other graphical formats is essential. Again, this is a continual process, rather than just one to be carried out at the end of the data collection.

3. *Conclusion drawing/verification:* In the final part of the procedure, your analysis should allow you to begin to develop conclusions regarding your study. These initial conclusions can then be certified. That is, their validity can be examined through reference to your existing field notes, further data collection, or even critical discussion with your colleagues.

More recently, qualitative researchers have moved to an analysis format based upon *integration of data collection with qualitative analysis*. This approach recognises that data collection is not separate from the analysis process and that these two elements work hand in hand with each other. This approach consists of three overlapping stages: (1) *Data documentation;* (2) *Data coding;* (3) *Interpreting and presenting the data.* These stages form the basis for our discussion on data analysis.

DATA DOCUMENTATION

Data documentation is the process through which the raw data from either personal interview, focus grouped discussion, observation, or other form of qualitative data collection is recorded. This process occurs at the same time as data collection (Easterby-Smith, Golden-Biddle, & Locke 2008). Data documentation is meant to serve the purpose of documenting simultaneously the data collected through every form of data collection, the researcher's description, feelings, view, and insights as well as assumptions and ongoing ideas about the subject matter. Some suggested ways for the researcher to engage the data from the outset are through *anecdotes, vignettes, or memos*.

- *Anecdotes:* Khan (2008) sees anecdotes as the chronological sequence of transformation actions. This guides the researcher in generating feelings and building the themes.

- *Vignettes:* A vignette is a useful term in qualitative research to represent narrative or story investigations on the interpretation of person, knowledge or circumstances that the researcher describes. The in-depth description of the setting, participants, and themes of qualitative research are the focus of vignettes to establish the credibility of the study. It is a deeper step further from anecdotes and reorganises the multifarious dimensions of its subject for capturing, in a brief representation of the information that needs to be gathered over a period of time. Vignettes therefore allow higher level of interpretation beyond mere description, provide a higher sense of understanding about the phenomenon and allow the capturing of themes

- *Memos:* These are immediate ideas or thoughts arising from familiarisation that can be noted down in a *memo* (ideally dated and with reference to the transcript(s) that prompted the thoughts). They can feed into the coding at a later stage when exploring themes.

An important component of the data documentation process is transcription. *Transcription* is the process of converting audio recorded data or handwritten fieldnotes obtained from interviews and observations into verbatim form (i.e. written or printed) for analysis. The value of transcribing has been defined as the ability to produce highly detailed and accessible accounts of interactions or phenomena, in a format that is largely transparent and immediate for the researcher to use in analysis (Nikander, 2008). Roberts (2007) states that transcription is a *"construction of knowledge rather than a transmission of knowledge"* (p. 19), and as such the creative role of the transcriber in the research process is identified, and must be reflected upon. In planning and conducting transcription, there are a series of decisions to be made about how and what data to capture, as well as reflecting practical and theoretical questions (Nikander, 2008). We suggest the following transcription process to ensure accurate representation of data:

1. Number each line of the transcript to facilitate referencing and quotation within the analysis phase (Roberts, 2007).

2. If transcribing data from multiple speakers, it is ideal to be able to identify each speaker each time they speak. Familiarisation with multiple voices can be done with reference to "ice-breaker" activities.

3. It is important for the transcriber to be conversant in nonstandard terminology and to be able to give a brief indication of the meaning of nonstandard words in brackets if it is not clear (Witcher, 2010).

4. Revisit transcripts to check for missed or misheard words, ideally using different members of the research team (Witcher, 2010).

5. Be aware that approaches to transcription may alter slightly through the research process, as interests change or knowledge is produced. This should be reflected upon and discussed when evaluating findings and drawing conclusions (Davidson 2009).

DATA CODING

Codes are tags that categorise the data collected during a study to assign meanings to them. Coding is the first stage to providing some form of logical structure to the data. Saldaña (2016) suggests:

> a code in qualitative inquiry is a word or a short phrase that symbolically assigns a summative, salient, essence-capturing, and/or evocative attribute for a portion of language-based or visual data. (p. 4)

Coding makes it easier to search the data, make comparisons, and identify patterns that require further investigation. Codes can be based on themes, topics, ideas, concepts, terms, phrases, or keywords found in the data, but they can also correspond to passages of audio or video recordings and to parts of images. Codes should be valid, that is they should accurately reflect what is being researched, where possible they should be mutually exclusive (in that codes should be distinct, with no overlap) and they should be exhaustive, that is, all relevant data should fit into a code.

Coding helps in separating data into *categories* (nodes) or *themes* so that data from different sources can be easily organised and compared. With significant themes coded in this manner, researcher can later examine and retrieve motivating sections and look at them as distinct files. *Themes* and *categories* are core concepts that are commonly confused in the analysis sections of qualitative studies. Morse (2008) published a simple editorial differentiating the two. A **theme** in qualitative research is something that runs through all the interviews as a persistent issue or experience. Creswell (2012) categorised a theme as ordinary, unexpected, hard-to-classify, and major and minor. He suggests, *ordinary themes* are those a researcher might assume to find, *unexpected* are the surprised themes that are not anticipated to surface during a study, while *hard-to-classify* themes are those that contain ideas that overlap with several themes. Typically, most qualitative studies have three to five themes emerging from the data. More than five themes may occur with highly heterogenous samples or large sample. A **category** occurs in qualitative research when codes can be grouped under a single title (Morse, 2008). They appear as distinct units of research data. Categories can often morph or transfer easily into quantifiably measurable variables in future quantitative studies, whereas themes are less transferable into a variable. Categories can also group together under certain themes, but they may also cross between themes due to how experiences of participants manifest themselves. Rigorous studies make clear differentiation between the two when presenting findings.

A suggested framework for undertaking coding includes:

1. To begin, the data is carefully read, all statements relating to the research question are identified, and each is assigned a code or category. These codes are then noted, and each relevant statement is organised under its appropriate code, either manually or via computer software, along with any notes or memos that the researcher wishes to add of their own. Strauss and Corbin (1990) identified three types of coding: *open coding, axial coding, and selective coding*. During *open coding*, the researcher must identify and tentatively name the conceptual categories into which the phenomena observed will be grouped. The goal is to create descriptive, multidimensional categories that form a preliminary framework for analysis. For example, when working with transcripts from interviews on sport for development in rural communities, some open codes might include "raising awareness", "connection", "driver of change", and "quality of life".

Words, phrases, or events that appear to be similar can be grouped into the same category. These categories may be gradually modified or replaced during the subsequent stages of analysis that follow. As the raw data are broken down into manageable chunks, the researcher must also devise an *audit trail* – that is, a scheme for identifying these data chunks according to their speaker and the context. Qualitative research is characterised by the use of "voice" in the text; that is, participant quotes that illustrate the themes being described.

2. The next stage of analysis involves re-examination of the categories identified in stage 1 to determine how they are linked, a complex process sometimes called *axial coding* (Strauss & Corbin, 1990). The discrete categories identified in open coding are compared and combined in new ways as the researcher begins to assemble the "big picture". In the sport for development example, open codes of "raising awareness" and "driver of change" may be linked through common passages in the transcripts. The purpose of coding is to not only describe but, more importantly, to acquire new understanding of a phenomenon of interest. Therefore, causal events contributing to the phenomenon, descriptive details of the phenomenon itself and the ramifications of the phenomenon under study must all be identified and explored. During axial coding the researcher is responsible for building a conceptual model and for determining whether sufficient data exists to support that interpretation. Two common types of axial coding are: *Non-hierarchical* or *Hierarchical*.

   ■ *Non-Hierarchical*: For example, a researcher asks a group of sport managers how they deal with stress in their normal work. The responses are grouped in a non-hierarchical manner (also called flat coding).

   ■ *Hierarchical*: In this type, several codes group together as types or kinds of something. You need to put some of the codes or labels into a group of their own or make them sub-codes – a hierarchical arrangement of codes, like a tree, a branching arrangement of sub-codes. Ideally, codes of the tree relate to their parents by being examples of… or contexts for….or causes of…. or setting for….etc. For example, a researcher studying doping asks a group of sport manager their views on the topic and creates a classification model that reflects the relationship between the codes.

3. Once the first two stages of coding have been completed, the researcher should become more analytical, and look for patterns and explanation in the codes. Questions should be asked such as: Can I relate certain codes together under a more general code? Can I organise codes sequentially? Can I identify any causal relations?

Table 8.1	What can be coded

What can be coded

- Behaviours – specific acts

- Events – short once in a lifetime events or things people have done that are often told as a story

- Activities – these are of a longer duration, involve other people within a particular setting

- Strategies, practice, or tactics

- States – general conditions experienced by people or found in organisations

- Meanings – A wide range of phenomena at the core of much qualitative analysis. Meanings and interpretations are important parts of what directs participants actions. What concepts do participants use to understand their world?

- Participation – adaptation to a new setting or involvement

- Relationships or interaction

- Conditions or constraints

- Consequences

- Settings – the entire context of the events under study

- Reflexive – researcher's role in the process, how intervention generated the data

4. The fourth stage is that of *selective coding*. This involves reading through the raw data for cases that illustrate the analysis, or explain the concepts. The researcher should also look for data that is contradictory, as well as confirmatory. For example, selective coding can include finding direct quotes from participants that relate how sport first raises awareness of a development issue through meaningful gatherings, then raising awareness becomes a catalyst for changing that issue by ongoing education tied to the sport events.

Lewins, Taylor, and Gibbs (2005) provide a detailed list of the kinds of things that can be coded (see Table 8.1).

CODING PROCESS

The coding process usually follows of a two-cycle process. First cycle coding involves the initial coding of data – e.g. *open coding* as discussed previously. A few transcripts can be selected to develop an initial coding framework to be applied to other transcripts. Second cycle coding is where more analytic skills required (e.g. classifying, prioritising, integrating, synthesising, conceptualising, theory building). A code structure emerges that is a compilation of emerging codes. This cycle includes definitions/descriptions of each code (usually also illustrative quotes). Guidance for using the codes is challenged and the code structure changes (evolves) throughout the analysis. In summary, you begin the process by reading the manuscript freely and making notes (memos). Then create the initial codes and describe the code properties. Code 2-3 transcripts, negotiate and then revise. A final code structure is then created and applied to all transcripts. You then combine concepts and themes to generate your own explanation of your data. Table 8.2 provides an example of coding qualitative data and illustrates the process, whereby the participants' comments are coded and categorised. After an interview in a sport organisation which asked *"What specific problems need immediate action in your sport organisation?"* The

Tables 8.2 Example of coding qualitative data
Participants responses to specific problems in their sport organisation

- There is not enough space for everyone.
- Our office is dated and needs replacing.
- We need a better cleaning service for the office.
- We need more objective recruitment and hiring standards.
- We need objective performance appraisal and reward system.
- We need consistent application of policy.
- There are leadership problems.
- Unproductive staff should not be retained.
- Each department stereotypes of other departments.
- Decisions are often based on inaccurate information.
- We need more opportunities for advancement here.
- Our product is not consistent because there are too many styles.
- There is a toxic culture too much gossiping and criticising.
- Responsibilities at various levels are unclear.
- We need a suggestion box.
- There is a lot of "us and them" sentiment here.

- There is a lack of attention to individual needs.
- There is favouritism and preferential treatment of staff.
- More professional development training is needed at all levels.
- There need to better assessment of employee ability and performance can be more objectively based.
- Training is needed for new employees.
- Many employees are carrying the weight of other untrained employees.
- This office is "turf" oriented.
- There is a pecking order at every level and within every level.
- Communication needs improving.
- Certain departments are put on a pedestal.
- There are too many review levels for our products.
- Too many signatures are required.
- There is a lot of overlap and redundancy.
- The components of our organisation office work against one another rather than a team.
- We need more computer terminals.

(Continued)

Themes	Data
Management issues	■ There are leadership problems.
	■ We need a suggestion box.
	■ There is a lack of attention to individual needs.
	■ There is favouritism and preferential treatment of staff.
	■ Decisions are often based on inaccurate information.
	■ We need consistent application of policy.
Physical environment	■ We need a better cleaning service for the office.
	■ Our office furniture is dated and needs replacing.
	■ We need more computer terminals.
	■ There is not enough space for everyone.
	■ We need more objective recruitment and hiring standards.
	■ We need objective performance appraisal and reward systems.
	■ Non-productive staff members should not be retained.
	■ There need to be better assessment of employee ability and performance so that promotions can be more objectively based.
Employee development	■ More training is needed at all levels.
	■ Training is needed for new employees.
	■ Many employees are carrying the weight of other untrained employees.
	■ We need more opportunities for advancement here.
Intergroup and interpersonal relations	■ The organisation is "turf" oriented.
	■ There is a lot of "us and them" sentiment here.
	■ There is pecking order at every level and within every level.
	■ Communication needs improving.
	■ There is too much gossiping and criticising.
	■ Certain departments are put on a pedestal.
	■ Each department has stereotypes of the other departments.
Work structure	■ There are too many reviews for our product.
	■ Too many signatures are required.
	■ Responsibilities at various levels are unclear.
	■ The components of our office work against one another rather than as a team.
	■ There is a lot of overlap and redundancy.
	■ Our product is not consistent because there are too many styles.

following responses from staff members were recorded in narrative form and then coded into themes.

These themes then formed the basis for an examination of the issues within the sport organisation.

Memoing

Whilst coding data, the researcher can aid in the maximisation of the validity and reliability of the modes of analysis process by writing memos. These are the ideas that occur to the researcher whilst coding the data, for example concerning explanation, theorising, or other ideas about the data. They can be extremely helpful in trying to make sense of the data at a later date. Memos can be written directly on the transcripts, or else the researcher can keep a record of them elsewhere. Making memos as detailed as possible can help with later analysis.

The limitations of coding

Although coding makes data more manageable, it also deflects attention away from phenomena that don't seem to fit anywhere. However, there may be potentially useful information so they need to be incorporated somehow. One way is to construct a coding system that allows the researcher to account for uncategorised ideas and activities. Another strategy is to reject a coding system altogether and attempt to carefully tease out the subtle and various meanings of words, coupled with an informed understanding of the broader structures within the data, similar to the process used in discourse analysis. This takes account of another problem of coding, which is the loss of the context of what is said when you fragment data minutely and in great detail through coding.

In addition, coding may not always be suitable for particular type of analysis, for example *discourse analysis*. Certain traditions of discourse which might include the micro-analysis of small amounts of data (e.g. Conversation Analysis), which rely much more on the patterns, structures, and language used in speech and the written word. For particular types of discourse analyses handling large amounts of data, there may be a place for coding of a kind as a data management device though usually not for the purposes of thematic analysis and managing "interpretive" annotations to the data as described in the discussion above. Similarly, it may not be suitable for *the analysis of narrative*. This is where the researcher needs to track sequences, chronology, stories, or processes in the data, coding in these cases is often too clumsy a tool as it disregards the backwards and forwards nature of much narrative.

Recursive abstraction

Some qualitative datasets are analysed without coding. A common method here is *recursive abstraction*, where datasets are summarised, those summaries are then further summarised, and so on. The end result is a more compact summary that would have been difficult to accurately discern without the preceding steps of distillation. A frequent criticism of recursive abstraction is that the final conclusions are several times removed from the underlying data. While it is true that poor initial summaries will certainly yield an inaccurate final report, qualitative analysts can respond to this criticism. They do so, like those using coding method, by documenting the reasoning behind each summary step, citing examples from the data where statements were included and where statements were excluded from the intermediate summary.

INTERPRETING AND PRESENTING THE DATA

Interpreting is the analytical process of ascribing meaning to data, explaining to others what the data means in order to help them understand what it is that has been have discovered in an investigation. Making selections of certain ideas, readings or quotations in order to confirm or challenge concepts is part of the process of analysing and interpreting. Although it is important to preserve participants' perspectives on their social realities, the researcher is also construing and conferring their own understandings about the analysed data, comparing them with the conclusions of other researchers who have published similar or related relevant studies. This process of transcending the data – or *interpreting* – involves arriving at an assessment of what the findings mean in relation to appropriate knowledge in sport management. In qualitative research, it also involves generating theory or new conceptual models or making theory-based generalisations that can be further developed in later comparative studies.

Generating theory

At the same time, as a researcher is concentrating on discovering relationships within the data, they are also seeking to explore relationships between their data and the relevant literature. This involves tacking back and forth between the evidence collected from fieldwork and the literature. This helps the researcher find a coherent theoretical framework that is informed by and which fits with their interpretation of the data. As Weick (1995) puts it: "The process of theorising consists of activities like abstracting, generalising, relating, selecting, explaining, synthesising, and idealising. These are ongoing activities" (p. 389).

The emphasis of grounded theory is on generating theory from data – "from the ground upwards" - rather than imposing theory on the data by forcing data into a pre-defined structure. This approach builds upon the flexible coding and comparative analysis techniques described above. The objective is to go beyond describing and categorising the "what" and "how" of data in thematic content analysis, to questioning "why", concentrating on phenomena in the data as examples of more generalisable concepts. This is explored in more detail in Chapter 17 on Grounded Theory.

Not all qualitative research involves generating theory. For instance, some studies seek to be endeavour to provide a link between data and theoretical knowledge in order to recontextualise a particular case or issue to a more universal sphere so that readers can identify more readily with it. In ethnographic studies, for instance, theorising often involves identifying beliefs and values in the data and then comparing them with established theory. Through this process of analysing and interpreting, new models or theories are developed. As discussed in Chapter 3, much qualitative research involves small samples and therefore attempts at *generalisation* will be tenuous.

Presenting the data

There are many ways to diagrammatically portray relationships in qualitative date and to be effective in this requires creativity on behalf of the researcher. Some examples include: (1) schematic diagrams; (2) cause and effect diagrams; and (3) sociograms.

Reflexivity

Confidence in the conclusions from a field research study are strengthened by an honest account about how the researcher interacted with participants in the field, what problems they encountered, and how these problems were or were not resolved. Such a "natural history" of the development of the evidence enables others to evaluate the findings and reflects the interpretivist philosophy that guides many qualitative researchers.

Research brief

Title: As the lights fade: A grounded theory of male professional athletes' decision-making and transition to retirement
Author: Eggleston, D., *Texas Tech University*, Hawkins, L. G., *Texas Tech University*, & Fife, S. T., *Texas Tech University* (2019)
Reference: Eggleston, D., Hawkins, L. G., & Fife, S. T. (2019). As the lights fade: A grounded theory of male professional athletes' decision-making and transition to retirement. *Journal of Applied Sport Psychology*, 1–18.
The purpose of this study was to examine how American male professional athletes make the decision to retire and how that decision process affect transition in retirement. The researchers used constructivist grounded theory to analyse personal accounts from professional athletes who wrote about retirement, and a model on the decision making and transition process of retirement was developed. The findings showed that athletes struggle in retirement, but by relying on their social support, they can accept the conclusion of their career as a professional athlete.

TRIANGULATION

Qualitative research exercises multiple methods, something that Denzin and Lincoln (1998, pp. 3–5) called bricolage. They referred to the qualitative researcher as a bricoleur, "a practical person who works with whatever strategies, tools, and materials are available to piece together an emergent solution to a puzzle or problem" (Bazeley, 1999, p. 279). It is an array of interpretative techniques that seek to describe, decode, translate, and subsequently come to terms with the meaning, not the frequency of certain naturally occurring phenomena in the social world (Gilmore & Carson, 1996).

Denzin and Lincoln (1998) introduced and then popularised this concept as triangulation into qualitative study. Triangulation involves examining the consistency of information generated by different data collection techniques, or by examining different data gathered by the same collection technique. Triangulation has been generally considered as the way to reduce the likelihood of misinterpretation with the target to clarify meaning and verifying the repeatability of an observation or interpretation (Stake, 2000). By using multiple methods, for example, different kinds of data can emerge from the same topic so that it will involve more data that will likely improve the quality of the research (Denscombe, 1998). Albeit the initial aim of triangulation is to test the validity of qualitative research, recently its role has been put into practice to ensure comprehensiveness and encourage a more reflexive analysis of data (Pope, & Mays, 2000). Seale (1999) suggests that "triangulation offers a way of explaining how accounts and actions in one setting are influenced or constrained by those in another" (p. 60). Silverman (1993) supports the idea by saying that this can assist "to address the situated work of accounts" more willingly than "using one account to undercut the other" (p. 158).

Burns (1997) postulated that triangulation leads to verification and validation of qualitative analysis in two ways: First, by examining the consistency of information generated by different data collection techniques, and second by examining the consistency of different information within the same technique. In other words, conforming to one method could have the tendency to bias the researcher's perspective of a "particular slice of reality being investigated" (Burns 1997, p. 325), but could be "neutralised when used in conjunction with other data sources, investigators and methods" (Jick cited Creswell, 1994, p. 174). Denzin and Lincoln (1998, p. 46) identified four basic types of triangulation and are explained as:

1. Data-source triangulation: The use of different types of data sources in a study, for example, time, space and person, and each occurrence or social interaction is unique.

2. Investigator triangulation: The use of different researchers or evaluators. The main purpose is to eliminate any bias inherent in using a single observer.

3. Theory triangulation: The use of multiple perspectives to interpret a single set of data.

4. Methodological triangulation: Involves the use of multiple techniques to study a single problem.

When analysing data, ensuring that the triangulation methods above are covered will give the researcher an added measure of validity and reliability in the final reporting of results.

CRYSTALLISATION

Crystallisation is proposed by Richardson (2000) to replace triangulation. Crystallisation refers to the process of suspending the modes of analysis process in order to reflect on the analysis experience. Richardson states:

> Rather, the central imaginary is the crystal, which combines symmetry and substance with an infinite variety of shapes, substances, transmutations, multidimensionalities, and angles of approach. Crystals grow, change, alter, but not amorphous. Crystals are prisms that reflect externalities and refract within themselves, creating different colours, patterns, and arrays, casting off in different directions. What we see depends upon our angle of repose. Not triangulation, crystallization. Crystallization without losing structure, deconstructs the traditional idea of 'validity' (we feel how there is no single truth, we see how texts validate themselves), and crystallization provides us with a deepened, complex, thoroughly partial, understanding of the topic. Paradoxically, we know more and doubt what we know. Ingeniously, we know there is always more to know. (p. 934)

Commonly associated with research that embraces a postmodern frame, an integral part of the crystallisation process is "immersion", where the researchers immerse themselves in the data they have collected by either reading or examining it in detail. By suspending this immersion, the researcher can "crystallise" – reflect on the analysis experience and attempt to identify and articulate patterns or themes noticed during the immersion process.

COMPUTER-ASSISTED QUALITATIVE DATA ANALYSIS SOFTWARE

Computer-Assisted/Aided Qualitative Data Analysis (CAQDAS) is the use of computer software to aid qualitative research such as transcription analysis, coding and text interpretation, recursive abstraction, content analysis, discourse analysis, grounded theory methodology, etc. CAQDAS can assist the sport

Table 8.3	Advantages and disadvantages of CAQDAS

Advantages

- Efficient
- Uniform
- Prestige in using computing
- Allows for focused and detailed analysis
- Facilitates rigour and transparency
- Makes qualitative data more scientific
- Time saving
- Ability to analyse larger sets of data
- More substantive analysis
- Data analysis remains the intellectual, interpretive, and creative work of the researcher

Disadvantages

- Inflexible
- Not hands-on
- Distracts from ideas, emphasises words
- Reification of the researcher and data
- Advocates the positivist or quantitative approach
- CAQDAS should support rather than replace manual data analysis
- Segments of text are removed from the whole, thus creating a loss of perspective
- Considerable time constraint in mastering the software in order to free the researcher to perform in-depth analyses and interpretation of the data
- CAQDAS is for coding, not analysis

management researcher in the modes of analysis process by searching, organising, categorising, and annotating textual and visual data. CAQDAS saves time and effort in data management by extending the ability of the researcher to organise, track and manage data. The transparency and reliability of the data analysis processes may enhance the credibility of the research processes. The use of CAQDAS is not without controversy. Table 8.3 summarises some of the contentious issues of CAQDAS by listing its advantages and disadvantages.

CAQDAS has also been criticised for favouring the grounded theory approach (Coffey, Holbrook & Atkinson, 1996). In the grounded theory approach, the process of coding is the fundamental task that needs to be satisfied first before any further processes can be carried out. Table 8.4 compares the ground theory approach through CAQDAS with manual coding.

Table 8.4	Comparative analysis coding process	

Comparative coding analysis process

Grounded theory method	CAQDAS	Manual
Open coding	Creation of codes as free nodes by sentence or paragraph description/ summary of sentences or paragraph	Creation of codes based by paragraph description/ summary of paragraph
Axial coding	Re-reading of codes/free nodes and re-arrangement according to theme/ categories/tree nodes. Creation of hierarchies by "drag" and "drop"	Re-reading of codes generated and rearrangement according to theme/ category – cutting and pasting
Selective coding	Re-reading of codes and categories and selection of category that most represents the cumulated categories. Higher hierarchies of the tree nodes are established to show the selected codes	Re-reading of codes and categories and selection of category that most represent the cumulated categories

Despite ongoing debate around the advantages and disadvantages of CAQDAS, many researchers now use CAQDAS, but often only for the purpose of coding alone, and go back to the manual methods for the theory-building stage; thus ensuring that the benefits of automation are reaped and its shortcomings are avoided.

CAQDAS SELECTION

Weitzman and Miles (1995) classified this software into five categories. These are: (1) text retrievers; (2) textbase managers; (3) code and retrieve programmes; (4) code-based theory builders; and (5) conceptual network builders. Fielding and Lee (2002) later identified three generations of CAQDAS. *First generation* software consisted of word processing and database software that allowed a researcher to search for specific text strings, but did not allow for encoding the data. *Second generation* software provided additional capability to encode the data, retrieve data by those codes and add memos to the encoded text. Second generation CAQDAS is commonly referred to as code and retrieve software. *Third generation* CAQDAS has added the ability to create complex families or networks of codes to support theory building. In most cases, third generation CAQDAS packages are represented by the latest versions of the industry leading products such as ATLAS.ti and are classified as code-based theory builders. Other prominent CAQDAS products, classified as conceptual network builders, provide linking, and graphic capabilities, but may lack coding and database management features. Third generation CAQDAS is very complex software and a significant learning curve is necessary for mining its full potential for qualitative research. The CAQDAS networking project lists the following tools a CAQDAS programme should have: content searching tools; coding tools; linking tools; mapping or networking tools; query tools; writing and annotation tools.

Selection of a suitable CAQDAS package requires the researcher to understand the purpose of the study, expected results and the available timeline in which to perform the study. Once CAQDAS becomes applicable to a particular study or research problem, various packages must be evaluated and an appropriate CAQDAS package is selected. Selection criteria may be different depending on the group in which a specific qualitative researcher resides. Students and other qualitative researchers may be directed to use a particular CAQDAS package as part of a university's standard software application suite. Some researchers may require more than one CAQDAS package. Training on the software is recommended. Appropriate usage of CAQDAS can then free the researcher from the burden of managing the raw data and allow him or her time to delve into the data and observe emergent themes and patterns as they develop.

There are a number of well-known CAQDAS packages. Some of the packages take some time to learn, even with specialised instruction. The sport management researcher needs to weigh up the pros and cons of taking the time to learn such a package before deciding on a particular approach. The software packages range in the level of sophistication, and if intending to utilise a CAQDAS package, the sport management researcher should seek a package that has the tools that suit the research style, rather than just the package that offers the greatest functionality. If a sport management researcher is likely to be undertaking a considerable amount of qualitative research over a reasonable period of time, then it may be worthwhile learning one of the packages. On the other hand, if the researcher is engaged in a one-off piece of research, then manual analysis might be more appropriate.

CAQDAS PACKAGES FOR SPORT MANAGEMENT RESEARCH

The following discussion examines some popular CAQDAS packages utilised in Sport Management Research.

Qualitative data analysis with ATLAS.ti

ATLAS.ti is a computer software programme that supports the qualitative analysis of large bodies of textual, graphical, audio and video data. It offers a variety of tools for accomplishing the tasks associated with any systematic approach to "soft" data. For example, material that cannot be analysed by formal, statistical approaches in meaningful ways. In the course of such a *qualitative analysis*, ATLAS.ti helps to uncover the complex phenomenon hidden in data in an exploratory way. The main strategic modes of operation can be termed "VISE": visualisation, integration, serendipity, and exploration.

Qualitative data analysis with NVivo

NVivo is a multifunctional software system for the development, support and management of QDA projects. It is used in a wide range of research for handling non-numerical unstructured data by processes of indexing, searching, and theory building. NVivo transforms the way data is viewed (from static to dynamic) in a way that makes relationships between categories more visible by using text formatting and hyperlinks to other documents and categories.

Qualitative data analysis with Leximancer

Leximancer is a sophisticated qualitative analysis of textual data. This software tool automates the analysis of concepts in the text, creating visualisation maps of the concepts and the relationships between them. The key capabilities of the Leximancer software provides a means for generating and recognising themes, including themes that might otherwise have been missed or overlooked if the data had been manually coded (Crofts & Bisman, 2010).

SUMMARY ON CAQDAS

The final decision on using CAQDAS is left to the confidence and expertise of the sport management researcher. If a researcher does reject the use of CAQDAS for analysis, then it should not immediately be assumed that the quality of analysis is inferior. Provided the mode of analysis is carried out correctly then there should be little difference in the quality of analysis.

Research brief

Title: 2022 Qatar world cup: impact perceptions among Qatar residents
Author: Al-Emadi, A., *Qatar University*, Kaplanidou, K., *University of Florida*, Diop, A., *Qatar University*, Sagas, M., *University of Florida*, Le, K. T., *Qatar University*, & Al-Ali Mustafa, S., *Qatar University* (2017)
Reference: Al-Emadi, A., Kaplanidou, K., Diop, A., Sagas, M., Le, K. T., & Al-Ali Mustafa, S. (2017). 2022 Qatar world cup: Impact perceptions among Qatar residents. *Journal of Travel Research, 56*(5), 678–694.
The purpose of this study was to evaluate how the impacts from the 2022 World Cup preparations in Qatar influenced local residents' attitudes, personal and community quality of life perceptions, excitement about hosting the event, and support toward the event. The examination of the way mega sport event impacts influence residents' perceptions of personal and community quality of life is lacking in the literature. Data were collected using systematic sampling in October 2014 from Qatari nationals and white-collar expatriates. Overall, 2,163 interviews with Qatari nationals (1,058) and white-collar expatriates (1,105) were completed. The results revealed that eight years before the event, sociocultural impacts were the most influential type of impact for residents' attitudes toward the event, community and personal quality of life, excitement about the event, and support of the FIFA decision to host the event in Qatar.

CONCLUSION

This chapter has explained the principles and techniques that should underpin modes of analysis. It began by discussing the phases of modes of analysis and an appropriate framework that can be used in organising that analysis. It identified the importance of coding and provided a detailed discussion of open, axial, and selective coding approaches to analysing data and provided an example of how this might be undertaken. Triangulation and crystallisation were then discussed and an example of how triangulation could be applied in the modes of analysis phase presented. The chapter concluded by discussing Computer-Assisted Qualitative Modes of Analysis Software (CAQDAS) and how it can assist the sport management researcher in the modes of analysis process.

REVIEW AND RESEARCH QUESTIONS

The process of modes of analysis aims to provide the sport management researcher with the opportunity to make sense of the data so that evidence can be obtained that can then be used to answer the research question. With a basic understanding now of the modes of analysis process, attempt to answer the following questions:

1. What are the three types of coding, and at what stage of the coding process would they be employed?

2. Identify some advantages and disadvantages to the use of CAQDAS over completely manual modes of analysis processes.

3. Using the web, research the different electronic packages that are available for QDA and find out what their advantages and disadvantages are.

REFERENCES

Bazeley, P. (1999). The bricoleur with a computer: Piecing together qualitative and quantitative data. *Qualitative Health Research, 9*(2), 279–287.

Bleicher, J. (1980). *Contemporary hermeneutics: Hermeneutics as method, philosophy, and critique.* London: Routledge & Kegan Paul Books.

Bogdan, R. C., & Biklen, S. K. (1982). *Qualitative research for education: An introduction to theory and methods.* Toronto: Allyn & Bacon.

Burns, R. B. (1997). *Introduction to research methods.* Melbourne: Longman.

Coffey, A., Holbrook, B., & Atkinson, P. (1996). Qualitative data analysis: Technologies and representations. *Sociological Research Online, 1*(1). Available at http://www.socresonline.org.uk/socresonline/1/1/4.html.

Creswell, J. W. (1994). *Research design: Qualitative and quantitative approaches.* Thousand Oaks, CA: Sage.

Creswell, J. W. (2009). *Research design: Qualitative, quantitative and mixed method approaches* (3rd ed.). Los Angeles, CA: Sage Publications.

Creswell, J. W. (2012). *Qualitative inquiry and research design: Choosing among five approaches.* London: Sage Publication.

Crofts, K., & Bisman, J. (2010). Interrogating accountability: An illustration of the use of Leximancer software for qualitative data analysis. *Qualitative Research in Accounting & Management, 7*(2), 180–207.

Davidson, C. (2009). Transcription: Imperatives for qualitative research. *International Journal of Qualitative Methods, 8*(2), 36–52.

Denscombe, M. (1998). *The good research guide for small scale social research projects.* Milton Keynes: Open University Press.

Denzin, N. K., & Lincoln, Y. S. (1998). *Strategies of qualitative inquiry.* Thousand Oaks, CA: Sage Publications.

Easterby-Smith, M., Golden-Biddle, K., & Locke, K. (2008). Working with pluralism: Determining quality in qualitative research. *Organizational Research Methods 11,* 419–29.

Fielding, N. G., & Lee, R. M. (2002). New patterns in the adoption and use of qualitative software. *Field Methods, 14*(2), 197–216.

Gadamer, H. G. (1976). *Philosophical hermeneutics.* Berkeley, CA: University of California Press.

Gilmore, A., & Carson, D. (1996). Integrative qualitative methods in a services context. *Marketing Intelligence and Planning, 14*(6), 21–26.

Khan, K. (2008). Evaluation challenges in Pakistan and establishment of Pakistan evaluation network (PEN). In *Evaluation South Asia.* Nepal: UNICEF.

Krippendorff, K. (2013). *Content analysis. An introduction to its methodology.* London: Sage Publications.

Lacey, A., & Luff, D. (2001). *Qualitative data analysis.* Nottingham: Trent Focus

Lewins A., Taylor C., & Gibbs G. R. (2005). *What is qualitative data analysis* (QDA)? Retrieved from http://onlineqda.hud.ac.uk/Intro_QDA/

Madill, A., & Gough, B. (2008). Qualitative research and its place in psychological science. *Psychological Methods, 13*(3), 254–271.

Miles, M. B., & Huberman, A. M. (1994). *Qualitative data analysis: An expanded sourcebook.* Thousand Oaks, CA: Sage Publications.

Morse, J., (2008). Confusing categories and themes. *Qualitative Health Research, 18*(6), 727–728.

Nikander, P. (2008). Working with transcripts and translated data. *Qualitative Research in Psychology, 5*(3), 225–231

Palmer, R. E. (1969). *Hermeneutics.* Evanston, IL: Northwestern University Press.

Parlett, M., & Hamilton, D. (1976). Evaluation as illumination: A new approach to the study of innovatory programs. *Evaluation Studies Review Annual, 1,* 140–157.

Patel, R., & Davidson, B. (2003). *Basic research methodology* (3rd ed.). Lund: Studentlitteratur.

Patton, M. Q. (2002). Two decades of development in qualitative inquiry: A personal, experimental perspective. *Qualitative social work, 1*(3), 261–283.

Pope, C., & Mays, N. (2000). *Qualitative research in health care.* London: Blackwell.

Radnitzky, G. (1970). *Contemporary schools of metascience* (2nd ed.). Goteborg: Akademiforlaget.

Richardson, L. (2000). Writing: A method of inquiry. In N. K. Denzin & Y. S. Lincoln (Eds.). *Handbook of Qualitative Research* (2nd ed.), pp. 923–948. Thousand Oaks, CA: Sage Publications.

Ricoeur, P. (1974). *The conflict of interpretation: Essays in hermeneutics.* Evanston, IL: Northwestern University Press.

Roberts C. (2007). *Qualitative Data Analysis. Transcribing Spoken Discourse.* FDTL Data Project 2004. http://www.kcl.ac.uk/schools/sspp/education/research/projects/dataqual.html.

Saldaña, J. (2016). *The coding manual for qualitative researchers* (3rd ed.). Thousand Oaks, CA: Sage Publications.

Seale, C. (1999). *The quality of qualitative research*. London: Sage.

Silverman, D. (1993). *Interpreting qualitative data*. London: Sage.

Stake, R. (2000). Case studies. In N. K. Denzin, Y. S. Lincoln (Eds.). *Handbook of qualitative research* (2nd ed.) pp. 435–454. Thousand Oaks, CA: Sage Publications.

Stake, R. E. (1995). *The art of case study research*. Thousand Oaks, CA: Sage Publications.

Strauss, A., & Corbin, J. (1990). *Basics of qualitative research: Grounded theory procedures and techniques*. Newbury Park, CA: Sage Publications.

Taylor, C. (1990). *Philosophy and the human sciences*. Cambridge: Cambridge University Press.

Thompson, J. B. (1981). *Critical hermeneutics: A study in the thought of Paul Ricoeur and Juergen Habermas*. Cambridge: Cambridge University Press.

Weick, K. E. (1995), What theory is not, theorizing is. *Administrative Science Quarterly*, 40, 385–90.

Weitzman, E., & Miles, M. (1995). *A software source book: Computer programs for qualitative data analysis*. Thousand Oaks, CA: Sage Publications.

Witcher, C. S. G. (2010). Negotiating transcription as a relative insider: Implications for rigor. *International Journal of Qualitative Methods*, 9(2), 122–132.

Wynn, E. (1979). *Office Conversation as an Information Medium*. Unpublished doctoral dissertation, University of California, Berkeley.

PART 5

Paradigms used in sport management research

CHAPTER 9

Action research and sport management research

LEARNING OUTCOMES

By the end of this chapter, you should be able to

- Identify the origins of Action Research as a means of understanding variation in the contemporary literature.

- Define, compare, and contrast the distinguishing bases of Action Research.

- Develop a review of the key features associated with Action Research.

- Describe the range of practical methods associated with Action Research.

- Consider the ethical challenges associated with Action Research.

KEY TERMS

1. The Action Research cycle: the steps of plan, act, observe, and reflect.

2. Emancipatory Action Research: seeks to bring together action and reflection, theory and practice through a participatory democratic process aimed at developing practical solutions to issues.

3. Participatory Action Research: a type of Action Research that involves the participation of those who may be affected by the outcomes of research in decision making in all stages of the research process.

KEY THEMES

- How is Action Research self-reflective?

- What are the key differences between emancipatory and participatory Action Research?

CHAPTER OVERVIEW

This chapter explores the various methodologies of Action Research, particularly Emancipatory Action Research (EAR) and Participatory Action Research (PAR), both of which have features that make them applicable to the field of sport management research. Action Research in general is cyclic in nature, with the researcher working from within the organisation to plan, act, observe, reflect, and plan again based on the outcome of the first cycle. This chapter will provide some methods from which the sport management researcher can start the process of Action Research within a sport management organisation.

INTRODUCTION

Action Research is based on a philosophical stance that focuses on the way knowledge is acquired, interpreted, and what outcomes can be expected. It is grounded on the foundations of naturalistic inquiry and phenomenology. Through the systematic participatory approach of Action Research, the lived experiences of participants are explored to find meaning and understanding that, with reflection, can translate to learning that is a basis for action.

Considered qualitative research, Action Research seeks action to improve practice and study the effects of the action that was taken. In Action Research, the implementation of solutions occurs as an actual part of the research process. There is no trying to generalize the findings of the study, as is the case in quantitative research studies According to Heron and Reason (1997), Action Research is similar to constructivist research methods but it adds the important ontological components of cooperation and experiential knowing, affirming "the primary value of practical knowing in the service of human flourishing" (p. 274). This framework acknowledges self-reflection as part of a participatory worldview (Heron & Reason, 1997). They further suggest that "to experience anything is to participate in it, and to participate is both to mould and encounter; hence, experiential reality is always subjective–objective" (p. 278). Action Research also increases accountability and quality (Catelli & Carlino, 2001; Schön, 1991). Hart suggests that Action Research is problem focused, context specific, participative, involves change, and intervention geared to improvement, and is a process based on a continuous interaction between research, action, reflection, and evaluation. Having an understanding of this allows for the appreciation of the lived experience and insights of all research participants or stakeholders of a system.

Through an Action Research methodology, meaning is constructed by participants in a social context. The constructivist epistemology is based on knowledge being created by the participants and it is an outcome of the collaboration and a subjective product of the context in which it occurs. (Brand, 2009). Constructivists challenge the notion that research should be undertaken by impartial, detached, value-neutral participants, who seek to discover discernible objects or phenomena. Rather, they view researchers as part of a network that creates knowledge and ultimately guides practice (Mir & Watson, 2000). Here we see the definitive link between Action Research and social constructivism.

ACTION RESEARCH DEFINED

Action Research can be defined in various ways. Since the method is applicable in many different research areas, it is seldom that the definition follows a universal format. This leads to many different definitions.

Action Research is a practice for the systematic development of knowing and knowledge, but based in a rather different form from traditional academic research. It has different purposes, is based in different relationships, it has different ways of conceiving knowledge and its relation to practice. We use the definition of Reason and Bradbury (2001) who it broadly as:

> ... a participatory, democratic process concerned with developing practical knowing in the pursuit of worthwhile human purposes, grounded in a participatory worldview... It seeks to bring together action and reflection, theory and practice, in participation with others, in the pursuit of practical solutions to issues of pressing concern to people, and more generally the flourishing of individual persons and their communities. (p. 1)

This definition brings together five dimensions of Action Research: (1) it is pragmatic, concerned with addressing practical issues, and making links between theory and practice; (2) it is democratic both in the sense of involving people and in being liberationist – seeking to enable all people to create their own knowledge in learning organisations and communities of inquiry; (3) it draws on an "extended epistemology" (Heron, 1996) of many ways of knowing, valuing the experiential, narrative, and aesthetic, alongside the propositional and conceptual; (4) it is value oriented, asking how we can contribute to the flourishing – economic, political, psychological, spiritual – of human persons, communities, and of the wider ecology of the planet; (5) and it is developmental, evolving over time from tentative beginnings toward more significant influence (Reason & Bradbury, 2001).

THE EVOLUTION OF ACTION RESEARCH

The origins of Action Research can be traced to two independent sources, John Collier and Kurt Lewin (Reason & Bradbury, 2001). John Collier was commissioner of Indian Affairs from 1933 to 1945 in President Franklin D. Roosevelt's administration, and had the role of developing programmes to improve race relations. He used the term "Action Research" to describe his collaborative method

Research brief

Title: Scaffolding student–coaches' instructional leadership toward student-centred peer interactions: A yearlong action-research intervention in sport education
Author: Farias, C., *University of Bedfordshire*, Hastie, P. A., *Auburn University*, & Mesquita, I. *University of Porto* (2018).
Reference: Farias, C., Hastie, P. A., & Mesquita, I. (2018). Scaffolding student–coaches' instructional leadership toward student-centred peer interactions: A yearlong action-research intervention in sport education. *European Physical Education Review, 24*(3), 269–291.
This study provided a yearlong, in-depth examination of the scaffolding processes used by a teacher during student participation in four consecutive seasons. The authors placed a strong focus on the preparation of the students in the role of team coaches to conduct instructions in

student-centred interactions (active engagement of teammates in problem-solving, discovery, and the construction of knowledge). Twenty-six seventh grade students participated in four consecutive seasons of sport education (basketball, handball, soccer, and volleyball). The research involved four action-research iterative cycles of planning, acting, monitoring, and reflecting. Data collection involved semi-structured interviews with teams and exclusively with the student–coaches, lesson observations, and a field diary kept by the first author, who assumed the role of practitioner–researcher. Findings showed the scaffolding of the student–coaches' instructional leadership was a non-linear process contingently adjusted in reference to aspects such as student–coaches' progress in the mastery of instructional processes, the complexity of the domain-specific content, and the nature of the sports.

of researching important practical problems in order to be able to take effective action (French & Bell, 1990). Some authors attribute the origins of Action Research solely to the German social psychologist Kurt Lewin who used the term in the mid-1940s (Reason & Bradbury, 2001; Schwandt, 1997). His idea was that researchers would enter a situation to attempt change and monitor the results. Lewin's contribution to change in the workplace began shortly after World War 1 when at Harwood Manufacturing Company he helped to explore ways to enhance productivity by using Action Research methods in which workers participated in experimental changes in methods. To Lewin (1948), Action Research was:

> *comparative research on the conditions and effects of various forms of social action and research leading to social action. (it is) a big spiral of steps, each of which is composed of a circle of planning, action and fact-finding about the result of the action. (p. 202)*

When Lewin died in 1947, his Action Research theory was still being developed. Many people have contributed to the body of knowledge on Action Research. Some Action Researchers have emphasized experimentation, others have been concerned with feedback, planning, or learning and theory building. For example, the staff at the Tavistock Institute of Human Relations emphasized collaborative problem solving and joint learning. Lewin and his associates at the Center for Group Dynamics were more concerned with theory building and experimentation (Cunningham, 1993; Lewin, 1952).

The process begins, according to Lewin (1948), with the researcher setting down a general idea of what he or she wants to achieve. The next step involves gathering information about the present situation, which allows the researcher to formulate "an 'overall plan' of how to reach the objective, and [to make] a decision in regard to the first step of action" (p. 205). This stage is followed by a series of phases, each involving "circles" of action, evaluation, reflection, fact-finding, modifying the original plan, and planning the next action. Lewin likens the process to a spiral staircase, where the steps ultimately lead to achievement of the desired outcome.

McTaggart (1991) identified Lewin's work as *first-generation Action Research*, which developed through the late 1950s in the educational sphere in America. McTaggart discusses how the process evolved with *second generation Action Research* developing within Britain from the 1960s through to the 1980s. *Third generation Action Research* originated in the 1980s with a call for a more critical basis within Australia and Europe. Finally, the *fourth generation Action Research* emerged in Australia with emancipatory Action Research (EAR) as the culmination of the previous three generations. It was here that the influences of the work of the German philosopher and sociologist Jurgen Habermas began to filter into Action Research. The *fourth generation of Action Research* owes much of its origins to the previous generations.

Kemmis (1995) a fourth-generation Action Researcher identified the following elements of Action Research. These were as follows:

1. Action Research is a social process: It deliberately explores the relationship between the realms of the individual and the social. It recognizes that "no individuation is possible without socialization, and no socialization is possible without individuation" (Habermas, 1972, p. 26).

2. Action Research is participatory: It engages people in examining their knowledge (understandings, skills, and values) and interpretive categories (the ways they interpret themselves and their action in the social and material world).

3. Action Research is practical and collaborative: It engages people in examining the acts that link them with others in social interaction.

4. Action Research is emancipatory: It aims to help people recover an awareness of and release themselves from the constraints of irrational, unproductive, unjust, and unsatisfying social structures, which limit their self-development and self-determination.

5. Action Research is critical: It aims to help people recover an awareness of and release themselves from the constraints embedded in the media through which they interact. Their language (discourses), their modes of work, and the social relationships of power (in which they experience affiliation and difference, inclusion and exclusion – relationships in which, grammatically speaking, they interact with others in the first or second or third person).

Table 9.1	Features of action research
Feature	**Explanation**
Problem Aimed	Research focuses on a special situation in practice. Action Research is aimed at a specific problem recognizable in practice.
Collective	All participants (for instance the researchers and persons standing in the participation practice) form an integral part of Action Research with the exclusive aim to assist in solving the identified problem.
Type of empirical Action Research	Is characterized as a means to change the practice while research the research is going on.
Outcome of Action Research	Is characterized by the fact that problem solving, seen as Action Research renewed corrective actions, cannot be generalized, because it should comply with the criteria set for scientific character.

Action Research has not been without its criticisms (see later in this chapter). The most significant being the challenge of *defining the term* and the lack of consistent approaches. The lack of consistent methodology enables such a wide range of interpretations to be made that it becomes difficult to evaluate and critique the rigour of an Action Research project. Practitioners can have difficulties applying a methodology that can be used in a number of different ways, which poses potential problems for the practitioner and may lead to lack of confidence in the results by those who are interested in the outcomes. Despite these criticisms it is now generally accepted that Action Research has a number of key features, which are outlined in Table 9.1.

PHILOSOPHICAL FOUNDATIONS

Action Research is based on a philosophical stance that focuses on the way knowledge is acquired, interpreted and what outcomes can be expected. It is grounded on the foundations of naturalistic inquiry and phenomenology. Through the systematic participatory approach of Action Research, the lived experiences of participants are explored to find meaning and understanding that, with reflection, can translate to learning that is a basis for action.

Naturalistic inquiry

Naturalistic inquiry provides the methodological grounding for Action Research by focusing on participants' meaning and understanding rather than looking for causal relationships. Naturalistic inquiry, often referred to as qualitative research, uses a diverse set of tools to study social and cultural phenomena and to explore meaning. People interpret their experiences in different ways and make meaning according to social and cultural norms and experiences. Where a group of individuals develop similar patterns of behaviour with similar experience and learning, they may develop a better understanding of the world in which they live and work. Naturalistic inquiry aims to explore the world of others and bring meaning to the combined worlds of interacting individuals. Stringer and Genat (2004) explain:

> It is this understanding that is at the heart of Action Research – the need to clarify and understand the meaning implicit in the acts and behaviours of all people involved in events on which research is focused, and the need to use those extended understandings as the basis for resolving the problems investigated. (p. 22)

By comparison, objective science or positivism is often more focused on quantitative research. It operates according to an agreed set of assumptions and beliefs about how we acquire knowledge and seeks to describe features of our world and relationships between features. Positivism uses a specific set of tools to measure variables and to determine the nature and extent of relationships between variables, often seeking to find causal relationships (Grbich, 1999). The accurate definition and measurement of variables and relationships, the aim of much objective science, has provided a powerful body of knowledge, particularly in biological and physical sciences. Research into social or cultural contexts, which are the foundations of human social life, are often studied more effectively with the help of naturalistic inquiry.

Phenomenology   3

A phenomenological perspective underpins an Action Research orientation by seeking meanings inherent in participant lived experiences. Phenomenology stems from the work of Edmund Husserl (1859–1938) and seeks to find how individuals understand and interpret "things" or phenomena. Other writers, including Gribich (1999), Jean-Paul Sartre (1960, 1963), Maurice Merleau-Ponty (1962), and Martin Heidegger (1962), seek to identify, understand, and describe the subjective experiences of participants. The emphasis is on identifying and describing the participants' "lived experiences" (Grbich, 1999) through rigorous analysis, rather than a subjective interpretation by a researcher. In research, everyday experiences are studied from the point of view of the participants as they describe their view of their world. An interpretive approach to qualitative inquiry describes and gives meaning to events and situations as described by the participants and enhances our understanding or comprehension of experiences.

Phenomenology suggests that if researchers put aside prevailing, accepted understandings of phenomena and revisit individuals' immediate experience of them, it is possible that new meaning will emerge or that current meaning will be reinforced (Crotty, 1998). It requires that usual (previous) understandings are set aside and a fresh look is taken at things that we "know". Sadler (1969) cited in Crotty (1998) describes phenomenology as "an attempt to find a fresh perception without prejudice or acculturation" (p. 80). Phenomenology may question what we take for granted and is viewed as a critical methodology, involving critical reflection and reinterpretation. Benner (1994) supports the use of interpretive phenomenology to study what is described as everyday aspects of the world, where the researcher seeks to understand the world of concerns, habits, and skills presented by participants. It uses a stringent set of disciplines to give the best possible account of the text, guided by an ethic of "understanding responsiveness", so that the researcher does not read into the text what is not there. The interpreter does not place his or her own world onto the text, rather, listens carefully and hears "the voices" and concerns within the text to give a full account. By taking an interpretive phenomenology approach, Action Research:

- Identifies different definitions of the problem.

- Reveals the perspectives of the various interested parties.

- Suggests alternative points of view from which the problem can be interpreted and assessed.

- Identifies strategic points of intervention.

- Exposes the limits of statistical information by furnishing materials that enable the understanding of individual experiences (Stringer & Genat, 2004).

ACTION RESEARCH ASSUMPTIONS

To summarize the above views, Action Researchers believe that complex social systems and social situations cannot be reduced for meaningful study; and as such, Action Research is a process of making sense of and understanding complex interactions and systems. Action Research is therefore highly suitable to sport managers as sport organizations inherently involve unique and complex interactions and systems. The cycle of plan, act, observe, and reflect represents actions that any sport manager should be engaging with on a regular basis to allow them to draw out understandings for others to learn from.

A major difference between Action Research and other forms of research is that Action Researchers insist that research processes, research outcomes, and the application of results to problem solving are inextricably linked (Greenwood & Levin, 1998). Action Researchers accept that a particular outcome is realized through the intersection of environmental conditions, a group of people and a variety of historical events, including the actions of the participants (Greenwood & Levin, 1998). From this perspective, all explanations of present situations are actually accounting of historical moments and particular causes acting on particular organizations in specific contexts. The Action Researcher understands the uniqueness of an Action Research project and is aware of the limitations of generalizing outcomes to other situations and organizational contexts.

✰ The role of theory in Action Research is to explain how what happened was possible and took place, to lay out possible scenarios for the future and give good reasons for the ones that seem to be probable outcomes. As Bate, Khan and Pye (2000) note, the methodology of Action Research doesn't emphasize prediction; it focuses instead on allowing what needs to happen, to happen. From a political perspective, Action Researchers believe that research results should be useful for participants in gaining increased control over their own situation, and that the research questions should be influenced by everyone involved in the study (Greenwood & Levin, 1998). For example, empowering concussion sufferers and medical personnel with knowledge of concussion treatment and prevention increases their ability to pressure sport bodies to change policies. Furthermore, it is critical to involve those groups in each stage of the Action Research, from research question development to interpretation of results to enacting the outcomes. It is preferable that participants be involved in the research process as it is not a technique applied by one person on others, but a process that is co-managed by the interested parties (Dick, 2002). This is what makes Action Research a particularly useful tool for sport organizational research. The characteristics that underpin the approach (see Table 9.2) lend themselves to its application in sport organisations as sport organisations are complex social settings with numerous stakeholders with an inherent interest in its organizational practices.

Table 9.2	Characteristics of action research

Characteristics of action research

- Focus on a particular social setting
- Collaboration/dialogue with others to identify the issues and to collect and analyse data
- Deliberate intervention into the operation of the status quo
- Processes of research lead to the construction of knowledge and theory (and political action)
- Testing of knowledge and theory by feeding information back into changes in practice
- Evaluation of changes through further cycles of action and reflection
- Opening of theories and knowledge to wider scrutiny through publication, information dissemination, and application by others in their own situations

ESTABLISHING A STRATEGY FOR ACTION RESEARCH

According to McLean (1995), a strategy for Action Research involves three stages: (1) conceptualization; (2) implementation; and (3) interpretation. While the conceptualization and interpretation stages demand skills that are part of the researcher's general skills, the implementation stage is dependent on the other stages.

Conceptualization

The first stage in the Action Research process is conceptualization, which requires that the specific process to study is selected. Moreover, it is important to consider what results are expected from the process, the outcome, and how the input might promote the outcome. In this perspective, Action Research is the process of determining whether the conceptualization was achieved. McLean (1995) stressed that the process of carefully considering the input and outcome brings up a clearer understanding that leads to new ideas of how the process can be improved.

Implementation

The stage of implementation consists of three components: (1) measurement of the outcomes; (2) identifying a standard of comparison; and (3) comparing current performance with the standard (McLean, 1995). This is the most technical phase of the Action Research process; and through the participation of the researcher, the implementation will be smoother.

Interpretation

Interpretation is the final stage in the Action Research process (McLean, 1995). In this phase, judgements are made about the effectiveness of the observed organisation. Here, findings of the implementation stage are brought together with the findings from the conceptualization stage. Furthermore, it is during the interpretation stage that judgements can be made about the effectiveness of the practice and whether it produces better results than the theories involved in the topic. In order to achieve the best results possible in the interpretation stage, it is crucial that the research effectively evaluates the implementation phase.

Despite Action Research having three clearly defined stages, sport managers; however, can have difficulties with Action Research because as a methodology it lacks a consistency in its approach. Applying a methodology that can be used in a number of different ways poses potential problems that may lead to lack of confidence in the results by those who are interested in the outcomes. Sport managers therefore need to consider a raft of issues before embarking on an Action Research project. An overview of these issues is presented in Table 9.3.

Table 9.3	Issues of action research for the sport management researcher to consider

Issues of action research for the sport management researcher to consider

- Who will you involve?
- What issues/questions will you focus on?
- What steps in the process will you put in place next?
- How will you collect data/information?
- How will you track/analyse it/identify emerging issues?
- What resources do you need?
- What skills/knowledge do you need?

Research brief

Title: Reinventing youth sport: Formative findings from a state-level action research project
Author: Chalip, L., *University of Illinois* & Hutchinson, R., *University of Illinois* (2017)
Reference: Chalip, L., & Hutchinson, R. (2017). Reinventing youth sport: Formative findings from a state-level action research project. *Sport in Society, 20*(1), 30–46.

This paper conducted a state-level action research in the United States in order to foster changes and promote participation in youth sport. The reasons for this research was the increasing scrutiny of challenges concerning building and maintaining youth sport participation. This paper reported the first phase of an action research approach, which has been dubbed "The Illinois Youth Sport Initiative". At its formative phase, the project began with a series of working sessions for 64 youth sport programme administrators from throughout the state whose responsibilities included youth sport programming. The sessions combined nominal group and dialectical decision-making techniques to enable them to identify youth sport problems, explore their causes, and suggest possible directions for solving those problems. Two sport management faculty members who were not part of the research team and six doctoral students were trained to be facilitators and recorders for the conversations that took place at the workshop. The two authors and an industry consultant who helped to plan the research outline moved among the tables also taking notes, and then facilitated and took notes when the groups at each table reported to the entire room after each working session. The authors used standard protocols for the analysis and their coding approach was initially open ended, with ideas sharing similar bases or foci grouped together and then labelled. Groupings were collated into categories, which were relabelled to represent the new aggregate. Those categories were again compared, and the process continued until the resulting themes were fully saturated and were sufficiently differentiated that they could not be further aggregated. In order to assure that the resulting themes were adequately representative, the two authors each worked through the notes separately. Each author identified six themes, and the content for each theme was consistent between the two authors. Differences in naming the themes and the minor differences in coding data from the notes were resolved by consensual discussions. The themes and the data assigned to each theme were then shared with the industry consultant, who evaluated the adequacy and representativeness of the themes. The results of the research laid a foundation for work to improve youth sport provision by examining the needs and experiences of those who are responsible for youth sport programming in their communities. The work concluded six thematic directions for improving youth sport: design and implement child-centred programming; build status for participatory youth sport programmes; creatively develop and manage resources; train coaches to be sport and life skill mentors; improve programming for traditionally underserved populations; and manage parents.

THE ACTION RESEARCH PROCESS

According to Kemmis and Grundy (1997), there are three conditions necessary for Action Research to exist:

1. A project takes as its subject matter a social practice, regarding it as a strategic action susceptible to improvement.

2. The project proceeds through a spiral of cycles of planning, acting, observing, and reflecting with each of these activities being systematically and self critically implemented and interrelated.

3. The project involves those responsible for the practice in each of the moments of the activity, widening participation in the project gradually to include others affected by the practice and maintaining collaborative control of the process.

Two criteria appear as fundamental to Action Research: the cyclic process and the research partnership. Noffke and Stevenson (1995) discuss the cyclical nature of Action Research:

As a research method, Action Research is cyclical, that is, it does not progress from an initial question to the formulation of data collection, analysis and conclusion... The process does not end, as with traditional notions of research, with richer understandings of education for others to implement; rather it aids in the ongoing process of identifying contradictions which, in turn, help to locate spaces for ethically defensible, politically strategic action. (pp. 4–5)

Action Research also emphasises the concept of co-researchers and stresses the notion of partnership as fundamental to achieving more democratic research processes and realization of practical and relevant outcomes. Research is "done with" not "done to" participants. The researcher does not presume a position of power nor participate as an expert, but rather as an equal partner in a process of discovery. Knowledge and power are balanced; the sport management researcher may have knowledge of the process but the participants have knowledge of the setting. Changes in position may occur as participants gain more understanding of the situation and participate in finding solutions. Action Research calls for reflection and analysis of knowledge and action by all participants and, consequently, has an educational function.

THE ACTION RESEARCH CYCLE

In its simplest form the cyclical process of Action Research is outlined in Figure 9.1 and is presented as:

■ Plan – develop a plan of critically informed action to improve what is already happening;

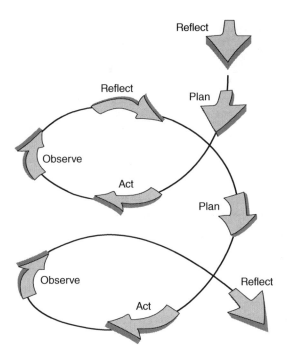

Figure 9.1 The cyclical process of action research

- Act – act to implement the plan;

- Observe – observe the effects of the critically informed action in the context in which it occurs;

- Reflect – reflect on these effects as the basis for further planning, subsequent critically informed action, [etc.] through a succession of stages (Kemmis & McTaggart, 1988, p. 10).

In the cycle of "plan, act, observe, and reflect" of Action Research, reflection is a key theoretical component (see Figure 9.1). From an analytic perspective the methodology endorses a reflective analytical approach. Gall, Borg and Gall (1996) note the analysis of data within an Action Research or critical theoretical research approach is reflective, rather than structural or interpretive. They state that, "reflective analysis is largely subjective and it is not possible to specify standard procedures for doing this type of data analysis" (p. 571). Moreover, critical researchers do not view data as something that contains facts that need to be "discovered" or "uncovered", but rather "data is constructed during research, and if reflected upon is somewhat self-validating because it grasps and reflects reality" (Reid, 1997, p. 56). Returning to an earlier example, Action Research for concussion prevention and treatment is not about discovering a link between head impacts and brain damage, but rather finding amicable solutions to how concussions are perceived and implementing policy changes in dealing with concussion injuries.

Reason (1990) describes a cycle or loop of reflective analysis as "moving to and fro between reflection and experience" (p. 45). This he suggests can be individually based, where each person operates individually and reflects upon their individual experiences, with ideally a group reflection at the very beginning or very end. Alternatively, it can be collective, where the researcher and participants "always reflect together; and they always experience together ... interacting as a group ... What is essential here is to ensure that each person has a say in the reflective phase and is fully involved in the experience phase" (p. 45).

Reason (1990) suggests that the balance between reflection and experience be seen as critical in relation to validity. Too much experience will result in a "supersaturated inquiry" or too much reflection can result in "intellectual excess". After each experience phase, Reason suggests three lines of thought for reflection: (1) the descriptive; (2) the evaluative; and (3) the practical. In the descriptive phase, the researcher describes "what went on", framing lucid descriptions. When evaluating, they are judging how sound and well-founded these descriptions are; that is, "how well they cohere with the recollected, presented content of the experience phase" (p. 49). The practical phase entails – in light of the description and evaluation – "what sort of content to explore in the next experience phase" (p. 50).

Streubert and Carpenter (1999, pp. 266–267) utilized five steps in the Action Research process. These steps include: (1) planning; (2) action; (3) evaluation; (4) reflection; and (5) conclusions, implications, and recommendations. Within each step are a number of stages the researcher must follow; these are identified below.

1. *Planning*

   - Describe the procedures for selecting participants;

   - Describe the extent of collaboration between researchers and participants during the analysis phase;

   - Describe strategies for data analysis;

   - Involve participants in the interpretation;

   - Description should reflect understanding of the educational situation;

   - Action planning;

   - Describe the planned change in detail;

   - Describe the change implementation methods;

   - Describe the method to evaluate the planned change;

   - All participants should be included in the action planning.

2. *Action*

  ■ Implement the change in the practice setting where the problem occurred;

  ■ Specify the implementation period.

3. *Reflection*

  ■ Specify methods for facilitating reflection;

  ■ Describe the results of reflection.

4. *Evaluation*

  ■ Describe the strategies for evaluating the change;

  ■ Evaluate the process for implementing the change and the outcomes of the change;

  ■ Evaluate the data evaluation methods for appropriateness to factors evaluated;

  ■ Include participants in the evaluation;

  ■ Address the validity and reliability of quantitative findings and the trustworthiness of qualitative findings.

5. *Conclusions, implications, and recommendations*

  ■ Conclusions must reflect the findings;

  ■ Formulate theory from the findings;

  ■ Describe findings in sufficient detail;

  ■ Discuss ethical and moral implications;

  ■ Include recommendations for research, education, and practice;

  ■ Describe the benefits participants gain from the study.

An alternative cyclic model of Action Research is provided by Dick (2000) who prefers the simple approach of: (1) action; (2) critical reflection; (3) action; and (4) critical reflection. For Dick, these are the essential features of Action Research. The reflection consists of a review of what has happened so far and deliberate planning for what will be done next. These cycles occur over a variety of time spans, ranging from entire programmes and beyond, down to moment-by-moment action. Dick emphasizes that there are cycles within cycles within cycles.

   While the full range of Action Research models cannot be discussed in detail here, those developed by Lewin (1948), Greenwood and Levin (1998), and

Gummesson (2000) will be touched on. Lewin's original Action Research model consisted of the steps of planning, fact-finding, and execution (Lewin, 1946, 1952). One feature of the Lewinian approach is that the participants under investigation are to be involved in every stage of the Action Research cycle (Kemmis, 1988). Greenwood and Levin (1998) highlight the diversity and complexity of the intellectual and political streams that feed into the different Action Research models and the different approaches to practice. They emphasize that there is no one right way to do Action Research and claim that what defines Action Research is the combination of research, action and democratization rather than adherence to a particular methodology (Greenwood & Levin, 1998). They observe that Action Research has five core characteristics: First, Action Research is context bound and addresses real-life problems. Second, Action Research is inquiry where participants and researchers co-generate knowledge through collaborative communicative processes in which all participants' contributions are taken seriously. Third, Action Research treats the diversity of experience and capacities within the local group as an opportunity for the enrichment of the research-action process. Fourth, the meanings constructed in the inquiry process lead to social action and reflections on action lead to the construction of new meanings. Finally, the credibility validity of Action Research knowledge is measured according to whether actions that arise from it solve problems and increase participants' control over their situation.

Greenwood and Levin (1998) and Gummesson (2000) share similar views regarding the aims and values of Action Research. Gummesson prefers to use the term "action science" (Argyris, 1985), recognizing that the term "Action Research" has been inappropriately used at times to describe activities that do not demonstrate the core components of Action Research. Gummesson is one of the few authors who refers to Action Research as being the most demanding and far-reaching method of doing case study research. He suggests that action science always involves two goals: (1) (to solve a problem for the participants; and (2) to contribute to science. During an action science project, those involved should learn from each other and develop their competencies. Gummesson notes that action science requires co-operation between the researcher and the client personnel, feedback to the parties involved, and continuous adjustment to new information and new events. Another characteristic of action science, according to Gummesson is that it is primarily applicable to the understanding and planning of change in social systems. He also maintains that there must be a mutually acceptable ethical framework within which action science is used.

REFLECTIVE PRACTICE AND ACTION RESEARCH

Action Research models mentioned in the previous section include reflection as a step in the process. Reflective practice has developed as a specialty area of its own with its own body of knowledge and is not always associated with

Action Research. Coghlan and Coghlan (2002) claims that it is the dynamics of the reflection cycle in Action Research that incorporates the learning process and enables Action Research to be more than everyday problem solving. The goal of reflection in Action Research is to create the possibility of new action, now informed by these insights and potentially transformed by the questioning of one's own assumptions and intentions (Watkins, 2000). The stage of critical reflection in Action Research focuses on both the outcomes and process (Swepson, 1995). The reflection looks for both confirming and disconfirming evidence (Dick, 1999; Swepson, 1995) and for agreements and disagreements that need to be tested and explained. Dick (2000) suggests that critical reflection underpins both action and understanding in Action Research by asking "what" questions and "why" questions. He comments that critical reflection that follows action and precedes planning identifies what has been learned from prior actions and can reinforce understanding.

Research brief

Title: Embedding experiential learning in HE sport coaching courses: An action research study
Author: Croning, C.J., *Liverpool John Moores University* & Lowes, J., *University of Cumbria* (2016)
Reference: Cronin, C.J., & Lowes, J. (2016). Embedding experiential learning in HE sport coaching courses: An action research study. *Journal of Hospitality, Leisure, Sport & Tourism Education, 18*, 1–8.
The paper analysed the integration of experiential learning within a UK Higher Education Institution (HEI) context. Sport coaches were provided with coaching opportunities with local school-children. Data were collected over three years through student interviews, coach educator reflections, and discussions with a critical friend. From this action research project, experiential learning presented two key challenges; (1) dealing with difficult emotions and competence awareness by students and the coach educator and (2) ensuring children received appropriate coaching practice.

MANAGING THE PRACTICAL NATURE OF THE RESEARCH PROCESS

In most practical terms, efforts have been made to define the practical elements required in the undertaking of the Action Research process. Kemmis and McTaggart (1988) list a range of "principles of procedure" that have strong ethical components; these include:

- Observing protocol;

- Involving participants;

- Negotiating with those affected;

- Reporting progress;

- Obtaining explicit authorization before observation starts;

- Obtaining explicit authorization before files or data are examined;

- Negotiating descriptions and others' point of view;

- Obtaining explicit authorization before using quotations;

- Negotiating reports for various levels of publication;

- Accepting responsibility for maintaining confidentiality;

- Assuming authorization has been gained, retain the right to report your work;

- Making your principles of procedures binding and known (pp. 106–108).

They also offer a range of observations in getting started in Action Research, including:

- Participate yourself in the Action Research process;

- Get organized when initiating the process;

- Be content to start small;

- Articulate the main theme and establish agreement around it;

- Establish a time-line that sets the time period for the work;

- Arrange for supportive work-in-progress discussions;

- Be tolerant and supportive of all involved;

- Be persistent about recording and monitoring;

- Plan for the longer haul in bigger issues of change;

- Register progress;

- Write up throughout the project;

- Be explicit about all progress made.

THE ROLE OF THE RESEARCHER IN ACTION RESEARCH

According to Webb (1990), traditional approaches to research involve "smash and grab" – the researcher enters a situation, grabs the required data, and leaves again. The Action Researcher attempts to work with participants on an equal basis. Action Researchers act as facilitators and are integral to the process. The participant status of the researcher is acknowledged in Action Research and is treated as a resource for the process. Action Researchers achieve a balance of critique and support through a variety of actions, including direct feedback, written reflections, pointing to comparable cases, and citing cases from the professional literature where similar problems, opportunities or processes have occurred. The Action Researcher needs to open up lines of discussion and be able to make evident the tacit knowledge that guides the local conduct.

Gronhaug and Olson (1999) observe that there are several challenges faced by Action Researchers. They must be able to make adequate observations and select and make use of other available data; interpret and make sense of the observations, which requires conceptualization and theory-building skills; plan and execute actions; and plan, collect, analyse, and interpret data to examine the outcome of the action. This shows that Action Research presumes important skills regarding observing and interviewing (and other data collection techniques), adequate theoretical knowledge that allows for observation and interpretation, creativity and ability to construct explanations, and methodological skills to examine outcomes of proposed action.

The types of roles that researchers take in their settings are a function of four factors (Adler & Adler, 1987). First, the conditions inherent in the setting that may affect the researcher's obtaining and maintaining access to the research setting. For example, if conducting Action Research on fair athlete recruiting practices in the NCAA, the researcher may need access to private information on scouting at several institutions; and, if any foul play was occurring then that information might be even more difficult to access. Second, the researcher's abilities, identities, theoretical orientations, demographics, and other personal factors can influence the research process. This includes the researcher's prior knowledge of the group members and degree of comfort with the people. Third, field researchers' roles may be affected by changes in the setting itself during the research period, including changes to group membership. Finally, researchers may undergo changes within themselves and therefore seek out new ways of collecting data (Adler & Adler, 1987).

ADDRESSING BIAS IN ACTION RESEARCH

Action Research is concerned with working toward practical outcomes, and also about developing new types of understanding, since action without reflection and some understanding is blind, just as theory without action can be considered meaningless (Reason & Bradbury, 2001). As part of the search for practical knowledge, Action Research involves working with people in their everyday lives (Reason & Bradbury, 2006). In Action Research, the researcher's values become manifested in how the research is carried out and reflected upon, as well as the actions taken. Values inspire and provide the reasons for the research, as well as its purposes. They also act as the basis for the researcher's conceptual frameworks (McNiff & Whitehead, 2006). In such a context, it can be seen how an

Action Researcher becomes immersed in the research and therefore bias from the researcher is inevitable. The researcher is an "insider" within the organisation that is a member of the collaboration that is the unit of analysis. It is therefore necessary to address how the researcher's bias will be dealt with in the research. The researcher acknowledges that there is present a perspective from their own unique experiences and it will therefore be necessary to articulate these perspectives or biases and build a critical reflexivity into the Action Research cycle.

VARIETIES OF ACTION RESEARCH

Organizational change

There is a longstanding tradition of Action Research in organizational settings that aims to contribute both to more effective work practices and better understanding of the processes of organizational change. This approach draws on a variety of forms of information gathering and feedback to organization members, leading to problem solving dialogue. This tradition is well represented in recent publications, such as Toulmin and Gustavsen (1996), Greenwood and Levin (1998), and Coghlan and Brannick (2001).

Co-operative inquiry

A co-operative inquiry group consists of people who share a common concern for developing understanding and practice in a specific personal, professional or social arena. All are both co-researchers, whose thinking and decision-making contributes to generating ideas, designing and managing the project, and drawing conclusions from the experience; and also co-participants, participating in the activity which is being researched. Co-operative inquiry groups cycle between and integrate four forms of knowing: (1) experiential: (2) presentational; (3) propositional; and (4) practical (Heron, 1996; Heron & Reason, 2001).

Action science and action inquiry

These related disciplines offer methods for inquiring into and developing congruence between our purposes, our theories and frames, our behaviour, and our impact in the world – to put it colloquially, they ask us "do we 'walk our talk'?". These practices can be applied at individual, small group, and organizational level. Their overall aim is to bring inquiry and action together in more and more moments of everyday life, to see inquiry as a "way of life" (Friedman, 2001; Marshall, 2001; Torbert, 2001).

Learning history

It is a process of recording the lived experience of those in an Action Research or learning situation. Researchers work collaboratively with those involved to agree the scope and focus of the history, identify key questions, gather information through an iterative reflective interview process, distil this information into a form which the organization or community can "hear", and facilitate dialogue with organization members to explore the accuracy, implications, and practical outcomes that the work suggests (Roth & Kleiner, 1998).

Appreciative inquiry

Practitioners of appreciative inquiry argue the extent that Action Research maintains a problem-oriented view of the world diminishes peoples' capacity to produce innovative theory capable of inspiring the imagination, commitment, and passionate dialogue required for the consensual re-ordering of social conduct. Devoting attention to what is positive about organizations and communities, enables us to understand what gives them life and how we might sustain and enhance that life-giving potential. Appreciative inquiry begins with the "unconditional positive question" that guides inquiry agendas and focuses attention toward the most life-giving, life-sustaining aspects of organizational existence (Ludema, Cooperrider, & Barrett, 2001).

Whole systems inquiry

Large group interventions or processes are events designed to engage representatives of an entire system, whether it be an organization or a community, in thinking through and planning change (for descriptions see Bunker and Alban, 1997). What distinguishes them is that the process is managed to allow all participants an opportunity to engage actively in the planning (Martin, 2001). Rather than aim at a single outcome, in dialogue conference design (Gustavsen, 2001) and whole system designs (Pratt, Gordon, & Plamping, 1999), the role of the researchers is to create the conditions for democratic dialogue among participants.

TYPES OF ACTION RESEARCH

There are a number of Action Research approaches available; however, there are two main ones that are applicable to sport management research. These are EAR and PAR.

Emancipatory action research

Lather (1991) and Smith (1993) both contend that Action Research should be an attempt to translate critical thought into emancipatory action. To accomplish this, they suggest that Action Research needs to be deliberately interventionist, and not compromise this intervention by strictly adhering to a prescribed approach. Smith recognizes these two alternative directions that critical educational theory may follow. The first direction encompasses the aim of empowerment through utilizing research methods such as critical ethnography, policy analysis, and text analysis (Smith, 1993, p. 84). The second direction includes approaches that encompass the notions of participation, but also includes and makes explicit the commitment to action. Smith terms this "Emancipatory Action Research" to differentiate it from Participatory Action Research. EAR therefore seeks to empower participants in identifying problems and making them explicit by raising their collective consciousness.

An objective of emancipatory research is therefore to enable the researcher and researched to work collaboratively in relation to the design, direction and conduct of the research (Kemmis & McTaggart, 1988). According to McTaggart (1991), EAR could be defined in two ways: first, as "involving a group of practitioners accepting responsibility for its "own emancipation" from the dictates of irrationality, injustice, alienation, and unfulfillment'; and second, as "the activity of a self-leading group aimed at developing new practices and/or changing the constraints with a shared radical consciousness" (p. 30). Moreover, MacTaggart suggests EAR extends beyond the interpretation of meanings for participants to an understanding of the social, political, and economic conditions, which allow meanings to be as they are. In terms of knowledge and human interests, EAR is clearly aimed at criticism and liberation through a process of critical reflection. The human interest served by such practices is that of "collective emancipation" (p. 30).

Carr and Kemmis (1986) suggest the main points of EAR of equal importance, these include:

- Bridging the gap between theory and practice.

- The epistemological understanding that the practitioners possess valid knowledge.

- Participation and equality of those involved within the situation.

- Practitioners critically reflecting on their own practices.

- The empowerment of the practitioners.

- Democratically chosen actions are implemented.

- Communication, which implies dialogues between participants.

- A cyclic process of planning, action, observation, and reflection (p. 17).

The methodology is selected and employed by the practitioners themselves, implying it is situation specific. Accordingly, EAR is more than simple radical critique – it demands action.

Participatory action research

PAR is research in which there is collaboration between the study participants and the researcher in all steps of the study, these include: (1) determining the problem; (2) the research methods to use; (3) the analysis of data; and (4) how the study results will be used. The participants and the researcher are co-researchers throughout the entire research study. Early developments in PAR transpired in the 1950s in America; however, it was not really taken seriously until the 1980s. The purpose of PAR is to minimize power differences between researchers and constituents, increase the knowledge of participants and promote social change. PAR is associated with two aspects of learning theory: Kurt Lewin's (1951) Action Research principles (knowledge flows from taking action) as well as the work of Paulo Freire (Pedagogy of the Oppressed, 1970) in which he described a process of education for marginalized groups that involved mutual learning among teachers and students. The basic assumption of these approaches is that academic research should be used to reduce the harmful effects of oppression by involving members of powerless groups in the construction of knowledge, a critical examination of the world around them, and action to address social problems (Stringer, 1999). PAR also draws upon social constructionism and the work of postmodern theorists such as Michel Foucault who maintain that scientific knowledge often has little relevance in people's everyday lives, but instead serves to maintain existing institutional arrangements that limit power to members of economic, social, and political elites (Rodwell, 1998).

PAR is participatory in that it expects and encourages the researcher and research participants to collaboratively engage in a strong degree of involvement and participation in the research process. It also questions the inequalities that are produced and maintained by the unequal power relations in our society (Pierce, 1995). In recognizing itself as a way to improve the social situation through intellectual effort (Popkewitz, 1984), the research approach therefore needs to be openly and explicitly committed to a more just social order and attempt to critique and question the status quo (Lather, 1986).

Smith (1997) describes a PAR model in which an external researcher/facilitator uses a five-stage process for goal attainment:

1. The researcher collects information about the community and its problems.

2. The researcher uses dialogue to engage the group in a process of problem identification.

3. Group members develop an understanding of the social, economic, and political context or origins of the problem. They identify questions that they want answered.

4. The group identifies theories about problem origins, designs data collection methods, and generates possible solutions to address the problem.

5. The group takes action.

CRITICISMS OF ACTION RESEARCH

Although we have noted that one of the key criticisms of Action Research is the lack of consistent approaches, it is important to address some of the other criticisms of Action Research. Badger (2000) identifies that Action Research is limited in its effectiveness as a strategy to manage change because of the lack of methodological rigour in this research method. She points to the fact that Action Research is not generalizable, and is basically a reflective, quality improvement strategy rather than research. There are also criticisms because each unique setting or organization requires a unique research method utilizing the researchers interpersonal and communication skills rather than a strict operationalized format (Badger, 2000). Issues of reliability and validity are also raised by Badger. Action Research depends upon congruence of others' interpretations with that of the researcher to protect against bias and error. Bellman (2003) discusses this issue and also the debate about whether or not Action Research is scientific. She concludes that the most important aspect of validity in Action Research is "catalytic validity" (Lather, 1991 cited in Bellman, 2003). According to Bellman, this "points to the degree to which research moves those it studies to understand the world and the way it is shaped in order to transform it" (p. 28). Other common criticisms are outlined in Table 9.4.

CREDIBILITY AND RIGOUR IN ACTION RESEARCH

Greenwood and Levin (1998) define credibility in Action Research as the arguments and the processes necessary for having someone trust the research results. One type of credibility is when knowledge generated by a group is credible to that group. This is fundamentally important to Action Research because of the

Table 9.4 Criticisms of action research
■ No external or internal validity
■ Findings are context specific
■ Lack of impartiality by researchers and dual role of researcher/participant
■ Difficult to publish Action Research results
■ Tendency for inexperienced researchers to focus entirely on planning, acting and observing phases and less upon theorizing
■ Ethical responsibilities to other participants
■ Length of projects – ongoing and evolutionary
■ As Action Research has become an accepted and legitimate methodology, its potential for action may be diluted by applying processes, structures, stages and so forth
■ Action Research that is non-participatory and non-interventionist is unable to measure up to its political, empowering or emancipatory purposes

collaborative nature of the research process. Another type is external credibility which means knowledge capable of convincing someone who did not participate in the inquiry that the results are believable. Credibility is established through prolonged engagement, persistent observation, triangulation, diverse case analysis, participant debriefing, referential adequacy, and member checking.

Stringer and Genat (2004) argue that credibility of an Action Research project may be further enhanced by the participation of stakeholders. Engaging sport managers as participants in the research minimizes the impact of the likelihood that the researcher will interpret events through their own interpretive framework. Bray, Lee, Smith, and Yorks (2000) report on the merits of participative inquiry as a means of establishing validity, in which participants collaborate (work together), cooperate (accommodate each other), and actively engage in a process of inquiry to answer questions of importance to them.

Rigour in Action Research refers to how data are generated, gathered, explored and evaluated, and how events are questioned and interpreted through multiple Action Research cycles. According to Coghlan and Brannick (2001), the Action Researcher needs to show four things in order to demonstrate rigour: first, how the researcher engaged in the steps of multiple Action Research cycles and how these were recorded to reflect that they are a true representation of what was studied; second, how the researcher challenged and tested his or her own assumptions and interpretations of what was happening continuously through the project, by means of content, process, and premise reflection; third, how the researcher accessed different views of what was happening, which may have produced confirming and contradictory interpretations; and fourth, how the researcher's interpretations and diagnoses are grounded in scholarly theory and rigorously applied.

This perspective is supported by Dick (2000) who also acknowledges that it is the balance between critical reflection and flexibility that allows adequate rigour in Action Research to be achieved. Dick emphasizes that the most important source of rigour in research, including Action Research, is the vigorous and continuous search for disconfirming evidence. If an Action Research project is attempting to shift physical activity programme from a competitive sport platform to a theoretically "ideal" participatory fitness platform, then the researchers (including the participants) should actively seek evidence that supports the competitive platform as ideal. Dick explains that there are several features of Action Research that allow it to pursue rigorous understanding. First, there is the involvement of all interested parties to provide more information about a situation. The information in the physical activity programme study might come from health professional, members of the public, physical education educators, policy makers and academics, and no group should be treated with less regard than another. Second, the critical reflection in each cycle provides many chances to correct errors, especially when there are cycles within cycles. It should occur after initial interviews and conversations with each group, during and after test cycles of both competitive sport and participatory fitness platforms, and as a whole during the analysis of those tests. Third, within each cycle the assumptions underlying the plans are tested in action, which adds to the achievement of rigour. These cycles allow further opportunities to seek out disconfirming evidence. Dick (2014) summarizes by stating that:

> with access to these sources of rigor, Action Research is not a second-best methodology to be used when other methods don't suit. It is a rigorous alternative in its own right, better for some applications, worse for others. (p. 55)

Reason and Bradbury (2001) have identified five choice points for assessing the rigour of an Action Research. They are:

1. Relationship: The Action Research should be explicit in developing a praxis of relational participation; that is whether the Action Research group is set up to ensure maximum participation, whether best decisions are those that ensure maximum participation, and whether less powerful people are helped by their participation in the inquiry.

2. Practical outcome: The Action Research should be guided by reflexive concern for practical outcomes. That is, the research is validated by participants' new way of acting in light of the work. At the end the participants should be able to say, "That was useful. I am able to use what I have learned".

3. Extended ways of knowing: The Action Research should be inclusive of a plurality of knowing. That is:

   - The Action Research should ensure conceptual–theoretical integrity. A well-written Action Research study should be such that it can be used by fellow inquirers with similar concern to "see as if" and illuminate their own situation.

   - It should embrace ways of knowing beyond the intellect, that is, artful ways of expression such as song and dance, video, poetry, and photography.

   - The Action Research should intentionally choose appropriate research methods. The choice of methods should be ecologically sensitive to the context in which it is being used.

   - Pay attention to what is worthy of attention: How do we decide where to put our effort?

4. At the heart of this process is to always ask the question "What values do we hold vis-à-vis the value of work with which we engage?" Reason and Bradbury (2001) believe that:

   > Since the AR community is committed to bring an attitude of inquiry towards questions of fundamental importance, we would do well to find ways to address the question of what purposes are

*worthy of more direct attention. It is worthwhile to articulate pos-
itive, life enhancing qualities in a situation and to amplify these
than to seek problems and try to solve them. It is thus better to
ask appreciative questions than critical questions. The emphasis
should be to ask the right research questions so that we are con-
vening a process that will generate the outcome we want. (p. 453)*

5. Enduring consequences: The Action Research should emerge towards a
new and enduring infrastructure. This means that the dyadic, small group
micro engagement of people should manifest into an ongoing new pattern-
ing of behaviour at a macro level even after the Action Researchers have
left the scene (Reason & Bradbury, 2001). It should be noted however that
Reason and Bradbury acknowledge that a given Action Research project
cannot address all these points.

VALIDITY OF ACTION RESEARCH METHODS

Researchers have identified a number of assumptions underlying the term "validity". Denzin and Lincoln (1998) cited in Stringer and Genat (2004) interpret validity in Action Research as, "a text's call to authority and truth" (p. 49). Waterman,
Tillen, Dickson, and de Konig (2001) further suggest that Action Research needs
to be judged according to its own terms: participatory work, aimed at change,
and movement between reflection, action, and evaluation. Badger (2000) claims
that Action Research is not amenable to critique by the strategies used for other
methodologies. He explains that "the design of Action Research is led by the
research problem rather than the requirements of a particular methodology, and
may be affected by the dynamics of the situation itself" (p. 201).

Action Research seeks to construct an understanding of a dynamic, complex social world, situation or agency and, being essentially qualitative and
naturalistic, it reveals subjective experiences of the participants and how they
assess meaning in their world or situation. Taking a set of criteria proposed by
Lincoln and Guba (1985) and Stringer and Genat (2004), they suggest validity is
demonstrated through trustworthiness and is established by attaining *credibility, transferability, dependability, and confirmability*. Stringer and Genat view
validity as a question of quality and address issues of validity when they say:

*the truths emerging from naturalistic inquiry are always contingent (i.e.
they are 'true' only for the people, the time and setting of that particular
study). We are not looking for 'the Truth' or 'the causes', but 'truths-in-
context'. (p. 49)*

They go on to explain that there are no objective measures of validity, so the
underlying issue is trustworthiness, "the extent to which we can trust the
truthfulness or adequacy of a research project" (p. 50).

Table 9.5	Methods for determining levels of validity of action research findings

Methods for determining levels of validity of action research findings

- Action Research uses different measures of validity and reliability than other forms of research.

- Action Research values responsiveness over replicability meaning that credibility, validity, and reliability in Action Research are measured by the willingness of local stakeholders to act on the results of the Action Research.

- Documentation of an Action Research undertaking takes the form of a case study, and thus becomes a resource that other organisations can learn from and apply in their own contexts.

Coghlan and Brannick (2001, p. 10) have said that Action Research is evaluated within its own frame of reference and that questions of reliability, replicability, and universality do not pertain to the Action Research approach. For them, an Action Researcher should be able to answer three questions:

1. What happened? The relating of a good story.

2. How do you make sense of what happened? This involves rigorous reflection on that story.

3. So what? This most challenging question deals with the extrapolation of usable knowledge or theory from the reflection on the story.

Table 9.5 identifies how the Action Researcher determines the level of validity in their findings.

Waterman (1998) suggests three types of validity critique in Action Research; *"dialectical, critical, and reflexive validity"* (p. 101). Waterman discusses the tensions between practice, theory and research in Action Research as *dialectical validity*. She notes that there are often tensions that arise when moving from theory to practice and the seemingly simplistic models of Action Research belie the complexity of practice/research settings. She also acknowledges that synthesis of findings from various perspectives can be obtained over a period of time and even subconsciously. She recommends that the complexities of the research situation/context be revealed to aid the understanding of tensions between practice, theory and research. *Critical validity* is associated with the "moral responsibilities" of the Action Research researcher. Waterman suggests that given the emancipatory element associated with Action Research there is an ethos that is geared towards "improving the justice of people's situations" (p. 103). Moreover, she suggests that:

> *The validity of an action research project ought not be judged by its ability to effect change; the degree of change is not the measure of its validity....sometimes the only moral way to act may be not to act. (p. 103)*

Reflexive validity is achieved by the researcher reflecting on what was found in the research study. Waterman suggests that Action researchers need to be reflexive about how they create and construct their reports, considering how they frame their work and how this led to their interpretations.

ETHICAL ISSUES IN ACTION RESEARCH

Three major positions can be detected on the ethics of Action Research: First, there is a perception that it raises no additional or different ethical challenges to those raised by traditional research; Waterman Webb, and Williamson (1995), for example, suggests that the same ethical principles apply (i.e. respect for participants, prevention of harm, assurance of confidentiality or anonymity, and maintenance of privacy). In such circumstances, Action Research is not ethical per se and it would be possible to have ethical traditional research and unethical Action Research. Second, as a product of its inclusive and emancipatory nature, there is an implicit assumption within some elements of the Action Research literature that it is either in itself more ethical or more cautiously is undertaken on stronger ethical grounds than other less participatory forms of research (Williams, 1995). Within this context, a number of writers have proposed a range of rather idealistic and aspirational ethical guidelines, for example, Winter (1996) proposes the principles that Action Research should aspire toward including a situation of "transparency" where all participants should be involved in the formulation of a consensus on the nature of the research problem, the choice of methods, and subsequent data analysis. McNiff, Lomax, and Whitehead (1996) identify "keeping good faith" as an ethical talisman and list various steps that would be involved in an "ethical" Action Research project, including: "negotiating access sensitively and honestly; promising confidentiality of information, identity and data; ensuring the right to withdraw; and keeping all informed at regular points in the work" (p. 24). Third, beyond these aspirations, on the basis that by its nature Action Research is bound to encounter ethical issues, many have begun to provide a more thorough analysis of the ethical implications of activities associated with Action Research (Balogh & Beattie, 1987). Fundamentally, contrary to the perception promoted above of an unproblematic relationship, Lincoln (2001) contends there has been to this point, little specific ethical guidance for Action Researchers and more significantly, she suggests that the complexity of this type of work raises ethical concerns not encountered in "conventional" research work; in other words, a contrary view to that which suggests that Action Research is implicitly ethical.

Kemmis and McTaggart (1988) list a range of "principles of procedure" that have strong ethical components; these include the following:

■ Observing protocol.

■ Involving participants.

- Negotiating with those affected.

- Reporting progress.

- Obtaining explicit authorization before observation starts.

- Obtaining explicit authorization before files or data are examined.

- Negotiating descriptions and others' point of view.

- Obtaining explicit authorization before using quotations.

- Negotiating reports for various levels of publication.

- Accepting responsibility for maintaining confidentiality.

- Assuming authorization has been gained, retain the right to report your work.

- Making your principles of procedures binding and known (pp. 106–108).

APPLICATION OF ACTION RESEARCH IN SPORT MANAGEMENT

Action Research is based on the premise that other types of research that are based on empirical positivism are, by design, outside of the process. For example, to be able to understand the workings of a sport organisation and to initiate change based on evaluation, research has to be done inside the sports. This requires participation on the part of the internal and external stakeholders themselves. This method encourages involvement and buy-in by those most affected by potential system changes. With the researcher being a part of the social reality being studied, interpretations are subjective but can be confirmed by other participants (Zuber-Skerritt, 1992). From this perspective the sport management practitioners not only pose the research questions but search for and try out their own answers to those questions. Because the research is practitioner driven, it promotes the development of professionals and the body of knowledge on which they base their actions. In today's rapidly changing and dynamic sport management environment, it is important that sport managers study their own practice and construct the new knowledge needed to answer their current questions and solve their own problems.

The notion of conducting Action Research within sport management organizations could be considered to be mutually antagonistic in many ways (McTaggart & Garbutcheon-Singh, 1988). Institutional practices and the values of the organisation can be questioned during the implementation of Action Research, and resistance can be expected. Although evidence-based practice requires sport management practitioners to think about practice in a constructively critical manner, reviewing the best evidence to inform the process of change, changes brought about by conducting Action Research can be problematic for the sport organisation and cause loss of credibility to those undertaking Action Research if they are seen to be radical. As such, the co-participation and co-construction of knowledge needs to be evident in the development of the research questions, the building of trust, the collecting and analysing of data, and communicating the results for action. If these practices are transparent, Action Research approaches to sport management research can be mutually beneficial.

Research brief

Title: Preparing Maltese Football Players for Migratory Based Transitions
A thesis submitted in partial fulfilment of the requirements of Liverpool John Moores University for the degree of Doctor in Philosophy May 2017
Author: Muscat, A., *Liverpool John Moores University* (2017)
Reference: Muscat, A. (2017). Preparing Maltese Football Players for migratory based transitions. *A thesis submitted in partial fulfilment of the requirements of Liverpool John Moores University for the degree of Doctor in Philosophy May 2017.* The thesis outlined a collaborative research project that was undertaken between the Malta Football Association (MFA), the Malta National Sports School (NSS), and Liverpool John Moores University (LJMU). Drawing on transition frameworks, models, and contemporary literature, the research adopted an action research methodology to examine the psycho-social and cultural challenges that young Maltese football players and parents experienced within migratory-based transitions. The author adopted the role of practitioner researcher to understand, plan, and support a range of key stakeholders during the transition process. Specifically, Study One (Reconnaissance Phase) examined the challenges experienced by Maltese footballers that had migrated to European professional football. Individual semi-structured interviews were conducted with 12 male Maltese players who had experienced migration to a foreign club. Results evidenced that players experienced homesickness and lacked psycho-social knowledge and skills for an effective transition. Players also experienced culturally based challenges. The findings are framed around a unique and deeply embedded Maltese cultural identity. Study Two (Reconnaissance Phase) utilised a focus group methodology with parents of players from the MFA Academy, parents of young players that had previously experienced migration, head coaches from top Maltese nurseries, and coaches from the NSS and MFA. Findings of Study One were disseminated to facilitate reflection, discussion, and to identify issues that required consideration in order to better prepare young players for future migratory-based transition. Study Three (Action Planning) used focus groups to disseminate the findings of Study One and Two with the Headmaster of the NSS, and parent representatives of the school. A number of change strategies were developed to improve the school's programme of preparation for students who may migrate to foreign clubs. A separate action meeting was conducted with the Technical Director of the MFA to discuss and highlight change strategies to improve the MFA's programme of preparation for young footballers seeking a career abroad in professional football. The Implementation and Monitoring phases focused on applying the action strategies agreed. These were: (i) to experience migration and independent living, (ii) psycho-social and cultural support and development of young players, and (iii) parental education. Regular evaluation of change strategy activities evidenced positive change and also continued to enhance the efficacy of the strategies being implemented. Young players who have migrated overseas over the past year and who had engaged in a programme of preparation prior to migration have coped well with the challenges they have so far faced.

CONCLUSION

Conducting Action Research within a sport management organisation can be seen as problematic in relation to issues around conflict of interest, the positioning of the researcher in relation to membership of the organisation, issues of credibility, rigour and validity, and ethical considerations. Despite this, there is evidence to suggest that Action Research, by dealing with the realities of practice, is more likely to represent the "truth" as compared to other research methods.

REVIEW AND RESEARCH QUESTIONS

With a general understanding of the emancipatory and participatory models of Action Research now:

1. Identify the steps in conducting an Action Research study.

2. Distinguish between EAR and PAR.

3. List three examples of how you believe action research approaches could be used in sport management settings. You must include an example of emancipatory and participatory approaches.

4. Explain why reflective practice is such an important component of action research?

REFERENCES

Adler, P. A., & Adler, P. (1987). *Membership roles in field research*. Thousand Oaks, CA: Sage Publications.

Argyris, C. (1985.) *Action science*. San Francisco, CA: Jossey-Bass.

Badger, T. G. (2000). Action research, change and methodological rigour. *Journal of Nursing Management, 8*, 201–207.

Balogh, R., & Beattie, A. (1987). *Performance indicators in nursing education*. London: University of London, Institute of Education.

Bate, P., Khan, R., & Pye, A. (2000). Towards a culturally sensitive approach to organization structuring: Where organization design meets organization development. *Organization Science, 11*(2), 197–211.

Bellman, L. (2003). *Nurse led change and development in clinical practice*. London: Whurr.

Benner, P. (Ed.) (1994). *Interpretive phenomenology: Embodiment, caring, and ethics in health and illness*. Thousand Oaks, CA: Sage Publications.

Brand, V. (2009). Empirical business ethics research and paradigm analysis. *Journal of Business Ethics, 86*, 429–449.

Bray, J., Lee, J., Smith, L. L., & Yorks, L. (2000). *Collaborative inquiry in practice: Action, reflection, and making meaning*. Thousand Oaks, CA: Sage Publications.

Bunker, B., & Alban, B. (1997). *Large group interventions: Engaging the whole system for rapid change*. San Francisco: Jossey-Bass.

Carr, W., & Kemmis, S. (1986). *Becoming critical: Education, knowledge and action research* (Rev. ed.). Geelong, Australia: Deakin University.

Catelli, L. A., & Carlino, J. (2001). Collaborative action research to assess student learning and effect change. *Academic Exchange Quarterly, 5*(1), 105–112.

Crotty, M. (1998). *The foundations of social research.* Sydney, Australia: Allen and Unwin.

Coghlan, D., & Brannick, T. (2001). *Doing action research in your own organisation.* London: Sage Publications.

Coghlan, P., & Coghlan, D. (2002). Action research for operations management. *International Journal of Operations & Production, 22* (2), 220–240.

Cunningham, J. B. (1993). *Action research and organizational development.* Westport, CT: Praeger.

Denzin, N. K. & Lincoln, Y. S. (1998). *Strategies of Qualitative Inquiry.* Thousand Oaks, CA: Sage Publications.

Dick, B. (1999). *Rigour without numbers: The potential of dialectical processes as qualitative research tools.* Brisbane: Interchange.

Dick, B. (2000). A beginner's guide to action research. Available at http://www.aral.com.au/resources/guide.html (Accessed 27 May 2020).

Dick, B. (2002). *Action research: Action and research (online).* Lismore, Australia: South Cross University.

Dick, B. (2014). Action research. In J. Mills, & M. Birks (Eds.), *Qualitative methodology: A practical guide,* pp. 51–65. London: Sage Publications.

French, W. L., & Bell Jr., C. H. (1990). *Organization development: Behavioral science interventions for organization improvement* (4th ed.). Englewood Cliffs, NJ: Prentice Hall.

Friedman, V. J. (2001). Action Science: Creating communities of inquiry in communities of practice. In P. Reason, & H. Bradbury (Eds.), *Handbook of action research: Participative inquiry and practice.* London: Sage Publications.

Gall, M. D., Borg, W. R., & Gall, J. P. (1996). *Educational research: An introduction.* New York: Longman.

Greenwood, D. J., & Levin, M. (1998). *Introduction to action research.* California: Sage Publications.

Grbich, C. (1999). *Qualitative research in health: An introduction.* London: Sage Publications.

Gronhaug, K., & Olson, O. (1999). Action research and knowledge creation: Merits and challenges. *Qualitative Market Research: An International Journal, 2*(1), 6–14.

Gummesson, E. (2000). *Qualitative methods in management research* (2nd ed.). Thousand Oaks, CA: Sage Publications.

Gustavsen, B. (2001). Theory and practice: The mediating discourse. In P. Reason & H. Bradbury (Eds.), *Handbook of action research: Participative inquiry and practice,* pp. 17–26. London: Sage Publications.

Habermas, J. (1972). *Knowledge and human interests.* London: Heinemann.

Heidegger, M. (1962). *Being and time.* New York: Harper & Row.

Heron, J. (1996). *Co-operative inquiry.* London: Sage Publications.

Heron, J. & Reason, P. (1997). *Qualitative inquiry.* London: Sage.

Heron, J. & Reason, P. (2001). The practice of co-operative inquiry: Research 'with' rather than 'on' people. In P. Reason, & H. Bradbury (Eds.), *Handbook of action research: Participative inquiry and practice,* pp. 179–188. London: Sage Publications.

Kemmis, S. (1988). *A study of the batchelor college remote area teacher education program: 1976–1988: Final Report.* Geelong, Victoria: Deakin Institute for Studies in Education.

Kemmis, S. (1995). Research and communicative action. Paper presented at the Invited Address: National Forum of the Innovative Project, Melbourne (May 26, 1995).

Kemmis, S., & Grundy, S. (1997). Educational action research in Australia: Organization and practice. In S. Hollingsworth (Ed.), *International action research: A casebook for educational reform*, pp. 40–48. London: Falmer Press.

Kemmis, S., & McTaggart, R. (1988). *The action research reader*. Geelong: Deakin University Press.

Lather, P. (1986). Issues of validity in openly ideological research: Between a rock and a soft place. *Interchange, 17*, 63–84.

Lather, P. (1991). Deconstructing/deconstructive inquiry: The politics of knowing and being known. *Educational Theory, 41*(2), 153–173.

Lewin, K. (1946). Action research and minority problems. *Journal of Social Issues, 2*(4), 33–46.

Lewin, K. (1948). *Resolving social conflicts*. New York: Harper & Row.

Lewin, K. (1951). *Field research in social sciences*. New York: Harper & Row.

Lewin, K. (1952). Group decision and social change. In G. E. Swanson, T. M. Newcomb, & E. L. Hartley (Eds.), *Readings in social psychology*, pp. 459–473. New York: Henry Holt.

Lincoln, Y. S. (2001). Engaging sympathies: Relationships between action research and social constructivism. In P. Reason, & H. Bradbury (Eds.), *Handbook of action research: Participative inquiry and practice*, pp. 124–132. Thousand Oaks, CA: Sage Publications.

Lincoln, Y. S., & Guba, E. G. (1985). *Naturalistic inquiry*. Beverley Hills, CA: Sage Publications.

Ludema, J. D., Cooperrider, D. L., & Barrett, F. J. (2001). Appreciative inquiry: The power of the unconditional positive question. In P. Reason, & H. Bradbury (Eds.), *Handbook of action research: Participative inquiry and practice*, pp. 189–199. London: Sage Publications.

Marshall, J. (2001). Self-reflective inquiry practices. In P. Reason, & H. Bradbury (Eds.), *Handbook of action research: Participative inquiry and practice*, pp. 433–439. London: Sage Publications.

Martin, A. (2001). Large group processes as action research. In P. Reason, & H. Bradbury (Eds.), *Handbook of action research: participative inquiry and practice*, pp. 200–208. London: Sage Publications.

Merleau-Ponty, M. (1962), *Phenomenology of perception* (C. Smith, Trans.). London: Routledge and Kegan-Paul.

McLean, J. E. (1995). *Improving education through action research*. Thousand Oaks, CA: Corwin Press.

McNiff, J., Lomax, P., & Whitehead, J. (1996). *You and your action research project*. London: Routledge.

McNiff, J., & Whitehead, J. (2006). *All you need to know about action research*. Thousand Oaks, CA: Sage Publications.

McTaggart, R. (1991). Principles for participatory action research. *Adult Education Quarterly, 41*(3), 168–87.

McTaggart, R., & Garbutcheon-Singh, M. (1988). Fourth generation action research: Notes on the 1986 Deakin Seminar. In S. Kemmis, & R. E. McTaggart (Eds.), *The action research reader*, pp. 409–428. Geelong: Deakin University Press.

Mir, R., & Watson, A. (2000). Strategic management and the philosophy of science: The case for a constructivist methodology. *Strategic Management Journal, 21*, 941–953.

Noffke, S. E., & Stevenson, R. B. (1995). *Educational action research: Becoming practically critical*. New York: Teachers College Press.

Pierce, J. (1995). Reflections of fieldwork in a complex organization. In R. Hertz, & J. Imber (Eds.), *Studying elites using qualitative methods*, pp. 94–110. Thousand Oaks, CA: Sage Publications.

Popkewitz, T. S. (1984). *Paradigm and ideology in educational research: The social functions of the intellectual.* Philadelphia, PA: The Falmer Press.

Pratt, J., Gordon, P., & Plamping, D. (1999). *Working whole systems: Putting theory into practice in organizations.* London: King's Fund.

Reason, P. (1990). *Human inquiry in action: Developments in new paradigm research* (2nd ed.). London: Sage Publications.

Reason, P., & Bradbury, H. E. (2001). *Handbook of action research: Participative inquiry and practice.* London: Sage Publications.

Reason, P., & Bradbury, H. (2006). *A handbook of action research: Participative inquiry and practice* (2nd ed.). Thousand Oaks, CA: Sage Publications.

Reid, L. (1997). Exploring the ways that dialogue journaling affects how and why students write: An action research project. *Teaching and Change, 5*(1), 50–57.

Rodwell, M. (1998). *Social work constructivist research.* New York: Garland.

Roth, G. L., & Kleiner, A. (1998). Developing organizational memory through learning histories. *Organizational Dynamics, 27*(2), 43–61.

Sartre, J. P. (1960). *Critique de la raison dialectique.* Paris: Éditions Gallimard.

Sartre, J. P. (1963). *Preface, in Frantz Fanon. The wretched of the earth* (C. Farrington, Trans.). New York: Grove Weidenfeld.

Schön, D. A. (1991). The theory of inquiry: Dewey's legacy to education. *Curriculum Inquiry, 22*(2), 119–139.

Schwandt, D. R. (1997) 'Integrating Strategy and Organisational Learning', In J. P. Walsh & A. S. Huff (Eds) *Advances in Strategic Management, Organisational Learning and Strategic Management, 14*(1) pp. 337–59, Greenwich, CT: JAI Press.

Smith, R. (1993). Potentials for empowerment in critical education research. *The Australian Educational Researcher, 20*(2), 75–93.

Smith, S. E. (1997). Deepening participatory action research. In S.E. Smith, D. G. Willms, & N. A. Johnson (Eds.), *Nurtured by knowledge: Learning to do participatory action research*, pp. 173–264. New York: Apex Press.

Stringer, E. (1999). *Action research* (2nd ed.). Thousand Oaks, CA: Sage Publications.

Stringer, E., & Genat, W. J. (2004). *Action research in health.* Columbus, Ohio: Person Prince Hall.

Streubert, H. J., & Carpenter, D. R. (1999). *Qualitative research in nursing: Advancing the humanistic imperative* (2nd ed.). Philadelphia, PA: Lippincott.

Swepson, P. (1995). *Action research: Understanding its philosophy can improve your practice.* Available at http://www.scu.edu.au/schools/ gcm/ar/arp/philos.html (Accessed 4 March 2008).

Torbert, W. R. (2001). The practice of action inquiry. In P. Reason, & H. Bradbury (Eds.), *Handbook of action research*, pp. 250–260. London: Sage Publications.

Toulmin, S., & Gustavsen, B. (1996). *Beyond theory: Changing organisation through participation.* Amsterdam: John Benjamins.

Waterman, H., Webb, C., & Williamson, A. (1995). Parallels and contradictions in the theory and practice of action research and nursing. *Journal of Advanced Nursing, 22*, 779–784.

Waterman, H. (1998). Embracing ambiguities and valuing ourselves: Issues of validity in action research. *Journal of Advanced Nursing, 28*, 101–105.

Waterman, H., Tillen, D., Dickson, R., & de Konig, K. (2001). Action research: A systematic review and guidance for assessment. *Health Technology Assessment, 5*(23), iii–157.

Watkins, K. E. (2000). Learning by changing: Action science and virtual organization development, *Adult Learning/Action Research,* 20–22.

Webb, C. (1990). Partners in research. *Nursing Times,* 86(32), 40–44.

Williams, A (1995) The relationship between ethnography and feminist research. *Nurse Research,* 2(3), 34–54.

Winter, R. (1996). Some principles and procedures for the conduct of action research. In O. Zuber-Skerritt (Ed.), *New directions in action research,* pp. 13–27. London: Falmer Press.

Zuber-Skerritt, O. (1992). *Action research in higher education: Examples and reflections.* London: Kogan Page.

CHAPTER 10

Deconstruction in sport management research

LEARNING OUTCOMES

By the end of this chapter, you should be able to:

- Understand the basic concepts of deconstruction.

- Identify some of the key strategies that are required to apply with deconstruction in sport management research.

KEY TERMS

1. **Deconstruction:** the attempt to take apart and expose the underlying meanings, biases, and preconceptions that structure the way a text conceptualises its relation to what it describes.

2. **Nihilism:** the belief that all values are baseless and that nothing can be known or communicated.

3. **Sign:** What is written.

4. **Signifier:** Is the visual mark, acoustic expression, or sound-image of the sign.

5. **Signified:** The concept of mental image associated with the sign.

6. **Canonical:** Conforming to well-established patterns or rules.

KEY THEMES

- What is deconstruction?

- Can deconstruction be used as a research methodology in sport management research?

- What are the implications for applying the process of deconstruction to sport management literature?

CHAPTER OVERVIEW

This chapter explores Jacques Derrida's strategy of deconstruction as a way of understanding and critiquing sport management theory and practice. Deconstruction looks primarily at existing literature as opposed to direct interaction with an organisation. Deconstruction seeks to locate and identify multiple interpretations within texts and to then dislocate the dominant discourse by examining the language and structure of the text – by what has been selected, and not selected, to create the structure.

WHAT IS DECONSTRUCTION?

According to Saukko (2003), deconstruction is a theoretical perspective, a methodology and a method. Deconstructionism is closely associated with the work of Jacques Derrida. Derrida's work demonstrates a constant critical interrogation of texts. As Denzin (1994) asserts, deconstruction "involves the attempt to take apart and expose the underlying meanings, biases, and preconceptions that structure the way a text conceptualises its relation to what it describes" (p. 185). Deconstruction is often associated with postmodernism. We argue that it is useful and relevant as a way of challenging the dominant paradigm of any discipline, including sport management.

Because deconstruction is notoriously difficult to define, we offer a number of examples of deconstruction in action. Deconstructionist features include: (1) *close reading of text* to demonstrate that any given text has irreconcilably contradictory meanings rather than a unified, logical whole; (2) the *aim* of deconstruction is *to criticise Western logic* but it arose as a response to *structuralism* and *formalism*; (3) seeing text as more radically *heterogeneous* than in a formalist way; (4) seeing works in terms of their *undesirability*; (5) regarding language as a *fundamentally unstable medium*; (6) the text is based only on *the author's intentions*; and (7) language and logic always being ruled by *hierarchical oppositions*.

In sport management, deconstruction can facilitate further scholarly discussion by challenging the legitimacy and validity of those precepts and ideas generally accepted within the sport management academic community to be irrefutable. Think about Western culture's generalisable assumptions about women as sport fans and compare that to men as sport fans. In practice and in academia, sport managers and/or sport management researchers often use these stereotypes when exploring fan affiliation. These inherent attitudes and assumptions can be isolated and inferred using deconstructionist methodologies.

DEFINING DECONSTRUCTION

One of the difficulties that many have with deconstruction is its unwillingness to be pinned down and precisely defined. We can see its elusive nature in Derrida's (1996) constant refusal to offer a definition: "Deconstruction doesn't consist in a set of theorems, axioms, tools, rules, techniques, methods ... There is no deconstruction, deconstruction has no specific object" (p. 218). Deconstruction challenges an author's attempt to privilege a theory, technique or model as a superior way to arrive at closure around knowledge. For example, deconstructing institutionalism (a common organisational change theory used in sport management research) may reveal major limitations with an author's attempt to explain a national sport organisation's response to change in board members, thus finding that institutionalism cannot explain the actions of the board to the extent the author argues. Thus, deconstruction particularly holds nothing sacred, seeks to question every assumption and presupposition offered under the rubric of "knowledge", and, most importantly, challenges any authority's claim to a "method" of knowledge production that is privileged over others.

THE DECONSTRUCTION METHOD

Deconstruction has often been presented and defended by its best proponents as neither a traditionally constituted philosophical system tending towards its own coherence and closure, nor an easily reproducible, stable method of inquiry or analysis (Wortham, 1998). Derrida himself refused to characterise deconstruction as a method, referring to it at different times as an "experience" or a "movement". It has in innate exploratory nature. The experience of deconstructing a text is to work through the structured genealogy of its concepts, to determine from a certain external perspective that it cannot name or describe what this history may have concealed or excluded, constituting itself as history through this repression in which it has a stake.

Deconstruction cannot be sought in an instruction manual. It is a method to be followed regardless of context, discourse, and purpose. Derrida's theoretical notions inform us of the broad purpose of deconstruction and of a general outline of its practice but there is no one way to "do" it. Derrida's writings supply some general rules, some procedures that can be transposed by analogy, but these rules are taken up in a text that is each time a unique element and that does not let itself be turned totally into a method. The experience of deconstructing a text is to "work through the structured genealogy of its concepts" to determine from a certain external perspective that it cannot name or describe what this history may have concealed or excluded, constituting itself as history through this repression in which it has a stake.

The goal of the deconstructor is to challenge the text's claims to coherence, neutrality, and objectivity. Then what can be perceived as deconstruction's methodology? Often in the literature that attempts to explain Derrida's approach it is described as a "disturbance", which we then conceptualise in our typical intellectual mind frame as though it were an experience of a movie, as in, "oh my, that was disturbing"! Deconstruction is not a compartmentalised disturbance that one leaves within the text. For part of what Derrida releases is the transcendental signifier which enables the limitless text. Deconstruction is the ultimate disturbance.

How are these ideas to be translated into action? It is not a method to be followed regardless of context, discourse and purpose. Derrida's theoretical notions inform us of the broad purpose of deconstruction and of a general outline of its practice but there is no one way to "do" it. Derrida's writings supply "some general rules, some procedures that can be transposed by analogy, but these rules are taken up in a text which is each time a unique element and which does not let itself be turned totally into a method". Each deconstructive inquiry is unique as reading is a mixed experience of the other in his or her singularity as well as philosophical content, information that can be torn out of this singular context.

The challenge of deconstruction is that it locates its understanding within a "language game" of textual analysis, and discovers multiple interpretations within texts (signifiers) which challenge meaning and identity. Deconstruction seeks to extrapolate signs and significations from a text which operate within written texts but conform to language as their regulated function (Derrida, 1976). In this language game, the text acts as a signifier in which language becomes a chain of significations and the author is seen as inscribed within the text. Basically, this implies that multiple interpretations of the text are valid, and in Derrida's terms, *"ll n'y a pos hors-texte"* (p. 158) – there is nothing outside the text.

By questioning the organising principles of canonical texts, Derrida aimed to place these principles in new relation to each other, suggesting the possibility that interpretations can be debated rather than suppressed. Thus, deconstruction is used not to abolish truth, but to question how these interpretations evolve from texts and how they are employed to systematically support categories of thought and communication. The implications of a deconstructive reading are therefore not limited to the language of the text itself but can be extended to the political and social context in which the text is placed. This allows the reader to understand the extent to which the objectivity and persuasiveness of the text is dependent on a series of strategic interpretations.

Though much has been referred to in recent years regarding deconstruction in postmodern research there is a noticeable scarcity of deconstruction strategies. Martin (1990, p. 355) provides a useful framework from which to begin the process of deconstruction:

- Dismantling a dichotomy, exposing it as a false distinction;

- Examining silences – what is not said;

- Attending to disruptions and contradictions, places where the text fails to make sense;

- Focusing on the element that is most alien to a text or a context as a means of deciphering implicit taboos – the limits to what is conceivable or permissible;

Table 10.1	Advantages and disadvantages of deconstruction

Advantages and disadvantages of deconstruction

Advantages	Disadvantages
■ Subverts the privileged position of positivist theory. ■ Holds theory intellectually accountable. ■ Makes clear the fact that knowledge production is always a political act. ■ Examines silences – what is not said.	■ Accusation of nihilism. ■ Derrida refuses to characterise deconstruction as a method. ■ Lack of definition. ■ Not a method of analysis.

- ■ Interpreting metaphors as a rich source of multiple meanings;

- ■ Analysing "double-entendres" that may point to an unconscious subtext, often sexual in content;

- ■ Separating group-specific and more general sources of bias by "reconstructing" the text with iterative substitution phrases;

- ■ Exploring, with careful "reconstructions" the unexpected ramifications and inherent limitations of minor policy changes;

- ■ Using the limitations exposed by "reconstruction" to explain the persistence of the status quo and the need for more ambitious change programmes.

As a method, however, it is not without its advantages and disadvantages. These are outlined in Table 10.1.

Research brief

Title: Troubling Dominance in Sport: Deconstructing Curling Culture(s) through Narrative Inquiry
Author: Norman, R., *University of Waterloo* (2020)
Reference: Norman, R. (2020). *Troubling Dominance in Sport: Deconstructing Curling Culture (s) through Narrative Inquiry. UWSpace.* http://hdl.handle.net/10012/15671
The purpose of this inquiry was to explore the role of dominant narratives in curling culture(s) as revealed through the experiences of its participants. Curling, with its deep history and colonial legacy offered a rich context to the author to explore how dominant narratives within a sport may continue to affect diversity and inclusion. The author further aimed to understand how dominant narratives may reinforce conditions limiting curling's ability to achieve a vision of a fully inclusive and truly diverse sport. The inquiry used semi-structured interviews to gather participant accounts that were analysed to detect tensions and stresses. The inquiry revealed that persistent questions of "race", lack of diversity, and of the possibility of decolonising curling's past continues to affect curling today.

THE IMPORTANCE OF DECONSTRUCTION IN SPORT MANAGEMENT RESEARCH

Our purpose of introducing deconstruction to sport management is twofold. First, we believe that in the practice of sport management, and theorising about that practice, deconstruction offers a pedagogy for the critical reading of texts. It tends to be assumed, once a text achieves a canonical status, that the business of commentary is to seek out coherence and intelligibility, to justify the text on its own argumentative terms. Deconstruction, of course, does exactly the opposite and calls into question the "coherence and intelligibility" of a text precisely on its own argumentative terms. Just because institutionalism is widely accepted in sport management, does it justly argue the points the sport management researcher has used it to argue?

Our second purpose is to subvert the privileged position of positivist theory as a theory of knowledge production. This influence is due to many factors; among them: (1) the unwillingness of some sport management scholars' to critically examine the political, ontological, metaphysical, and epistemological assumptions that underlie research; and (2) specific institutional arrangements for the production and dissemination of sport management knowledge that form a "market" for sport management research that is driven by factors beyond the intellectual competence of the research. Thus, sport management research is less expensive and less intellectually rigorous than it could be. Our dual purposes, then, are designed to hold positivist theory intellectually accountable and to make clear the fact that knowledge production is always a political act. We find deconstruction a useful praxis for these purposes. What deconstruction attempts to destroy is the claim of any rule-bound system of knowledge production to unequivocally dominate another, the attempt to close off the scholarly conversation by privileging one's own discourse over others.

Research brief

Title: Deconstructing comparative sport policy analysis: Assumptions, challenges, and new directions
Author: Dowling, M., *Anglia Ruskin University*, Brown, P., *Plymouth Marjon University*, Legg, D., *Mount Royal University*, & Grix, J., *Manchester Metropolitan University* (2018)
Reference: Dowling, M., Brown, P., Legg, D., & Grix, J. (2018). Deconstructing comparative sport policy analysis: assumptions, challenges, and new directions. *International Journal of Sport Policy and Politics*, 10(4), 687–704.

Despite progress within comparative sport policy analysis over the past two decades and advancements within the broader comparative sociology literature, comparative analysis within sport policy/management remains limited. Furthermore, there is a dearth of literature that explicitly addresses the philosophical, methodological, and practical challenges of comparing sporting nations. The authors therefore argued to address this shortcoming by developing a framework to interrogate the philosophical assumptions and methodological approaches of comparing sporting nations. In doing so, they reviewed the current state of comparative sport policy research and elaborated on the challenges and limitations of conducting comparative sport policy analysis. The authors further deconstructed the theory and method of comparative sport policy research by exploring its underlying assumptions and challenges. Ultimately, their broader intention was to reengage and reinvigorate scholarly debate surrounding the philosophical and methodological approaches of comparing sporting nations.

The authors' intention to conduct a comparative research project demanded them to consider the unit of analysis and the specifics of how this will be pursued. In the paper, they identified a number of common challenges and themes from the comparative sociology, management and sport policy literature. Based upon their assessment of the dominant approaches to comparing sporting nations, the first decision was deciding what data to measure. The second was then trying to ensure equivalence (including construct, sample, and function) among the nations being studied. The third was how to collect data and the fourth was how to present data once it has been collected. Overall, the paper concluded advancement of the comparative sport policy research can only occur through further questioning of the distinctive characteristics of comparative analysis.

CONCLUSION

By introducing deconstruction to sport management it is possible to subvert the pretensions of positive theory as a theory of knowledge production. Therefore, by supporting deconstruction it is possible to hold positive theory intellectually accountable and to make clear the fact that knowledge production is always shaped by political, ontological and epistemological assumptions. The challenge of deconstruction as a research approach is that no one *narrative* is considered dominant or superior over another. As such, deconstruction is often viewed as more a form of critique than of conclusive analysis.

REVIEW AND REVIEW QUESTIONS

Deconstruction seeks to locate and identify multiple interpretations within text that challenge meaning and identity. With a basic understanding now of deconstruction as an alternative to the more traditional methodologies associated with sport management research, attempt to answer the following questions.

1. Is there any place within sport management research for deconstruction?

2. Identify those key features of the frameworks suggested here that you believe would enable an effective "deconstruction" of a sport management text.

3. Discuss the advantages and disadvantages of "deconstruction" as a "method".

REFERENCES

Denzin, N. K. (1994). Postmodernism and deconstruction. In D. R. Dickens, & A. Fontana (Eds.). *Postmodernism and Social Inquiry*, pp. 182–202. London: Guilford Press.

Derrida, J. (1976). *Of grammatology* (G. C. Spivak, Trans.). Baltimore: John Hopkins University Press.

Derrida, J. (1996). *Deconstruction and pragmatism.* New York: Routledge.

Martin, J. (1990). Deconstructing organizational taboos: The suppression of gender conflict in organizations. *Organization Science, 1*(4), 339–359.

Saukko, P. (2003). *Doing research in cultural studies.* London: Sage.

Wortham, S. M. (1998.) *Counter-institutions: Jacques Derrida and the question of the university.* New York: Fordham University Press.

CHAPTER 11

Case study in sport management research

LEARNING OUTCOMES

When you have completed this module, you will be able to:

- Define what is a case study.

- Justify the use of the case study method.

- Differentiate between single and multiple cases.

- Explain the steps in using the case-study method.

KEY TERM

1. *Case study:* An empirical inquiry that investigates a contemporary phenomenon within its real-life context.

KEY THEMES

- What does case study research represent in sport management research?

- Is it a qualitative research strategy?

- Does it involve theory testing instead of theory building or both?

CHAPTER OVERVIEW

This chapter maps the value of case study in sport management research. In particular, it deals with the paradigmatic aspects of case study as a research strategy. We argue that case study is a comprehensive research strategy. It has the capacity to embrace paradigm plurality representing both inductive and deductive strategies. Because of its epistemological, ontological, and methodological flexibility, case study has become one of the established research approaches in sport management. There is no fixed set of methods for the case study research. This depends on the ontological presuppositions of the researchers. The significance of the ontology becomes apparent depending on the nature of the case and the types of the research questions. As case study research is reflexive, flexible, and context specific, it allows emerging contexts to shape methods.

INTRODUCTION

The case study method is the investigation of a phenomenon in its real-world context using multiple empirical methods (Yin, 2003). Case studies are highly contextual in that they cover a specific time period of the phenomenon and involve a small number of participants. Researchers have typically used the case study method to analyse how and why particular events unfold or to compare how similar groups were impacted by a particular change. The rationale behind using the case study method is that it allows the researcher to delve into a real-life context and produce a rich description from which to understand the situation, which then allows for the opportunity to build theory. Case studies may be utilised for qualitative, quantitative, and mixed methods research. This chapter will focus on the application of case study to qualitative research.

DEFINING CASE STUDY ∿

The term case study is often used interchangeably with "field research", "qualitative research", "direct research", "ethnographic studies", or "naturalistic research". Yin (1994) defines a case study as: "an empirical inquiry that investigates a contemporary phenomenon within its real-life context, especially when the boundaries between phenomenon and context are not clearly evident" (p. 13). He argues that the case study "allows an investigation to retain the holistic and meaningful characteristics of real-life events" (p. 3). Stake (1995) focuses on the case as an object of study, derived from Smith's (1979) notion of the case as a bounded system. The case is "an integrated system", a "specific, a complex functioning thing" (p. 2). Merriam (1998) supports Stake's view, concluding that "the single most defining characteristic of case study research lies in delimiting the object of study, the case" (p. 27). For Creswell (1998), a case study is an exploration of a bounded system, which may be a programme, an event, an activity, or a group of individuals. Similarly, Miles and Huberman (1994) define a case as "a phenomenon of some sort occurring in a bounded context" (p. 25). Case study research also involves situating the research phenomena within their context: The context of the case involves situating the case within its setting, which may be a physical setting or the social, historical, and/or economic setting for the case (Creswell, 1998). Merriam further characterises the case study as par-ticularistic, descriptive, and heuristic. *Particularistic* allows for a focus on a particular individual, group, event, programme, or phenomenon. *Descriptive* case studies can illustrate the complexities of a situation, influence of people, and influence of time on the phenomenon. They produce a "rich 'thick' descrip-tion of the phenomena under study" (p. 29). A *Heuristic* case can explain the reasons for a problem or issue (i.e. what happened and why). Case studies are particularistic in that they "focus on a particular situation, event, programme, or phenomenon. They are descriptive in that they produce a rich, 'thick' descrip-tion of the phenomena under study" (p. 29).

CASE STUDY AS A RESEARCH METHOD

Case studies usually define their methods of data gathering as descriptive, qual-itative, interpretive, particularistic, heuristic, and naturalistic (Cohen, Manion, & Morrison, 2000). Four different applications for case studies have been identi-fied by Yin (1984), these include:

1. To *explain*: (1) the causal links in real-life interventions that were too complex for the survey or experimental strategies; and (2) the particular case at hand with the possibility of coming to broader conclusions.

2. To *describe* the real-life context in which an intervention had occurred.

3. To *evaluate* an intervention in a descriptive case study.

4. To *explore* those situations where the intervention being evaluated has no clear, single set of outcomes.

The essence of a case study, and the central tendency among all types of case study, is that it tries to illuminate a decision or set of decisions, why those decisions were taken, how they were implemented, and with what result. Yin (2003) lists five components that are especially important for case studies: (1) a study's question; (2) its propositions, if any; (3) its unit(s) of analysis; (4) the logic linking the data to the propositions; and (5) the criteria for interpreting the find-ings (p. 21). When research is aimed at developing a theory rather than verifying one, then the use of the case study methodology is the most appropriate one. Moreover, the case study methodology suits both theory building and data anal-ysis, as they interact with each other, through the multiple sources and flexible nature of the process of data collection.

Research brief

Title: The cultural production of a successful sport tradition: A case study of Icelandic Team Handball
Author: Thorlindsson, T., *University of Iceland* & Hallordsson, V., *University of Iceland* (2019)
Reference: Thorlindsson, T., & Halldorsson, V. (2019). The cultural production of a successful sport tradition: A case study of Icelandic team handball. In *The Interaction Order*. Emerald Publishing Limited.
In this study, the authors analysed sport as a cultural product of a particular place. They used the concept of "tradition" to highlight the collective (as opposed to individual) aspects of sport, emphasising the importance of temporality, emergence, and novelty in social processes. The authors conducted a case study of internationally successful Icelandic men's team handball that provided an interesting topic in this respect. Their findings challenged decades of research on sport that had stressed innate talent, individual qualities or physiological processes rather than the sociocultural processes. The paper supported the interactionist approach to culture showing how local culture, rooted in specific interaction settings, influences the formation and development of a successful sport tradition.

EPISTEMOLOGICAL AND ONTOLOGICAL DIMENSIONS OF THE CASE STUDY

In their discussion of the epistemological and ontological assumptions that undergird case study methodology, Guba and Lincoln (1981) say that case study methodology operates within a naturalistic perspective whose epistemology assumes that there is interaction between the inquirer and the subject of his/her inquiry, and an ontology which assumes that reality in the situation being studied is "multiple, divergent and with inter-related elements" (Scott & Usher, 2004, p. 94). While acknowledging that we cannot fully know reality, although we can make judgements about it, Scott and Usher advise that these assumptions are important because of their implications about the relationship between the researcher's values, conceptualisations, knowledge frameworks, and his/her construction of knowledge in the case study.

Generally, these assumptions associate the sport management researcher with the different ways by which he/she can gain some understanding of some aspects of the nature of reality in his/her research setting (the epistemological dimension), and the different ideas the researcher holds about the nature of reality in the research phenomenon (the ontological dimension). The implication of the epistemological assumption is that "the inquirer and his/her subject interact" (Scott & Usher, 2004, p. 94). When the data was "analysed", the use of the case study methodology allows the researcher to classify, compare and describe the findings, in a more meaningful way (Shipman, 1997). For example, Perry, Riege, and Brown (1998) note that case studies allow for the: "classification into categories and the identification of inter-relationships between these categories of the data acquired" (p. 12). This use of multiple sources of data has particular value, as it increases the construct validity of the research in question. Yin (1989) notes that the use of multiple sources of evidence are "convergent lines of enquiry" that allows a process of triangulation to take place (Parkhe, 1993). Denzin (1978) suggests "the combination of methodologies used in the study of the same phenomenon" (p. 291) is a practice used to verify the findings. Eisenhardt (1989) adds weight to Denzin's approach arguing that "triangulation made possible by multiple data collection methods provides stronger substantiation of constructs" (p. 291). Thus, using multiple sources of evidence makes the findings of the case study method both more convincing and accurate and thus shows that consistent levels of validity and generalisability were achieved (Shipman, 1997).

CHARACTERISTICS OF A CASE STUDY

The "characteristics" of a case study have been defined in many ways. The categories of intrinsic, instrumental, and collective are used by Stake (1995). Merriam (1988) defines "a qualitative case study as an intensive, holistic description and analysis of a single instance, phenomenon, or social unit: (p. 21). The case study can be a: (1) *descriptive;* (2) *interpretive; or* (3) *evaluative.* Yin (1984) employs the terms: (1) *descriptive;* (2) *exploratory;* and (3) *explanatory.* The similarities of the terms may be grouped as: (1) *intrinsic and descriptive;* (2) *instrumental, interpretive, and explanatory; and* (3) *exploratory and evaluative.* In essence *intrinsic and descriptive* case studies describe in detail a particular case without forming hypotheses, making judgements or pitting against a theory. As stated by Stake (1995): "....the study is undertaken because one wants better understanding of this particular case.... not because the case represents other cases .... but because, in all its particularity and ordinariness, this case itself is of interest" (p. 88). The *intrinsic and descriptive* case can provide a basis for future comparison and theory building but it is not the primary reason for the study, the narrative account is. *Instrumental, interpretive or explanatory* case studies are more about interpreting or theorising about the phenomenon (Merriam, 1988). The *instrumental, interpretive, or explanatory* case study is more likely to look at the "why" question and contain a far greater level of analysis and conceptualisation than a descriptive case study. *Exploratory and evaluative* case studies, according to Merriam (1988), involve "description, explanation and judgement" (p. 28). Although Yin (1994) does not ascribe evaluation as a specific type of case study he does state the value and place of case study in evaluative research because case studies can explain, describe, illustrate, and explore to form judgements about a programme, event, or intervention.

TYPES OF CASE STUDY DESIGNS

Case study research may be conducted using single or multiple designs. The *single case study design* is intrinsic in nature and is useful for testing the "applicability of existing theories to real world data" (Willig, 2001, p. 74). A single case design may have multiple units of analysis and would be used when the focal case is used to test a well-formulated theory or the case represents an extreme or unique case. For example, studying the impact of changing the dates of FIFA World Cup in Qatar on a single nation's (e.g. England) professional football season. Single case study designs can also be used for a *"revelatory case"* – a situation that occurs when the researcher has an opportunity to observe and analyse a phenomenon previously inaccessible to scientific investigation. Benefits with a single case study are that they are not as expensive and time-consuming as multiple case studies. A researcher can create a high-quality theory, because this type produces extra and better theory. It also makes the researcher to have a deeper understanding of the exploring subject and can richly describe the existence of the phenomenon (Gustafsson, 2017). The types of singular case studies in relation to their time duration (Gustafsson, 2017; Thomas, 2011) are as follows:

- **Retrospective case study:** It is the simplest type of study that involves the collection of data relating to a past phenomenon of any kind. The researcher looks back on a phenomenon, situation, person, or event, and studies it in its historical integrity.

- **Snapshot study:** The case is being examined in one particular period of time, such as a current event, a day in the life of a person, a diary, etc. Here a month, a week, a day, or even a period is as short as an hour, the analysis is aided by the temporal combination of events. As the snapshot develops, the picture presents itself as a gestalt over a tight timeframe.

- **Diachronic study:** The phenomena changes over time, similar to longitudinal studies.

Research brief

Title: Tensions in stakeholder relations for a Swedish football club – a case study
Author: Junghagen, S., *Copenhagen Business School* (2018)
Reference: Junghagen, S. (2018). Tensions in stakeholder relations for a Swedish football club – a case study. *Soccer & Society, 19*(4), 612–629. This paper identified important stakeholders in Swedish football and discussed the multitude of objectives in managing these relations. The empirical base of the study was founded in a case study of Malmö FF, one of the dominant clubs in Sweden, with a qualitative single case research approach. Data were collected by means of semi-structured interviews and participant observations. The results of the study showed a number of tensions as paradoxes for stakeholder management, suggested management dispositions to reconcile these paradoxes, and suggested areas for further research.

The *multiple case study design* differs from the single case in that it does not just test existing hypotheses, but allows the sport management researcher to generate new hypotheses. That is, through the comparison of individual cases, the sport management researcher has the opportunity to develop and refine these new formulations. This means that the same study has two or more cases. What would the impact of changing the dates of the FIFA Qatar World Cup have on professional competitions in Europe, Asia, and America? If it is found to have similar negative impacts in several global competitions, then the case against moving the dates is much more significant. As such, the evidence from multiple cases is often considered more compelling, which makes the overall study more robust. Undertaking a multiple case study, however, can require extensive resources and time beyond the means of a single researcher. A multiple case design means that the same study has two or more cases and has the following implications:

■ The evidence from multiple cases is often considered more compelling, which makes the overall study more robust.

■ Undertaking a multiple case study can require extensive resources and time beyond the means of a single researcher.

■ Each case must be chosen carefully and specifically

■ The framework needs to state the conditions under which a particular phenomenon is likely to be found (literal replication) and the conditions under when it is not likely to be found (theoretical replication).

■ It is important in a replication process to develop a rich theoretical framework.

■ The individual cases within a multiple-case study design may be either holistic or embedded.

Multiple case studies are considered strong and reliable as they allow for a greater theoretical evolution and emergence of research questions. As they are intensely grounded in different empirical evidence they are able to create a more convincing theory (Gustafsson, 2017). The types of multiple case studies (Thomas, 2011; George & Bennett, 2005; Gustafsson, 2017) are as follows:

■ **Nested studies:** These involve the comparison of elements within one case, and the breakdown is within the principal unit of analysis. A nested study is distinct from a straightforward multiple studies in that it gains its integrity; its wholeness from the wider case. For example, a researcher might observe three teams within one football academy. He/she can then take interviews from the players' experience of the training.

■ **Parallel studies:** The cases are all happening and being studied concurrently.

- **Sequential studies:** The cases happen consecutively and there is an assumption that what has happened at one time point or in an intervening period will in some way affect the next incident.

- **Theoretical idiographic case studies:** These are illustrative case studies that do not accumulate or contribute directly to theory.

- **Disciplined configurative case studies:** These are used to establish theories to explain the cases.

- **Heuristic case studies:** These identify new, unexpected paths; for such studies, marginal, deviant, or outlier cases may be particularly useful.

- **Theory-testing case studies:** The studies that assess the validity and scope conditions of single or competing theories.

A number of variations of case studies have also been proposed, as such, Table 11.1 presents a typology of case study types.

Another typology of case studies is presented in Table 11.2, based upon the work of Roche (1999) and Patton (1990).

Table 11.1 Types of case study typology	
Case study type	**Description**
Illustrative case studies	Illustrative case studies describe a domain; they use one or two instances to analyse a situation. This helps interpret other data, especially when researchers have reason to believe that readers know too little about a program. These case studies serve to make the unfamiliar familiar, and give readers a common language about the topic. The chosen site should typify important variations and contain a small number of cases to sustain readers' interest.
Exploratory case studies	Exploratory case studies condense the case study process: researchers may undertake them before implementing a large-scale investigation. Where considerable uncertainty exists about programme operations, goals, and results, exploratory case studies help identify questions, select measurement constructs, and develop measures; they also serve to safeguard investment in larger studies.
Critical instance case studies	Critical instance case studies examine one or a few sites for one of two purposes. A very frequent application involves the examination of a situation of unique interest, with little or no interest in generalisability. A second, rarer, application entails calling into question a highly generalised or universal assertion and testing it by examining one instance. This method particularly suits answering cause-and-effect questions about the instance of concern.
Programme effects case studies	Programme effects case studies can determine the impact of programmes and provide inferences about reasons for success or failure.

(*Continued*)

Case study type	Description
Prospective case studies	In a prospective case study design, the researcher formulates a set of theory-based hypotheses in respect to the evolution of an on-going social or cultural process and then tests these hypotheses at a pre-determined follow-up time in the future by comparing these hypotheses with the observed process outcomes using "pattern matching" or a similar technique.
Cumulative case studies	Cumulative case studies aggregate information from several sites collected at different times. The cumulative case study can have a retrospective focus, collecting information across studies done in the past, or a prospective outlook, structuring a series of investigations for different times in the future.
Narrative case studies	Case studies that present findings in a narrative format are called narrative case studies. This involves presenting the case study as events in an unfolding plot with actors and actions.
Embedded case studies	A case study containing more than one sub-unit of analysis is referred to as an embedded case study.

Table 11.2 Typology of case study types

Types of case	Usefulness
Unusual, extreme, or deviant cases	Useful in understanding puzzling cases which seem to break the rules, and why certain people or organisations seem to achieve particularly good or bad results. Useful in understanding the reasons for exceptionally good or bad performance.
Typical or average cases	Useful in understanding the situation of most people, communities, and organisations. Findings maybe replicable in other "normal" situations.
Homogenous or similar cases	Useful in looking at particular sub-groups in depth, which may be important when many different types of people or activities are involved.
Varied or heterogeneous cases	Useful in exploring common or distinct patterns across great variance. Common patterns in such cases are likely to indicate core and central impacts of wider relevance, precisely because they occur across diverse groups.
Critical cases	Useful when a single case study can dramatically make a point; statements such as "if it happens here it can happen anywhere" or "if it doesn't work here it won't work anywhere" indicate that a case is critical.
Snowballing cases	One starts with a few cases and then selects others on the basis of the findings. Useful when the information to select all case studies is not available or are dependent on a greater understanding of the situation.
Convenience cases	Where case studies are chosen solely because it is easy – the information already exists, the site is very close, and so on. Generally, a bad idea if these are the only or most important reasons for choosing case studies.

SELECTION OF CASES FOR STUDY

Case studies and qualitative research, generally, however, do not aim to be statistically representative in the manner of the formal random samples typical of quantitative studies. Rather, case studies "draw a purposive sample, building in variety, and acknowledging opportunities for intensive study" (Stake, 2000, p. 446). Purposive sampling, or criterion-based selection (Maxwell, 1996; Ritchie, Lewis, & Elam, 2003), bases the selection of study settings and participants on features and characteristics that will enable the researcher to gather in-depth information on the areas of research interest. This form of sampling is therefore purposeful and strategic (Maxwell, 1996), with considerations of convenience and ease of access to study situations and participants given only secondary importance.

Case study

Title: Peace, sports diplomacy and corporate social responsibility: A case study of Football Club Barcelona Peace Tour 2013
Author: de-San-Eugenio, J., *University of Vic*, Ginesta, X., *University of Vic*, & Xifra, J., *Pompeu Fabra University* (2017)
Reference: de-San-Eugenio, J., Ginesta, X., & Xifra, J. (2017). Peace, sports diplomacy and corporate social responsibility: A case study of Football Club Barcelona Peace Tour 2013. *Soccer & Society, 18*(7), 836–848.

The aim of this article was to analyse the initiative FC Barcelona Peace Tour 2013 in Israel and Palestine. The article defined the nature of FC Barcelona Peace Tour 2013 as an exercise in sports diplomacy inspired by civil society and articulated through the club. In terms of primary sources, both institutional and journalistic information were used. Information was obtained from FC Barcelona's press office and communications department. In addition, two lengthy interviews were conducted with professionals who have worked with FC Barcelona in the field of sports diplomacy and were associated with the initiative. These were Xavier Mas de Xaxàs – former correspondent for La Vanguardia in Israel and ideologue of the initiative under analysis

in this article, and the secretary general of Diplocat, Albert Royo.

With respect to secondary sources, after reviewing the scientific literature most relevant to this case, the authors used journalistic accounts of the initiative. They carried out a discursive analysis of journalistic sources linked to the Catalonian club's tour of Israel and Palestine. All the published articles related to the tour between August 2 and 5 were analysed (informative, interpretive, and op-ed pieces) from the principal Catalonian newspapers (La Vanguardia, El Periódico, El Punt Avui, Ara, El 9 Esportiu, El Mundo Deportivo, and Sport) and Spanish newspapers (Marca, AS, El País, Abc, and La Razón). In total, there were 78 published articles, from which the authors extracted the excerpts which best illustrated the concept of sports diplomacy as applied to their research work.

The article concluded that in the context set out, Barça functioned as a universal, civil religion insofar as it received popular devotion from the Palestinian and Israeli people. The authors further argued that the club is thus constituted as a common denominator or element of shared heritage within a public ritual, which was transformed into an act of faith, from which attempts were made to create bonds of peace in the Middle East.

PROCEDURES FOR CONDUCTING A CASE STUDY

Several procedures are available for conducting case studies (see Merriam, 1998; Stake, 1995; Yin, 2003). This discussion will rely primarily on Stake's (1995) approach to conducting a case study. First, researchers should determine if a case study approach is appropriate to the research problem. A case study is a good approach when the inquirer has clearly identifiable cases with boundaries and seeks to provide an in-depth understanding of the cases or a comparison of several cases. Researchers next need to identify their case or cases. These cases may involve an individual, several individuals, a programme, an event, or an activity. In conducting case study research, we recommend that sport management researchers first consider what type of case study is most promising and useful. The case can be single or collective, multi-sited or within-site, focused on a case or on an issue (intrinsic, instrumental) (Stake, 1995; Yin, 2003). In choosing which case to study, an array of possibilities for **purposeful sampling** is available. We suggest, if possible, that the sport management researcher selects cases that show different perspectives on the problem, process, or event you want to portray but you also may select ordinary cases, accessible cases, or unusual cases.

The data collection in case study research is typically extensive, drawing on multiple sources of information, such as observations, interviews, documents, and audiovisual materials. For example, Yin (2003) recommends six types of information to collect: (1) documents; (2) archival records; (3) interviews; (4) direct observations; (5) participant-observations; and (6) physical artefacts. The type of analysis of these data can be a **holistic analysis** of the entire case or an **embedded analysis** of a specific aspect of the case (Yin, 2003). Through this data collection, a detailed description of the case (Stake, 1995) emerges in which the researcher details such aspects as the history of the case, the chronology of events, or a day-by-day rendering of the activities of the case. After this description, the researcher might focus on a few key issues (or **analysis of themes**), not for generalising beyond the case, but for understanding the complexity of the case. One analytic strategy would be to identify issues within each case and then look for common themes that transcend the cases (Yin, 2003). This analysis is rich in the **context of the case** or setting in which the case presents itself (Merriam, 1988). When multiple cases are chosen, a typical format is to first provide a detailed description of each case and themes within the case, called a **within-case analysis**, followed by a thematic analysis across the cases, called a **cross-case analysis**, as well as **assertions** or an interpretation of the meaning of the case. In the final interpretive phase, the researcher reports the meaning of the case, whether that meaning comes from learning about the issue of the case (an instrumental case) or learning about an unusual situation (an intrinsic case). As Lincoln and Guba (1985) mention, this phase constitutes the "lessons learned" from the case.

USING THE CASE STUDY METHODOLOGY TO BUILD A THEORY

Case study research can be useful in *theory building*. Theories are initially based on a particular case or object. Mintzberg (1979) states that for a researcher to effectively build a theory, it needs to be clearly specified what kind of data is to be collected and how that data is to be systematically gathered. As highlighted by Eisenhardt (1989): "The definition of the research questions, within a broad topic, permit the researcher to specify the kind of organization to be approached...and the kind of data to be gathered" (p. 536). This is in accordance with Yin's (1989, 1993) thinking, which confirms the importance that the research question plays in the overall design of the research. However, what about the role of developed theory or the lack of one, within the research design?

While Eisenhardt (1989) is not wholly in favour of developing a theory prior to the data collection phase, Yin (1989) argues that: "...theory development prior to the collection of any case study data is an essential step in doing case studies" (p. 36). Yin highlights a number of steps in the process, including:

1. Developing a theory from the reviewed literature;

2. Then define the relationship between the variables within the theory;

3. Then define the units of analysis;

4. The process of analysis; and

5. The criteria for interpreting the findings (pp. 33–35).

By doing this, the researcher can be assured of the robustness of the findings, once they have been interpreted and the soundness of the research design as a whole (Yin, 1989, 1994). In contrast to Yin (1989), Eisenhardt (1989) argues that: "investigators should formulate a research problem and possibly identify some of the potential variables, with some reference to extant literature" (p. 536). Eisenhardt further elaborates, noting that: "the investigator should avoid thinking about specific relationships between variables and theories as much as possible, especially at the outset of the process since such attempts will bias and limit the findings" (p. 536). Similarly, Eisenhardt sets out a way of approaching this process, suggesting that: "the research problem is formulated from which only some of the variables are identified. This allows for an appropriate research design to be chosen, allowing the data to be specified and synthesised to then, build a theory/model" (p. 537). However, Eisenhardt uses a more inductive approach to theory building than does Yin, by using induction, which concerns inferring a general law from a particular set of circumstances.

Research brief

Title: The challenges of the semi-professional footballer: A case study of the management of dual career development at a Victorian Football League (VFL) club
Author: Pink, M. A., *Australian Catholic University*, Lonie, B. E., *Australian Catholic University*, & Saunders, J. E., *Australian Catholic University* (2018)
Reference: Pink, M. A., Lonie, B. E., & Saunders, J. E. (2018). The challenges of the semi-professional footballer: A case study of the management of dual career development at a Victorian Football League (VFL) club. *Psychology of Sport and Exercise, 35,* 160–170.

The purpose of this study was to examine the challenges semi-professional VFL footballers experienced managing a dual career and the factors in the club environment that facilitated and impeded their dual career development. Data were collected over a three-month period and comprised interviews, participant observations, and casual conversations with players and staff. A non-linear process of description, analysis, and interpretation framed the analysis, which focussed on the interaction between personal and environmental variables related to the management of footballers' career development. Analysis of the findings suggested that in addition to the development of personal skills such as time management, developing an approach to dual career development that is: player driven, using existing sources for mentorship and support, and recognising the specific challenges facing semi-professional footballers and their portfolios of work has the potential to support athletes in the development of their dual careers.

Case study protocol

Prior to the commencement of case study research, it is recommended that a research protocol be established. The protocol should include: (1) an overview of the case study project (project, substantive issues, relevant reading); (2) field procedures (how to gain access to interviewees, planning for sufficient resources, providing for unanticipated events etc.); and (3) case study questions (about individuals, multiple cases, entire study, normative questions about policy recommendations, and conclusions). Yin (1994) identified the following steps in conducting any case study:

1. The first relates to the *research questions* which most likely to be "how" and "why" questions.

2. Second relates to the *unit of analysis* which could be an individual, a group of individuals, or an organisation.

3. Third relates to *linking the data* collected with the research questions.

4. Fourth relates to the *interpretation* of findings. A useful technique is "pattern-matching" where data collected from the case may be related to some theoretical proposition.

Tellis (1997), however, proposed the following steps in using the case study method and we shall explore these in more detail as they relate to the sport management researcher.

Step 1. Determine and define the research questions

In the initial stage of planning, the sport management researcher establishes a clear research focus by forming *research questions* about the problem (or situation) to be studied. This research focus could be a programme, an entity, a person, or a group of people. The key purpose is to find answers to questions which begin with "how" or "why". It is important also that the sport management researcher checks with literature review when formulating the research questions and checks what has been done previously to help determine how the study will be designed, conducted, and reported. Research does not occur in a vacuum and it is the responsibility of the sport management researcher to connect the research question to political, social, historical, and personal issues.

Step 2. Select the cases and determine data gathering and analysis techniques

a. *Selection of cases*

The objective of case studies and qualitative research is not to be statistically representative in the manner of the formal random samples typical of quantitative studies. Alternatively, case studies "draw a purposive sample, building in variety and acknowledging opportunities for intensive study" (Stake, 2000, p. 446). Purposive sampling, or criterion-based selection, (Maxwell, 1996; Ritchie, 2003) bases the selection of study settings and participants on features and characteristics that will enable the sport management researcher to gather in-depth information on the areas of research interest. This form of sampling is therefore purposeful and strategic (Maxwell, 1996), with considerations of convenience and ease of access to study situations and participants given only secondary importance. Sport management researchers need to decide whether to: (1) select "single" or "multiple" cases to study in depth; (2) relate the selection of the case or cases back to the purpose of the study; and (3) identify the boundary around the case.

b. *Data gathering techniques*

The key decision for a sport management researcher is to determine in advance what evidence to gather and what analysis techniques to use with the data to answer the research questions. The case study approach uses a range of techniques appropriate to a given context. It is important to note that this is unlike some other forms of research, that employ a particular method of data collection or data analysis, a case study may employ a wide variety of data collection methods. Generally case studies will use qualitative methods of data collection. Stake (1995) and Yin (1994) suggest these include:

- Interviews: The interview is an important technique for data collection and there are two forms of interview: Closed or Structured Interviews and Open-Ended Interviews. Open-ended interviews allow subjects to express themselves more freely and insight into events.

- Observations: This could be direct observation of events and behaviours as well as participant-observation where the researcher is an active participant in the events being studied.

- Documents: These could be letters, memos, agendas, administrative documents, newspaper articles, and any other relevant documents. Documents are useful for making inferences about events. Documents are communications between persons in the study.

- Physical artefacts: These are objects collected from the setting which could be products made by students and other individuals, the objects used such as tools or instruments.

The sport management researcher must make sure the data gathering tools are used systematically and properly to ensure: (1) construct validity; (2) internal validity; (3) external validity; and (4) reliability (Tellis, 1997). These positivist terms (Yin, 2003, p. 4) are defined in Table 11.3.

The use of the terms validity and reliability however is deemed by Sandelowski (1996) to be inappropriate in case study research in the qualitative paradigm. Klein and Myers (1999) attempted to overcome this criticism of case study by using interpretivist criteria for judging case study quality, these criteria are shown in Table 11.4.

Table 11.3 Positivist criteria for judging case study quality		
Construct validity	■ Multiple sources of evidence	■ Data collection
	■ Establish chain of evidence	■ Composition
	■ Have key informants review draft case study reports	
Internal validity	■ Do pattern matching	■ Data analysis
	■ Do explanation building	
	■ Address rival explanations	
	■ Use logic models	
External validity	■ Use theory in single case designs	■ Research design
	■ Use replication logic in multiple-case designs	
Reliability	■ Use case study protocol	■ Data collection
	■ Develop case study database	

Table 11.4 Interpretivist criteria for judging case study quality		
Principles	**Case study tactic**	**Phase of research**
Hermeneutic	Long periods of time between conducting cases, preparing drafts and drawing conclusions	Data collection
Contextualisation	Sufficient time to reconsider the context, check alternative interpretations, and maintain an overall suspicion of the findings	Data collection
Interaction	Researcher places themselves and subjects into a historical perspective, socially engaging in the process	Data collection

Step 3. Prepare to collect the data

A key element in data collection is the use of *multiple sources* of evidence. The opportunity to use multiple sources of evidence in case studies far exceeds that in other research methods such as experiments or surveys and an allows the sport management researcher to address a broader range of historical and observational issues in order to gain a better understanding of a case and contribute to theorisation. Furthermore, the use of multiple sources of evidence enables better triangulation of findings. Maintaining *a chain of evidence* in the collection of data allows an external observer – the reader of the case study for example – to follow the derivation of any evidence from initial research questions to ultimate case study conclusions. The sport management researcher also needs to prepare letters of introduction, establish rules for confidentiality, and be prepared to revisit and revise the research design and the original set of research questions.

Step 4. Collect data in the field

An important role for the sport management researcher is to collect and store multiple sources of evidence comprehensively and systematically through the creation of a *case study database*. Four components should be contained in a *database* created for case study research: (1) notes (including interview data); (2) documents; (3) tabular materials (e.g. from surveys; structured interviews); and (4) narrative (stories; diaries). Based on field notes the researcher may be able to identify patterns emerging or alternatively may need to reformulate or redefine the data collection strategy. Yin (2003) suggests that when a researcher is in the field they need to: (1) ask good questions; (2) be a good listener; (3) be adaptive and flexible; (4) have a firm grasp of the issues being studied; and (5) do not show bias towards preconceived notions.

Step 5. Evaluate and analyse the data

Gall, Borg, and Gall (1996) outlined three approaches of case data analysis:

1. Interpretational analysis: When employing this strategy, the sport management researcher is looking for patterns (threads, constructs, commonalities, etc.) within the data to explain the phenomenon.

2. Structural analysis: Investigating patterns that may be found in conversations, text, activities, etc., with little or no explication as to pattern meaning.

3. Reflective analysis: The description and evaluation of the studied phenomenon based on judgement and intuition by a highly qualified expert.

Yin (2003) explained that high quality evaluation and analysis requires the sport management researcher to:

- Attend to all the evidence.

- Address all major rival interpretations.

- Address the most significant aspect of your case study.

- Use their own prior expert knowledge.

- Examine the raw data using many interpretations in order to find linkages with the original research questions.

- Categorise, tabulate, and recombine data to address the initial research questions.

- Treat the evidence fairly to produce analytic conclusions answering the original "how" and "why" research questions.

Step 6. Prepare the report

The report of case studies should convince the reader that the researcher has examined all aspects of the subject studied and the boundaries of the case. The aim of the written report is to transform a complex issue into one that the reader can understand. It is also hoped that by reading the report, a reader will arrive at their understanding independent of the researcher. The different case study reporting styles include:

1. Linear-analytic: Follows the sequence – Problem, methods, findings of data collection and analysis, and conclusion.

2. Comparative: The same kind of case is repeated two or three times. Alternative descriptions or explanations can be compared.

3. Theory building: Where case evidence is used to construct/ground a new theory.

4. Chronological case: Studies investigates a phenomenon over a period of time but it uses a temporal dimension. The case is normally very specific, large scale, and involves complex phenomenon.

5. Suspense: This style inverts the linear analytical structure. The direct answer or outcome of a case study and its substantive significance is paradoxically presented in the initial chapter, unlike linear where it is at the end.

CASE STUDY FOR SPORT MANAGEMENT

Despite some interesting and novel case studies on the whole sport management research has there is some hesitancy to offer a primary or central role to case studies, or to apply the approach rigorously and innovatively. We would argue that the potential of the case study for providing insights into managed sport management topics has not been fully exploited. To some extent, the preference of many sport management researchers comes down to the fact that the term "case study" is not used consistently. There are an abundance of reasons to embrace case study designs in sport management research, these include: (1) they can provide a description of the complex environment within which sport management is situated; (2) they can provide a holistic view of the research process; (3) they are able to provide an understanding of complex social phenomena and real life events; (4) they are suitable for generating and testing theories; (5) they allow for an exploration of "how" and "why" questions; (6) they are suitable for an analysis of process.

CASE STUDY AND ETHICS

Because of the intense nature of involvement and participatory observation by the researcher in a case study over a prolonged period of time, there is the possibility of revealing or encountering issues that could be harmful to the participants (Ball, 1984; Stake, 1995). The risk of exposure and embarrassment to the participants can be high and it remains the responsibility of the sport management researcher to ensure that the participants are comfortable with all stages of reporting, be it interview transcripts, anecdotal evidence, initial interpretations or the final public document. Merriam (1988) in her summary of ethical considerations concludes:

> the burden of producing a study that has been conducted and disseminated in an ethical manner lies with the individual investigator. the best that an individual researcher can do is be conscious of the ethical

issues that pervade the research process, from conceptualizing the problem to disseminating the findings. (p. 184)

Case study

Title: The community impact of football pitches: A case study of Maidstone United FC
Author: May, A., *Manchester Metropolitan University* & Parnell, D., *Manchester Metropolitan University* (2017)
Reference: May, A. & Parnell, D. (2017). The community impact of football pitches: A case study of Maidstone United FC. *Sport in Society*, 20(2), 244–257.

This article analysed ways in which the installation of an artificial grass pitch (AGP) can boost revenue and improve football clubs' community engagement and participation, using a detailed case study from the National League South club Maidstone United. The club has installed an AGP at their stadium and are able to utilise it for up to 80 hours a week. All the club's 45 teams are able to train and play on the AGP, and other local sport clubs have hired it, arguably increasing Public Health opportunities. This means that youth teams, first team club players and community participants alike have access to a high-quality playing surface.

Data for this article were gathered using Maidstone United's own website and 3G4US's archive of news articles about AGPs. Observations of matches played at the Gallagher Stadium was also carried out in order to independently ascertain the depth of community engagement in Maidstone

United. The first author attended a number of matches at the stadium from 2012 to 2015 and had first-hand knowledge of the size and nature of the club's support. Further, a detailed interview with one of the directors and co-owner Oliver Ash was conducted by the lead first author on April 27, 2015. Details given by Mr Ash have been checked against available material and corroborated independently. Ash told the first author that it is hard to say definitively at this stage whether the cost of installing the surface has already been paid off. Nevertheless, he confirmed that the club have experienced "growth season upon season" and said that given the need for a significant outlay on the new stadium, the installation of the AGP surface was ultimately the "only way for the club to survive". The club have met their aim of bringing the local community into the stadium and the pitch that they have installed has played a significant part in that.

As the case study of Maidstone United demonstrated, there are benefits to installing an AGP, which go beyond the on-field performance of the first team squad. Whilst more research is needed to fully understand the potential, there remains an interesting and reasonable opportunity for successful outcomes from a financial perspective through a Public Health perspective.

CONCLUSION

The aim of case study research is generalising to theoretical propositions but not to populations. Sport management case studies may be epistemologically in harmony with experiences of others, and a natural basis for generalisation. Although the case study method is valuable to sport management it is infrequently used as a method in sport management research. Encouragement for its use in sport management research as a method is given in order to investigate the day-to-day observations and interventions that constitute sport management practice. The benefits of using case study include: (1) the research can be conducted in the natural setting; and (2) because of this it is grounded or embedded and this allows for rich description. Case study as a research method can and does provide rich narrative data gathered by a variety of both qualitative and quantitative methods. Bounding or defining the case strengthens the methodology, design, and validity. Inherent in the characteristics of case study is the sport management researchers' depth of interest and focus on the specificity or uniqueness of the case. This makes possible or allows for a detailed study of all aspects of an individual case or cases.

REVIEW AND RESERARCH QUESTIONS

1. Describe the different types of case study designs and how you might use them in sport management research.

2. Discuss some of the obstacles you may confront in case study research and how you might overcome these.

3. Case Study as a method can be used to investigate the day-to-day observations and interventions that constitute sport management practice. With this in mind:

   ■ Provide an example of how a case study approach could be used in a sport management setting. Identify the limitations that may exist and how those limitations may be overcome.

REFERENCES

Ball, S. (1984). Beachside reconsidered; reflections on a methodological apprenticeship. In R. Burgess (Ed.), *The Research Process in Educational Settings: Ten Case Studies*, pp. 69–96. London: Falmer Press.

Cohen, L., Manion, L., & Morrison, K. (2000). *Research methods in education* (5th ed.). London: Routledge/Falmer.

Creswell, J. W. (1998). *Qualitative inquiry and research design: Choosing among five traditions.* Thousand Oaks, CA: Sage Publications.

Denzin, N. K. (1978). *Sociological methods: A sourcebook.* New York: McGraw-Hill.

Eisenhardt, K. M. (1989). Building theories from case study research. *Academy of Management Review, 14*(4), 532–550.

Gall, M. D., Borg, W. R., & Gall, J. P. (1996). *Educational research: An introduction.* New York: Longman.

George, A. L., Bennett, A. (2005). *Case studies and theory development in the social sciences.* Cambridge, MA: The MIT Press.

Guba, E. G. & Lincoln, Y. S. (1981). *Effective evaluation.* San Francisco, CA: Jossey-Bass.

Gustafsson, J. (2017). Single case studies vs. multiple case studies: A comparative study. Available at https://www.diva-portal.org/smash/get/diva2:1064378/FULLTEXT01.pdf (Accessed 29 May 2020).

Klein, H. K., & Myers, M. D. (1999). A set of principles for conducting and evaluating interpretive field studies in information systems. *MIS Quarterly, 23*(1), 67–93.

Lincoln, Y. S. & Guba, E. G. (1985). *Naturalistic inquiry.* Newbury Park, CA: Sage

Maxwell, J. A. (1996). *Qualitative research design: An interactive approach.* Thousand Oaks, CA: Sage Publications.

Merriam, S. B. (1988). *Case study research in education: A qualitative approach*. San Francisco, CA: Jossey-Bass.

Merriam, S. B. (1998). *Qualitative research and case study applications in education*. San Francisco, CA: Jossey-Bass.

Miles, M. B., & Huberman, A. M. (1994). *Qualitative data analysis: A sourcebook of new methods* (2nd ed.). Thousand Oaks, CA: Sage Publications.

Mintzberg, H. (1979). An emerging strategy of 'direct' research. *Administrative Science Quarterly, 24*, 580–589.

Patton, M. Q. (1990). *Qualitative evaluation and research methods*. Newbury, CA: Sage Publications.

Parkhe, A. (1993). 'Messy' research, methodological predispositions, and theory development in international joint ventures. *Academy of Management Review, 18*(2), 227–268.

Perry, C., Riege, A., & Brown, L. (1998). Realism rules OK: scientific paradigms in marketing research about networks. *Conference Proceedings of the 28th Australian and New Zealand Marketing Academy*. Dunedin: University of Otago.

Roche, C. (1999). *Impact assessment for development agencies: Learning to value change*. Oxford: Oxford University Press.

Ritchie, J., Lewis, J., & Elam, G. (2003). Designing and selecting samples. In J. Ritchie & J. Lewis (Eds.), *Qualitative Research Practice: A Guide for Social Sciences Students and Researchers*, pp. 77–109). London: Sage Publications.

Sandelowski, M. (1996). Using qualitative methods in intervention studies. *Research in Nursing & Health, 19*, 359–364.

Scott. D., & Usher, R. (2004). *Researching education: Data, methods, and theory in educational enquiry*. New York: Continuum.

Shipman, M. (1997). *The limitations of social research*. London: Longman.

Stake, R. E. (1995). *The art of case study research*. Thousand Oaks, CA: Sage Publications.

Tellis, W. (1997). Application of a case study methodology. *The Qualitative Report, 3*(3). Available at: www.nova.edu/ssss/QR/QR3-2/tellis1.html (Accessed February 4, 2014).

Thomas, G. (2011). A typology for the case study in social science following a review of definition, discourse, and structure. *Qualitative Inquiry, 17*(6), 511–521.

Willig, C. (2001). *Introducing qualitative research in psychology: Adventures in theory and method*. Buckingham: Open University Press.

Yin, R. (1984). *Case study research: Design and methods* (1st ed.). Beverly Hills, CA: Sage Publications.

Yin, R. (1989). *Case study research: Design and methods* (Rev. ed.). Beverly Hills, CA: Sage Publications.

Yin, R. (1994). *Case study research: Design and methods* (2nd ed.). Thousand Oaks, CA: Sage Publications.

Yin, R. K. (2003). *Case study research: design and methods* (3rd ed.). Newbury Park, CA: Sage Publications.

CHAPTER 12

Discourse and critical discourse analysis in sport management research

LEARNING OUTCOMES

By the end of this chapter, you should be able to:

- Understand the basic concepts of discourse analysis;

- Identify some of the key strategies with which to apply discourse analysis in Sport Management Research;

- Understand the basic concepts of discourse, discourse analysis, and critical discourse analysis;

- Identify the implications of the use of discourse analysis and critical discourse analysis methodology in sport management;

- Reflect on what these approaches offer for research and practice.

KEY TERMS

1. **Discourse:** refers to the attitudes, rules, "ways of being", actions, and language used to construct a particular knowledge. Language, power, and knowledge are joined. Discourse ultimately serves to control not just *what* a subject/phenomenon is but *how* they are constructed.

2. **Discursive practices:** discursive practices are the translation of discourses into social action; they are the enactment of discourse.

KEY THEMES

- Can discourse analysis be used as a research methodology in sport management research?

- What is "discourse", "discourse analysis", and "critical discourse analysis"?

- There is no just one discourse but a polyvalence of discourses that are simultaneously occurring and sometimes even contradicting each other.

CHAPTER OVERVIEW

This chapter explores the methodology of discourse, discourse analysis, critical discourse analysis (CDA), and their possible applications to the field of sport management research. Discourses are the conversations and the meanings behind those conversations of groups of people who hold certain ideas and beliefs in common. In the context of sport management research, the analysis of discourses can provide new and exciting insights into the reasons behind the adoption of certain sport policies, and the acceptance of certain research outcomes as "truth". This chapter will provide an introduction and overview of the concept of discourse and provide some suggestions to possible frameworks from which to start the process of discourse analysis in the reading of sport management literature.

INTRODUCTION

Developed since the 1970s, discourse analysis has its roots in linguistics, psychology, cultural studies, and sociology. As a field of study, it comprises diverse perspectives and approaches, two of which we discuss in this chapter. The *first*, informed by psychology and sociology, was initially based on the work of Potter and Wetherell (1987) and Gilbert and Mulkay (1984). They see the speaker as an active agent, with language used as a tool to give meanings to experiences. The *second* has its roots in critical theory. Wodak (2001) and Fairclough (2004 and earlier editions) were early proponents of this approach. While critical discourse analysts use the same techniques as the first version of discourse analysis, they give their attention to the impact of ideology, seeking to uncover how power relations are reproduced through everyday talk and social practice. A number of critical scholars frame their analyses in the ideas of the philosopher Foucault (discussed later in this chapter).

As its name suggests, discourse analysis is primarily concerned with the nuances of conversation (Potter, 1996). The term "discourse" can cover anything related to our use of language whether a single utterance or moment of speech (speech fragment) through to a conversation between two people, or the delivery of a political speech. It may refer to how language may be systematically ordered as in language "rules" or different conventions such as medical jargon or legal terminology (Tonkiss, 2012, p. 406). The "turn to language" in researching society and in the discursive psychology field has been inspired by theories emerging from other disciplines and consideration of speech use as both communication and performance (Seale, 2012). As Willig (2008) observes discourse analysis is more than a methodology, since social scientists have become interested both in how we use language in communication and also how we "socially construct" our environment and lived experience by the use of language (see Bruner, 1986; Gergen, 2001). It has become more of a critique of how we describe the world and the nuances of the discourse and language we use.

DEFINING DISCOURSE AND DISCOURSE ANALYSIS

The term "discourse" is taken up by contrasting theoretical perspectives and so has come to mean very different things. As Potter and Wetherell (1987) suggest: "the only thing that commentators are agreed on in this area is that terminological confusions abound" (p. 6). According to Shapiro (1987), "discourse" can be "any systematic or disciplined way of constituting subjects, objects, and relationships" (p. 365). Parker (1992), for example, defined discourse as "a system of statements that construct an object" (cited in Burr, 1995, p. 48). For Burr discourse analysis is "the analysis of a text in order to reveal either the discourses operating within it or the linguistic and rhetorical devices that are used in its construction" (p. 184).

In addition to the notion of discourse, the notion of *"discursive practices"* developed by Foucault describes the linguistic practices and the use of socially charged language to produce dominant fields of knowledge. Foucault's analysis highlights the struggle between dominant social, cultural and political power groups within society. Discursive practices are the translation of discourses into social action; they are the enactment of discourse. They are the discursively inscribed, ordered regularities of behaviour that underscore discourses as social action (Fairclough, 1989).

Discursive analysis is an important technique that could be used by the sport management researcher if trying to identify the hidden meaning that may exist in a text. A number of discursive devices can be used to unpack the text, these discursive devices are identified in Table 12.1.

These discursive devices are then applied by following a number of steps, these include:

1. Read through the data several times to become familiar. What jumps out as you read? Think about what is "going on" in the text; what are the speakers/writers involved in (e.g. blaming, justifying, describing, etc.)?

2. Ask yourself "why this word, why now?" Try mentally replacing words with others to see how the construction changes; such as "athlete" to "gay athlete"). Is the narrative structure of the text important? How does the constructed meaning of the talk/text change as the words change?

3. Look for "discursive devices" such as 3-part lists, extreme case formulations, etc. What are these doing? What psychological issues are they attending to?

4. Start to think about possible themes or research questions that you could use to focus your analysis. These can be very simple, such as "how are categories used to manage identity?" or "how are issues of blame and accountability dealt with in the text?"

5. Note down anything at all that interests you – work on your intuitive hunches – and list your ideas down the margins of the transcript.

Table 12.1 Discursive devices
Extreme case formulations: Using words like "very" or "the worst" strengthen an argument or account. Can also be treated ironically.
Emotion categories: Not referring to underlying emotional states, but as a resource for holding others accountable, and useful for setting up rhetorical contrasts (e.g. versus "rational").
Active voicing: This is when speakers report the words of others as if they were spoken directly. Used to add authenticity and credibility.
Script formulations: Formulating an action as routine or usual – does "being normal".
Assessments and second assessments: These are usually organised in preference terms (i.e. agree with someone as preferable for smooth interaction).
Affect displays: E.g. sighing, crying, sniffing – often these are organised alongside talk; not separate to interaction.
Pronoun use and footing: Using "I", "we", "you", etc. Used to distance or align oneself with others.
Detail in narrative/generic vagueness: Often used to make accounts more plausible. Vagueness can be used as a distancing tool (i.e. "this is not my story...").
3-part lists: These are common in much talk and esp. in political speeches – adds credibility and authenticity. Examples include: "Government of the people, by the people, for the people"; "Blood, sweat, and tears"; "Location, location, location".

6. Once you've gone through the transcript in this way, do it again! Then start to make more detailed notes, relating to your theme or research question.

Research brief

Title: Toward a typology for negotiating layered identities: An oppositional discourse analysis of girls' youth sport
Author: Zanin, A. C., *Arizona State University*, Shearer, E.T., *Arizona State University*, & Martinez, L. V., *Arizona State University* (2020)
Reference: Zanin, A. C., Shearer, E. T., & Martinez, L. V. (2020). Toward a typology for negotiating layered identities: An oppositional discourse analysis of girls' youth sport. *Communication Monographs*, 1–23.
The authors of the paper aimed to study how participants in an all-female youth sport organisation negotiated oppositional discourses of identity. The study documented the context of girls' youth sport presented in a case of voluntary organising, multi-layered identities, and several different types of oppositional discourses reinforced by individuals inside (e.g. coaches, participants) and outside (e.g. parents, non-participant peers) the sports team. The analysis revealed two major categories of identity discourse in an all-female youth sport context: oppositional discourses about gendered identity (i.e. boys and girls are different and boys and girls are the same) and oppositional discourses about a nested female athlete identity (i.e. collaborative vs. competitive, insecure vs. confident.

THE NATURE OF DISCOURSE ANALYSIS

Discourse analysis has similarities with conversation and narrative analysis but is more flexible because there is less of an emphasis on naturally occurring talk. Researchers who follow this approach are preoccupied with the idea that discourse occurs within a social context, which both influences and is influenced by discourse. Therefore, in their research they examine three key aspects, and the relationships between them:

1. The form and content of the language in use.

2. The ways in which people use language in order to communicate ideas and beliefs.

3. Institutional and organisational factors, as well as wider political, social, cultural, or economic contexts surrounding the discourse under investigation, and how these might shape the discourse and also be changed to some extent by it.

Discourse analysis is based on certain assumptions about the social world. While most other qualitative approaches are concerned with an understanding of the meanings which people attribute to their experience, discourse analysis examines the process through which meanings are generated and maintained. Discourse analysis, therefore, moves beyond textual examination to explore how language is used, why, when, and by whom. Discourse analysis however has been criticised in a number of areas. Table 12.2 lists some of these criticisms.

DISCOURSE ANALYSIS

Discourse analysis focuses on language as a social practice in its own right and is concerned with how individuals use language in specific social contexts. It

Table 12.2 Criticisms of discourse analysis

Criticisms of discourse analysis

- Accusations of moral nihilism: unethical acts are dismissed as having no material reality.

- Countered by argument that discourse analysis does not deny material reality, but focuses on the way our understandings of such practices are constructed through discourse.

- Voicing concerns for groups who do not consider themselves to be oppressed or disadvantaged.

- Subversion of oppressive discourses may lead to alternative suppressive discourses for other social groups.

- Difficulty of identifying interpretative repertoires when research is not independent of linguistic resources needed to construct discourse.

enables researcher to gain an understanding of *how* individuals use language to construct themselves and the world around them. It is an approach that provides a way for the researcher to understand *why* individuals use language to construct themselves and the world around them and to understand the ideological effects of individuals constructions. Discourse analysis works on the assumption that individuals construct the world in order to make sense of it whilst also reproducing or challenging ideological systems of belief that exist in society at large (Dick 2004).

MAPPING THEORIES OF DISCOURSE

Various forms of discourse analysis exist. The most common are Foucaultian discourse analysis and CDA. These will now be discussed.

FOUCAULTIAN DISCOURSE ANALYSIS

Foucault viewed discourse analysis as revealing relations of power/knowledge encoded in the social processes of language and action. Foucaultian style discourse analysis has also been referred to as genealogy, power analytics, critical hermeneutics or critical ethnography, although there are those who maintain that there are differences among these approaches. Foucault argued that discourse, knowledge and power are so closely interrelated that a field of discourse is co-extensive with a field of power. In fact, Foucault often used the phrase "power/knowledge" with respect to discourse. Thus, using a Foucaultian perspective, it is possible to explore the links among knowledge, power, and resultant discourses. An analysis of these links reveals that claims to knowledge by exponents of certain dominant discourses are, in fact, claims to power (Foucault, 1980).

All discourses, in the Foucaultian view, contain internal contradictions. Analysis of the contradictions and silences in a discourse are important elements in a Foucaultian discourse analysis. Because of the historically situated nature of all discourses, the internal contradictions "make sense" only with respect to a specific context. This makes it problematic to claim that a discourse analysis describes:

> what is really going on' within a discourse because the analyst coexists with the discourse she or he is analysing. Consequently, the purpose of discourse analysis is to describe the contradictions and puzzles as they become apparent, as a 'tool for radical political action'. (Foucault, 1980, p. 205)

A Foucaultian style discourse analysis is sometimes referred to as an analytic because it seeks the conditions that make possible the analyses practiced in the discipline (Kusch, 1991). Discourse analysis decomposes statements and their context-dependent interpretation into context-dependent categories called *subjects, concepts,* and *strategies.* Foucault (1983) stressed that a discourse analysis concerns itself with the following five power/knowledge issues, which can be highlighted by reference to the sport media. First, *the system of differentiations or privileged access to the discourse* – more powerful sport media entities, such as Entertainment and Sports Programming Network (ESPN), may control access to discourse by selecting topics and interviewees or the time and place of the texts. Second, *the types of objectives of one group of adherents over another* – discourses may reflect an ESPN objective to market sports that are broadcast on its networks rather than sports contracted to a competitor's network. Third, *the means of bringing power relations into being that reveals surveillance systems, threats and dismissals* – an example could be ESPN's influence in the collegiate sports conference realignment in the USA, as colleges were under threat of losing media coverage depending on what conference they participate in. Fourth, *"forms of institutionalisation" such as the bureaucratic structures* – ESPN engages sports properties in, pressuring textual conformity to ESPN's agenda. Finally, *the degree of rationalisation required to support power arrangements* – as more sports are contracted to the ESPN network, sport governing bodies tend to rationalise that they need to be on ESPN in order to attain the desired coverage.

The process of a Foucaultian style discourse analysis involves careful reading of entire bodies of text and other organising systems (such as taxonomies, commentaries, and conference transcriptions) in relation to one another, in order to interpret patterns, rules, assumptions, contradictions, silences, consequences, implications, and inconsistencies. The product of a discourse analysis shows how discourses are constructed, circulated and played out. Discourse analysis includes a focus on oppression and also identifies potential discourses of resistance through which people may construct subject positions that challenge the dominant discourses. Discourse analysis may involve identification of several related discourses available to people in a given social context at a given time.

Research brief

Title: Student-athletes' experiences with racial microaggressions in sport: A Foucauldian discourse analysis

Author: Lee, S. M., *West Virginia University* (2017)

Reference: Lee, S. M. (2017). Student-athletes' experiences with racial microaggressions in sport: A Foucauldian discourse analysis. *Graduate Theses, Dissertations, and Problem Reports.*

The purpose of this study was to examine U.S. collegiate student-athletes-of-colours' experiences with racial microaggressions in sport through a new theoretical lens, Foucauldian poststructuralist theory. The author theorised microaggressions as an example of the daily panoptic gaze that leads to self-surveillance and the production of normalised individuals. Eight student-athletes-of-colour participated in two interviews: a two-person focus group interview followed by an individual interview. A Foucauldian discourse analysis was further conducted to identify the discourses that student-athletes-of-colour drew upon to make sense of their microaggression experiences. The various racial microaggressions shared by the participants illustrated how student-athletes-of-colours' experiences and subjectivities were racialised.

DISCOURSE ANALYSIS AND SPORT MANAGEMENT

Edwards and Skinner (2009) suggested that the potential contribution of a Foucaultian style discourse analysis to the discipline of sport management is twofold: first, discourse analysis would provide an approach suitable for addressing such notions as the taken-for-granted nature of specific sport management practices; the history of sport management practices; the vested interest of authorised voices; the rules of evidence used to formulate and structure discussions; the rules of evidence used to produce explanations; and the rules of which topics are dismissed from inquiry. Second, from Foucault's perspective, all discourses are merely perspectives. The aim of Foucaultian analysis is to examine the legitimacy of claims to truth by such groups as policy makers, editorial boards, and researchers. Foucaultian discourse analysis constantly asks questions about how and why knowledge is constructed and by whom. From this perspective all sport management knowledge is under constant scrutiny. There are no absolute truths that are above or exempt from examination.

When applied to sport management, the discourse analyst should consider the historical, sociocultural, spatial, and institutional context within which the discourse was assembled, legitimised, and disseminated. The process of a Foucaultian style discourse analysis involves careful reading of entire bodies of text and other organising systems (such as taxonomies, commentaries, and conference transcriptions) in relation to one another, in order to interpret patterns, rules, assumptions, contradictions, silences, consequences, implications, and inconsistencies (Weedon, 1987). The product identifies and names language processes and social practices that people use to construct their understanding of social life that necessarily serves either to reproduce or challenge the distribution of power as it currently exists (Weedon, 1987).

Discourse analysis can contribute to the discipline is by providing a way to analyse power in sport management. Examples of issues that would benefit greatly from the power perspective provided by discourse analysis, include the discourses of theory, professionalism, practice, gender, sport management communication to name a few. An examination of these issues would contribute to the further development of sport management as an academic discipline.

Moreover, Foucaultian analysis can illuminate the mechanisms and techniques used by sport management to legitimise its own knowledge claims and the various, often competing, discourses embedded in sport management knowledge. It could reveal the nature of the interplay between sport management "experts" and practitioners. For example, in sport management the technocratic discourse operates in such a way as to limit the sport mangers' perception of the nature of management practice. The power afforded to the technocratic/managerial discursive framework is such that it is very difficult for sport management practitioners to move away from a management approach to a reflective practitioner. As such, the discursive formation of the managerial model both legitimises this approach to sport management practice and limits other forms of possibility.

The product of a discourse analysis includes a description of the internal rules and ideological elements of a particular discourse, plus documentation of the "conditions of its existence". Questions that would illuminate the conditions of existence for the discourse of sport management theory could include the following:

1. What kinds of practices or discourses had to be in place before the discourse of sport management theory could be constructed?

2. What social practices and power arrangements are necessary for the discourse of sport management theory to continue?

3. What implicit rules are there in the discourse of sport management theory that help to validate its existence?

In such analysis, there is a dynamic relationship between power and "truth" where truth is a product of dominant discursive frameworks shaped and defined by power, whilst power is legitimated on the basis of expert ownership of such "truth". For example, the scientific/management model is regularly described as neutral and value free. So hegemonic is this notion of objectivity, that the underlying relations of power embedded in "true" concepts such as objectivity and neutrality are not exposed. Foucault extends the conceptualisation of power from the realm of the ideological, to figuring in the very production of the instruments for the formation and accumulation of knowledge. In such an analysis, knowledge is not identical to ideology but in fact precedes ideology. Further, dominant discourses figure in both the development and the continuation of social truths. From Foucault's perspective, all discourses are merely perspectives. If one discourse has more value than another, this is not because of its intrinsic properties as truth but because of the role that discourse plays in constituting practices. Discourses produce not "truth" but "truth effects" (i.e. they organise and constitute the world in particular ways). These effects are not contingent on whether the discourse is oppressive or liberating. Any discursive regime (and human existence is unthinkable without one) implies a particular exercise of power. Power not only represses but it also makes possible the knowledge that constitutes culture – any culture. Foucault argues for the power effect of knowledge rather than its truth value. The notion of ideology critique is misleading in that it promises a truth not distorted through the effects of domination. For Foucault such a notion is an impossibility.

Discourse analysis draws attention to the discursive construction of sport management knowledge and practices; the point is not to replace one set of categories with another, but to focus on differences and marginality, thus expanding different theoretical understandings and facets of experience. Post structural sport management discourses of inquiry do not propose a new "paradigm" in the sense of value-free truth seeking, the concern is with "intertextualism", which involves the generation of new positions to resist or question existing discourse. Clearly, there are numerous ways in which discourse analysis has been applied in various contexts whether it be for critical social commentary, empowerment, or to further reform agendas. However, we suggest for the purposes of sport management Foucaultian analysis has much to offer.

Case study

Title: Children's stories about team selection: A discourse analysis

Author: Lindgren, E. C., *University of Gothenburg*, Hildingh, C., *Halmstad University*, & Linnér, S., *Linneus University* (2017)

Reference: Lindgren, E. C., Hildingh, C., & Linnér, S. (2017). Children's stories about team selection: A discourse analysis. *Leisure Studies*, *36*(5), 633–644.

The aim of this study was to identify and problematise messages and value principles visible in children's stories about team selection in sport. To achieve this, the authors have adopted a discourse analysis approach. The study interpreted norms and values that determined what is considered to be important in children's team sports, how the teams are constructed, and what general experience children derive from this. Semi-structured face-to-face interviews were conducted with 24 children aged 10–11 years who participated in four team sports in 12 different Swedish sports clubs. Based on the children's stories, the findings revealed two discourses of team selection: one participation/inclusion-oriented and one performance/exclusion-oriented discourse in which four different forms of team selection work. The participation/inclusion-oriented discourse constructed sport as a fun game that involves all participating children. The performance/exclusion-oriented discourse showed that coaches select the best children in the team to obtain the best

chance of winning games. Some of the coaches have given conflicting messages that align with both discourses which were revealed by both the girls' and the boys' voices in varying degrees. The analysis of discursive practice was utilised by the authors to examine the complexity of power relationships between children and adults and between different groups of children. The authors further focused on the discourses of sport that legitimise knowledge and on the practice of power by adults (Johns & Johns, 2000). Depending on children's talk about their reasons for playing sport and their coaches' selection procedures, the meaning and issues of power were conveyed. The findings concluded that children's reasons for playing sport are in harmony with the participation/inclusive-oriented discourse. This discourse represented a child's perspective, promoting every child's right to participate under the same conditions. However, the selection procedure in both discourses exhibited strong classification, since coaches are the ones who possess the power to select.

References in this case study

Winther Jørgensen, M., & Phillips, L. (2002). *Discourse analysis as theory and method.* London: Sage

Johns, D., & Johns, J. (2000). Surveillance, subjectivism and technologies of power. *International Review for the Sociology of Sport, 35*, 219–234.

FAIRCLOUGH'S APPROACH TO CRITICAL DISCOURSE ANALYSIS

According to Fairclough (1993), CDA is:

> ....discourse analysis that aims to systematically explore the often opaque relationships of causality and determination between (a) discursive practices, events, and texts, and (b) wider social and cultural structures, relations and processes; to investigate how such practices,

events and texts arise out of and are ideologically shaped by relations of power and struggles over power; and to explore how the opacity of these relationships between discourse and society is itself a factor in securing power and hegemony. (p. 135)

The theoretical underpinnings of CDA bring together a wide variety of critical social theories, the Frankfurt school and other neo-Marxist scholars (Blommaert & Bulcaen, 2000). Collectively, these theories have influenced many facets of CDA including the way power is conceptualised. Fairclough's (1993) model focuses on discourse as text. It is centred on the pivotal point that text is a concrete manifestation of discourse. Given this focus, Fairclough analyses structural and stylistic aspects within documents (e.g. paragraphs, sentences, phrases, clauses, grammar, speech acts, and vocabulary) and their interactions and ties these discursive constructions (or elements of orders of discourse) to social relations. Figure 12.1 provides an overview of these aspects.

Fairclough (1992) believes there are three dimensions to a discursive event: (1) it is spoken or written language *text*; (2) it is an *interaction* between people involving processes of producing and interpreting the text (discursive practice); and (3) it is part of a piece of *social action* (social practice). As such, he believes there should be three dimensions to CDA: (1) *description* of the text; (2) *interpretation* of the interaction processes and their relationship to the text; and (3) *explanation* of how the interaction process relates to the social action (p. 11).

The *description* dimension consists of examining the organisation of the text, its structure, and vocabulary while "framing" the language of the text

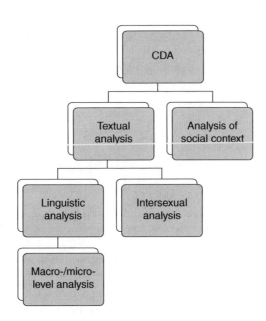

Figure 12.1 Elements of orders of discourse to social relations

within the other dimensions of the analysis (since one cannot separate description and interpretation). The aim in the *interpretation* dimension is to give a moment-by-moment analysis of how the participants produce and interpret the texts by specifying the discursive practices that are being used and in which combinations. This process relates the discourse event to the order of discourse used. The aim in the *explanation* dimension is to explain the properties of the interaction by referring to its social context and assessing its contribution to social action (its effectiveness in constituting or helping to reconstitute different dimensions of the social in the interpretation phase). In this social action dimension, Fairclough's (1993) focus is political and ideological: political in that it establishes, sustains, and changes power relations and ideological in that it constitutes, naturalises, sustains, and changes significations of the world. The two are not independent of each other "for ideology is significations generated within power relations as a dimension of the exercise of power and struggle over power" (p. 67). In sum, he focuses on the discursive event within relations of power and domination. For a summary of Fairclough's (1993) three-dimensional analysis see Table 12.3.

Fairclough's (1995) CDA is based on the premise that power operates through discourse to structure social relations. This method analyses how stylistic properties of the text are linked to material relations. For example, the method assists in examining how the communications and organisational documents from an international sports federation contribute to the power relationship with national sports federations. In this way, CDA moves beyond the content of a text to examine the effect of discourse on reality. By firmly centring the analysis of discourse within the field of political action, CDA does not reduce its analysis to "merely the markings of textuality", but also examines the physicality of its effects in the materiality of its practices (Foucault, 1981, p. 66; as cited in Hook, 2001, p. 537). Fairclough's method is also political for its goal is not only deconstruction but also social change. The objective of his approach is to transform society by exposing how material relations of force are linked to discourse. CDA is not without its critics. Table 12.4 indicates some of the strengths and weaknesses of this approach.

CDA AND SPORT MANAGEMENT

There is no set questioning through which a CDA takes place. The questions asked in an analysis of a particular text depend on the research aims and the nature of the debate under analysis (Fairclough, 2003). CDA presents a structured methodology for analysing any text and is useful for sport management researchers who require a set approach to the analysis of discourse. The utility of the textual analysis offered by CDA lies in the depth that it can add to issues related to sport management practice. One area in which CDA could

Table 12.3 Fairclough's three-dimensional analysis

1. **Description** of the text: examine the organisation of the text, its structure and vocabulary.

   ■ Vocabulary – individual words

   ■ Grammar – words combined into clauses and sentences

   ■ Cohesion – how clauses and sentences are linked together

   ■ Text structure – large scale organisational properties of texts

   ■ Force of utterances – types of speech acts used (promise, request, threat)

   ■ Coherence of texts – connections based on ideological assumptions

   ■ Intertextuality – connections to other texts, may be explicit or implicit

2. **Interpretation** of the interaction processes and their relationship to the text: give a moment-by-moment analysis of how the participants produce and interpret the texts by specifying the discursive practices that are being used and in which combinations.

   ■ Who is the producer (the animator, author, and/or principal) of the text?

   ■ What are the social constraints as to how it is produced?

   ■ What aspects of members' resources are used to understand the text?

3. **Explanation** of how the interaction process relates to the social action: explain the properties of the interaction by referring to its social context and assess its contribution to social action (its effectiveness in constituting or helping to reconstitute different dimensions of the social in the interpretation phase).

   ■ Ideology – how the text constitutes, naturalises, sustains, and changes significations of the world

   ■ Hegemony – the implicit practices that become naturalised or automated, and expose the constant struggle

   ■ Political – how the text establishes, sustains, and changes power relations

Table 12.4 CDA strengths and weaknesses

CDA strengths and weaknesses

Strengths	Weaknesses
■ Links discourse to material relations.	■ Not specific enough in explaining how people reconcile contradictions by creating new discourses.
■ It is political; it focuses on power relations.	
■ Reveals the impact on social relations, not the "truth".	■ Critical research projects develop a social critique without developing a theory of action that people can draw upon to develop "counter-hegemonic" practices in which dominant structures can be challenged.
■ Does not grant privileged status to the content of a discourse.	

have particular relevance within the sport management research domain is sport policy. Policies can be broadly defined and include directives for action, or the responsibilities for action and the processes guiding the implementation of action. CDA aims to expose sources of domination, repression, and exploitation that are entrenched in, and legitimated by policy. Thus a policy analysis goes beyond analysing the content and implementation of policies to examine how those policies reflect certain understandings of reality in the first instance.

A CDA of sport policy should have the following characteristics: (1) situates the policy in its discursive context; (2) examines the multiple voices present in policy discourse, i.e. the policy actors/stakeholders and their power relationships; (3) identifies multiple discourses exposing their relationships and interactions with each other; (4) highlights predominant discourses; (5) conducts multi-levelled analysis of texts. Analyses detailed structural aspects within the textual document (e.g. paragraphs, sentences, phrases, clauses, grammar, speech acts, and vocabulary) and their interactions; (6) exposes ideology operating through discourse (i.e. how discourse orchestrates a version of truth that structures reality); and (7) proposes a theory of action through the development of counter discourses as forms of resistance.

VALIDITY IN DISCOURSE ANALYSIS

Because discourses are reflexively related to situations that make them meaningful, they do not as such reflect "reality", but rather the meanings as constructed by people in a particular context (Gee & Green, 1998). It is important, therefore, for the discourse analyst to show that the findings are not just his or her opinion but are grounded in the data. Gee and Green argue that validity for discourse analysis is based on three elements:

1. *Convergence*: the more the same data yields similar results from the use of different methods, or from multiple analysis, the more the study can be considered valid.

2. *Agreement*: this is when both "native" speakers of the social languages in the data and other discourse analysts (i.e. insiders and outsiders) agree that the analysis reflects how such social languages actually can function in the settings under interrogation.

3. *Coverage*: a study is valid "when the analysis can be applied to related sorts of data. This includes being able to make sense of what has come before and after the situation being analysed and being able to predict the sorts of things that might happen in related sorts of situations" (p. 159).

To ensure that a sport management study constitutes these three elements, the sport management researcher would need to apply other methods (such as interviews and observations) in order to introduce other forms of text, or would need to undertake a member check after the first round of analysis. In addition, in order to contextualise the analysis, the sport management researcher would need to draw connections between the historical and current settings and the wider social context in which the data is situated by, for example, examining media archives or other documents in the public domain.

A NOTE ON BIAS

Similar to criticisms, mentioned previously in the critique of discourse analysis, critics of CDA have commented that CDA researchers read what they want to find in the texts they analyse (Schegloff, 1991; Stubbs, 1997). This is a common criticism made against critical social scientists in many disciplines and is not necessarily seen as a criticism by CDA researchers. Far from being a problem for CDA, however, Chouliaraki and Fairclough (1999) suggest that this is one of the important understandings of a CDA. They comment that CDA takes the view that any text can be understood in different ways – a text does not uniquely determine a meaning, though there is a limit to what a text can mean. Different understandings of the text result from different combinations of the properties of the text and the properties (social positioning, knowledges, values, etc.) of the interpreter.

When sport management researchers use a CDA analysis, it is important they acknowledge the bias inherent in any research methodology but minimise this bias through the use of a consistent methodological approach. The sport management researcher needs to analyse the utterances of all speakers within the debate, using the same questioning, and to be up-front concerning overt personal biases. For example, if a sport management practitioner were undertaking this analysis, it would be important that he or she acknowledge this so that the research could be understood in light of this influence.

Case study

Title: What can Foucault tell us about fun in sport? A Foucauldian critical examination of the discursive production and deployment of fun within varsity coaching contexts
Author: Whitehouse, L. E., *University of Chester* (2019)
Reference: Whitehouse, L. E. (2019). What can Foucault tell us about fun in sport? A Foucauldian critical examination of the discursive production and deployment of fun within varsity coaching contexts. *Master Thesis for the fulfilment of the degree at University of Chester.*

This research investigated the discourses that have impacted recreational women's hockey players' perspectives and experiences surrounding sexual identity. Furthermore, the participants' engagement with sexual identity discourses and through what discursive practices and disciplinary techniques sexual identities became dominant or alternative was examined. The experiences of and towards non-heterosexual sportspeople is a developing area of research, though little research focuses on recreational level sport that is not identified as a "gay sport space". This

(Continued)

study contributed to sexuality and sport research by investigating a recreational women's team, which is not restricted to the "gay sport space" label to develop understandings of the dynamics and complexities that sexual identity discourses have on both heterosexual and non-heterosexual sportspeople. A post structural, Foucaultian theoretical framework underpinned this study with the utilisation of Foucault's work on discourses, techniques of power and the technologies of the self. Data was generated from semi-structured interviews with seven hockey players, who discussed their experiences regarding sexual identity at Castle Ladies Hockey Club. By analysing the participants' talk through discourse analysis, discourses of acceptance and inclusivity towards non-heterosexual identities were found. Firstly, non-heterosexual identities were regarded as "normal"; secondly, the focus was on if the player was a good team player rather than sexual identity; and thirdly, there was an increased acceptance of sexual fluidity leading to decreased tolerance towards homophobia. This research highlighted that players engage with multiple discourses associated with sexual identity. This raised questions surrounding the dominance of heteronormativity, as non-heterosexual identities are not presented as marginal.

CONCLUSION

The discipline of sport management exists globally without a long history of allegiance to an established philosophical perspective or social theory. Sport managaement is therefore in the enviable position of having a widely informed choice among philosophical approaches as models for teaching, practice and research. The application of discourse analysis as a methodology for sport managerment inquiry provides the discipline with the opportunity to construct alternative perspectives on power/knowledge. Such an addition to sport managerment inquiry would therefore seem justified.

REVIEW AND RESEARCH QUESTIONS

Discourses are conversations and the meanings behind those conversations. With a basic understanding now of discourse analysis and CDA and attempt to answer the following questions:

1. Identify two key features of CDA that would have particular relevance for sport management research.

2. What factors should the sport management researcher take into consideration before deciding to adopt critical discourse as a research approach?

REFERENCES

Blommaert, J., & Bulcaen, C. (2000). Critical discourse analysis. *Annual Review of Anthropology, 29,* 447–466.

Bruner, J. (1986). *Actual minds, possible worlds.* Cambridge, MA: Harvard University Press.

Burr, V. (1995). *An introduction to social constructionism.* London: Routledge.

Chouliaraki, L., & Fairclough, N. (1999). *Discourse in late modernity: rethinking critical discourse analysis.* Edinburgh: Edinburgh University Press.

Dick, P. (2004). Discourse analysis. In C. Cassell, & G. Symon (Eds.), *Handbook of Qualitative Methods: The Essential Guide*, pp. 203–213. London: Sage Publications.

Edwards, A., & Skinner, J. (2009). *Qualitative research in sport management.* Oxford: Elsevier.

Fairclough, N. (1989). *Language and power.* London: Longman.

Fairclough, N. (1992). *Discourse and social change.* Cambridge, UK: Polity Press.

Fairclough, N. (1993). Critical discourse analysis and the marketization of public discourse: The universities. *Discourse and Society, 4*(2), 133–168.

Fairclough, N. (1995). *Critical discourse analysis: The critical study of language.* New York: Longman.

Fairclough, N. (2003). *Analyzing discourse: Textual analysis for social research.* New York: Routledge.

Fairclough, N. (2004) *Critical Discourse Analysis in researching language in the New Capitalism: Overdetermination, Transdisciplinarity, and Textual Analysis.* In L. Young and C. Harrison (eds), *Systemic Functional Linguistics and Critical Discourse Analysis* (pp, 103–122). London: Continuum.

Foucault, M. (1980). *Power/knowledge selected interviews and other writings, 1972–77* (C. Gordon, Trans.). New York: Harvester Wheatsheaf.

Foucault, M. (1981). The order of discourse. In: *Untyping the Text* (Ed. by R. Young), pp. 48–78. London: Methuen.

Foucault, M. (1983). The subject and power. In D. Dreyfus, P. Rabinow, & M. Foucault (Eds.), *Beyond Structuralism and Hermeneutics* (2nd ed.), pp. 208–226. Chicago: University of Chicago Press.

Gee, J. P., & Green, J. L. (1998). Discourse analysis, learning, and social practice: A methodological study. *Review of Research in Education, 23*, 119–169.

Gergen, K. J. (2001). *Social construction in context.* London: Sage Publications.

Gilbert, N. G., & Mulkay, M. (1984). *Opening Pandora's box: A sociological analysis of scientist's discourse.* Cambridge: Cambridge University Press.

Hook, D. (2001). The disorders of discourse. *Theoria, 1*(97), 41–68.

Kusch, M. (1991). *Foucault's strata and fields: An investigation into archaeological and genealogical science studies.* Dordrecht, The Netherlands: Kluwer Academic Publishers.

Parker, I. (1992). *Discourse dynamics: Critical analysis for social and individual psychology.* London: Routledge.

Potter, J. (1996) *Representing reality.* London: Sage Publications.

Potter, J., & Wetherell, M. (1987). *Discourse and social psychology: Beyond attitudes and behavior.* London: Sage Publications.

Schegloff, E. (1991). Reflections on talk and social structure. In D. Boden, & D. H. Zimmerman (Eds.), *Talk and Social Structure: Studies in Ethnomethodology and Conversation Analysis*, pp. 44–70. Berkeley, CA: University of California Press.

Seale, C. (2012). *Researching society and culture* (3rd ed.). Thousand Oaks, CA: Sage Publications.

Shapiro, M. J. (1987). *Educational theory and recent political discourse: A new agenda for the left?* Teachers College Record, Winter.

Stubbs, B. (1997). Whorf's children: Critical comments on critical discourse analysis (CDA). In A. Wray, & A. Wray (Eds.), *Evolving Models of Language. British Studies in Applied Linguistics*, pp. 100–116. Clevedon: BAAL/Multilingual Matters.

Tonkiss, F. (2012). Discourse analysis. In C. Seale (Ed.), *Researching Society and Culture* (3rd ed.), pp. 405–423. Thousand Oaks, CA: Sage Publications.

Weedon, C. (1987). *Feminist practice and poststructuralist theory*. Oxford: Blackwell.

Willig, C. (2008). Foucauldian discourse analysis. In C. Willig (Ed.), *Introducing Qualitative Research in Psychology*, pp. 112–131. Buckingham: Open University Press.

Wodak, R. (2001). The discourse-historical approach. In R. Wodak, & M. Meyer (Eds.), *Methods of Critical Discourse Analysis*, pp. 63–95. London: Sage Publications.

CHAPTER 13

Ethnomethodology and sport management research

LEARNING OUTCOMES

By the end of this chapter, you should be able to:

1. Understand the basic concepts of ethnomethodology.

2. Identify some applications of the use of ethnomethodology in sport management.

3. Identify some strategies to apply the key analytic tools of ethnomethodology to sport management research.

KEY TERMS

1. *Ethnomethodology:* a form of discourse analysis that aims to study, understand, and articulate how people make sense of themselves and each other in everyday life.

2. *Conversation analysis:* examines order as it is produced through talk in an achieved manner in situ, accomplished in and through the actual practices of social members.

3. *Membership categorisation device:* an analytic tool or device that describes the culturally available sets of categories into which we commonsensically divide persons.

4. *Membership categorisations analysis:* how social structures are articulated in the talk-in-interaction of everyday life.

5. *Indexicality:* the meaning of a work, which takes into account its context and sequence.

6. *Turn-in interaction:* the sequencing of conversation whereby participants to a conversation engage in a turn-in method of conversation.

7. *Praxis:* the process of using a theory a practical way.

KEY THEMES

- What is ethnomethodology?

- What are some of the implication of applying the analytic tools of conver-

sation analysis and member categorisation devices to sport management research?

CHAPTER OVERVIEW

This chapter aims to explore a qualitative research methodology that aims to study, understand, and articulate how people make sense of themselves and each other in everyday life – ethnomethodology. Simply stated, ethnomethodology is a form of discourse analysis (refer to the chapter on discourse analysis). In the field of sport management research, ethnomethodology has to date been largely ignored. In this chapter, we explore some of the basic tenets of ethnomethodology and how these can be applied to the field of sport management research in useful and practical ways that can facilitate the development of practices that enhance sport management education. This will aid in the positive development of praxis within the sport management community that can enhance in a positive way the experience and engagement of members of the sport management community.

WHAT IS ETHNOMETHODOLOGY?

Garfinkel (1967) coined the term and was the founder of ethnomethodology. In his text discussing Garfinkel's work, Heritage (1984) defines ethnomethodology as the study of:

> … *the body of common-sense knowledge and the range of procedures and considerations by which the ordinary members of society make sense of, find their way about in, and act on the circumstances in which they find themselves. (p. 4)*

The ethnomethodological perspective views social actors as accomplishing their social worlds through interaction, by means of a continuous process of intersubjective adjustment. Social realities are, therefore, regarded as action in process (Garfinkel, 1967). Ethnomethodological studies investigate social life *in situ*, in ordinary settings, examining "the most routine, every-day, naturally occurring activities in their concrete details" (Psathas, 1995, pp. 1–2). Lee (1991, pp. 224–225) outlines five axioms that characterise the way that an ethnomethodological approach gives a new orientation to the study of social life and social activity. The axioms are:

1. Suspending general questions (e.g. about class, socioeconomic status, cultural differences) until those characteristics of people and activities have occurred as activity or interaction that can be understood and observed by participants in (members of) the culture or language of the community: for example, ignoring the preconceived knowledge of sport rivalry until actions depicting rivalry among fans of different teams are observed and then understood.

2. Treating social activities, such as talk (e.g. conversation, social interaction, interviews), as jointly constructed social events that are observable,

rather than as the result of cognitive or linguistic choices or cultural attributions.

3. Translating the conceptually unanalysed notion of "language forms" into an exploration (scrutiny) of how people organise their activities in and through talk and local routines of that talk without pre-empting notions of what these structures look like.

4. Accepting that the ways in which people coordinate their activities in and through talk will show the orderliness of their culture and how that is achieved, day by day, in ordinary activities. For example, the daily activities and interactions of athletes and coaches may provide an illustration of team culture.

5. Regarding culture as implanted in and built by the course of everyday actions, because that is how members of a culture experience it, not as something "external" to and "constraining on language". Culture is present in ordinary activities, in knowledge and skills used and available in talk and action.

Ethnomethodology studies the specific interactions among participants and acknowledges that interactions are actually agents for constituting social order and reality. Gubrium and Holstein (2000) suggest that ethnomethodologists focus on how members actually "do" social life, aiming in particular to document how they concretely construct and sustain social entities, such as gender, self, and family. The five concepts are central to ethnomethodology; these are shown in Table 13.1.

Table 13.1 Concepts that are central to ethnomethodology

Concepts that are central to ethnomethodology

Indexicality	The meaning of a word – indeed of all words – is dependent on its context of use.
Reflexivity	This is the process in ordinary conversation by which we build up meaning, order, and rationality by both describing and producing action simultaneously.
The documentary method of "interpretation"	The meaning of a word is indexical, but at the same time, we seek patterns method of to compensate for this indexicality of language that make sense.
The notion of "member"	The term member is used in ethnomethodology to describe a member of group who has mastered the natural language of that group and does not have to think about what he or she is doing as the routines of everyday social practice are known.
Accountability	Accountability means that the activities whereby members produce and manage settings of organised everyday affairs as observable and reportable.

Research brief

Title: Complicity, performance, and the 'doing' of sports coaching: An ethnomethodological study of work
Author: Corsby, C. L. T., *Cardiff Metropolitan University* & Jones, R. L., *Cardiff Metropolitan University*
Reference: Corsby, C. L., & Jones, R. L. (2019). Complicity, performance, and the 'doing' of sports coaching: An ethnomethodological study of work. *The Sociological Review*, 0038026119897551
Recent attempts to "decode" the everyday actions of coaches have furthered the case for sports coaching as a detailed site of "work". Adhering to Harold Garfinkel's ethnomethodological project, the aim of this article was to deconstruct contextual actors' interactions, paying specific attention to the conditions under which such behaviours occur. The article thus explored the dominant taken-for-granted social rules evident at Bayside Rovers Football F.C. (pseudonym), a semi-professional football club. A 10-month ethnomethodologically informed ethnography was used to observe, participate in and describe the Club's everyday practices. The findings comprised two principal "codes" through which the work of the Club was guided: "to play well" and "fitting-in".

METHODOLOGY

According to Schegloff (1991), the basic task of the ethnomethodologist is "to convert insistent intuition, however correct, into empirically detailed analysis" (p. 66). Lee's (1991) five principles of ethnomethodology summarise the researcher's position. *First*, an ethnomethodologist suspends belief or acceptance of social relationships between categories of people. An ethnomethodologist understands that members continually display the "lived" reality of their relationships and their world to themselves and to others (Schegloff, 1991). *Second*, the ethnomethodologist's task is to treat interactive situations as scenes that are jointly and sequentially produced by all participants. *Third*, the ethnomethodologist sets aside formats of talk or interaction that given participants would or should use in favour of the structures of talk and interaction that they do use. *Fourth*, the assumption that the orderliness of social structures and social organisation is achieved in the day-to-day ordinary activities of members and will, therefore, be available in the details of everyday events, is maintained by the ethnomethodologist. *Finally*, the ethnomethodologist understands that, for members of a society, society's traditions, customs, and more are not sequestered from the talk and interaction, nor do they limit and constrain what those members do and say.

Case study

Title: Mental health disclosure in the public eye: Accounting for and managing absences from professional sporting competition
Author: Elsey, C., *De Montfort University* (2019)
Reference: Elsey, C. (2019). Mental health disclosure in the public eye: Accounting for and

managing absences from professional sporting competition. *Qualitative Research in Sport, Exercise and Health*, *11*(4), 435–459.

The purpose of this paper was to consider how professional sports players and their sporting clubs and associations publicly managed the disclosure of mental health issues that resulted in a players' enforced absence from competition. The paper focused on official or authorised press statements, press conferences (and transcripts thereof), social media posts, and official websites, to consider public discourses and media coverage of mental health in professional sport. The research was informed by the principles and methods of ethnomethodology and conversation analysis (CA). In this paper, two retrospective "mental injury" timelines were presented from two professional sports players in the UK (namely Sarah Taylor, cricketer and Aaron Lennon, footballer), starting with the initial announcement that the player will not be participating and ending with the announcement of their reintegration into their team's routine match day activities.

In particular, the research used the analytical techniques of membership categorisation analysis (MCA), derived from ethnomethodology and CA, to examine interactions or media sources and how members of society reference particular social categories or identities to describe, classify and, ultimately, divide people within specific social settings (e.g. Eglin & Hester, 2003). These approaches were particularly suited to visual/verbal materials and methods, as well as the embodied nature of sport as work (Evans, 2017; Groom, Cushion, & Nelson, 2012; Phoenix, 2010).

Several important findings have emerged, including whether the original announcement was (in)voluntary; the categorisation of mental health conditions employed; the details made public in press statements and what is added in subsequent press conferences and interviews; and the open-ended return time frames.

References in this case study

Eglin, P. & Hester, S. (2003). *The Montreal Massacre: A study of membership categorization analysis.* Waterloo, Ontario: Wilfrid Laurier University Press.

Evans, B. (2017). Sports coaching as action-in-context: Using ethnomethodological conversation analysis to understand the coaching process. *Qualitative Research in Sport, Exercise and Health*, 9(1), 111–132.

Groom, R., Cushion, C.J., & Nelson, L.J. (2012). Analysing coach–athlete 'Talk in Interaction' within the delivery of video-based performance feedback in elite youth soccer. *Qualitative Research in Sport, Exercise and Health*, 4(3), 439–458.

Phoenix, C. (2010). Seeing the world of physical culture: The potential of visual methods for qualitative research in sport and exercise. *Qualitative Research in Sport and Exercise*, 2(2), 93–108.

THE ANALYTIC TOOLS OF ETHNOMETHODOLOGY

The key analytic tools of ethnomethodology are CA and membership categorisation devices (MCDs). CA is concerned with explicating the practices social actors (e.g. sport managers, athletes, coaches, fans, etc.) use to understand, and exhibit understanding of, everyday discourse (e.g. social media posts, team meetings, stadium cheers and jeers, etc.). CA goes beyond a grammatical analysis of statements and relies on detailed transcripts of conversation (naturally occurring or interviews).

CA is characterised by three main features or assumptions: *first*: interaction is structurally organised; *second*: contributions to interaction are contextually oriented; and *third*: as a result of these two characteristics, no

Table 13.2 Comparing discourse analysis and conversation analysis

Discourse analysis vs. conversation analysis	
Discourse analysis	**Conversation analysis**
Rules, formulas, more typical of linguistics.	More rigorously empirical and inductive and philosophers.
Categories, contingencies, grammars.	Focus on what is found in data, not on what is expected to be found or would sound odd.
Use of a small but strategic amount of data.	Hesitant to make generalisations/accused of being atheoretical.
Accused of "premature" theory construction.	Questions about whether the rules "work" on real data.

order of detail in interactions can be dismissed as disorderly, accidental, or irrelevant (Heritage, 1984). These features are the basic foundations on which CA is built. As a branch of ethnomethodology, CA examines order as it is produced through talk in an achieved manner *in situ*, accomplished in and through the actual practices of social members. Hallmarks of conversation analytic work are: (1) commitment to naturally occurring discourse; (2) usage of a particularly detailed transcription system; (3) an inductive theoretical stance; (4) a strong reliance on the conversational text; and (5) avoidance of non-discourse data (e.g. participant interviews) or predetermined category information (e.g. team affiliation) that is unavailable in the interaction itself. The distinctions between discourse analysis and CA are identified in Table 13.2.

The MCD is an analytic tool or device that describes the culturally available sets of categories into which we commonsensically divide persons. These categories are fundamental sense-making resources for members in everyday interaction. We do not argue that all the approaches to textual, conversational and pictorial analysis are, in fact, similar or interchangeable. Indeed, there are certain ways in which they are divergent. Silverman (1993), for example, argues that discourse analysis and critical discourse analysis are different from ethnomethodology and CA in that the former two analytic approaches possess the following three features: (1) they are concerned with a far broader range of activities, often related to more conventional social science concerns (e.g. gender relations, social control, etc.); (2) they do not always use analysis of ordinary conversation as a baseline for understanding talk in institutional settings; and (3) discourse analysis and critical discourse analysis work with far less precise transcripts than CA (p. 121). A summary of the terminology used in MCD is highlighted in Table 13.3.

Table 13.3 MCD terminology
Membership categorisation devices (MCDs)
Category: any person can be labelled in many "correct" ways.
MCD: categories are seen as grouped together in collections.
Economy rule: a single category may be sufficient to describe a person.
Consistency rule: if one person is identified from a collection, then another person may be identified from the same collection.
Duplicative organisation: when categories can be heard as a "team" hear them that way.
Standardised relational pairs (SRPs): pairs of categories are linked together in standardised routine ways.

Research brief

Title: Sports coaching as action-in-context: Using ethnomethodological conversation analysis to understand the coaching process
Author: Evans, B., *Auckland University of Technology* (2016)
Reference: Evans, B. (2017). Sports coaching as action-in-context: Using ethnomethodological conversation analysis to understand the coaching process. *Qualitative Research in Sport, Exercise and Health*, *9*(1), 111–132.
This paper explored the turn to context within contemporary studies of sports coaching, observing that the theoretical progress in reconceptualising coaching as complex and contextually shaped social activity had not yet been matched by empirical studies explicating how coaching actually transpired as situated action. It argued that this imbalance is attributable, at least in part, to a research practice predominant within sociological research on coaching that involved mobilising theorised conceptualisations of context to specify the significance of social actions. The paper outlined an alternative understanding of context, shared by the perspectives of ethnomethodology and CA, under which actions and contexts were treated as being reflexively configured by participants in and as their ongoing accomplishment of intersubjectively intelligible social activities.

QUALITY CRITERIA

The quality criteria for carrying out research using CA are set out in Table 13.4. The criteria for quality investigation (assumptions) have been adapted from a number of authoritative sources (Boden, 1994; Have, 1999; Heritage, 1997; Hutchby and Wooffitt, 1998; Psathas, 1995; Silverman, 1998). The right-hand column shows, for each of the criteria, how the methods of CA were put into practice in a research study. Table 13.4 demonstrates that ethnomethodology is an emerging body of scholarship that is directed at promoting a more rigorous and theoretically informed understanding of the conduct and reporting of fieldwork.

Table 13.4 The methodological perspective of conversation analysis

The methodological perspective of conversation analysis

Assumptions	Practice in study
CA methods were seen by Harvey Sacks as "methods anyone could use" (Silverman, 1998) though familiarity and practice is essential for quality data transcription and analysis.	Recordings must be able to be repeatedly played and transcribed for verification and re-examination.
Data should be derived from naturally recurring conversation.	
CA tries to describe and analyse phenomena and not explain phenomena by drawing on a theoretical framework other than the frameworks of CA itself.	

Data-transcription assumptions

Data is recorded by audio-recordings. This original data is the only evidence from which all analysis derives.	The original recordings were used throughout the analysis in preference to transcripts.
Transcription seeks to capture the "machinery" of conversation using the transcription.	
Practice was guided by practitioner handbooks (e.g. Have, 1999; Hutchby & Wooffitt, 1998) and skills developed during the transcription and analysis.	
The researcher did not impose any order.	
Members were selected randomly by other than the researcher. Places were determined by where the conversations were to take place. Research settings were natural	

Data analysis: Analytical assumptions

CA research adopts a stance of "unmotivated looking".	Phenomena are analysed in accordance with CA theory and conventions.
No assumptions are made regarding members' motivations, intentions, purposes; nor about their ideas, thoughts or understandings; except in so far as these can demonstrably be shown.	
The researcher's analysis of what participants are doing is never based on some constructive analytic interpretation such as: "taking the role of the other" "presenting a self" "being deviant" "managing impressions" "defining the situation"	
These are set aside because they interfere with the direct examination of the phenomena of talk-in-interaction.	

(*Continued*)

Assumptions	Practice in study
Data analysis: practical assumptions	
Existing knowledge of the "machinery of conversation", established through research on CA over the last 30 years, is accepted as a faithful description of recurrent phenomena that can be used for analysis.	A single instance is not usually taken as evidence of structure. Repeated instances of demonstrably similar empirical structures are admissible.
The analytical task is, initially, to provide a wholly adequate analysis of how a single instance (utterance, individually or in sequence) is organised. The aim is to "recover the machinery" that produced the interaction "as it happened".	
This principle, or assumption, was followed so that the researcher was not part of the interpretive framework. The question of setting aside analytical interpretations such as these did not arise as they were not used.	
Data sessions and reporting	
Written reports must include transcripts of the data from which the report was written.	Transcription conventions were used but some additional notations were devised to transcribe phenomena for which there is no existing symbol.

RIGOUR

The essential problem for ethnomethodological research is not operationalising some theory, but in making the world able to be investigated in terms of the phenomena that the theory of ethnomethodology specifies (Benson & Hughes, 1991). This places a methodological constraint on the researcher in that nothing can be assumed to be known about the phenomena specified in advance of investigating the world through the theory. Benson and Hughes suggest that "to do otherwise would transgress the requirements of rigor in failing to establish that the world can be investigated by the theory to produce findings about the phenomena. Rigour, then is "adhering to the methodological election to treat the social order as a member's accomplishment through and through" (p. 129).

POSSIBLE APPLICATIONS OF ETHNOMETHODOLOGY TO SPORT MANAGEMENT RESEARCH

CA, as an analytic tool of Ethnomethodology, can be used to examine order as it is produced through talk in an achieved manner *"in situ"*, accomplished in and through the actual practices of social members. Conversational practices are instrumental to human sociality, and enable the construction of social reality.

This construction extends to institutions whereby restrictive codes of conduct, which establish the context and content, serve to distinguish it from everyday talk. In the context of sport communication and public relations, the sports interview is one such institution, which involves the construction of turn taking through sequence design, lexical choice, and asymmetry. Additionally, the sports interview requires first, the management of success in order to maintain the loser's "face", and second, the use of text to sustain the opposition's sporting abilities. Heritage (1997) provides "tools" to analyse sport interviews such as: "sequence organisation, turn design, lexical choice, and asymmetry which may provide an insight into the institutional practices of the sports interview" (p. 164).

Another area of investigation could involve the role of women in sport management. Limited research has been conducted on the impact of psycho-social development (how women grow, develop, and are socialised) and its influence on their career choices, specifically their decision to be involved in sport management. This type of research could explore the psychosocial developmental experiences and critical factors leading women to choose sport management as a career option. This effort is significant for the following reasons:

1. Discovering and understanding the factors that lead women to study sport management.

2. Increasing the overall number of women sport managers.

3. Hearing the stories of how other women made their choices to become sport managers, will provide affirmation to those in the profession and motivation to others to make this career choice.

Ethnomethodology may also draw Bourdieu's (1973) conceptions of "habitus, cultural and symbolic capital". Bottomley (1991) claims that, within one's everyday world, power relations are both structured and symbolically formed, giving meaning to everyday practice. From this perspective, the sport manager engages in action that supports power within the sport organisation but at the same time may resist oppression. The dialectics of oppression and resistance become obvious in the taken-for-granted terrain of practice. The power relationship in sport organisations can be analysed using the ethnomethodological tools of CA and MCD.

Ethnomethodology can also treat social interactions such as sporting team training sessions primarily as organised interactional events. The goal of ethnomethodology is to explore how people coordinate their everyday courses of action in and through the routines of their talk, without pre-empting what the structure of those routines might look like. Ethnomethodology can be useful in exploring the cultural practices we see in sporting clubs and sporting teams and examines how they are embedded in and built by the everyday discourses and conversations that occur between members.

Ethnomethodologists understand this shared common-sense and experienced world to be constituted by orderly social practices evidenced in texts and talk. The task of ethnomethodologists is to investigate the recurrent practices found within members' interactions that constitute their shared common-sense worlds, and make them orderly.

In ethnomethodological studies, people's *reports* of what they did or did not do and say in a particular situation cannot be substituted for what they did or did not do. Similarly, interviews of interactants about a particular incident cannot stand in the place of observations, recordings, and transcriptions of the incident. This is not to say reports and interviews are not potentially interesting data per se. For example, in the case of interviews of sport managers about their management practices, the interviews would count as data in the question of what sport managers say in interviews about what they do, but they would not count as data that answers the question of what those sport managers actually do when "managing" the sport organisation.

Case study

Title: Video gaming as practical accomplishment: Ethnomethodology, conversation analysis, and play

Author: Reeves, S., *University of Nottingham*, Greiffenhagen, C., *The Chinese University of Hong Kong*, & Laurier, E., *The University of Edinburgh* (2017)

Reference: Reeves, S., Greiffenhagen, C., & Laurier, E. (2017). Video gaming as practical accomplishment: Ethnomethodology, conversation analysis, and play. *Topics in Cognitive Science*, 9(2), 308–342.

Accounts of video game play developed from an ethnomethodological and conversation analytic (EMCA) perspective remained relatively scarce. This study collected together an emerging body of research that focused on the material, practical "work" of video game players. The study offered an example-driven explication of an EMCA perspective on video game play phenomena. The materials were arranged as a "tactical zoom." The authors started very much "outside" the game, beginning with a wide view of how massive-multiplayer online games were played within dedicated gaming spaces; here, the authors found multiple players, machines, and many different sorts of activities going on (besides playing the game). Still, remaining somewhat distanced from the play of the game itself, the authors took a closer look at the players by examining a notionally simpler setting involving pairs taking part in a football game at a games console. As they drew closer to the technical details of play, the authors narrowed their focus further still to examine a player and spectator situated "at the screen" but jointly analysing play as the player competed in an online first-person shooter. Finally, they went "inside" the game entirely and looked at the conduct of avatars on-screen via screen recordings of a massively multiplayer online game. Having worked through specific examples, the authors provided an elaboration of a selection of core topics of ethnomethodology and CA that were used to situate some of the unstated orientations in the presentation of data fragments. In this way, recurrent issues raised in the fragments were shown as coherent, interconnected phenomena. In closing, the paper suggested caution regarding the way game play phenomena have been analysed in this study, while remarking on challenges present for the development of further EMCA-oriented research on video game play.

CONCLUSION

This chapter has introduced the research method of ethnomethodology. Ethnomethodology, a form of discourse analysis, is offered as a contribution to an emerging body of scholarship that is directed at promoting a more rigorous and theoretically informed understanding of the conduct and reporting of field-work. The method aims to study, understand, and articulate how people make sense of themselves and each other in everyday life. It clearly has unexplored potential in the field of sport management research.

REVIEW AND RESEARCH QUESTIONS

Ethnomethodology is a form of discourse analysis that aims to study, understand, and articulate how people make sense of themselves and each other in everyday life. With an understanding of ethnomethodology, attempt to answer the following questions:

1. What factors should the sport management researcher take into consideration before deciding to adopt ethnomethodology as a research approach?

2. How can ethnomethodology be applied to sport management research?

3. Discuss the various *membership categorisation devices* and how they would be applied in sport management research.

REFERENCES

Benson, D., & Hughes, J. (1991). Method: Evidence and inference – Evidence and inference for ethnomethodology. In G. Button (Ed.), *Ethnomethodology and the Human Sciences*, pp. 109–136. New York: Cambridge University Press.

Boden, D. (1994). *The business of talk: Organizations in action*. Cambridge: Polity Press.

Bottomley, G. (1991). Representing the 'second generation. In G. Bottomley, M. de Lepervanche, & J. Martin (Eds.), *Intersexions: Gender/Class/Culture/Ethnicity*. Sydney, Australia: Allen & Unwin.

Bourdieu, P. (1973). Cultural reproduction and social reproduction. In R. Brown (Ed.), *Knowledge, Education and Cultural Change*, pp. 71–112. London: Tavistock.

Garfinkel, H. (1967/1999). *Studies in ethnomethodology*. Englewood Cliffs, NJ: Prentice-Hall.

Gubrium, J., & Holstein, J. (2000). Analyzing interpretive practice. In N. K. Denzin, & Y. S. Lincoln (Eds.), *Handbook of Qualitative Research* (2nd ed.), pp. 487–508. Thousand Oaks, CA: Sage Publications.

Have, P. T. (1999). *Doing conversation analysis: A practical guide*. London: Sage Publications.

Heritage, J. (1984). *Garfinkel and ethnomethodology*. Cambridge, MA: Polity Press.

Heritage, J. (1997). Conversation analysis and institutional talk: Analyzing data. In D. Silverman (Ed.), *Qualitative Analysis: Issues of Theory and Method*, pp. 161–181. London: Sage Publications.

Hutchby, I., & Wooffitt, R. (1998). *Conversation analysis*. Cambridge: Polity Press.

Lee, J. R. E. (1991). Language and culture: The linguistic analysis of culture. In G. Button (Ed.), *Ethnomethodology and the Human Sciences*, pp. 196–226. Cambridge: Cambridge University Press.

Psathas, G. (1995). *Conversation analysis: The study of talk-in-interaction*. Thousand Oaks, CA: Sage Publications.

Schegloff, E. (1991). Reflections on talk and social structure. In D. Boden, & D. H. Zimmerman (Eds.), *Talk and Social Structure: Studies in Ethnomethodology and Conversation Analysis*, pp. 44–70. Berkeley, CA: University of California Press.

Silverman, D. (1993). The machinery of interaction: Sacks' lectures on conversation. *Sociological Review, 41*(4), 731–752.

Silverman, D. (1998). *Harvey sacks: Social science and conversation analysis*. Cambridge: Polity Press.

Ethnography and sport management research

CHAPTER OVERVIEW

This chapter examines the qualitative research approach of ethnography. For many years traditional ethnography has been applied to the field of sport. From the late 1990s, sport management researchers began to embrace ethnographic frameworks underpinned by critical and postmodern theories. The advantage for sport management researchers in applying critical and postmodern thought to ethnographic approaches is that it strengthens their own critical consciousness. This chapter will provide an introduction and overview to the concepts of ethnography, and provides some examples of critical and postmodern frameworks that ethnographic researchers can use in the sport management research.

WHAT IS ETHNOGRAPHY?

Ethnography is a qualitative design in which the researcher describes and interprets the shared and learned patterns of values, behaviours, beliefs, and language of a culture-sharing group (Harris, 1968). As both a process and an outcome of research (Agar, 1980), ethnography is a way of studying a culture-sharing group as well as the final written product of that research. As a process, ethnography involves extended observations of the group, most often through participant observation, in which the researcher is immersed in the day-to-day lives of the people and observes and interviews the group participants. Ethnographers study the meaning of the behaviour, the language, and the interaction among members of the culture-sharing group.

Ethnographic studies involve the collection and analysis of data about cultural groups. Ethnography means: "to write about people or cultures" from the Greek words *"ethnos"* (people) and *"graphein"* (write). It is influenced by other theories, such as phenomenology, feminism, grounded theory, and postmodernism. Sometimes ethnography is used (inappropriately) as an umbrella term for many types of qualitative research. According to Cameron (1990), ethnography is "learning from people". Leininger (1985) suggests ethnography can be defined as: "the systematic process of observing, detailing, describing, documenting, and analysing the lifeways or particular patterns of a culture (or subculture) in order to grasp the lifeways or patterns of the people in their familiar environment" (p. 35). Hammersley and Atkinson (1995) indicate that:

> The ethnographer participates, overtly or covertly, in people's daily
> lives for an extended period of time, watching what happens, listening
> to what is said, asking questions; in fact collecting whatever data are
> available to throw light on the issues with which he or she is concerned.
> (p. 2)

What does become clear is that in contemporary research usage, there is a lack of consensus over its definition.

ORIGINS OF ETHNOGRAPHY

Ethnography had its beginning in the comparative cultural anthropology conducted by early 20th-century anthropologists, such as Boas, Malinowski, Radcliffe-Brown, and Mead. Although these researchers initially took the natural sciences as a model for research, they differed from those using traditional scientific approaches through the first hand collection of data concerning existing "primitive cultures" (Atkinson & Hammersley, 1994). In the 1920s and 1930s, sociologists such as Park, Dewey, and Mead at the University of Chicago adapted anthropological field methods to the study of cultural groups in the United States (Bogdan & Biklen, 1992). Recently, scientific approaches to ethnography have expanded to include "schools" or subtypes of ethnography with different theoretical orientations and aims, such as structural functionalism, symbolic interactionism, cultural and cognitive anthropology, feminism, Marxism, ethnomethodology, critical theory, cultural studies, and postmodernism (Atkinson & Hammersley, 1994). This has led to a lack of orthodoxy in ethnography and has resulted in pluralistic approaches. Many excellent books are available on ethnography, including Van Maanen (1988) on the many forms of ethnography; Wolcott (1999) on ways of "seeing" ethnography; LeCompte and Schensul (1999) on procedures of ethnography presented in a toolkit of short books; Atkinson, Coffey, and Delamont (1999) on the practices of ethnography; and Madison (2005) on critical ethnography.

Research brief

Title: Corruption and public secrecy: An ethnography of football match-fixing
Author: Numerato, D., *Loughborough University* (2016)
Reference: Numerato, D. (2016). Corruption and public secrecy: An ethnography of football match-fixing. *Current Sociology, 64*(5), 699–717. The topic of corruption has recently moved from the periphery to the centre of social scientific attention. Notwithstanding the increased interest, research into corruption has been empirically limited and under theorised. This study addressed that gap by providing an ethnographic account of football match-fixing in the Czech Republic. By qualitatively analysing both primary and secondary data, this study examined match-fixing and corruption through the lens of the concept of public secrecy. Three different, narrowly intertwined forms of match-fixing were identified: direct corruption, mediated corruption, and meta-corruption. By conceptualising match-fixing as a public secrecy, the study explored how the publicly secret nature of match-fixing is normalised and how the match-fixing complex is reinforced by a compromising complicity of social actors who are both victims and principals.

CHARACTERISTICS OF ETHNOGRAPHY

Hammersley (1990, p. 1) points out that the term ethnography typically relates to social research, which comprises most of the following features, in that:

- People's behaviours are studied in everyday context, rather than under experimental situations developed by the investigator.

- Data are collected from various sources, with observation and interviews being the primary aspects.

- Data are gathered in an "unstructured" manner in that it does not follow a plan. This does not imply that the research is unsystematic, rather data is collected in as raw a form, and on as wide a front, as feasible.

- The focus is commonly a single setting or group and on a small scale.

- Data analysis entails interpretation of the meanings and functions of human actions and is primarily conducted in the form of verbal descriptions and explanations.

These characteristics make ethnography very applicable to many sport management research contexts or settings. Tables 14.1 highlights the characteristics of ethnographic research.

Ethnography is an appropriate research tool for researchers seeking an in-depth understanding of the practices and professions of sport management.

Table 14.1 Characteristics of ethnographic research

Features of ethnographic research

- Conducted in a natural context

- Involves intimate face-to-face interactions with participants

- Reflects participants' perspectives and behaviours

- Uses inductive, interactive, and recursive collection of unstructured data

- Data is collected primarily through fieldwork experiences

- Uses multiple data sources including both quantitative and qualitative

- Frames all human behaviour and beliefs within a socio-political and historical context

- Uses the concept of culture as a lens through which the results are interpreted

- Places an emphasis on exploring the nature of particular social phenomena

- Investigates a small number of cases in detail

- Uses data analyses that involve the explicit interpretation of the meanings and functions of human actions that are presented through the description of themes and interpretations within the context or group setting

- Offers interpretations of people's actions and behaviours that are uncovered through the investigation of what they actually do and the reasons for doing it

- Offers a representation or interpretation of people's lives and behaviours that is neither the researcher's or the participants' but is built on the points of understanding and misunderstanding that occur between the researcher and participants

- Is necessarily partial, bound by what can be handled within a certain time under certain specific circumstances, and from a particular perspective

Table 14.2	Applications of ethnography to sport management research

Applications of ethnography to sport management research

- To know "why" people behave in a certain way over a period of time

- To understand a phenomenon in its natural setting

- To know *how, when,* and *why* people behave the way they do when they interact with others in a particular setting or situation (i.e. social interaction)

- To obtain data to support your understanding of the complexity of society

- To focus on studying the culture of the sport community – socio-cultural interpretation

- To focus on natural, ordinary events in natural settings – understand better the latent or hidden or non-obvious aspects of people's behaviours, attitudes, feelings, and so forth

- To use multiple data collection methods over a sustained period

- The emphasis on lived experiences – locating the meanings people place on events, processes, and patterns of their lives

Possible areas of sport management research

- Lived day-to-day experiences of sport managers

- Fan experiences on game day

- Community sport organisational behaviour

This is because ethnographic researchers study the lived experiences of participants in the study, seeking to see the world as they do and gain an understanding of the cultural meanings and social formations (and their inter-relationships) of a group – such as an organisation, profession, community, or society. Tables 14.2 highlights the potential applications of ethnographic research to sport management.

DEVELOPMENT OF ETHNOGRAPHY

Traditional ethnography has been a research tool used for many years and emerged from a close relationship with anthropology to study traditional and non-Western societies (Chambers, 2000). Early studies associated with traditional ethnography were the work of "Malinowski and Evans-Prichard in social anthropology and with the classic Chicago studies in urban sociology" (Chambers, 2000, p. 406). Chambers claims the usefulness of ethnographic data grasped what is sometimes called "the native point of view" (p. 853) with an emphasis on the "slice of life approach" (Atkinson, Coffey, & Delamont, 1999). American ethnography, however, was derived largely on the understanding of events whereas the use of ethnography in Britain was associated more with anthropology. Skinner and Edwards (2005) purported that: "in this tradition, emphasis has been more about understanding relationships rather than activities, and research has been based more explicitly on sociology theory" (p. 407).

Regardless of its theoretical origins, ethnography is used to understand the culture of a particular group from the perspective of the group members (Tedlock, 2000; Wolcott, 1995). Tedlock described ethnography "as an attempt to place specific encounters, events and understandings into fuller, more meaningful context" (p. 455). Many researchers portray ethnographic fieldwork involving living both with and like those who are being studied – taking part or being in a group's activities, problems, language, knowledge, rituals, and social relations (Hammersley, 1992; Pedersen, 1998; Tedlock, 2000; Van Maanen, 1988), for example, volunteering in a sport franchise for several months, or long enough to understand how the sport managers, athletes, coaches, and other staff interact and behave. Ethnography provides the opportunity for exploration and investigation of the data via progressive focusing (Burns, 1997) and allows for the "development of theory" (Hammersley & Atkinson, 1983, p. 23). Critics of traditional ethnography (Skinner & Edwards, 2005; Fay, 1975; Habermas, 1978) are concerned about the exclusion of power from the field of study and lack of theoretical relationship that may bring about liberation of the people being investigated. It is also argued that conventional ethnography contains a certain element of neutrality in that a sport management researcher may only observe behaviours in the sport organisation, and not attempt to challenge, change, or fix issues uncovered in the observation. Tedlock (2000) denotes that interpretive ethnographers deny the voice of the researcher-as-author. Moreover, the tenets of traditional ethnography have been brought into question for their validity and worth hence the emergence of other forms of ethnographic research such as critical ethnography (Skinner & Edwards, 2005).

CRITICAL THEORY AND ETHNOGRAPHY

Critical theory is represented to a certain degree in the work of Marx, Freud, and the Frankfurt School (Hammersley, 1992). The Frankfurt School allied critical theory with social theory (Gingrich, 2002). According to Edwards, Gilbert, and Skinner (2002), critical theory challenges societal beliefs to achieve positive changes due to exhibited differences in status and power. Hammersley concludes that critical theory is "grounded in an emancipatory interest in overcoming social oppression, which is clearly the category critical ethnography is intended to fall" (p. 99). This emancipation was achieved through "enlightenment thus enabling members of oppressed groups to recognise their interests" (Hammersley, 1992, p. 100). Hammersley denotes that: "advocates of critical ethnography criticise conventional ethnography for adopting an inappropriate theoretical perspective that neglects oppression and its causes and for not being closely related to political practices designed to bring about emancipation" (p. 96). Table 14.3 highlights the features of critical ethnography.

Table 14.3	Features of critical ethnography

Features of critical ethnography?

- Used by politically minded people
- Advocate for the emancipation of marginalised groups
- Seek to change society
- Identify and celebrate research bias: all research is value laden
- Challenge status-quo and ask "why is it so?"
- Create literal dialogue with participants
- Social issues include: power, empowerment, inequity, dominance, repression, hegemony, victimisation
- Collaborate actively with participants and negotiate final report
- Self-conscious about their own interpretation
- Reflexive and self-aware of their role
- Non-neutral
- Addresses issues of power, authority, emancipation, oppression, and inequity
- Advocates against inequities and domination of particular groups
- Uses contradiction, imponderable, and tension

Adapted from Denzin (1997).

Critical ethnography emphasises the use of power by the power hold-ers and the raising of consciousness. If it was uncovered through ethno-graphic investigation that a certain group (e.g. women sport managers) were oppressed in a sport organisation then a critical ethnographer would seek to empower that group. Through this enlightenment it is believed "eman-cipation and empowerment occurred to allow marginalised individuals and groups to become autonomous and responsible for themselves" (Hammersley, 1992, p. 100). Examples of critical theoretical approaches to ethnography that address hegemonic practices in sport can be seen in the work of Birrell and Theberge (1994), Edwards, Skinner, and O'Keefe (2000), and Sykes (1996). In an analysis of the leadership experience of women, Edwards et al. con-ducted a critical ethnography of dominant practices and discourses that exist within sporting organisations that restrict women from managing effectively. This approach provided the participants with empowerment to enable greater insights into the hegemonic practices to improve managerial techniques.

Although critical ethnography talks about empowerment of individuals in the research process and alerts us to particular types of issues and injustice, Skinner and Edwards (2005) argue "it does not actually involve the researcher in empowering the research participants' understanding of the research issue" (p. 411). Ethnography based on postmodern thought claims to do this.

POSTMODERN ETHNOGRAPHY

The idea of a "postmodern" ethnography is a hotly debated one. Denzin (1997) dismisses critics who claim that, because of their inherent narrative and cohesive features, ethnographies can never be effectively fragmented while still telling the story of a culture. According to Lindlof and Taylor (2002), a postmodern ethnography is one that blurs genres of writing and embraces marginalised voices through a disruption of institutional narratives. Denzin and Lincoln (2000) deem that "the emergence of postmodernism in ethnographic research was useful in adding greater theoretical weight to the ethnographic research because epistemologies from previously silenced groups emerged to offer solutions to representational concerns" (p. 17). Fay (1975) suggests that there is a need for a theory that would lead people to seek to change the way they think about what others are doing. Skinner and Edwards (2005) concur that such a theory would "contribute to the interrelationship between knowledge as beliefs and attitudes, actions, and power relations, and by doing so offer a social rather than individualistic approach to the study of sport and sport organizations" (p. 408).

Gottschalk (1998) argues that a postmodern ethnography is more or *differently* demanding because, in addition to the essential tasks of collecting, organising, interpreting, validating, and communicating "the data", the author needs to remain constantly and critically attentive to issues such as subjectivity, rhetorical moves, problems of voice, power, textual politics, limits to authority, truth claims and unconscious desires. A sport management researcher might alleviate this demand by paying attention to all levels and groups within a sport organisation under investigation, actively seeking to empower those with the smallest voice. Postmodern researchers are interested "in pointing out signs of postmodern changes in the world that is still largely under modern influences" (Markula, Grant, and Denison, 2001, p. 260). Markula et al. agree with other postmodernists' argument that "today's society is constituted of multiple meanings and prefers qualitative research that allows multiple voices to emerge from the research text" (p. 260). An important aspect in incorporating postmodern ethnography as a methodology is that it favours social analyses that incorporates practical or moral interests with local narratives being preferred to grand narratives, for example telling local stories of female surfers, "as opposed to general stories" (Edwards & Skinner, 2009). Skinner and Edwards (2005) believe that the researcher in postmodern ethnography also becomes "encapsulated in the research, not only in the research process but also in the empowerment of the research participants" understanding of the research issue under investigation" (p. 412).

A review of sport research by Sparkes (2003), cited in Skinner & Edwards, 2005, p. 405) suggests that "it was only in the 1990s that the influence of critical and postmodern ethnographic frameworks began to touch on the sub-disciplines of sport". Packwood and Sikes (1996) believe that:

> postmodernism not only focuses on the narrative of the individual but breaks down the meta-narratives into micro-narratives. This serves to allow the voices denied in meta-narrative to be heard, and the taken-for-granted truths and realities of the meta- narratives to be made problematic and thereby verified. (p. 337)

This also permits others, for example, the sponsored female surfers, voices, and opinions to be heard, not just those of the surfing industry. Packwood and Sikes (1996) summarise the underlying assumptions of postmodernism by Docherty (1993) and Smart (1992) as follows:

> Postmodernism rejects a single cosmological theory – an absolute truth in the definitive story. In this type of work, there is no single story, no meta-narrative. Instead, there is a series of stories that, when put together, constitute one individual version of the myth of the research, and the situation, phenomenon, or event addressed through a postmodernist perspective is made sense of by its particularity within both its immediate context and its historicity. (p. 342)

This implies that texts do not have absolute meaning in postmodern research. Rather their meanings reside in the reality that the interpreter brings to the text by which it is read. Packwood and Sikes (1996) believe this type of research results in a "deep reading of the text context rather than merely accepting what it is saying" (p. 343). Semerjian and Waldron (2001) agree and state that there is "more than one way to tell a story about what we see in the world and a number of possible perspectives" (p. 440).

Critics of traditional ethnography concerned about the exclusion of power from the field of study (Edwards & Skinner, 2009, p. 262). The application of postmodern theory within an ethnographic framework in a study by Dunbar (2003) demonstrates the successful use of a postmodern approach in highlighting contradictory images of masculinity. Both these studies enable the researcher to question and disrupt taken-for-granted notions of masculinity, *empowering* the research participants in both studies to revisit their understanding of "what it means to be masculine through critical reflection" (cited in Skinner & Edwards, 2005, p. 412).

Postmodernism compels sport management researchers to examine their theoretical accomplishments, question their epistemological assumptions, and continually challenge the appropriateness of their methodological procedures. In sum, ethnographic research that embraces postmodern thought must address the methodological concerns raised through postmodern inquiry. These include the following:

1. Acknowledgement of the researchers' values, interests, interactions, and interpretations within the research process.

2. Acknowledgement of the reasons for undertaking research.

3. Research is a mutually participative, creative process, wherein the "voice" of the participants is valued and recognised in the research process.

4. Acknowledgement is made of the authorial self as intrusive, but as indispensable to the research process.

5. Encouragement is given to facilitate and allow individuals to tell their own stories, to identify their own issues, and find their own solutions beyond the activities of the researcher.

Regardless of the which ethnographic approach you chose to use, as with other qualitative methods, ethnographic approaches have advantages and disadvantages. Table 14.4 outlines some of these advantages and disadvantages.

Table 14.4 Advantages and disadvantages of ethnographic research

Advantages and disadvantages of ethnographic research

Advantages

■ Provides the researcher with a much more comprehensive perspective than other forms of research

■ Appropriate to behaviours that are best understood by observing them within their natural environment (dynamics)

■ Looks at the situation holistically

■ May arrive at greater understanding of the problem than other research processes

■ Can generate theories

Disadvantages

■ *Highly dependent on the researcher's observations and interpretations*

■ *No way to check the validity of the researcher's conclusion, since numerical data is rarely provided*

■ *Observer bias is almost impossible to eliminate*

■ *Generalisations are almost non-existent since only a single situation is observed, leaving ambiguity in the study*

■ *Researcher's familiarity with the field site may have an impact*

■ *Researcher needs to be familiar with cultural jargon/language*

Case study

Title: Being women in a male preserve: An ethnography of female football ultras
Author: Pitti, I. (2019), *Örebro University* (2019)
Reference: Pitti, I. Being women in a male preserve: An ethnography of female football ultras. *Journal of Gender Studies, 28*(3), 318–329.

This article investigated the characteristics of contemporary sports audiences from the perspective of gender, focusing on the phenomenon of female *ultras* or "professional" football fans. Drawing on ethnographic research conducted in an Italian football *ultras* group composed of male and female fans, this paper offered an analysis of female participation in communities of organised supporters. In examining the role and position of women inside the considered group, the paper paid attention to their perception of the existing gender differences showing how female *ultras* explained inequalities on the basis of "natural" and "innate" differences and capacities between men and women.

The materials considered in this article have been collected between September 2015 and December 2016. The research started with a semi-structured interview conducted with the head of the group in September 2015, which focused on the *ultras* subculture and the *ultras* community. Following this first meeting, participant observations were carried out in several settings and in relation to a variety of events involving the group (126 single observations for about 620 hours spent in the field). In a first phase, observations took place mostly at the group's "headquarter", a formerly abandoned bowl court located in front of the stadium, which the group occupied at the beginning of 2015. Observations at the centre were conducted both during organised special events (i.e. music events, book presentations, pre and post-matches parties, beer, and food festivals) and in "standard" days: since the occupation, the centre has progressively become a familiar place for the members of the core group who meet there almost every evening after work to chat and have a drink together. In a second phase, other observations were conducted in conjunction with matches (both away and played at home games) and events in public domains (i.e. sport festivals) where the author has been invited to participate together with the group. In the last phase, some observations took place in "private" settings and events, such as dinners and parties at the *ultras*' houses.

In total, 23 in-depth interviews were conducted with the *ultras*, of which 6 were with the women involved in the group. The interviews focused on the interviewees' paths of participation into the group, on the relationship between their private life and their *ultras* identity, and on the meanings they associate to the participation in the *ultras* community.

The author concluded that existing patterns of male dominance were supported by female fans' own discourses and performance of their gender identity in the "male preserve". Rather than questioning male dominance and gender hierarchies, female supporters' efforts appeared to be aimed at being recognised as *ultras* "despite being women".

ETHNOGRAPHIC RESEARCH STEPS

According to Spradley (1980), there are five tasks in ethnographic research design, although appearing sequential are actually cyclical in design (Spradley, 1980). These tasks are: (1) selecting an ethnographic project; (2) collecting ethnographic data; (3) analysing ethnographic data; (4) asking ethnographic questions; and (5) writing the ethnography.

Wolcott (1995) states that ethnographic procedures require three things: (1) a detailed description of the culture-sharing group being studied; (2) an analysis of this group in terms of perceived themes or perspectives, and (3) some interpretation of the group by the researcher as to meanings and generalisation about the social life of human beings, in general.

The tasks outlined by Spradley (1980) and procedures suggested by Wolcott (1980) provide a framework for ethnographic research. However, as with all qualitative inquiry, there is no single way to conduct the research in an ethnography. The main issue prior to ethnography is to first determine if ethnography is the most appropriate design to use to study the research problem. Ethnography is appropriate if the needs are to describe how a cultural group works and to explore the beliefs, language, behaviours, and issues, such as power, resistance, and dominance. We propose that the ethnographic process shares many similarities with phenomenological research. As such, we suggest nine (9) steps that can be used to conduct an ethnographic (Gay, Mills, & Airasian, 2009). These are:

1. *Identify the purpose of the research study.* This section should describe and explain a facet or segment of group social life as it relates to sport management.

2. *Frame the study as a larger theoretical, policy, or practical problem.* Framing the question presents a contextual framework for the research.

3. *Pose initial ethnographic research questions.* Although research questions may change in the course of the research as more is learned it is suggested that having guiding questions is a good idea.

4. *Describe the overall approach and rationale for the study.* During this stage it is recommended that a research plan be established.

5. *Describe the site and sample selection.* The site and its characteristics are described to provide context to the study. The following steps are proposed in selecting a sample: (a) define the population (the population consists of every individual case that possesses the characteristic that is of interest to the researcher; and (b) determine the sampling method.

6. *Describe the researcher's role.* The role of the researcher in qualitative research has been identified elsewhere in this book (refer to Chapter 19 on Phenomenology). According to Bryman (2004), the role of the researcher is different in ethnography according to: (a) open field site and covert role; (b) open field site and overt role; (c) closed field site and overt role; and (d) closed field site and covert role. Ethics issues are less problematic where the research takes an overt role, where the people being studied are aware the research is occurring.

7. *Describe the data collection methods.* Data collection and analysis occur simultaneously in ethnography. As understanding of the data occurs, new

questions emerge. The end purpose of ethnography is the development of cultural theories. The *fieldwork* researcher gathers data in the setting where the participants are located and where their shared patterns can be studied. This may be in the head office, the sport facilities, in and around the sport event area, or even in online forums and chat rooms. Types of data that can be collected includes:

i. Emic data (data supplied by the participants);

ii. Etic data (ethnographer's interpretation of participants' perspectives);

iii. Negotiation data (information participants and researcher agree to use in a study).

There are two main methods of collecting data through ethnographic research:

i. Interviewing is the most important tool.

ii. Participant observation is crucial to effective fieldwork, which requires an immersion in the culture, the use of other tools are also required to ensure data reflexive accuracy, these include:

   ■ Field notes are used to check the accuracy of an ethnographer's observations;

   ■ Other forms of writing used are field jottings, field diary, and field logs.

Spradley (1980) suggests a checklist should be used when is extensive field-work is being completed by the researcher. When attempting to seek out rich detailed description the researcher should not attempt to summarise, generalise, or hypothesise. Fieldnotes capture and describe what happened to permit interpretations, and most of all, to later convey cultural meaning.

8. *Describe appropriate strategies for the analysis and interpretation of data.*
   The data analysis follows many of the processes recommended previously for qualitative research:

   ■ Triangulation (checking the validity by comparing sources of information).

   ■ Patterns (checking reliability by revealing consistencies and describing matches).

   ■ Key events (a lens through which to view a culture).

   ■ Visual representations (maps, charts, sociograms).

   ■ Statistics (use of non-parametric techniques).

- Crystallisation (when everything falls into place).

- Ethnographic saturation.

- Managing the process.

9. *Write the ethnographic account.*

The ethnographic account: From the beginning of the research, the researcher will need to record what goes on "in the field". This includes making notes of early impressions as well as detailed descriptions of events and behaviour. There are four different types of fieldnotes in ethnography, according to Spradley (1979), all of which should be written as the researcher proceeds:

1. The condensed account;

2. The expanded account;

3. The fieldwork journal;

4. Analysis and interpretation notes.

Condensed accounts are summary descriptions made in the field, while *expanded accounts* are written up later, with the detail filled in and the short notes extended. In the *fieldwork journal*, the researcher needs to be reflexive, noting their own assumptions and reactions, as well as the problems which they encounter. *Fieldwork proceeds* in stages. Initially, the researcher gains an overview of the site, later focusing on issues that seem important to them. Finally, writing becomes detailed *analysis and interpretation*.

Research brief

Title: The geopolitics of sport beyond soft power: Event ethnography and the 2016 cycling world championships in Qatar
Author: Koch, N., *Syracuse University* (2018)
Reference: Koch, N. (2018). The geopolitics of sport beyond soft power: Event ethnography and the 2016 cycling world championships in Qatar. *Sport in Society*, 21(12), 2010–2031.
State leaders in the Arabian Peninsula have increasingly sought to host globalised sporting events to broadcast a cosmopolitan and modern image of the region. These efforts are typically interpreted as examples of states exercising "soft power". This article challenged the state-centric assumptions built into the soft power approach by employing an event ethnography of the 2016 UCI Road Cycling World Championships in Doha. Advancing a more grounded geopolitics of elite sport in the Gulf, the author examined how geopolitical identity narratives about Qatar, and the Gulf region more broadly, circulate at various scales and through countless contingent encounters at the event. More specifically, the author explored how these identity narratives were constructed and challenged, both materially and discursively by athletes, spectators, and urban residents.

REFLEXIVITY, VALIDITY, AND RELIABILITY IN ETHNOGRAPHIC DESIGNS

Reflexivity

Reflexivity is a process that has been identified previously as fundamental to qualitative research. In ethnography this means that researchers: (1) openly discuss respect for participants and sites; (2) talk about themselves; (3) share their experiences; and (4) identify how their interpretations shape their discussions about sites and groups.

Validity in ethnography

According to Burns (1997), the data collection and analysis strategies used by ethnographers in ethnographic studies maintain high internal validity for a number of reasons. First, the long-term living relationship with participants in the setting allows continual data analysis and comparison to "refine constructs and to ensure the match between scientific categories and participant realities" (p. 324). Second, interviews with participants, which constitute a primary ethnographic data source, must be solely derived from experience or observation and "are less abstract than many instruments used in other research designs" (p. 324). Third, the researcher's role as participant–observer, in order to acquire the reality of life experiences of participants, is found in the natural settings. Finally, ethnographic analysis embodies a process of ethnographer self-monitoring known as disciplined activity, in which the researcher continually questions and re-evaluates information and challenges his/her own opinions or biases.

Reliability in ethnography

The scale of reliability in ethnographic research is based on replication of the study, and that two or more individuals can have comparable explanations by conforming to categories and procedures in the study (Burns, 1997). Despite replication in social sciences not always being achievable (due to changes in the setting or behaviours of members), the possibility to replicate ethnographic findings does not undermine assessments of their validity, though it may make the task more difficult. Moreover, Burns (2000) notes that qualitative research does not pretend to be replicable. The researcher "purposely avoids controlling the research conditions and concentrates on recording the complexity of changing situational contexts" (p. 417).

The threat to reliability in ethnographic studies can be overcome if ethnographers can: (1) provide a profile for the research together with major question(s) they wish to address; (2) describe their views on the question(s) and explain the research assumptions and biases; and (3) explain the data collecting process in view of timing and parameters of the study, interviews, relationships with members and categories to be developed for analysis (Burns, 1997). The quality of data is also improved when the participant observer establishes and sustains trusting and co-operative relationships with people in the field. In a sense, validity and reliability are closely associated issues that "acquire a distinct character for the methodology of participant observation" (p. 325).

TRUST AND INTEGRITY IN ETHNOGRAPHIC RESEARCH

Definite guidelines for researchers in order to gain trust and integrity in ethnographic research do not exist, and according to Neuman (1994) "a genuine concern for and interest in others, being honest, and sharing feelings are good strategies" (p. 342). A researcher's long-term period in this study interacting with members, listening and understanding their concerns, their verbal and non-verbal language, and acknowledging their cultural rules helps to develop rapport, trust, integrity, and cooperation. As a sport management researcher spends more time within the sport organisations and around sport managers, coaches, players, etc., the higher the degree of trust builds, allowing the data to be checked over and over. The degree of the relationship between researcher and members is very useful in obtaining "accurate and dependable information" (Jorgensen, 1989, p. 70).

ETHICAL PRINCIPLES

It is important to note that participants are human beings who have interests, concerns and problems, and researchers' values are not necessarily similar to those of participants. Fieldwork is an essential component of ethnography and researchers in the field frequently confront conflicting values and a broad range of possible choices. As a result, it is important for ethnographers to protect the physical, social and psychological welfare and to honour the dignity and privacy of their participants. Ethnography also entails interaction with other people such as sponsors and gatekeepers, who may have the power to grant or withhold permission to conduct interviews. The researcher must also safeguard the artefacts that are collected. When considering the ethics of ethnographic research the sport management researcher should ask number of ethical questions, these are:

- How is the research problem defined?
- Is the work justified?
- What are the risks/benefits to participants? Social, psychological, physical.
- How will participants be selected?
- Will privacy, confidentiality, and anonymity be assured? How?
- How will informed consent be established?
- How can a researcher be involved yet still maintain her/his capacity for analytical scrutiny?

- Should a researcher conduct an interview in an everyday setting, even very informally, if consent is not obtained?

- How will study participants be able to control the researcher's interpretations of their experiences?

- How will the researcher handle a situation where they are asked to take sides?

- How will the researcher manage situations where antagonistic views, violence, racism, or sexism threaten their presence/values?

- How will results be disseminated?

Case study

Title: From boys to men: An interpretive ethnography of college football
Author: Mays, J. R., *University of Kansas* (2017)
Reference: Mays, J. R. (2017). *From boys to men: An interpretive ethnography of college football*, Doctoral dissertation, University of Kansas.

This dissertation approached an interpretive ethnography grounded in a circuit of culture framework. The ethnography was conducted on and written about the Midwest State Mustang's (a pseudonym) football programme, one of the most successful programmes at the Football Championship Subdivision (FCS) level over the past half-decade. The researcher immersed himself within the culture of Mustang football for an entire calendar year, attending team functions such as practices, workouts, meetings, social events, and games. The term, culture, within college football programmes has been used as an all-encompassing buzz word; the present dissertation aimed to apply academic theory and definition to the complex concept of culture. Using the circuit of culture model as a guide to understand culture as a fluid process occurring through the production, representation, and consumption of cultural products, the researcher further implemented a multi-level (institutional, organisational, and individual) exploration of culture based in various academic research areas. Literature from institutional theory, organisational culture, organisational politics, organisational justice, political skill, and motivation and inspiration are all implemented to support the circuit of culture framework.

This dissertation aimed to identify ways in which members of Mustang football produce, represent, and consume cultural products, in addition to the process of cultural learning that new members experience. The results were conveyed in the form of narrative ethnography, written in the first person to convey to the reader the lived experience of the researcher during his year-long research endeavour. The unprecedented access granted to the researcher allowed for rich and plentiful data that granted an extensive and comprehensive analysis of a captivating and complex cultural setting.

CONCLUSION

Traditional ethnography's approach to such areas of study as sport management has a number of criticisms and weaknesses. More recent discourses such as critical and postmodern theories can be applied to the ethnographic method to broaden the field of ethnography by accentuating awareness of research practices, drawing attention to the role of power relations in the construction of reality, problematising the role of the researcher as subject, and providing the potential to empower the research participants' understanding of the research issue under investigation. In endeavouring to emulate rigorous standards of research sport management researchers should be encouraged to take more methodological "risks" and embrace more eclectic research approaches. Critical and postmodern research approaches offer these opportunities. Moreover, if sport management researchers embrace critical and postmodern thought it provides them with a theoretical framework to question the social, historical, and political forces that play a role in shaping social reality.

REVIEW AND RESEARCH QUESTIONS

Ethnography is a qualitative research methodology aimed at describing and analysing the practices and beliefs of cultures and communities. With a basic understanding now of ethnography, attempt to answer the following questions:

1. Is there any place within sport management research for ethnography underpinned by critical and postmodern theories?

2. Discuss some of the ethical challenges that ethnographic researchers confront and how you would address them. Pay particular attention to how your values may be comprised during the research.

REFERENCES

Agar, M. (1980). *The professional stranger: An informal introduction to ethnography.* New York: Academic Press.

Atkinson, P.A., Coffey, A., & Delamont, S. (1999). Ethnography: Post, past and present. *Journal of Contemporary Ethnography, 28*, 460–471.

Atkinson, P., & Hammersley, M. (1994). Ethnography and participant observation. In N. Denzin & S. Lincoln (Eds.), *Handbook of Qualitative Research*, pp. 248–261. Thousand Oaks, CA: Sage Publications.

Birrell, S., & Theberge, N. (1994). Feminist resistance and transformation in sport. In M. Costa & S. Guthrie (Eds.), *Women and Sport: Interdisciplinary Perspectives,* pp. 361–376. Champaign, IL: Human Kinetics.

Bogdan, R. C., & Biklen, S. K. (1992). *Qualitative research for education.* Needham Heights, MA: Allyn & Bacon.

Burns, R. B. (1997). *Introduction to research methods* (3rd ed.). Melbourne: Longman.

Burns, R. B. (2000). *Introduction to research methods* (4th ed.). Melbourne: Longman.

Bryman, A. (2004). *Social research methods* (2nd ed). Oxford: Oxford University Press.

Cameron, C. (1990). The ethnographic approach: Characteristics and uses in gerontological nursing. *Journal of Gerontological Nursing, 16*(9), 5–7.

Chambers, E. (2000). Applied ethnography. In N.K. Denzin, & Y. S. Lincoln (Eds.), *Handbook of Qualitative Research* (2nd ed.), pp. 851–869. Thousand Oaks, CA: Sage Publications.

Docherty, T. (1993). Authority, history and the question of the postmodern. In M. Biriotti, & N. Miller (Eds.), *What is an Author?* Manchester: Manchester University Press.

Denzin, N. (1997). *Interpretive ethnography.* Thousand Oaks, CA: Sage Publications.

Denzin, N. K., & Lincoln, Y. S. (Eds.). (2000). *Handbook of qualitative research* (2nd ed.) Thousand Oaks, CA: Sage Publications.

Fay, B. (1975). *Social theory and political practice.* London: Allen & Unwin.

Edwards, A., Gilbert, K., & Skinner, J. (2002). *Extending the boundaries: Theoretical frameworks for research in sport management.* Melbourne, Victoria: Common Ground Publications.

Edwards, A., & Skinner, J. (2009). *Qualitative research in sport management.* Oxford: Elsevier.

Edwards, A., Skinner, J., & O'Keefe, L. (2000). Women sport managers. *International Review of Women and Leadership, 6*(2), 48–58.

Gay, L. R., Mills, G. E., & Airasian, P.. (2009). *Educational research: Competencies for analysis and applications* (9th ed.). Upper Saddle River, NJ: Pearson Merrill.

Gingrich, A. (2002). When ethnic majorities are 'dethroned'. In A. Gingrich & R. G. Fox (Eds.), *Anthropology, by Comparison,* pp. 225–232. London: Routledge.

Gottschalk, S. (1998). Postmodern sensibilities and ethnographic possibilities. In A. Banks, & S. P. Banks (Eds.), *Fiction and Social Research: By Ice or Fire,* pp. 205–233. Walnut Creek, CA: AltaMira.

Habermas, J. (1978). *Knowledge and human interests* (J. J. Shapiro, trans.). Cambridge: Polity. (Original work published 1965).

Hammersley, M., & Atkinson, P. (1983). *Ethnography: Principles in practice.* London: Routledge.

Hammersley, M. (1990). *Reading ethnographic research: A critical Guide.* New York: Longman.

Hammersley, M. (1992). *What's wrong with ethnography: Methodological explorations.* London: Routledge.

Hammersley, M., & Atkinson, P. (1995). *Ethnography: Principles in practice* (2nd ed). London: Routledge.

Harris, M. (1968). Emics, etics, and the new ethnography. In Marvin Harris (Ed), *The rise of anthropological theory. A history of theories of culture,* (pp, 568–604). New York: Thomas Crowell.

Jorgensen, D. L. (1989). *Participant observation.* Newbury Park, CA: Sage Publications.

LeCompte, M. D., & Schensul, J. J. (1999). *Designing and conducting ethnographic research.* New York: Altamira Press.

Leininger, M. M. (1985). *Qualitative research methods in nursing.* Philadelphia: W.B. Saunders.

Lindlof, T. R., & Taylor, B. C. (2002). *Qualitative communication research methods* (2nd ed.). Thousand Oaks, CA: Sage Publications.

Madison, D. S. (2005). *Critical ethnography: Method, ethics, and performance.* Thousand Oaks, CA: Sage Publications.

Markula, P., Grant, B., & Denison, J. (2001). Qualitative research and aging and physical activity: Multiple ways of knowing. *Journal of Aging and Physical Activity, 9,* 245–264.

Neuman, D. L. (1994). *Social research methods: Qualitative and quantitative approaches.* Boston: Allyn & Bacon.

Packwood, A., & Sikes, P. (1996). Adopting a postmodern approach to research. *International Journal of Qualitative Studies in Education, 9*(3), 335–346.

Pedersen, K. (1998). Doing feminist ethnography in the wilderness around my hometown. *International Review for the Sociology of Sport, 33*(4), 393–402.

Semerjian, T. Z., & Waldron, J. J. (2001). The journey through feminism: Theory, research, and dilemmas from the field. *The Sport Psychologist, 15,* 438–444.

Skinner, J., & Edwards, A. (2005). Inventive pathways: Fresh visions for sport management research. *Journal of Sport Management, 19*(4), 404–421.

Smart, A. (1992). *Making room: Squatter clearance in Hong Kong.* Hong Kong: Centre of Asian Studies.

Sparkes, A. C. (2003). Bodies, identities, selves: Autoethnographic fragments and reflections. In J. Denison and P. Markula (eds) *Moving writing: Crafting writing in sports research,* (pp. 51–76). New York: Peter Lang.

Spradley, J. (1979). *The ethnographic interview.* New York: Holt, Rinehart and Winston.

Spradley, J. P. (1980). *Participant observation.* New York: Holt, Rinehart & Winston.

Sykes, H. (1996). Constr(i)(u)cting lesbian identities in physical education: Feminist and poststructural approaches to researching sexuality. *Quest: Journal of the National Association for Physical Education in Higher Education, 48*(4), 459–469.

Tedlock, B. (2000). Ethnography and ethnographic representation. In N. K. Denzin, & Y. S. Lincoln (Eds.), *Handbook of Qualitative Research* (2nd ed., pp. 455–486). Thousand Oaks, CA: Sage Publications.

Van Maanen, J. (1988). *Tales of the field: On writing ethnography.* Chicago: The University of Chicago Press.

Wolcott, H. (1980). How to look like an anthropologist without really being one. *Practicing Anthropology, 3*(1), 56–59.

Wolcott, H. F. (1995). *The art of fieldwork.* Walnut Creek, CA: AltaMira Press.

Wolcott, H. (1999). *Ethnography: A way of seeing.* Walnut Creek, CA: AltaMira Press.

CHAPTER 15

Emerging ethnographies and sport management research

KEY TERMS

1. **Autoethnography:** a form of self-narrative that places the self within a social context.

2. **Ethnodrama:** transformation of data into theatrical scripts and performance pieces.

3. **Phenomenography:** a process that is concerned with identifying peoples' ideas about a phenomenon, rather than proving that the actual phenomenon exists.

4. **Netnography:** a written account resulting from fieldwork studying the cultures and communities that emerge from online, computer mediated, or Internet-based communications.

KEY THEMES

- What is Autoethnography?

- What is Ethnodrama?

- What is Phenomenography?

- What is Netnography?

CHAPTER OVERVIEW

This chapter will highlight some emerging ethnographical methodologies and demonstrate how they can be situated in the sport management research field. Autoethnography, ethnodrama, phenomenography, and Netnography may appear on the surface to have little relation to sport management research; however, this chapter will briefly cover each of these methodologies and discuss their potential applications to the field of sport management.

AUTOETHNOGRAPHY

This section explores the emerging ethnographic research approach of autoethnography. Although not a mainstream methodological approach, it is becoming more accepted (although still viewed suspiciously) because it offers a way of uncovering, which previously has been taken for granted; "hidden, taboo or otherwise shrouded in secrecy" (Bochner & Ellis, 2006, p. 119). It is likely to be useful in sport management, where those currently employed in the professions seek to scrutinise and explain the centrality of their current and historical personal experiences and identities in relation to cultural and political contexts.

Autoethnography emerged in the 1980s in the social sciences and more recently in the study of sport and physical education (Holt, 2003). Many evolving research methods fall under the umbrella of autoethnography: personal narratives, narratives of the self, and ethnographic short stories (Ellis & Bochner, 2000). One way of understanding autoethnography is to deconstruct the components of the word. In this fashion, *auto* refers to the self or the autobiographical (Reed-Danahay, 1997), *ethno* to a social group, and *graphy* to the process of researching and writing (Ellis & Bochner 2000; Reed-Danahay, 1997). Ellis and Bochner characterise autoethnography as follows:

> *Autoethnography is an autobiographical genre of writing and research that displays multiple layers of consciousness, connecting the personal to the cultural. Back and forth autoethnographers gaze, first through an ethnographic wide-angle lens, focusing outward on social and cultural aspects of their personal experience; then they look inward, exposing a vulnerable self that is moved-by and may move through, refract, and resist cultural interpretations. As they zoom backward and forward, inward and outward, distinctions between the cultural and personal become blurred, sometimes beyond distinct recognition. Usually written in first-person voice, autoethnographic texts appear in a variety of forms: short stories, poetry, fiction, novels, photographic essays, personal essays, journals, fragmented and layered writing, and social science prose. In these texts, concrete action, dialog, emotion, embodiment,*

spirituality and self- consciousness are featured, appearing as rela-
tional and institutional stories affected by history, social structure, and
culture, which themselves are dialectically revealed through action,
feeling, thought, and language. (p. 739)

There are several distinctions among type, meaning, methodological strategies, and application of autoethnography (Ellis & Bochner, 2000), ranging from
personal narratives (Bochner, 2001) to autoethnographic performance (Slattery,
2001). Common among the more than 60 variations of autoethnographic application is the interconnectedness between the researcher and the research.
Researcher emphasis varies between the self, the culture, and the form their
research will take (Ellis & Bochner, 2000).

In an autoethnography, the observer is part of the subculture studied. For
example, a coach may conduct an autoethnography of the coaching culture in
a local basketball league. Van Maanen (1995) suggests that this type of research
is carried out by a native who reveals his or her own group. Autoethnography
has close ties to phenomenology and hermeneutics. Ellis (2004) describes a more
specific placement of autoethnography as a form of impressionistic or interpretive ethnography. Indeed, autoethnography may be viewed as both, with narrative being the more general description.

As an outgrowth of the interpretive turn (postmodernism), autoethnography is considered a form of autobiographical narrative combining evocative
writing and research that display multiple levels of consciousness, generally written in first person (Denzin & Lincoln, 1994; Ellis, 2000, 2004).
Autoethnography has been acknowledged as a method of inquiry since the
mid-1970s and was shaped by the ideas of feminism, post-structuralism, and
postmodernism (Ellis & Bochner, 2000). Much like hermeneutics, autoethnography circles among the social and cultural aspects of personal experience; and
the inner self, feelings, emotions, and experience, with the primary purpose
of understanding a singular or multiple self, through lived experience (Ellis &
Bochner, 2000).

Ellis and Bochner (2000) advocated the use of autoethnography suggesting personal experience as an opportunity to move beyond a passionless and
objective authoritative voice; autoethnography presents an opportunity to connect the personal to the cultural. The research becomes a personal account
(e.g. coach) of experiences within and in relation to a particular culture (e.g.
local basketball coaches) that also draws on others' lived experiences (e.g.
other coaches in the league); the completed text seeks to engage the readers
and draws them into the experiences of the author and other participants. The
coach has the opportunity to relay both his/her personal feelings and experience as part of the local basketball culture and other coaches' perspectives
through discussions and interviews. Ellis and Bochner have also suggested
that autoethnography asks readers "to become co-participants, engaging the

storyline morally, emotionally, aesthetically, and intellectually: (p. 745). Other scholars have also suggested that autoethnography must be considered a valid form of reporting the social (Denzin & Lincoln, 2002); this same plea has been made specifically within the study of sport (Denison & Rinehart, 2000; Holt, 2003; Sparkes, 2000). Spry (2001) writes that: "Autoethnography can be defined as a self-narrative that critiques the situatedness of self with others in social contexts" (p. 710).

Blurring the distinction between self and other, autoethnography is a form of research that provides opportunity for the researchers to incorporate their own life experiences with the experiences of those being studied (Reed-Danahay, 1997). Autoethnography moves beyond self-reflexivity within an ethnographic study, encouraging researchers to write about their own experiences of the social phenomena and not solely their experiences of recording the culture. As Reed-Danahay (1997) argues:

> Autoethnography is defined as a form of self-narrative that places the self within a social context. It is both a method and a text, as in the case of ethnography ... [Autoethnography] can be done by an autobiographer who places the story of his or her life within a story of the social context in which it occurs. (p. 9)

While providing unique opportunities to share personal experiences, autoethnography can be extremely difficult to undertake for a number of reasons not the least of those being the willingness of the researcher to self-analyse. As Ellis and Bochner (2000) state:

> The self-questioning autoethnography demands is extremely difficult. So is confronting things about yourself that are less than flattering ... Honest autoethnographic exploration generates a lot of fears and doubts – and emotional pain. (p. 738)

Sparkes (2002) has suggested that in autoethnography it is made clear that the author "was "there" in the action, that the story is based on "real" people, "real" events, and "data" that were collected in various ways" (p. 3). Furthermore, a critical analysis of one's own experiences of the social phenomenon under study works to locate the writer/researcher as a living and breathing participant, a researcher that physically coached in the local basketball league under investigation.

One goal of autoethnography is to bring forward conversations through stories about personal, emotional experiences. What distinguishes autoethnography from other types of narratives is the intent to write about self (or multiple selves in the context of culture) (Ellis, 2004; Richardson, 2000). Sparkes (2002) argues that alternative representation practices, such as autoethnographies, poetic representations, and ethnodramas offer insight into sport by privileging the lived body.

Research brief

Title: Autoethnography as a critical approach in sport management: Current applications and directions for future research
Author: Cooper, J. N., *University of Connecticut* (2017)
Reference: Cooper, J. N., Grenier, R. S., & Macaulay, C. (2017). Autoethnography as a critical approach in sport management: Current applications and directions for future research. *Sport Management Review, 20*(1), 43–54.
The purpose of this paper was to highlight the value of autoethnography as a qualitative methodology, document the current literature using autoethnographic approaches, and explore the possibilities for future research in the field of sport management. Using a critical lens to counter dominant ideologies that marginalise certain groups of people through the sustainment of existing power structures and inequities, the authors sought to address the following inquiries: What is autoethnography and how can it be applied to the critical study of sport management? In doing so, the authors explored the benefits of the methodology to the field of sport management as well as the challenges and opportunities created in this form of reflexive study.

Methodology

There is much debate regarding the methodology of autoethnography and whether it constitutes scientific research. The use of self as the only data source can be problematic in this regard. Ellis (1995) argues that a story could be considered scholarly if it makes the reader believe that the experience is authentic, believable, and possible. The intended purpose of autoethnography is to provide the opportunity for the reader and author to become co-participants in the recorded experience. There are also multiple warning signs, skills and difficulties that are experienced or needed in writing ethnography (Ellis & Bochner, 2000). Sport management researchers must be adept at identifying pertinent details, introspection, descriptive and compelling writing, and confronting things about themselves that may be less than flattering. What if the coach, as the researcher, discovers they are a source of oppressing minority coaches in the same league? Will he or she be completely forthcoming in the write-up? Also, the sport management researcher must handle the vulnerability of revealing oneself to a greater audience. The use of self as the source of data can be restrictive, yet a powerful aspect of unpacking the many layers involved in the study of a particular culture or social context. Tierney (1998) explains that autoethnography is intended to confront dominant forms of representation and power in an attempt to reclaim marginalised representational spaces.

Data collection

Autoethnographic data collection subscribes to the dualistic nature of exploring oneself within culture, and then reflective introspection of the expressed embodiment of that culture in oneself (Foley, 2002). In autoethnographic research, the researcher may begin with the question, what is it that I really want to know and why? This framework provides a more concise description and direction for the type of data to collect, where to collect it, and whom to collect it from. In autoethnographic data collection, all of the considerations of ethnographic field-work are applicable as long as it adds useful information to the study (Nilan, 2002). Interviews, artefacts, sketches, field notes, and photographs can all be part of autoethnographic research (Tomasell, 2003).

The ultimate goal of self-study research is to produce literary representa-tions and to add value to readers of our research. With this in mind, data collec-tion tools vary greatly in self-narrative research and autobiographical studies. To ensure proper validity in an autoethnography, Feldman (2003, pp. 27–28) has developed four criteria upon which data collection are based:

1. Provide clear and detailed description of how we collect data and make explicit what counts as data in our work.

2. Provide clear and detailed descriptions of how we constructed the rep-resentation from our data. What specifics about the data led us to make this assumption?

3. Extend triangulation beyond multiple sources of data to include explora-tions of multiple ways to represent the same self-study.

4. Provide evidence that the research changed or evolved the educator and summarise its value to the profession. This can convince readers of the study's significance and validity.

Research brief

Title: Body classification in sport: A collaborative autoethnography by two female athletes
Author: McMahon, J. A., *University of Tasmania*, Franklin, R., *Southern Cross University* & McGannon, K. R., *Laurentian University* (2016)
Reference: McMahon, J. A., Franklin, R., & McGannon, K. R. (2016). Body classification in sport: A collaborative autoethnography by two female athletes. *Psychology of women section review, 18*(2), 48–58.
The paper examined two female athletes and their embodied experiences in two different aquatic nature-based sports. The approach chosen was a collaborative autoethnography in conjunction with Foucault's theory of the body as a site of discipline. The first section of the paper provided an overview of literature addressing body practices occurring in sport as a means of better contextualising how sporting sites have come to privilege female athletes' bodies that are "fatless", "fit", "idealised", and "feminine", over those who did not meet such body standards. In the second part of the paper, collaborative autoethnography was used as a means of presenting and analysing two female athletes' embodied experiences in aquatic nature-based sport. The two female athletes' stories revealed how their bodies were "classified" according to the idealised female athletic body shape for their specific sport. The two female athletes' stories also revealed that as a result of their bodies being classified in the sporting context, a fractured body-self relationship resulted.

Data analysis

In autoethnography, reflective analysis is an ongoing part of the data collection process (Ellis, 1999). The lived experience of the researcher is fundamental to understanding the experience as lived. The difficulty with this "anything goes" approach to data analysis fuels the ongoing debate between traditional positivistic qualitative inquiry and postmodern, contemporary qualitative research. Other methods of data analysis specifically useful in autoethnography include collaboration, emotional recall, and reflective field notes.

The analysis of data begins the moment the researcher perceives the information. In an autoethnography, the analysis of data is an ongoing event, developing and crystallising over time. With each rereading of the personal reflexive journal, each examination of a written artefact, and with further introspection and self-analysis, the process and clarity of the research is enriched. These processes form the analysis of data in a qualitative study of an autoethnographical nature. The gathering and analysis of data go hand in hand as theories and themes emerge during the study. The reflection involved by the researcher consistently shapes and forms the articulation of the experiences of the researcher in a self-study.

Nevertheless, autoethnography has ethical implications for others appearing in the narrative, as Ellis (2007) notes:

> When we write about ourselves, we also write about others. In so doing, we run the risk that other characters may become increasingly recognisable to our readers, though they may not have consented to being portrayed in ways that would reveal their identity; or, if they did consent, they might not understand exactly to what they had consented. (p. 14)

Ellis and Bochner (2000) assert that the analysis of data in a personal narrative involves a process where the researcher emotionally recalls the events of the past. The researcher looks back on specific, memorable episodes, and experiences paying particular attention to the emotions and physical surroundings during the recollection. Emotional recall is expressed through writing that includes thoughts, events, dialogue, and physical details of the particular event. Methods of data analysis specifically utilised in autoethnography include collaboration, emotional recall, and reflective field notes. Collaboration in autoethnographic research relates to understanding the phenomenon studied by those involved. Reflective journals are also a key element.

Reliability

Reliability within an autoethnographic study can be sought through feedback from the other participants included in the research: for example, the coach sharing the field notes with other coaches and allowing them to provide input. Ellis and

Bochner (2000) have suggested that "when other people are involved, you might take your work back to them and give them a chance to comment, add materials, change their minds, and offer their interpretations" (p. 751). With inclusion of the "self" in the research, reliability is unorthodox as compared to traditional, positivist definitions that have previously been applied to qualitative research. To a certain degree, there must be some "letting go" of traditional, evaluative approaches to the notions of validity and reliability. As Holt (2003) has argued:

> *Describing investigator responsiveness during the research process would be a constructive approach to validity, as opposed to the inclusion of evaluative checks to establish the trustworthiness of completed research (e.g. an external audit) … Constructive approaches to validity and reliability would be more appropriate criteria to judge autoethnography than the post-hoc imposition of evaluative techniques associated with the parallel perspective. (pp. 11–12)*

Ellis (2004) suggested that validity is still important in interpretive ethnography, and requires some conceptual reframing for autoethnographic inquiry. For her, the question is how to judge interpretive or impressionist inquiry. She suggests several questions for assessing quality including:

1. Do the stories "ring true" to the audience?

2. Do the stories resonate with the lives of the researcher and readers?

3. Are the accounts plausible and coherent?

4. Does the author make claim to a single standard of truth or leave open the possibility of multiple interpretations and truths as is inherent in autoethnography?

5. Is the whole person taken into account?

6. Does the work communicate with others?

7. Is the resulting story useful in helping others?

Autoethnography is not concerned with generalisability, but rather with understanding the unique experiences of cultural groups or members. As a methodology autoethnography has number of advantages; however, it not without its critics who point to its disadvantages. Table 15.1 outlines some of the advantages and disadvantages of autoethnography.

Case study: *Autoethnography*

Title: Basketball officiating as a gendered arena: An autoethnography

Author: Schaeperkoetter, C. C., *University of Kansas* (2017)

Reference: Schaeperkoetter, C. C. (2017). Basketball officiating as a gendered arena: An autoethnography. *Sport Management Review*, *20*(1), 128–141.

In this study, an autoethnographic methodological approach was used to examine the author's basketball officiating experience as a female. Over the course of one year, Schaeperkoetter officiated more than 250 basketball games within a 300 mile radius of her current location, including games at officials' training clinics, parks and recreation, recreational and competitive youth leagues, varsity and sub-varsity games sanctioned by the state's high school activities association, Amateur Athletic Union (AAU) competitive travel team tournaments, summer league games organised by local high school coaches, and games as part of an Olympic-style sport contest (in which basketball was not the only sport competition taking place at the particular tournament). Age groups of games officiated ranged from Kindergarten all the way through 19-and-over men's tournaments.

The data were compiled via electronic field notes based on in-game experiences, discussions with other officials, athletes, coaches, and game assignors, and through the author's personal reflections. Specifically, representative examples were all detailed in electronic field notes entered into a smartphone immediately after each game (or set of games). Field notes were then combined into one Microsoft Word document and analysed in comparison to previous sport-specific autoethnographies. The findings were presented in the form of specific representative examples in comparison to previous sport-specific autoethnographies. A discussion of the findings examined the current autoethnography in comparison to previous literature on officiating and gender representation in the sport management field and also through an examination of the role of autoethnography in sport management research.

Table 15.1   Advantages and disadvantages of autoethnography

Advantages and disadvantages of autoethnography

Advantages

- Rather than maintaining a disconnected objective position, the narrative and subjectivity of the researcher fashion autoethnographic writing as "creative non-fiction".
- The reader is granted permission into the intricate life of another and in adding their own life experience the study becomes more personal and effective.
- In autoethnographic research, the author commits to researcher subjectivity and uses an introspective lens in writing personal narrative history, often confronting hidden emotional content.

Disadvantages

- The author must skillfully capture and communicate a narrative voice.
- Shallow introspection will directly influence the impact and persuasiveness of the narrative and can undermine the credibility of proposed conclusions.
- Narcissistic use of "I" in social science discourse.
- Difficulty in any autoethnographic study lies in the attempt to reclaim or recollect self and story reflexively.
- Autoethnography is still a contested methodological approach.
- Autoethnographic study is more fiction than fact.
- Autoethnography is self-indulgent, narcissistic, and academic "navel-gazing".

Adapted for Sparkes (2000).

ETHNODRAMA

Ethnodrama is also known as *"performance ethnography"* (Denzin, 2003) or *"performed ethnography"* (e.g. Brunner, 1999; Gallagher, 2006; Mienczacowski, 1997; Sykes & Goldstein, 2004). Saldaña (2011) identifies over 80 other terms that can be used for this type of study (pp. 13–14). From docudrama to meta-theatre, from performance inquiry to transcription theatre, whatever it is called, ethnodrama is "solidly rooted in nonfictional, researched reality, or an individual's own experience "(Saldaña, 2011, p. 14). Many professional organisations embrace and endorse the arts as legitimate interests of members who integrate traditional research with human participants and expressive forms of documentation and reportage. Saldaña cites the American Educational Research Association, the American Counselling Association, and the American Anthropological Association as examples.

The purpose of an ethnodrama is not to entertain, but to encourage critical thinking and questioning. Denzin (1991) outlines five forms of performance text:

1. Dramatic texts (rituals, poems, and plays meant to be performed).
2. Natural texts (transcriptions of everyday conversations).
3. Performance science texts (fieldwork notes and interviews).
4. Improvisational.
5. Critical ethnodramas (the merging of natural script dialogues with dramatised scenes and the use of composite characters).

According to Saldana (2005), Ethnodrama consists of "dramatised, significant selections of narrative collected through interviews, participant observation, filed notes, journal entries, and/or print and media artefacts such as diaries, television broadcasts, newspaper articles, and court proceedings" (p. 2). Coffey and Atkinson (1996) go further to say that the "idea of ethnodrama is to transform data (dialogue, transcripts, etc.) into theatrical scripts and performance pieces" (p. 126). The primary function of ethnodrama is to tell the stories of the participants, as true to their words and actions as possible. As Saldana suggests: "ethnodrama maintains 'close allegiance' to the lived experiences of real people while presenting their stories through an artistic medium" (p. 3). The goal of ethnodrama, however, is to "investigate a particular facet of the human condition for purposes of adapting those observations and insights into a performance medium" (p. 1).

Ethnodrama has been promoted as a means of communicating the emotional and contextual complexities of lived experiences (Gilbourne, 2007). It has also been described as "a new form of theatre", that seeks to translate research into reflective performances to effect meaningful change

(Mienczakowski & Morgan, 2001). The aim is to promote empathetic understanding and learning by providing circumstances where individuals recognise themselves in the scenarios, and are confronted by the multiple interpretations and ramifications of those representations (Mienczakowski & Morgan, 2001). The theoretical focus of ethnodrama is based on nascency; embryonic moments of insight or enlightenment (Saldana, 2005). The power of this form of theatre, therefore, lies in its presentation of the detail and depth of human experience including the sub-texts of thought and emotion through vocal and physical pretence (Llewellyn, Gilbourne, & Triggs, 2011). It is a form of theatre that has the responsibility to create entertainingly informative experiences that are emotionally evocative, aesthetically sound and intellectually rich (Saldana, 2005). The performance allows text to "come alive" through voice, gesture, and posture, making what might be challenging in written form even more powerful via the skills of actors and the prompting of the director.

Key assumptions about research in ethnodrama

The ethnodramatic researcher believes that we claim knowledge in a subjective, interpretive, and interactive way. For example, in the act of creating a play out of data from an interview, there is reaffirmation in the interactional nature of the interview. Moreover, there is an interactive nature to the genre itself, that is, through the transformative and catalytic inner dialoguing that exists between the audience, the participants and the researcher (the latter two are usually part of the cast). The ethnodramatic researcher also believes that we come to know knowledge in a realist way because the genre itself "attracts those with a predominantly realist perspective" (Sparkes, 2002, p. 133). According to Sparkes, this means that ethnodrama has advantages over purely textual reports in terms of validity because it remains true to lived reality. In fact, Conrad (2004) suggests there is no better way to study lived experience than to re-enact it.

Ethnodrama and the research process

Traditionally, qualitative research involves note taking, observations, interviews, transcripts, coding, triangulation, etc. and the transformation, selection, interpretation, and perceptions of the researcher. These methodological approaches and issues readily transfer into the ethnodrama research design. Ethnodrama works at two levels: (1) in the creation of the ethnodrama with the participants as they learn to communicate the meaning of their experiences; and (2) in the performance of ethnodrama to an audience that responds to the play and ideally after the performance can further interact with the performers to examine the issues presented.

Scripting an ethnodrama

The process of scripting an ethnodrama involves including as much verbatim narrative as possible (Mienczakowski & Morgan, 1993). This allows the performance text to attempt to create a high degree of *"vraisemblance"* or *"semblance of truth"* (Mienczakowski, 2001). By inviting "informants" to validate the research by attending scripting sessions, rehearsals, group readings, and preview performances, Mienczakowski used feedback from the "informants" to edit and rewrite the script. Post-performance discussions with the audience also allow the researcher to "renegotiate" the ethnodrama's meaning after every performance. According to Mienczakowski (2001), this high level of communication and cooperation among researcher, informant, and audience make an ethnodrama approach reflexive, polyvocal, and accessible to a broad audience.

The role of the audience in an ethnodrama

The ethnodrama is the culminating piece to the research. In recent years, various researchers have recognised that they are pursuing the same ends – voicing the marginalised experience – albeit through different lenses. In the late 1980s and early 1990s, sociologists began turning ethnographic research into performances while theatre artists began to turn to ethnographies for performance material (McCall, 2000).

The next step is to develop the material beyond its ethnodrama format into a Theatre-In-Education (TIE) programme. TIE is an effective educational tool that invites audience members to interact with the characters on stage in a variety of ways and often through creative drama methods. For example, the audience members may become a part of the scene being acted out, or may be allowed to interview characters to learn more about their lives. The audience can give the characters advice, which may in turn influence the outcome of the play. The actors can also freeze a scene, allowing the audience the chance to analyse the conflict, and rewind it to playback the same scene for further clarification. The TIE programme often involves its audience physically as well as mentally. This involvement is intrinsic to the plot and the pupils become an essential part of the action, either as participants, or as critical observers whose opinions are sought and valued. In the work of Mienczakowski (2001), one finds a form of TIE techniques. During an after-performance discussion, Mienczakowski's performers "rework scenarios, reinterpret events, and thereby reconstruct and negotiate the individual's understanding of the play's outcomes" (p. 361).

Ethical concerns and limitations of ethnodrama

According to Saldana (2005), theatre's primary goal is neither to educate nor to enlighten. Theatre's primary goal is to *"entertain"* (p. 141). This poses a dilemma for the ethnodramatist. Is it possible for ethnodrama to be widely accepted as a valid and viable methodology for data presentation or is it just entertainment? There are also ethical concerns surrounding the participants themselves, relating to issues of confidentiality and anonymity. It is essential, therefore, that all participants consent to all the content in the performance, and that they are fully aware of the implications of being in the performance, if that is the approach taken (Saldana, 2005).

Validity

Richardson (2000) calls for five criteria to assess the validity and quality of ethnographic texts: (1) Substantive contribution: Does this piece contribute to our understanding of social-life? (2) Aesthetic merit: Does this piece succeed aesthetically? (3) Reflexivity: How did the author come to write this text? (4) Impact: Does this affect me? Emotionally? Intellectually? Generate new questions? (5) Express a reality: Does this text embody a fleshed out, embodied sense of lived experience? (p. 254).

Ethnodrama and sport management research

Sparkes (2002) notes how it is surprising that scholars in sport have made little use of this genre. He believes that ethnodrama permits a more embodied way of knowing for both the researcher and the audience and that it "would seem particularly attractive to fields like sport where the body is taken to be central, but for the most part has been curiously missing, absent, or invisible" (p. 146). Sparkes (2002) suggests that transforming data into ethnographic drama is a "way to extend our understanding of bodies beyond abstract theorising, by including not just the bodies of our research participants, but also our own bodies as researchers–performers–audience" (p. 142).

Ethnodrama has the potential to demonstrate that the embodiment of human experience through artistic means can enhance the understanding of the experiences of sport managers, and can situate the experience within a recognisable context that also has the facility to satisfy the "entertainment" component of theatre. The personal reflections of a sport manager, especially one with connections to high profile clubs, teams, or athletes, will have the voyeuristic component that will attract a certain audience membership, as well as the educational component that other sport managers, sporting purists, and a wider segment of society will find attractive. The sport management researcher has the opportunity to use ethnodrama to discover, discuss, and explore previously untouched areas of sport management by creating a "real world" presentation of the "real life" experiences of sport managers in such a way that will engage the audience in critical reflection and debate on the issues and situations presented in the ethnodrama.

Case study: *Ethnodrama*

Title: Slim to Win: An Ethnodrama of Three Elite Swimmers' 'Presentation of Self' in Relation to a Dominant Cultural Ideology
Author: McMahon, J., *University of Tasmania*, McGannon, K. R., *Laurentian University*, & Zehntner, C., *University of Tasmania* (2017)
Reference: McMahon, J., McGannon, K. R., & Zehntner, C. (2017). Slim to win: An ethnodrama of three elite swimmers' 'presentation of self' in relation to a dominant cultural ideology. *Sociology of sport journal*, *34*(2), 108–123.

In this paper, the authors used an ethnodrama approach combined with Goffman's "presentation of self"" to explore three elite swimmers" "presentation of self" in relation to the dominant ideology of "slim to win". The "presentation of self" of three swimmers was analysed according to their front stage (e.g., posting of specific images; direct media quotes) and backstage (e.g., an autoethnographic representation) performances. Goffman's concepts of expressions "given" and "given off" were used to highlight how the ideology comes to be presented to others and whether the swimmer negotiated and/or contested it. As an analysis and representation, ethnodrama afforded the opportunity to reveal the extent an athlete might go to avoid a failing "presentation of self" in relation to "slim to win", highlighting potential health effects (e.g., physical, emotional).

During the data collection process, a selection of material was collected that was invariably used by the directors to create the ethnodrama. This selection included three sources of material:

(1) Visual images that in turn will be enacted through poses with the support of various props. (2) Direct quotes made by the swimmers to the media; and (3) Autoethnographic accounts. It took the directors over 12 months to collect, sort, collate, and dissect the enormous amount of material that was gathered. The directors commenced this process in May 2014 and completed it in June 2015. Material such as images posted on Instagram and Twitter as well as direct quotes made to the media was specifically collected from the timeframe of 2011–2014.

This ethnodrama also revealed how the three swimmers generated a specific public output that not only reflected on their self but also reflected the values of the culture (Birrell, 1981). In doing so, "slim to win" as an ideology was enacted through social interactions and the "presentation of self" of all three swimmers. This ethnodrama highlighted the potential health implications for athletes that may occur as a result of dominant sporting ideologies (Kalleberg, 2009). Specifically, this ethnodrama made known the detrimental effects that came to result in an attempt to uphold a certain "presentation of self" in relation to the cultural ideology of "slim to win."

References in this case study

- Birrell, S. (1981). Sport as ritual: Interpretations from Durkheim to Goffman. *Social forces*, *60*(2), 354–376.

- Kalleberg, A.L. (2009). Precarious work, insecure workers: Employment relations in transition. *American sociological review*, *74*(1), 1–22.

PHENOMENOGRAPHY

Phenomenography attempts to identify and describe, as faithfully as possible, the individual's conceptions of some aspect of reality (Sandberg, 1995). In this way, it attempts to bring all conceptions to light and tries to describe them. The phenomenographer seeks to understand, systematise and order these conceptions in relation to each other, thus arriving at a view of the whole picture of the phenomenon, by describing the range of variation among its subjects (Svensson, 1994). For Bruce (1997, p. 5), phenomenography is able to:

- Provide direct descriptions of a phenomenon.

- Describe conceptions in a holistic and integrated way.

- Capture a range of conceptions, due to its focus on variations in people's experiences.

- Produce descriptions of conceptions that are useful in teaching and learning.

- Focus on groups of people, rather than on individuals.

Phenomenography was recognised as a research approach in the 1970s at the University of Gothenberg, where the focus of study was to examine what people learn rather than how or why they learn (Saljo, 1988). It is the what question that differentiates phenomenography from other ethnographies. Marton and Booth (1997) believe that phenomenography also looks at how:

people handle problems, situations, the world, we have to understand the way in which they experience the problems, the situations, and the world that they are handling or in relation to the way they are acting. Accordingly, a capability for acting in a certain way reflects a capability of experiencing something in a certain way. The latter does not cause the former, but they are logically intertwined. You cannot act other than in relation to the world as you experience it. (p. 117)

Phenomenographic research

Phenomenographic research is centred on the variation in experiencing phenomena, and describing phenomena as others see them (Hasselgren & Beach, 1996). The variations in experiences are teased out from individual conversations, and used to exemplify different "categories of description", which are collectively expressed as "conceptions". Conceptions have been variously described as a "way of seeing something, a qualitative relationship between an individual and some phenomenon" (Johansson, Marton & Svensson, 1985, p. 236), as the ways in which individuals experience the meaning of something (Svennson, 1994), and as "people's ways of experiencing a specific aspect of reality" (Sandberg, 1995, p. 203). The central aim of phenomenographic research is its attempt to uncover and describe qualitatively different ways people perceive, experience, and understand various aspects of phenomena in the world as they see it. Phenomenography is therefore primarily concerned with identifying and understanding the relationship between the person and the phenomenon being studied.

Phenomenography and sport management research

The methods for conducting phenomenographical research may vary depending on the phenomena under investigation. The researcher will research and adopt those methods appropriate to the research study. This said, in phenomenography, sport management researchers should try to describe, analyse and understand how people think about particular phenomena. This is not about describing how reality "is", but how reality is perceived by that person. For the sport management researcher, the opportunities are boundless. For example, the following could be considered:

1. How does the sport manager perceive their organisation's performance in the hosting of a major sporting event?

2. How does the sport manager evaluate their performance as manager of a major sporting event?

3. Did the sport manager identify problems in the event that were not recognised elsewhere?

Phenomenographic approaches are appropriate for research in the field of sport management however, to date they have not been applied. The challenge for sport management researchers is to engage with the method and demonstrate that new sport management knowledge can be generated from this approach.

NETNOGRAPHY

Netnography is defined by Kozinets (1998) as:

a written account resulting from fieldwork studying the cultures and communities that emerge from online, computer mediated, or Internet-based communications, where both the field work and the textual account are methodologically informed by the traditions and techniques of cultural anthropology. (p. 6)

A main difference between netnography and traditional ethnography is that netnography "is based primarily upon the observation of textual discourse, an important difference from the balancing of discourse and observed behaviour that occurs during in-person ethnography" (Kozinets, 2002, p. 7). This raises some significant issues, mainly: how does the netnographer determine the trustworthiness – not to mention the age, gender, race, true sport team affiliation, etc. – of their informants?

In essence, this approach turns a potential problem of netnography (lack of access to informants' non-verbal cues, including their physical appearance) into a potential asset. If, as mentioned above, ethnographic studies always reflect "differences and similarities between participants and scholars in terms of class, gender, race, culture or subculture, educational background, age, etc." (Seiter, Borchers, Kreutzner, & Warth, 1989, p. 227), then netnography's tendency to obscure these variables may produce research uncomplicated by issues of class, gender, and race. Most Internet and Usenet posts betray no information about the poster's age, gender, or race. Therefore, the focus of netnography is on what is written, not on who does the writing. It is suggested that one way for dealing with netnography's reliance on textual discourse as opposed to observed behaviour is simply to develop an understanding of the online community and its leaders, its rank-and-file members, its rhetorical style and its codes and mores. After extensive exposure, a netnographer will develop a sense of whether a particular posting is valid and reliable. As Kozinets (1998) suggests, netnographers must always be aware that:

> the limitations and requirements of producing and communicating textual information obviously structure virtual relationships in many ways, including: eliminating and simulating physicality and body (e.g. body language has been virtually replaced by (deliberately) shared (emot)icons), privileging verbal-rational states and skills over non-verbal-emotional ones, and allowing more 'pre-editing' of expressed thoughts and thus more opportunities for strategic self-presentation efforts. (p. 3)

He adds that in the end, good netnography is built on the same foundation as good ethnography: "persistent observation, gaining rapport and trust, triangulating across sites and sources, using good interview techniques, and researcher introspection" (p. 7).

Ethics and netnography

Research ethics may be one of the most significant disparities between traditional ethnography and netnography. Ethical concerns over netnography turn on contentious and still largely unsettled concerns about whether online forums are to be considered a private or a public site, and about what constitutes informed consent in cyberspace (see Paccagnella, 1997). In a major shift from traditional methods, netnography uses cultural information that is not given specifically, and in confidence, to the sport management researcher. The sport consumers who originally created the data do not necessarily intend or welcome its use in research representations.

Research brief: *Netnography*

Title: Netnography on football: Fans online attitudes towards football
Author: Xavier, B. M. T. D. G., *Catholic University of Portugal* (2019)
Reference: Xavier, B. M. T. D. G. (2019). *Netnography on football: fans online attitudes towards football*, Doctoral dissertation.
This study aimed to understand the behaviour of football fans within online communities. The author intended to understand how people live the daily life of clubs, what influence sports have in their well-being and how they interact with each other using online platforms. The approach used to conduct the study was netnography. The data collected during the study were treated using a thematic approach in which it was possible to disclose the main themes of the research based on the collected volumes of information. The results suggested that there is a quasi-religious nature in football: Clubs appear to be as cults followed by legions of loyal fans.

Advantages and limitations of netnography

Compared to surveys, experiments, focus groups, and personal interviews, netnography is a far less obtrusive method. It is conducted using observations in a context that is not fabricated by the sport management researcher. Netnography also is less costly and timelier than focus groups and personal interviews. It is a naturalistic and unobtrusive technique – a nearly unprecedented combination.

The limitations of netnography draw from its narrower focus on online communities, its inability to offer the full and rich detail of lived human experience, the need for researcher interpretive skills, and the lack of informant identifiers present in the online context that leads to difficulty in generalising results to groups outside the online community sample. Sport management researchers wishing to generalise the findings of a netnography of a particular online group to other groups must apply careful evaluations of similarity and consider using multiple methods for research triangulation. Netnography is still a relatively new method, and awaits further development and refinement at the hands of a new generation of Internet-savvy ethnographic sport management researchers. Table 15.2 outlines some of the advantages and disadvantages of using netnography.

Applications of netnography to sport management research

The sport management researcher interested in applying netnographical methodologies to their research first needs to determine whether or not a viable and functioning online community exists from within which to conduct the research study. A search of Yahoo groups, which claims to host millions of online groups, fails to find a single hit with the keyword search "sport management". "Management" secures over 63,000 results.

The sport management researcher must obviously first focus on who are the target participants for the research study. If sport managers themselves are the

Table 15.2 Advantages and disadvantages of netnography

Advantages and disadvantages of netnography

Advantages

- Large sample possible quickly

- Less obtrusive compared to surveys, focus groups and personal interviews

- Performed using observations in a context that is not fabricated by the sport management researcher

- Less costly and timelier than focus groups and personal interviews

- It is a naturalistic and unobtrusive technique

- Immediate analysis

- Transcripts easily available

- Sensitive topic can be researched

Disadvantages

- The lack of informant identifiers present in the online context that leads to difficulty generalising results to groups outside the online community sample

- Narrow focus on online communities

- Inability to offer the full and rich detail of lived human experience

- The need for researcher interpretive skills

- Loss of non-verbals

- Loss of intangibles (silence, tone of voice)

- Compensate with emoticons :-)

- Cookies controversy

- Reliability and integrity of information

- Shoulder surfing distortions

- Information overload

- Netnography is still in its infancy

- Ethical concerns

desired participants, then it is likely that another source will need to be found other than Yahoo groups. The question then needs to be asked whether sport managers are likely to utilise online forums, groups, etc. to exchange information, share resources, seek solutions to problems from other sport managers, and even vent to others with a shared interest/profession. If no online community exists for the target participant group, then the sport management researcher may even consider establishing such a group, although the time involved to cultivate members, build trust, and establish a network of members beyond a localised area would probably be prohibitive.

One of the advantages of online communities is their ability to link people with a shared interest who would otherwise never have connected due to differences in culture, language, and geographical distance. The sharing of information, opinions and even life stories from seemingly disparate groups of people who may on the surface have only one obscure thing in common can make for a rich source of data for the budding netnographer. Whilst online communities of sport managers may be few and far between (or even completely missing), the netnographer will still find a rich source of potential research participants among the possibly millions of online groups dedicated to particular sports, sporting teams, and individual athletes. Membership of these groups will vary, from die-hard fans to the merely curious fan looking for a specific piece of information, to support teams, and family and friends of athletes looking for an easy way to maintain contact and share information.

Depending on the particular focus of the research study, online communities have the potential to offer the sport management researcher access to a pool of participants eager and willing to share information and their opinions. The very fact of their active membership in a particular online community demonstrates their interest in the topic. Active participation in discussions within the community demonstrates the willingness of members to share information. The sport management researcher will need to proceed with caution however, as long-standing online communities will usually take action against perceived "lurkers" or "trolls" (by eviction from the community), and will need to take the time to build trust within the community. This may involve being completely upfront about the purpose of the researcher's membership of the community.

Research brief: *Netnography*

Title: Building international relationships through social media marketing: A netnography of football communities
Author: Fenton, A., *University of Salford* (2016)
Reference: Fenton, A. (2016). Building international relationships through social media marketing: A netnography of football communities. In *Contemporary Issues in International Marketing Conference*.
This paper used empirical evidence using a netnography approach to explore and evaluate the phenomenon of digital marketing and its relation to football clubs. Understanding the benefits and challenges of digital marketing and communications for sports clubs in the digital age is an important aspect of the evolving discipline. Football clubs are examples of high impact brands with loyal customers who are using social media to reach out to international audiences. This study used the blended qualitative methods of online participant observation, interviews and social network analysis to evaluate the effect of relationships between international football fans and the clubs that they support.

CONCLUSION

The research methodologies discussed in this chapter may have different output and appearance, but they are related in their connection to ethnography and its focus on the experience of the research participant. In many ways, these are research approaches that will be taken on by the next generation of sport management researchers. The discipline can only benefit by sport management researchers embracing these new and emerging ethnographies to understand sport management practice.

REVIEW AND REVIEW QUESTIONS

Each of the emerging ethnographies discussed in this chapter embraces this as a basic tenet while adopting a unique methodological approach that has significant relevance to Sport Management Research. With a basic understanding now of these emerging ethnographies, attempt to answer the following questions:

1. Is there any place within sport management research for autoethnography?

2. Discuss the positive and negative features of an ethnodramatic approach to a sport management research question.

3. Provide other examples of how phenomenographic approaches to sport management research could be applied.

4. What are the ethical considerations associated with "netnography" and how do you mitigate for these concerns?

REFERENCES

Bochner, A. (2001). Narrative's virtues. *Qualitative Inquiry, 7*(2), 131–157.

Bochner, A., & Ellis, C. (2006). Communication as autoethnography. In G. J. Shepherd, J. S. John, & T. Striphas (Eds.), *Communication as Perspectives on Theory*, pp. 110–122. Thousand Oaks, CA: Sage Publications.

Bruce, C. (1997). *The seven faces of information literacy*. Adelaide: Auslib Press.

Brunner, D. (1999). Challenging representations of sexuality through story and performance. In J. Sears, & W. Williams (Eds.), *Overcoming Heterosexism and Homophobia: Strategies that Work*, pp. 169–181. New York: Columbia University Press.

Coffey, A., & Atkinson, P. (1996). *Making sense of qualitative data: Complementary research strategies*. Thousand Oaks, CA: Sage Publications.

Conrad, D. (2004). Exploring risky youth experiences: Popular theatre as a participatory, performative research method. *International Journal of Qualitative Methods, 3*(1), 12–25.

Denzin, N. K. (1991). The reflexive interview and a performative social science. *Qualitative Research, 1*(1), 23–46.

Denzin, N. (2003). *Performance ethnography: Critical pedagogy and the politics of culture*. Thousand Oaks: Sage Publications.

Denzin, N. K., & Lincoln, Y. S. (Eds.) (1994). *Handbook of qualitative research*. London: Sage Publications.

Denzin, N. K., & Lincoln, Y. S. (Eds.) (2002). *The qualitative inquiry reader*. Thousand Oaks, CA: Sage Publications.

Denison, J., & Rinehart, R. (2000). Imagining sociological narratives. *Sociology of Sport Journal, 17,* 1–4.

Ellis, C. (1995). *Final negotiations.* Philadelphia: Temple University Press.

Ellis, C. (1999). Heartful autoethnography. *Qualitative Health Research, 9*(5), 669–683.

Ellis, C. (2000). Creating criteria: An ethnographic short story. *Qualitative Inquiry, 6*(2), 273–277.

Ellis, C. (2004). *The ethnographic I: A methodological novel about autoethnography.* Walnut Creek, CA: AltaMira Press.

Ellis, C. (2007). Telling secrets, revealing lives: Relational ethics in research with intimate others. *Qualitative Inquiry, 13,* 3–2.

Ellis, C., & Bochner, A. P. (2000). Autoethnography, personal narrative, reflexivity. In N. K. Denzin, & Y. S. Lincoln (Eds.), *Handbook of Qualitative Research* (2nd ed.), pp. 733–779. Thousand Oaks, CA: Sage Publications.

Feldman, A. (2003). Validity and quality in self-study. *Educational Researcher, 32,* 26–28.

Foley, D. (2002). Critical ethnography: The reflexive turn. *International Journal of Qualitative Studies in Education, 15,* 469–490.

Gallagher, K. (2006). Sexual fundamentalism and performances of masculinity: An ethnographic scene study. *Journal of Gay and Lesbian Issues in Education, 4*(1), 47–76.

Gilbourne, D. (2007). *Self-narrative: illustrations of different genre and explorations of the underlying rationale for writing.* In Paper presented at 12th European Congress of Sport Psychology, Halkidiki, Greece.

Hasselgren, B., & Beach, D. (1996). Phenomenography – *a 'good-for-nothing brother' of phenomenology?* Outline of an analysis. Available at: https://www.tandfonline.com/doi/pdf/10.1080/0729436970160206?casa_token=jiJ69Sdary4AAAAA:LTh-DE-Nxr4QffJrlVrKASq0oRWHn5yQWjFq_9UWhYQFINW6xi5CAFH1PA_KZFhKhhql8dk09JwppZw (Accessed 19 June 2020).

Holt, N.L. (2003). Representation, legitimation, and autoethnography: An autoethnographic writing story. *International Journal of Qualitative Methods, 2,* 1–22.

Johansson, B., Marton, F., & Svensson, L. (1985). An approach to describing learning as change between qualitatively different conceptions. In L. West (Ed.), *Pines Cognitive Structure and Conceptual Change.* New York: Academic Press.

Kozinets, R. V. (1998). On netnography. Initial reflections on consumer investigations of cyberculture. In W.H. Alba (Ed.), *Advances in Consumer Research* (vol. 25), pp. 366–371. Provo, UT: Association for Consumer Research.

Kozinets, R. V. (2002). The field behind the screen: Using netnography for marketing research in online communities. *Journal of Marketing Research, XXXIX,* 61–72.

Llewellyn, D., Gilbourne, D., & Triggs, C. (2011). Representing applied research experiences through performance: Extending beyond text. In D. Gilbourne, & M. Andersen (Eds.), *Critical Essays in Applied Sport Psychology,* pp. 23–38. Champagne, IL: Human Kinetics.

Marton, F., & Booth, S. (1997). The learner's experience of learning. In D. R. Olson, & N. Torrance (Eds.), *The Handbook of Education and Human Development: New Models of Learning, Teaching and Schooling,* pp. 534–563. Oxford: Blackwell.

McCall, M. M. (2000). Performance ethnography: A brief history and some advice. In N. K. Denzin, & Y. S. Lincoln (Eds.), *Handbook of Qualitative Research* (2nd ed.), pp. 412–433. Thousand Oaks, CA: Sage Publications.

Mienczacowski, J. (1997). Theatre of change. *Research In Drama Education, 2*(2), 159–171.

Mienczakowski, J. (2001). Ethnodrama: Performed research – Limitations and potential. In P. Atkinson, A. Coffey, S. Delamont, J. Lofland, & L. Lofland (Eds.), *Handbook of Ethnography,* pp. 468–476. London: Sage Publications.

Mienczakowski, J., & Morgan, S. (2001). Ethnodrama: Constructing participatory, experiential and compelling action research through performance. In P. Reason, & H. Bradbury (Eds.), *Handbook of Action Research*, pp. 227–291. London: Sage Publications.

Mienczakowski, J., & Morgan, S. (1993). *Busting: The challenge of the drought spirit*. Brisbane: Griffith University Reprographics.

Nilan, P. M. (2002). 'Dangerous fieldwork' re-examined: The question of researcher subject position. *Qualitative Research, 2*(3), 363–386.

Paccagnella, L. (1997). Getting the seats of your pants dirty: Strategies for ethnographic research on virtual communities. *Journal of Computer-Mediated Communication, 3*(1). Available at http://jcmc.indiana.edu/vol3/issue1/paccagnella.html (Accessed 10 January 2008).

Reed-Danahay, D. E. (1997). Introduction. In D. E. Reed-Danahay (Ed.), *Auto/Ethnography. Rewriting the Self and the Social*, pp. 1–17. New York: Berg.

Richardson, L. (2000). Writing: A method of inquiry. In N. K. Denzin, & Y. S. Lincoln (Eds.), *Handbook of Qualitative Research* (2nd ed.), pp. 923–948. Thousand Oaks, CA: Sage Publications.

Saldana, J. (2005). *Ethnodrama: An anthology of reality theatre*. Walnut Creek, CA: Alta Mira Press.

Saldaña, J. (2011). *Ethnotheatre: Research from page to stage*. Walnut Press, CA: Left Coast Press.

Saljo, R. (1988). Learning in educational settings: Methods of inquiry. In P. Ramsden (Ed.), *Improving Learning: New Perspectives*, pp. 32–48. London: Kogan Page.

Sandberg, J. (1995). Are phenomenographic results reliable? *Nordisk Pedagogik, 15,* 156–164.

Seiter, E., Borchers, H., Kreutzner, G., & Warth, E. (1989). Don't treat us like we're so stupid and naive: Toward an ethnography of soap opera viewers. In E. Seiter, H. Borchers, G. Kreutzner, & E. Warth (Eds.), *Remote Control*, pp. 223–247. New York, NY: Routledge.

Svensson, L. (1994). Theoretical foundations of phenomenography. In R. Ballantyne, & C. Bruce (Eds.), *Phenomenography: Philosophy and Practice*, pp. 9–20. Brisbane: Queensland University of Technology.

Slattery, P. (2001). The educational researcher as artist working within. *Qualitative Inquiry, 7*(3), 370–398.

Sparkes, A. C. (2000). Fictional representations: On difference, choice, and risk. *Sociology of Sport Journal, 19,* 1–24.

Sparkes, A. C. (2002). *Telling tales in sport and physical activity: A qualitative journey*. Champaign, IL: Human Kinetics.

Spry, T. (2001). Performing autoethnography: An embodied methodological praxis. *Qualitative Inquiry, 7*(6), 706–732.

Sykes, H., & Goldstein, T. (2004). From performed to performing ethnography: Translating life history research into anti-homophobia curriculum for a teacher education program. *Teaching Education Journal, 15*(1), 31–56.

Tierney, W. G. (1998). Life history's history: Subjects foretold. *Qualitative Inquiry, 4,* 49–70.

Tomasell, K. G. (2003). "Dit is die here se asem": The wind, its messages, and issues of auto-ethnographic methodology in the kalahari. *Cultural Studies-Critical Methodologies, 3*(4), 397–428.

Van Maanen, J. (1995). Style as theory. *Organization Science, 6,* 133–143.

CHAPTER 16

Gender theories and sport management research

LEARNING OUTCOMES

By the end of this chapter, you should be able to:

- Understand the basic concepts of feminism.

- Identify the implications of the use of feminist methodology in sport management.

- Recognise some key features of "queer theory".

- Identify some strategies with which to apply feminist and queer methodology to sport management research.

KEY TERMS

1. **Feminism:** theories and philosophies concerned with issues of gender difference and which advocate women's rights and interests.

2. **Feminist theory:** Feminist theory extends feminism into theoretical and philosophical grounds. It aims to understand the nature of inequality and focuses on gender politics, power relations, and sexuality.

3. **Standpoint theory:** A standpoint is a position from which a human being views the world, and influences how they construct their position in the world.

4. **Queer theory:** It calls into question "essential" sexed, gendered, and sexual identities, striving to destabilise discursive constructions of sexuality that come to be accepted as "natural" and that maintain a dominant/subordinate power relationship.

KEY THEMES

- Is there a distinctive feminist methodology?

- What is queer theory?

CHAPTER OVERVIEW

This chapter explores gender research methodologies and their application to sport management research, in particular feminist and queer theories. The first section argues that feminist methodologies offer the sport management researcher scope to investigate issues specifically related to gender, and the impact these issues may have on the sport management environment. The second section of this chapter discusses how queer theory has the potential to be utilised in sport management research.

ORIGINS OF FEMINIST THEORY

Feminist theory has its origins in the political activism of the 1960s and 1970s, generally referred to as the second wave of feminism; the first wave being centred in the suffrage movement of the late 19th and early 20th centuries. The second wave of feminism sought equality and an end to discrimination. Although the activism of the 1970s has been somewhat tempered, feminism, as an academic focus, has developed throughout the 1980s and 1990s, and into the 21st century, coexisting alongside what has been called the third wave of feminism, which arose as a result of perceived failures of the second wave. This third wave of feminism, with its origins in the 1980s, seeks to challenge existentialist definitions of femininity and accepted views of what is or is not good for women. Table 16.1 outlines briefly this development of feminist theory.

WHAT IS FEMINIST METHODOLOGY?

According to Mies (1991), the emergence of feminist methodology "arose out of women's frustration at the realisation that women's lives, their history, their struggles, their ideas constitute no part of dominant science" (p. 66). Defining feminist research is far from clear-cut, with van Zoonen (1994) noting "the issue

Table 16.1 Stages of the development of feminist theory

Stages of the development of feminist theory

- First wave: rights
- Second wave: anti-essentialism, equality
- Third wave: beyond gender, class, power
- Neo-Marxist: materialist feminisms
- Queer theory: othered spaces
- Womanism and third-world feminism: beyond gender, race, class, power

of what exactly constitutes feminist research has been a subject of debate since the late 1970s" (p. 127). Feminist research is in "an emergent state" (Olesen, 2000, p. 215). It has also proven to be resistant to definitions revealing itself as "highly diversified, enormously dynamic" with competing models of thought and divergent methodological and analytic approaches jostling and at times blurring and merging (Olesen, 2000, p. 215). This stems from the differing strains of feminism that have evolved in the contemporary period embracing a multitude of variants ranging from liberal feminism to radical feminism. Consequently, feminist research has attempted to seek out methods receptive to the diversity of female experience, the multiple identities women take on (Olesen, 2000) and the plurality of subjectivities women experience. Feminist researchers and theorists draw on a range of methodologies from the social sciences, the humanities, and literary theory. Postmodernism, deconstruction theory, and poststructuralist theory have also led to a re-examination of the researcher's role, calling upon them to exercise "unremitting reflexivity" (Olesen, 2000). According to DeVault (1996):

> feminist methodologists do not use or prescribe any single research method; rather, they are united through various efforts to include women's lives and concerns in accounts of society, to minimize the harms of research and to support changes that will improve women's status. (p. 29)

Feminist research has thus evolved along with feminism to be characterised by diversity and complexity with no specific methodological or research orthodoxy prevailing. It is, however, marked by a number of fundamental precepts. Of fundamental importance in feminist research is a direct engagement with the question of gender such that research phenomena are "studied in a 'gendered', rather than a gender-blind or gender-neutral perspective" (Lundgren, 1995, p. 3).

Fine (cited in Gatenby & Humphries, 1996, pp. 77–78) details five epistemological and methodological commitments of feminist research. The *first* of Fine's precepts was labelled **"women's problematic"** by which she means that for research to be considered feminist it must not only focus on gender but it must make women's experiences central to the research and seek to understand the way in which women make sense of concepts relevant to the research. For example, taking women's perspective when investigating the portrayal of women in sport media. The *second* of Fine's precepts for feminist research is "**women's ways of knowing**", which is a twofold process. In the first instance the research must value women's ways of knowing by encouraging women to describe their own experiences and must respect their truths. Asking woman sport figures their opinion on how they are perceived and how they perceive other women in sport media helps to satisfy this precept. But second, researchers must address their own experiences and knowledge, and as van Zoonen (1994) terms it, radically politicise the research process by reflexively interrogating their own role, standpoint epistemologies, research praxis, and the position of power. Therefore, a sport management researcher must openly and honestly explore and explain any preconceptions and perceptions they have about women in sport media. Fine's *third* requirement of feminist research is a focus on **"feminist synalytics"**, which she describes as a blend of analysis and synthesis to facilitate new understanding that supersedes "the usual male-defined definitions" (cited in Gatenby & Humphries, 1996, pp. 77–78). Her *fourth* tenet is that of **"revolutionary pragmatism"** – a call for research that is of practical value and that is either the basis for a call for change or can, as Olesen (2000) argued, "set the stage for other research, other actions, and policy that transcend and transform" (p. 215). It may at its most basic be simply "helping the silent to speak and consciousness raising" (Dervin, cited in van Zoonen, 1994, p. 128), but whatever the desired outcomes, there is clear agreement that a feminist methodology entails a commitment to change, be that at the micro or at the macro level. The end result may be a reduction in the sex appeal of women in sport media, moving towards depicting woman as athletes. This commitment aligns with the fact that, "feminism is first and last a political movement concerned with practical issues" (Alcoff & Potter, 1993, p. 2). The *final* "epistemological and methodological" commitment from Fine is that of **"methodological integrity"**, which refers to the necessity to utilise diverse methods and perspectives (cited in Gatenby & Humphries, 1996). In this criterion, Fine is in agreement with numerous other theorists such as Reinharz (cited in McCarl Nielsen, 1990), for example, who describe feminist research as multi-methodological. Ever conscious of the epistemological issues at play in feminist methodology and sensitive to all stages of the research process, Stanley and Wise (1993) suggested that:

> There are a number of key areas of the research process in which we think precepts drawn from feminist epistemology need to be integrated: in the researcher/researched relationship; in emotion as an aspect of the research process that, like any, other aspect, can be analytically interrogated; in critically unpacking conceptualizations of 'objectivity' and 'subjectivity' as binaries or dichotomies; in the processes by which 'understanding' and 'conclusions' are reached; in the existence and management of the different 'realities' or versions held by researchers and researched and in issues surrounding authority and power in research, but also and perhaps more crucially in written representations of research. (p. 189)

FEMINIST ETHICAL CONCERNS AS THEY RELATE TO METHODOLOGY

Thompson (1992) summarises ethical concerns in feminist research into two areas. She believes we should first ask whether the research is either exploitative or empowering of participants and others, and then ask how oppressive objectification of participants can be avoided given that any method has the potential to be oppressive. Meeting these ethical concerns is not simple or straightforward, and feminist researchers have sometimes reported the challenges of carrying out completely ethical research on feminist terms (Maguire, 1987).

Research brief

Title: "If people are wearing pink stuff they're probably not real fans": Exploring women's perceptions of sport fan clothing
Author: Sveinson, K., *University of Regina*, Hoeber, L., *University of Regina*, & Toffoletti, K., *Deakin University* (2019)
Reference: Sveinson, K., Hoeber, L., & Toffoletti, K. (2019). "If people are wearing pink stuff they're probably not real fans": Exploring women's perceptions of sport fan clothing. *Sport Management Review, 22*(5), 736–747.
Given the growth in the female sport fan base of North American major league sports and the development and expansion of women's team-related apparel, the purpose of this study was to examine women sport fans' perceptions of team apparel. The authors collected data through in-depth interviews with 16 Canadian women who self-identified as fans of professional sport teams. They perceived a lack of options in team apparel, despite the development of women's clothing lines. Analysis of the aesthetics, symbolism, and instrumentality of team apparel using a third-wave feminist approach provided socio-cultural explanations for women fans' dissatisfaction with existing offerings.

FEMINIST THEORY MAKING

Maria Lugones and Elizabeth Spelman (Lugones & Spelman, 1983) suggest that the following criteria are important in feminist theory making: (1) the theory or account can be helpful if it enables one to see how parts of one's life fit together; (2) a useful theory will help one locate oneself concretely in the world; (3) a theory or account not only ought to accurately locate one in the world, but also enable one to think about the extent to which one is responsible for not being in that location; (4) a theory that is useful will provide criteria for change and make suggestions for modes of resistance that don't merely reflect the situation and values of the theoriser (p. 482). The criteria of Lugones & Spelman are captured within "standpoint theory".

STANDPOINT THEORY

Feminist standpoint theory assumes that there is no single objective truth and that class, race, gender, and sexual orientation structure a person's understanding of reality. To survive, less powerful groups must be attuned to the culture of the dominant group. In fact, these individuals have the potential for a more complete and less distorted view of social reality precisely because of their disadvantaged position (Nielsen, 1990). By living out their lives in both the dominant culture and in their own culture, members of stigmatised groups can develop a type of double vision, and hence a more comprehensive understanding of social reality (Hartsock, 1987, 1998; Westkott, 1990). This standpoint, however, must be developed by appropriating one's experiences through intellectual and political struggles against gender, race, class, and sexual orientation inequalities (Allen & Baber, 1992; Harding, 1987; Hartsock, 1987, 1998).

The social location of oppressed groups vis-a-vis their oppressors creates the potential for critical social analysis, but such a standpoint only emerges through consciousness raising experiences, such as those utilised by the feminist movement of the 1960s and 1970s. According to feminist standpoint theory, women's lives, in general, differ systematically and structurally from men's lives. Women and men are expected to engage in distinct activities, and the two groups are accorded different rights and opportunities. Wood (2005) suggests that some feminist standpoint theorists assert that knowledge from subordinated social locations is more complete than knowledge from dominant social locations. They believe that members of subordinated groups are likely to understand both their own group's perspective and the perspective of members of the dominant group, but that members of the dominant group are not as likely to understand – or have a motive to understand – the perspective of members of subordinate groups. This reasoning leads to the conclusion that members of dominant groups have less complete knowledge of the social world than members of subordinate groups. However, not all feminist standpoint theorists accept this claim. Patricia Hill Collins (1997), for instance, expresses scepticism that some knowledge is more complete or accurate than others. Studying subordinated locations and the knowledge they foster not only provides insight into the lives of members of subordinated groups, but also casts light on dominant group practices, especially those that create and reproduce inequality. This explains why feminist standpoint theorists claim that, while it is easier for women than men to achieve a feminist standpoint, it is possible for men to do so if they engage in the intellectual struggle to recognise and reject established power relations, including male privilege (Wood, 2005).

In summary, individuals hold a standpoint when they: (1) grasp the arbitrary and unfair nature of power relations that structure social life; and (2) are critical of the uneven consequences of those power relations for members of different groups. A feminist standpoint grows out of encountering oppositional knowledge and is unapologetically political because it aims to identify and challenge established social hierarchies and their consequences (Wood, 2005). In addition, feminist standpoint researchers must reflect upon (and share with their readers) how their own social group status influences their interpretations of their data, which leads us to a discussion of the importance of the researcher in feminist research.

THE ROLE OF THE FEMINIST RESEARCHER

Most researchers recognise that they bring a unique history, connection, value, and interpretation to the research they are conducting, and as such is an important and vital part of the research process. Gergen (1988) agrees, saying that "feminist meta-theory and methodology would thus incorporate the tenet that the investigator and the subject are interdependent" (p. 90). Harding (1987) also discusses the importance of positioning by the researcher. The researcher is located in the "same critical plane" as the subject. Class, race, culture, gender, beliefs, and assumptions of the researcher provide important and real information. The articulation of the researcher's unique relationship to the research not only identifies the limitations of the research, but will also strengthen the quality of the findings.

Research brief

Title: Playing like a girl? The negotiation of gender and sexual identity among female ice hockey athletes on male teams
Author: DiCarlo, D., *University of Toronto* (2015)
Reference: DiCarlo, D. (2016). Playing like a girl? The negotiation of gender and sexual identity among female ice hockey athletes on male teams. *Sport in Society*, *19*(8–9), 1363–1373.
While no one can deny the rich history of girls and women in sport, they continue to face obstacles to their full participation and representation in mixed-sex sport environments. Sex integration in sport is often contentious for those female athletes who participate in sports traditionally played by men, such as ice hockey. The authors argued that there is too little known about the lived experiences of girls and women who navigate these gendered sport spaces. This study therefore qualitatively explored how seven female ice hockey athletes negotiate their identities as female athletes, in such a way that focused on the social constructions of gender and sexuality. Findings of this study highlighted the tensions and contradictions of being a female athlete in a traditionally male sport and the rigid categories used by the women interviewed in negotiating their gendered and sexual identities while playing on male ice hockey teams.

FEMINIST THEORY AND SPORT MANAGEMENT

Sport management related feminist research studies have covered a diversity of topics. Brown (2007) utilised socio-legal, legal-geographic, and feminist sports theory to examine increased participation of women in elite sport in a patchwork case study on four nations: Canada, the United States of America, the Islamic Republic of Iran and Australia. Vander Kloet (2005) utilised feminist post-structuralism to explore lifeguarding, subjectivity, equity, and the public provision of public leisure through interviews with lifeguards. Scrogum (2005) explored the experiences of women who played rugby. Women took part in three focus groups to discuss their experiences in rugby and the meanings they attributed to them. Although not explicitly utilising feminist theory, Farrell (2006) investigated female consumption of women's basketball through the voices and perspectives of female spectators of men's basketball.

Case study

Title: An examination of women in leadership positions in sport: A case study of Australian Rules Football
Author: Richards, K., *Charles Sturt University* (2018)
Reference: Richards, K. (2018). An examination of women in leadership positions in sport: A case study of Australian Rules Football. A thesis submitted in fulfilment of the requirement of the degree of Doctor of Philosophy Charles Sturt University.

Sport is considered as a platform that both reinforces and challenges gendered stereotypes and it is often seen to privilege men over women. However, women are becoming more visible in roles and positions that have traditionally been held by men in sport (such as roles in sports departments, sports journalism, and managerial positions). These changes have challenged the traditional gender hierarchy in sport and are gradually changing the perception of women working in sport.

This thesis highlighted the lived experiences, beliefs and opinions of 26 women working and volunteering in leadership positions in Australian

rules football. Using methods such as in-depth interviews, case study analysis and thematic analysis, this thesis investigated whether these women "fit in" or challenge the traditionally male environment. The extent to which Australian rules football practices gender inclusivity and equality is also explored. Participants shared both positive and challenging experiences within their respective workplaces. These women shared experiences where they were proud to forge a pathway for women following in their footsteps. They also believed they brought diversity to their workplace and for the most part, did not feel there were gendered barriers in place. However, participants also faced challenges, such as institutional barriers, sexism and a pressure to conform to gender stereotypes. At times, females were also held to higher standards and expectations (compared to males) and showed a hesitancy to advocate for gender equality. Adopting a third wave feminism perspective, this research concluded that the environment of Australian rules football is both empowering and oppressive for women in leadership positions.

QUEER THEORY AND SPORT MANAGEMENT RESEARCH

Queer theory seeks to deconstruct hegemonic notions of sexuality and gender. Queer theorists examine how traditional definitions of gender identity (masculine vs. feminine) and sexuality (heterosexual vs homosexual) break down, overlap, misrepresent or do not adequately explain the dynamic range of human sexuality in a text. It calls into question the "naturalness" of heterosexuality and the notion of stable sexualities. Jagose (1996) suggests that the evolution of queer theory is "a product of specific cultural and theoretical pressures with increasingly structured debates … about questions of lesbian and gay identity" (p. 76). Though difficult to define as it is ever evolving, queer theory calls into question "essential" sexed, gendered and sexual identities, striving to destabilise discursive constructions of sexuality that come to be accepted as "natural" and that maintain a dominant/subordinate power relationship (Halperin 1995; Jagose 1996).

Queer theory also claims diversity through its intended inclusion of gay, lesbian, bisexual, transgendered, and transsexual persons, and really any subject (even heterosexual) that somehow deviates from normative definitions of (sexual) desire; it purports to be inclusive of any one who feels marginalised from the norm – be it a result of sexuality, intellect, culture, etc. (Giffney, 2004). Queer theory is a contested term that is sometimes used as a catchall for marginalised sexual groups, or as a radical new theory that has emerged out of lesbian and gay studies. Queer theory has been critiqued by some as not being inclusive of other forms of difference, for example, race or gender. Gamson (2000) argues that "queer studies is largely a deconstructive enterprise, taking apart the view of a self-defined by something at its core, be it sexual desire, race, gender, nation, or class" (p. 348). He goes on to say, "Queer marks an identity that, defined as it is by a deviation from sex and gender norms either by the self- inside or by specific behaviors, is always in flu" (p. 349).

The distinction between queer identity and queer theory is important. We understand queer as a way of reading an action, behaviour or characteristic, so that queer can remain a fluid, dynamic term. Beemyn and Eliason (1996) write that queer theory must "be flexible enough to accommodate all people who identify as queer" (p. 3). Beemyn and Eliason (1996) go on to argue "queer theory has the potential to be inclusive of race, gender, sexuality, and other areas of identity by calling attention to the distinctions between identities, communities, and cultures, rather than ignoring these differences or pretending that they don't exist" (p. 165). Krane (2001) argues that queer theory has moved beyond lesbian and gay studies because, "queer theory seeks to avoid privileging one component of identity over another" (p. 404).

This may also be the opinion of Tierney (1997) who sees queer theory as seeking "to interrogate terms such as gender and race so that the norms of our lives are reconfigured" (p. 37). Queer theory calls into question understandings of identity categories and operations of power; it seeks to destabilise accepted gender and identity constructs through individual acts of resistance/subversion. Queer theorists raise questions that other researchers may not about identity categories. Table 16.2 lists some of the generally accepted features of queer theory while examples of the types of questions research may raise about identity categories are presented in Table 16.3.

CRITICISMS OF QUEER THEORY

Critics of queer still find it problematic that queer is used. Butler (1991) argues that it remains politically necessary to lay claim to "women", "queer", "gay", and "lesbian", precisely because of the way these terms, as it were, lay their claim on us prior to our full knowing. Laying claim to such terms in reverse will be necessary to refute homophobic deployments of the terms in law, public policy, on the street, in "private" life. Other criticism of Queer theory are identified in Table 16.4.

Table 16.2 Features of queer theory

Queer theory features

- Gender and sex are socially constructed.
- Deconstructs gender and sexuality/gender norms.
- Rejects biological theories of sexual identity.
- Questions the usefulness of sexual and gender categories.
- Challenges the taken-for-granted binaries of gender and sexuality.
- Opens up for debate and discussion the very notions of what constitutes maleness and femaleness as well as sexualities.
- Gender and sex binary serve to *acknowledge* sexual differences and also operates to *contain* and *regulate* these identities.
- Once such categories are formulated, various institutions – parents, families, medicine, social work, the law, mental health, and criminal justice systems – regulate and police them.
- Identity politics and social movements.

Table 16.3 Questions asked by queer theorists

Questions queer theorists ask?

- What do these categories serve?
- Who do these categories include and who do they exclude?
- Who has the power to define the categories?
- How are the categories policed?
- How do these categories change over time and over cultures?

Table 16.4 Criticisms of queer theory

Criticisms of queer theory

- It fails to consider the reality of structural power (class, patriarchy, race/ethnicity, ability.
- It simply (re)named and then (re)constructed typical power relations despite its claims of diversity.
- While some writers argue that queer theory is actually too inclusive because it renders difference invisible, others argue that it is not inclusive enough.
- Sexual identity is a false construct created to categorise deviant behaviour and to promote a dominant sexuality.
- Existing queer theory, despite attempts to avoid normativity, harbours a normative discourse around race, sexuality, and class.
- It must provide a framework in which to challenge racist, misogynist, and other oppressive perspectives/discourse/norms, as well as those that are heterosexist and homophobic.

SPORT AND QUEER THEORY

Although not yet used in a sport management context queer theory as a research method has been applied in sport studies. Davidson and Shogan (1998) urge scholars to consider a queer theoretical perspective that would deconstruct sexuality and dominant ideologies within sport. Abdel-Shehid (2005) has explored the possibility of analysing sport through a queer lens, and more specifically of deconstructing black masculinity, its link to heterosexuality and the sexualisation of black athletes. Abdel-Shehid has proposed that deconstructing sport using "black queer theory" would engage questions of visibility and recognition and would provide an alternative reading of sport culture and black masculinity.

Research brief

Title: The queer sport of failure: Representations of female athletes in Korean Sport Films
Author: Kim, S. Y., *Hankuk University of Foreign Studies* & Park, S., *Kookmin University* (2017)
Reference: Kim, S. Y. & Park, S. (2017). The queer sport of failure: Representations of female athletes in Korean sport films. *Sociology of Sport Journal, 34*(4), 354–363.
This article aimed to update the discourse on female Korean athletes by illuminating the radical change of their imagery and reality over the last three decades, from sexless victims of patriarchy to sportswomen asserting their strength, femininity, and even "queerness." Insofar as sport films provide a felicitous site through which to examine popular and evolving representations of gender and sport, the article analysed a variety of Korean sports films which reproduced, or posed a challenge to conventional portrayals of female athletes.

CONCLUSION

Gender approaches have much to offer the sport management researcher. The overarching goal of this form of research is to identify the ways in which multiple forms of oppression impact the lives of women and those of alternate sexual orientation. From a feminist's perspective the goal is to seek emancipation, whereas "standpoint theory" aims to provide an understanding of the perspective of others. Queer theory seeks to address issues associated with sexuality and provide a vehicle for greater inclusivity. All three approaches have a place in sport management research.

Case study

Title: "Some are gay, some are straight, no one actually cares as long as you're there to play hockey": Women's field hockey players' engagement with sexual identity discourses
Author: Whitehouse, L. E., *University of Chester* (2019)

Reference: Whitehouse, L. E. (2019). "Some are gay, some are straight, no one actually cares as long as you're there to play hockey": Women's field hockey players' engagement with sexual identity discourses. Master Thesis University of Chester.

(Continued)

This research investigated the discourses that have impacted recreational women's hockey players' perspectives and experiences surrounding sexual identity. Furthermore, the participants' engagement with sexual identity discourses and through what discursive practices and disciplinary techniques sexual identities became dominant or alternative was examined. The experiences of and towards non-heterosexual sportspeople was claimed to be a developing area of research, though little research focuses on recreational level sport that has not been identified as a "gay sport space". This study contributed to sexuality and sport research by investigating a recreational women's team, which was not restricted to the "gay sport space" label to develop understandings of the dynamics and complexities that sexual identity discourses had on both heterosexual and non-heterosexual sportspeople. A post structural, Foucaultian theoretical framework underpinned this study with the utilisation of Foucault's work on discourses, techniques of power, and the technologies of the self. Data was generated from semi-structured interviews with seven hockey players, who discussed their experiences regarding sexual identity at Castle Ladies Hockey Club. By analysing the participants' talk through discourse analysis, discourses of acceptance and inclusivity towards non-heterosexual identities were found. Firstly, non-heterosexual identities were regarded as "normal"; secondly, the focus were shifted to whether the player was a good team player rather than sexual identity, and thirdly, there was an increased acceptance of sexual fluidity leading to decreased tolerance towards homophobia. This research highlighted that players engaged with multiple discourses associated with sexual identity, often complexly. This raised questions surrounding the dominance of heteronormativity, as non-heterosexual identities were not presented as marginal.

REVIEW AND RESEARCH QUESTIONS

With a basic understanding now of feminist and queer theories, attempt to answer the following questions:

1. Is the gender of the researcher important in feminist research?

2. Standpoint theory is about the different ways each person experiences situations. Our perceptions are influenced by our position in society, and by power relations. Watch the following video and discuss how their "standpoints" influence their perception: https://www.youtube.com/watch?v=zmBMcTVXgrk

3. Provide some examples of how "queer theory" could be applied to sport management research.

REFERENCES

Abdel-Shehid, G. (2005). *Who da man? Black masculinities and sporting cultures.* Toronto: Canadian Scholars.

Alcoff, L., & Potter, E. (1993). *Feminist epistemologies.* New York: Routledge.

Allen, K. R., & Baber, K. M. (1992). Ethical and epistemological tensions in applying a postmodern perspective to feminist research. *Psychology of Women Quarterly, 16,* 1–15.

Beemyn, B., & Eliason, M. (1996). *Queer studies: A lesbian, gay, bisexual, and transgender anthology.* New York: New York University Press.

Brown, D. M. (2007). *Communicating design: Developing web site documentation for design and planning.* Berkeley, CA: Peachpit.

Butler, J. (1991). *Gender trouble: Feminism and the subversion of identity.* New York, NY: Routledge.

Collins, P. H. (1997). African American women and economic justice: A preliminary analysis of wealth, family, and African American social class. *University of Cincinnati Law Review, 65*(3), 825–852.

Davidson, J., & Shogan, D. (1998). What's queer about studying up? A response to messner. *Sociology of Sport Journal, 15*(4), 359–366.

Devault, M. L. (1996). Talking back to sociology: Distinctive contributions of feminist methodology. *Annual Review of Sociology, 22,* 29–50.

Farrell, K. (2006). HIV on TV: Conversations with young gay men. *Sexualities, 9*(2), 193–213.

Gamson, J. (2000). Sexualities, queer theory, and qualitative research. In N. K. Denzin, & Y. S. Lincoln (Eds.), *Handbook of Qualitative Research* (2nd ed.), pp. 347–365. Thousand Oaks, CA: Sage Publications.

Gatenby, B., & Humphries, M. (1996). Feminist commitments in organisational communication: Participatory action research as feminist praxis. *Australian Journal of Communication, 23*(2), 73–87.

Gergen, K. J. (1988). Feminist critique of science and the challenge of social epistemology. In M. Gergen (Ed.), *Feminist Thought and the Structure of Knowledge,* pp. 27–48. New York: New York University Press.

Giffney, N. (2004). Denormatizing queer theory: More than (simply) lesbian and gay studies. *Feminist Theory, 5*(1), 73–78.

Halperin, D. M. (1995). *Saint-foucault: Towards a gay hagiography.* New York: Oxford University Press.

Harding, S. (1987). *Feminism and methodology.* Bloomington, IN: Indiana University Press.

Hartsock, N. (1987). Rethinking modernism. *Cultural Critique, 7,* 187–206.

Hartsock, N. C. M. (1998). *The feminist standpoint revisited and other essays.* Boulder, CO: Westview.

Jagose, A. M. (1996). *Queer theory: An introduction.* New York: New York University.

Krane, D. (2001). Disorderly progress on the frontiers of policy evaluation. *International Journal of Public Administration, 24*(1), 95–123.

Lugones, M., & Spelman, E. (1983). Have we got a theory for you! Feminist theory, cultural imperialism and the demand for 'the woman's voice. *Women's Studies International Forum, 6,* 573–581.

Lundgren, C. (1995). *Feminist theory and violent empiricism* (Trans. Linda Schenck). Aldershot: Avebury.

Maguire, P. (1987). *Doing participatory research: A feminist approach.* Amherst, MA: University of Massachusetts.

Mies, M. (1991). Women's research or feminist research: The debate surrounding feminist science and methodology. In M. M. Fonow, & J. A. Cook (Eds.), *Beyond Methodology: Feminist Scholarship as Lived Research,* pp. 60–84. Bloomington: Indiana University Press.

Nielsen, M. C. (1990). *Feminist research methods exemplary readings m the social sciences.* Boulder, CO: Westview Press.

Olesen, V. L. (2000). Feminisms and qualitative research at and into the millennium. In N. Denzin, & Y. Lincoln (Eds.), *Handbook of Qualitative Research* (2nd ed.), pp. 215–256. London: Sage Publications.

Scrogum, J. (2005). *Binaries and Bridging: A Feminist Analysis of Women's Rugby Participation*. Unpublished master's thesis. University of North Carolina at Greensboro.

Stanley, L., & Wise, S. (1993). *Breaking out again*. London: Routledge.

Tierney, W. (1997). *Academic outlaws: Queer theory and cultural studies in the academy*. London: Sage Publications.

Thompson, D. (1992). Against the dividing of women: Lesbian feminism and heterosexuality. *Feminism and Psychology, 2*, 387–398.

Vander Kloet, M. A. (2005). *Baywatch babes as recreation workers: Lifeguarding, subjectivity, equity*. Masters Dissertation, University of Toronto, Canada

van Zoonen, L. (1994). *Feminist media studies*. Thousand Oaks, CA: Sage Publications.

Westkott, M. (1990). Feminist criticism of the social sciences. In J. M Nielsen (Ed.), *Feminist Research Methods: Exemplary Readings in the Social Sciences*, pp. 58–68. Boulder, CO: Westview Press.

Wood, J. T. (2005). Feminist standpoint theory and muted group theory: Commonalities and divergences. *Women and language, 28*(2), 61–72.

CHAPTER 17

Grounded theory and sport management research

LEARNING OUTCOMES

By the end of this chapter, you should be able to:

- Understand the basic concepts of grounded theory.

- Identify some sport management phenomena to which the application of the grounded theory methodology would be suited.

- Apply the process of grounded theory in sport management research.

KEY TERMS

1. **Symbolic interactionism:** The theory that people have developed conventionalised signs that have become organised into language which, in turn, is the vehicle for the transmission of culture, which provides the major means for carrying on social interaction.

2. **Theoretical coding:** It is dealing with conceptual codes, which are derived from the open codes and form the link between the data and the theoretical findings.

3. **Theoretical sampling:** The process of choosing new research sites, participants or targets, based on an analysis of the data already collected, and the theories gleaned from that data.

KEY THEMES

- What is Grounded Theory?

- What are some of the weaknesses of the Grounded Theory method for Sport Management research?

- What are some of the strengths of the Grounded Theory method for Sport Management research?

CHAPTER OVERVIEW

This chapter explores the research approach of grounded theory. It examines the debates surrounding the application of grounded theory to research and identifies and discusses the principles that underpin grounded theory approaches to research in sport management settings. The chapter notes that: grounded theory is both a set of research procedures and the theory that develops from that research; theory is generated or modified from the data rather than from pre-existing theoretical frameworks; procedures and specific techniques are carried out systematically in a step by step fashion; the approach is built upon specific procedures and techniques, including; "constant comparison" between data and emergent theory, "theoretical sampling", and progressive focusing; it is a particularly suitable approach for sport management research because it allows practice-based theories to be built that extend or modify existing theory.

INTRODUCTION

Grounded Theory is frequently considered to offer researchers a suitable qualitative method for in-depth exploratory investigations (Charmaz, 1995; Strauss & Corbin, 1990; Willig, 2008). It is a rigorous approach that provides the researcher with a set of systematic strategies (Charmaz, 1995). While this method shares some features with phenomenology, Grounded Theory assumes that the analysis will generate one over-arching and encompassing theory. Grounded theory is a research approach in which the researcher develops a theory that is grounded in the data. It shares some procedures and strategies with ethnography, phenomenology, and discourse analysis. Although a research approach in its own right, it also can be used in combination with other approaches, such as case studies.

Grounded theory is an open, reflexive form of research where data collection, analysis, the development of theoretical concepts, and the literature review occur in a cyclical and interactive process. While these features apply to some of the other qualitative research orientations, grounded theory has *three* distinguishing features. First, researchers follow systematic, analytical procedures: grounded theory is more structured in its process of data collection and analysis than other forms of qualitative research, even though their strategies are similar (such as analysis of interview transcripts, observations and written documents). Second, researchers do not aim merely to describe but also to conceptualise and explain: the purpose of grounded theory is to generate and develop theory. Without doing this, researchers may have done research in the grounded theory style but will not have employed grounded theory per se. Finally, researchers carry out theoretical sampling where decisions about the data to be collected are determined by the concepts they discover, both in the early stages and then later as the theory is in the process of being constructed. Hence data are collected, analysed, and theory is developed in parallel and interactively through a process of "constant comparison". Researchers attempt to enter the research process without prior assumptions. This means eschewing pre-existing theories and a detailed literature review in order to concentrate on discovery and emergent knowledge. Grounded theory studies, therefore, are based on the premise that the strategies and products of research are shaped from the data rather than from any preconceived theoretical frameworks and hypotheses that you might bring to the research.

DEFINING GROUNDED THEORY

Grounded theory was developed in 1967 by two sociologists, Barney Glaser and Anselm Strauss, in their book "The Discovery of the Grounded Theory". This is an approach to theory development grounded/rooted in the data rather than empirical testing of the theory, that is, data are collected and analysed, and then a theory is developed which is grounded in the data (Glaser & Strauss, 1967). These two authors defined the grounded theory as "The theory that was derived from data, systematically gathered, and analysed through the research process" (Strauss & Corbin, 1990, p. 12). They took the idea from symbolic internationalist that meaning is constructed through the use of sign, languages, and symbols. The grounded theory approach is different from the "framework approach" in analysing qualitative data. The grounded theory approach emphasises "theory" as the final output of research (Strauss & Corbin, 1998). The word "theory" is used to mean the relationships that exist among concepts that comes from the data and helps us understand our social world more clearly (Strauss & Corbin, 1998). The framework approach in data analysis may "stop" at the level of description or simple interpretation. The aim of grounded theory is "theoretical development". Creswell (2009) indicates that in the grounded theory research approach the researcher attempts to derive a general, abstract theory of a process, action, or interaction grounded in the views of participants in a study. The basic principles of this theory are; (1) the task of research is to discover new methods of understanding or investigating the social processes and interactions; and (2) the purpose of the analysis is to generate or discover a theory based on possibility fundamental patterns in life (Glaser & Strauss, 1967). The sport management researcher utilising the grounded theory of qualitative research therefore must understand the world and their interpretation of it, as the research participants understand it (Marshall & Rossman, 1995).

Grounded theory aids the researcher seeking to study social phenomena in a range of different fields, in its natural setting. For the sport management researcher, this could be a study of athletes at a competition, specific consumers attending a sporting event, or even the management team within a sporting organisation. The researcher will engage in a data collection process of field observation, in-depth interviews, and document analysis (Glaser & Strauss, 1967). Following analysis of one set of data, the researcher then decides what data to collect next and where to find them from other participants, sites, and/or events or incidents. Therefore, the grounded theory researcher develops the theory as it emerges in this ongoing process – referred to by Glaser and Strauss, as "grounding" the theory in the data. Because of this continual "grounding" process, the theory accurately reflects the data. It takes a researcher both time and the ability to think conceptually about the data in order to develop a grounded theory. Wilson (1989) asserts that the time is essential to allow for both a component of creativity and comprehensive analysis of the data, the end result of which is a theoretical explanation of the phenomenon being studied. This theoretical explanation is enough to provide differing accounts while at the same time allowing generalisations.

THE GROUNDED THEORY DEBATE

The literature provides discussion of an ongoing debate initiated by the original researchers and augmented by differing schools of thought on the "correct" method and interpretation of grounded theory. The two popular approaches to grounded theory are the systematic procedures of Strauss and Corbin (1990, 1998) and the constructivist approach of Charmaz (2005, 2006). The method of grounded theory as originally proposed by Glaser and Strauss (1967) has more recently been presented in densely codified and structured format (Strauss & Corbin, 1990). However, this later version has been criticised by Glaser (1992) on the grounds that it deviates from the original method in that it is orientated toward "forcing" the data into a codified frame rather than allowing the theory or concepts to emerge from the data.

This debate is further elaborated on by Kendall (1999) who suggests that Strauss and Corbin (1990) perceived the need to address what they viewed as the limitation caused by a lack of detail in the literature surrounding the processes involved in generating meaningful theories grounded in qualitative data. The main criticism of their approach is the apparent contradiction to the original assumptions, in particular the emphasis on conceptual description rather than emergent theory. Kendall (1999) proposes that the crux of the issue in differences between the two approaches is the use of axial coding. There is no argument regarding the importance of coding (Glaser, 1978, 1992; Strauss & Corbin, 1990) in that it is essential to transform the raw data into theoretical constructions of social processes. Glaser and Strauss (1967) and Glaser (1978) describe two types of coding, substantive or open and theoretical coding, whereas Strauss and Corbin (1990) articulate three types, open, axial, and selective coding.

While the versions of open coding are espoused to be similar (Kendall, 1999), there are nonetheless, differences. The controversy was created when Strauss and Corbin (1990) added "axial" coding to the coding process, which they define as a set of procedures whereby data is put back together in new ways after open coding has occurred, by making connections between the categories. Specifically, conditions, contexts, action, and interactional strategies and consequences are articulated. Glaser (1978) emphasises the need to allow codes and theoretical underpinnings to "freely" emerge. It would appear that Glaser's (1978) main concern with axial coding is the act of placing labels on the codes which should be guided by conceptual interests emergent from the data, and not interpreted as belonging to, or being representative of particular scheme as proposed in Strauss and Corbin's (1990) paradigm model.

Glaser (1978) identifies 18 coding elements that could be used to guide the researcher to connect categories. These elements are not exclusive, and therefore, because there is no pre-set framework, there is an increased guarantee of a unique emergence of the data, rather than fitting it to a framework (Kendall, 1999). In a counterclaim, Strauss and Corbin (1990) argue that their process allows the researcher to be guided by a more complex, systematic, and accurate method. The key difference in the two approaches was formalised when Strauss co-published a text on grounded theory (Strauss & Corbin, 1990). Glaser went public with allegations that the method espoused in this text was not true to the original notion of grounded theory, and he articulated two major reasons for this: (1) researchers are required to ask questions of the data which varies from the original purpose to ask "what is the main concern or problem and what accounts for most of the variation in processing the problem?"; and (2) a preconceived framework for asking questions of the data is used rather than allowing the categories to emerge from the data itself.

CHARMAZ APPROACH

A second variant of grounded theory is found in the constructivist writing of Charmaz (see Charmaz, 2005, 2006). Instead of embracing the study of a single process or core category as in the Strauss and Corbin (1998) approach, Charmaz advocates for a social constructivist perspective that includes emphasising diverse local worlds, multiple realities, and the complexities of particular worlds, views, and actions. Constructivist grounded theory, according to Charmaz (2006), lies squarely within the interpretive approach to qualitative research with flexible guidelines, a focus on theory developed that depends on the researcher's view, learning about the experience within embedded, hidden networks, situations, and relationships, and making visible hierarchies of power, communication, and opportunity. Charmaz places more emphasis on the views, values, beliefs, feelings, assumptions, and ideologies of individuals than on the methods of research, although she does describe the practices of gathering rich data, coding the data, memoing, and using theoretical sampling (Charmaz, 2006). She suggests that complex terms or jargon, diagrams, conceptual maps, and systematic approaches (such as Strauss & Corbin, 1990) detract from grounded theory and represent an attempt to gain power in their use. She advocates using active codes, such as gerund-based phrases like "recasting life" (Gerund phrases always function as nouns, so they will be subjects, subject complements, or objects in the sentence). Moreover, for Charmaz, a grounded theory procedure does not minimise the role of the researcher in the process. The researcher makes decisions about the categories throughout the process, brings questions to the data, and advances personal values, experiences, and priorities. Any conclusions developed by grounded theorists are suggestive, incomplete, and inconclusive (Charmaz, 2005). Although Charmaz's interpretive approach has many attractive elements, as a novice researcher we recommend Strauss and Corbin (1990, 1998) to illustrate grounded theory procedures because their systematic approach is helpful to individuals learning about and applying grounded theory research.

Research brief

Title: Educating and supporting tennis parents: A grounded theory of parents' needs during childhood and early adolescence
Author: Thrower, S. N., *Loughborough University*, Harwood, C. G., *Loughborough University*, & Spray, C. M., *Loughborough University* (2016)
Reference: Thrower, S. N., Harwood, C. G., & Spray, C. M. (2016). Educating and supporting tennis parents: A grounded theory of parents' needs during childhood and early adolescence. *Sport, Exercise, and Performance Psychology*, 5(2), 107.
The purpose of this study was to identify British tennis parents' education and support needs across contexts and developmental stages. Data were collected in 2 high-performance tennis centres and consisted of 6 months of fieldwork and interviews with parents, coaches, and 29 ex-youth players. The authors applied a grounded theory methodology and data were analysed through a process of open coding, axial coding, and theoretical integration. The resulting grounded theory highlighted the need to provide tennis parents with education that covers their introductory needs, organisational needs, development needs, and competition needs during childhood/mini tennis (5–10 years) and early adolescence/junior tennis (11–14 years).

ASSUMPTIONS UNDERPINNING GROUNDED THEORY METHOD

Eaves (2001) was able to identify seven assumptions about the method from *Glaser's and Strauss'* writings. These assumptions are as follows:

1. Grounded theory method assumes the emergence of a substantive theory from the research process, rather than verifying pre-existing theories. According to Glaser and Strauss (1967), the development of theories that are grounded on data is an important process that many social scientists ignored.

2. The systematic application of grounded theory method analytical techniques (constant comparative analysis) lead progressively to more abstract theories.

3. A third assumption, therefore, is that the process and products of grounded theory studies are shaped from data rather than a preconceived theoretical framework.

4. Grounded theory methodology assumes that discovery of a core category(ies) and a core process (substantive theory) is the ultimate focus of grounded theory studies. For instance, a basic social process is one type of core category that provides the building blocks of a theory (Glaser, 1978).

5. The aim of grounded theory methodology is not only to study processes, but also to assume that making theoretical sense of social life through a systematic study is itself a process.

6. Rigour of the related study is enhanced by simultaneous data collection and analysis in a grounded theory study.

7. Finally, theoretical sampling in the grounded theory method maximises the coverage of variations within the phenomenon being studied.

According to Glaser and Strauss (1967), the major uses of grounded theory include the following:

1. Preliminary, exploratory, and descriptive studies, where little research has been done and further investigation may be required.

2. The provision of a different perspective in areas where a substantial amount of research utilising other research methodologies has been completed.

3. The clarification and explanation of some of the major components of a social and psychological process, for example, implementing change.

4. The sharpening of sensitivities to the problems, dilemmas, and issues that are facing people who work in some area of social life, for example, sport managers implementing change.

5. The prediction and explanation of behaviour, thus allowing understanding and control over some situations (p. 27).

PHILOSOPHICAL UNDERPINNINGS OF GROUNDED THEORY

According to Crotty (1998), the researcher should articulate a philosophical position, consisting of the ontological, epistemological, and methodological assumptions that underlie a research study. Since the choice of a research methodology is linked to the researcher's philosophical position or basic belief system (Crotty 1998; Guba & Lincoln, 1994), researchers are advised to adopt a "...research paradigm that is congruent with their beliefs about the nature of reality" (Mills, Bonner & Francis, 2006, p. 26) in relation to the study. Such a clarification is important in light of the considerable debate over the philosophical paradigm upon which Grounded Theory fits into, that is, whether it arises from a positivist–objectivist or an interpretivist–constructionist epistemology.

GROUNDED THEORY METHODOLOGY

The essential features of the grounded theory methodology are firstly that the data itself is used to identify and interrelate the abstract concepts which drive theory and secondly that the resultant theory is the product of the data collection and analysis process. As previously mentioned, this is the process whereby the data drives the theory and is what Glaser and Strauss (1967) refer to as "grounding" the theory in the data. Because of this continual "grounding" process, the theory accurately reflects the data. Eaves (2001) suggests also that one aim of grounded theory methodology is not only to study processes, but also assume that making theoretical sense of social life through a systematic study is itself a process. Although Glaser and Strauss did not specifically articulate the basic tenets of grounded theory, subsequent theorists have articulated such tenets as follows:

1. The theory must be generated from praxis.

2. The theory must be interesting and useful, or have what is called "grab".

3. The resultant theory must fit, that is, demonstrate relevance and be able to explain, predict, and be modified by the social phenomenon under study.

4. Data collection and analysis are undertaken simultaneously, that is both processes are interwoven, concepts, and propositions that emerge guide the subsequent data collection.

5. The substantive theory should be able to transcend a particular setting and extend to a wider scope of circumstances.

6. The emergent theory must be able to incorporate other theories, rather than existing in opposition.

7. The approach of grounded theory presumes the possibility of discovering fundamental patterns in all social life, specifically the emergency of variability of the core category of basic social processes (Wilson, 1989, p. 19).

In addressing all of these tenets, what results is a theoretical explanation of the phenomenon which: (1) fits the substantive area under study; (2) is appropriately dense and thereby provides an adequate variational account; (3) abstract enough to allow generalisation; and (4) allows for a degree of control over structures and processes seen in the everyday account of the phenomenon (Wilson, 1989, p. 21). Additionally, grounded theory methodology assumes that discovery of a core category(ies) and a core process (substantive theory) is the ultimate focus of grounded theory studies (Eaves, 2001).

THE GROUNDED THEORY METHOD

This section outlines the key principles in "Classic Grounded Theory" and describes the various procedures of the methodology. The researcher needs to begin by determining if grounded theory is best suited to study their research problem. Grounded theory is a good design to use when a theory is not available to explain a process. The literature may have models available, but they were developed and tested on samples and populations other than those of interest to the qualitative researcher. Also, theories may be present, but they are incomplete because they do not address potentially valuable variables of interest to the researcher. On the practical side, a theory may be needed to explain how people are experiencing a phenomenon, and the grounded theory developed by the researcher will provide such a general framework. The research questions that the researcher asks of participants will focus on understanding how individuals experience the process and identifying the steps in the process (What was the process? How did it unfold?).

Annells (1997a, 1997b) asserts that the following 10 elements are essential to any approach utilising the grounded theory method. These are presented below:

1. The asking of theoretically orientated questions.

2. Theoretical sampling.

3. Constant comparative analysis.

4. Theoretical coding – this includes open, theoretical, and selective coding.

5. Theoretical sensitivity.

6. Memoing.

7. Theoretical saturation.

8. Identification of a core category(ies), for example, a BSP.

9. The production of theory from the core category(ies) (the core process).

10. The grounding of theory upon data through data-theory interplay.

These elements will now be considered in relation to the method of grounded theory.

METHOD

Theoretical sampling

The first step in the grounded theory method is theoretical sampling. Theoretical sampling is the "... process of data collection for generating theory whereby the analyst jointly collects, codes, and analyses his data and decides what data to collect next and where to find them, in order to develop his theory as it emerges" (Glaser & Strauss, 1967, p. 45). This principle requires that the emerging theory dictates the sampling and data collection process, with the aim of generating hypothesis with "...evidence enough only to establish a suggestion" (Glaser & Strauss, 1967, p. 40). Unlike pre-planned samples in quantitative research, theoretical sampling requires the researcher not to know in advance what to sample for and where it will lead (Glaser, 1992), but to go "...to the most obvious places and the most likely informants in search of information" (Goulding, 2001, p. 25). The sampling process was allowed to develop during the research process itself, that is, analysis of an initial case would lead to examination of further cases and sources of data pertinent to the forming theory.

Data analysis through constant comparison

Constant comparison is the central analytical process in Classic Grounded Theory. It consists of two coding stages, namely an initial Substantive Coding stage, which consists of Open Coding and Selective Coding, and a latter Theoretical Coding stage. In the constant comparative method, each piece of data or item of information gleaned from the data collection process is repeatedly compared with all other data, so that theoretical concepts are generated that will include as much behavioural variation as possible. The purpose of comparative analysis is to determine the accuracy of data collected, establish the generality of a fact, specify a concept, and thereby generate a theory (Glaser & Strauss, 1967).

Coding

Glaser (1998) described coding as assigning categories to incidents in the data. He explained that incidents were identified in a phrase or a sentence in the interviews. Joint coding and analysis lifted the data from an empirical or descriptive level to a conceptual or theoretical level (Glaser, 1978). The path from the empirical to conceptual level was not linear but creative in nature, and Glaser (1998, 1978) warned of using pathways that were too prescriptive. Coding is carried out on three levels: *Open coding, theoretical coding, and selective coding*. These coding methods will now be described.

Open coding

Glaser (1978) described open coding in detail. Open coding was defined as "running the data open" or coding "different incidents into as many categories as possible" (p. 56). He stated that data collection and open coding were completed when no new properties of categories or the same properties were identified in further interviews. Open coding aims at expressing data and phenomena in the form of concepts. For this purpose, data are first disentangled (segmented). Basic questions in doing open coding include;

- What? Which phenomenon is mentioned?
- Who? Which persons and roles?
- How? Which aspects are mentioned?
- When? How long? Where? Time, course, location.
- How much? How strong? Aspects of intensity.
- Why? Which reasons are given or can be constructed?
- What for? With what intention, to which purpose?
- By which? Means, tactics, and strategies for reaching the goal.

Theoretical coding

Glaser (1978) described theoretical coding as dealing with conceptual codes, which were derived from the open codes and formed the link between the data and the theoretical findings. Theoretical codes form the basis for the theoretical findings and are important that they emerge from the data and not from extraneous sources (Glaser, 1998).

Selective coding

In selective coding, as described by Glaser (1978), the researcher "selectively code[s] for a core variable and cease[s] open coding" (p. 61). Once the core category is identified the researcher delimits their coding and data collection to gather properties related to the core variable only.

Theoretical sensitivity

It is the ability of the researcher to move beyond the mere description of the data to see theoretical possibilities, to see the variables in the data and recognise the meanings attributed to them by the participants in the study that Glaser and Strauss (1967) referred to as theoretical sensitivity. This sensitivity can guide the researcher to recognise and conceptualise a theory as it emerges from the data – thus ensuring that the theory is "grounded" in the data.

Memoing

Memos are an essential part of data analysis in the grounded theory method. They are the "theorising write-up of ideas about codes and their relationships as they strike the analyst while coding" (Glaser, 1978, p. 83). Another goal of memo writing was to allow the researcher the freedom to develop ideas as they arise because the contents of the memos do not have to be in logical order. The analysis, through the use of memos, can then be justified because it is grounded in the data (Glaser, 1978).

Theoretical saturation

Data collection is complete when saturation is reached. Theoretical saturation occurs when no new or relevant data seem to emerge regarding a category, the category is well developed with a variation of its properties and dimensions, and the relationships among categories are well established and validated (Strauss & Corbin, 1998).

The core category

The end product of developing theory is the core category (Glaser & Strauss, 1967). Glaser and Strauss describe the emergence of a "core category" as follows: As categories and properties emerge, develop in abstraction, and become related, their accumulating interrelations form an integrated central theoretical framework – the core of the emerging theory. This "core of the emerging theory" is, therefore, not only the substantive theory, but also is more commonly known as the "core category". The emergence of a core category occurs after extensive analysis of the data using the constant comparative method. The purpose of a core category is to conceptualise the basic social psychological process; or the basic social problem which is addressed by the theory. Glaser (1978) states that: "the core category must account for most of the variation in a pattern of behaviour" (p. 93). Glaser further suggests that for a core category to be effective it must be central, stable, complex, integrative, incisive, powerful, and highly variable.

The mandate of grounded theory is to strive for the verification of its resulting hypothesis which is attained as part of the research method. Grounded theory aims to be a rigorous method through the provision of detailed and systematic procedures for data collection, analysis, and theorising, along with the quality of the emerging theory (Strauss & Corbin, 1994). More specifically, the most important criteria for maintaining and determining rigour in a grounded theory study is following the systematic grounded theory process and procedures. These include those that comprise the constant comparative method: concurrent collection of data and analysis; theoretical sampling; theoretical sensitivity; and memoing and diagramming (Glaser & Strauss, 1967; Strauss & Corbin, 1990). Four central criteria for a good grounded theory are that it should:

1. Reflect the phenomenon being studied.

2. Be easily understood by both the researcher and those involved in the phenomenon.

3. Provide generality and applicability to a diverse range of contexts.

4. Provide control by stating the condition that the theory applies.

Strauss and Corbin (1990) provide their own interpretation of criteria for rigour in response to their re-worked version of grounded theory, which was primarily to allow for a more structured way to undertake grounded theory. These criteria include plausibility; generalisability; concept generation; systematic conceptual relationships; density; variation; and the presence of process and broader conceptions.

Theory production

The result of the process of data collection and analysis is a theory, a substantive-level theory, written by a researcher close to a specific problem or population of people. The theory emerges with help from the process of memoing, a process in which the researcher writes down ideas about the evolving theory throughout the process of open, axial, and selective coding. The substantive-level theory may be tested later for its empirical verification with quantitative data to determine if it can be generalised to a sample and population. Alternatively, the study may end at this point with the generation of a theory as the goal of the research. The theory production process is represented in Figure 17.1.

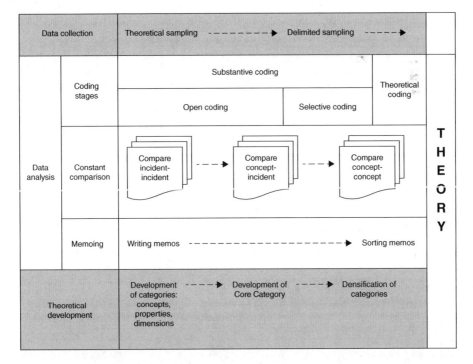

Figure 17.1 Graphical description of the grounded theory approach to qualitative data

LIMITATIONS AND PROBLEMS IN GROUNDED THEORY-BUILDING

The process of grounded theory building has been accused of being bewilderingly complex. Many find it difficult to follow in practice except in "a loose, non-rigid, non-specifiable fashion" (Partington, 2000, p. 95). One problem is linked to theoretical sampling. Often researchers use sampling procedures that they decide on before they start collecting the data, forgetting that "sampling in grounded theory proceeds on theoretical grounds" (Corbin & Strauss, 1990, p. 8). Theoretical sampling is necessary because of the inductive–deductive nature of the research. This is linked to the emerging theories which you are trying to advance through theoretical sampling. Many researchers produce good categories and interesting narratives but often neglect underlying social processes, or they fail to develop abstract concepts. The aim of grounded theory is expressly to develop new theory or modify existing theory. This means providing explanation and conceptualisation, not mere description. It is not enough to describe the perspectives of participants to develop a "grounded" theory. Researchers need to move on to the next stage, where you advance concepts.

Although the grounded theory approach is particularly appropriate for research in sport management, there are few examples where this methodology has been applied successfully. Certainly, some of the methodology sections of studies in the sport management journals, which claim to have applied the approach, fail adequately to articulate the systematic steps through which the authors developed theory. In many cases, theory has not been developed and there is no evidence of how coding actually occurred. It seems likely that in these cases the term "grounded theory" has been inappropriately purloined to describe what is primarily research of an inductive nature. However, it is understandable that the difficulty of operationalising a grounded theory approach leads many researchers to follow a simplified version of its principles and procedures. For instance, the various stages in coding and categorising may be condensed, or the sample may be selected in advance of data collection, or the development of a conceptual framework may precede data collection. If such research has developed theoretical concepts that are grounded in the data, it can be said to have employed a grounded theory style and, despite neglecting a full-blown grounded theory approach, such research may still hold value for knowledge in the field of sport management.

Research brief

Title: A grounded theory of music use in the psychological preparation of academy soccer players

Author: Karageorghis, C. I., *Brunel University London*, Bigliassi, M., *Brunel University London*, Tayara, K. *Brunel University London*, Priest, D.

L., *City College Norwich*, & Bird, J. M., *Brunel University London* (2018)

Reference: Karageorghis, C. I., Bigliassi, M., Tayara, K., Priest, D. L., & Bird, J. M. (2018). A grounded theory of music use in the psychological preparation of academy soccer players. *Sport, Exercise, and Performance Psychology, 7*(2), 109. The main objectives of the study were (a) to examine soccer players' use of music to psychologically prepare for performance and (b) to present a grounded theory to illuminate this phenomenon. Thirty-four academy soccer players were selected from a U.K. Premier League soccer club. Individual- and group-based questionnaires, reflective journals, and interviews were administered. The findings documented the use of music as a stimulant and regulator of emotion prior to performance, as well as its propensity to develop shared meanings and contribute to a sense of group identity.

THE ROLE OF THE RESEARCHER IN GROUNDED THEORY

A grounded theory study challenges researchers for the following reasons. The researcher needs to set aside, as much as possible, theoretical ideas or notions so that the analytic, substantive theory can emerge. Despite the evolving, inductive nature of this form of qualitative inquiry, the researcher must recognise that this is a systematic approach to research with specific steps in data analysis, if approached from the Strauss and Corbin (1990) perspective. The researcher faces the difficulty of determining when categories are saturated or when the theory is sufficiently detailed. One strategy that might be used to move toward saturation is to use discriminant sampling, in which the researchers gathered additional information from individuals similar to those people initially interviewed to determine if the theory holds true for these additional participants. The researcher needs to recognise that the primary outcome of this study is a theory with specific components: a central phenomenon, causal conditions, strategies, conditions and context, and consequences. These are prescribed categories of information in the theory, so the Strauss and Corbin (1990, 1998) approach may not have the flexibility desired by some qualitative researchers. In this case, the Charmaz (2006) approach, which is less structured and more adaptable, may be used.

Issues of validity and truth rely on the interpersonal skills of the researcher to obtain the perspective of the participant, as the researcher is the instrument, or conduit for, receiving and interpreting the narrative. Importantly, therefore, the researcher should utilise the following stratagems: acknowledgment of involvement and subsequent "inseparability" from the research; use of the first person; use of reflexive accounts about the research process and decisions made.

Strauss (1978) alerts the researcher to the fact that they can shape the interview by the way they probe for detail, clarity or explanation, and non-verbal gestures and associated responses. The grounded theory researcher has to consider specific strategies when interviewing to suit grounded theory methods. Specifically, how to ask questions and what to ask based on: (1) what is being said in the interview; (2) questions predetermined as dictated by theoretical sampling; and (3) the development of hypotheses or relational statements. The grounded theory researcher "conducts" the interview in a highly alert state – the interview although recorded and transcribed is a one-off opportunity to engage with the source of data and participate in the collection of data that could be missed without an in-depth awareness of what is being said, the nuances of the narrative and an understanding of what questions to ask. Additionally, where the researcher is relying on observation, they need to be alert to nuances in behaviour and reactions of those being observed, and to accurately record the evidence they are observing, so that the next stage of the comparative analysis and theoretical sampling process can effectively occur.

GROUNDED THEORY AND SPORT MANAGEMENT RESEARCH

In Grounded Theory, the theories relevant to a particular event, situation or phenomena emerge from the data following a continual process of comparative analysis. As such, it is particularly applicable to research areas that have heretofore been ignored or even not identified at all. It does not require a pre-formulated theory for testing, and as such allows the sport management researcher great scope to investigate, observe, interview – and then to engage in the methodology of grounded theory to draw sometimes surprising or unexpected theories from the data collected at the site of the phenomena under study.

Grounded theory is a complex and difficult approach and many sport management researchers who claim to have employed it have done so incorrectly, taking merely an inductive route to analysis instead. The core activities in the grounded theory method, the continual interplay of comparative analysis and theoretical sampling, require the study of a phenomena "in action" or "in situ" as the theories develop and evolve over a period of time as the sport management researcher engages continually with the phenomena and the data collected from it. As the theories are generated from praxis, grounded theory is therefore particularly relevant for the sport management researcher. In addition to developing the theories, grounded theory enables the sport management researcher to go beyond a mere description or statistical analysis of the phenomena, to describe the how and the why, and situate the phenomena within specific contexts. As sport management often functions in complex social and physical situations and with a wide variety of human interactions both internal and external to the sport management event or organisation, grounded theory can provide a useful and functional approach to the sport management researcher.

The case study is a frequently used research and reporting tool of the sport management researcher, and grounded theory works to enhance the strengths of the case study. Grounded theory ensures that the data are collected in the setting in which the case study is set, and can be gathered in a variety of ways including observation and interviewing. Moreover, as the sport management researcher engages in the processes of comparative analysis and theoretical sampling, the issues being investigated or studied in the case study can be reviewed and clarified at many different times over the duration of the study. In a sport management setting, a case study looking at operational issues with a sport management organisation can utilise grounded theory methods to look at attitudes and performance over a period of time, and the grounded theory method can facilitate the development of theories that before the start of the study, had not even been considered.

A variety of data collection methods often utilised by the sport management researcher are intrinsically suited to the grounded theory method. Observations, interviews, questionnaires, document analysis, and even the sport management researcher as active participant in the research process are all methods familiar to the sport management researcher, and which suit the method of grounded theory. Grounded theory gives the researcher the opportunity to observe and eventually formulate unanticipated results and theories derived from the data collected. Despite the advantage of grounded theory in enabling the sport management researcher to insinuate himself/herself into the research study to facilitate a greater understanding of participants and their view of the phenomena being studied, the limitations of the sport management researchers' knowledge and analytic ability in relation to the phenomena can also lead to questions about the validity or reliability of the emergent theories derived from the data. As each sport management researcher may have a unique perspective on the phenomena being studied, and their levels of the study theoretical sensitivity will vary, it can therefore be difficult to replicate the findings generated from a grounded theory study.

Theorists also disagree on the importance of cultural difference in the grounded theory method. Whilst Glaser (1978) did not believe that variables such as age, sex, race, etc. should not be considered relevant until the relevance emerged from an analysis of the data, other researchers such as Barnes (1996) believe that the responses of participants should be analysed from the participant's own cultural perspective, given that language is the symbolic representation of the participant's views and ideas, and these views and ideas are shaped by the cultural context from which the participant and by extension, the sport management researcher, operates.

Three recent studies provide an indication of the application of grounded theory in various sport management contexts. Sotiriadou, Shilbury, and Quick (2008) examined the impact of the Australian Federal Government involvement with sport policy on the sport development processes at a national level. In doing so, she explored the roles of the key sport development players and the ways sport policies shape sport development processes. Sotiriadou et al. utilised constant comparison and coding of data from the Annual Reports of 35 National Sporting Organizations in Australia. Dunphy (2006) investigated the perceptions of the two parties associated with an event bid: the event bidders and the event owners. The event management research also compared and contrasted the international findings with the New Zealand findings and a model of the event bidding process (Targeted Model). Using the grounded theory methodology, common success factors and a model of the event bidding process emerged from the data. A common success factor that was frequently mentioned by event owners and event bidders included the need for government support.

Jones and Bee (2003) examined (1) what it means to be a sport fan, (2) the factors and conditions that influence an individual to become a sport fan, and (3) how sport fans interpret sport-related events. Grounded theory methodology was selected as a means of exploring this previously unexamined phenomenon. Jones' study relied on interpretations of interviews with 14 highly committed sport fans and excerpts submitted by sports fans on two popular sport-related websites (www.SportingNews.com and www.ESPN.com). Perhaps the most comprehensive application of grounded theory is illustrated in Roy (2004). Roy utilised a qualitative, hermeneutic approach to expand the sport commitment model (SCM). He incorporated concepts from diverse theoretical backgrounds to provide a richer, more complex understanding of the factors that affect sport enjoyment and sport commitment. Roy also enhanced the generalisability of the model by extending it to athletes actively competing at the intercollegiate, national, international, or Olympic level. They competed in the following sports: wrestling, basketball, soccer, football, track and field, and triathlon.

CHALLENGES AND ISSUES RELATED TO THE GROUNDED THEORY

According to Stern (1985), in grounded theory research, a detailed pre-study literature search is disadvantageous for three reasons: (1) the search may lead to pre-judgement and affect premature closure of ideas and research inquiry; (2) the direction may be wrong; and (3) the available data or materials used may be inaccurate. In other words, some knowledge of the literature is required, yet an exhaustive review before data collection may increase the chance of a researcher's bias or pre-conceptions which may lead to insufficient interpretation of the phenomenon. Although a detailed pre-study literature search is disadvantageous in grounded theory research, the question of just how much literature review or reading is sufficient before commencing a ground theory study still remains a matter of debate. A criticism of not conducting an extensive literature review is that without doing this the researcher may not be able to identify gaps in existing research or the implications of research already conducted in the topic. The researcher may not know how extensive the phenomenon has been researched and whether or not the use of a grounded theory method might add to the existing knowledge about it. However, when the researcher considers literature as a slice of data (Glaser & Strauss, 1967) that is concurrently used to compare with the emerging categories from the data, it makes sense that more relevant and appropriate literature specific to the emerging categories will be used to rigorously complete the analysis. The use of literature as a slice of data for the analysis of emerging categories from data minimises the risk of the researcher's pre-conceptions about these categories. Furthermore, in a grounded theory study, technical (academic), and non-technical (common publications and media reports) literature are also used as slices of data during the process of constant comparative analysis. These data trigger new questions and further data collection, and provide the basis of verification for the researcher to draw conclusions, until data saturation occurs (Strauss & Corbin, 1998).

Case study

Title: A grounded theory of inspirational coach leadership
Author: Figgins, S. G., *University of Chichester*, Smith, M. J., *University of Winchester*, Knight, C. J., *Swansea University*, & Greenlees, I. A., *University of Chichester* (2019)
Reference: Figgins, S. G., Smith, M. J., Knight, C. J., & Greenlees, I. A. (2019). A grounded theory of inspirational coach leadership. *Scandinavian Journal of Medicine & Science in Sports, 29*(11), 1827–1840.

The purpose of this study was to develop a grounded theory of the process of inspirational coach leadership in sport. Semi-structured interviews and focus groups were conducted with 22 athletes and 15 coaches. Athletes who had experience of being inspired by a coach were sampled. As data collection progressed, theoretical sampling was used to further explore concepts identified within the initial data collection and analysis. Phases of theoretical sampling included interviewing: (a) coaches (at grass roots, county, and regional level) to identify athlete characteristics which impact upon the potential for athletes to be inspired; (b) high-level coaches (e.g., coaches who had experience of coaching at national and international level) to explore how group factors influence trust in the coach; and (c) participants who had experiences of a coach who did not inspire them (i.e., negative cases). According to the authors, negative cases are consistent with grounded theory methodology and were used to gain a deeper understanding of inspirational coach leadership (i.e., to understand what was lacking from their experiences). In addition to the specific negative cases that were sought, participants who detailed inspirational cases compared these experiences with coaches who had not inspired them.

Data were analysed through a process of open and axial coding, and theoretical integration. Through the process of analysis, data were broken down into smaller units (concepts), relationships between concepts were identified, and a substantive grounded theory was developed. The grounded theory of inspirational coach leadership was built around the core category of "athlete(s) inspired through changed awareness of their capabilities". The core category was underpinned by three categories: (a) establishment of mutual trust and respect with athletes, whereby coaches need to establish trust with athletes in order to inspire athletes; (b) conditions under which inspiration has the potential to occur, which highlighted that athletes are inspired in situations where they are vulnerable or ignorant regarding their potential; and (c) coach acts to change athlete's awareness of their capabilities, which denotes the specific behaviours coaches should display to inspire athletes in such conditions. The theory also highlighted that a range of contextual factors relating to the coach, athletes, and performance–environment interact to impact upon the process. The theory predicts that consistency between coach behaviour and the conditions in which inspiration can occur will lead to athlete inspiration, but only if the coach has established a foundation of trust and respect with the athlete.

CONCLUSION

Grounded theory is an under-utilised but potentially important research approach for sport management. Despite some identified weaknesses in the grounded theory approach, there are certainly some distinct advantages in the approach for the sport management researcher. The grounded theory approach is generally compatible with the aims of sport management researchers because it enables the research to capture and explicate on a theoretical level the complexity of organisational situations and processes. Because by its nature grounded theory requires a basis in praxis, the organisational elements and participants can recognise and relate to the aims of the sport management researcher following this particular methodology. Finally, and probably most importantly, because the continual process of comparative analysis facilitates the emergence of theories grounded in the data, some theories may emerge that lead to the investigation of new areas, and also give a refreshed perspective to previously research areas.

REVIEW AND REVIEW QUESTIONS

1. How can grounded theory approach be used in sport management research?

2. What insights can a grounded theory approach provide that a positivist approach could not?

REFERENCES

Annells, M. (1997a). Grounded theory method, part I: Within the five moments of qualitative research. *Nursing Inquiry, 4*(2), 120–129.

Annells, M. (1997b). Grounded theory method, part II: Options for users of the method. *Nursing Inquiry, 4*(3), 176–180.

Barnes, D. M. (1996). An analysis of the grounded theory method and the concept of culture. *Qualitative Health Research, 6*(3), 429–441.

Charmaz, K. (1995). Grounded theory. In J. A. Smith, R. Harré, & L. V. Langenhove (Eds.), *Rethinking Methods in Psychology*, pp. 27–48. London: Sage Publications.

Charmaz, K. (2005). Grounded theory in the 21st century: A qualitative method for advancing social justice research. In N. K. Denzin, & Y. S. Lincoln (Eds.), *Handbook of Qualitative Research* (3rd ed.), pp. 507–35. Thousand Oaks, CA: Sage Publications.

Charmaz, K. (2006). *Constructing grounded theory: A practical guide through qualitative analysis*. London: Sage Publications.

Corbin, J., & Strauss, A. (1990). Grounded theory research: Procedures, canons, and evaluative criteria. *Qualitative Sociology, 13*(1), 3–21.

Creswell, J. W. (2009). *Research design: Qualitative, quantitative and mixed method approaches* (3rd ed.). Los Angeles: Sage Publications.

Crotty, M. (1998). *The foundations of social research: Meaning and perspective in the research process*. Crows Nest, New South Wales, Australia: Allen & Unwin.

Dunphy, A. P. (2006). *Common Success Factors When Bidding for Sporting Events in New Zealand*. Unpublished Master's thesis, Auckland University of Technology, New Zealand.

Eaves, Y. D. (2001). A synthesis technique for grounded theory data analysis. *Journal of Advanced Nursing, 35*(5), 654–663.

Glaser, B. G. (1978). *Theoretical sensitivity.* Mill Valley, CA: Sociology Press.

Glaser, B. G. (1992). *Basics of grounded theory analysis.* Mill Valley, CA: Sociological Press.

Glaser, B. G. (1998). *Doing grounded theory: Issues and discussions.* Mill Valley, CA: Sociology Press.

Glaser, B. G., & Strauss, A. S. (1967). *The Discovery of grounded theory: Strategies for qualitative research.* New York: Aldine de Gruyter.

Goulding, C. (2001). Grounded theory: A magical formula or a potential nightmare. *Marketing Review, 2*(1), 21–34.

Guba, E. G., & Lincoln, Y. S. (1994). Competing paradigms in qualitative research. In N. K. Denzin, & Y. S. Lincoln (Eds.), *Handbook of Qualitative Research,* pp. 105–117. Thousand Oaks, CA: Sage Publications.

Jones, S. A., & Bee, C. C. (2003). *Interpreting athletic endorsements from a persuasion knowledge framework.* Proceedings of the Sport Marketing Association Conference, Gainesville, FL.

Kendall, J. (1999). Axial coding and the grounded theory controversy. *Western Journal of Nursing Research, 21*(6), 743–757.

Marshall, C., & Rossman, G. B. (1995). *Designing qualitative research* (2nd ed.). Thousand Oaks, CA: Sage Publications.

Mills, J., Bonner, A., & Francis, K. (2006). The development of constructivist grounded theory. *International Journal of Qualitative Methods, 5*(1), 25–35.

Partington, D. (2000). Building grounded theories of management action. *British Journal of Management, 11*(2), 91–102.

Roy, R. J. E. (2004). *A Grounded Theory Approach to the Extension and Revision of Scanlan's Sport Commitment Model.* Unpublished doctoral dissertation, Simon Fraser University, British Columbia, Canada.

Sotiriadou, K., Shilbury, D., & Quick, S. (2008). The attraction, Retention/Transition, and nurturing process of sport development: Some Australian evidence. *Journal of Sport Management, 22,* 247–272.

Stern, P. N. (1985). Using grounded theory method in nursing research. In M. Leininger (Ed.), *Qualitative Research Methods in Nursing,* pp. 149–160. Orlando, FL: Grune & Stratton.

Strauss, A. L. (1978). *Negotiations: Varieties. Contexts. Processes and social order.* London: Jossey-Bass.

Strauss, A., & Corbin, J. (1990). *Basic qualitative research: Grounded theory procedures and techniques.* Newbury Park, CA: Sage Publications.

Strauss, A., & Corbin, J. (1994). Grounded theory methodology. In N. K. Denzin, & Y. S. Lincoln (Eds.), *Handbook of Qualitative Research,* pp. 273–285. Newbury Park, CA: Sage Publications.

Strauss, A., & Corbin, J. (1998). *Basics of qualitative research: Techniques and procedures for developing grounded theory.* Thousand Oaks, CA: Sage Publications.

Willig, C. (2008). *Introducing qualitative research in psychology: Adventures in theory and method* (2nd ed.). New York: Open University Press.

Wilson, H. S. (1989). Family caregiving for a relative with Alzheimer's dementia: Coping with negative choices. *Nursing Research, 38,* 94–98.

CHAPTER 18

Narrative inquiry in sport management research

LEARNING OUTCOMES

By the end of this chapter, you should be able to:

- Understand the basic principles associated with narrative inquiry.

- Articulate the purpose of narrative research.

- Outline the narrative research process and its key characteristics.

- Outline narrative research data collection techniques.

- Identify some strategies with which to apply a narrative methodology to sport management research.

KEY TERMS

1. **Narrative:** the consciously formulated, premeditated, and coherent account of an experience.

2. **Story:** a more informal, provisional, and exploratory narrative.

3. **Voice:** sometimes "voice" is used synonymously for "story", at other times it means "professional knowledge or orientation". When one calls writing a "voice" one is enlisting the residual power of this tradition to give power to the group or individual concerned.

KEY THEMES

- What is the relationship between narrative and critical reflection?

- What are the implications for utilising narrative in the field of sport management research?

CHAPTER OVERVIEW

This chapter explores the qualitative research methods of "narrative", "story", and "voice" and highlights how they can provide rich descriptions of the sport management environment and at the same time provide an alternative research approach. The chapter notes that in combination with the process of reflection, narrative inquiry as a qualitative research methodology has the capacity to bring to the field of sport management research an understanding of the unique experiences of sports managers. By sharing narratives, the sport management researcher and sport manager can ultimately aim to understand the complex nature of the practitioner's world, with a resultant improvement in practice and leadership qualities.

DEFINING NARRATIVE AND ITS CHARACTERTICS

Starting in the late 1960s, the concept of narrative has spread across many disciplines and professions, and draws on varied epistemologies, theories, and methods. Paley and Eva (2005) distinguish between narrative and story, saying that narrative is variously assumed to be a naive account of events, a source of subjective truth, intrinsically fictional or a way of explaining. A story contains an interweaving of plots and character organised to elicit a certain emotional response; narrative refers to the sequence of events and the (claimed) causal connexions.

There appears to be some disagreement about a precise definition of narrative (Riessman, 1993). There are those who suggest that narratives are simply stories about past experiences; for example, Labov (1972) described it as a partial reliving of past experiences: "We define narrative as one method of recapitulating past experiences" (p. 359). Notably, Labov made a point of bringing his narratives to life and not allowing his audience to question his interpretation of the story. Unlike more traditional research methods, narrative inquiry captures aspects of personal and human lives that cannot be "quantified into facts and numerical data" (Clandinin & Connelly, 2000, p. 19). Advocates of narrative research claim that it is a tool that arranges experiences to make them comprehensible, memorable and shareable (Gudsmundsdottir, 1991, p. 1996; Casey, 1995; Clandinin & Connelly, 2000). To give their definition to narrative inquiry, Clandinin and Connelly proffer some of its characteristics:

> narrative inquiry is a way of understanding experience. It is collaboration between researcher and participants, over time, in a place or series of places, and in social interaction with milieu. An inquirer enters this matrix in the midst and progresses in this same spirit, concluding the inquiry still in the midst of living and telling, reliving and retelling,

the stories of the experiences that make up people's lives, both individual and social. Simply stated ... narrative inquiry is stories lived and told. (p. 20)

The key element is that meaning resides within the individual, capturing, and recognising their meaning. Some will do this in chronological order, some will do it by themes. Similarly, Gartner, Latham, and Merritt (2003) propose that: "Narrative inquiry, gives permission to learners to tap into the tacit knowledge embedded in their experience as well as to learn from each other in the process. It serves as a springboard for dialogue about the deeper issues of their professional discipline that may not be easily illuminated through other methods" (p. 2). Perhaps the most concise definition of narrative research is that proposed by Smith (1981) who notes that: narratives are "verbal acts consisting of someone telling someone else that something happened" (p. 228). Polkinghorne (1988), while acknowledging that the term narrative generally can refer to any spoken or written presentation, confines his usage to the kind of organisational scheme that is expressed in story form. He uses the term to describe the process of creating a story, the internal logic of the story (its plot and theme), and also the product – the story, tale, or poem as a unit.

In narrative research, researchers describe the lives of individuals, collect and tell stories about people's lives and write narratives of individual experiences. As a distinct form of qualitative research, a narrative typically focuses on studying a single person, gathering data through the collection of stories, reporting individual experiences and discussing the meaning of those experiences for the individual (Creswell, 2003). For example, a narrative inquiry on Tiger Woods might reveal his perceptions and meanings of his quick rise to the top of golf, his transgressions, and their personal effects on himself, and his rise back to the top. Table 18.1 provides examples of when a narrative design could be used in sport management research.

Table 18.1 When to use narrative designs

When do you use narrative designs?

- When individuals are willing to tell their stories.
- When you want to report personal experiences in a particular setting.
- When you want a close bond with participants.
- When participants want to process their stories.
- When you have a chronology of events.
- When you want to write in a literary way and develop the micro picture.

Research brief

Title: Disability sport and activist identities: A qualitative study of narratives of activism among elite athletes with impairment
Author: Smith, B., *University of Birmingham*, Bundon, A., *The University of British Columbia*, & Best, M., *University of Wolverhampton* (2016)
Reference: Smith, B., Bundon, A., & Best, M. (2016). Disability sport and activist identities: A qualitative study of narratives of activism among elite athletes with impairment. *Psychology of Sport and Exercise, 26*, 139–148.
Sport and exercise psychology has recently expanded into how it can be utilised to enable social missions like activism. According to the author, no research has examined activist identities among disabled, elite athletes. This paper therefore aimed to engage with this new and complex issue by examining narratives of activism amongst elite athletes with impairment and their adoption/rejection of various activist identities. Data was collected using interviews and fieldwork observations (e.g., observation and social media material). The large data set was rigorously analysed using a narrative thematic analysis.

TYPES OF NARRATIVE STUDIES

One approach to narrative research is to differentiate types of narrative research by the analytic strategies used by authors. Polkinghorne (1995) takes this approach and distinguishes between "analysis of narratives" (p. 12), using paradigm thinking to create descriptions of themes that hold across stories or taxonomies of types of stories, and "narrative analysis", in which researchers collect descriptions of events or happenings and then configure them into a story using a plot line. Chase (2005) presents an approach closely allied with Polkinghorne's "analysis of narratives". Chase suggests that researchers may use paradigmatic reasons for a narrative study, such as how individuals are enabled and constrained by social resources, socially situated in interactive performances, and how narrators develop interpretations.

A second approach is to emphasise the variety of forms found in narrative research practices (see, e.g., Casey, 1995, 1996). A *biographical study* is a form of narrative study in which the researcher writes and records the experiences of another person's life. **Autobiography** is written and recorded by the individuals who are the subject of the study (Ellis, 2004). A *life history* portrays an individual's entire life, while a personal experience story is a narrative study of an individual's personal experience found in single or multiple episodes, private situations, or communal folklore (Denzin, 1989). An *oral history* consists of gathering personal reflections of events and their causes and effects from one individual or several individuals (Plummer, 1983).

Mishler (1995) has organised narrative studies according to three types of central research issues. First, reference and temporal order refers to the relationship between the order in which events actually happened and the order in which they are told in narration. Second, textual coherence and structure concerns the

Table 18.2 Advantages and disadvantages of narrative research

Advantages and disadvantages of narrative research

Advantages of narratives

1. Through narratives individuals connect experiences in a meaningful way via temporal ordering, emplotment, and evaluation

2. Through narratives people share experience because they are built on the basis of social dialogue (they are always produced for an audience)

3. Because narratives are a natural and common way to construct experience they are seen as useful to:

   ■ facilitate empathy between interviewers and interviewees

   ■ allow interviewees to find their voice through a dialogue with the interviewer that is largely based on the interviewees' own experience

Disadvantages of narratives

1. Very little safeguard against bias

2. Rigorous appraisal methods are not used

3. Analysis of collected information is often subjective

4. Researchers' opinions may be mixed together with evidence

linguistic and narrative strategies on which the story is constructed. Finally, narrative functions deal with the broader place of the story within the greater society or culture. Labov (1972, 1982) suggested that a "fully formed" (narrative) includes six common elements: (1) an abstract (summary of the substance of the narrative); (2) orientation (time, place, situation, participants); (3) complicating action (sequence of events); (4) evaluation (significance and meaning of the action, attitude of the narrator); (5) resolution (what finally happened); and (6) coda (returns the perspective to the present). With these structures a teller constructs a story from a primary experience and interprets the significance of events in clauses and embedded evaluation (Reissman, 1987). In sum, narrative studies may have a specific contextual focus or the stories told about organisations. Narratives may be guided by a theoretical lens or perspective; however, a narrative study brings advantages and disadvantages, and these are highlighted in Table 18.2.

COLLECTION AND ANALYSIS OF NARRATIVE DATA

Researchers draw upon many techniques and sources for the collection and analysis of narrative data. For example, the Internet, autobiographies, letters, journals, ethnographic field notes, diaries, obituaries, photograph albums, poetry, newspapers, magazines, television, and participant observation can be used. Any of the following may produce narrative data that require analysis.

- Open-ended questions and written comments on questionnaires may generate single words, brief phrases, or full paragraphs of text.

- Testimonials may give reactions to a programme in a few words or lengthy comments, either in person or in written correspondence.

- Discussion group or focus group interviews often involve full transcripts and notes from a moderator or observer.

- Logs, journals, and diaries might provide structured entries or free-flowing text that you or others produce.

- Observations might be recorded in your field notes or descriptive accounts as a result of watching and listening.

- Documents, reports and news articles or any published written material may serve as evaluation data.

- Stories may provide data from personal accounts of experiences and results of programmes in people's own words.

- Case studies typically include several of the above.

Undoubtedly the most pervasive source of data is the interview. Reissman (1987) distinguished several genres in interviews: among these, she includes: (1) habitual narratives (events happen over and over, and consequently, there is no peak in the action) such as the routine of team practice; (2) hypothetical narratives (which depict events that did not happen) such as what would have happened if a championship was won or lost; and (3) topic centred narratives (snapshots of past events that are linked thematically) such as a player switching teams several times over his or her career.

Case study

Title: Adjusting to retirement from sport: Narratives of former competitive rhythmic gymnasts
Author: Cavallerio, F., *Anglia Ruskin University*, Wadey, R., *St Mary's University*, & Wagstaff, C. R., *University of Portsmouth* (2017)
Reference: Cavallerio, F., Wadey, R., & Wagstaff, C. R. (2017). Adjusting to retirement from sport: Narratives of former competitive rhythmic gymnasts. *Qualitative Research in Sport, Exercise and Health, 9*(5), 533–545.
This study used narrative inquiry to understand the retirement experiences of rhythmic gymnasts. Eight female former competitive gymnasts each participated in four life-history interviews. In line with narrative inquiry, interviews were deemed the most appropriate method to collect participants' stories of

gymnastics and life after gymnastics. The authors adopted short life history interviews (Plummer, 2001), which focused on key moments in the life of the interviewee that were linked with the topic of the research. Following dialogical narrative analysis, three narrative typologies were outlined: Entangled Narrative, Going Forward Narrative, and Making Sense Narrative. The entangled narrative shows an individual with a monological athletic identity, who is unable to develop a new identity following her retirement to the detriment of her well-being, and wishes to return to being a gymnast. The going-forward narrative describes those former gymnasts who were able to develop multiple identities during their gymnastics career, and are now flourishing in their life post-retirement. The making sense narrative is an emergent narrative, which transcends the previous two narratives. The authors have used a narrative inquiry in order to collect and analyse data that offers the chance to explore an individual's stories and allows for consideration of the relational and cultural construction of them (Smith, 2016). The authors suggest that narrative inquiry had the capacity of offering information about the personal world of athletes and the meanings behind their experiences, but it also offered insights on how people create their stories. The findings of the paper expanded narrative research by providing new narrative resources to understand the experience of retirement from gymnastics. These narrative resources might assist gymnasts to expand their narrative repertoire by raising awareness of different narratives available in their culture.

References in this case study

- Plummer, K. (2001). Documents of life 2. Thousand Oaks, CA: Sage.

- Smith, B. (2016). Narrative analysis. In E. Lyons, & A. Coyle (Eds.), *Analysing Qualitative Data in Psychology* (2nd ed.), pp. 202–221. London: Sage.

PROCEDURES FOR CONDUCTING NARRATIVE RESEARCH

Clandinin and Connelly (2000) developed a general procedural guide. They proposed that the methods of conducting a narrative study do not follow a lock-step approach, but instead represent an informal collection of topics. These topics include:

1. Determine if the research problem or question best fits narrative research. Narrative research is best for capturing the detailed stories or life experiences of a single life or the lives of a small number of individuals.

2. Select one or more individuals who have stories or life experiences to tell, and spend considerable time with them gathering their stories through multiples types of information. Clandinin and Connelly (2000) refer to the stories as "field texts". Research participants may record their stories in a journal or diary, or the researcher might observe the individuals and record field notes. Researchers may also collect letters sent by the individuals; assemble stories about the individuals from family members; gather documents such as memos or official correspondence about the individual; or obtain photographs, memory boxes (collection of items that trigger memories), and other personal–family–social *artefacts*. After examining these sources, the researcher records the individuals' life experiences.

3. Collect information about the context of these stories. Narrative research-ers situate individual stories within participants' personal experiences (their jobs, their homes), their culture (racial or ethnic), and their histori-cal contexts (time and place).

4. Analyse the participants' stories, and then "restory" them into a frame-work that makes sense. **Restorying** is the process of reorganising the sto-ries into some general type of framework. This framework may consist of gathering stories, analyzing them for key elements of the story (e.g., time, place, plot, and scene), and then rewriting the stories to place them within a chronological sequence (Ollerenshaw & Creswell, 2000). Often when individuals tell their stories, they do not present them in a chronological sequence. During the process of restorying, the researcher provides a causal link among ideas. Cortazzi (1993) suggests that the chronology of narrative research, with an emphasis on sequence, sets narrative apart from other genres of research. One aspect of the chronology is that the stories have a beginning, a middle, and an end. A chronology further may consist of past, present, and future ideas (Clandinin & Connelly, 2000), based on the assumption that time has a unilinear direction (Polkinghorne, 1995). In a more general sense, the story might include other elements typically found in novels, such as time, place, and scene (Connelly & Clandinin, 1990).

5. Collaborate with participants by actively involving them in the research (Clandinin & Connelly, 2000). As researchers collect stories, they negoti-ate relationships, smooth transitions, and provide ways to be useful to the participants. In narrative research, a key theme has been the turn toward the relationship between the researcher and the researched in which both parties will learn and change in the encounter (Pinnegar & Daynes, 2006). In this process, the parties negotiate the meaning of the stories, adding a validation check to the analysis (Creswell & Miller, 2000). Within the par-ticipant's story may also be an interwoven story of the researcher gaining insight into her or his own life (see Huber & Whelan, 1999).

ROLE OF RESEARCHER

In their article, "Working in the Interpretive Zone", Wasser and Bresler (1996) commented on the importance of the researcher's presence and how the inter-actions of the researcher with the participants serve to shape study outcomes. This shift, they say, is occurring in tandem with the increasing recognition of the collective nature of knowing and our greater attention to social theories of development. By working in "the interpretive zone" (Wasser & Bresler, 1996), multiple voices and viewpoints were encouraged, and participants had an oppor-tunity to bring together their different kinds of knowledge, experiences, and beliefs, hopefully forging new meanings through the process of joint inquiry.

The concept of "voice" is a central controlling metaphor in much of the writing in narrative inquiry. Syrjala and Estola (1999) for example use the term "telling and retelling", while Connelly and Clandinin (1990), prominent in contemporary works in this field, argue narrative to be the process by which researchers insert themselves into the story of another, for the purpose of giving that other a "voice". Viewed in this light, narratives are seen as mutual constructions, in which the researcher and participant work together, to produce a story, which is authentic. Chase (2005) took up the issue of researcher voice in narrative inquiry. She identifies three types of voices that narrative researchers may use: (1) an "authoritative voice"; (2) "a supportive voice"; and (3) an "interactive voice". Authoritative voices separate researcher voice from the voices of the researched and usually follow the pattern of a textual presentation of "data" or narrative followed by a set of interpretations. Supportive researcher voices foreground the researcher's voice over the voices of the researched. Chase suggests that "because the goal of this narrative strategy is to bring the narrator's story to the public, researchers do not usually dwell on how they engaged in the interpretive process" (p. 665). Finally, interactive researcher voices seek to disrupt the notion of the all-knowing observer and author. It is with the interactive voice that all aspects of the research process, from the intriguing insights to the downright embarrassing moments are fully exposed. Chase notes that the interactive voice "displays the complex interaction – the intersubjectivity – between researchers' and narrators' voices" (p. 666).

When engaged in narrative inquiry researchers have often been accused of using prior knowledge by reminiscing about their own life experiences. Sparkes (1995) refers to this process as "narrative of self" (p. 175). Porter and Washington (1993) remark: "the individual is not admitting to the self that he/she is denying the existence of things prior" (p.149). However, the self should be prepared to accept a situation of neutrality before the research begins. For example, the sport managers' life could be interpreted in the context of a narrative report and the act of reminiscing also becomes an important tool for representing the narrative of their life. In other words, the act of reminiscing can have a major effect on the final production of the narrative. Furthermore, and perhaps more importantly, reminiscing is the precursor to reflection which requires a deeper form of thought.

Another form of interference in the narrative comes from the acceptance of nostalgia. This can also function as an important perspective in the act of reminiscing. Thus, the nostalgic or positive thoughts of the past may lead some respondents to reminisce and over-emphasise the nature of certain points in the narrative. If the researcher has experienced similar occurrences the passage of narrative might take on a stronger significance than warranted within the text. Porter and Washington (1993) go further and argue that: ... "the very implicitness of nostalgia' leads one to assume that, previous knowledge and experience must affect the context and overall development of the narrative account of an individual's life or voice" (p. 151). In short, sport management researchers should be aware that nostalgia may have some influence over the "truth" of the narrative. On a reflective note, Clandinin and Connelly (2000) remind the researcher that in doing narrative inquiry research we continually meet ourselves in past remembrances, present experiences and future dreams and, perhaps, even daydreams. In essence, they are saying:

> *.... as narrative inquirers we work within the space not only with our participants but also with ourselves. Working in this space means that we become visible with our own lived and told stories. Sometimes, this means that our own unnamed, perhaps secret, stories come to light as much as so those of our participants. This confronting of ourselves in our narratives past makes us vulnerable as inquirers because it makes secret stories public. In narrative inquiry, it is impossible (or if not impossible, then deliberately self-deceptive) as researcher to stay silent or to present a kind of perfect, idealised, inquiring, moralising self. (p. 62)*

Research brief

Title: Are mental toughness and mental health contradictory concepts in elite sport? A narrative review of theory and evidence
Author: Gucciardi, D. F., *Curtin University*, Hanton, S., *Cardiff Metropolitan University*, & Fleming, S., *Cardiff Metropolitan University* (2017)
Reference: Gucciardi, D. F., Hanton, S., & Fleming, S. (2017). Are mental toughness and mental health contradictory concepts in elite sport? A narrative review of theory and evidence. *Journal of Science and Medicine in Sport, 20*(3), 307–311.
Within elite sport, multidisciplinary sport science and medicine teams play an important role in achieving an optimal balance between preventing athlete ill-health and optimising health and performance. The psychological aspects of athlete health and performance have gained increased attention over the past two decades, with much of this research concerned with the mental health of athletes and the concept of mental toughness. Recently, it was proposed that mental health and mental toughness are contradictory concepts in the world of elite sport. Thus, the purpose of this narrative review was to evaluate theory and evidence regarding the thesis that mental health and mental toughness are contradictory concepts in the world of elite.

VALIDATING NARRATIVES

Riessman (1993) acknowledged that there is no single way of evaluating narrative research. She wrote: "There is no canonical approach in interpretive work, no recipes and formulas, and different validation procedures may be better suited to some research problems than others" (p. 69). Even so, she offered a few criteria for evaluation. First, she suggested that validation be conceived of as trustworthiness of the text. If the reader finds the text to be honest (perhaps no elaborations or misguiding in telling the story of Lance Armstrong's doping

Table 18.3 How to evaluate narrative studies

Criteria for the evaluation of narrative studies

1. Width: The Comprehensiveness of Evidence. This refers to the amount of evidence that is provided to allow the reader to make an informed judgement on the evidence and its interpretation.

2. Coherence: The Way Different Parts of the Interpretation Create a Complete and Meaningful Picture. There is a distinction between internal coherence (how the parts fit together) and external coherence (how the research compares to existing theories and previous research).

3. Insightfulness: The Sense of Innovation or Originality in the Presentation of the Story and Its Analysis. Does this research move the reader to greater insight into his or her own life?

4. Parsimony: The Ability to Provide an Analysis Based on a Small Number of Concepts, and Elegance or Aesthetic Appeal. This refers to the literary merits of oral or written presentation of the story.

Source: Adapted from Lieblich *et al.* (1998).

scandal), it is a starting point for a positive evaluation. Riessman further notes the persuasiveness, coherence, and the pragmatic usefulness of the text as standards for evaluating the research. Noting the difficulty of establishing criteria for evaluating qualitative work, Sparkes (2002) recommends verisimilitude, rather than validity, as a starting point. The extent to which a story evokes a sense of truth within its readers is the foundation for the story's worth. Sparkes (2000) reviewed other scholars' views on evaluation as well, and included in his list of possible evaluative criteria items such as coherence, insightfulness, parsimony (Lieblich, Tuval-Mashiach, & Zilber, 1998); fairness and authenticity (Lincoln & Guba, 2000); substantive contribution, aesthetic merit, reflexivity, impact and expression of a reality (Richardson, 2000). A summary of some of these criteria to evaluate narrative research is provided in Table 18.3.

NARRATIVE ETHICS

Narrative ethics as an ethical approach has begun to garner attention in a small but vibrant body of literature that has begun to emerge over the past few decades (Nelson, 2001). While there is no agreed upon definition of narrative ethics, nor any one academic discipline that can lay claim to it, many scholars concur that a central tenant of narrative ethics is the idea that narratives "figure importantly into the moral life" (Nelson 2001, p. 36). Moreover, as Nelson elaborates, narrative ethics, "accords a central role to stories" (p. 36). But what does it mean to say that narratives figure into the moral life? Nelson (1997, 2001) claims that, from a philosophical perspective, it often means assigning moral significance to stories, not simply as examples or illustrations (although these are legitimate uses of stories for moral purposes as well as for narrative ethics), but rather as a "necessary means to some moral end" (p. 36).

DATA MANAGEMENT

Hollway and Jefferson (2000) warn against fragmenting narratives. The tendency to handle large amounts of unstructured data by coding passages thematically and retrieving them to form a new text breaks narratives to pieces. This is undesirable within Hollway and Jefferson's narrative approach in so much as it "often leads researchers to overlook the form of their data" (p. 68). Instead, they offer suggestions for data management. They begin approaching their data by taking detailed notes and identifying a few key passages. From those notes they created a "pro forma" summary of those notes to convey some sense of the whole narrative. Additionally, they create "pen portraits" of each participant that were intended to make the narrator "come alive for a reader" (p. 70). This approach allows readers and researchers to grasp some sense of the whole narrator, complete with incoherence, inconsistency, and unpredictability. This self-consciousness in writing or "researcher reflexivity" speaks directly to the notion of multiple truths' or "realities".

NARRATIVE AND SPORT MANAGEMENT RESEARCH

Lysaght (2001) captures the fundamental place of the narrative in our society, saying "narratives are said to fashion our lives, providing the structure for our day-to-day existence and they propel us into a future that is shaped by our lived experiences of them" (p. 64). While narratives are the fundamental means of making ourselves intelligible to one another, they provide the framework by which humans convey valuable cultural information. Values and norms on doping, cheating, and other sport scandals can be passed on to future generations by storytelling or narratives. Barthes (1996) summarises this state of affairs thus:

> *The narratives of the world are without number, the narrative is present at all times, in all places, in all societies; history of narrative begins with the history of mankind, there does not exist, and never has existed, a people without narratives. (p. 1)*

Narratives, therefore, bind the facts of our existence together, to enable people to find meaning and continuity in seemingly complex lives (Beattie, 2000). In a similar vein and a sport management context, Rinehart (2005) argues that narratives examine how lives are lived into existence, and it provides models for practitioners and scholars of sport management to model, discover, experience, and use. He further suggests that: The possibilities for use of personal narrative within sport management are expanding all the time, as formerly discrete academic disciplines borrow from one another, creating new forms and new uses for old forms. As was pointed out earlier, sport management scholars and practitioners might gain knowledge and understanding from personal experience narratives. This type of research can "provide deep understanding that could lead to structural changes in human resource management, marketing, advertising, policy studies, and leadership training for practitioners of sport management (p. 517). Smith and Weed (2007) propose the following orienting propositions for narrative inquiry in general, and for sport research: (1) meaning is central to being human, and being human entails actively construing meaning; (2) meaning is created through narrative, and thus is a storied effort; (3) narratives are created within relationships, and thus storytelling relations are a vital condition for making narrative meaningful; (4) narratives are constructed within relationships as a result of human agency; and (5) narratives are a constitutive force. These propositions could be specifically applied to the sport management context.

Case study

Title: Psychological Effects of Sport Injury on NCAA Division I Student Athlete: A Qualitative Case Study
Author: Gilbert, K. C., *Oregon State University* (2019)
Reference: Gilbert, K. C. (2019). *Psychological Effects of Sport Injury on NCAA Division I Student Athlete: A Qualitative Case Study*. A thesis submitted for the degree of Honours Baccalaureate of Science in Kinesiology Oregon State University.
Negative emotional states are common for injured athletes, yet a 2016 survey suggested that only 38.3% of NCAA institutions had a full or part-time mental health professional (Kroshus, 2016). In considering the lack of support for mental health conditions in NCAA institutions, and the mental and psychological issues that come with injury, there is a gap in the psychological treatment of injured student athlete. To date, the extant literature suggests that sport medicine professionals (SMPs) play a critical role in the psychology of injury recovery, yet lack formal training in psychological interventions (Clement et al., 2013). Moreover, research examining athlete and SMPs experiences of the psychological aspects of injury rehabilitation is largely limited to retrospective accounts (e.g., Clement

et al., 2015; Tatsumi & Takenouchi, 2014). The purpose of the current study was to prospectively examine the psychological challenges of injury rehabilitation in an NCAA athlete. A qualitative case study grounded in narrative methodology, and an interpretive epistemology, was conducted (Smith & Sparkes, 2009). Research interviews were conducted with an injured athlete, the athlete's SMP, and a member of the athlete's social support team at baseline (i.e., post-injury and prior to the start of rehabilitation) and during the rehabilitation process before the sport-specific phase. Additionally, the athlete kept a journal to document the psychological and emotional struggles that took place during the rehabilitation process. Data analysis was iterative through each phase of the study and followed Polkinghorne's (1995) seven stages of narrative analysis. The results suggested that issues with identity are central to the injury–rehabilitation–return to play process. Notably, data suggested an ongoing struggle between the loss of identity in the present, the fear of identity loss in the future, and a desire to maintain a positive outlook on current circumstances, and ongoing tensions between cognitive appraisals and emotional reactions. The work of SMPs and sport psychology professionals working with

(Continued)

injured athletes seemed to be highly linked to the cognitive appraisals and behavioural responses and emotional responses, respectively. According to the author, while cognitive appraisal and behavioural responses seemed to be congruent, cognitive appraisals and emotional responses appeared to lack this dynamic. Suggested in this case, psychological interventions (specifically support groups) seemed to be helpful in working through emotional stresses that come up throughout the rehabilitation process.

References used in this case study

- Kroshus, E. (2016). Variability in institutional screening practices related to collegiate student- athlete mental health. *Journal of Athletic Training, 51*(5).

- Clement, D., Granquist, M. D., & Arvinen-Barrow, M. M. (2013). Psychosocial aspects of athletic injuries as perceived by athletic trainers. *Journal of Athletic Training, 48*(4).

- Clement, D., Arvinen-Barrow, M., & Fetty, T. (2015). Psychosocial responses during different phases of sport-injury rehabilitation: a qualitative study. *Journal of Athletic Training, 50*(1), 95–104.

- Tatsumi, T., & Takenouchi, T. (2014). Causal relationships between the psychological acceptance process of athletic injury and athletic rehabilitation behavior. *Journal of Physical Therapy Science, 26*(8), 1247–1257.

- Smith, B., & Sparkes, A. C. (2009). Narrative inquiry in sport and exercise psychology: What can it mean, and why might we do it? *Psychology of Sport and Exercise, 10*(1), 1–11.

- Polkinghorne, D. E. (1995). Narrative configuration in qualitative analysis. *International Journal of Qualitative Studies in Education, 8*(1), 5–23.

CONCLUSION

Unlike more traditional research methods, narrative inquiry captures aspects of personal and human lives that cannot be "quantified into facts and numerical data" (Clandinin & Connelly, 2000, p. 19). Narrative inquiry is a tool that arranges lived experiences to make them comprehensible, memorable, and shareable. As a research methodology can engage the researcher in reflective practice of lived experiences and can provide a means for sport management researchers to understand the complex nature of the sport practitioner's world. The narrative process of writing, sharing, reflecting and then analysis can work to improve sport management knowledge and practice.

REVIEW AND RESEARTCH QUESTIONS

With a basic understanding now of the key elements of narrative inquiry, attempt to answer the following questions:

1. Identify two ways in which narrative inquiry can be used in Sport Management Research.

2. Discuss the importance of reflection to the narrative inquiry process.

3. Identify the different forms of "voice that can be present in narrative research".

REFERENCES

Barthes, R. (1996). Introduction to the structural analysis of narratives. In S. Onega and J. A. G. Landa (eds), *Narratology* (pp. 45–60). New York: Longman.

Beattie, M. (2000). Narratives of professional learning: Becoming a teacher and learning to teach. *Journal of Educational Enquiry, 1*(2), 1–23.

Casey, K. (1995). The new narrative research in education. *Review of Research in Education, 21*, 211–253.

Casey, K. (1996). The new narrative research in education. In M. W. Apple (Ed.), *Review of research in education* (vol. 21), pp. 211–253. Washington, DC: American Educational Research Association.

Chase, S. E. (2005). Narrative inquiry: Multiple lenses, approaches, voices. In N. K. Denzin, & Y. S. Lincoln (Eds.), *Handbook of qualitative research* (3rd ed.), pp. 651–680. Thousand Oaks, CA: Sage Publications.

Clandinin, D. J., & Connelly, F. M. (2000). *Narrative inquiry: Experience and story in qualitative research.* San Francisco: Jossey-Bass.

Connelly, F. M., & Clandinin, D. J. (1990). Stories of experience and narrative inquiry. *Educational Researcher, 19*(5), 2–14.

Cortazzi, M. (1993). *Narrative analysis.* London: Falmer Press.

Creswell, J. W. (2003). *Research design: Quantitative, qualitative and mixed methods approaches* (3rd ed.). Thousand Oaks, CA: Sage Publications.

Creswell, J. W., & Miller, D. L. (2000). Determining validity in qualitative inquiry. *Theory into Practice, 39*(3), 124–130.

Denzin, N. K. (1989). *Interpretive interactionism.* Newbury Park, CA: Sage.

Ellis, C. (2004). *The ethnographic I: A methodological novel about autoethnography.* Walnut Creek, CA: Altamira Press.

Gartner, A., Latham, G., & Merritt, S. (2003). The power of narrative: transcending disciplines. Available at: http://ultibase.rmit.edu.au/Articles/dec96/gartn1.htm# (Accessed March 3, 2011).

Gudsmundsdottir, S. (1991). Story maker, story teller: Narrative structures in the curriculum. *Journal of Curriculum Studies, 23*(3), 207–221.

Hollway, W., & Jefferson, T. (2000). *Doing qualitative research differently: Free association, narrative and the interview method.* London: Sage Publications.

Huber, J., & Whelan, K. (1999). A marginal story as a place of possibility: Negotiating self on the professional knowledge landscape. *Teaching and Teacher Education, 15*(4), 381–396.

Labov, W. (1972). The transformation of experience in narrative syntax. In W. Labov (Ed.), *Language in the Inner City: Studies in the Black English Vernacular,* pp. 354–396. Philadelphia, PA: University of Pennsylvania Press.

Labov, W. (1982). Speech actions and reactions in personal narrative. In D. Tannen (Ed.), *Georgetown university round table on languages and linguistics 1981: Analyzing discourse: Text and talk,* pp. 219–247. Washington, DC: Georgetown University Press.

Lieblich, A., Tuval-Mashiach, R., & Zilber, R. (1998). *Narrative research.* Thousand Oaks, CA: Sage Publications.

Lincoln, Y. S., & Guba, E. G. (2000). Paradigmatic controversies, contradictions, and emerging confluences. In N. K. Denzin, & Y. S. Lincoln (Eds.), *Handbook of Qualitative Research* (2nd ed.), pp. 163–188. Thousand Oaks, CA: Sage Publications.

Lysaght, P. (2001). *Intelligent profiles: A model for change in women's lives.* Unpublished doctoral thesis, University of Wollongong, Australia.

Mishler, E. G. (1995). Models of narrative analysis: A typology. *Journal of Narrative and Life History, 5*(2), 87–123.

Nelson, H. L. (1997). *Stories and their limits: Narrative approaches to bioethics.* New York: Routledge.

Nelson, H. L. (2001). *Damaged identities: Narrative repair.* Ithaca: Cornell University Press.

Ollerenshaw, J. A., & Creswell, J. W. (2000). *Data analysis in narrative research: A comparison of two "restorying" approaches.* Paper presented at the annual meeting of the American Educational Research Association, New Orleans, LA.

Paley, J., & Eva, G. (2005). Narrative vigilance: The analysis of stories in health care. *Nursing Philosophy, 6,* 83–97.

Pinnegar, S., & Daynes, J. G. (2006). Locating narrative inquiry historically: Thematics in the turn to narrative. In D. J. Clandinin (Ed.), *Handbook of narrative inquiry.* Thousand Oaks, CA: Sage Publications.

Plummer, K. (1983). *Documents of life.* London: Allen & Unwin.

Polkinghorne, D. E. (1988). *Narrative knowing and the human sciences.* Albany, NY: State University of New York Press.

Polkinghorne, D. E. (1995). Narrative configuration in qualitative analysis. *International Journal of Qualitative Studies in Education, 8*(1), 5–23.

Porter, J. R., & Washington, R. E. (1993). Minority identity and self-esteem. *Annual Review of Sociology, 19,* 139–161.

Rinehart, R. E. (2005). 'Experiencing' sport management: The use of personal narrative in sport management studies. *Journal of Sport Management, 19*(4), 497–522.

Reissman, C. K. (1987). When gender is not enough: women interviewing women. *Gender and Society, 1*(2), 172–207.

Riessman, C. K. (1993). *Narrative analysis.* London: Sage Publications.

Richardson, L. (2000). Writing: A method of inquiry. In N. K. Denzin, & Y. S. Lincoln (Eds.), *The handbook of qualitative research* (2nd ed.), pp. 923–948. Thousand Oaks, CA: Sage Publications.

Smith, B. (1981). Narrative versions, narrative theories. In W. J. T. Mitchell (Ed.), *On Narrative,* pp. 209–232. Chicago, IL: University of Chicago.

Smith, B., & Weed, M. (2007). The potential of narrative research in sports tourism. *Journal of Sport and Tourism, 12*(3–4), 249–269.

Sparkes, A. (1995). Writing people: Reflections on the dual crises of representation and legitimation in qualitative inquiry. *Quest, 47*(2), 158–195.

Sparkes, A. C. (2000). Fictional representations: On difference, choice, and risk. *Sociology of Sport Journal, 19*(1), 1–24.

Sparkes, A. C. (2002). *Telling tales in sport and physical activity: A qualitative journey.* Champaign: Human Kinetics.

Syrjala, L., & Estola, E. (1999). *Telling and retelling stories as a way to construct teachers' identities and to understand teaching.* Paper presented at the European Conference on Educational Research, Lahti, Finland. Retrieved February 27, 2008 from http://www.leeds.ac.uk/educol/documents/00001311.htm

Wasser, J. D., & Bresler, L. (1996). Working in the interpretive zone: Conceptualizing collaboration in qualitative research teams. *Educational Researcher, 25*(5), 5–15.

CHAPTER 19

Phenomenology and sport management research

LEARNING OUTCOMES

By the end of this chapter, you should be able to:

- Understand the basic concepts of phenomenology.

- Recognize the implications for adopting a phenomenological approach to sport management.

KEY TERMS

1. **Phenomenology:** is a method of philosophical inquiry that lays stress on the impressions of a reader.

2. **Transcendental phenomenology:** each experience must be taken in its own right as it shows itself and as one is conscious of it.

3. **Existential phenomenology:** a perspective that insists that the observer cannot be separated from the world.

4. **Hermeneutic phenomenology:** a phenomenological interpretation that seeks to unveil hidden meanings in phenomena.

5. **Descriptive phenomenology:** a direct description of phenomena aimed at maximum intuitive content.

6. **Bracketing interview:** to identify interviewer presuppositions from the very outset of the research project.

KEY THEMES

- What is "Phenomenology"?

- What is the difference between Husserl and Heidegger's interpretations of phenomenon?

- Can phenomenology be used as a research methodology in sport management research?

CHAPTER OVERVIEW

Phenomenology aims to investigate and comprehend the lived experience of its participants. In sport management literature, phenomenology offers researchers a different perspective while providing the opportunity to explore previously unchartered waters. This chapter will provide an introduction and overview to the major concepts of phenomenology, as well as provide some suggestions as to possible frameworks from which to apply the phenomenological methodology to sport management research.

INTRODUCTION

Defining phenomenology is complex. Phenomenology is a method of philosophical inquiry that lays stress on the impressions of a reader. The reader is the main figure to determine the meanings of a given text. The name Husserl (1931) gave to his philosophical method is phenomenology. As a methodology, phenomenology has become increasingly employed in social science research, and has the potential to be used with great effectiveness in the field of sport management research. Whereas other qualitative research approaches also attempt to see things through the eyes of the people they study, phenomenology goes further because it provides a means for you to set aside your own preconceived ideas about an event or an experience in order to understand it from the world in which research participants exist; in this way, you can illuminate human thinking and behaviour from the inside.

WHAT IS PHENOMENOLOGY?

Phenomenology describes "how one orients to lived experience". From a phenomenological point of view, to do research is always to "question the way we experience the world, to want to know the world in which we live as human beings" (Van Manen, 1990, p. 5).

Phenomenology as a philosophy/history

This can be viewed as three forms: (1) *transcendental*; (2) *existential*; and (3) *hermeneutic Transcendental phenomenology* as methodology began with Husserl (1931) who presented an alternative way of thinking offered by positive philosophy. Instead of trying to explain minds in terms of matter, or vice versa, Husserl demanded that each experience must be taken in its own right as it shows itself and as one is conscious of it. Husserl reflected that to truly understand a phenomenon one needed to bracket oneself or suspend all biases and assumptions. He used the term Epoche to describe this bracketing of prior assumptions. In Husserl's conception, phenomenology is primarily concerned with making the structures of consciousness, and the phenomena that appear in acts of consciousness, objects of systematic reflection and analysis. Such reflection was to take place from a highly modified "first person" viewpoint, studying phenomena not as they appear to "my" consciousness, but to any consciousness whatsoever. For example, examining values associated with professional sports (competitiveness, commercialisation, player development, etc.) from as many viewpoints as possible to encompass all readers' viewpoints. Husserl believed that phenomenology could thus provide a firm basis for all human knowledge, including scientific knowledge, and could establish philosophy as a "rigorous science".

Husserl (1931) hoped to develop a philosophy that would deepen our understanding of how objects, or phenomena, are experienced and present themselves to our consciousness. He looked to answer the question "how do we know?" by examining and describing the world-as-experienced by the participants of the inquiry. Husserl referred to this world of lived experience as the life-world *(Lebenswelt)* (Spiegelberg, 1982). It is in this world that much is considered commonplace and taken for granted. Husserl believed that we need to explore the "essential" features of this experienced world. He argued that lived experience should be used as a tool to gain access to experiences of phenomena in their original form, as part of an individual's everyday physical reality.

Heidegger's existential phenomenology reinterpreted phenomenology and its methods. His phenomenology is existential, a perspective that insists that the observer cannot be separated from the world, and that an understanding of the person cannot occur in isolation from the person's world. Heidegger (1962) saw humans as beings that experience objects in particular and individual ways, and proposed a particular form of *hermeneutic phenomenology* in his pursuit of the meaning of being. This new approach had a considerable influence on the development of *existential phenomenology*. In his hermeneutical work, Heidegger employed two notions, the *hermeneutic circle* and *historicity of understanding*. Heidegger's emphasis is on *being-in-the-world (dasein)* and how phenomena present themselves in lived experience, in human existence (Van Manen, 1990). Heideggerian phenomenology asks "what does it mean to be a person?" and holds that the answer to this is found in *dasein* or being already in the world. As such, it deals with questions of human existence by seeking the meaning of being. Heidegger was concerned with what he considered the essential philosophical (and human) question: what is it "to be"?

Hermeneutic phenomenology concerns how one orients to the lived experience, and Van Manen (1994) suggested that it is, in a broad sense, a philosophy or *theory of the unique*. Van Manen was strongly influenced by Merleau-Ponty's philosophy. He explains how phenomenology differs from almost every other science in that it attempts to gain insightful descriptions of the way we experience the world. How do sport fans from all over the world each experience a World Cup? Max Van Manen (1990) proposed:

> *phenomenology does not offer us the possibility of effective theory with which we can now explain and/or control the world but rather it offers us the possibility of plausible insight, which brings us in more direct contact with the world. (pp. 37–38)*

Rather than seeking a judgement about facts or reality, the aim of phenomenology is to gain people's understanding, opinions, and expressions of feelings. In other words, rather than generating theories or general explanation, phenomenology aims to describe the experience as it exists. The World Cup experience will likely exist differently for different people, based on their cultural and personal experiences and interpretations of those experiences. It is about expressing thoughts and perceptions of phenomena in the form of language in speech or writing (Van Manen, 1990). It is about describing the essence of the experience and a fuller understanding of the nature of the experience.

Based on the philosophical works of Heidegger, hermeneutic phenomenology, as outlined by Van Manen (1990), is a process of exploring one's interests and understandings of a phenomenon, uncovering the essence of that phenomenon by gathering and interpreting "raw data" from those living it, and offering implications for practice. The "raw data" of a phenomenological study are personal experiences, often complemented with poetry, biography, art or literature. Hence the remark that hermeneutic phenomenology is "both descriptive and interpretive" (p. 180). Van Manen outlined the essentials of phenomenological research as: the study of lived experience; the explication of phenomena as they present themselves to consciousness, rather than as conceptualised, categorised or theorised; the study of essences of experience that asks, not "how", but rather, what is the "nature" of the experience; the description of experiential meanings we live as we live them, examples of which are designed to enable us to see the structure or the deeper significance of the experience being described; the human scientific study of phenomena in that it is systematic, explicit, intersubjective, self-critical, and examines structures of the lived human world (rather than the natural world); the attentive practice of thoughtfulness whose language awakens a person to the meaning of the experience; a search for what it means to be human, which may be achieved by more deeply understanding human experience; and a poetising activity insofar as its language reverberates in the world rather than speaking "of" it. In this sense, the poem itself is the result rather than a conclusion or summary of the phenomenological study. Table 19.1 outlines what phenomenologists "do".

In general it is proposed that there are a number of *strengths* and *weaknesses* associated with phenomenological research. Some of these have been summarised in Table 19.2.

Table 19.1 What phenomenologists do

Phenomenologists

- REJECT scientific realism (objects exist independently of our knowledge of their existence).
- DISAGREE that the empirical sciences are better methods to describe the features of the world.
- DESCRIBE the ordinary, conscious experience of things.
- OPPOSE the acceptance of unobservable things.
- REJECT naturalism and positivism.
- BELIEVE objects in the natural world, cultural world, and abstract objects (like numbers and consciousness) can be made evident and thus known.
- RECOGNISE the role of description prior to explanation by means of causes, purposes, or grounds.
- DEBATE whether Husserl's transcendental epoche and reduction is useful or even possible.
- STUDY the "life-world" (the taken-for-granted pattern of everyday living).

PHENOMENOLOGY AS A RESEARCH METHODOLOGY

The differences between the philosophies of Husserlian and Heideggerian phenomenology impact their use as research methodologies are compared and contrasted in Table 19.3.

While Husserlian phenomenology is a descriptive methodology, Heideggerian phenomenology rests on an interpretive (hermeneutic) process.

Descriptive phenomenology

Descriptive phenomenology emphasises descriptions of human experience. It insists on the careful description of ordinary conscious experience of everyday life – a description of "things" as people experience them. These "things" include hearing, seeing, believing, feeling, remembering, deciding, evaluating, acting, etc. A descriptive phenomenology of a participant's experience in a charity marathon may detail as many "things" as possible in order to provide a holistic capture of the experience. The steps in descriptive phenomenological studies are:

1. Bracketing: the process of identifying and holding in abeyance preconceived beliefs and opinions about the phenomenon.

2. Intuiting: the researcher remains open to the meanings attributed to the phenomenon by those who have experienced it.

3. Analysing: extracting significant statements, categorising, and making sense of the essential meanings of the phenomenon.

4. Describing: researchers come to understand and define the phenomenon.

Table 19.2 Strengths and weaknesses of phenomenology

Strengths of phenomenology	Weaknesses of phenomenology
■ Efficient and economical data generation	■ Findings are difficult to generalise to a larger population
	■ Small number of participants (3–10) only
	■ Individual responses are not always independent of one another
	■ Dominant or opinionated members may overshadow the thoughts of the other group members if group interviews are conducted
■ Direct interaction with participants	■ Data is often difficult to analyse and summarise
■ Allows the researcher to ask for clarification and to ask immediate follow-up/probing questions	■ Enormous amount of data, difficult to organise and interpret
■ Allows the researcher to observe nonverbal responses that can be supportive or contradictory to the verbal responses	
■ Rich, first person accounts in conversation and interviews	■ Researcher may give too much credit to the results (immediacy of a personal opinion)
■ Participants react to and build upon the responses of other participants.	■ It is a philosophy not a research method
■ Research tool is applicable to a wide range of settings and individuals.	■ Difficulty in describing the unique experiences AND make generalisations about the experiences at the same time
■ Results are easy to understand (in terms of people's direct opinions and statements)	■ Ethical issues occur due to the close relationship of participants and researcher
■ Uncovers taken-for-granted assumptions	■ Can be difficult to gain trust of participants
■ Writing of stories creates rich text to recreate "lived experience"	■ Can be useful in reporting individual cases, but must be tentative when suggesting their extent to a general population
	■ A form of ideal abstraction detached from the world of concrete experience

Interpretive/hermeneutic phenomenology

Interpretive phenomenology stresses the interpretation and understanding, and not just description of, human experience. An interpretive phenomenologist would go beyond describing the "things" of the marathon participant, and

Table 19.3 Comparing and contrasting two theories of phenomenology interpretation	
Husserlian phenomenology	**Heideggerian phenomenology**
Transcendental phenomenology	Philosophical hermeneutics Hermeneutic phenomenology
Epistemological	Existential-ontological
Epistemological questions of knowing	Questions of experiencing and understanding
How do we know what we know?	What does it mean to be a person?
Cartesian duality: mind–body split	Emphasis is on being-in-the-world (Dasein)
A mechanistic view of the person	Person as self-interpreting being
Mind-body person lives in a world Objects	Person exists as a "being" in and of the world
A historical	Historicality
Unit of analysis is the meaning giving subject	Unit of analysis is the transaction between the situation and the person
What is shared is the essence of the conscious mind	What is shared is culture, history, practice, language
Starts with a reflection of mental states	We are already in the world in our pre-reflexive selves
Meaning is unsullied by the interpreter's own normative goals or view of the world	Interpreters participate in making data
Participants' meanings can be reconstituted in interpretive work by insisting that the data speak for themselves	Within the fore-structure of understanding interpretation can only make explicit what is already understood
Claim that adequate techniques and procedures guarantee validity of interpretation	Establish own criteria for trustworthiness of research
Bracketing defends the validity or objectivity of the interpretation against self-interest	The hermeneutic circle (background, co-constitution, pre-understanding)

Source: Adapted from Koch, 1995

elaborate on the meanings and connections of certain "things" (e.g. the importance of seeing family members cheering along the marathon course).

- Hermeneutic generally refers to the art and philosophy of interpreting the meaning of an object.

- The goals of interpretive phenomenology are to enter another's world and to discover the practical wisdom, possibilities, and understandings found there.

Table 19.4 Features of phenomenology as a methodology

Descriptive	Interpretive
Believe it is possible to suspend personal opinion to arrive at a single, essential, descriptive presentation of a phenomena	There are endless number of realities.
Think that if there is more than one reality, that leaves doubt, ignorance, and a lack of clarity.	Interpretations are all we have, because description is an interpretive process
Husserl followers	Heidegger followers

- Interpretive phenomenology relies primarily on in-depth interviews with individuals who have experienced the phenomenon of interest. Sometimes uses supplementary texts, such as novels, poetry, or other artistic expressions – or the use of such materials in their conversations with the study participants.

Table 19.4 lists some of the contrasts the features between descriptive and interpretive phenomenology.

Research brief

Title: Parental stress and coping in elite youth gymnastics: an interpretative phenomenological analysis
Author: Burgess, N. S., *Swansea University*, Knight, C. J., *Swansea University*, & Mellalieu, S. D., *Cardiff Metropolitan University* (2016)
Reference: Burgess, N. S., Knight, C. J., & Mellalieu, S. D. (2016). Parental stress and coping in elite youth gymnastics: An interpretative phenomenological analysis. *Qualitative Research in Sport, Exercise and Health*, 8(3), 237–256.
This study sought to understand how parents of elite youth gymnasts cope within youth sport. Interpretive Phenomenological Analysis (IPA) was used to facilitate an in-depth exploration of parents' experiences. Seven parents of national and international level gymnasts aged 11–14 years participated in semi-structured interviews and data were analysed according to the guidelines set out by IPA. The results suggested that parents face numerous organisational, competitive, and developmental stressors in youth gymnastics including time and travel demands, child's competition nerves, schooling, finances, and injury. The findings suggested that parents' stress experiences are dynamic and complex, with parents utilising different coping strategies to manage different stressors in different situations.

EXISTENTIAL PHENOMENOLOGICAL RESEARCH

Kerry and Armour (2000) argue that researchers who choose to employ an *existential phenomenological research* approach must provide sound conceptual rationale for using this specific method of inquiry. Existential phenomenological research consists of a sequence of interrelated steps.

Step 1: Choosing a topic

As described by Thomas and Pollio (2002), the first step is the researcher's decision regarding the topic of investigation.

Step 2: The bracketing interview

Once a topic has been chosen and the phenomenological method has been determined to be the most appropriate approach for addressing it, the focus shifts to the participant. In order to sharpen this focus, a bracketing interview is conducted. During this interview the primary investigator is interviewed by another researcher familiar with the phenomenological research process. The goal of the bracketing interview is for the primary investigator to identify his or her presuppositions from the very outset of the research project (Dale, 1996). Does the sport management phenomenologist have biases towards certain sports, teams, competitions, etc. that may tarnish the investigation? By making biases visible, the sport management researcher is positioned to be a good listener during the interview process and is less likely to mix his or her own beliefs with the experience of the participant.

Step 3: Interviewing participants

The third step in the phenomenological research process is the actual phenomenological interviews. The researcher poses a single open-ended question or statement for the participants to ponder and respond to. Following this initial open-ended question, the interview follows the direction given it by the participant. The interview concludes once the participant agrees that he or she has described his or her experience in as much detail as possible and that there is nothing else that "stood out" to him or her about the experience.

Step 4: Data analysis

After conducting and audiotaping the interview, the researcher uses analysis procedures to thematise the data. The steps of data analysis include transcribing and the hermeneutic circle.

Step 4.1 – Transcribing

The audiotaped interviews are transcribed verbatim, paying close attention to pauses, laughter or other noticeable phenomena during the interview. Transcribing the interviews enables the researcher to begin the process of data analysis by trying to interpret parts of the text in relation to other parts.

Step 4.2 – The Hermeneutic Circle

The hermeneutic circle is implemented in three ways during the interpretation of phenomenological interviews. *First*, the primary researcher brings his/her own interpretation of an interview to an interpretative research group, where the interview is read aloud. While the primary researcher sits and takes notes, two other members of the group take turns reading the questions and statements by the interviewer and the participant, respectively. The group provides feedback as to whether the presented thematic structures are supported by the interview data and represent clear descriptions of the participants' experiences. *Second*, the hermeneutic circle functions in an *"idiographic"* way, where the group or the primary researcher continuously relates parts of a single interview to the whole text. This methodological procedure is used to ensure that all parts of the text are always understood in terms of their relationship to the larger whole. Thematic descriptions of passages of a participant's interview lead to the formation of an overall thematic structure of that individual's unique experience. The *third* function of the hermeneutic circle is in the analysis of each transcript in the context of all the other transcripts. This application is referred to as the *"nomothetic"* (in contrast to the *"idiographic"*) level of hermeneutic analysis (Pollio, Henley, & Thompson, 1997). During this step, the researcher attempts to develop a single general or overall thematic structure for all of the interviews.

Step 5: Reporting findings to participants

During the last step of the phenomenological research process, the focus shifts back to the participant. Here the researcher gives participants an opportunity to review the thematic structure describing their experience and provide feedback as to how accurately and completely the structure does so. This step is important in securing the study's validity (Dale, 1996).

PHENOMENOLOGICAL "TRADITION"

In contrast to both Husserl and Heidegger, Van Manen (1990) spoke of there being no *"method"* as such if this is understood as a set of procedures, but rather of "ways" or "paths" leading to "clearings". These paths cannot be determined by fixed signposts – they need to be discovered or invented as a response to the question in hand. He spoke, however, of a "tradition" – a set of guides and recommendations that form the basis of a principled form of enquiry. This tradition is presented as "methodological structure" in which hermeneutic phenomenological research is seen as a dynamic interplay among six research activities. Van Manen lists these six activities as:

1. Turning to a phenomenon that seriously interests us and converts us to the world.

2. Investigating experience as we live it rather than as we conceptualise it.

3. Reflecting on the essential themes that characterise the phenomenon.

4. Describing the phenomenon through the art of writing and rewriting.

5. Maintaining a strong and oriented pedagogical relation to the phenomenon.

6. Balancing the research context by considering parts and the whole (pp. 30–31).

From this perspective the source of phenomenological research is the life-world. The aim is to create a dialogue between practical concerns and lived experience through engaged reasoning and imaginative dwelling in the immediacy of the participants' worlds (Van Manen, 1990).

RESEARCH ISSUES

Data saturation

Many qualitative researchers use the term "data saturation" to suggest when enough data have been collected. Saturation is a term that refers to the repetition of discovered information and confirmation of previously collected data. An inquirer does not involve an exhaustive number of participants, but identifies when the data has revealed itself to be rich, diverse, and significant enough to illuminate for readers an experience that leads to a deeper understanding of the phenomenon. The phenomenologist knows that one's own experiences are also the possible experiences of others' (Van Manen 1990).

Phenomenological sampling

In phenomenological inquiry, purposeful sampling is commonly used. This method of sampling selects individuals for study participation based on their particular knowledge of a phenomenon, for the purpose of sharing that knowledge: for example, asking black athletes about racism in sport to describe the situation over asking any athletes (regardless of race) to describe the situation.

Issues of validity and reliability in phenomenology

In phenomenological research the term *validity* is used in a general sense. According to Polkinghorne (1989), the issue concerns the question; "does the general structural description provide an accurate portrait of the common features and structural connections that are manifested in the examples collected?" (p. 57). The challenge for the phenomenological researcher is to convince the reader that their findings are accurate. To achieve that goal, the researcher must show that their method has been applied rigorously and appropriately, and that the results are plausible and illuminating. Pollio et al. (1997) point out that "only when both criteria are met does phenomenological description attain the rigour and insight that it aspires to attain" (p. 56). One way to ensure the validity of phenomenological interview data is to send participants the thematic structure that emerged from the data analysis and ask them to confirm that it accurately represents their experience.

Giorgi (1975) argued that findings from a phenomenological research project are *reliable* "if a reader, adopting the same viewpoint as articulated by the researcher, can also see what the researcher saw, whether or not (s)he agrees with it" (p. 93). Thus, it is the researcher's responsibility to provide the reader with as much information as possible in order to allow the reader to understand the researcher's perspective. A phenomenological researcher expects that an overall thematic structure and understanding of participants' experiences that might emerge from another study examining the respective experience would be commensurate with the structure found in the original study. Summing up their notions about the reliability of phenomenological studies, Thomas and Pollio (2002) point out that "in a sense, the aim of replication is to *extend*, not *repeat*, the themes and relations obtained in the original study" (p. 40).

Research brief

Title: A phenomenological interpretation of the parent–child relationship in elite youth football
Author: Clarke, N. J., *Leeds Beckett University*, Harwood, C. G., *Loughborough University*, & Cushion, C. J., *Loughborough University* (2016)
Reference: Clarke, N. J., Harwood, C. G., & Cushion, C. J. (2016). A phenomenological interpretation of the parent–child relationship in elite youth football. *Sport, Exercise, and Performance Psychology, 5*(2), 125–143.
Youth sport parenting research, in psychology, has methodologically prioritised individual level analysis of the behaviours, perceptions, or needs of parents and young athletes. However, an exploration of parenting in youth sport from a dyadic, interindividual perspective has received far less attention. Accordingly, the purpose of this research was to explore parent's and children's experience of their interaction and relationship in the context of elite youth football. Eight parent-player dyads, recruited from English professional football club youth academies, participated in phenomenological interviews. A two-stage analysis process was performed to explore individual parent and player experiences and examine how accounts related dyadically. Findings presented a detailed description and interpretation of the parent–player relationship as one constituted by relations with other family members, an embodied sense of closeness, the temporal significance of football transitions, and gender relations.

PHENOMENOLOGY IN SPORT MANAGEMENT

Phenomenology in the field of sport management serves as a theoretical framework that privileges participants' lived experience. As such, phenomenological sport management researchers seek to learn what is central to the phenomena being studied. Research conducted from a phenomenological perspective allows participants to communicate their experience without the meaning being significantly altered by the sport management researcher, and can aid in the empowerment of participants by encouraging them to speak about their own experiences.

Phenomenological research is important in sport management because sport managers are interested in human experiences and phenomenological research is a way to study human experiences. Phenomenology involves developing relationships with participants of the research process. It is believed that phenomenological research is a way for sport managers to enhance their knowledge about lived experiences, which can lead to the development or enhancement of sport management knowledge, and stimulate changes in the sport management process. Phenomenological research is seen as a co-creation between researcher and participants rather than an observation of objects or behaviours. It is also said that phenomenology strives to bring language, perceptions, and descriptions of human experience, with all types of phenomena, to enhance understanding. Sport management researchers have already effectively utilised the phenomenological hermeneutic research method when studying human experiences. For example, McAllister (2006) utilised phenomenology to explore how women administrators perceive the benefits of competitive sport experiences. More recently, O'Halloran, Littlewood, Richardson, Tod, and Nesti (2018) provide theoretically informed practical guidelines for researchers who wish to employ the descriptive phenomenological interview in their research; arguing that descriptive phenomenology holds in creating new knowledge through rich description. Bradshaw (2020) applied a phenomenological lens to understand why high-performance organisations were innovating, what caused them to be innovative, in what way they were innovating and what the consequences of being an innovative organisation were. The study provided insight into the innovation capabilities of organisations and added to the paucity of research on innovation in sport.

METHOD AND SPORT MANAGEMENT

Below is an example of a phenomenological research approach to a sport management topic using a phenomenological method. The topic is: The experiences of a Team Manager at the Tokyo Olympic Games.

Step 1: *Choosing a topic*

The topic is chosen. *The experiences of team managers at the Tokyo Olympic Games.*

Step 2: *The bracketing interview*

Once a topic has been chosen and the phenomenological method has been determined to be the most appropriate approach for addressing it, the focus shifts to the participant. To sharpen this focus, a bracketing interview is conducted. During this interview, the primary investigator is interviewed by another researcher familiar with the phenomenological research process. The purpose of the bracketing interview is to explore possible personal biases of the sport management researcher. Bracketing should be considered as an ongoing process during the research project where the sport management researcher continually reflects upon, brackets, and intuits his/her biases. Hector (2003) points out that a bracketing interview is only a first step in an attempt to achieve a suspension of the natural attitude. Besides being aware of his or her own presuppositions and biases regarding the topic, the researcher brackets those biases by using the participant's words, rather than his/her own, when interviewing participants and summarising their experience. In summary, the goal of the bracketing interview is for the sport management researcher to identify his or her presuppositions from the very outset of the research project. By making biases visible, the sport management researcher is positioned to be a good listener during the interview process and is less likely to mix his or her own beliefs with the experience of the participant (Thomas & Pollio, 2002).

Step 3: *Interviewing participants*

The third step in the phenomenological research process is the actual phenomenological interviews (Thomas & Pollio, 2002). Here, the focus is on the participants and their first-person description of the specific lived experience of being a Team Manager at the Tokyo Olympic Games. Following an initial open-ended question regarding the participant's recollection of the experience, the interview follows the direction given by the participant. The dialogue between the interviewer and participant is more circular than linear in nature (Dale, 1996). Thus, it resembles a conversation more than a question and answer session (Thompson, Locander, & Pollio, 1989). To achieve this conversational dialogue, the sport management researcher asks probing follow-up questions to clarify statements or to obtain a more detailed description of certain experiences. Whenever possible, the interviewer uses the participant's own vocabulary when asking these questions. As noted earlier, this is another way the sport management researcher can assure the bracketing of his/her biases (Hector, 2003). The sport management researcher might also summarise what the participant has said as a way of obtaining clarification (Thomas & Pollio, 2002). The interview concludes once the participant agrees that he or she has described his or her experience in as much detail as possible and that there is nothing else that "stood out" to him or her about the experience. The researcher then summarises once more what he/she has heard the participant say regarding his or her experience in order to obtain final confirmation.

Step 4: *Data analysis*

After conducting and audiotaping the interview, the sport management researcher uses analysis procedures, such as those described by Dale (1996), Thomas and Pollio (2002), and Polkinghorne (1989) to thematise the data. As Polkinghorne points out, "the aim of phenomenological inquiry is to reveal and unravel the structures, logic, and interrelationships that obtain in the phenomenon under inspection" (p. 50). Dale (1996) suggests that the researcher maintain a methodological log throughout the duration of the study, making notes on his/her thought processes, reasoning, and specific actions undertaken throughout the research project. The steps of data analysis include transcribing and the hermeneutic circle.

Step 4.1: *Transcribing*

The audiotaped interviews are transcribed verbatim, paying close attention to pauses, fluctuations in voice tone or other noticeable phenomena during the interview (Thomas & Pollio, 2002). Whenever possible, the sport management researcher should transcribe the audiotaped interviews himself or herself. This allows the sport management researcher to engage the data, containing participants' descriptions of their experiences. Transcribing the interviews himself or herself also enables the sport management researcher to begin the process of data analysis by trying to interpret parts of the text in relation to other parts.

Step 4.2 – *The hermeneutic circle*

In general, the concept of the hermeneutic circle helps to overcome "the seemingly linear character of reading by having an interpreter understand earlier portions of the text in relation to latter portions and, conversely, understand latter portions in the context of preceding ones" (Pollio et al., 1997, p. 49). Smith (1998) notes continuous bracketing by the researcher facilitates the hermeneutic process. Valle, King, and Halling (1989) point out that "the ability to deepen one's understanding of the text has to do with one's willingness and ability to reflect one's own *pre-understanding* of the text" (p. 15). Valle et al. suggest that such reflection should lead researchers/readers to ask themselves questions like: "What have I already assumed which may account for my failure to make sense of this section" (p. 16)? By continuously asking and answering such questions, the sport management researcher maintains a more heightened self-awareness when interviewing participants and also when interpreting the interviews.

Step 5 – *Reporting findings to participants*

During the last step of the phenomenological research process, the focus shifts back to the participant (Thomas & Pollio, 2002). Here the sport management researcher gives participants an opportunity to review the thematic structure describing their experience and provide feedback as to how accurately and completely the structure does so. This step is important in securing the study's validity (Dale, 1996). Put another way, the sport management researcher is asking each participant "How do my descriptive results compare with your experiences" (Polkinghorne, 1989, p. 53)? Any requests from the participants to add or delete something from the thematic structure are honoured and the changes are incorporated into the thematic structure.

Issues of reliability of data need to be addressed. There are some methods phenomenological researchers can use to ensure the reliability of their data. Giorgi (1975) argues that findings from a phenomenological research project are reliable "if a reader, adopting the same viewpoint as articulated by the researcher, can also see what the researcher saw, whether or not he agrees with it" (p. 93). Thus, it is the sport management researcher's responsibility to provide the reader with as much information as possible to allow the reader to understand the researcher's perspective. This information should consist of a thorough bracketing statement outlining the sport management researcher's biases and presuppositions. It should also include a detailed description of the thematic structure, along with many examples and excerpts from participants' interviews that support the themes. Although identical word-for-word replication is not possible in dialogic studies, Thomas and Pollio (2002) point out that thematic consistency is as much a goal of phenomenological research projects as it is of quantitative studies.

Case study

Title: 'It's not about sport, it's about you': An interpretative phenomenological analysis of mentoring elite athletes
Author: Sandardos, S. S., *Australian College of Applied Psychology* & Chambers, T. P., *Australian College of Applied Psychology* (2019)
Reference: Sandardos, S. S., & Chambers, T. P. (2019). "It's not about sport, it's about you": An interpretative phenomenological analysis of mentoring elite athletes. *Psychology of Sport and Exercise*, *43*, 144–154.

The need to support the well-being of elite athletes in a holistic manner is becoming increasingly evident with the rise of reported mental health issues in this context. Surprisingly, mentoring as a support mechanism for athlete well-being has yet to be explored. The purpose of this exploratory study was to develop a contextualised perspective of the experience of mentoring within sport, and investigate whether athletes perceived benefits to their well-being as a consequence of engaging in mentoring. An IPA was adopted (Smith, Flowers & Larkin, 2009). Semi-structured interviews were conducted with eight mentors and three athlete-mentees, who had been mentored for at least 6 months.

Data analysis of participant narratives were conceptualised into five high-order themes: (1) role; (2) attributes; (3) experience and training; (4) relationship structure; and (5) agenda. Higher-order themes were embedded into three superordinate themes: critical elements of mentoring, effective relationships, and perceived benefits to psychological well-being. Overall, this study has shown that mentoring plays a pivotal role in protecting elite athletes from an all-encompassing sport life, in terms of their identities, lifestyles, values, and future visions. Although athletes were highly passionate about sport, it did not restrict their ability to explore other non-sport related aspects of their internal and external lives. Mentees' athletic and personal development were facilitated by a mentor, which was perceived as beneficial to psychological well-being. These findings lend support to the notion that mentoring is a promising and appropriate social support mechanism for elite athletes.
References in this case study
Smith, J.A., Flowers, P., & Larkin, M. (2009). *Interpretative phenomenological analysis: Theory, method and research.* Sage, London, UK.

CONCLUSION

This chapter has explored and examined the concepts and methods of phenomenology. With the aim of studying and understanding the "lived experience", phenomenology offers sports management researchers the opportunity to delve into previously under-researched phenomena. A phenomenological research approach has value in that it critically analyses phenomena as they present in sport and sport management for deeper understanding of the universal meanings of the phenomena that occur in these fields. Phenomenology can be used to address some of the more under-explored areas in sport management research such as the lived experiences of athletes attempting to excel in a non-traditional gender-specific sport, or the daily experiences of a sport manager operating at a senior executive level in a global sporting event, where the sport management researcher seeks to understand the human condition as much as the lived experience of the phenomenon itself. For this reason, such research can lead one in the direction of uncovering the meaning of lived experience from the subjective perspectives of the persons who participate. This approach therefore has the ability to foster understanding of many of the complex and perplexing conditions in which sport managers find themselves.

REVIEW AND REVIEW QUESTIONS

Phenomenology seeks to identify and understand the lived experience of individuals. With an introductory understanding of phenomenology, an alternative to the more traditional methodologies associated with sport management research, attempt to answer the following questions:

1. Is there any place within sport management research for phenomenology? Explain your reasons.

2. Identify those key methodological features of Husserl's, Heidegger's, and Van Manen's approach to phenomenology that you believe would enable an effective analysis of the lived experience of a sport manager.

3. Develop a bracketing interview that you would use to explore possible personal biases of a sport management researcher that was investigating the lived experiences of fans in relation to "racism in football".

REFERENCES

Bradshaw, L. (2020). *'It's Not Rocket Science': A Phenomenological Study of Innovation in Elite Sport*. Unpublished doctoral dissertation draft, Loughborough University, UK.

Dale, G. A. (1996). Existential phenomenology: Emphasizing the experience of the athlete in sport psychology research. *The Sport Psychologist, 10*(4), 307–321.

Giorgi, A. (1975). An application of the phenomenological method to psychology. In A. Giorgi, C. Fisher, & E. Murray (Eds.), *Duquesne studies in phenomenology* (vol. 2), pp. 82–103. Pittsburgh: Duquesne University Press.

Hector, M. A. (2003). Phenomenology, research, and counselling psychology. *Tennessee Education, 32/33*(1/2), 25–31.

Heidegger, M. (1962). *Being and time*. New York: Harper & Row.

Husserl, E. (1931). *Ideas: General introduction to phenomenology*. New York, NY: Macmillan.

Kerry, D. S., & Armour, K. M. (2000). Sports sciences and the promise of phenomenology: Philosophy, method, and insight. *Quest, 52*(1), 1–17.

Koch, T. (1995). Interpretive approaches in nursing research: The influence of Husserl and Heidegger. *Journal of Advanced Nursing, 21*, 827–836.

McAllister, S. L. (2006). *Women Administrators' Perceptions of the Contribution of Competitive Sport Experiences to Their Career Paths and Leadership Practices*. Unpublished doctoral dissertation, Illinois State University, Bloomington.

O'Halloran, L., Littlewood, M., Richardson, D., Tod, D., & Nesti, M. (2018). Doing descriptive phenomenological data collection in sport psychology research. *Sport in Society, 21*(2), 302–313.

Pollio, H. R., Henley, T. B., & Thompson, C. B. (1997). *The phenomenology of everyday life*. Cambridge: Cambridge University Press.

Polkinghorne, D. E. (1989). Phenomenological research methods. In R. S. Valle, & S. Halling (Eds.), *Existential phenomenological perspectives in psychology*, pp. 41–60. New York: Plenum Press.

Smith, C. P. (1998). *The hermeneutics of original argument: Demonstration, dialectic, and rhetoric*. Evanston: Northwestern University Press.

Spiegelberg, H. (1982). *The phenomenological movement: A historical introduction*. Dordrecht, The Netherlands: Kluwer: Academic Publishers.

Thomas, S. P., & Pollio, H. R. (2002). *Listening to patients: A phenomenological approach to nursing research and practice*. New York: Springer.

Thompson, C. B., Locander, W. B., & Pollio, H. R. (1989). Putting consumer experience back into consumer research: The philosophy and method of existential-phenomenology. *Journal of Consumer Research, 16*(2), 133–146.

Valle, R., King, M., & Halling, S. (1989). An introduction to existential phenomenological thought in psychology. In R. Valle, & S. Halling (Eds.), *Existential-Phenomenological Perspective in Psychology*, pp. 3–16. New York: Plenum Press.

Van Manen, M. (1990). *Researching lived experience: Human science for an action sensitive pedagogy*. Ontario: The University of Western Ontario.

Van Manen, M. (1994). Pedagogy, virtue, and narrative identity in teaching. *Curriculum Inquiry, 24*(2), 135–170.

New directions for sport management research

KEY TERMS

1. **Social network:** is a social structure made of nodes (which are generally individuals or organisations) that are tied by one or more specific types of interdependency, such as values, visions, ideas, financial exchange, friendship, kinship, dislike, conflict, or trade.

2. **Actor network theory:** delineation of a set of actors that influence, shape, or determine an action, which facilitates the identification of relationships within and between actors in the same or different networks.

3. **Race/critical race theory:** investigates the social constructions of race and discrimination that are present in society.

4. **Whiteness studies:** a process of making white culture and political assumptions and privileges visible so that whites do not assume that their own position is neutral or normal.

5. **Postcolonialism:** challenges Western science as the unique source of knowledge production and uncovers inequities related to gender, race, and class resulting from the process of colonisation and post-colonisation.

6. **Disability studies:** an interdisciplinary field of study that is focused.

7. **Visual sociology:** a research approach concerned with the visual dimensions of social life.

8. **Participant authored audio–visual stories:** deal with qualitative research methodology based on sound and image data, in particular with audio–visual stories authored by the research participants.

9. **Historical studies:** the investigation of elements from history.

10. **Diaspora studies:** is an academic field that was established in the late twentieth century to study dispersed ethnic populations.

11. **Globalisation:** in general terms it is a means to explain the intricacy and variability of the ways in which the world is restructuring.

KEY THEMES

- What is social network theory?
- What is actor network theory?
- What are race theory and critical race theory?
- What is whiteness studies?
- What is postcolonialism?
- What is disability studies?
- What is visual sociology?

- What are participant authored audio–visual stories?
- What is historical studies?
- What is diaspora studies?
- What is globalisation?
- What are the potential benefits from applying these research designs to sport management contexts?
- What are the implications for applying postcolonialism and globalisation theories to sport management research processes?

CHAPTER OVERVIEW

This chapter provides an outline of some new direction that are evolving in sport management research and demonstrates how they can be situated in the sport management research field. Social network theory, actor network theory (ANT), race and critical race studies, whiteness studies, postcolonialism, disability studies, visual sociology, participant authored audio–visual stories (PAAS), historical studies, diaspora studies, and globalisation are research methods that need to be considered for future research projects. Each in its own way presents opportunities for sport management knowledge to be extended through its application. This chapter briefly outlines the basic principles that underpin these approaches and suggests how they might be applied in the field of sport management.

INTRODUCTION

Research in the field of sport management is still perceived as neutral and apolitical, which explains why sensitive issues related to race, gender, and class need to evolve. A diversity of perspectives such as those outlined in this chapter equip us to meet the epistemological imperative of giving voice to subjugated knowledge and the social mandates of uncovering existing inequities and addressing the social aspects of sport. To varying degrees, sport management researchers have been slow to embrace approaches utilised in the social sciences; however, these research approaches are gaining traction and have the potential to become acceptable forms of research within sport management.

SOCIAL NETWORK THEORY

A social network is a social structure made of nodes that are generally individuals or organisations. The nodes are tied by one or more specific types of interdependency, such as values, visions, ideas, financial exchange, friendship, kinship, dislike, conflict, or trade. The resulting structures are often very complex. Social network analysis (SNA) views social relationships in terms of nodes and ties. Nodes are the individual actors (athlete, fan, administration, etc.) within the networks, and ties are the relationships between the actors. There can be many kinds of ties between the nodes. Research in a number of academic fields has shown that social networks operate on many levels, and play a critical role in determining the way problems are solved, organisations are run, and the degree to which individuals succeed in achieving their goals. In its simplest form, a social network is a map of all of the relevant ties between the nodes being studied. The network can also be used when determining the social capital of individual actors. These concepts are often displayed in a social network diagram where nodes are the points and ties are the lines.

SNA (related to network theory) has emerged as a key technique in a range of disciplines: modern sociology, anthropology, sociolinguistics, geography, social psychology, communication studies, information science, organisational studies, economics, and biology, as well as a popular topic of speculation and study. For over a century, people have used the social network metaphor to connote complex sets of relationships between members of social systems at all scales, from interpersonal to international. In 1954, J. A. Barnes started using the term systematically to denote patterns of ties that cut across the concepts traditionally used by the public and social scientists: bounded groups (e.g. tribes, families) and social categories (e.g. gender, ethnicity) (Barnes, 1954). Over time, other scholars expanded the use of social networks.

Research brief – *Social network analysis*

Title: A social network analysis of the goal scoring passing networks of the 2016 European Football Championships

Author: Mclean, S., *University of the Sunshine Coast*, Salmon, P. M., *University of the Sunshine Coast*, Gorman, A. D., *University of the Sunshine Coast*, Stevens, N. J., *University of the Sunshine Coast*, & Solomon, C., *University of the Sunshine Coast* (2018)

Reference: Mclean, S., Salmon, P. M., Gorman, A. D., Stevens, N. J., & Solomon, C. (2018). A social network analysis of the goal scoring passing networks of the 2016 European Football Championships. *Human movement science, 57,* 400–408.

The aim of the study was to determine the goal scoring passing networks (GSPN) characteristics for the European Football Championships 2016, between the group and knock out stages and for the successful and unsuccessful teams. The authors applied SNA and notational analysis (NA) methods to examine the GSPN for all goals scored at the overall tournament. The results indicated that the GSPN had low values for network density, cohesion, connections, and duration. The networks were direct in terms of pitch zones utilised, where 85% of the GSPN included passes that were played within zones or progressed through the zones towards the goal.

The benefits of social network analysis

SNA has diverged from being a suggestive metaphor to an analytic approach to a paradigm. It has its own theoretical statements, methods, SNA software, and researchers. Analysts reason from whole to part; from structure to relation to individual; from behaviour to attitude. They either study whole networks (also known as complete networks), all of the ties containing specified relations in a defined population, or personal networks (also known as egocentric networks), the ties that specified people have, such as their "personal communities". The analytic tendencies that distinguish SNA are identified as follows:

- There is no assumption that groups are the building blocks of society: the approach is open to studying less-bounded social systems, from non-local communities to links among web sites.

- Rather than treating individuals (persons, organisations, states) as discrete units of analysis, it focuses on how the structure of ties affects individuals and their relationships.

- In contrast to analyses that assume that socialisation into norms determines behaviour, network analysis looks to see the extent to which the structure and composition of ties affect norms.

The shape of a social network helps determine a network's worth to its individuals. Networks that are smaller can be less useful to their members than networks with lots of loose connections (weak ties) to individuals outside the main network. On the other hand, more open networks with many weak ties and social connections are more likely to introduce new ideas and opportunities to their members than closed networks with many redundant ties. In other words, a sport organisation that discusses things with each other or hires from the same network of people already shares the same knowledge and opportunities. A sport organisation with connections to other social worlds is likely to have access to a wider range of information. A sport organisation may be more successful if they have connections to a variety of networks rather than many connections within a single network. Similarly, individuals can exercise influence or act as brokers within their social networks by bridging two networks that are not directly linked. This process is known as filling structural holes.

The power of SNA stems from its difference from traditional social scientific studies, which assume that it is the attributes of individual actors that determine whether they are friendly or unfriendly. SNA produces an alternate view, where the attributes of individuals are less important than their relationships and ties with other actors within the network. This approach has turned out to be useful for explaining many real-world phenomena, but leaves less room for individual agency, the ability for individuals to influence their success, because so much of it rests within the structure of their network.

Social networks have also been used as a method for exploring ways in which organisations interact with each other, characterising the many informal connections that link sport executives together, as well as associations and connections between individual employees at different sport organisations. To illustrate, power within sport organisations often comes more from the degree to which an individual within a network is at the centre of many relationships than an actual job title. Social networks also play a key role in recruiting in sport organisations, in business success and in job performance. Networks also provide ways for organisations to gather information, deter competition, and collude in setting prices or policies.

Applying social network theory to sport management research

According to Quatman (2006), studies using SNA are limited in the discipline of sport management. She argues that while the idea of social influence is often implied or referred to in sport management literature on consumer behaviour, conceptual, and empirical studies specifically integrating the role others play in influencing others' behaviours and attitudes are limited. Although consumer behaviour is used as the primary example here, the same critique can be applied to many of the topics of interest in the field.

Quatman (2006) identified that sport management research traditionally focuses on identifying and measuring the personal attributes, attitudes, and perceptions of individuals. Similarly, individuals conforming to social norms (i.e. gender, race, or ethnic variables) are often used as explanatory elements for many sport management studies. Paradoxically then, Quatman suggests that individuals are often assumed to be acting in complete isolation of one another, while at the same time, individuals are construed as strong conformers to social norms. Individuals' behaviours are therefore automatically believed to be a relative function of deliberate choice based on reason, serendipitous contact or "socially constraining factors" (p. 11). However, Quatman highlights that individuals do not function in vacuums, whether social or environmental, and are driven to action by "both conscious and subconscious motives" (p. 11), yet "decision making, attitudinal formation, and other processes of interest in sport management research often embrace one of these two extreme approaches taking on either an over-socialised or an under-socialised view of the world" (p. 11).

Quatman (2006) argues that the capabilities of traditional methods of research have not allowed for sufficient integration of social influence into measurement and interpretation techniques. Although sport management studies often explain philosophical and paradigmatic approaches that incorporate social interaction and processes as necessary components, conventional analytical instruments have been insufficient for testing a social reality of such complexity. She suggests:

> by providing analytical tools for overturning some of the under-socialized and over- socialized limitations of the more conventional research methods, social network techniques may indeed prove to be a valuable methodological approach for investigating even more diverse topics and domains in the field of sport management. (p. 11)

Case study – *Social network analysis*

Title: Understanding effective tactics in Australian football using network analysis
Author: Young, C. M., *Deakin University*, Luo, W., *Deakin University*, Gastin, P., *La Trobe University*, Lai, J., *Deakin University*, & Dwyer, D. B., *Deakin University* (2019)
Reference: Young, C. M., Luo, W., Gastin, P., Lai, J., & Dwyer, D. B. (2019). Understanding effective tactics in Australian football using network analysis. *International Journal of Performance Analysis in Sport*, *19*(3), 331–341. The authors of this study aimed to (1) assess if measures of teamwork varied between teams and between seasons, (2) identify whether there are differences in teamwork between winning and losing performances, (3) determine whether teamwork is related to score margin, and (4) determine whether teamwork is also related to whole-of-season performance using SNA. SNA has been applied in soccer and basketball to assess how a team shares possession of the ball, which could be considered as an aspect of teamwork. The analysis of teamwork could provide the opportunity to identify tactical characteristics of team performance that are associated with winning.
In this paper, ball possession data from 1,516 Australian Football League (AFL) matches (3,032 analyses) in the 2009–2016 AFL seasons were analysed with an SNA approach. The characteristics of teamwork for each AFL team were analysed separately for every match. The data used in this study were comprised of every pass and the type of pass (kicking the ball by foot and handballing by punching the ball with a closed fist), team in possession, and players involved. Interactions where a player both passed or received the ball with no other player involvement were removed as these events did not include interaction between teammates (i.e. passing the ball ineffectively where no player received the ball and it resulted in a turnover or resulted in an out of bounds). The ball could also be received from an opponent or from an umpire where no interaction has occurred with a teammate. As a result, seven network measures (edge count, edge density, transitivity, average path length, degree centrality, betweenness centrality, and eigenvector centrality) were derived. The results of the paper suggested that effective passing within a team is important and that a team should maximise the number of trios in their passing network. This work provided novel insights regarding optimal teamwork strategies in AFL.

ACTOR NETWORK THEORY (ANT)

In the 1980s, the ANT approach emerged within the sociological research of science and technology, having its roots in French philosophy and semiotics. Since then, ANT has spread into various contexts of sociological inquiry (Jóhannesson, 2005; Rhodes, 2009). It is seen as a socio-philosophical approach that seeks to understand complex social circumstances by paying attention to relational factors referred to as associations (Alcadipani & Hassard, 2010; Arnaboldi & Spiller, 2011).

ANT enables the delineation of a set of actors (the network) that influence, shape, or determine an action (Rhodes, 2009), which facilitates the identification of relationships within and between actors in the same or different networks. It comprises four main components, the first being the actor or the actant, who is not just seen as a "point object" but rather as an association of various factors, themselves forming an actor-network (Tatnall & Burgess, 2002). An actor or actant may be an individual, a group, an idea, a piece of software, a material object, a plant, natural capital or an animal that acts towards something. It may not inevitably be the source of an action but instead may modify and enhance the state of affairs by making a significant difference (Latour, 1996; cited in Dolwick, 2009). The second component relates to the "links" or relationships that exist between the actors, and may include money transfers, verbal or written communication, publications sent to subscribers, friendships, or resource exchange, including information and overlapping memberships of networks (Timur & Getz, 2008). The third element is the "network", which may be an individual, a group, an idea, a physical object, a plant, or an animal. It could also be an interactive assembly of entities, or a group or "series of actions" including a number of potential mediators (Dolwick, 2009). The fourth component is the action itself (Dolwick, 2009), and relates to agency, or taking seriously what the actors (human or non-human) have to say.

According to Van der Duim (2007), ANT seeks to examine the tools by which relationships emerge, and how the roles of subjects and objects, and intermediaries, human actors (i.e. people, organisations, and groups) and non-humans (the natural environment, software, and computers) are attributed and stabilised. The point of interest is how these and other categories come into existence via the processes involved in constituting a network. ANT supposes that collective action is made up of a series of human and non-human actors, and a translation carried out through a translator or an interpreter will create various relationships between these heterogeneous actors, which then become networked. The process of translation is a concatenation of successive stages, transformations, and redefinitions of the collective project, through which actors (human and non-human) are mobilised in various ways. ANT is centred around four important points:

1. Networks are always being gathered and re-gathered for specific projects; they are constantly in flux.

2. Networks are interim entities; their existence depends essentially on the action of ongoing relationships.

3. ANT, in contrast to other network theories, ascribes power to non-human actors in the network, such as the natural environment, objects, technologies, software, machines, implements, and computers.

4. Contrary to mediators, translators are the dynamic element of networks, which effect the changes that lead towards the recognition of specific projects (Ren, 2011; Cohen & Cohen, 2012).

ANT is based on three methodological principles (Tatnall & Gilding, 1999). The first principle is *agnosticism*, which is the requirement of impartiality regarding the actors involved in the network (Rodger, 2007). ANT compels dispassion and holds that all interpretations should be unbiased (Callon, 1986). The second ANT principle is *generalised symmetry*, which offers a counterbalance to the principle of agnosticism as it continues the idea of equivalence between human and non-human actors (McLean & Hassard, 2004). Symmetry refers to the idea of networks being formed where human and non-human actors have equally important roles (Callon, 1986). The conflicting viewpoints of these heterogeneous actors can be explained and interpreted through an abstract and impartial vocabulary that treats all actors fairly and in the same way, whether they are human or non-human based (Tatnall & Lepa, 2003). This principle asserts that everything merits explanation (Rodger, 2007). In other words, generalised symmetry implies using the same repertoire (or not changing the register) when describing both nature and society (or when moving between social and technological aspects) as both are mixed together as the ingredients of the controversies concerning them. ANT ensures the full recognition of the power and effect of entities in nature and the physical globe, instead of remaining hidden or being rejected as they are in much contemporary social theory (Burgess, Clark, & Harrison, 2000). The third principle, *free association*, argues that heterogeneous actors can be linked together through a number of conceptual divisions, such as national/international, cultural/natural, or social/natural (Burgess et al., 2000). Latour (1993, cited in Burgess et al., 2000) suggests that the world is composed of "hybrids" that contain complex relations of social, technological and natural features, and not of entities that are "purely social" or "purely natural". Free association supports abandoning any privilege or peculiarity between social and technical phenomena. This means that there can be no assumed distinctions between human and non-human actors in coming to recognise the phenomenon under investigation (Callon, 1986). Thus, actor-networks are made up of hybrids via relations between heterogeneous entities as they are formed into a particular network (Rodger, 2007).

Rodger (2007) argues that ANT looks at the transformation of heterogeneous networks into aligned networks, which can be composed of individuals, groups, organisations, technologies, animals, and more. It examines how the networks emerge, who or what is involved, how the networks are maintained, and how networks of actors compete with other networks. Moreover, ANT investigates the mechanics of power through the networks' construction and maintenance – both human and non-human (Rodger, 2007). ANT has also been called the process of translation or enrolment (Norbert & Schermer, 2003).

Rodger claims that actors become involved in networks through the process of translation.

The process of translation

The process of translation itself consists of a series of successive movements, transformations and redefinitions (Paget et al., 2010). It is employed to explain the methods through which power is ascribed and negotiated, and it also attempts to dissolve the classic dualism of technical and social, as the characteristics of all enrolled actors are derived from their relative value within an actor-network (Ruming, 2008). The process of translation can be divided into four moments (Cordella & Shaikh, 2003; Tatnall & Burgess, 2002), which we will now described.

Problematisation

Problematisation is the first step in the process of translation, in which an actor (the focal or principal actor) analyses a situation, defines the nature of the problem, proposes a solution and identifies the actors involved (human and non-human) who have similar aims and interests in forming a network to work together to resolve the identified problem (Huxford, 2010; Ibrahim, 2009).

Interessement

Interessement is the second moment of translation and relates to the involvement of other actors in resolving the identified problem (Brito & Correia, 2004). In other words, it refers to the actions and strategies taken by the principal actor to ensure that other actors accept the proposed solution to the problem, and the specific roles assigned to them (Huxford, 2010).

Enrolment

Callon (1986) defined enrolment, the third moment of translation, as the series of mutual negotiations, trials of strength and tricks that accompany interessement and help networks of actors to succeed in achieving their goals. Enrolment is when actors become involved in a network, and will only occur if interessement has already been successful (Van der Duim, 2005).

Mobilisation

Mobilisation is the fourth moment of translation and, according to Tatnall and Davey (2005), it is the phase during which the proposed solution to an identified problem gains wider acceptance, resulting in the formation of an even larger network of absent actors, formed through some actors acting as spokespersons for others. Ibrahim (2009) suggests that during this stage, the leader will line up a series of distinctive links to maintain the network. Huxford (2010) claims that the stage of mobilisation might never be reached, and is by no means a stable or fixed position even if it is reached. In many cases, a change will force a return to one of the earlier stages of translation.

Actor-network theory and sport management

Within the social sciences arena, the application of ANT has largely occurred within a business management context to map the stakeholders and non-human actors that may impact on the success of corporations. More recently, though, there has been increasing recognition of the relevance of ANT to sport management, perhaps reflecting the fact that the sport management industry is comprised of different kinds of networks that are often intertwined through collaborative arrangements. ANT can be a valuable tool for exploring the processes and complex interactions that are at work in sport management. Edwards and Skinner (2009) argue that ANT is particularly relevant to sport management since the latter is a phenomenon that comprises a collection of producing and consuming moments.

There is a strong relationship between sport management and ANT as the latter can be used as a theoretical and methodological lens through which to analyse sport. Sport management is a heterogeneous collective network of actors in continuous movement, and this network involves three key elements: (1) actors; (2) non-human entities; and (3) interactions. First of all, the actors include, on the one hand, the fans who consume sport management services and products, and on the other hand, the producers who provide these services and products. The second group, the non-human entities, is very diverse, and includes objects (stadiums etc.), natural environments (mountains, reefs, snow, etc.), means of communication (magazines, brochures, websites, newspapers, etc.), technologies, services (e.g., sports activities, financial services), and others. Third, there would be no sport management, without the interactions that connect these human and non-human entities.

Advantages and disadvantages of ANT

Advantages of ANT

ANT is a useful approach that can help the researcher to understand the complexity of reality (e.g. the complexity of organisations) and the collective and active role of non-human actors in this context. This can be useful for understanding how social (human actors) influences are created as a result of relationships between heterogeneous entities in a network. Of main importance in this regard is that ANT provides a lens through which to look at the role of natural (non-human) entities in the formation of social processes (Cresswell, Worth, & Sheikh, 2010; Elgali & Kalman, 2010).

ANT is also "useful in providing the ability to apply insights to storytelling and to empirical studies of technologies, power and actor-networks" (Corrigan & Mills, 2012, p. 262). Hence, ANT can be useful for thinking with regard to networks of associations, or more specifically, actor-networks (Williams-Jones & Graham, 2003). According to Cressman (2009), ANT can be employed as a tool for sampling by focusing on relevant participants/informants that are associated with the technology in question. Despite these advantages, however, there are some limitations to the use of ANT, as explained next.

Disadvantages of ANT

Cressman (2009) suggests that ANT is characterised by an exclusive emphasis on case studies and empirical observation, leading to situations where researchers simply report what they see and intangible elements like values and norms are not recognised. The theory has also been criticised by Huxford (2010) and Doolin and Lowe (2002) for failing to provide any means of differentiating between human and non-human actors. However, the purpose of considering social (human) and natural (non-humans) entities as symmetrical is to help provide a comprehensive description of the actor-network, and does not mean or entail that all actors must be treated as equal for all objectives, nor that the different associations between entities be similar. In fact, part of the advantage of building a network will be tracing the types of associations between entities and defining the flow of power or power relations and control. In addition, since each network is influenced by other networks in an actor network, it is quite difficult to completely explain the complexity of the network (Huxford, 2010).

Huxford (2010) describes ANT as overly descriptive, obscuring differences, and having a tendency to produce centred managerialist studies that focus on the powerful. Meanwhile, Ginn (2005) identifies that it can be difficult to attribute agency within networks whilst maintaining the principle of symmetry. ANT has also been accused of lacking political and critical content (Johannessen, 2005); Huxford comments on the lack of awareness of political agendas within ANT studies. Typically, the choice of which actor to follow is left up to the researcher, who may make the wrong decision. Furthermore, Cressman (2009) suggests that in many works in the literature, the ANT terminology is confusing. For example, the processes of translation, the sociology of translation and enrolment are all used interchangeably to refer to ANT. Moreover, ANT is criticised by Cresswell et al. (2010) for failing to reach any detailed propositions of how actors should be viewed, and their collective actions analysed, explained, and interpreted. Thus, it has been suggested that ANT can be best applied and employed in combination with other theoretical approaches, in particular with regard to analysis, explanation, and interpretation (Greenhalgh & Stones, 2010).

Research brief – *Actor-network theory*

Title: Unravelling legacy: A triadic actor-network theory approach to understanding the outcomes of mega events
Author: Dawson, J., *Loughborough University* & Jöns, H., *Loughborough University* (2018)
Reference: Dawson, J., & Jöns, H. (2018). Unravelling legacy: A triadic actor-network theory approach to understanding the outcomes of mega events. *Journal of Sport & Tourism*, *22*(1), 43–65.
This paper aimed to advance ongoing debates on the outcomes of sports mega events by bringing together the literatures on mega event legacy and actor-network theory. Drawing on a case study on the usage of the Queen Elizabeth Olympic Park, the main legacy of the London 2012 Olympic Games, the paper developed a novel conceptual framework for researching the multi-scalar outcomes of mega events and locating respective studies within the resulting wider research agenda. This paper aimed to contribute to both types of interdisciplinary debates about mega events by conceptualising their outcomes along a temporal spectrum of short-term effects, medium-term impacts, and long-term legacies using a practice-based approach.

RACE THEORY, CRITICAL RACE THEORY, AND SPORT MANAGEMENT RESEARCH

What are race theory and critical race theory?

Race theory and critical race theory (CRT) are fields of inquiry that examine the social construction of race and discrimination that are present in society. Both fields emphasise the socially constructed nature of race, consider the workings of power, and oppose the constitution of all forms of subordination. Most recent attention in the field of race studies has occurred in the field of CRT. Scholars have looked to CRT, as an epistemological and methodological tool, to help analyse the experiences of historically under-represented populations.

Critical Race studies could be defined as a critique of racism as a system of oppression and exploitation that explores the historic and contemporary constructions and manifestations of race in our society with particular attention to how these issues are manifested in society. Critical Race studies is ultimately concerned with employing multiple methods and borrowing from diverse traditions in the law, sociology, ethnic studies, and other fields to formulate a robust analysis of race and racism as a social, political, and economic system of advantages and disadvantages accorded to social groups based on their skin colour and status in a clearly defined racial hierarchy. Some of the key features of CRT include:

- Derived from critical legal studies in the 1960s

- Explores the role of race in society

- Questions racism and White privilege

- Provides a space for histories of people of colour
- Describes whiteness as a form of property
- Race goes beyond colour, it includes class
- Discussion of race: beyond semantics, back to class, and inequality
- CRT derivations: queer theory, critical Asian scholarship

Applications to sport management

CRT has evolved into a type of revolutionary project. Such a project unapologetically centres race and examines how this key sociohistorical construct affects all facets of daily life. CRT also problematises objectivity and exposes how colour-blind and post-racial ideologies, that envelope daily discourse, work to maintain privilege, and protect white supremacy. We suggest that while CRT offers us a strong lens to identify institutional racism it does not offer remedies. The role of sport management researchers in shaping the direction and driving the work of Critical Race work remains paramount. As CRT continues to evolve so does its potential potency. In recent years, Critical Race researchers have expanded the application and scope of critical race scholarship. New literature now exists that confronts the important and racialised components of heretofore unexamined sport experiences. For example, there have been a number of studies investigating under-representation of racial groups and racial stacking in sport, particularly in the USA context.

We believe that when aiming toward a CRT inspired revolutionary praxis in sport management, paying more attention to the institutional, not just individual, structures, and relationships would help facilitate larger scaled change. We applaud all the CRT inspired work done to date but are reminded that and rampant neoliberalism, complicate CRT's task of challenging white supremacy in sport and elsewhere. The core of sport management critical race research should be the task of advancing social justice.

WHITENESS STUDIES AND SPORT MANAGEMENT RESEARCH

What is whiteness studies?

Whiteness theory is a process of making white culture and political assumptions and privileges visible so that whites do not assume that their own position is neutral or normal. Whiteness studies is an interdisciplinary arena of academic inquiry focused on the cultural, historical, and sociological aspects of people identified as white. Whiteness emerged as a focus of academic study primarily in the United States as early as the 1980s. *White women, race matters: The social construction of whiteness*, by Ruth Frankenberg (1993) and; *The wages of whiteness* by David Roediger (1991) are two seminal books that highlight whiteness theory. Eminent feminist scholar Frankenberg (1993) on the one hand examines white women's thoughts "about interracial relationships as idea and the racialised constructions of masculinity, femininity, identity, and community that flow from a dominant discourse against interracial relationships" (p. 8). Roediger on the other hand writes on experiences of the white working class – principally men – through an analysis of "the role of race in defining how white workers look not only at blacks but at themselves; the pervasiveness of race; the complex mixture of hate, sadness and longing in the racist thought of white workers; the relationship between race and ethnicity" (p. 5).

Since the mid-1990s, a number of publications across many disciplines have analysed the social construction of *whiteness* as an ideology tied to social status. A central belief of whiteness is that race is said to have been constructed by a white power structure in order to justify discrimination against non-whites. Significant areas of research include the nature of white identity and white privilege, the historical process by which a white racial identity was created and the relation of culture to white identity. A reflexive understanding of such assumptions underpins work within the field of whiteness studies. Lipsitz (2000) argues there is more to whiteness than just attitude. The possessive investment in whiteness is about assets as well as attitudes; "it is about property as well as pigment. It does not stem primarily from personal acts of prejudice by individuals but from shared social structures that skew access to resources, opportunities, and life chances along racial lines" (p. 519).

No longer content with accepting whiteness as the norm, critical scholars have turned their attention to whiteness itself. In the field of *critical white studies*, numerous thinkers investigate such questions as:

- How was whiteness invented and why?

- How has the category of whiteness changed over time?

- Can some individual people be both white and non-white at different times and what does it mean to "pass for white"?

- At what point does pride for being white cross the line into white power and white supremacy?

- What can whites concerned over racial inequity or white privilege do about it?

Research brief – *Whiteness study*

Title: Applying white dialectics: Exploring whiteness and racial identity among white college athletes
Author: Vadeboncoeur, J. D., *University of Florida* & Bopp, T., *University of Florida* (2019)
Reference: Vadeboncoeur, J. D., & Bopp, T. (2019). Applying white dialectics: Exploring whiteness and racial identity among white college athletes. *Quest, 71*(1), 1–20.
This article aimed to synthesise and apply White racial identity theory and concomitant research to the interaction between athletic and racial identity, specifically as it relates to the experiential variations of how race impacts White athletes within the college sport environment. White dialectics, or the tensions that White Americans experience as dominant social group members, served as the guiding theoretical framework and provided a theoretical lens through which the experience of White college athletes was examined at each distinct dialectic. In this article, the application of White dialectics offered a theoretical foundation for developing a better understanding of how White college athletes made sense of their racial identity, as well as to understand their racialised experiences within intercollegiate athletics.

POSTCOLONIALISM AND SPORT MANAGEMENT RESEARCH

Postcolonial ideological discourse

The term postcolonialism is a challenging one. Just like post-structuralism and postmodernism, it has multiple meanings and implications when used. It is also highly criticised (Viruru & Cannella, 2001). Cannella and Bailey (1999) argue that postcolonial scrutiny and insights could have potential for influencing research, perhaps even challenging Western constructions of research. "Postcolonialism" continues to generate dissatisfaction among practitioners and detractors alike, of which some (most notably those who equate postcolonial studies with postmodernism) now suggest the term may have outlived its usefulness (see San Juan, 1998; Hardt & Negri, 2000).

Postcolonial study is a relatively recent ideological discourse. It represents a critical response by the former colonised to the various forms and processes of Western domination and subjugation resulting from the colonial encounter. The colonial enterprise has left former colonies suffering from wounds that appear to deepen rather than heal. In virtually every aspect of their lives, former colonised people contend with the repercussions of their encounter with European colonisers. In response, postcolonial theorists engage in discussions about a host of experiences relating to slavery and colonialism such as suppression, resistance, representation, difference, race, gender, and social class. Within these broader themes, specific issues such as the primacy of the coloniser's language, religion, cultural histories, knowledge, and other elements of identity over that of the local peoples is topical in the postcolonial conversation. Global sport, especially football, rugby, and cricket brought by the British Empire may have transcended some of the negativity left by colonisers, and can be studied as a positive change. Postcolonial studies, therefore, is an academic space in which to contest hegemonic ideologies and impositions, which continue to oppress and confuse formerly colonised peoples who now inhabit what is called the "developing world" (hereafter, Third World or postcolonial societies). McConaghy (2000) suggests that while postcolonialism draws on post-structuralism and postmodernism, it does not overlap neatly with them.

Defining postcolonialism

Postcolonialism challenges Western science as the unique source of knowledge production and uncovers inequities related to gender, race, and class resulting from the process of colonisation and postcolonisation. This discourse is especially pertinent to sport management as it brings to the forefront these issues and makes explicit how these socially constructed categories have been used in the colonising process, and the effect that this has had on people's lives and life opportunities.

Colonisation is defined by Said (2000) as: "the expansive force of a people; it is its power of reproduction; it is its enlargement and its multiplication through space; it is the subjugation of the universe or the vast part of it to that people's language, customs, ideas, and laws. Postcolonialism is the process of postcolonialising" (p. 135). Quayson (2000) suggests that to understand this process (postcolonialising), it is necessary to disentangle the term, postcolonial, from its implicit dimension of chronological supersession, that aspect of its prefix that suggests that the colonial stage has been surpassed and left behind. It is important to highlight instead a notion of the term as a process of coming into being and of struggle against colonialism and its after-effects.

More specifically, the postcolonial approach is directed at uncovering the exclusionary effects of dominant ideologies in "Othering" other forms of knowledge – the subjugated knowledge. Foucault (1980) defines subjugated knowledge as a whole set of knowledge that has been disqualified as inadequate to its task or insufficiently elaborated naïve knowledge, located low down in the hierarchy, beneath the required level of cognition or scientificity. According to Quayson (2000), postcolonialism focuses on dominant discourses and ideologies that shape the social world to look at the material effects of subjugation. Subjugation is the process by which imperialism and colonialism impose a condition of positional superiority over the colonised (Said, 2000). The process is to ground contemporary world phenomena such as immigration, unemployment, health problems, into the real world to unmask the interrelations between these phenomena and new colonial ideologies. Consequently, the researcher's aim is to "relate modern-day phenomena to their explicit, implicit, or even potential relations, to the heritage of colonialism" (Quayson, 2000, p. 11) while decolonising methodologies and methods (Tuhiwai Smith, 1999), aim to critique the marginalising effect of Western science on subjugated knowledge.

Applying postcolonialism to sport management research unveils the reductionist Western discourse of essentialising the "Other" in a unique, crystallised, neutral, rational, and objectivist cultural entity. As well, "decolonialising" methodologies and methods are directed at disrupting the power relations to voice subjugated knowledge. According to Hall (1997), subjectivities emerge from: "the different constellation of social, cultural and economic forces ... since we are, in part, constructed as subjects through the particular layering of historical discourses, which we inhabit, then new kinds of sensibilities begin to be clearly discernible" (p. 247). Postcolonial scholarship in sport management research is limited; however, important work has been produced in which issues and concerns of postcolonialism and sport are discussed.

How can postcolonialism be articulated in sport management research?

The development of postcolonial scholarship in sport management depends on our abilities to define new theories and methods to explore and understand cultural differences, and to challenge dominant culture stereotypes instead of trying to change the subaltern, as proposed by culturalist models. Also, sport issues related to racial, gendered, and class discrimination need to be part of the sport management social mandate. Given this era of increasing cultural intolerance, the harmful effects of racial, gendered and social discrimination on sport management must be recognised. Postcolonial research is a theoretical perspective that moves us away from the shortcomings of cultural essentialism, since culture cannot be isolated from the broader social context within which it comes into play together with a constellation of other structural factors. This theoretical approach provides the analytic lens to examine the extent to which sport management research and practice perpetuate dominance through our everyday practice. However, it should be remembered that research cannot be neutral, apolitical, or ahistorical since sport management is governed by normalising discourses and practices.

Furthermore, there is the complex question of political commitment and its relation to scholarly inquiry. Undoubtedly, it is a core issue to be addressed in sport management, and postcolonial research provides the analytical framework to perform such reflection. Nevertheless, postcolonial research warns us to distance ourselves from the expert role in acknowledging the anthropological construction of sport. Democratisation of sport management research can be realised by recognising "subjugated knowledge" as a legitimate source of theorisation, adapting sport management interventions to meet the needs of people located at the margins of pluralist societies. If social justice is ever to be achieved in the sport system, voices of the subaltern have to be heard. In this sense, postcolonialism questions the appropriateness of culturist theories to correct such issues as managerial imbalances stemming from social discrepancies and neocolonial ideologies. Finally, postcolonialism is not specifically directed at developing knowledge for the sake of knowledge. Giroux (2002) describes this strategy as the "most retrograde academic use" (p. 98) of knowledge since it evacuates the possibilities of challenging the status quo. Anderson (2000) emphasises that deconstructing and rewriting "taken-for-granted" knowledge, and redefining relations of power and privilege is a step towards achieving social justice.

FROM THEORY TO METHOD

Possibly the greatest challenge in our call for a postcolonial sport management scholarship lies in the translation of its theoretical tenets into a method of research. The following section describes a postcolonial research method that has evolved from an exploration of the dialectic between theory and research.

Framing the research

The first distinction of a postcolonial sport management research method lies in the way in which the entire research project is viewed through a political lens – a lens that attends to the micro politics and macro dynamics of power. While attending to power relations is certainly a methodological theme of other brands of research (e.g. feminist research may be the most overt example), a postcolonial framing rests on an overarching mindfulness of how domination and resistance mark intercultural encounters at individual, institutional, and societal levels. Thus, postcolonial sport management scholarship pursues matters of how contemporary constructions of race, ethnicity and culture continue to rely on colonialist images and patterns of inclusion and exclusion within sport management settings. Careful attention to the social and historical positioning of the sport management researcher vis-à-vis research participants also is paramount to the postcolonial project.

Linking self and society

Inherent in contemporary postcolonial efforts is the tension between self and society, the local and the global, the particularities of the hybrid moment and the universality of the colonial experience. It is our ability to understand and explain how the nature of the relationship between self and society, the contextualisation of subjectivity, is critical to the progress of sport management. We suggest, therefore, that a feature of postcolonial sport management scholarship is situating human experience (or everyday reality) in the larger contexts of mediating social, economic, political, and historical forces. Should ex-colonies (e.g. Kenya) continue with the same high-performance goals and strive to implement a Western high-performance structure, simply because the West has been successful? Or are resources better utilised elsewhere? What is the opportunity cost of Kenya funding high performance structures similar to Western society? Are gold medal marathoners actually benefiting Kenya from a Kenyan point of view, or just a Western point of view?

Giving voice

The third feature of a postcolonial research method suggested is the deliberate decentring of dominant culture so that the worldviews of the marginalised become the starting point in knowledge construction. A postcolonial commitment results in the weaving of the perspectives and experiences of those marginalised in our society into the very fabric of sport management. Core to the postcolonial movement is the question raised by Gayatri Chakrovorty Spivak's (1988) "Can the Subaltern speak?" At its most basic level postcolonialism demands the right to speak rather than being spoken for, and to represent oneself rather than being represented or, in the extreme cases, rather than being erased entirely. A further opportunity for giving voice to previously subjugated voices is the liberal use of polyvocality in research through strategies such as purposive sampling from diverse groups of participants with a range of experiences, listening carefully to the accounts of these participants, and liberally using their verbatim stories in written reports.

A basic question in postcolonial research has been posed as to whether or not white researchers can truly understand the experiences of issues such as racialisation and racism. Some argue that postcolonial studies in the field are best undertaken by minority scholars; others have argued that such matching of researchers with the researched results in marginalising certain types of research, making, for example, racism only a concern for racialised groups. We take the position that rather than pursuing the legitimacy of our roles as sport management researchers based on one aspect of one's social identity (e.g. whiteness), one's legitimacy as a sport management researcher is based on one's ability to explicate the ways in which marginalisation and racialisation operate. Furthermore, acknowledging the interrelatedness of race, class, and gender provides important insights for postcolonial sport management inquiry and guards against incomplete and simplistic analyses.

Emancipatory intent

The final feature of a postcolonial research method is its open commitment to critiquing the status quo and building a more just society. We make the case for emancipatory intent. Praxis- oriented research is research committed to social change. Thus, sport management inquiry within the larger genre of an emancipatory research paradigm is committed to moving beyond the description of what "is" to providing prescription for what "ought" to be, and raises our level of investigation from matters of the individual to consideration of larger socio-political forces impacting on the common good. The goal of emancipatory sport management researchers is to foster self-reflection and deeper understanding on the part of the researched at least as much as it is to generate empirically grounded theoretical knowledge.

Method

An important distinction of a postcolonial perspective is that there are no pre-scribed techniques for data collection or data analysis. In this research approach, different techniques can be drawn on depending on the focus of the inquiry, as long as they meet the criteria for scientific adequacy and rigour. The hallmark of postcolonial scholarship is a strong research-theory dialectic that brings a par-ticular interpretive lens to the sport management research that recognises that each life is shaped by history. This lens frames how questions are formulated, who is included in the study, how data are interpreted, the meanings derived from the data, and how research findings are communicated and applied. While we are not limited in the kinds of questions we ask, our questions are framed from a particular epistemological perspective. That is, the postcolonial lens always takes into account the context in which each life is situated, and anal-yses how gender, race, class, and historical positioning intersect at any given moment to organise experience in the here and now. The postcolonial meth-odology sketched out here promises us new and important tools for forms of transformative knowledge that have been largely overlooked within sport man-agement scholarship and practice. With such a commitment, postcolonial sport management scholarship will permit more thoughtful attention to the issues of equity and social justice.

DISABILITY STUDIES AND SPORT MANAGEMENT RESEARCH

What is disability studies?

People with disabilities have a long history of being seen as "other" or "not one of us". For many years they were kept "out of sight, and out of mind" on the margins of our communities. Yet, during the last few decades there has been a concerted effort to bring people with disabilities back into society. Policies of inclusion, normalisa-tion, and community living are vigorously pursued in many countries. Disability studies is an interdisciplinary field of study that is focused on the contributions, experiences, history, and culture of people with disabilities. The field of research in the area of disability is growing worldwide. It is based on the premise that dis-advantage typically experienced by those who are disabled reflects primarily on the way society defines and responds to certain types of difference. The definition of disability studies is contested by those coming from different epistemologies. A range of social theorists emphasise the various social processes that construct and shape the lives of people with disabilities and the meanings of disability within contemporary society. These two opposing arguments – the commonsense and the social – essentially underpin the two main intellectual traditions that have emerged around disability theory and research and that have, in turn, informed disability policies and practices. These are the *Naturalistic* and *Social* intellectual traditions. Some of the major features of disability studies include:

- Should be interdisciplinary/multidisciplinary.

- Should challenge the view of disability as an individual deficit or defect that can be remedied solely through medical intervention or rehabilitation by "experts" and other service providers.

- Should study national and international perspectives, policies literature, culture, and history with the aim of placing current ideas of disability within their broadest possible context.

- Should actively encourage participation in disabled students and faculty, and should ensure physical and intellectual access.

- Should make a priority to have leadership positions held by disabled people, at the same time it is important to create an environment where contributions from anyone who share the above goals are welcome.

Research brief

Title: Understanding which dimensions of organisational capacity support the vertical integration of disability football clubs
Authors: Kitchin, P. J., *School of Sport, Faculty of Life and Health Sciences, Ulster University, Newtownabbey, Northern Ireland* & Crossin, A., *Independent Scholar, Belfast, Northern Ireland* (2018).
Reference: Kitchin, P. J, & Crossin, A. (2018). Understanding which dimensions of organisational capacity support the vertical integration of disability football clubs. *Managing Sport and Leisure, 23* (1–2), 28–47.

Disabled people continue to face exclusion from full participation in community sports. Efforts to include disabled people in sports organisations have favoured structural solutions to make sport accessible. Our purpose was to understand which dimensions of a football club's organisational capacity assisted the vertical integration of disability football clubs. A theoretical framework combining organisational capacity and acculturation informed an exploratory and qualitative research design using semi-structured interviews. Findings indicate that the brand and the size of the organisation assisted the generation of integrative capacity. Following the acquisition of integrative capacity, two types of integration – assimilation and accommodation appeared. This study contributes to the extant literature on the vertical integration of disability sport and the management and organisation of disability football. Recommendations for policy makers and practitioners seeking to implement the vertical integration process as this study provides a theoretical and empirical perspective on how mergers can create inclusive organisations.

Disability studies is not without its critics. It has been suggested that the dominant social model, developed in the 1970s, has now been outgrown, and requires major developments. Disability studies has also been criticised for its failure to engage with multiple forms of oppression, such as racism, sexism or homophobia. As a relatively new discipline, it is true that as yet disability studies has seen little progress in this area. More recently, the concept of critical disability studies has started to emerge in the social sciences. Publications are now beginning to emerge though, and in time it is hoped that this issue will be fully engaged by researchers, including sport management researchers. Within sport management a few studies have examined disability. However, to date studies have not studied specific sport management issues from a disabilities studies perspective. Research in this area is urgently needed. The recent work of Paul Kitchin from Ulster university on the mainstreaming of disability cricket in England and Wales and the institutional perspectives on the implementation of disability legislation and services for spectators with disabilities in European professional football are examples of the important research that can be undertaken. The Special Olympics and Paralympics also provide important fertile ground for research.

Case study – *Disability study*

Title: Understanding Coach Learning in Disability Sport: A Bourdieusian Analysis
Author: Townsend, R. C., *Loughborough University* (2018)
Reference: Townsend, R. C. (2018). Understanding Coach Learning in Disability Sport: A Bourdieusian Analysis. *Submitted in partial fulfilment for the requirements for the award of Doctor of Philosophy of Loughborough University.*
The purpose of this research was to answer longstanding calls to explore the learning and development of coaches in disability sport. According to the author, it is very little known about coaches in disability sport. Although a growing body of work that has explored coach learning is emerging, the author argued that there is an absence of in-depth sociological research on disability coaching and coach education. In order to address this gap in the literature, this research sought to examine the nature of coach learning through analyses of coach education and coaching practice. Drawing upon a critical sociological framework, the research was conducted on the premise that understanding social practice can generate critical insights into the nature of coach learning. The research began to answer some of the criticisms levelled at previous research by operationalising the sociological framework of Pierre Bourdieu in conjunction with disability studies, to analyse data generated through a two-year case study evaluation of an impairment-specific mode of coach education, and ethnographic data generated from eighteen-months of fieldwork in a specific disability coaching context. Altogether, data were collected through in-depth observations, interviews, focus groups and qualitative surveys to generate data that had both breadth, gathering data from large numbers of participants, and depth, by understanding in detail a particular coaching culture. The findings revealed how knowledge about disability was often marginalised in coach education, with engagement in the field functioning as principle source of knowledge about coaching in disability sport. As a result, disability-specific coach education contributed marginally to coach learning and functioned as a platform for the transmission of medical model discourses about disability, in terms of the pedagogy adopted and its effects on coaches' knowledge. In the ethnographic study, analyses revealed how disability was assimilated into a high-performance coaching logic that structured coaches' learning according to high-performance ideals. Overall, the author argued that the research extended an understanding of coach learning, taking into consideration social structure and agency as a basis for further critical inquiry into coaching in disability sport.

VISUAL SOCIOLOGY AND SPORT MANAGEMENT RESEARCH

What is visual sociology?

Visual sociology is an emerging field in the social sciences. Despite this, its theoretical and methodological contributions are just becoming known. Visual sociology is a research approach concerned with the visual dimensions of social life. It includes the study of all kinds of visual material and the visual social world, and uses all kinds of visual material in its methodologies such as photographs, film, tape, and video to study society as well as the study of the visual artefacts of a society. Visual sociology is viewed as suited to data gathering technologies for small group interactions, ethnography, and oral history.

Theory and method

There are at least three approaches to visual sociology, there are:

1. *Data collection using cameras and other recording technology.* In this first sense visual sociology means including and incorporating visual methods of data gathering and analysis in the work of research. Visual recording technology allows manipulation of data because they make it possible to speed up, slow down, repeat, stop, and zoom in on things of interest. In a sport management context, this methodological approach is routinely utilised by venue managers as they collect visual data through security cameras, to monitor the behaviour of spectators and to observe behavioural patterns that may lead to security or safety issues. These "observations" could be the basis for a more formalised research inquiry, if ethically approved. In this way, new knowledge and understanding of facility management may evolve that assists the facility manager to better understand the behaviour of fans in their venues.

2. *Studying visual data produced by cultures.* The second approach of visual sociology is to study the visual products of society – their production, consumption, and meaning. Visual images are constructed and may be deconstructed and read as texts in a variety of ways. In a sport management context, Gilbert & Schantz (2008) utilised visual sociology methods for understanding the visual culture of the Olympic Games host city of Beijing. He examined a range of visual sub-cultures including architecture, space and place, landscape, art, ceremonies, cultural displays as well as people's lives and fashion. Gilbert suggests that the possibility of conceiving the visual culture of Olympic host cities as a holistic entity raises the problem of devising broader more encompassing visual-centric methodologies for Tokyo 2020 and beyond.

3. *Communication with images and media other than words.* A third approach of visual sociology is both the use of visual media to communicate sociological understandings to professional and public audiences, and also the use of visual media within sociological research itself. In a sport management context researchers could, for example, use a combination of narrative and photographs to seek a more effective way of understanding just how facility managers see and experience their environment on game day. The importance of subjecting routine understandings and practices to detailed analysis in this way allows the lives of these "social actors" to be analysed in a unique way and provide new understanding of their "lived experiences".

PARTICIPANT AUTHORED AUDIOVISUAL STORIES AND SPORT MANAGEMENT RESEARCH

What are participant authored audio–visual stories?

PAAS are controversial new approach that we believe has possibilities in sport management research particularly in the area of consumer behaviour and insider knowledge. PAAS deals with qualitative research methodology based on sound and image data, in particular with audio–visual stories authored by the research participants. As a research method, PAAS promises a sound platform from which to explore social phenomena, especially when what is at stake is an understanding of the relationship between the agency of subjects and their sociocultural contexts.

According to Harrison (2002), visual research is still viewed as a marginal practice. Despite its marginality, Ramella and Olmos (2005) argue that research methodologies based on sound and image data open up a vast field of opportunities, one that is rapidly capitalising on many of the twists and turns of societal change: from the fast development of audio–visual technologies, and the improvements in digital communications, to the growing case made in the social sciences against the hegemony of the written text and the incorporation of audio–visual languages into our everyday lives (p. 3).

Ramella and Olmos (2005) describe the process in the following way: research participants create their own stories around a more or less determined problem. For this purpose, they utilise audio-visual media, that is, video cameras or photo-cameras or a radio, just to cite some. Further, they draw on a variety of genre to organise their stories, for example, an autobiography, a documentary or a drama. According to the genre selected, stories may include personal testimonies, or fictional enactment of life episodes; they may also include stories by other people (e.g. street interviews by research participants to lay people). Here the list can be limitless. Also, being in possession of the audio–visual media provide participants ample latitude to situate themselves, and importantly, their stories. Situating a story should not be restricted to a physical location; it also means situating it socially (who else is there?), and culturally (what is in it?). PAAS has been successfully utilised in many projects and offers in particular the potential for research participants to own the story, to express it and articulate it in close relation to their everyday life social and cultural context (Ramella & Olmos, 2005).

Case study – *Disability study/Audio–visual study*

Title: An Embodied Approach to Disability Sport: The Lived Experience of Visually Impaired Cricket Players
Author: Powis, B. J., *University of Brighton* (2017)
Reference: Powis, B. J. (2017). *An embodied approach to disability sport: The lived experience of visually impaired cricket players*, Doctoral dissertation, University of Brighton.

This work investigated the England Visually Impaired Cricket Team, whose squad members comprised sixteen men aged 18–54 and their lived experiences' of playing visually impaired cricket. Through an embodied theoretical approach that accounted for the corporeal experience of impairment alongside the role of social institutions and discourse in the high-performance culture of modern disability sport, the author aimed to establish the significant aspects of this previously unexamined research "site", both on and off the pitch. This study consisted of ten months of ethnographic fieldwork using participant observation and semi-structured interviews shaped by a new method of recording and eliciting data. To capture the participants' sensorial experiences of playing visually impaired cricket, "soundscape elicitation", the process of composing auditory "tracks" of the players' participation and then using these recordings during semi-structured interviews to prompt sensorial discussions,

was utilised. This method was central to the production of previously unexamined knowledge and was argued to be a significant methodological advancement in the wider field of sensory studies. The findings presented a number of original contributions to knowledge regarding "sporting bodies", the sensorial experiences of sport, and the construction of identity through disability sport. The participants' embodied experiences of playing visually impaired cricket reveal an alternative way of "being" in sport and physical activity. However, it is the inescapable ocular centric value of "sight" that inhibits the resistive potential of the game. Instead of the presumed empowering experience, elite visually impaired cricket is disempowering for many participants due to the irreversible relationship of blind cricket institutions with mainstream cricketing bodies. Furthermore, a "hierarchy of sight" based upon the official sight classification process emerged that highly values those players with the highest sight classifications and marginalises the blind players. All of these factors inform visually impaired cricket players' construction of their own identities. Although many players viewed visually impaired cricket as a way of demonstrating their "normality", it actually accentuated the impairment that they are attempting to dissociate from and is one of the few social situations where they are "outed" as disabled or blind.

HISTORICAL RESEARCH

Historical research is referred to as historiography, that is, investigation of elements from history (Berg, 2012). Kerlinger (1972) defines historical research as "Critical investigation of events, development, and experiences of the past, careful consideration of past testimonies from the perspective of information sources validity and subsequent interpretation of the concerned testimonies" (p. 673). Historical research seeks not only to discover the events of the past but also to relate these past happenings to the present and to the future.

Historical research is an important but relatively under-developed approach to studying sport management. Historical research in sport management often employs mixed methods, although frequently qualitative methods are prominent. We focus here on qualitative historical research as a discrete or complementary approach. History is a discipline within the humanities field, although many historians consider themselves social scientists because they are interested in social lives within historical settings. In employing research techniques from history, historians of sport management often carry out their research in conjunction with a case study approach, collecting data about either an autonomous case or an example of a larger phenomenon. In some instances, the historical case becomes an intricate part of a larger comparative project or is a useful illustration in the development of theory (Moses & Knutsen, 2007).

There are two strands of historical research. The first strand seeks to *imaginatively reconstruct* the role of sport and the lives of people in other times and contexts. The focus of the study is on sport activities, issues, causes, and the people involved (such as communicators, organisations, and stakeholders). The second strand *involves producing a history of thought or ideas*. Here the researcher is interested in tracing and interpreting ideas, concepts, theories, or schools of thought about historical phenomena. There are a wide variety of contexts in which sport management histories can be explored. These are national, regional, cultural, governmental, institutional, organisational, and professional. The historical role of sport management might be studied in relation to broad political, economic, social, diplomatic, and international contexts. Within each of these settings, historical research has the potential to offer a range of perspectives, including those of the individual (through autobiography or biography), or from the perspectives of an organisation, industry, institution or society. For example, the life history of an individual (such as an influential sport manager) cannot be told without constant reference to social or organisational historical change. Therefore, historical research into the work life of an individual practitioner involved in sport could provide a useful window through which to widen understanding about how transformation occurs in a sport organisation. A major issue is that many sport management histories tend to present a gender bias towards men, with women's influential role in sport overlooked. There is a similar issue with respect to culture, race, and class.

Role of researcher

The stance of the researcher in the research process is a core aspect of historical research. As in other forms of qualitative interpretive research, the researcher is not "an impartial, value-free entity, unproblematically engaging in the research process to produce objective accounts of a reified truth" (Musson, 2004, p. 35), but instead they bring implicit and explicit theories to the research situation. These might involve "different philosophies of history, different social, political, and moral philosophies, and even different assumptions about epistemology and ontology" (Pearson, 2009, p. 93). Therefore, the position of the researcher is central to how historical research is conducted, interpret and recorded. An important part of this process is that the researcher should explain clearly the basic assumptions and theoretical framework on which the research is based. Such reflexivity and transparency not only aid the methodological rigour of research, but also helps you to better understand how the researchers thinking has informed the presentation of the historical account (that is, how the researcher's theoretical stance and views concerning have influenced your choices of data, methods and interpretation). L'Etang (2008) points to the necessity of the researcher being philosophically reflective about their own worldview, not only in relation to time and change, but also from a theoretical position because "historical explanations are not neutral and include ideological or moral components" (p. 322). If the lens through which the researcher views the world is feminist then what counts as relevant and how the researcher collects and uses data to support a particular argument will be different than for another researcher with a postmodern or traditional lens. Consequently, the historical accounts will differ.

Much historical writing is descriptive, although explanation is also involved. Historical narratives usually give emphasis to characters, settings and events, which include actions taken by the characters as well as happenings, that is, how settings impinge upon characters (Witkowski & Jones, 2006). There is some debate over the contribution of historical research to developing or appraising theory. Some argue that histories are an end in themselves because they illustrate events that have historical significance which are pertinent to their own time and place and therefore cannot be generalised. However, Scott, Chambers, and Sredl (2006) drew attention to the contentions of those who advocate the value of historical research as a cumulative theory-building strategy, especially in connection with ethnography and other approaches and methods. They provide a number of examples, including the work of Holt (2004), who undertook "painstaking historical research" (p. 227) across several important historical counterexamples. His findings led him to debunk and destroy the credibility of conventional theories of branding.

Limitations of historical research

A major problem evident in some theories and concepts derived from research into an imagined past is the "error of presentism" (Scott et al., 2006). This is where the assumptions and agendas of the present are projected onto the people and events of the past. Data sources should not be taken at face value. Often evidence is incomplete, contradictory or even faked. Oral histories may suffer from selective retention and perceptions. Documents may have been written to embellish the image and reputation of the writer. The quality of historical research, then, is based on what data are available and for this reason it is important to seek multiple sources of evidence. Much early evidence either has been deleted from archives or was simply never collected in the first place. Other available materials may have suffered from impression management whereby accounts seen as undesirable have been erased or – in the case of annual reports or the minutes of organisational meetings – invisible editors and concealed contributors have been influential in reshaping texts or images for purposes of self-presentation. This can lead, for example, to the obscuring of organisational politics or the real role that communications practitioners may have had, or the fact that sport management decisions and recommendations may have been ignored or over-ruled. Many official documents were originally created by elite males and therefore under-represent the experiences of stakeholders and publics characterised as lower classes, minorities, and women.

DIASPORA STUDIES AND SPORT MANAGEMENT RESEARCH

Diaspora studies is an academic field that was established in the late 20th century to study dispersed ethnic populations. These groups are referred to as diaspora peoples. The term diaspora implies forced resettlement, due to expulsion, slavery, racism, or war, especially national conflict. The recent proliferation of the discourse of diaspora but the relative lack of attempts to theorise the term might be more or less attributed to the very nature of its internal dynamics and multiplicity. Each ethnic group has a different narrative and trajectory of migration, and this complexity and multiplicity of experiences of dislocation cannot be unproblematically subsumed under the rubric of diasporas. Diasporas are not static or monolithic, but dynamic, changing, and ongoing constructions. Brubaker (2005) invites us to think of diaspora not as a bounded entity, but rather as an idiom, stance and claim. As a category of practice, diaspora is "used to make claims, to articulate projects, to formulate expectations, to mobilise energies, to appeal to loyalties. ... It does not so much describe the world as seek to remake it" (Brubaker 2005, p. 12). In a similar vein, Baumann (1999) posits that diasporic identities can be understood as acts of identification that are "frozen in time ... not an identity given by nature, but an identification created through social action" (p. 21).

A diaspora approach draws analytical attention to socio-cultural formations and performances that generate a collective consciousness which binds dispersed people to a homeland and to each other (Butler 2001). In Clifford's (1997) classic definition, diasporas are composed of "displaced peoples who feel (maintain, revive, invent) a connection with a prior home" (p. 255). Diasporas are thus viewed as people who are physically dispersed across the globe, yet are linked by "important allegiances and practical connections' to a common homeland" (p. 307). As Clifford's reference to the active verbs "maintain, revive, invent" suggests, diaspora formation involves agency and action in terms of, inter alia, the provision of transnational care and support, the maintenance of culture and language (Ben-Moshe, Pyke, & Kirpitchenko, 2016), and the production of a shared sense of identity through transnational connections to other places (Joseph, 2014; Vertovec, 2001). Joseph (2011) shows how sports spaces can act as sites for the maintenance of both a homeland (e.g. nation of origin) and a homespace (e.g. diasporic belonging) that unites dispersed people. Areas of interest in diaspora studies for sport management researchers could include sport in conflict zones such as Iraq and Afghanistan, and sport and refugees.

GLOBALISATION AND SPORT MANAGEMENT RESEARCH

What is globalisation?

Globalisation research can be classified in a number of ways. Specifically, it can be characterised based on its focus on specific phenomena of globalisation, i.e. economic, political or social. It is, however, important to note that in each of these categories, there are different perspectives, such as neoliberalism, Marxism, neo-Marxism, etc. Sklair (2002) identified that research on globalisation can be categorised into four broad approaches: (1) the global polity and society; (2) the world systems; (3) the global capitalism; and (4) the global cultural approaches.

The global polity and society approach maintain that global polity and society can be achieved only in the modern age with the advancement of science, technology, and industry. This body of literature is filled with discussions of the decreasing power and significance of the nation-state and the increasing significance, or actually power of, super-national and global institutions and systems of belief and value (Sklair, 2002). Global sport federations and governing bodies, such as World Rugby, have existed for over a hundred years, but have increased their power and influence over national governing bodies as the desire for global competitions (e.g. Rugby World Cups) has skyrocketed. The most desirable future, according to those theorists, is the organisation of global governance through some global civil society, while globalisation is the most potent and necessary drive for that future. Anthony Giddens (1990) is one of the principal voices of such arguments. Giddens characterises globalisation in terms of four dimensions: the nation–state system, the world military order, the international division of labour and the world capitalist economy. He believes globalisation is a consequence of modernity itself because "modernity is inherently globalising" (p. 63). The philosophical assumption of this approach is essentially neoliberalism.

The next approach to globalisation study is the world-systems perspective (Sklair, 2002). This approach is based on the distinction between core, semi-peripheral and peripheral countries in terms of their positions in the international division of labour demanded by the capitalist world-system. Based on the work of Immanuel Wallerstein (1974), social scientific research on world-systems has been developed since the 1970s. Unlike other approaches in which writers are grouped based on the tenets of their work, the world-systems school is a highly institutionalised academic enterprise. This school of thought has been the most systematic available for the analysis of the global system for more than 20 years. The world-system theory closely resembles dependency theory.

An approach that is more sophisticated than the world-system approach is the global capitalism approach (Sklair, 2002). For these theorists, the main driving force of globalisation is the structure of the ever-more globalising capitalism (e.g. Robinson, 1996; Ross & Trachte, 1990; Sklair, 2002). In contrast to the world-system approach that focuses on nation-state centred economics, the global capitalism approach strives toward "a concept of the global that involves more than the relations between nation-states and explanation of national economics competing against each other" (Sklair, 2002, p. 46). Similarly, many national governing bodies cannot thrive on their own, and rely on the economic value of international competition.

The final approach to globalisation research is the global culture approach (Sklair, 2002). Placing culture at the centre is inspired by Marshall McLuhan's (1964) notion of "the global village", the very rapid growth of the mass media in scale and scope that has taken place over the last few decades. As sociologist John Tomlinson (1999) puts it, "Globalization lies at the heart of modern culture; cultural practices lie at the heart of globalisation" (p. 1). Huntington (1993, 1996) predicts that the source of future international conflicts lies in the cultural, rather than the political and ideological. Appadurai (1996) developed a fivefold conceptual framework of empirical research on global cultural flows. His categories include: (1) ethnoscapes (flows of people); (2) mediascapes (flows of images and information); (3) technoscapes (development and flows of technology); (4) finanscapes (flows of global capital); and (5) ideoscapes (flows of ideologies and movements). The most widespread form of research within sport and cultural studies as well as sociology is identified as the global culture approach. Edwards and Skinner (2006) suggested that this is a self-limiting form of research inquiry and explored the conceptions of a new world order and implications for sport management in the book entitled Sport Empire. In this work, the explore some of the concepts in this new and controversial form of globalisation research.

Globalisation: decentred?

Michael Hardt and Antonio Negri (Hardt & Negri, 2000), in their influential work, Empire, argue that we experience the irresistible and irreversible globalisation of economic and cultural exchanges. These researchers suggest that with the development of a global market and global circuits of production, we also see the materialisation of a global order or a new form of sovereignty. Together with the processes of globalisation, sovereignty of nation-states has weakened. Now, the money, technology, people, and goods move easily across national borders and the nation–state has less power to regulate these flows. It is more and more common for athletes to seek work in overseas professional systems, and harder for domestic sport organisations to retain their services.

The governing terms of Hardt and Negri's (2000) discussion are "Empire" and "Multitude". It is suggested that along with the global market and global circuits of production a new global order has emerged, a new form of sovereignty based on a new logic and structure of rule. Empire is the political subject that effectively regulates these global exchanges, the sovereign power that governs the world. Empire does not refer to imperialism; it has no territorial centre of power and does not depend on fixed boundaries. The divisions among three Worlds (First, Second, and Third) have been unclear. It is a decentred and deterritorialising apparatus of rule that progressively incorporates the entire global realm with its open, expanding frontiers. Empire manages hybrid identities, flexible hierarchies, and plural exchanges through modulating networks of command (Hardt & Negri, 2000, p. xii). Multitude is opposed to Empire. Multitude is all those who labour and produce under capital, it is the "class of productive singularities, the class of the operators of immaterial labour" (Hardt & Negri, 2000). The Multitude however has power that is driven by its desire for liberation from Empire's global structures and networks.

Globalisation research approach

Essentially, qualitative globalisation research may be characterised by three commitments. First, researchers employing globalisation approaches seek to understand the world through interacting with, empathising with and interpreting the actions and perceptions of its actors. Consequently, globalisation research methods are used to explore the meanings of people's worlds – the myriad personal impacts of impersonal social structures, and the nature and causes of individual behaviour. Second, globalisation qualitative research involves the collection of data in natural settings, rather than in artificial contexts. Third, it tends to explore and generate theory rather than test it. Qualitative globalisation methods work inductively, i.e. building up theory from observations; rather than deductively, i.e. testing theories by trying to refute their propositions.

Data generated by qualitative globalisation research can provide powerful and critical insights into particular questions. It is, however, important to note that it depends on the theoretical or explanatory frames and the quality of interpretation. They can be used effectively with people or places we think are familiar to us, as well as in situations somewhat removed, geographically and otherwise, from our own. Given the interpenetrating contexts generated by globalising phenomena, together with associated mobile, trans-local, and diasporic communities, much research conducted using qualitative approaches includes the ways in which communities are both tied into and construct trans-local/ transnational networks and discourses, such that while people might be organising and acting at local spatial scales they are consistently framing their identities with reference to larger scale and global contexts.

Globalisation and sport management

The problematic that globalisation theorists seek to explain, while dynamic and open-ended, not invariant, may be gleaned from an emerging series of core linked propositions. Six propositions are highlighted as they relate to sport management research:

1. Many contemporary issues in sport management cannot be explained as local interactions and must be construed as global issues. Although this claim is not unique to globalisation studies, at issue is a series of sport problems e.g. doping in sport, the rise of organised crime in sport, global warming threats to sport, and the spread of infectious diseases – which are beyond the regulatory framework of the national sporting organisation.

2. Globalisation constitutes a structural transformation in world order. As such, sport does not exist in a vacuum separate from the social, economic and environmental context. Questions arise as to how national and international sport organisations respond to this new world order.

3. As a transformation, globalisation involves a series of continuities and discontinuities with the past. In other words, there is no escaping historiography. Modern conceptions of sport organisation have their foundation in the past.

4. The advent of globalisation is fluid. This implies that global sport is an actor in its own right. Transnational sport organisations, national sporting bodies, and local sport organisations all influence and are influenced by local and global issues. In opposition to most globalisation researchers, Hardt and Negri (2000) suggest we need to: "think globally and act globally".

5. Given shifting parameters, sport needs to adjust to evolving global structures. International sport organisations, however, are in varied positions vis-à-vis globalising structures, and need to reinvent themselves differently according to changing global circumstances.

6. Underpinning such differences is a set of new, or deeper, tensions in world sport. For example, the global trend to postmodern individualistic leisure pursuits poses a challenge for traditional sport organisations such as the World Athletics and the International Olympic Committee. The next generations of sport consumers are likely to challenge the hegemony of some Olympic sports with little consumer appeal. The challenge is how to respond to these global changes.

Globalisation and qualitative research method

There has been no change in research methods under contemporary globalisation processes. Sullivan and Brockington (2004) note that orientations to research and to the interpretation of "findings" – particularly in relation to certainty, to the implications of notions of difference and "the Other", and to aspirations of objectivity – have been much affected by the intertwined theoretical fields of post-structuralism, postcolonialism, and feminism. They add that by high-lighting the infusion of power in research praxis the globalisation researcher acknowledges the always politically constitutive role(s) of academic engagement. As a developing sport management research paradigm, globalisation is more a potential than a refined framework, kit of tools and methods, and mode of resolving questions. The efforts to theorise sport globalisation have produced an intellectual move rather than a methodological movement to investigate global sport. Globalisation research does not have a clearly defined methodology. There is no one correct approach. Qualitative globalisation research utilises many of the approaches mentioned previously in this book.

Research brief – *Globalisation*

Title: A comparative analysis of the policy process of elite sport development in China and the UK (in relation to three Olympic sports of artistic gymnastics, swimming and cycling)
Author: Zheng, J., Loughborough University (2015)
Reference: Zheng, J. (2015). A comparative analysis of the policy process of elite sport development in China and the UK (in relation to three Olympic sports of artistic gymnastics, swimming and cycling). *Submitted in partial fulfilment of the requirements for the award of the degree of PhD of Loughborough University.* This work aimed to analyse the policy making and policy implementation processes of elite sport in China and the UK, covering the period 1992–2012. Three sports were selected for detailed cases studies: artistic gymnastics, swimming, and cycling. They represented a wide range of sports in two countries, based on their varying competiveness, weights, and traditions. Key areas including organisational structure, financial support, talent identification, athlete development, coaching, training, competition opportunities, scientific research, and others (including international influence and other sport- and country-specific areas) were identified to lead the discussion. The aim was to present key characteristics of the development of each sport in China and the UK respectively, as well as to form a basis for the discussion of policy making, policy implementation, and policy changes.

REVIEW AND RESEARCH QUESTIONS

Each of the new directions discussed in this chapter embrace a unique methodological approach that has significant relevance to sport management research. With a general understanding of these emerging issues, attempt to answer the following questions:

1. Is there any place within sport management research for these approaches to sport management research? Justify your answer.

2. Discuss the positive and negative features of each approach.

3. Provide examples of how two of these approaches could be applied to sport management research.

REFERENCES

Alcadipani, R., & Hassard, J. (2010). Actor-network theory, organizations and critique: Towards a politics of organizing. *Organization, 17*(4), 419–435.

Anderson, J. M. (2000). Gender, race, poverty, health and discourses of health reform in the context of globalization: A postcolonial feminist perspective in policy research. *Nursing Inquiry, 7,* 220–229.

Appadurai, A. (1996). *Modernity at large: Cultural dimensions of globalization.* Minneapolis, ME: University of Minnesota Press.

Arnaboldi, M., & Spiller, N. (2011). Actor-network theory and stakeholder collaboration: The case of cultural districts. *Tourism Management, 32*(3), 641–654.

Barnes, J. (1954). Class and committees in a Norwegian Island parish. *Human Relations, 7,* 39–58.

Baumann, G. (1999). *The multicultural riddle: Rethinking national, ethnic and religious identities.* London: Routledge.

Ben-Moshe, D., Pyke, J., & Kirpitchenko., L. (2016). The Vietnamese diaspora in Australia: Identity and transnational behaviour. *Diaspora Studies, 9*(2), 112–127.

Berg, B. L. (2012). *Qualitative research methods for the social science.* Long Beach: Allyn & Bacon.

Brito, C., & Correia, R. F. (2004). A model for understanding the dynamics of territorial networks: the case of tourism in the Douro Valley [online]. IMP- Bocconi University. Available at: http://hdl.handle.net/10198/5834 (Accessed June 16, 2020).

Brubaker, R. (2005). The 'diaspora' diaspora. *Ethnic and Racial Studies, 28,* 1–19.

Burgess, J., Clark, J., & Harrison, C. (2000). Knowledges in action: An actor network Analysis of a wetland agri-environment scheme. *Ecological Economics, 35,* 119–132.

Butler, K. D. (2001). Defining diaspora, refining a discourse. *Diaspora, 10,* 189–219.

Callon, M. (1986). Some elements of a sociology of translation – domestication of the scallops and the fishermen of St-brieuc Bay. In J. Law (Ed.), *Power, action and belief: A new sociology of knowledge?,* pp. 196–223. London: Routledge.

Cannella, G. S., & Bailey, C. (1999). Postmodern research in early childhood education. In S. Reifel (Ed.), *Advances in early education and day care* (vol. 10), pp. 3–39. Greenwich, CN: Jai Press.

Clifford, J. (1997). *Routes: Travel and translation in the late twentieth century.* Cambridge, MA: Harvard University Press.

Cohen, E., & Cohen, S. A. (2012). Authentication: Hot and cool. *Annals of Tourism Research, 39*(3), 1295–1314.

Cordella, A., & Shaikh, M. (2003) Actor Network Theory and After: What's New For IS Research? Available at: http://personal.lse.ac.uk/shaikh/ANT%20ECIS%20FINAL%20VERSION%2031%20March.pdf (Accessed June 22, 2020).

Corrigan, L. T., & Mills., A. J. (2012). Men on board: Actor-network theory, feminism and gendering the past. *Management & Organizational History, 7*(3), 251–265.

Cressman, D. (2009). A Brief Overview of Actor-Network Theory: Punctualization, Heterogeneous Engineering & Translation. Centre for Policy Research on Science and Technology. Avaiable at: http://summit.sfu.ca/item/13593 (Accessed June 12, 2020)

Cresswell, K. M., Worth, A., & Sheikh, A. (2010). Actor-network theory and its role in understanding the implementation of information technology developments in healthcare. *BMC Medical Informatics and Decision Making, 10*(67), 2–11.

Dolwick, J. (2009). The social and beyond: Introducing actor-network theory. *Journal of Maritime Archaeology, 4*, 21–49.

Doolin, B., & Lowe, A. (2002). To reveal is to critique: actor–network theory and critical information systems research. *Journal of Information Technology, 17*, 69–78.

Edwards, A., & Skinner, J. (2006). *Sport empire*. Oxford: Meyer & Meyer Sports.

Edwards, A., & Skinner, J. (2009). *Qualitative research in sport management*. Oxford: Elsevier.

Elgali, Z., & Kalman, Y. M. (2010). Using actor network theory to analyse the construction of the failure concept in a K-12 ICT integration program. *Proceedings of the Chain Conference in Instructional Technologies Research 2010: Learning in the Technologies Era.* Raanana, Israel: The Open University of Israel.

Foucault, M. (1980). *Power/Knowledge*. Hemel Hempstead, Herts: Harvester Wheatsheaf.

Frankenberg, R. (1993). *White women, race matters: The social construction of whiteness*. Minnesota: University of Minnesota Press.

Giddens, A. (1990). *The consequences of modernity*. Cambridge: Polity Press.

Gilbert, K., & Schantz, O. J. (2008). *The paralympic games: Empowerment or Side Show?* Maidenhead: Meyer & Meyer.

Giroux, H. (2002). Neoliberalism, corporate culture, and the promise of higher education: The university as a democratic public sphere. *Harvard Educational Review, 72*(4), 425–463.

Greenhalgh, T., & Stones, R. (2010). Theorising big IT programmes in healthcare: Strong structuration theory meets actor–network theory. *Social Science & Medicine, 70*, 1285–1294.

Hall, S. (1997). *Representation: Cultural representation and signifying practices*. London: University of Minnesota Press.

Hardt, M., & Negri, A. (2000). *Empire*. Cambridge, MA: Harvard University Press.

Harrison, B. (2002). Seeing health and illness worlds using visual methods in A sociology of health and illness: A methodological review. *Sociology of Health and Illness, 24*(6), 856–872.

Holt, D. B. (2004). *How brands become icons: The principles of cultural branding*. Boston: Harvard Business School Press.

Huntington, S. P. (1993). The clash of civilizations. *Foreign Affairs, 72*(3), 22–49.

Huntington, S. P. (1996). *The clash of civilizations and the remaking of world order*. New York: Simon & Schuster.

Huxford, K. M. L. (2010). *Tracing Tourism Translation: Opening the Black Box of Development Assistance in Community-based Tourism in Viet Nam*. Unpublished MSc Dissertation, Geography, University of Canterbury.

Ibrahim, A. B. (2009). *Creating Collaborative Platform for Knowledge Transfer Based on Actor-network Theory.* Unpublished MSc Thesis, IT, University of Malaysia, Malaysia.

Jóhannesson, G. T. (2005). Tourism translations: Actor-network theory and tourism research. *Tourist Studies, 5*(2), 133–150.

Joseph, J. (2011). A diaspora approach to sport tourism. *Journal of Sport and Social Issues, 35*(2), 146–167.

Joseph, J. (2014). Culture, community, consciousness: The Caribbean sporting diaspora. *International Review for the Sociology of Sport, 49*(6), 669–687.

Kerlinger, F. N. (1972). *Základy výzkumu chování. Pedagogický a psychologický výzkum. (Foundations of behavioural research. Pedagogical and psychological research.* Praha: Academia.

L'Etang, J. (2008). Writing PR history: Issues, methods and politics. *Journal of Communication Management, 12*(4), 319–335.

Lipsitz, G. (2000). The White 2K problem. *Cultural Values, 4*(4), 518–524.

MacLean, C., & Hassard, J. (2004). Symmetrical absence/symmetrical absurdity: Critical notes on the production of actor-network accounts. *Journal of Management Studies, 41*(3), 493–519.

McConaghy, C. (2000). *Rethinking indigenous education: Culturalism, colonialism and the politics of knowing.* Flaxton: Post Pressed.

McLuhan, M. (1964) *Understanding media: The extensions of man.* New York: McGraw-Hill.

Moses, J. W., & Knutsen, T. L. (2007). *Ways of knowing: Competing methodologies in social and political research.* Basingstoke: Palgrave Macmillan.

Musson, G. (2004). Life histories. In C. Cassell, & G. Symon (Eds.), *Essential Guide to Qualitative Methods in Organizational Research*, pp. 34–44. London: Sage Publications.

Norbert, G., & Schermer, M. (2003). *The use of actor network theory to analyze the impact of organic marketing initiatives on regional development.* University of Innsbruck: Centre for Mountain Agriculture.

Paget, E., Dimanche, F. & Mounet, J. (2010). A tourism innovation case: An actor-network approach. *Annals of Tourism Research: A Social Sciences Journal, 37*(3), 828–847.

Pearson, R. (2009). Perspectives on public relations history. In R. L. Health, E. L. Toth, & D. Waymer (Eds.), *Rhetorical and critical approaches to public relations II*, pp. 92–109. Routledge: London.

Quatman, C. (2006). *The Social Construction of Knowledge in the Field of Sport Management: A Social Network Perspective.* Unpublished doctoral dissertation, The Ohio State University, Columbus.

Quayson, A. (2000). *Postcolonialism: Theory, practice or process?* Cambridge: Polity Press.

Ramella, M., & Olmos, G. (2005). *Participant authored audio-visual Stories (PAAS). Giving the camera away or giving the camera a way?* Papers in social Research Methods: Qualitative Series no. 10, June (London School of Economics and Political Science Methodology Institute).

Ren, C. (2011). Non-human agency, radical ontology and tourism realities. *Annals of Tourism Research, 38*(3), 858–881.

Rhodes, J. (2009). Using actor-network theory to trace an ICT (telecenter) implementation trajectory in an African Women's micro-Enterprise development organization. *Information Technologies & International Development, 5*(3), 1–20.

Robinson, W. (1996). *Promoting polyarchy. Cambridge*: Cambridge University Press.

Rodger, K. J. (2007). *Wildlife Tourism and Natural Science: Bringing them Together.* Unpublished doctoral dissertation, Murdoch University, Perth, Western Australia.

Roediger, D. (1991). *The wages of Whiteness: Race and the making of the American working class.* London: Verso.

Ross, R. J. S., & Trachte, K. C. (1990). *Global capitalism: The new leviathan.* Albany, NY: SUNY Press.

Ruming, K., (2008). *Negotiating development control: using actor-network theory to explore the creation of residential building policy, City Futures Research Centre,* University of New South Wales, Sydney, Australia

Said, E. (2000). *Reflections on exile and other essays.* Cambridge, MA: Harvard University Press.

San Juan, E. (1998). *Beyond postcolonial theory.* London: Macmillan.

Scott, L. M., Chambers, J., & Sredl, K. (2006). The monticello correction: Consumption in history. In R. W. Belk (Ed.), *Handbook of qualitative research methods in marketing,* pp. 219–229. UK, Cheltenham: Edward Elgar.

Sklair, L. (2002). *Globalization: Capitalism and its alternatives.* Oxford: Oxford University Press.

Spivak, G. C. (1988). Can the subaltern speak? In C. Nelson, & L. Grossberg (Eds.), *Marxism and the Interpretation of Culture,* pp. 24–28. London: Macmillan.

Sullivan, S., & Brockington, D. (2004). *Qualitative methods in globalisation studies: or, saying something about the world without counting or inventing it.* CSGR Working Paper, 139/04.

Tatnall, A., & Burgess, S. (2002), *Using Actor-Network Theory to Research the Implementation of a B-B Portal for Regional SMEs in Melbourne, Australia,* 15th Bled Electronic Commerce Conference, eReality: Constructing the eEconomy, June 17–19, Bled, Slovenia.

Tatnall, A., & Davey, B. (2005). An actor network approach to informing clients through portals. *The Journal of Issues in Informing Science and Information Technology, 2,* 771–780.

Tatnall, A., & Gilding, A. (1999). *Actor-network theory and information systems research.* Paper presented at the 10th Australasian Conference on Information Systems (ACIS), University of Wellington, Wellington.

Tatnall, A., & Lepa, J. (2003). The internet, E-commerce, and older people: An actor network approach to researching reasons for adoption and use. *Logistics Information Management, 16*(1), 56–63.

Timur, S., & Getz, D. (2008). A network perspective on managing stakeholders for sustainable urban tourism. *International Journal of Contemporary Hospitality Management, 20*(4), 445–461.

Tomlinson, J. (1999). *Globalization and culture.* Chicago, IL: University of Chicago Press.

Tuhiwai Smith, L. (1999). *Decolonizing methodologies.* London: Zed Books.

Van der Duim, R. (2005). *Tourismscapes. An Actor–Network Perspective on Sustainable Tourism Development.* Unpublished PhD Dissertation, Wageningen University, Wageningen.

Van der Duim, R. (2007). Tourismscapes. An actor-network perspective. *Annals of Tourism Research, 34*(4), 961–976.

Vertovec, S. (2001). Transnationalism and identity. *Journal of Ethnic and Migration Studies, 27*(4), 573–582.

Viruru, R., & Cannella, G. S. (2001). Postcolonial ethnography, young children and voice. In S. Grieshaber, & G. S. Cannella (Eds.), *Embracing identities and early childhood education,* pp. 158–172. New York: Teachers College Press.

Wallerstein, I. (1974). *The modern world-system, I: Capitalist agriculture and the origins of the European world-economy in the sixteenth century.* London: Academic Press.

Williams-Jones, B., & Graham, J. E. (2003). Actor-network theory: A tool to support ethical analysis of commercial genetic testing. *New Genetics and Society, 22*(3), 271–296.

Witkowski, T. H., & Jones, D. G. B. (2006). Qualitative historical research in marketing. In R. W. Belk (Ed.), *Handbook of qualitative research methods in marketing,* pp. 70–82. Cheltenham: Edward Elgar.

PART 6

Digital tools for qualitative research

CHAPTER 21

Social media research methods in sport management

<table>
<tr><td>

KEY THEMES

- The Social Media Research Opportunity.
- Understanding Social Media as a Research Site.
- Defining Qualitative Social Media Research.

</td><td>

- Special Aspects of Social Media Data Methods.
- Challenges and Opportunities with Qualitative Social Media Methods.
- Issues in Qualitative Social Media Research Validity and Reliability.

</td></tr>
</table>

CHAPTER OVERVIEW

Sport, and its myriad of associated products and services, incorporate physical and social experiences at its core. In fact, most sport experiences invoke sufficient personal investment that they become what Scott and Harmon (2016, p. 492) described as "multiphasic experiences"; that is, experiences that transgress the immediate temporal and social boundaries of the actual consumption. Sport, of course, exemplifies the multiphasic experience as it generates an endless supply of discussion, debate, controversy, reflection, analysis, and conjecture both before and well after its performance. No other product or service can rival sport's command of the social tongue, so it is no surprise that its presence in social media (SM) is commensurately vast. The result of sport's comprehensive diffusion into SM content is that it has become almost incomprehensibly complex and difficult to follow. Not only is the commentary on and around sport prolific, it is also now swiftly changeable, highly personalised, and to a growing extent, deeply engrained in the social lives of fans and the organisational lives of brands. This chapter explores the opportunities and barriers associated with SM research, paying particular attention to the features that differentiate it from traditional qualitative methods.

THE SOCIAL MEDIA RESEARCH OPPORTUNITY

Undeniably, much of the excitement for sport researchers about the potential within SM comes as a consequence of its sheer volume and newfound cultural status. Scholars can extract literally billions of lines of text for analysis from platform giants like Facebook and Twitter, as well as from seemingly countless, ever expanding platforms celebrating niche interests and audiences. For the qualitative researcher, however, the greatest excitement has less to do with the volume of content and more to do with its context. In research nomenclature, SM can be described as "natural" (Bail, 2017); it records not only the naturally occurring, time-relevant, and event-specific commentaries by individual sport commentators, but also their interactions with other fans and with sport brands. These data provide a rich and textured tapestry of authentic narratives, which are for the most part unavailable or at least difficult to access via conventional surveys, interviews, or observations. Some of the most powerful SM platforms include comparatively little text, instead allowing users to prioritise images and videos, neither of which lend themselves to quantitative analysis. In addition, SM data does not suffer from poor memory or from the unconscious filtering that accompanies the reflections of interview respondents long after the event under study occurred. Rather, SM captures opinions, emotions and thoughts at the very moment of impact. Moreover, by reviewing a longitudinal series of SM content, it is possible to create an understanding of how ideas and views have formed, transmitted, and fizzled.

UNDERSTANDING SOCIAL MEDIA AS A RESEARCH SITE

As a first step, we must accept that SM has introduced an unprecedented quantity of data. However, the qualitative researcher should not become distracted by sheer size of SM when their focus should remain on the potential quality that it also contains. Thus, the second step in successful qualitative SM research is to remember that the tools and techniques of conventional qualitative methods remain essential. In other words, we should still keep focussed on sound choices about pertinent research questions, selecting an appropriate population, honing in on a critical sample, collecting credible data, and conducting a robust analysis of its contents. It is true that the virtual world of SM is a separate sphere from the "real world", but like Quan-Haase and Sloan (2017a, 2017b), we argue that SM data need to be treated as part of a broader social fabric. SM does not operate in a vacuum removed from other social forces; it is an intractable part of the sporting experience and cannot be separated from a historical, social, political, and economic context. However, SM data does present some unique research challenges such as the increased likelihood of fabricated, deceitful or "fake" material. In addition, the technological presentation of SM data can displace the human element, leading researchers to forget that there are individuals behind every pattern and code. Conversely, it is just as easy to lose track of the importance of technical aspects of a platform that affect the way that contributors engage and respond (Weller, 2015). After all, one study could review a single user's lifetime of posts while another could skim across hundreds or more.

We take an inclusive view of SM and define it accordingly as cloud-based mobile platforms and applications dedicated to large-scale personal, user-generated content, and communication. Put simply, SM uses technology to allow users to communicate content to others. Like Carr and Hayes (2015), we also point out that SM is characterised by social identification where users deploy their content under personal profiles as well as within the hosted domains of other users or groups like sport organisations.

Some important characteristics of SM are worth highlighting as they have a material influence on the nature of the data that can be yielded. SM has at its core the generation and sharing of user content. This means that communication is conversational in nature involving not just the expression of views, but their exchange through interaction. It is also worth keeping in mind that although most users are individuals, groups and organisations can post content too, as representatives of larger entities. Kaplan and Haenlein (2010) provided a useful classification of SM platforms based on functionality.

- Blogs and microblog sites (e.g. Twitter, Tumblr)
- Social networking sites (e.g. Facebook, MySpace)
- Content communities (e.g. YouTube, Daily Motion, Pinterest, Instagram, Flickr, Vine)
- Collaborative projects (e.g. Wikipedia)
- Virtual game worlds (e.g. World of Warcraft)
- Virtual social worlds (e.g. Second Life, Farmville)

The above classifications and examples are undoubtedly a useful start, but the swiftly changing SM landscape means that hasty and constant re-definitions are critical in order to remain current.

Research brief

Title: Football Players' Popularity on Twitter Explained: Performance on the Pitch or Performance on Twitter?
Author: Vergeer, M., *Radboud University* & Mulder, L., *Radboud University* (2019)
Reference: Vergeer, M., & Mulder, L. (2019). Football Players' Popularity on Twitter Explained: Performance on the Pitch or Performance on Twitter? *International Journal of Sport Communication, 12*(3), 376–396.

This study tested football players' performance on the pitch against their performance on Twitter as explanations for Twitter popularity. Guided by network theory, social-identity theory, and basking in reflective glory and using data of all players of all teams in the Dutch premier league ("Eredivisie"), the multilevel models showed that players with a Twitter account were more popular when they scored more goals, were non-Dutch, were on loan at another club, and were networkers actively following others on Twitter.

DEFINING QUALITATIVE SOCIAL MEDIA RESEARCH

In this chapter, we are interested in any form of research derived from SM data sources and employing qualitative techniques. This includes when SM is used as a research site to gather data, and also when the nature, activity, and content of SM sites themselves are investigated. As researchers we can therefore study sport via SM, or study sport SM itself.

Although different to other forms of digital and online research, SM does not necessarily have well-defined boundaries as it can have different characteristics depending upon the user's engagement, the device employed, whether it is accessed through an online platform or a mobile application, and the degree to which it is embedded into other digital technologies. For example, a user's experience might be significantly different if he or she accessed a SM site though a desktop computer at work compared to through a wearable device during a sporting event (Creighton, Foster, Klingsmith, & Withey, 2013). Access affects interaction as well as the disposition of the content a user contributes. Researchers need to remain keenly aware of the unique effects that each platform and application have upon users, along with the implications of uploading content via different forms of access. Nevertheless, irrespective of the interface, what makes SM different from other forms of media – which are all social in one way or another – is that it focusses on connecting via mobile technology (Bruns, 2015).

According to Quan-Haase and Sloan (2017a, 2017b), SM possesses three distinguishing characteristics. First, it has the technological capability to support user-generated content. Depending upon the platform and its specialty, the content may be text, images, videos, or even geographical status, either directly created by the posting user, or previously posted content forwarded or re-posted by a user. Second, SM pivots around interactions where users connect with each other, or with a larger group or organisation. One unique dimension of many SM platforms is that they include a (usually binary) mechanism to express interest or support in a post by "liking" or "following". These forms of support can provide interesting evidence to a researcher seeking to understand the social dynamics of a group within a platform. Third, SM encourages users to coalesce into collaborative communities where informal, self-organised groups share, link, collaborate, and participate around a common interest. For the sport management researcher, collaborative communities delivery ready-made study populations as they often form around common team fandom, or specific sporting interests, and even much prized sporting products and brands, from the Facebook giants like Manchester United to the cult following for sport fashion brand Lululemon on Flickr.

To the above three characteristics, we add the following given their centrality to sport management and its research:

- SM users and content are ephemeral, coming and going without warning, shifting and transient in terms of frequency, interesting and vigour;

- Although SM content often clusters around shared interests, the opinions and backgrounds of users can be diverse;

- SM users have the freedom to create and curate their own content, which means that they delete, modify, update and discard, making the data fluid and changeable;

■ The inexhaustible supply of SM content tends to encourage outlier contributions with intentionally provocative posts, in turn distracting from the majority shared opinion.

Sport management researchers seeking to use qualitative techniques need to remain mindful of these additional elements and incorporate strategies for maintaining focus on their key questions (Andreotta et al., 2019), while avoiding disruptions from "trolls" and bored teenagers. It is also important to keep in mind that SM networks give individuals the chance to re-create and re-shape their own identities by manipulating the content they post (Reich, 2015). The result is the potential for SM content to manifest augmented representations of the individuals doing the posting, which might in turn be affected by the content from the posts of key influencers.

The distinctive characteristics of SM and the data it generates presents some specific challenges to sport management researchers. A helpful way to summarise the features was presented by Burnap et al. (2015) under six categories. We have adapted and added four additional categories to the first six from Burnap et al. (2015), as displayed in Table 21.1. It is worth noting that the 10 features also constitute opportunities because they reflect the unique features of the data that SM can create.

Table 21.1 Social media research features		
Category	**Description**	**Sport research context**
1. *Volume*	The immense quantity and detail of content	Focus on sampling parameters and ensuring that the selection focuses on the specific research questions under investigation
2. *Variety*	The multimodal and diverse nature of the data	Opportunity to focus on one mode, or compare and/or triangulate data from multiple modes; different sport contexts can be contrasted, while in-group perceptions can be examined from multiple modes of data
3. *Velocity*	The speed at which data content is generated as well as responded to	Focus on current issues and consumer/fan responses to specific events
4. *Veracity*	The accuracy, reliability, and authenticity of the data	Select sport communities cautiously, emphasising "official", endorsed, and moderated groups

(Continued)

Table 21.1	Social media research features	
Category	**Description**	**Sport research context**
5. *Virtue*	The ethics associated with access, analysis, and reproduction of personal content	Exercise the same ethical sensitivities as with other qualitative techniques, with particular awareness on the difference between making passive observations and making active contributions as researchers
6. *Value*	The possible access to difficult to reach and sensitive data	The opportunity to locate fan perceptions and experiences that are impossible to access via conventional techniques
7. *Visuality*	The presence of imagery and videos that are difficult to analyse and interpret with consistency and rigour	Sport's physical nature lends itself to the analysis of visual materials from participants, fans, and product users, thus offering a potent new avenue to acquire insightful, non-textual data
8. *Virtuality*	The potential for social media to become disjoined from reality due to technology, anonymity, the use of hyperbole, and the desire for attention	Insight into consumer and fan identification, especially via over-emotive content
9. *Vicissitude*	The potential for social media content to change swiftly, often towards confrontational or adversarial circumstances	Unusual opportunity to understand consumer responses to sport organisation actions, especially those that inspire dissatisfaction
10. *Vehemence*	The possibility that outlier comments receive a disproportionate amount of attention due to their controversial contents	Avoid distraction by outliers and focus on mainstream consensus; opportunity to study outliers to gain an insight into extreme fanatical beliefs

Qualitative research is particularly well designed to leverage the content contained in sport-related SM, mainly because the conversations that occur in the platforms demand the recognition of deep patterns and themes. Shared understandings – particularly around issues that are typically difficult to access under other research circumstances – require the kind of dynamic, flexible, and integrative techniques that qualitative research wields. Not only can SM analysis deliver important insights into the social lives of fans, followers, and participants, but it can also help reveal the underlying perceptions, motives, and complex consumer relationships with sporting brands (Branthwaite & Patterson, 2011).

Title: "Gateway to the sideline": Brand communication on social media at large-scale sporting events
Author: Vann, P. L., *Queensland University of Technology* (2018)
Reference: Vann, P. L. (2018). *"Gateway to the Sideline": Brand Communication on Social Media at Large-Scale Sporting Events.* Doctoral dissertation, Queensland University of Technology.

SM platforms have become an essential component of a transmedia sport experience for fans. This has significant implications for sport organisations, which now need to strategically incorporate SM platforms into a communications plan alongside their traditional media counterparts. The emergence of SM as a popular form of communication in sport also provides opportunities for sport organisations, as they no longer rely on one-way methods of distribution through mainstream media platforms, and instead can connect with fans directly via SM. Initially, sport organisations took an ad hoc approach to SM strategy, yet as the use of SM in sport becomes increasingly normalised, and the affordances of SM platforms present opportunities to engage with new and existing sport fans, approaches to SM communications have become more strategic. Existing research has examined many aspects of the role SM plays in the transmedia sport experience, from the perspectives of fans and organisations. However, the approaches and strategies SM teams use within sport organisations remain largely unexamined from an inside perspective. Thus, the aim of this research was to document exactly how sport organisations use SM for communication, the motivations, and considerations behind this use, and the tensions between sport fans and organisations that arise on SM surrounding the discussion of sport. This research was an inductive study, which used a qualitative multiple case study design and included both within-case and cross case analysis to explore the phenomenon of SM communication in the sport industry. Specifically, drawing on first-hand insight through participant observation in combination with interviews, this work documented, analysed, and compared the creation and implementation of SM strategy by the SM teams of two events: The Asian Football Confederation's (AFC's) Asian Cup (AC) and Netball World Cup (NWC). The author was embedded within each organisation throughout these events (both held in Australia in 2015), observing, assisting staff and participating in SM communications.

The results of this study revealed that organisations take a strategic approach to SM communications that depends on their market position (which sits on a mainstream–niche continuum) and target audience.

UNIQUE QUALITATIVE SOCIAL MEDIA RESEARCH ELEMENTS

Big data to deep data

SM has converted the usually hidden opinions and interactions between individuals and groups into publically available, searchable and downloadable data (Felt, 2016). Moreover, the data represents not only content from a networked community but also a barometer of current social discourses (Papacharissi, 2014). Research can centre around questions concerning the nature and behaviour of people participating in SM networks, or it can seek to understand more general sport issues through SM platforms (Quan-Haase and Sloan 2017a, 2017b).

In relation to the former, research can pertain to SM as a social instrument in its own right. For example, hundreds of millions of sports fans congregate and communicate through SM, transgressing geography, and background. Exactly what effect SM has had on sport remains uncertain, and the investigation of SM as a cultural institution sits at the top of the list of significant under-explored topics in sport management. Concerning the latter, SM can be employed as a tool to access data relevant to non-SM specific issues, simply providing access to handy clusters of opinions and experiences about aspects of sport.

NON-CONTENT DATA

One of the unique features of SM is its self-organisation, where users cluster their contributions under self-identified categories of content like hashtags. For researchers, hashtags can provide a useful insight into the shared themes, domains, and topics that a group focuses on. Presently, hashtags are regularly employed as encouraged destinations for posts organised around specific topics, the most common being sporting events, clubs and teams, sponsors, and product manufacturers. Hashtags have become so ubiquitous that they can play critical galvanising and information distribution functions during social upheavals, political crises, and natural disasters, not to mention the World Cup finals. Unlike other qualitative population and sampling procedures, sport management researchers can access respondents already self-subscribed to specific sport identifications, whether in the form of support for a club, or interest in a sport equipment brand. In addition, platforms like Instagram allow users to "tag" their images with descriptive keywords, which makes it quite easy for researchers to zero in on themed content.

As a starting point, hashtags give researchers a head start for two reasons. First, SM users identify themselves as part of specific groups based on hashtags. It is more likely that the members of a hashtag-based community hold some shared beliefs, and exchange content pivoting around some consistent topics. Second, hashtags encourage SM users to locate each other based on the likelihood of a favourable reception due to common interests and opinions. These two aspects allow researchers to shortcut onerous sampling procedures where suitable respondents are difficult to find or contact. They further increase the chances that the data will be relevant to the research question because the hashtag will signal the nature of the content. At the same time, it is important that researchers investigate hashtag-labelled groups thoroughly because hashtags can either change over time, or the focus of the communities they have come to represent can shift. It should be kept in mind that some hashtags are introduced by individuals or organisations with specific agendas, or have been devised to maximise popularity, attention, memorability, or commercial exploitation.

The fluid nature of "hashtagged" communities means that some groups can come and go quickly; a reflection of the responsiveness inherent in SM platforms to current issues and debate (Bruns & Burgess, 2011). As a result, researchers can focus in on specific, topical niches without having to lose valuable time finding respondents after the hot issue has dissipated. In a sport context, such immediate accessibility to data can prove decisive, especially around significant on-field events or dramatic match build-ups. The power of short-lived communities has been documented, a consequence of their potent efficiency and timing (Bruns & Highfield, 2013).

Although qualitative research tends not to be associated with counting and numbers, all researchers can benefit from the careful notation of platform and content data, some of which can provide critical information about users and their activities. For example, many platforms include profile data about the users and their networks of friends and followers. Further, aggregated data can sometimes specify frequency and volume of content generation, interactions, and keywords. Certain SM platforms indicate geographical data as well, tagging users' whereabouts and movements, often relative to locations of shared interest. For the sport management researcher, such information can provide valuable clues about venues, events, local communities, and essential services. Even at its simplest, geographical data can indicate a potential user's country or locality; an essential piece of information for sampling.

Research brief

Title: Does Social Media Engagement Affect National Basketball Association Game Attendance?

Author: Macklin, S., *Virginia State University* & Wynn, M., *Virginia State University* (2019)

Reference: Macklin, S., & Wynn, M. (2019). Does Social Media Engagement Affect National Basketball Association Game Attendance? *Presentation Session 'Posters' Virginia State University.*

This study investigated the relationship between SM engagement on Instagram, Facebook, and YouTube and attendance to home games during regular basketball seasons from 2013 to 2018. The number of posts made on each of the 30 National Basketball Association (NBA) teams' respective SM accounts from April 15 to September 30 of the years before the upcoming basketball seasons were counted, reviewed, sorted into categories including team and player information, promotional posts, and miscellaneous posts, and then compared to each teams' home game attendance statistics for each season. Results indicated that SM engagement did not have a significant impact on basketball game attendance.

FOLLOWERS, LIKES, AND INFLUENCERS

Numerous SM networks encourage users to follow others' posts through automated updates, as well as "like" them as symbol of reinforcement, acceptance or endorsement. In this way, researchers can acquire a rapid measure of content popularity, peer attention, and validation (Chua & Chang, 2016).

The content provided by key users – usually "influencers" – can also become the focal point of a study. For example, not only can their history of text and images be examined, but they can also be interviewed via SM (or through digital or analogue means) in order to secure their own interpretations of the material they have posted. Such a "scroll back" (Robards & Lincoln, 2017) method can assist the researcher in understanding the motivations and intentions behind posts, bringing into sharp focus the assumptions and expectations held by individuals who wield substantive influence over the collective direction and perceptions of a community. To add another layer of data, a researcher can further interact with followers in order to assess the effect of the same material. "Trace" interviews enhance the vibrancy of data as it allows for its contours and context to emerge from the participants' direct reports as well as though their posts.

SPECIAL ASPECTS OF SOCIAL MEDIA DATA METHODS

Ethnographic methods

Qualitative methods for collecting and analysing SM content mirror the conventional options that are outlined in detail throughout this text. Drawing upon the long-standing and robust techniques of anthropological ethnography, specific refinements have been developed to suit the digital and virtual environments, with added subtleties incorporated for observations made in SM platforms. All ethnographies revolve around either observing, and/or participating in, specific bounded groups or communities. Thus, ethnographic observations and participation can be targeted at SM platforms by carefully identifying communities, groups, or individual constituents. For example, SM ethnographers can focus on observing the content posted by members under certain hashtags, or as part of an emerging cluster of individuals particularly interested in a sport, club, product, event, or issue.

Unlike conventional "analogue" environments, SM platforms like Twitter can prove difficult to narrow into practical chunks for analysis due to the complexity of group and hashtag membership, and the overlap with other topics and hashtags. In addition, groups and communities on SM are notoriously fluid; they can appear almost instantaneously in response to a crises, issue or topic of potent interest, change radically in composition over a short period of time, shift their emphasis in a direction unrelated to the original topic or hashtag, or disappear altogether virtually overnight.

Thematic, content, and discourse analysis

Like with all text-based data, qualitative coding techniques can be employed to analyse content on the basis of themes or other hierarchical structures. In this chapter, our emphasis has been on where SM research deviates from the conventions. To that end, we shall not provide another repetition of how to conduct thematic coding here, as it is thoroughly described elsewhere in this text. Moreover, once the text for analysis has been selected, the actual coding process using SM generated text is no different to any other kind of text. Thus, SM data can be coded in order to specify the character of the content or to classify the data into hierarchical relationships and order. The data can be removed and manually analysed or dropped into ready-made qualitative data management software such as NVivo. Depending upon the approach taken by the researcher, codes will be created based on literature or through emergent frequency, or a combination of both (Chan, Wang, Lacka, & Zhang, 2016).

Where SM diverges from other data such as interviews or document analysis, is its dynamic and fluid nature. For example, by the time a researcher has systematically extracted a data set for coding, the contributors, opinions, focus, and issues could have all transformed. For this reason, we re-emphasise the importance of sampling a bounded data set, including a clear timescale. Conversely, real time studies can prove immensely insightful, revealing how opinions and perspectives regarding current issues can evolve and escalate exponentially, or regress and dissipate unexpectedly. Researchers pursuing a real time study in SM tend to do so as participants in order to gain an appreciation for a sampled community's dynamics from within. Of course, participation observation cannot work when researchers sample historical channels of data.

SM textual analysis would typically begin by selecting a data set constrained to a particular community or as a sample from a hashtag. The data set would then be extracted for either manual or software-assisted textual analysis focused on categorising the content under pre-determined conceptual themes, or identifying common emergent themes. Other approaches to coding can be based on the frequency or contextual importance of keywords, names, events, topics, or hashtags (Papacharissi, 2012).

Visual analysis

SM content may take numerous forms, but the most rapid growth has been in the rise of platforms accommodating and encouraging visual materials like images and videos, as well as general trend towards pictures rather than words. A consequence of the shift towards non-textual content is that the word-based analytical techniques dominating qualitative research's history have become less relevant. The surge in platforms such as Instagram has brought a major research opportunity to access rich, visual data at the same time as instigating a methodological conundrum (Hutchinson, 2016). Instagram's remarkable, exponential growth as a mobile application wherein users upload images and video footage taken on their phones, has pushed researchers to develop robust methods for studying visual material.

A serious challenge frustrating visual SM research comes as a result of a posted image's multiple sites of interaction. According to Hand (2017), visual content can be examined from production, image, and audience perspectives. For example, a "selfie" can be analysed as a contrived event, in terms of the apparent contents of the image itself, and in terms of its impact on and reception by a communal audience. Working out the relationships between these three elements is complex, and explains why the best qualitative approaches involve the triangulation of data, such as with the scroll back and tracing methods. Sport-related visual content provides a good example. In analysing a single posted image, a researcher might consider the context in which the image was taken, the composition including what was not captured and why, and the meaning-making that the image precipitates amongst a receiving community. Hand (2017) noted that visual data are produced, circulated, reflected upon, negotiated, deleted, and analysed by both its owners and its recipients.

We recommend that sport management researchers begin with a clear position on their approach to the interpretation of visual SM content. Three options – to be used independently or in combination – are worthy of consideration (Munk, Abildgaard, Birkbak, & Petersen, 2016). A first approach views images as units of analysis that can be counted, coded, and themed. From this viewpoint, visual content constitutes photographic representations of a sporting context, environment, or experience. They can be categorised, counted, compared, and classified as verbal summaries of the image composition.

A second approach uses visual data to reflect the daily practices, experiences, and perceptions of users. For example, images are interpreted as depictions of the routine responses that sport fans consider worthy of sharing. They reveal what is considered important to fans and expose how sport plays a role in their daily lives.

A third approach views visual data as a SM-specific version of the phenomenon or issue under investigation. Thus, the data is not considered a proxy or representation of the sport domain, but a separate and independent social instrument where an interest in sport is expressed. Here, the SM platform exists as its own social reality where the rules and boundaries surrounding the experience of sport and its communication are entirely specific to the SM context. Sport researchers using this approach would assume that the behaviours and attitudes they encounter are connected only and exclusively to SM. It is possible, however, that images can be coded in multiple categories, or from different perspectives (Tiggemann & Zaccardo, 2018).

The interpretation of visual data can create complications for researchers used to the more literal understanding of text. Visual aesthetics are inevitably subject to more severe diversity of response, so researchers need to find a consistent way of coding. For example, some researchers rely heavily on the descriptive text that accompanies most imagery in order to understand the image context. Furthermore, questions need to be raised concerning authenticity, especially with regard to how a user is positioning him or herself. Image manipulation is common and may be employed to reinforce a user's self-identity, or even to help sell a fitness product. While artistic interpretation has less bearing on a user's illustration of a personal experience, it has greater implications if presented as objective photo-journalism (Highfield & Leaver, 2016).

Added to the above considerations are first, the ever-present SM challenge of temporality, and second, the possibility that any given visual image can embed multiple levels of meaning (Poulaki, 2015). Regarding the former, visual SM can work outside conventional expectations of timelines and points of beginning and ending. Consider, for example, an uploaded image of young fan who has "Photoshopped" herself onto the balance beam next to Nadia Comaneci during her Montreal Olympic performance.

Regarding the latter, visual images and objects can inspire different meaning to different observers. As a result, it is troublesome to assume that an image or object is meant in the way a researcher infers. For example, what if an image of Muhammed Ali were posted. Does it represent victory, or does it have to do with bravado. Alternatively, perhaps the image relates to race? Context remains pivotal with visual data coding and must be triangulated with other data such as textual descriptors. One additional complication is that even hashtags can prove ambiguous when they are represented in a visual form like an emoji (Highfield & Leaver, 2016).

CHALLENGES AND OPPORTUNITIES WITH QUALITATIVE SOCIAL MEDIA METHODS

Populations and sampling

The unprecedented success and growth of SM emanates from its remarkable and unique ability to connect people in ways that would never be possible through conventional, analogue means of personal contact. Unlike almost every normal social contact, which tend to pass by unrecorded, SM leaves a trace. Not only that, conversations are sometimes helpfully labelled according to audience and content.

In response to the previous challenges in locating and studying a consistent group on SM, sport management researchers are advised to consider the following tactics (see Marwick (2013) for detailed Twitter examples). First, a researcher can focus on following a prescribed number of participants sampled within a specified group. Second, researchers can ensure that their sample of participants all have an active history including historical posts for a minimum, shared period, ensuring that they can be compared against the same context. Third, researchers can choose to begin with a particularly pertinent conversation stream and then focus their observations in a reverse chronological order to track the stream's antecedents (some platforms allow for a "conversation view", which can assist).

Fourth, although available and useful only on some platforms, the search function can be employed to sample posts that refer exclusively to significant keywords. Fifth, a predetermined number of participants can be sampled on the basis of aspects common in their profiles (or, if diversity is desired, a heterogeneous set of profiles can be sampled). Finally, a researcher (assuming appropriate ethics protocols have been observed) can post a request for participants to join a study, which subsequently allows for more interactive data collection. Similarly, a researcher can request permission to participate in a group as a way of better understanding its dynamics. However, since most groups do not have a single authority moderating inclusion, researchers conducting participant observation typically have to either hide their research agendas, or declare them outright and risk marginalising the group. Both can introduce ethical concerns.

Most SM and networking sites provide information pertinent to the content that can be extremely useful to a researcher's sampling decisions. For example, the Instagram Application Programming Interface (API) allows queries to be performed on user-generated tags, providing extensive information about relevant images and videos. Similarly, the Twitter API can be used to conduct searches around hashtags and keywords. All of this data can be advantageous in establishing patterns of use concerning publication times, content types, and other key features. In general, these data come in six types:

1. Social (e.g. hashtags, fan pages)

2. Temporal/spatial (e.g. timestamps, geotags)

3. Subject (e.g. hashtags, URLs)

4. Group (e.g. hashtags, community labels)

5. Events (e.g. photos, calendar)

6. Evaluations (e.g. likes, follows, shares)

Most researchers would be well advised to begin with hashtags, aware that they can come in two major forms (Yang, Sun, Zhang, & Mei, 2012). In the first instance, a hashtag represents a content bookmark describing and summarising the theme of the conversations it contains. In the second instance, hashtags are more subtle and complex when they act as a marker, symbol, or signal of a virtual community. Of course, the two types overlap. Communities of users can come together due to numerous intersecting factors including, club membership, interest in a sport, attendance at an event, or a shared disposition towards an issue. Hashtags label the content while at the same time signalling it to others as a beacon to join. Researchers can benefit from being able to reference descriptive concepts and summary labels that are not necessarily readily accessible amidst the details of a community's content (Wills, 2016).

Research brief

Title: Social media in relationship marketing: The perspective of professional sport managers in the MLB, NBA, NFL, and NHL
Author: Abeza, G., *Southern Methodist University*, O'Reilly, N., *University of Ohio*, & Seguin, B., *University of Ottawa* (2019)
Reference: Abeza, G., O'Reilly, N., & Seguin, B. (2019). Social media in relationship marketing: The perspective of professional sport managers in the MLB, NBA, NFL, and NHL. *Communication & Sport*, *7*(1), 80–109.

This study aimed to obtain an in-depth understanding of the use, opportunities, and challenges related to SM in achieving relationship marketing (RM) goals in professional sport. Semi-structured interviews were conducted with 26 managers of professional sport teams from the four major leagues in North America.

MIXED METHODS

Although it is beyond the scope of this text to provide an inventory of possible mixed methods approaches involving both qualitative and quantitative procedures, it is relevant that we acknowledge the increasingly common practice of marrying approaches. For example, Andreotta et al. (2019) recommended that researchers automate some aspects of data collection and consolidation with the aim of reducing the material for qualitative analysis to a manageable and precise volume. During such a process the researcher can extract an initial dataset of SM content, and then apply a quantitative procedure in order to narrow it down to the most relevant posts. A large dataset can therefore be conflated to issues of greater and more direct salience to the research questions. Keywords can be used, as can hashtags, causal relations, and broader content analysis. APIs can also be employed, if accessible.

Sometimes sport management researchers can employ some rudimentary text analysis to help locate a rich data set for subsequent qualitative focus. After all, if a researcher can eliminate material that is not directly relevant to the study before the time-consuming work of qualitative coding begins, they can maximise their efficiency as well as the project outcomes. For example, Santarossa, Coyne, Lisinski, and Woodruff (2019) used a mixed methods approach to study fitness perceptions on Instagram. They started by downloading 10,000 records comprising 229,000 unique words. The 30 most commonly used words were then employed to help manually identify 10 thematic categories. In this instance, some simple content analysis provided the researchers with guidance on the qualitative response. Further, the researchers used a SM network analysis to quantitatively reveal the links between the nearly 10,000 users, which showed where the main conversations were happening. Again, this head-start from using a SM network software programme allowed the researchers to better concentrate their qualitative energies. Table 21.2 provides a summary of how quantitative methods can be employed to optimise qualitative analysis.

Table 21.2 Summary of social media mixed methods

Method	Data and access	Advantages	Disadvantages	Approach
Case	Multiple sources Public and non-public	Reveals fan responses to specific events Tracks behavioural change of consumers or effects of action Comprehensive and defined boundaries in context, time, participants Lessons become evident	Results specific to case and context Difficult to generalise Comparison of cases difficult on the basis of similar variables due to unique context	Mixed, can employ all methods Multiple data sources about an event or situation are used to explain and interpret
Content	Social media, user generated content	Highlights key themes and issues Can be used to delimit data sample or to analyse final sample Can be used to summarise key qualitative themes on the basis of keywords and frequencies	Can overemphasise frequencies and the presence of keywords Can lead to the removal of data on the basis of quantitative analysis rather than in-depth coding	Employed to identify rich data by constraining volume or eliminating extraneous material
Netnography	Social media user generated content	Immersive and detailed within the social media platform context Best employed when focused on a narrow community or small group of users Deeper understandings of attitudes, behaviours, and motivations can be exposed Embedded nature provides intrinsic knowledge of community	Difficult to quantify and generalise Only small communities or a narrow group of users can be studied Time consuming Requires considerable researcher experience	Multiple and mixed methods based on sociological and anthropological techniques Researcher is immersed in the platform community Based on observations, interactions with community and interviews. Surveys may be used to supplement Observations are contextualised within social structures Analysis employs conventional qualitative techniques, but can also take advantage with retrospective analysis like the scroll back technique

(Continued)

Table 21.2 (*Continued*)

Method	Data and access	Advantages	Disadvantages	Approach
Predictive	Social media, user generated content	Links data to events, such as likely increases in match attendance or consumption Can be used to classify sport consumers into different lifestyle groups based on their demographic or psychographic characteristics	Tends to focus on short term and immediate effects rather than long term patterns Can be simplistic and miss deeper, underpinning motivations and attitudes	Mostly relies on quantitative content analyses including data analytics, sentiment analysis and machine learning algorithms. Aims to establish connections between consumer social media content and their collective behaviours. Can be used to predict future consumer behaviours based on previous relationships between social media sentiment contents and subsequent changes in purchase or other behaviours. At its most simple, predictive analytics attempt to link volume or strong sentiments with later action. Most attention is placed on patterns in historical content that precedes major change
Search	Search data information Mainly private but available from search engine providers on a fee for service basis	Reveals trends and patterns behind information searching and retrieval Shows consumer intentions Links fan responses to events Useful to platform host or content provider to understand consumer behaviour drivers, especially converting visits to sales	Requires a social media or website owner's permission to access data Generally undertaken internally by site or platform owner or host Not always possible to distinguish between human and bot traffic	Statistical summary of platform / site analytics, including visits, content review, click throughs, time on content, keywords, traffic movement and flow direction, likes, responses to advertising, etc., depending upon the platform. Often linked to a hashtag or similar keyword descriptor or identifier Uses data provided through internally installed server software or external analytics tools to understand user behaviour (*Continued*)

Method	Data and access	Advantages	Disadvantages	Approach
Sentiment	Social media, user generated content, mostly in the public domain	Reveals attitudes and responses, usually in positive or negative terms Helps to understand consumer and fan responses to events or issues Show where consumers want change as well as their levels of support Can reveal influencers and/or influencing issues Can provide a broad analysis of consumer sentiment covering vast amounts of data	Automated natural language analysis is a form of content analysis and can miss subtle but important nuances in the data Data filtering to eliminate the "noise" is often essential Sentiment analysis can remove the variations that occur in fan responses Does not necessarily reveal the causes for sentiments	Keyword analysis of user generated content. Can be interpreted inductively to generate categories of sentiment summarising the responses of users, or can be used deductively by matching or coding against a predetermined list of words which have already been assigned a sentiment Can employ complex algorithms and machine learning to identify patterns within big data sets Smaller data sets can be examined manually using qualitative coding methods, particularly when studying a narrow issue

CROSS-PLATFORM ANALYSIS

Sport management SM research is only just emerging in popularity as a productive method. As a result, researchers have not yet fully explored its methodological opportunities, particularly as new SM platforms and modalities are exploding into the mainstream more quickly than their research implications can be fully grasped. Amidst this inevitable clutter and learning on the job, one area of immense possibility for sport management researchers lies in conducting cross-platform studies; that is, research that collects data from numerous SM platforms at the same time.

A first advantage of cross-platform analysis is that it can add tremendous richness and diversity to the data set. For example, different platforms attract different users, so the combination can immediate enhance the demographic and profile heterogeneity (dissimilarity) of samples. Added to this, a second advantage is that the same issue, topic, or question can be addressed within different platforms, offering the researcher with different angles to investigate. Further to the opportunities for superior sampling, third, cross-platform analysis can also mean that different kinds and forms of data concerning the research question can be gathered, such as lengthy textual conversations, images, and short summaries. It is easy to see how the study of a major sport event's fan experience could be enriched through the combined examination of images, comments, conversations, and impressions. Fourth, cross-platform analysis exposes how the content and character of SM data can be platform specific, in line with the structures and modes each one allows and encourages (Burgess & Matamoros-Fernández, 2016). Sport management researchers can discover how each platform itself channels certain forms of responses. A key implication is that qualitative researchers must remain mindful of the effects of each platform's medium, including its architecture, displays, data types, policies, rules, hashtags and labels, advertising, and moderation or censorship (Pearce et al., 2018). Qualitative researchers should be naturally attuned to such contextual variables anyway, but SM tends to amplify the effect. Furthermore, researchers need to be aware of how each platform presents it data, including the prioritisation of content based on certain metrics such as likes, retweets, followers, friends, and upvotes (Rogers, 2017); all of which can potentially influence the perceptions and responses of subsequent users.

ISSUES IN VALIDITY AND RELIABILITY

As with all qualitative research methods, ensuring validity and reliability can be demanding. In addition to the conventional qualitative research validity and reliability issues, here we specify a handful that pose particular challenges when dealing with SM methods. These problems have contributed to the incorrect perception that qualitative SM methods are a less legitimate form of research. It is not that the method is less valid but that the issues surrounding validity are more complex and not yet well understood. However, if a researcher can adequately address the aspects below, then they can be confident that a robust account of validity and reliability has been made.

1. *Social media users* present an obstacle to validity and reliability because from a sampling viewpoint they tend not to be representative of populations. Making generalisations from the sample to the population can therefore be problematic due to bias. After all, SM users are self-appointed; they need to be interested, engaged, motivated and opinionated in order to participate in the first place. To add to the complexity, user interactions vary in character immensely even on the same platform, which makes pinpointing a singular or dominant theme like trying to hit a moving target (Weller, 2015). On the other hand, inherent biases can also allow a researcher to more easily engage with a homogenous (similar) group of users all sharing a common outlook, like being "one-eyed" supporters of a certain club. Such groups can be impractical, if not impossible, to locate through conventional, analogue contacts.

2. *Data volume and volatility* makes SM validity and reliability trickier due to the sheer size and the swift changeability of the content. To begin with, the volume of data can mask or clutter the key issues that a researcher wishes to address. In qualitative research data, volume cannot be quickly "crunched" in order to sidestep the irrelevant parts. As a result, researchers must assume the burden of delimiting – cutting down – the data into a sample of a practical size to deal with. However, the process of delimitation comes with the supplementary onus of justifying the decisions taken, including how the researcher has accounted for personal biases, assumptions about what is relevant and what is not, and how the resulting data set can be relied upon to return confident answers about the research questions. SM content also transitions so quickly that topical issues come and go faster than researchers can track them. Inevitably, real-time analysis becomes historical, while real-time longitudinal studies are inherently challenging. Not only does the content change swiftly, but new platforms gain ascendency while others falter, and even the most popular ones can add and remove features that make the comparison of different time periods more difficult.

3. *User content authenticity* can prove troublesome to validity and reliability because it cannot be assumed that user behaviour in SM aligns with the same user's behaviour in the material world. Emotive and deliberately controversial or sensationalist language and images are commonplace in SM, a side-effect of the desire for users to cut through the volume

and attract attention. Exaggeration and over-statement can therefore bias results. For example, a researcher cannot necessarily be confident that a user's report of their opinions, actions and intentions are authentic. An "echo effect" can also skew findings where dominant and popular views are repeated in a version of a group think. Hashtags tend to attract like-minded users, so it is essential that researchers sample with careful thought given to the need for diversity. Finally, some user groups pursue political or commercial agendas vigorously, sometimes with less interest in facts and evidence than is desirable. Conversely, the emotionally charged, instant and direct nature of SM commentary and conversation can yield important insights into fan thinking that otherwise remain personal.

4. *Social media content private ownership* can add another complication to the process of securing a valid and reliable set of results. In the first instance, some SM content is unavailable for public viewing, again meaning that what is available will reflect a bias towards those users who want their opinions heard. Another problem is that some SM companies do not release information about the content on their platforms in a transparent way. SM companies make decisions about their rules and policies on the basis of commercial imperatives, such as the distracting presence of advertisements and click throughs. Platforms can change in functionality and search algorithms can shift opaquely. Some companies provide selective fee-for-service access to key data statistics, leaving researchers subordinate to their profit seeking. Users can also delete their content and even entire accounts, while the companies can manage historical data in any way they wish. Researchers cannot rely on the long-term preservation or storage of SM archives unless they have a way of downloading it.

5. *Issues of privacy and ethics* have not been as fully reconciled for qualitative SM methods as they have for its traditional, analogue counterpart. For example, SM ethnography can raise ethical challenges when researchers want to take advantage of the insights that accompany participant observation or action research. Researchers must identify themselves and their intentions to the participants with whom they wish to interact. Due to the inherent caution users have about authenticity and the prevalence of "trolls", the very act of moving from observer to participant can skew the following content significantly, as some users disengage while other take the opportunity to deliberately provide misleading or fabricated content for amusement. If these obstacles can be overcome, however, the transition from observer to participant can lead to a rich vein of data through access to a wide range of individuals inaccessible via other avenues.

Case study

Title: Social media and not-for-profit sport organizations
Author: Naraine, M. L., *University of Ottawa* (2017)
Reference: Naraine, M. L. (2017). *Social Media and Not-for-Profit Sport Organizations.* Thesis submitted to the Faculty of Graduate and Postdoctoral Studies in partial fulfilment of the requirements for the Doctorate in Philosophy degree in Human Kinetics University of Ottawa. The purpose of this dissertation was to address the degree to which SM can be utilised as a tool for stakeholder communication by not-for-profit sport organisations. Delimited to national sport organisations, specifically those in a Canadian context, and using a stakeholder theory approach, the project advanced three major research objectives: (1) determine what not-for-profit sport organisations are communicating to their stakeholders via SM, including identifying forces and pressures that impact content and messaging; (2) identify which stakeholders are positioned and advantaged in the social network of not-for-profit sport organisations; and (3) uncover the contextual factors that have enabled the use of SM channels by not-for-profit sport organisations. In order to accomplish these objectives, the dissertation was structured into three interconnected stages parsed into three research articles – each with its own supporting theoretical framework (i.e., institutional theory, network theory, and the contextualist approach to organisational change) – providing findings discussed using a stakeholder perspective. In the first article, the results found SM communication was predominantly used for promoting, reporting, and informing purposes, attributable to the coercive (e.g., funding partners), mimetic (e.g., salient organisation routines), and normative (e.g., best practices) pressures at play. In the second article, fans, elite athletes, photographers, competing sport organisations, and local sport clubs were identified as key stakeholders with significant advantage given their position in the SM network of not-for-profit organisations. The final article revealed SM has yet to radically impact the operations of these organisations, highlighting some of the challenges related to SM communication.

Cumulatively, the findings illustrated not-for-profit sport organisations can improve upon their current use of SM as a stakeholder communications tool. Through the implementation of a unique SM strategy composed of multiple philosophies, not for profit sport organisations could consider the variance in stakeholder groups while incorporating the immediacy and engagement SM requires. In doing so, organisations may create the conditions to satisfy stakeholder expectations and increase organisational capacity simultaneously.

CONCLUSION

An upside to the immense scale of sport's SM content is an opportunity for researchers to access a smorgasbord of valuable information about sport consumers' opinions, attitudes, experiences, consumption behaviours, preferences, desires, and frustrations. Never before has such a rich vein of potential data been available to sport management researchers, especially when it comes to questions that demand deeper, more nuanced insights than can be yielded from quantitative techniques applied to word content analyses. A new era has brought with it a new kind of data that echoes the engaged, interactive, asynchronous and unique character of the sport consumption experience. Qualitative analysis of SM presents researchers with a potent tool to expose some of the deeper mysteries of sport's ubiquitous impact.

RESEARCH AND REVIEW QUESTIONS

1. Why is social media research growing in popularity amongst sport management researchers?

2. In what ways is social media different or unusual compared to other research and data sites?

3. How would you define qualitative social media research?

4. Identify and explain the special aspects of social media research methods.

5. What are the main challenges and opportunities associated with qualitative social media research?

6. Explain the key issues in qualitative social media research validity and reliability?

REFERENCES

Andreotta, M., Nugroho, R., Hurlstone, M. J., Boschetti, F., Farrell, S., Walker, I., & Paris, C. (2019). Analyzing social media data: A mixed-methods framework combining computational and qualitative text analysis. *Behavior Research Methods, 51*(4), 1766–1781.

Bail, C. A. (2017). Taming big data: Using app technology to study organizational behavior on social media. *Sociological Methods & Research, 46*(2), 189–217.

Branthwaite, A., & Patterson, S. (2011). The power of qualitative research in the era of social media. *Qualitative Market Research: An International Journal, 14*(4), 430–440.

Bruns, A. (2015). Making sense of society through social media. *Social Media + Society, 1*(1), 1–2.

Bruns, A., & Burgess, J. E. (2011). #ausvotes: How twitter covered the 2010 Australian federal election. *Communication, Politics and Culture, 44*(2), 37–56.

Bruns, A., & Highfield, T. (2013). Political networks on twitter: Tweeting the Queensland state election. *Information, Communication & Society, 16*(5), 667–691.

Burgess, J., & Matamoros-Fernández, A. (2016). Mapping sociocultural controversies across digital media platforms: One week of #gamergate on twitter, YouTube, and tumblr. *Communication Research and Practice, 2*(1), 79–96.

Burnap, P., Williams, M. L., Rana, O., Edwards, A., Avis, N., Morgan, J. ... Sloan, L. (2015). Detecting tension in online communities with computational twitter analysis. *Technological Forecasting & Social Change, 7*, 96–108.

Carr, C. T., & Hayes, R. A. (2015). Social media: Defining, developing, and divining. *Atlantic Journal of Communication, 23*, 46–65.

Chan, H. K., Wang, X., Lacka, E., & Zhang, M. (2016). A mixed-method approach to extracting the value of social media data. *Production and Operations Management, 25*(3), 568–583.

Chua, T. H. H., & Chang, L. (2016). Follow me and like my beautiful selfies: Singapore teenage girls' engagement in self-presentation and peer comparison on social media. *Computers in Human Behavior, 55*, 190–197.

Creighton, J. L., Foster, J. W., Klingsmith, L., & Withey, D. K. (2013). I just look it up: Undergraduate student perception of social media use in their academic success. *Journal of Social Media in Society, 2*(2), 26–46.

Felt, M. (2016). Social media and the social sciences: How researchers employ Big data analytics. *Big Data & Society, 3*(1), 1–15.

Hand, M. (2017). Visuality in social media: Researching images, circulations and practices. *The SAGE handbook of social media research methods*, 217–231.

Highfield, T., & Leaver, T. (2016). Instagrammatics and digital methods: Studying visual social media, from selfies and GIFs to memes and emoji. *Communication Research and Practice, 2*(1), 47–62.

Hutchinson, J. (2016). An introduction to digital media research methods: How to research and the implications of new media data. *Communication Research and Practice, 2*(1), 1–6.

Kaplan, A. M., & Haenlein, M. (2010). Users of the world, unite! The challenges and opportunities of social media. *Business Horizons, 53*(1), 59–68.

Marwick, A. (2013). Ethnographic and qualitative research on twitter. In K. Weller, A. Bruns, C. Puschmann, J. Burgess, & M. Mahrt (Eds.), *Twitter and society*, pp. 109–122. New York: Peter Lang.

Munk, A. K., Abildgaard, M. S., Birkbak, A., & Petersen, M. K. (2016). (Re-) appropriating Instagram for social research: Three methods for studying obesogenic environments. In *Proceedings of the 7th 2016 International Conference on Social Media & Society*, ACM, pp. 1–10.

Papacharissi, Z. (2014). Affective publics: Sentiment, technology, and politics. In Z. Papacharissi (Ed.), *Affective publics: Sentiment, technology, and politics*, pp. 64–94. Toronto, ON: Oxford University Press.

Papacharissi, Z. (2012). Without you, I'm nothing: Performances of the self on twitter. *International Journal of Communication, 6*(18), 1989–2006.

Pearce, W., Özkula, S. M., Greene, A. K., Teeling, L., Bansard, J. S., Omena, J. J., & Rabello, E. T. (2018). Visual cross-platform analysis: Digital methods to research social media images. *Information, Communication & Society, 23*(2), 161–180.

Poulaki, M. (2015). Featuring shortness in online loop cultures. *Empedocles: European Journal for the Philosophy of Communication, 5*(1), 91–96.

Quan-Haase, A., & Sloan, L. (2017a). *The SAGE handbook of social media research methods*. London: Sage Publications.

Quan-Haase, A., & Sloan, L. (2017b). Introduction to the handbook of social media research methods: Goals, challenges and innovations. In A. Quan-Haas, & L. Sloan (Eds.), *The SAGE handbook of social media research methods*, pp. 1–8. London: Sage.

Reich, J. A. (2015). Old methods and new technologies: Social media and shifts in power in qualitative research. *Ethnography, 16*(4), 394–415.

Robards, B., & Lincoln, S. (2017). Uncovering longitudinal life narratives: Scrolling back on facebook. *Qualitative Research, 17*(6), 715–730.

Rogers, R. (2017). Digital methods for cross-platform analysis. In J. Burgess, A. Marwick, & T. Poell (Eds.), *The SAGE handbook of social media*, pp. 91–110. London: Sage Publications.

Santarossa, S., Coyne, P., Lisinski, C., & Woodruff, S. J. (2019). #fitspo on instagram: A mixed-methods approach using netlytic and photo analysis, uncovering the online discussion and author/image characteristics. *Journal of Health Psychology, 24*(3), 376–385.

Scott, D., & Harmon, J. (2016). Extended leisure experiences: A sociological conceptualization. *Leisure Sciences, 38*(5), 482–488.

Tiggemann, M., & Zaccardo, M. (2018). Strong is the new skinny: A content analysis of #fitspiration images on instagram. *Journal of Health Psychology, 23*(8), 1003–1011.

Weller, K. (2015). Accepting the challenges of social media research. *Online Information Review*, 39(3), 281–289.

Wills, T. (2016). Social media as a research method. *Communication Research and Practice*, 2(1), 7–19.

Yang, L., Sun, T., Zhang, M., & Mei, Q. (2012). We know what@ you# tag: does the dual role affect hashtag adoption? In *Proceedings of the 21st international conference on World Wide Web*, pp. 261–270. ACM.

PART 7

Writing the sport management research report

CHAPTER 22

Research preparation and the sport management research report

LEARNING OUTCOMES

By the end of this chapter, you should be able to:

- Understand the basic steps involved in formulating a research plan.

- Identify the research problem.

- Describe the process for conducting a literature review.

- Identify key chapters in the research report.

- Identify strategies with which to begin writing the research report.

KEY TERMS

1. **Research problem:** a concise and clear statement that provides the context for the research study, and that generates specific research questions that the research study aims to answer.

2. **Research Plan:** a detailed description of the procedures that will be used to investigate your topic or problem.

3. **Literature review:** a critical comprehensive reporting of any existing literature that is relevant to the study being conducted by the researcher.

KEY THEMES

- What is the research report?

- What is a research problem?

- Where does the sport management research their get research ideas from?

- What is a literature review?

- Why is it important to have a systematic approach to the research report?

CHAPTER OVERVIEW

An important part of the research process for the sport management researcher to precisely identify is the area they want to investigate. To do this, they must first critically examine what has been published in the area, and this process will help them to work out how they should go about conducting the investigation (and why). This chapter identifies that from the initial idea that sparks the sport management researcher's interest, the conduct of the literature review, refining the research problem, formulating the questions to be answered through to the design of the research plan, the sport management researcher must carefully review, and plan each step of the research journey. This process requires careful and methodological planning on the part of the sport management researcher as the study is only complete once the findings have been written up and possibly published. There is no definitive format for a qualitative research report; however, this chapter seeks to guide the new researcher in writing up a report in a systematic way.

INTRODUCTION

Many sport management problems may not be appropriate for a research study. They may simply be trivial issues that do not require further investigation – such as, are there more blonde-haired football players than those with brown hair in the draft? It is very unlikely that answering this question would provide meaningful insight into sport management. The sport management researcher should avoid trivial research problems, as well as those studies that lack any theoretical relevance. If there is no theoretical framework to inform or guide a study (deductive) and any study designing one (inductive) would struggle to fit alongside existing research, then we need to ask serious questions about the benefit of doing the study. For example, many wristbands that claim to improve performance would require an entirely new branch of physics to explain how they work – so should a sport management researcher concern themselves with this?

The final type of problems that the sport management researcher will *avoid* are those where a research topic is "saturated" and any new studies are either purely replication or do not add meaningful knowledge to the body of literature. With a literature base that is still emerging in sports management it can sometimes seem that the harder a researcher tries to think of a research topic/question, the more the researcher might feel that their study has already been done. This frustrating experience is the reason why the success of research depends largely on taking a great deal of care during the preliminary preparation of the project (i.e. you'd rather solve this issue early on than find out you've been beaten to the punch after you've collected and analysed your data).

THE QUALITATIVE RESEARCH PROCESS

Performing research can be challenging, and the sport management researcher beginning a research project with only a blank sheet of paper might feel quite overwhelmed. "Getting organised" and developing a process can provide a clear pathway that will both guide the research project and offer the researcher some peace of mind. The following section will provide a model research process that can be used as a guide for accomplishing your research project or dissertation. It will discuss research methods and provide a comprehensive graphical model that can be used as a guide to quick-start your research effort.

A research process can be defined as a detailed description of the procedures that will be used to investigate your topic or problem. In general, a research plan will include the following two key elements that, between them, encapsulate the ideas and methods the sport management researcher may use: (1) a detailed presentation of the steps to be followed in conducting the study – i.e. an overall view of what, when, where, how, and why for performing the research; and (2) a strong idea of how each step will inform the next – i.e. how the literature review will frame neat research questions and formulate. Crotty (1998) suggests an approach to the research process that involves the posing and answering of four associated questions. These are as follows:

1. What methods do we propose to use?

2. What methodology governs our choice and use of methods?

3. What theoretical perspective lies behind the methodology in question?

4. What epistemology informs this theoretical perspective?

Within these four questions are embedded the basic elements of the research process:

- Methodology: the strategy, plan of action, process or design lying behind the choice, and use of particular methods and linking the choice and use of methods to the desired outcomes.

- Methods: the techniques or procedures used to gather and analyse data related to a research question(s) or hypothesis.

- Theoretical perspective: the philosophical stance informing the methodology and thus providing a context for the process and grounding its logic and criteria.

- Epistemology: the theory of knowledge embedded in the theoretical perspective and thereby in the methodology.

THE RESEARCH PLANNING PROCESS

In most universities, students enrolled in a dissertation or thesis complete a course on research methods or research planning in the semester prior to writing of the project. During this time, students are introduced to various research methods as well as given advice on research and writing the project. Substantial online and library resources are usually available to ensure that students have the best possible background prior to commencement of the dissertation or thesis. The research planning process can involve the following steps:

1. **Identify a research topic and draft research questions**
   - Browse literature
   - Talk to supervisor
   - Talk to colleagues/peers

2. **Preliminary literature review**
   - Scholarly journals
   - Books (not textbooks)
   - Professional publications
   - Google scholar and professional websites

3. **Narrow the literature review**
   - Examine scholarly articles and books
   - Examine references scholarly in articles and books
   - Examine related subjects
   - Examine sub-disciplines

4. **Plan data collection and gather data**
   - Establish methods for collecting data
   - Gain access
   - Address ethical issues
   - Collect data

5. **Organise information and analyse data**
   - Refine methods for analysis
   - Analyse data
   - Refine literature review

6. Reflect and write

- Reflect and write draft

- Edit

- Final critique and polish

A number of textbooks provide a highly similar overview of a typical research methodology and, in some cases, the philosophical assumptions underpinning it (see Creswell & Plano Clark (2010).

Research brief

Title: Development of school and sport burnout in adolescent student-athletes: A longitudinal mixed-methods study
Author: Sorkkila, M., *University of Jyväskylä*, Ryba, T. V., *University of Jyväskylä*, Selänne, H., *University of Jyväskylä*, & Aunola, K., *University of Jyväskylä* (2018)
Reference: Sorkkila, M., Ryba, T. V., Selänne, H., & Aunola, K. (2018). Development of school and sport burnout in adolescent student-athletes: A longitudinal mixed-methods study. *Journal of research on adolescence.*
The paper investigated the development of school and sport burnout in adolescent student-athletes during their first year in upper secondary school using an embedded mixed-methods design. The questionnaire-based data were analysed with growth mixture modelling and four burnout profiles were identified among student-athletes. From the found burnout profiles, two were typical for the interviewed subsample of elite athletes, that is, burnout risk and non-risk profiles. The authors generated rich descriptions of well-being and ill-being, showing that elite athletes in two burnout profiles differed in their experienced demands and resources related to individual and environmental factors.

PREPARING THE RESEARCH PROPOSAL

The *research proposal* is a document one typically writes with a view to gaining funding, supervision, or to have one's project formally approved (e.g. by an ethics board). Typically, once a research proposal is completed and approved the researcher will be required to follow the proposal submitted just like a contractual obligation. Developing a written research proposal forces the sport management researcher to think through every aspect of the study. However, "best laid plans" don't always survive exposure to reality, particularly the more exploratory forms of research mentioned above, and with the approval of supervisors or funders, it can be acceptable to change the plan in response to new and interesting findings.

The purposes of the *proposal* are threefold: (1) the plan forces the researcher to think through every aspect of the study; (2) it facilitates the evaluation of the proposed study; and (3) it provides detailed procedures to guide the conduct of the study.

Research proposal purpose

In light of the above requirements to gain supervision, funding and ethical approval, the research proposal has several core purposes:

1. A research proposal should contain all the key elements involved in the research process and include sufficient information for the readers to evaluate the proposed study.

2. A research proposal is a planning tool: a map or sketch of activities to be executed, resources to be employed and a time frame to be adhered to.

3. A research proposal serves the function of convincing people of the value of the proposed work by showing them how the research will make a difference to the world, or by identifying a dilemma in existing theory that the research will help resolve.

4. A research proposal demonstrates the expertise of the researcher in a particular area of study by summarising, comparing, and integrating all the relevant theory and existing research pertaining to a specific topic.

5. A research proposal seeks to demonstrate competency to carry out the proposed study by describing an appropriate and feasible research method.

Research proposals come in different formats, as different universities, funders, and governing bodies will place a different emphasis on certain elements of the research process. For example, some will emphasise scientific rigour, while others might emphasise accessibility and dissemination of findings. Likewise, the process may vary for qualitative and quantitative projects. Table 22.1 outlines a generic proposal and then potential variations when writing qualitative and quantitative methods research proposals.

Table 22.1 Typical differences between qualitative and quantitative research proposals

Qualitative research proposal	Quantitative research proposal
■ Identify the general research issue.	■ State the hypothesis.
■ Explain how the researcher intends to gain entry to the research site.	■ Determine the participants.
■ Identify the participants.	■ Select measuring instruments.
■ Estimate the time that will be spent in the field.	■ Choose a specific research design.
■ Determine the best ways to collect data.	■ Specify procedures to conduct the study.
■ Identify appropriate ways to analyse the data.	■ Stipulate the statistical techniques.

Writing the proposal

Working up a proposal to a minimum of 3,000 words (or whatever length your institution requires) can take about one month for an undergraduate proposal or up to 12 months for a PhD proposal. Whether you are writing a proposal to be read by a potential supervisor, members of a proposal review committee or a funding body, your proposal should contain the elements shown in the *Generic Template for Writing a Research Proposal.* Because qualitative research is flexible, the following outline is indicative only, as you may choose to structure your proposal differently, depending on the aims of your research.

A Generic Template for Writing a Research Proposal:
1. Overview of the study

    a. Introduction to the study

    b. Background to the study

2. Statement of the research problem

    a. The qualitative paradigm format

3. Research objectives/aims

4. Research questions

5. Research rationale

6. Scope of the study

7. Literature review

8. Conceptual process

9. Definitions, delimitations, and limitations

10. The nature of the necessary evidence

11. Selecting a research methodology

    a. The qualitative paradigm

12. Results and their dissemination

13. Budgeting

14. Referencing

In most cases, the University usually requires students to submit a research proposal prior to the commencement of a dissertation/thesis. This ensures that the student has examined the issue and developed a plan to complete the project. Once the thesis or dissertation proposal is submitted, the supervisor will give guidance on whether or not the study is suitable in terms of its size and scope, given the academic degree toward which the student is working.

DISSERTATION OR THESIS

Although a dissertation or thesis should both offer original and significant contributions to the sport management field there are differences in requirements of both. A *dissertation* will normally be submitted as just one of the requirements of a Bachelors or Master's degree (BA, BSc, MA, MSc, MPhil) and may well be the product of just a few months' work. A dissertation is shorter than a thesis (typically 10,000 to 15,000 words), and has a simpler design and methodology. In contrast, a Masters or PhD *thesis* is generally the product of a longer period of work (up to three or more years' full-time work in a PhD). It will normally extend to at least 100,000 words and can constitute the sole written requirement for the PhD degree. A thesis will be more in-depth, the design, and methodology much more sophisticated, and the data richer than those of a dissertation. Once accepted into a dissertation or thesis research programme, researchers are urged to familiarise themselves with your university's rules and regulations.

DISSERTATION/THESIS STRUCTURE

This section looks at the various chapters of a Dissertation/Thesis, each of which serves a unique and important function. Although the final structure may vary in different Universities the following provides a guideline of universally accepted sections. Table 22.2 provides an outline of a typical qualitative thesis; it is important to note that the structure of a thesis can vary and is dependent on the topic and what is most appropriate.

As Table 22.2 identifies, each of these sections/chapters/requires different content. An overview of what each section/chapter should include will now be discussed.

ABSTRACT

An abstract is a brief overview, not an evaluative summary, of a longer piece of writing. The abstract should be no more than about 500 words and take no more than one page of space. It should, very briefly, provide a description of the nature of the work, how it was undertaken and its main findings. There are different kinds of abstracts which contain different information. Social science and scientific abstracts contain a statement of the research problem or purpose, the method and methodology, the findings, and the conclusions. Humanities

Table 22.2 A typical qualitative research format

Qualitative thesis format

Abstract: Brief overview of a longer piece of writing.

Chapter 1: *Introduction:* Orientation of the study, stating the research problem and placing it into theoretical and/or historical context.

Chapter 2: *Literature review:* Comprehensive review of articles relevant to the study, justifying, to some degree, the researcher's own methodology.

Chapter 3: *Methodology:*

- ■ Explanation of how research was accomplished: what the data consisted of; how the data were collected, organised, and analysed. Justification for the analytic strategy.

- ■ Participants: who the subjects were, how they were selected, what steps were taken to protect them from risks.

- ■ Nature of data: e.g. interview, ethnography, videotapes, etc., and how data was selected.

- ■ Description of research setting: validity and reliability of the research data may depend on the appropriateness of the setting selected.

Chapter 4: *Findings and Results:*

- ■ Findings refer to what the data actually are.

- ■ Results offer interpretations and analyses of these data.

Chapter 5: *Conclusion:* Contributions, limitations of the study, and recommendations for further research.

References: Referencing format normally applied is American Psychological Association (APA) style.

Appendices: This may include the interview/survey protocol, ethics forms, confidentiality agreements, etc.

abstracts contain a description of the problem, the main position or "argument" and an overview of the contents.

The abstract provides further information about the problem or aim, the methodology, findings, and conclusions. It provides a framework and prepares the reader to read the paper more closely. One important aspect of abstract writing is therefore to ensure that the abstract provides an accurate description of the paper and does not leave anything important out. The other main purpose of abstracts is to provide key words for information searches. Librarians, and other information managers, use abstracts and the key words contained within them to develop indexing systems. Researchers use key words within online data bases to retrieve relevant information. This prevents searches of full texts, which would be too broad to be useful, and titles alone, which often do not provide enough information. Another important consideration in abstract writing is therefore to ensure that the abstract includes the key words that are applicable to the field or topic area. The *informative abstract* is most common. It is used within the social sciences and the sciences. This kind of abstract describes what happened during the research process. The key elements of an informative abstract are: (1) reason for writing; (2) research question/aim; (3) method and methodology; (3) findings/results; and (4) conclusions or implications.

How to write an abstract

Abstracts are usually written after the longer paper is complete. The first step in abstract writing is to re-read the longer paper, perhaps highlighting important facts, and conclusions.

Next write a sentence or two for each of the key elements within the abstract. Check that each sentence summarises the key element and does not leave anything important out. Then put the sentences together and work towards a unified paragraph. Pay particular attention to key words and transitions to ensure the ideas flow from sentence to sentence. The last step is to edit the abstract and to check that it fits within the word limit. Whilst the final part of the writing process is writing an abstract for the paper, the abstract will actually appear at the front of the paper. This is the piece of the work that will represent the researcher on bibliographic search engines and it may be all that many readers know of the work. Once you have completed this process your abstract should include:

- Describe the overall research problem being addressed and indicate why it is important.
- Identify the purpose and theoretical foundations, if appropriate.
- Summarise the key research question(s).
- Describe, briefly, the overall research design and methods.
- Identify the key results, one or two conclusions, and recommendations that capture the heart of the research.
- Briefly interpret the results with a statement on the implications for positive social change.

CHAPTER 1: INTRODUCTION

The introduction sets the scene of the study and puts the research in context. It should aim to start with a sentence that describes exactly what the paper is about. If the research is about the experiences of fans at sporting events, then the reader will want to know why the study was done, and how it relates to other research in the area. It should contain the following elements: the purpose of the research, i.e. the research "problem" (expanding on the abstract) and reasons why it was under- taken, a summary of the research design, a clear statement of the overall aim and specific objectives of the research, define key concepts/ terms, present the delimitations of the study and provide an outline of the main points within the middle chapters of the thesis. Whichever style or structure chosen, the first step of the research story line is to persuade the reader that the question or argument posed in the thesis is justified and "significant".

Statement of the problem

Thesis writing opens with an unresolved problem or paradox, or an explanation of something important that we need to know. This is done in order to grab the reader's attention, establish the significance of the research, and signal the literature/s that the research will contribute to. In some theses, this is accomplished in a few sentences or paragraphs. In others it may take several pages or even an entire chapter. The problem statement presented in the introduction should be brief; a more detailed description of the problem should be placed before your research questions after the review of the literature. The key points here are: (1) clearly and un-ambiguously explain the nature of the problem; (2) summarise what is already known about the problem by briefly reviewing its history; and (3) explain why the problem is worth investigating. The research problem provides the context for the research study and typically generates questions, which the research hopes to answer. In considering whether or not to move forward with a research project, the researcher will generally spend some time considering the problem. The statement of the problem is the first part of the paper to be read (we are ignoring the title and the abstract). The problem statement should "hook" the reader and establish a persuasive context for what follows. It is important for the researcher to be able to clearly answer the question: "what is the problem"? and "why is this problem worth my attention"? At the same time, the problem statement limits scope by focusing on some variables and not others. It also provides an opportunity for you to demonstrate why these variables are important.

Selecting the research problem

A research problem involves accurately capturing a key issue regarding existing knowledge – for example, a gap, a deficiency, a contradiction, or an uncertainty. As a good rule of thumb, the sport management researcher should ensure that their statement of the problem captures the *who*, the *what*, the *where*, the *when*, and the *why* of the problem situation. Good studies often establish the *how* as well. The statement of the problem is a specific and accurate synopsis of the overall purpose of the study, and having read it, any interested reader should immediately understand the relevance and importance of your proposed study.

There are certain criteria that should be taken into consideration when selecting a research problem:

- *Workability*: Is the contemplated study within the limits and range of your resource and time constraints? Will you have access to the necessary sample size to generate the rich insights required (e.g. in a quantitative study this may be to enable statistical comparisons)? Is there reason to believe you can come up with an "answer" to the problem? Is the methodology that you have planned appropriate, manageable and understandable?

- *Critical mass*: Is the problem of sufficient magnitude and scope to fulfil the requirements of your course and level of study? Will it deliver findings of sufficient significance? Will it "fill" your specified word limit?

- *Interest*: Are you interested in the problem area, specific problem and potential solution? Does it relate to your background and career interest? Does it "turn you on"? Will you learn useful skills from pursuing it? Generally, if you are going to spend 6–12 months (or more) investigating a problem, you had best be interested in the answer.

- *Theoretical value*: Does the problem fill a gap in the literature? Will others recognise its importance? Will it contribute to advancement in your field? Does it improve the "state of the art"? Is it publishable?

- *Practical value*: Will the solution to the problem improve sport management practices? Are real-life sports managers and CEOs likely to be interested in the results? Will future research be changed or informed by the outcomes? Will your own research practices be likely to change as a result?

Finding a problem

There are many problem situations that may give rise to research. Bless, Higson-Smith, and Kagee (2006) suggest that research problems can be classified according to the motives or interests that drive them, using the following criteria: (1) observation of reality; (2) theory; (3) previous research; (4) practical concerns; (5) personal interest; (6) public issues; and (7) funding opportunities.

1. *Observation of reality* denotes that research questions may be developed by researchers' observations of everyday life, usually observations that require exploration and explanation.

2. *Theory and research literature*: Whilst reviewing the current available literature on a particular topic, the sport management researcher may identify other topics or areas that warrant further investigation, or which pose unanswered questions and opportunities for further study. For example,

an article documenting the experiences of disabled athletes at a major sporting event may pose questions for the sport management researcher around the event or organisational management that are not covered in the original study. Useful sources are journal articles and books (at the end of these, you will usually find suggestions and implications for further research), unpublished theses and dissertations, conference proceedings and reports, reports from government sponsored bodies and research institutions, and reviews and overviews of the field of study.

3. *Previous research* can also identify conflicting findings and observations, leading to uncertainty about which theory or management practice is "best". Rather than leaving such conflicts unresolved, such contradictory (or "equivocal") findings present ideal opportunities for sport management researchers.

4. *Practical concerns* usually arise from sport managers and practitioners. Practical concerns are generally driven by problems experienced in the everyday practice of sports managers, rather than being motivated by conflicts between theories or findings.

5. *Personal interest* describes the very real and normal situation that researchers have their own special areas of interest, and that their interest inspires their research topics – for example, the desire to follow a career in that field, or a friend or family member who has been affected in some way.

6. *Public issues*: The media is quick to report or sensationalise news about sporting stars – either in a positive or negative way. Publicity around favourable sporting outcomes, for example successful medal wins in an Olympic Games is certainly of major appeal to the sporting public. But is there something in the reporting of a successful or favourable outcome for the sport management researcher to investigate further?

7. *Funding opportunities*: Government authorities or sporting organisations may at times identify topics of specific interest that it is determined warrant investigation. These topics may be deemed to be of public interest or concern – such as illicit drug taking, behaviour of sporting stars, or of particular interest to a sporting organisation, such as in the organisation of a major sporting event. Such research opportunities will often have funding attached, which is of significant advantage to the sport management researcher.

Additionally, as a researcher in sport management you should be aware of the research being done at their institution. If possible be aware of research being undertaken by colleagues or fellow researchers at other institutions. Be alert to any controversial issues that may arise in your area of interest. Be aware of what is *big* in sport management at the moment – e.g. drugs in sport, salary cap, corruption? Discuss the potential research with your peers, lecturers and PhD students. Where they exist, read a review paper covering your topic (i.e. a paper that uses other research findings as its "data") and from there read any relevant research studies from the reference list. From the search you should make a list of research questions that appear unanswered. Try to balance your research question with your capabilities and experience. It shouldn't be too hard or too easy. A general process for developing a research problem may involve the following processes:

1. Outline the general context of the problem area.

2. Highlight current key theories, concepts and ideas in this area.

3. Establish what appear to be the underlying assumptions of this area.

4. Question why the issues identified are important/relevant.

5. Establish whether there is anything that needs to be solved.

Read around the area (discipline/sub-discipline) to get to know the background and to identify unanswered questions or controversies, and/or to identify the most significant issues for further exploration.

Problem importance

Clearly specifying the problem is important because it provides a foundation for the research objectives, the methodology, the work plan, budget, etc. (e.g. how much money can you justifiably request for the project?). Additionally, a clearly stated research problem makes it easier to find information and reports of similar studies and enables the researcher to clearly explain why the proposed research project should be undertaken. The research problem is a key element of research, and Table 22.3 contains several questions that help determine the feasibility of the research problem.

Role of your supervisor

Your academic supervisor usually has an understanding of "hot topics" in sport management and may be able to assist in refining your thoughts. Likewise a chat with sport management professionals could provide potential areas of investigation. Supervisors are not there to tell you what to do. Their role is to guide and advise rather than direct. This means that, in most cases, you are expected to work with a measure of independence. However, both you and your supervisor have a common aim, that is, to achieve a study of a high standard which will be completed on time. To accomplish the goal, both of you should be committed to the contract of respectively doing and supporting your research. Supervision is based on a framework of ground rules and a process of negotiation

Table 22.3 Criteria for testing the feasibility of the research problem
Criteria for testing the feasibility of the research problem

- Is the problem of current interest in sport management research? Will it be possible to apply the results in sport management practice? Does the research contribute to sport management theory?
- Will the research identify new problems and lead to further research for sport managers? Is the research problem important for sport managers?
- Will it be practically possible to undertake the research?
- Will it be possible for another researcher to repeat the research? Is the research free of any ethical problems and limitations?
- Will it have any value to the field of sport management?
- Do you have the necessary knowledge and skills to do the research? Are you qualified to undertake the research?
- Is the problem important to you and are you motivated to undertake the research? Is the research viable in your situation?
- Do you have the necessary support for the research?
- Will you be able to complete the project within the time available?
- Do you have access to the facilities and support the research requires?

(Deuchar, 2008). This means that you and your supervisor need to come to an agreement about the following areas:

- The staff/student relationship.
- The routine aspects of the relationship.
- The agenda for each supervisory meeting.
- The outcome of each meeting.
- The nature and timing of written material to be submitted.

Generating research questions

Once you have a clear aim (purpose) and have established the need for research to help address it, the next task is to refine your research questions. A research question can be simply defined as the questions the research needs to address in order to help answer the business question. Your research questions will shape the whole design and approach, so it's essential that you are clear on what you want to achieve from the outset. Creswell (2009) suggested the following guidelines for writing qualitative research questions: (a) present one or two central research questions followed by sub-questions; (b) relate the central research question to the specific qualitative strategy of inquiry; (c) begin the research question with "what", "how", "why", "what if"; (d) where possible, focus on a single phenomenon or concept; (e) use exploratory verbs: discover, seek to understand, explore a process; (f) use non-directional language (delete words that suggest quantitative study with a directional orientation: affect, influence, impact, determine, cause, etc.); (g) be open, and expect that the research questions will evolve and change during the study consistent with the emerging design.

Significance of the study

Significance of the study comes from the uses that might be made of the results – how they might be of benefit to theory, knowledge, practice, policy, and future research.

Theoretical perspective

Many dissertation papers are not based on a theory, but if it is, the researcher will need to make that clear early in the paper. The researcher should briefly describe the theory that is being investigated by describing its key propositions and concepts, as well as the important relationships described in the theory. It is important to also indicate who created the theory and why the theory is important in sport management. In a PhD thesis, the theoretical perspective has greater importance and is often included as a separate chapter. Typically, a PhD researcher will discuss the problem to be addressed in the research – the gaps, perplexities, or inadequacies in existing theory, empirical knowledge, practice, or policy that prompted the study. The problem may be a theory that appears inadequate to explain known phenomena, the lack of empirical data on a potentially interesting relationship between X and Y, or a common practice that appears ineffective.

Delimitations of the study

Delimitations are primarily concerned with external validity, which is the extent to which the results of a study can be generalised to people (population validity) or settings (ecological validity) other than the one studied. In Chapter 1 researchers must consider the ways in which specific variables, participants, settings, designs, instruments, time, and analyses are used in your study and how they limit its generalisability. For example, in a study dealing with the attitude of individual sport athletes to doping, the researcher may choose to restrict the selection of subjects to just two or three sports, simply because all individual sports cannot be included in one study. Thus the researcher delimits the study.

Limitations

Limitations are possible shortcomings or influences that cannot be controlled or are the results of the delimitations imposed by the researcher. If we limit the previous study of individual-sport athletes to just two sports, there is an immediate limitation with respect to how well these represent all individual sports and therefore the generalisations that can be made from the research. The researcher should not be overzealous in searching for limitations as it may devalue the study too much in the eyes of the research community. An example of a limitation is that a sport organisation might only allow the researcher to collect data during a certain time of the regular season, or that selected participants might not answer truthfully or at all. In setting out the limitations, Pajares (2007) suggested that the researcher should think about one's analysis, the nature of self-report, one's instruments, and the sample. In other words, one should think about threats to internal validity that may have been impossible to avoid or minimise and explain.

Definition of concepts/terms

Key concepts/terms in the research are included in the introduction chapter so as to provide context and understanding for readers. When the meaning of a concept/term is unclear or contested, it must be defined the first time it is used. This often occurs in the introduction of the thesis, though other terms can be defined as they arise in the flow of the writing. Technical, theoretical, or other concepts/terms can be defined by referring to a previously published definition. Alternatively, aim to provide a precise, unambiguous definition, and to use the term in this sense throughout the main body of the writing.

The chapter outline

The chapter outline is often the last section of the thesis introduction, and usually follows after the description of the research design. The chapter outline within a research thesis aims to summarise the main ideas from each of the middle chapters of the thesis, and to show how they link with the main argument or research aim/purpose. Introductory and concluding chapters do not need to be summarised because they are themselves summary chapters. For the other chapters, the objective is to integrate the summaries into the flow of the writing, to avoid repetition of content, and to be clear about how each chapter supports the key objectives of the research. You can write the chapter outline by re reading each of the middle chapters and noting down the key points in a few sentences on a separate piece of paper. Then go back to the introduction and incorporate your summary in the introduction. Be sure to make a note of the main sub-headings or themes discussed in each chapter, but try to be as concise as possible. Each chapter is discussed in the order in which it appears in the thesis. In summary, after reading an introduction, the reader should know:

1. What problem, issue or controversy the research relates to?

2. What bodies of literature and fields of practice the research relates to?

3. Why the research is significant?

4. For question/answer theses, the central question, proposition or research aim.

5. For descriptive theses, the central argument, idea, theory (your "thesis").

6. The definitions of any key concepts/terms.

7. The rationale underpinning the method (methodology).

8. How the answer or evidence was attained (research methods)?

9. The chapter contents; and how each chapter supports the thesis objective or argument?

CHAPTER 2: LITERATURE REVIEW

Purpose of the literature review in identifying the problem

A major part of developing the research problem is reading what has already been published about the problem. As indicated earlier, the first step in identifying a problem is locating a series of studies from the literature, and then deciding which studies relate to your chosen topic. To do this successfully, the sport management researcher must know how to locate information and then how to use it. If the researcher does this correctly then the knowledge generated can stimulate inductive reasoning – that is, the researcher may attempt to locate and synthesise all relevant literature on a topic to develop a more general explanation or a theory to explain certain phenomena. For example, the sport management researcher might induce that participation in sport leads to greater social cohesion, which will create better communities. Once this has been accomplished, the researcher might also discuss their thoughts with peers and fellow researchers/experts to eliminate any unproductive or unpromising approaches. The task of the literature review within research writing is to:

- Take the reader from the broad topic to the research questions;

- Define the field/s of the research;

- Introduce and explain findings and theories that support the research;

- Draw together main conclusions of literature relevant to the topic;

- Highlight gaps or unresolved issues within the literature;

- Establish what is original, new or "significant" about the research.

What should the literature review do?

Apart from providing the answers to the previous questions, the review should enable you to sharpen and focus your initial research questions or even suggest new research questions.

It should provide you with a wide and deep knowledge of the theoretical, empirical, and methodological issues within your chosen research topic and provide a "bridge" between your research questions and your research findings. This will allow you to compare your research methods, theoretical framework and findings with work already done and enable you to set the scope and range of your research topic. When you have completed your review you should be able to speak with authority on your research topic and the wider subject area.

Basic literature search strategies

There is no single right way to undertake a literature search. The search will depend considerably on the researcher's familiarity with the topic. If the researcher has virtually no knowledge about a particular topic, the starting point and sequence will be different from that of somebody already quite familiar with the literature. Most researchers will go straight to a computer to start a literature search. This can certainly be useful, but there are two major weaknesses that the researcher must consider: (1) generally, only more recent references are available for computer searching, depending on the database used (and in many cases you might still need to go and find a paper copy for older "classic" references rather than simply clicking on a link); and (2) getting the necessary background and broad overview of the problem from individual studies can be difficult, as many database searches tend to only give individual studies – leaving you as the researcher to evaluate which studies are truly relevant to your own study.

Talk to the reference librarian at your library for guidance in undertaking the literature search. The review of literature is generally undertaken in two stages: *Stage one* involves a general overview of the relevant area using secondary sources (i.e. books, book chapters and reviews that will give you a broad overview of the area); while *Stage two* involves a more specific and structured review involving primary sources (i.e. to help identify specific research problems and opportunities to contribute). Primary sources are ultimately the most valuable tool for the researcher in that the information is first hand. Most primary sources in a literature review are peer reviewed journal articles. In sport management, some of these journals include: *Sport Management Review, Journal of Sport Management, European Sport Management Quarterly, International Journal of Sport Marketing and Sponsorship, International Journal of Sport Communication, Journal of Global Sport Management, Journal of Sport, Business and Management,* and the *International Journal of Sport Management and Marketing.* Dissertations are also primary sources; however dissertations may be difficult to locate as they are often only stored in a university library. Typical databases for searching sport management studies include: Index Medicus (medline); Psychinfo; ERIC; Sports Discus; and of course, the bibliographies of any good articles that you do find. Online search engines, such as

Google Scholar, are fast becoming a user-friendly online tool to search many databases at once.

Secondary sources of data

The difference between items in a literature review and sources of secondary data relate to how the information will be used. Secondary sources of data form part of the actual data collection. The "secondary" element indicates that the data have already been collected for another purpose. Sources of secondary data can be categorised as *internal secondary sources*. These are sources of data available from within an organisation. They can include minutes of meetings, reports from sales representatives, financial records, and internal review reports. There are also *external secondary sources.* There are a variety of external sources of secondary data which can include official government statistics on sport partic- ipation, etc., as well as other commercial documents that have been developed by allied organisations, for example, the annual review of football finance by Deloitte and the Sweeney sport report published in Australia. There are other commercial organisations who undertake surveys which researchers can sub- scribe to or purchase reports on.

Literature searching and the internet

There is no question that the Internet (and its associated hardware) has sig- nificantly changed the methodologies of qualitative research. Searching the Internet for resources; using software to manage citations; interviewing par- ticipants over the Internet; using dialogues and interactions online as data; and even using online software to analyse your data are all now part and parcel of much scholarship in sport management research. While the Internet can be a valuable and time-effective means of gathering information, sport management researchers must recognise that just because it is available on the Internet, and even if the website looks professional and authoritative, the information con- tained there is often unreliable or politically motivated. It is essential that the researcher determine the validity and authenticity of information retrieved via the Internet (Denzin & Lincoln, 2005).

Most government agencies have websites that offer copies of recent reports and policies, whether for free or at a cost. For example, the Australian Sports Commission and Sport England are two such websites. These websites can be a useful source of information as one can at least be sure that the source is original and, in all likelihood, quite influential. Electronic journals are gen- erally very useful, particularly if they are peer reviewed and receive "impact factors" and indexing. However, you should be wary of websites and blogs that seem to "replicate" the format of proper journals offering inaccurate, erro- neous, or fabricated information. As the primary researcher, it is your job to evaluate any and all documents that you use carefully. In general though when using the web as a source for information you may want to ask yourself the following questions:

1. Whose website is it? Is it a well-known and reputable organisation?

2. Is it a reputable individual's website? Be cautious and consider the credibility of the individual who is operating and maintaining the website.

3. Is the material dated? Can it be referenced formally using the Harvard system?

4. Can the information be corroborated?

SIX STEPS IN THE LITERATURE SEARCH

If we move away from the basics, there are relatively formal and specific steps to follow that will help to ensure a high-quality literature review, these include:

Step 1: Write the problem statement. As discussed previously, one can begin by trying to specify what research questions are being asked, and which are the most relevant/important. For example, a sport management researcher might want to find out whether the way that sport managers are trained influences their ethical attitudes. More specifically, the researcher wishes to examine the difference between the "traditional" management approach of focusing on the economic bottom line versus a triple bottom line management approach. By carefully defining the research problem, the researcher will be able to keep the literature search within reasonable limits. While you may progress through numerous drafts of a problem statement, always try to write the statement as completely (and as concisely) as you can very early in the literature review.

Step 2: Collate secondary sources. These will offer you a broad oversight of the area so you can begin to "get your bearings" and navigate around.

Step 3: Determine descriptors. What are some of the key words and phrases that relate to your research question?

Step 4: Search, evaluate, and collect primary sources. Original studies are those that have collected their own data, rather than reviewing the studies of others.

Step 5: Read and record literature. While arduous and sometimes very mundane, this is the "meat" of your task in preparing a literature review, and key tasks to guide your reading should include: forming a statement of problem; considering the characteristics of participants that you will need; the type of research design employed, the data collection methods you may use; the way you will analyse and report findings; and potential questions for further study.

Step 6: Write the literature review. A review of literature is not a mere list or summary of books and articles that the researcher has read. Instead, a literature review combines the most significant aspects of the works one has consulted. It is a *combination* and *synthesis* in the form of *an integrated description* of the field of study. In reviewing literature, the reviewer must show awareness of the most important and relevant theories, models, studies and methodologies, and should indicate how these are relevant to one's project, and evaluate how these works are similar to and/or different from one's own research.

The literature review therefore serves several important functions: (1) it ensures the production of original work; (2) it acknowledges the contribution of previous works; (3) it demonstrates critical ability to evaluate literal materials; (4) it rationalises the importance of the problem being studied; (5) it defines the boundaries of the research project; (6) it establishes the size and extent of the research project; (7) it considers the procedures and the instruments that can/should be used in the research project; (8) it casts the "problem" in a better perspective through a better understanding of the underlying theory in an attempt to render it "solvable"; (9) it helps to ensure you avoid the unnecessary (non-purposeful) repetition of research already undertaken.; (10) it assists you in evaluating the significance of your own findings (i.e. at the end of the study); (11) it helps to formulate and justify hypotheses and research questions; and (11) it allows the researcher to carry out work more purposefully. In fact a good literature review can be pretty inspirational, believe it or not!

Annotated bibliography

Developing an annotated bibliography is another procedure to organise research information. Many academic organisations/schools require this highly simplified literature review as part of the initial research process. What the annotated bibliography will display is that the researcher has read and understands the materials gathered. It also identifies critical research issues that directly support the study topic, such as research designs, methodology, samples and findings. For example, a sport management researcher may put together an annotated bibliography on organisational change. This may include the more generic studies on organisational change before eventually being narrowed to those research projects that have examined organisational change in sporting organisations.

Writing the review

When writing the literature review, the researcher should describe the work that has been done, and be critical where necessary. This can be done by using the following as a guide:

1. Summarise the main facts and conclusions, which emerge, synthesising the material to explicate the main themes, directions, contradictions, challenges, etc.

2. Point out the areas of the field that are still inadequately covered.

3. Organise your information carefully, summarise the salient details of the research, the conclusions, and any weaknesses in them.

4. Combine the information in ways that allow adequate description of the literature and insightful conclusions about its meaning for the context in which you are going to be researching.

5. Critically analyse and synthesise the material.

6. This synthesis becomes the foundation of the conceptual framework for your study.

When searching for the following is recommended.

- Look for source materials related to your topic in the library

- Ask a librarian for assistance

- Enrol in a library research help course

- Conduct an internet search of relevant topics

- Check indexes and databases

- Look at dissertations/theses stored in your University library

- Perform an internet search of dissertations/theses through internet sites such as Dissertations Abstract

- Read abstracts and bibliographies

- Look for sport management related journals

- Search sport management books

- Search for key authors in your research area

- Scan books or articles for key terms

Finally, remember a literature review normally has an introduction, a body (with relevant research organised and synthesised), a summary, and conclusions. It is important to include in the literature review a description of the work being done, being critical where necessary. Summarise the main facts and conclusions that emerge, synthesising to produce main themes, directions/trends, contradictions etc., and point out those areas in the field that are still inadequately covered. It is increasingly a good idea to use a software programme such as EndNote when conducting the literature review as this will assist you throughout the preparation of your final article or report, by managing your references and producing an "instant" reference list at the end.

CHAPTER 3: METHODOLOGY

Developing the method

The purpose of developing the method is to effectively address the research aim/questions. If the method is planned and pilot-tested appropriately, the study's outcome will allow the research aim/questions to be answered. One could even argue that the researcher has "failed" when the results of the study are blamed on methodological problems. A review of the literature is very helpful in identifying successful methods, for example recent studies examining the same topic, or other studies that have attempted to use the same research design. It is a good idea to pilot-test any unusual methods to determine whether the method answers the specific question asked, and delivers appropriate data. Otherwise the researcher may find out too late that their method does not answer the aim/question(s), and their contribution to sport management literature will be undermined.

There are many ways to answer most research questions and the approach that you eventually adopt can depend on a number of factors, such as your personal preferences, your knowledge of research methodology, the time you have available to complete the study, and your advisors' preferences. It may also depend on whether you take a pragmatic approach and adopt the research approach that seems most appropriate for your topic or a more philosophical approach in which the choice of research method is dictated by a particular view of reality. Qualitative research seeks answers to questions that are not easily quantified, such as those involving an individual's experience, different social settings, and the individuals who inhabit those settings. Qualitative researchers are most interested in how humans make sense of their surroundings through symbols, metaphors, rituals, social structures, social roles and so forth. Qualitative methods emphasise measures that are intentionally unobtrusive. We have discussed numerous research approaches in this book; four of these typical approaches are outlined in Table 22.4 for the purpose of this chapter.

Recent qualitative research has included approaches such as: case studies; observation of participants in natural settings; interviewing; historical analysis (historiography); and applying discourse analysis to documents/texts. We would however encourage you to embrace any of the methodological frameworks presented in this book if they allow you to address your research question(s).

Data collection method

Generally, sport management researchers will discuss the data collection methodology as it is located within the chosen theoretical framework. Qualitative approaches to research involve measures that do not use numerical data. As discussed throughout this book these kinds of data include

Table 22.4	Typical methodologies adopted within qualitative research projects
Research approach	**Description**
Narrative Approach	Focuses on the analysis of stories portrayed by an individual through text or discourse. It includes collecting stories, reporting experiences described and chronologically ordering the experiences.
Phenomenological Approach	Focuses on the common conscious experience of a phenomenon shared by multiple people. It describes the essence of how and what the participants experience without additional explanation or analysis.
Grounded Theory Approach	Focuses on a large sample of interpretations regarding a process, action or interaction. Interpretations provide the data from which to generate a theory about the phenomenon.
Ethnographic Approach	Focuses on the shared patterns of behaviour, beliefs and language developed among a group of people. Research describes how the culture works through the analysis of shared values.

observations, field notes that you have taken in order to describe a situation in detail, transcripts of face-to-face or telephone interviews with individuals or groups of people, public documents such as newspapers or official reports, or private documents such as personal diaries, letters or email, and audiovisual materials, such as photographs and audio and video recordings. Qualitative approaches are particularly well-suited when you are trying to generate new theories, achieve a deep understanding of a particular issue, present detailed narratives to describe a person or process, and as one component of a mixed-methods study.

The methods section informs readers about the who, what, when, where, and how of your research. Who are the participants, what variables are involved in the study, what did you do, when and in what order did you do it, where did the study take place, and how did you gather and analyse the data? A clearly written methods section allows readers to understand what you have done, evaluate the appropriateness of your methodology, and replicate your study if they wish to do so. The methods section typically includes a description of the participants, instruments, procedures, and the types of analyses that you will use.

Research participants

Identify the number, source, characteristics of the population and sample, and sampling procedures. Describing participants allows readers to interpret the results with greater confidence and to consider the generalisability of those results. Nowadays it is generally agreed that you should not refer to the people who took part in a qualitative study as *subjects*, instead use *participants*.

Sampling frame

For the qualitative researcher, sampling is based upon their relevance to the research topic as opposed to their representativeness, which determines the way in which the participants to be studied are selected. Sport management researchers will in general utilise techniques that are defined as "non-probability" sampling techniques, as they aim to select participants with a connection to, involvement in, or interest in the research topic under investigation. Decisions need to be made regarding how many people to question or interview, where and when to question or interview, and the length of the survey period. Again, the nature of the survey will determine sample size, for example, as well as the expected response rate for the data collection method and available resources.

Instrumentation

Qualitative studies describe interactive techniques (e.g. interviews and unstructured observations). The goal in this section should be to describe the procedures so that anyone can replicate the study. Each of the data collection methods should be discussed in this section. If interviews were used, then why interviews were chosen as an appropriate data collection method how the interviews were carried out should be discussed; however, this does not require a detailed critique of the interview process itself. The researcher should report what they did and how they did it.

Fieldwork

Depending on the nature of the project and the methods of data collection selected, there will be a variety of fieldwork to organise. At this stage in the planning process, it is a case of preliminary identification of what will be required. This may well include: (1) arranging permission to interview at a site; (2) gaining access to the names and addresses of potential respondents; (3) getting quotes for the printing of paper-based questionnaires or the cost of online surveys; (4) identifying any equipment that is required, for instance voice-recording technology; (5) establishing the training requirements of staff, or the need for the recruitment of staff; and (6) obtaining ethical approval from your university before research can take place.

CHAPTER 4: FINDINGS AND RESULTS

Framing findings

The researcher needs to analyse and explore the patterns, similarities, differences, and unusual aspects of the data. They need to explore ways to translate or interpret the data analysis into findings. Through interpretation of findings the researcher examines concepts, ideas, theories, arguments, models of explanations, so as to move analysis of the data to judgements that can be defended. This section is often the most difficult part of the study to write because it involves a great deal of analysis. The results should be interpreted in light of the full set of results, the applicable literature, the theoretical foundation or conceptual framework used, and the limitations of the study and literature. What do the results mean and what do they not mean? What are the possible causes of the results? What are the possible consequences of the results? The findings should directly answer the research questions and clearly indicate the answers to these research questions. These are some suggestions:

- *Relate results to previous research*: Compare and contrast your findings with those of previous researchers. What is the same? What is similar?

- *Discuss the theoretical consequences of your results*: If a theory or model has been used then it is important to frame the results by placing them in that theory or model. Where do they support, partially support or not support the theory?

- *Using tables and figures to present results*: Researchers should use tables and figures as needed, always remembering that they should be included in order to make the results easier for the readers to understand. In addition, figures should generally supplement rather than duplicate information provided in the text of the dissertation/thesis.

Beginning the findings section of a qualitative study requires a strong opening sentence clearly stating the study focus in a way that captures readers' interest, which can be a challenge to do well. Experienced qualitative researchers often start the findings section with a paragraph framing the study in the context of who participated in the study, highlighting basic participant demographics, and including any study-specific demographics of importance to the specific study area. The second paragraph should describe the themes that emerged from the analysis and provide evidence-based definitions for them. This helps set up the presentation of the themes (using subheadings) and the supporting quotes.

Presenting qualitative findings should tell the story of the phenomenon of interest and represent the participants' thoughts and experiences. Sandelowski and Leeman (2012) suggest qualitative research should be useful to the reader and help contribute to the evidence base. For individuals with similar experiences as study participants, reading the findings should resonate with their own experience and they should find "truth" in the results.

Choosing quotes

Throughout the data analysis process, certain quotes usually stand out as representative of participants' experiences and are important for articulately or succinctly explaining a phenomenon. Exemplar quotes should be noted when reading one-on-one or focus group transcripts for possible future inclusion in write-ups of study findings (Sandelowski & Leeman, 2012). When many good quotes are present, it can be difficult to choose which one(s) to include. It is important to note selecting too many quotes will not improve the trustworthiness of the results and may dilute the impact of the study findings. Qualitative researchers should create systematic ways of keeping track of exemplar quotes so when telling the participants' stories, the researchers can represent their voices appropriately.

Common mistakes with presenting the findings include:

- Introducing quotes with a single sentence, rather than establishing the context of the quote and how it links to the theme;

- Inserting overly long quotes to represent experiences or the phenomenon;

- Failing to transition between quotes and the next paragraph without an explanatory or transition sentence;

- Choosing quotes that do not represent the theme;

- Inserting too many quotes;

- Separating every quote, regardless of length (35 words or more should be in a separate paragraph), without integrating them into the paragraph for a seamless reading experience.

If the researcher focuses on telling the story of the participants with the phenomenon, avoiding the issues highlighted previously becomes easier. It is more important to choose a truly representative quote of participant experiences than it is to have a large number.

CHAPTER 5: CONCLUSION

This chapter clearly needs to be relevant to the "evidence" cited in the substantive analysis. It should clearly show which of the research questions have been achieved and which remain "unanswered" as they relate to the research aim/purpose. The conclusions should contain a discussion of the "limits" of the research in terms of; the research method and specific research instruments used, the theoretical framework used, the data analysed and the assumptions made. It is in this chapter that the researcher can both summarise their findings and suggest applications of those findings. Such applications should be realistic and not speculative and no attempt should be made to extrapolate beyond the data. When the evidence is overwhelming, the researcher should make statements authoritatively. When the evidence is only suggestive, then it is advised to add caveats to statements such as; "The results suggest ...," "It appears ...," or "It could be that ...." Informed speculations are appropriate and useful in the interpretations, as long as they signal to the reader that the researcher is speculating.

Clearly, there are many questions that researchers cannot answer and they need to be open to the possibility that the research project does not answer all that many questions – and never answers any conclusively. A common mistake in qualitative writing is when authors assume the findings are generalisable to the broader population. Qualitative findings are only applicable to the local context where the study took place. Aside from acknowledging this as a study limitation, a good technique is to highlight the importance of replicating the study with similar or more diverse populations affected by the same regulatory mechanism so the similarities and differences in experiences can be captured.

The conclusion chapter also needs to outline new theoretical contributions of your study and its practical implications. It is hopeful that the research has made a contribution to knowledge in the sport management field. Ensure that you make the unique and original contributions of the study clear. This is yet another section of your dissertation or thesis where consultation with your supervisor is strongly recommended. The practical implications of your results are important for the industry and sport managers. Document how your research might improve professional practice. This may include writing one or two paragraphs in which you make final recommendations. Each recommendation should be directly related to the study.

Although the researcher has no control over limitations they do have a responsibility to forewarn readers of the limitations and the reasons for them. The following questions help identify some common sources of limitations in qualitative research. What were the boundaries of the case or topic studied? What related phenomena, events, or questions were not examined – by original plan or due to unexpected barriers? What access did the researcher seek but was unable to gain? How were informants selected, and how might that have biased or limited the information that was collected from them? How did requirements for protection of humans perhaps adversely affect the study? How did the researcher's presence perhaps affect the phenomena being studied?

Typically in the final chapter, researchers make specific recommendations for future research. Recommendations are suggestions for action that are based upon the results and the applicable literature, with consideration for the limitations of both. The implications can be for modifications or new initiatives in theory, practice, and policy. They can also be for future research – new problems that have become apparent, new research questions raised by the results, and conceptual frameworks and methodologies that seem to hold promise or should be avoided in the future. Even though qualitative findings are not generalisable, there may still be implications for research, policy, practice, and education. Including a sentence or two about how the study's findings may influence each factor provides useful direction for others seeking to replicate the study in different contexts or with populations affected by the same regulation.

References

A list of references identifies all sources cited in the text of your thesis. It is an essential component of a dissertation or thesis because it provides the reader with an indication of the scope and depth of research reading. It's important, therefore, that when formatting a reference list that researchers follow the conventions accurately and provide all the necessary publication details. The introduction of bibliographic management software packages in recent years has made the process of creating a reference list far easier that it used to be. Popular packages currently available include *Endnote* (www.endnote.com), *Reference Manager* (www.refman.com), *ProCite* (www.procite.com), and *Ref Works* (refworks.com). These packages are integrated fully with word-processing packages such as Microsoft Word and allow the researcher to create their own database in which they can store and organise references, and from which they can format their reference list.

Appendices

Information that is not essential to explain your findings, but that supports your analysis (especially repetitive or lengthy information), validates researcher conclusions or pursues a related point should be placed in an appendix (plural appendices). You may also include a copy of the questionnaire and interview protocol.

Publishing in journals

Researchers who produce quality dissertations or theses are encouraged to publish in journals. PhD students are obliged to publish their work normally in partnership with their supervisor. It's not easy get your work published in journals, particularly the more prestigious ones; standards are high and the competition is strong. Everyone is trying to do the same thing in order to further their own careers and professional standing and you will therefore need to be as well prepared and strategic as possible if you are to maximise your chances of success. Almost all good journals are peer-refereed. This means that an editorial board has been set up to oversee and maintain the quality of the journal by ensuring that only the best articles get published. This is normally done through a system of blind refereeing whereby all articles submitted to the journal are sent out to reviewers to be assessed for their suitability for publication in the journal. Those reviewers are themselves respected individuals within the profession and well placed to comment on your contribution. An article will typically go to two reviewers and sometimes a third if those two reviewers have opposing views on whether or not the article should be published. From the time you submit your article it may well take three to six months for the review process to be completed and for you to hear back from the editor(s) notifying you of their decision. It may take up to 12–24 months for your work to be published from the time of submission. This timeframe is now reducing due to published work being placed online in the first instance.

Plagiarism

Plagiarism is the act of using someone else's work and passing it off as your own. In other words, when you plagiarise you fail to acknowledge the sources of those ideas that are not your own. This is one of the most serious offences you can commit as an academic and the punishment can consequently be severe. If your examiners feel you have a case to answer, you will probably be asked to explain yourself formally to a committee and you may be downgraded or even fail your dissertation or thesis should the committee determine that you are guilty of plagiarism.

The supervisor's role

The role of a supervisor is essentially supportive in nature. They are there to stimulate you, to keep you on the straight and narrow, and to provide encouragement during difficult periods when you may face challenges. Their role is not to lead you but to advance your own thinking by challenging your ideas, suggesting other avenues of enquiry or argument, and provoking you into thinking about things in alternative ways. They can also be a valuable repository of information and well positioned to direct you to relevant literature as well as potentially helpful professional connections – both individuals and institutions. It is expected that you will meet with your supervisor periodically to discuss your work and any progress made, to talk through any difficulties, and to obtain their feedback. It's quite common, prior to the supervision, for students to submit any written work they may have done in order to give their supervisor the opportunity to review it. That piece of work and the supervisor's response to it then constitutes a stepping off point for the discussion. How often supervisions take place will depend on a number of factors including the following:

- The nature of the project itself. If a project is intellectually demanding or particularly original – in its methodology, say – you may well need to meet with your supervisor more frequently in order to work through problems and discuss ways of overcoming unforeseen obstacles.

- The stage your project is at. If you are in the process of collecting your data, for example, you may have little need to meet with your supervisor.

- Your level of self-confidence. Students who lack self-confidence or who are cautious by nature may appreciate the guidance and reassurance that can come from supervisions. In these cases students they tend to schedule meetings more often. In contrast those with a good deal of self-confidence may not meet as regularly.

■ Your personal style of working. Some people relish autonomy and are quite happy to "go it alone" until they run into a snag. At that point, they may feel it's time to schedule a meeting with their supervisor.

■ Your supervisor's availability. Your supervisor may have limited availability. A busy schedule may mean that meetings with you may have to be fairly infrequent affairs.

■ The physical distance between you. Particularly in these days of quick and easy electronic communication, it's not uncommon for students to live in one country whilst being enrolled in a department located in another country. In extreme cases, where a student is jointly supervised by two academics from different institutions, three countries may be involved! Obviously, this makes supervisions in person far less practical and any arrangement of this kind would need to have been approved by the departments and supervisors concerned at the time of your enrolment.

■ There are two other reasons why there may be real physical distance between a supervisor and their student. First, the student may be out in the field collecting their data for an extended period – for example, in an anthropological study in a remote location. Secondly, visa regulations may mean that international students can only stay in their host department's country for a limited period. These are very real constraints and once again, they need to be ironed out at the time of enrolment in order to avoid, or at least minimise, misunderstanding, and frustration further down the line.

■ Your supervisor's own expectations. Your supervisor may well have their own ideas and expectations about how many times they should meet with their students. Some supervisors feel uncomfortable with the idea of seeing their supervisees only two or three times a year. This is particularly the case today, when universities are trying to improve research degree completion rates and avoid situations where students are taking in excess of four or five years to submit their theses.

It is important to be aware that your supervisor is not there to lead but to support. Conducting research is, in part, about finding and expressing your voice, about realising your ideas. It is about autonomy, initiative and taking control of your own project. That's why the letters "PhD" say as much about who you are as they do about what you have achieved. Finally, it is useful to use a self-evaluation checklist before submitting your thesis to confirm you have addressed all the necessary areas. Table 22.5 is an example of a checklist you could use.

Table 22.5 A self-evaluation checklist

Questions	Yes/No/Unsure

1. Dissertation topic

- Is the topic clear and well defined? Does it involve a problem, question, or hypothesis that sets the agenda and points precisely to what needs to be explored or discovered?

- Is the topic of genuine relevance or interest within your subject discipline? Does it pick up on important or interesting themes or subjects arising from your studies?

2. Literature review

- Have you accessed the most recent literature of relevance to your topic, as well as seminal sources from the past?

- Do you refer to major books, articles, artefacts? Since quality is more important than quantity – how well have you selected your material?

- Does the literature review hang together, to show how the ideas and findings have developed, or is it merely a shopping list of books and articles?

- Is the review critical? Does it briefly evaluate, showing how your dissertation fits into what is mistaken or lacking in other studies? The literature review should provide a critically appraised context for your studies.

3. Theoretical underpinnings

- Does theory permeate the structure from beginning to end, from statement of problem to conclusion? Are you asking yourself a key question, presenting a thesis, or defending a statement? Be clear about your approach.

- Theory is the framework of your study – not a luxury. Your dissertation will be judged, in part, by how well you express and critically understand the theory you are using, and how clearly and consistently it is connected with the focus and methodology of your dissertation.

4. Methodology
Two main criteria:

- Is your choice of methods and research techniques well suited to the kind of problem you are studying? Methods work if they provide a persuasive response to your question, positive or negative.

- Is your description of the methods you have adopted clear enough to take a blueprint and replicate?

(*Continued*)

Table 22.5 A self-evaluation checklist (*Continued*)	
Questions	**Yes/No/Unsure**

5. Results

■ Are your findings faithful to what you actually found – do you claim more than you should? Don't "massage" your evidence or findings…

■ Have you provided enough evidence to make a convincing case?

■ Have you presented everything directly relevant to the question in such a way that the reader doesn't have to flip back and forth to make her or his own connections?

■ Are results or findings clearly and accurately written, easy to read, grasp and understand?

6. Conclusions

■ Have you answered the question "So what?". What should we do with your findings and conclusions? What do they imply?

■ Findings don't speak for themselves – they need to be analysed. Have you explained what your findings mean and their importance, in relation to theory and practice?

Research brief

Title: An Inductive Thematic Analysis of Male Competitive Figure Skaters' Experiences of Weight Pressure in Sport
Author: Voelker, D. K., *West Virginia University* & Reel, J. J., *University of Utah* (2018)
Reference: Voelker, D. K., & Reel, J. J. (2018). An inductive thematic analysis of male competitive figure skaters' experiences of weight pressure in sport. *Journal of Clinical Sport Psychology*, *12*(4), 614–629.
The purpose of this qualitative investigation was to examine male competitive figure skaters' experiences of weight pressure in sport. Specifically, male skaters' perceptions of the ideal skating body, sources of weight pressure in elite figure skating, and the perceived role of their sport in shaping body image, athletic performance, eating, and exercise behaviours were explored. Through a social constructivist lens, an inductive thematic analysis was used to examine the contextual influences of the skating environment. Thirteen male figure skaters ages 16–24 with an average 10.38 years of skating experience were interviewed. Skaters identified the parameters for the ideal body in skating along with specific weight pressures, body image concerns, and weight management strategies.

CONCLUSION

This chapter discussed the processes that underpin a research study or investigation. It has identified that ideas for research can be obtained from numerous sources. Once the research topic has been identified the sport management researcher needs an understanding of research planning, what constitutes a literature review and strategies to complete one. The chapter also offered an overview of the stages involved in writing a qualitative research report. It is not intended to be definitive, but merely provides a roadmap to the sport management researcher. Whichever way researchers choose to structure their report – and this will generally depend on the final destination or audience of the paper – the sport management researcher should endeavour to take a systematic and structured approach to the process to ensure that their research findings are presented in the most effective way.

REVIEW AND RESEARCH QUESTIONS

It is an important part of the research process for the sport management researcher to identify the area they want to investigate. With a basic understanding of this process, answer the following questions:

1. Identify three ways in which the sport management researcher can determine suitable research topics.

2. Search and identify two articles that are based on your research topic. Now answer the following questions:

   - In what ways are the two studies different (excluding the research focus)?

- Which research perspective do the author/s take in their study (i.e. subjective or objective or in other words, interpretivist or positivist)?

- What elements (e.g. specific words, sentences, research questions) in the introduction reveal the approach taken by the authors?

3. How can the sport management researcher identify what has already been published in their area of interest?

4. Is the Internet a primary and reliable source of literature and/or information for the sport management researcher? Justify your answer.

REFERENCES

Bless, C., Higson-Smith, C., & Kagee, A. (2006). *Fundamentals of social research methods: An African perspective* (4th ed.). Cape Town, SA: Juta & Co.

Creswell, J. W. (2009). *Research design: Quantitative, qualitative and mixed methods approaches* (4th ed.). New York: Sage Publications.

Creswell, J. W., & Plano Clark, V. L. (2010). *Designing and conducting mixed methods research* (2nd ed.). Thousand Oaks, CA: Sage Publications.

Crotty, M. (1998). *The foundations of social research: Meaning and perspective in the research process.* Sydney, NSW: Allen & Unwin.

Denzin, N. K., & Lincoln, Y. S. (2005). *Handbook of qualitative research* (3rd ed.). Thousand Oaks, CA: Sage Publications.

Deuchar, R. (2008). Facilitator, director or critical friend? Contradiction and congruence in doctoral supervision styles. *Teaching in Higher Education, 13*(4), 489–500.

Pajares, F. (2007). Self efficacy information. In T. Urden, & F. Pajares (Eds.), *Self-Efficacy Beliefs of Adolescents*, pp. 339–367. Charlotte, NC: Information Age Publishing.

Sandelowski, M., & Leeman, J. (2012). Writing usable qualitative health research findings. *Qualitative Health Research, 22*(10), 1404–1413.

Index

Note: Locators in *italics* represent figures and **bold** indicate tables in the text.

517